INTRODUCTION TO

INFORMATION SYSTEMS

IN

BUSINESS MANAGEMENT

INTRODUCTION TO

INFORMATION SYSTEMS
IN
BUSINESS MANAGEMENT

SIXTH EDITION

JAMES A. O'BRIEN
College of Business Administration
Northern Arizona University

IRWIN
Homewood, Il 60430
Boston, MA 02116

The previous edition of this book was published under the title of *Information Systems in Business Management*.

Senior sponsoring editor: Lawrence E. Alexander
Project editor: Rita McMullen
Production manager: Carma W. Fazio
Cover illustrator: Sandra Dionisi
Artist: Rolin Graphics
Compositor: Better Graphics, Inc.
Typeface: 10/12 Caledonia
Printer: Von Hoffmann Press, Inc.

Library of Congress Cataloging-in-Publication Data

O'Brien, James A.,
    Introduction to information systems in business management / James A. O'Brien. —6th ed.
      p.   cm.
    Rev. ed. of: Information systems in business management.
    Includes index.
    ISBN 0-256-08855-1   ISBN 0-256-09880-8 (international ed.)
      1. Business—Data processing.   2. Management—Data processing.
I. O'Brien, James A.,   Information systems in business management. II. Title.
HF5548.2.O23   1991
658'.05—dc20   90–38637

Printed in the United States of America

3 4 5 6 7 8 9 0 VH 7 6 5 4 3 2

With love to my beautiful wife
Patsy Lee O'Brien
You make life's journey worthwhile

PREFACE

This text is written as an introduction to information systems for business students. Thus, it uses a business management focus, which has been the primary reason for its success over five editions. Of course, like previous editions, the Sixth Edition is a major revision which provides up-to-date coverage that reflects the dynamic changes occurring in information systems technology, theory, and pedagogy. However, the text continues to have one overriding goal: to help business students become knowledgeable end users who will use information systems concepts and technology to solve business problems and pursue business opportunities.

This text is designed for use in undergraduate courses that introduce information systems in a business management context. Such courses are required in many business administration or management programs as part of the *common body of knowledge* required of all business majors. Thus, this text treats the subject area known as information systems (IS), management information systems (MIS), or computer information systems (CIS) as a major functional area of business that is as important to management education as the areas of accounting, finance, operations management, marketing, and human resource management.

Like my other text, *Management Information Systems: A Managerial End User Perspective*, this text is designed to support **information system literacy** by students. That is, its objective is to build a basic understanding of the value and uses of information systems for business operations, management decision making, and strategic advantage. However, this text and its optional workbook can also be used to support student **computer literacy.** For example, Chapter 1 contains a section on *Computers: Past, Present, and Future*, while Module II, entitled "Information Systems Technology," contains four chapters on computer concepts and hardware, software, telecommunications, and database management which review the technological foundations of computer literacy. In addition, the text can be packaged with an optional workbook on productivity software packages and BASIC, entitled *Software Tools for Managing Information: A Hands-On Workbook*. This workbook can serve to introduce students to the hands-on use of computer hardware and software for business productivity.

INTRODUCING
INFORMATION
SYSTEMS TO
BUSINESS
STUDENTS

AN INFORMATION SYSTEMS FRAMEWORK

This text provides a teaching-learning resource that reduces the complexity of an introductory course in information systems by using a conceptual framework that organizes the knowledge needed by business students into five major areas:

☐ **Foundation concepts**—basic information systems concepts and the operational, decision making, and strategic roles of information systems (Chapters 1 and 2). Other behavioral, managerial, and technical concepts are presented where appropriate in other chapters.

☐ **Technology**—major concepts, developments, and managerial implications involved in computer hardware, software, telecommunications, and database management technologies (Chapters 3, 4, 5, and 6). Other technologies used in computer-based information systems are discussed where appropriate in selected chapters.

☐ **Applications**—how information systems support end user activities, business operations, managerial decision making, and strategic advantage (introduced in Chapter 2 and discussed in detail in Chapters 7, 8, 9, and 10).

☐ **Development**—developing information system solutions to business problems using a variety of systems development tools and methodologies (presented in Chapter 11 and in other chapters when discussing development issues for major types of information systems).

☐ **Management**—the challenges and methods of managing information systems technologies, activities, and resources (emphasized in each chapter, but discussed specifically in Chapters 12, 13, and 14).

REAL WORLD PROBLEMS AND CASES

This text makes extensive use of up-to-date, real world case studies and problems. These are not fictional stories, but actual situations faced by business firms and other organizations as reported in current business and IS periodicals. This includes two short real world case studies in each chapter that apply specifically to that chapter's contents, and eight real world problems provided at the end of every chapter. Hands-on software assignments are also provided at the end of selected chapters and in the optional workbook on software and BASIC. These can be used to demonstrate computer-based solutions to business problems. The purpose of this variety of assignment options is to give instructors and students many opportunities to apply information system solutions to real world business problems, in addition to reading and discussing the course material.

MODULAR STRUCTURE OF THE TEXT

The text is organized according to the five major areas of the framework for information systems knowledge mentioned earlier. Figure 1 illustrates how the chapters of the text are organized into four **modules.** Also, each chapter is organized into two or three distinct **sections.** This is done to avoid proliferation of chapters, as well as to provide better conceptual organization of the text and each chapter. This organization increases instructor flexibility in assigning course material since it structures the text into modular levels (i.e., modules, chapters, and sections) while reducing the number of chapters that need to be covered.

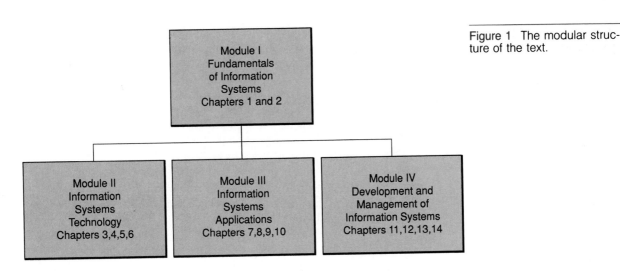

Figure 1 The modular structure of the text.

Each chapter starts with a Chapter Outline and Learning Objectives. The learning objectives can also be used as topics for class discussion or as essay questions for class assignments and examinations. Each chapter ends with a Summary, Key Terms and Concepts, a Review Quiz tied directly to the Key Terms and Concepts, Real World Problems, and Selected References. Real World Cases are also provided at the end of each section. These chapter components help students organize their reading and review of each chapter and demonstrate how the chapter material relates to the challenges of using information systems in the real world of business management.

Module I: Fundamentals of Information Systems

The first module of this text is designed as a **core module** of foundation IS concepts. It consists of two chapters that stress basic systems concepts and the major roles of information systems. Once instructors have covered this module, they can assign any other module, depending on their pedagogical preferences. Chapter 1 introduces students to the importance of information systems, a framework of information systems knowledge, and the generic components and properties of information systems. It then briefly introduces the major trends that have developed over five generations of computing. Chapter 2 introduces the major roles and types of information systems, emphasizing the strategic role that information systems can play in gaining competitive advantages for an organization.

Module II: Information Systems Technology

Module II contains four chapters on computer concepts, hardware, software, telecommunications, and database management. Its purpose is to give students an introduction to the technology used in modern computer-based information systems and its implications for end users. This material is consolidated in an independent module so instructors can selectively use the chapters and sections of this module, depending on the preparation of their students. This is especially useful in the case of the important topics of telecommunications and database management, in which many students have typically had only a brief exposure. Students need an adequate background in such topics in order to propose realistic information system solutions to business problems.

Module III: Information Systems Applications	Module III contains four chapters that discuss the basic components and major applications of computer-based information systems. It emphasizes how information systems support end user activities and the operations and management of business firms and other organizations. Thus, it includes coverage of concepts and applications in end user computing and office automation (Chapter 7); transaction processing and information reporting systems (Chapter 8); decision support and executive information systems, and expert systems (Chapter 9); and business function information systems (Chapter 10).
Module IV: Information Systems Development and Management	It is important that end users learn that although information systems can help them develop solutions to business problems, they also pose major managerial challenges. That is the focus of the four chapters of Module IV. Chapter 11 introduces the systems development and prototyping processes and includes an introduction to the use of systems development tools. Chapter 12 covers strategic, tactical, and operational information systems planning, as well as management issues in the implementation of information systems. The impact of information technology, the importance of information resource management, and the managerial implications of providing information services are covered in Chapter 13. Chapter 14 discusses the controls needed for information systems performance and security, as well as the legal and ethical implications of the control of computer crime and other societal impacts of information systems.
INTERNATIONAL AND ETHICAL DIMENSIONS	This text covers the international and ethical dimensions of information systems with both text material and case studies on such topics. For example, the necessity of telecommunications networks for competition in global markets is mentioned in Chapter 5, while their potential for causing violations of international law is discussed in Chapter 14. Computer crime and ethics are also discussed in Chapter 14, with an emphasis on what it takes to be a *responsible* end user. Finally, the text contains many cases and problems illustrating the international and ethical dimensions of IS. Examples include Nissan Motor Company, Grand Metropolitan (United Kingdom), Canadian Pacific, Unix in Europe, Citicorp Latin American Technology Group, United Parcel Service (Eastern Europe), and East India Hotels. These and other Real World Cases and Problems emphasize the role of information systems in businesses that must increasingly compete in government regulated domestic and international markets.
SUMMARY OF CHANGES	Major changes have been made to the former 5th Edition material that reflect curriculum demands for more MIS content, as well as developments in IS technology. Changes to the 5th Edition are incorporated in the following 6th Edition chapters:

Chapter 1: New material on the information systems area, systems concepts, and the information systems model. Color section moved to Chapter 3.

Chapter 2: New Chapter—Combines the overview of information systems material, formerly in Chapter 9, with new material on information systems for strategic advantage.

Chapter 3: New Chapter—Provides two full-color sections, which present updated material on types of computer systems and peripherals. Combines material on input, output, and storage hardware and processing methods, formerly in Chapters 4, 5, and 6.

Chapter 4: Updates material on system and application software, formerly in Chapter 3.

Chapter 5: Major change to a managerial emphasis on telecommunications in Section I, with technical telecommunications alternatives placed in Section II of the chapter.

Chapter 6: Major change to a managerial emphasis for data resource management in Section I, with more technical material on database management placed in Section II.

Chapter 7: New Chapter—New first section on end user computing combined with material on office automation, formerly in Chapter 12.

Chapter 8: New Chapter—Combines material on batch and realtime processing, formerly in Chapter 4, and data entry and output concepts, formerly in Chapter 5, with new material on transaction processing systems and information reporting systems.

Chapter 9: New Chapter—New material on decision making, decision support systems, executive information systems, artificial intelligence, and expert systems.

Chapter 10: New Chapter—Major revision of material on business function information systems, formerly in Chapters 13 and 14.

Chapter 11: Major revision of information systems development material, formerly in Chapter 10, with significant discussion and illustration of prototyping, CASE, and systems development tools.

Chapter 12: New Chapter—Adds new sections on information systems planning and implementation to IS resource acquisition material, formerly in Chapter 16.

Chapter 13: Major revision of former Chapter 15 material on the management of information systems resources and services.

Chapter 14: Major revision of material, formerly in Chapter 17, on the control of information systems performance and security, computer crime, and computer ethics.

The Use of Color

In an effort to reduce costs this text will continue to be printed in two colors with a full-color insert included as Sections I and II of Chapter 3. This 32-page insert contains text material and full-color photographs and illustrations that provide an attractive introduction to computer systems and their peripheral devices. This color insert avoids arbitrary interruption of text material and provides real working chapter sections, not just visual treats, as is sometimes the case in the multiple-color inserts found in other texts.

SUPPORT MATERIALS

A new **software workbook,** *Software Tools for Managing Information: A Hands-On Workbook,* by James N. Morgan of Northern Arizona University, accompanies the text. This optional workbook contains new and revised mate-

The Software Workbook

rial formerly in the 5th edition appendices on productivity software packages and BASIC. It includes a section on the use of PC and DOS, and sections on Wordperfect, Lotus 1-2-3, dBASE III Plus, and BASIC. The workbook continues the practice of demonstrating fundamental, generic activities that one does with productivity software packages. This is accomplished by using leading commercial software packages as specific examples in figures of typical displays and in tutorial discussions of typical types of activities. The workbook also provides an extensive number of hands-on exercises and cases that give students many opportunities to learn to use productivity software packages to solve realistic business problems.

BASIC

Introductory MIS courses are still being taught either with or without coverage of software development and a programming language. To accommodate these two approaches, the material in the 5th edition's chapter on the software development process has been condensed and included as the first section of the introductory coverage of BASIC in the optional workbook. Thus, instructors can better choose whether or not they want to cover such material.

Student Study Guide

The **Student Study Guide** that supplements the text is improved for this edition. It contains detailed chapter outlines, chapter learning objectives, chapter overviews, definitions of key terms and concepts, chapter test-yourself questions (true-false, multiple-choice, fill-in-the-blanks, matching), answers to test-yourself questions, and short chapter assignments. The study guide should thus be a valuable supplement to the main text.

Instructor's Manual and Lecture Guide

An **Instructor's Manual** is available to instructors upon adoption of the text. It contains instructional aids and suggestions, detailed annotated chapter outlines with page and figure references, and answers to chapter review quizzes, real world problems, and case study questions. Transparency masters of important figures in the text and a set of 60 color overhead transparencies are also provided to adopters.

A separate **Lecture Guide,** developed by Al Kagan of North Dakota State University, is also available to adopting instructors. It contains detailed notes designed to help instructors develop and present lectures to large class sections.

Test Bank

A **Test Bank** containing over 1,400 true-false and multiple-choice questions is available to adopting instructors as a separate test manual and in computerized form on floppy disk for use with the Irwin's CompuTest test generator software package or its TeleTest service.

ACKNOWLEDGMENTS

The author wishes to acknowledge the assistance of the following reviewers, whose constructive criticism and suggestions helped him shape the form and content of this text:

Johannes Aarsen   *The Wichita State University*
Connie Morris Fox   *West Virginia Institute of Technology*
Bruce J. McLaren   *Indiana State University*

Thomas A. Pollack   *Duquesne University*
John E. Powell   *University of South Dakota*
Rex Kelly Rainer, Jr.   *Auburn University*
Teresita S. Salinas   *Washburn University*
Todd Schultz   *Augusta College*
James B. Shannon   *New Mexico State University*

A special acknowledgment is owed to Jim Morgan of Northern Arizona University, who revised the Student Study Guide, Instructor's Manual, and Test Bank, and authored the software workbook that can be used with this text. Thanks also go to Al Kagan of North Dakota State University who developed the text's Lecture Guide. My thanks also extend to Jory Gerken for her word processing skills, and to the authors, publishers, and firms in the IS field who contributed ideas, illustrations, and photographs used in this edition. Finally, I wish to thank the many instructors who have used my texts in their MIS classes. Their comments and suggestions continue to help me improve each edition of this text.

Acknowledging the Real World of Business

A special acknowledgment is due the 145 business firms and other computer-using organizations that are the subjects of most of the Real World Cases and Problems in each chapter of this text. Their titles and the chapters and page numbers where they appear in the text begin on page xv. My industry experience with General Electric and IBM, and a variety of consulting assignments, have taught me to appreciate the value of emphasizing real-life situations faced by real people and organizations in my texts and classes. Such real world cases and problems provide students with invaluable examples of the problems and opportunities confronting companies that are using computer-based information systems to support business operations, managerial decision making, and strategic advantage.

James A. O'Brien

REAL WORLD CASES AND PROBLEMS

MODULE **III**

CONTENTS IN BRIEF

CONTENTS

MODULE **II**

INFORMATION SYSTEMS TECHNOLOGY   *71*

MODULE **III**

MODULE **IV**

INFORMATION SYSTEMS DEVELOPMENT AND
MANAGEMENT   *379*

CHAPTER 11   **DEVELOPING INFORMATION SYSTEM
SOLUTIONS**   *380*

CHAPTER 12   **PLANNING AND IMPLEMENTING INFORMATION SYSTEMS**   *420*

INTRODUCTION TO

INFORMATION SYSTEMS
IN
BUSINESS MANAGEMENT

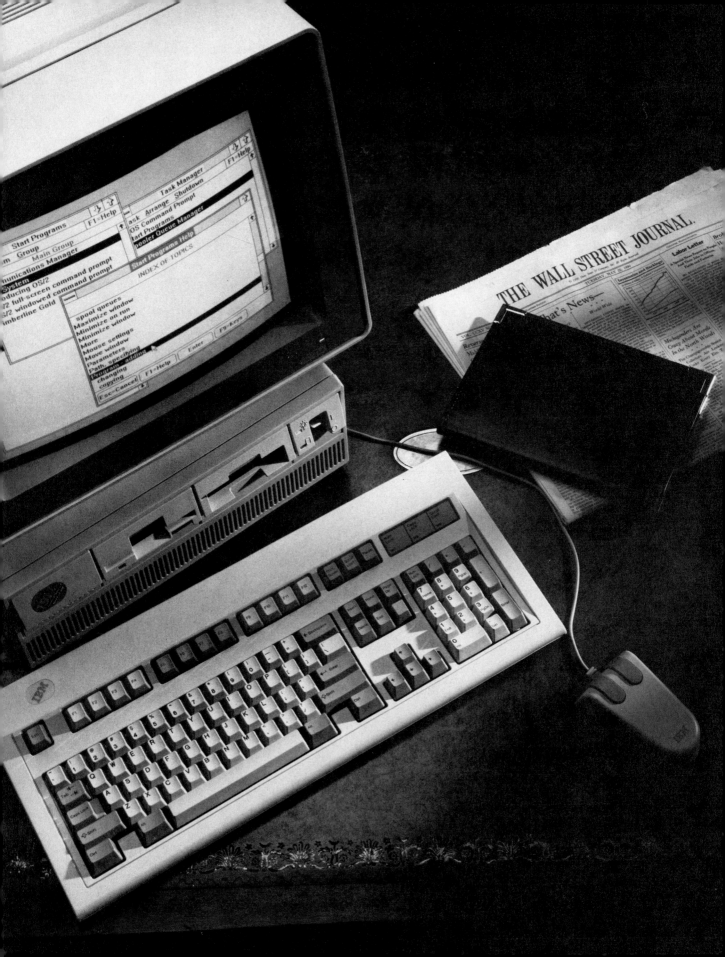

FUNDAMENTALS OF INFORMATION SYSTEMS

What are information systems and what is their role in business firms and other organizations? What should end users know about information systems? The two chapters of Module I are designed to begin answering these important questions.

Chapter 1, Introduction to Computers and Information Systems, introduces you to the importance of information systems, the framework of information systems knowledge needed by end users, and the conceptual system components and properties of information systems. It also briefly introduces you to the major trends that have developed over five generations of computing.

Chapter 2, Information Systems in Business Management, introduces the major operations and management roles of information systems and emphasizes the strategic role that information systems can play in gaining competitive advantages for an organization.

CHAPTER 1

INTRODUCTION TO COMPUTERS AND INFORMATION SYSTEMS

■ **Chapter Outline**

■ Learning Objectives

The purpose of this chapter is to give you an understanding of the use of computers in information systems by analyzing (1) fundamental system concepts used in information systems and (2) major trends in the development and use of computers.

Section I of this chapter discusses the importance to business end users of understanding the foundation concepts, technology, applications, development, and management of information systems.

Section II introduces basic concepts of systems theory, information processing, and information systems, including a fundamental conceptual framework or model of information system components and activities.

Section III presents brief summaries of the major generations in the development of computers and emphasizes the major trends that are expected to continue into the future.

After reading and studying this chapter, you should be able to:

1. Explain the importance of computers and information systems in today's organizations.

2. Identify five areas of information systems knowledge you need.

3. Explain and give examples from your experience of the concept of an information system as a system that uses the resources of hardware (machines and media), software (programs and procedures), and people (specialists and end users) to perform input, processing, output, storage, and control activities that transform data resources into information products.

4. Identify the major changes that have occurred in each generation of computers, the trends that will continue into the future, and their effect on computer users.

Section I: The Importance of Information Systems

WHY LEARN ABOUT COMPUTERS AND INFORMATION SYSTEMS?

Why should you learn about computers and information systems? To answer this question, we will briefly discuss the importance of information systems. Then, we will analyze a short example from the real world of business.

Information, along with energy and materials, is a basic resource in today's world. We are living in an *information society* whose economy is heavily dependent on **knowledge workers,** that is, people whose primary work activity is the creation, use, and distribution of information. We must learn to harness our information resources to benefit ourselves, our organizations, and all of society. This includes finding ways to use information to make better use of our limited supplies of material, energy, and other natural resources.

Computers are major tools in the production and use of information. The use of computers is vital to the operations and management of business firms, government agencies, and the rest of society. For example, banks, retail stores, stock exchanges, and airlines would not be able to process the millions of sales transactions, money transfers, stock trades, and travel requests made each day. Thousands of business firms in many other industries could not operate without the basic information concerning their customers, suppliers, inventories, and finances provided by their *computer-based information systems.*

The proper flow and management of information in an organization is vital to its success. Thus, the *information system (IS) function* represents:

- ☐ A major functional area of business that is as important to business success as the functions of accounting, finance, operations management, marketing, and human resource management.
- ☐ A major part of the resources of an organization and its cost of doing business, thus posing a major resource management challenge.
- ☐ An important factor affecting operational efficiency, employee productivity and morale, and customer service and satisfaction.
- ☐ A major source of information and support needed to promote effective decision making by managers.
- ☐ An important ingredient in developing competitive products and services that give an organization a strategic advantage in the marketplace.
- ☐ A vital, dynamic, and challenging career opportunity for millions of men and women.

Therefore, you can increase your opportunities for success by becoming a knowledgeable user (i.e., *end user*) of computers and information systems. Businesses and other organizations need people who can use computers to enhance their own personal productivity and the productivity of their work groups, departments, and organizations. For example, you should be able to use word processing and electronic mail to communicate more effectively, spreadsheet packages to more effectively analyze decision situations, and database management packages to provide better reports on organizational performance. You should also be aware of the management problems and opportunities presented by the use of computers, and how you can effectively

REAL WORLD CASE

Back Bay Hardware

Stuffed with 18,000 products to help make urban life more livable, the Back Bay Hardware store across from PC Week's office in downtown Boston is a wonderful place to visit. But it's been a nightmare to manage, says owner Bill Kruse. A nightmare, that is, until he put in a microcomputer.

Bill was lucky, though. Having spent 28 years in the Navy working with inventory systems and computers, he knew the right things to do. He just never had the time—or the money—to do them. Now the micro has changed all that.

It's changed Bill, too. Once the micro was installed over a year ago, Bill changed from stock clerk to store manager. In the transformation, he learned some valuable lessons about common-sense micro management. These principles hold up as well in the corridors of corporate computing as in the crammed aisles of the hardware store.

First of all, Bill dismissed any notion to buy the $30,000 deluxe system with all the hardware and software goodies. Instead, he focused on what was really important to him: store receivables and inventory control. He shopped around and assembled his own system, using an IBM AT microcomputer and $3,000 worth of software designed for hardware stores. A modest $7,500 investment. The big effort was going through the store, item by item, and assigning each a bin number for computer-based control.

"There were some surprises," he said. "The store actually ran differently in several ways than I'd imagined." Human error with the old cash registers rang up several hundred dollars per month—much more than he'd thought. Breakage and mistakes—such as mixing the wrong color paint or cutting the wrong length of chain—were both much higher than expected. And the amount of theft was a shock.

Bin numbers and the computer, however, have produced a pocketful of miracles. With the computerized system, all clerks use a common process of accounting for all items. And all items in the store are accounted for. No exceptions. Pricing strategy, Bill said, has been vastly improved. All information is easily at hand, and he can quickly select the margins he wants for each item. For the first time, Bill can do price comparisons and change his prices in a wink to outmaneuver the store up the street.

Bill now has 200 regular commercial customers in addition to the walk-in trade. Reflecting changes in the city, this part of the business is growing rapidly. And Bill knows exactly what these important customers want stocked and has plenty of the right inventory on hand. With the computer system, the commercial accounts are easily billed and effectively managed.

Application Questions

☐ How did a microcomputer improve Bill Kruse's management of his business?

☐ Why did the use of a PC prove successful at Back Bay Hardware?

Source: Adapted from Fritz Dressler, "Doing the Right Things or Doing Things Right?" *PC Week*, March 6, 1989, p. 59.

---

confront such challenges. Then you can play a major role in seeing that information system resources are used efficiently and effectively to benefit your career goals and the goals of the business firms or other organizations you may work for in the future.

The previous paragraphs may not have convinced you of the importance of learning about computers and information systems. That is understandable because your personal experiences with the successes and failures of computer

INFORMATION SYSTEMS IN THE REAL WORLD

use in business may be limited at this point. That's why this text provides at least two Real World Cases and eight Real World Problems in every chapter. The vast majority describe actual situations (not fictional stories) occurring in over 140 actual companies and organizations. This should give you a better appreciation of the problems and opportunities presented by computers and information systems in the real world of business and management. Let's analyze the case of Back Bay Hardware on page 7 right now.

Analyzing Back Bay Hardware

We can learn a lot about the importance of computers and information systems from the Real World Case of Back Bay Hardware. The installation of a microcomputer and business software packages changed owner Bill Kruse from a stock clerk to a store manager. What had been a nightmare to manage became an efficiently and effectively run business. The computerized information systems greatly reduced the amount of time spent in order entry, inventory control, and error correction activities. They have allowed Bill to fully account for all items in the store, to quickly set and adjust margins for all items, and to see at a glance what products his most important commercial customers want stocked.

So why did the PC prove so successful at Back Bay Hardware? Computers are not a magic solution to business problems. Bill could have become just another example of a failure to properly apply computers to business problems. However, Bill used computers to change his way of doing business. He knew the details of the business firsthand. And just as important, he knew about computers and how to use them for inventory control and other information system applications needed for efficient and effective management of his business.

WHAT YOU SHOULD KNOW ABOUT INFORMATION SYSTEMS

It would be easy for someone like Bill Kruse or yourself to feel overwhelmed by the complex technologies, abstract behavioral concepts, and specialized applications in the field of information systems. However, most people do not have to absorb all of this knowledge. Figure 1–1 illustrates a useful conceptual framework that outlines what you need to know about information systems. It emphasizes that as a business end user, you should concentrate your efforts in five areas of knowledge: foundation concepts, technology, applications, development, and management.

Foundation Concepts

What are information systems and why are they important to end users and their organizations? In order to answer this question, you should first have a knowledge of basic concepts about systems, information systems, and information processing. You should also understand the vital roles played by information systems in business firms and other organizations. Chapters 1 and 2 of Module I and other chapters of the text support this area of knowledge.

Technology

What should business end users know about the technologies used in computer-based information systems? The answer to this question is that you should have an understanding of major concepts, developments, and manage-

INFORMATION SYSTEMS

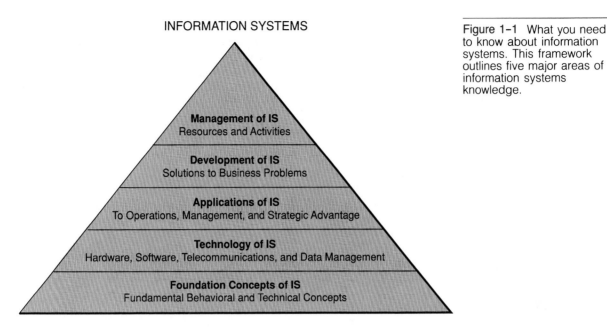

Figure 1-1 What you need to know about information systems. This framework outlines five major areas of information systems knowledge.

ment issues in hardware, software, telecommunications, database management, and other information processing technologies. Technology is so dynamic in this field that a factual knowledge that concentrates on detailed characteristics and capabilities would soon be outdated. Instead, you should focus on generic capabilities, major developments and trends, and management challenges in the use of information systems technology. Chapters 3, 4, 5, and 6 of Module II along with other chapters of the text support this area of information systems knowledge.

Applications

In what major ways can information systems support end users and organizations in accomplishing their activities and meeting their strategic objectives? Answering this question requires a knowledge of the major types of applications of information systems for end user activities and the operations, management, and strategic advantage of organizations. You should gain a basic understanding of information systems concepts and applications in areas such as end user computing, office automation, transaction processing, management reporting, decision support, executive support, artificial intelligence, and the functional areas of business. Chapters 7, 8, 9, and 10 of Module III support this learning objective.

Development

How should business end users work with information specialists to develop information system solutions to business problems? In order to answer this question you should learn some basic developmental concepts used in the information systems field. You should understand how methodologies such as the *systems development life cycle* and *prototyping* can be used to construct information system applications that successfully meet end user and organizational needs. The goal of Chapter 11 of Module IV is to help you learn how to propose information system solutions to business problems.

Management

How should end user managers meet the major challenge of managing the information systems of their organizations? Answering this question requires understanding the managerial challenges and appropriate methods involved in properly managing the resources, technologies, and activities of information systems. Developing and using information systems can be difficult and costly as well as beneficial to a firm. Thus, you should understand concepts such as *information resource management* and information systems planning, implementation, and control. Chapters 12, 13, and 14 of Module IV cover these important topics.

Section II: Fundamental Information System Concepts

Systems concepts underlie the field of information systems. Other disciplines may use the term *system* as an important concept or as a convenient way of describing the phenomena they must deal with. However, knowledge of systems concepts is vital to a proper understanding of the technology, applications, development, and management of information systems. Therefore, you should understand how generic systems concepts apply to information processing and information systems. This should provide you with a systems viewpoint which will help you understand many of the important information system concepts contained in this text.

What is a system? A system can be very simply defined as *a group of interrelated or interacting elements forming a unified whole.* Many examples of systems can be found in the physical and biological sciences, in modern technology, and in human society. Thus, we can talk of the physical system of the sun and its planets, the biological system of the human body, the technological system of an oil refinery, and the socioeconomic system of a business organization. However, the following generic concept of a system is widely used in the information systems discipline.

A system is a group of interrelated components working together toward a common goal by accepting inputs and producing outputs in an organized transformation process.

Such a system (sometimes called a *dynamic system*) has three basic functional components that interact to form a system:

- **Input** involves capturing and assembling elements that enter the system so they can be processed. *Examples:* Raw materials, energy, data, and human effort must be secured and organized for processing.
- **Processing** involves transformation processes that convert input into output. *Examples:* a manufacturing process, the human breathing process, data calculations.
- **Output** involves transferring elements that have been produced by the transformation process to their ultimate destination. *Examples:* Finished products, human services, and management information must be transmitted to their human users.

Examples A manufacturing system accepts raw materials as inputs and produces finished goods as output. An **information system** can be viewed as a system that accepts *data resources* as *input* and *processes* them into *information products* as *output*. See Figure 1–2.

The systems concept can be made even more useful by including two additional components: *feedback* and *control*. A system with feedback and control components is sometimes called a *cybernetic* system, that is, a *self-monitoring, self-regulating* system.

- **Feedback** is data or information concerning the performance of a system.

SYSTEMS CONCEPTS

Feedback and Control

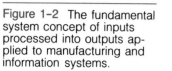

Figure 1–2 The fundamental system concept of inputs processed into outputs applied to manufacturing and information systems.

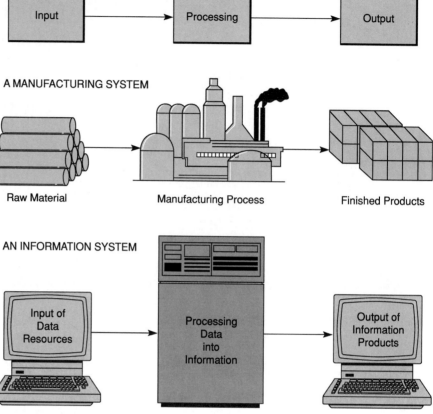

☐ **Control** is a major system function that monitors and evaluates feedback to determine whether the system is moving toward the achievement of its goal. It then makes any necessary adjustments to the input and processing components of the system to ensure that proper output is produced.

Feedback is frequently included as part of the concept of the control function because it is such a necessary part of its operation. Figure 1–3 shows the relationship of feedback and control to the other components of a system. The flow of feedback data to the control component and the resulting control signals to the other components are shown as dotted arrows. This emphasizes that the feedback and control functions play an important supportive role to assure that the other system components properly transform inputs into outputs and achieve the goal of the system.

Examples A familiar example of a self-monitoring and self-regulating system is the thermostatically controlled heating system found in many homes, which automatically monitors and regulates itself to produce a desired temperature. Another familiar example is the human body, which can be considered as a cybernetic system that automatically monitors and adjusts many of its functions, such as temperature, heartbeat, and breathing.

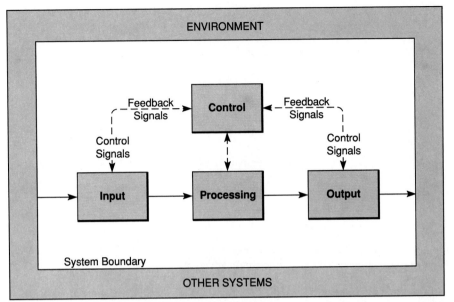

Figure 1–3 Fundamental components and charac- teristics of a system. This illustrates a generic concept of a system that has feed- back and control compo- nents and that exchanges inputs and outputs with its environment.

Other System Characteristics

Figure 1–3 illustrates several other characteristics that are important to under- standing information systems. Notice that a system does not exist in a vacuum. It exists and functions in an **environment** consisting of other systems. If a system is one of the components of a larger system, it is called a **subsystem,** and the larger system is its environment. Also, a system is separated from its environment and other systems by its system **boundary.**

Other systems may also exist in the same environment. Some of these systems may be connected to each other by means of a shared boundary, or **interface.** Figure 1–3 also illustrates the concept of an **open system,** that is, one that must interact with other systems in its environment to survive. In this illustration, the system exchanges inputs and outputs with its environment. Thus, we could say that it is connected to its environment by input and output interfaces. Finally, if a system has the ability to change itself or its environment in order to survive, it is known as an **adaptive system.**

Example An example can help to clarify these system concepts. Organiza- tions such as business firms or government agencies are *subsystems* of society, which is their *environment.* Society is composed of a multitude of systems, that is, individuals and their social, political, and economic insti- tutions. Organizations themselves consist of many subsystems, such as departments, divisions, and other work groups. Organizations are *open sys- tems* since they must interface and interact with other systems to survive in their environment. In addition, organizations are *adaptive systems* since they possess the ability to modify themselves to meet the demands of a changing environment.

A BUSINESS AS A SYSTEM

You should be able to visualize any organization as a system. For example, Figure 1–4 emphasizes that a business firm is an open, adaptive *organizational system* operating in a business environment. It consists of the following interre- lated system components:

Figure 1–4 A business is a system where *economic resources* (input) are transformed by various *organizational processes* (processing) into *goods and services* (output). *Information systems* provide information (feedback) on the operations of the system to *management* for the direction and maintenance of the system (control), as it exchanges inputs and outputs with its environment.

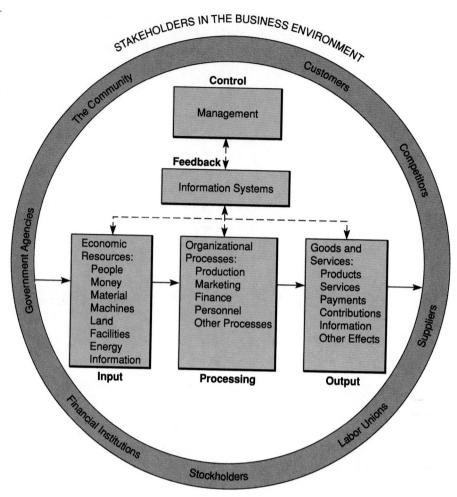

☐ **Input:** Economic resources such as people, money, material, machines, land, facilities, energy, and information are acquired by a business from its environment and used in its system activities.

☐ **Processing:** Organizational processes such as the business functions of marketing, manufacturing, and finance transform input into output. Other organizational processes include functions such as engineering, research and development, legal services, and so on.

☐ **Output:** Products and services and other outputs such as payments to employees and suppliers, dividends, interest, contributions, taxes, and information are produced by a business and exchanged or transferred to its environment.

☐ **Feedback:** A primary role of information systems is serving as the feedback component of an organizational system. They provide information to management concerning the performance of the business organization.

☐ **Control:** Management is the control component of an organizational system. Managers control the operations of a business so that its performance meets organizational goals such as profitability, market share, and social responsibility. Feedback about organizational performance is compared to standards of performance established by management. Managers then make decisions required to adjust performance to meet organizational goals.

☐ **Environment:** As we have just mentioned, a business is an open, adaptive system that exchanges inputs and outputs with other systems in its environment.

A business must maintain proper interrelationships with the other economic, political, and social subsystems in its environment. This includes *stakeholders*, such as customers, suppliers, competitors, stockholders, labor unions, financial institutions, governmental agencies, and the community, all of whom have a stake in the proper and successful operation of the business. Information systems must be developed to help a business shape its relationships to each of these stakeholders.

INFORMATION PROCESSING

It is important to understand information systems in the context of their use in **information processing,** which is also called **data processing.** We can define data or information processing as the processing of data to make it more usable and meaningful, thus transforming it into information. Let's take a closer look at the concepts involved.

Data versus Information

The word *data* is the plural of *datum*, though data is commonly used to represent both singular and plural forms. **Data** is commonly defined as *raw facts* or *observations*, typically about physical phenomena or business transactions. For example, a spacecraft launch or the sale of an automobile would generate a lot of data describing those events. More specifically, data are objective measurements of the *attributes* (the characteristics) of *entities* (such as people, places, things, and events). These measurements are usually represented by symbols such as numbers and words, or by codes composed of a mixture of numerical, alphabetical, and other characters. However, data commonly takes a variety of forms including numeric data, text, voice, and images.

The terms *data* and *information* are often used interchangeably. However, it is helpful to view data as raw material *resources* that are processed into finished information *products*. **Information** can then be defined as data that has been transformed into a meaningful and useful context for specific end users. Of course, data may not require processing before constituting information for a particular end user. However, data is usually not useful until subjected to a *value-added* process where (1) its form is aggregated, manipulated, and organized; (2) its content is analyzed and evaluated; and (3) it is placed in a proper context for a human user. Thus, you should view information as *processed data* placed in its proper context to give it value for specific end users. See Figure 1–5.

Example Names, quantities, and dollar amounts recorded on sales forms represent data about sales transactions. However, a sales manager may not consider them to be information. Only when such facts are properly organized and manipulated can meaningful sales information be provided, such as the amount of sales by product type, sales territory, or salesperson.

Data   **Information**

$35,000 12 Units		Processing		Salesperson: J. Jones
$12,000 J. Jones	→	Data	→	Sales Territory:
Western Region		into		Western Region
$100,000 100 Units		Information		Current Sales:
35 Units				147 Units = $147,000

Figure 1–5 Data versus information. Notice that information is processed data placed in its proper context to give it value for specific end users.

INFORMATION SYSTEM CONCEPTS

We can define an **information system** very simply as a set of people, procedures, and resources that collects, transforms, and disseminates information in an organization. Or as we said earlier, an information system is a system that accepts data resources as input and processes them into information products as output. But how does an information system accomplish this? What system components and activities are involved?

An Information System Model

Figure 1–6 illustrates an **information system model** that provides a fundamental conceptual framework, or *model,* of the major components and activities of an information system.

An information system uses the resources of hardware (machines and media), software (programs and procedures), and people (specialists and end users) to perform input, processing, output, storage, and control activities that transform data resources into information products.

This information system model helps tie together the major components and activities of all types of information systems. It provides a framework that emphasizes three major concepts:

☐ Hardware (machines and media), software (programs and procedures), and people (specialists and end users) are the primary resources needed to accomplish information processing activities in information systems.

☐ Data resources are transformed into a variety of information products by the information processing activities of information systems.

☐ Information processing consists of the basic system activities of input, processing, output, storage, and control.

Information System Activities

Let's take a closer look now at each of the basic information processing activities that occur in information systems. Then we will discuss the resources needed to accomplish them. Figure 1–7 lists business examples that illustrate each of the basic activities of information systems.

Input of Data Resources

Data about business transactions and other events must be captured and prepared for processing by the basic *data entry* activities of recording and editing. End users typically record data about transactions on some type of physical medium, such as a paper form, or enter it directly into a computer system. This usually includes a variety of editing activities to assure that they have recorded data correctly. Once entered, data may be transferred onto *machine readable media,* such as magnetic disk or tape, until needed for processing.

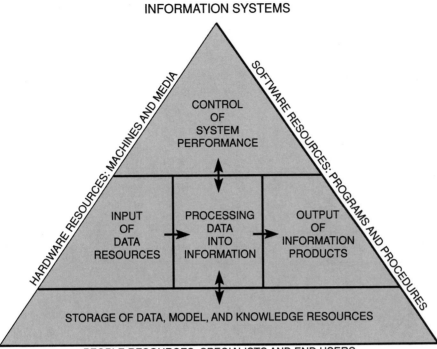

INFORMATION SYSTEMS

Figure 1-6 An information system model. Information systems use the resources of hardware (machines and media), software (programs and procedures), and people (specialists and end users) to perform input, processing, output, storage, and control activities that transform data resources into information products.

For example, data about sales transactions can be recorded on *source documents* such as paper sales order forms. (A **source document** is the original formal record of a transaction.) Alternatively, sales data could be captured by salespersons using computer keyboards or optical scanning devices who are visually prompted to enter data correctly by video displays. This provides them with a more convenient and efficient **user interface,** that is, methods of end user input and output with a computer system. Methods such as optical scanning and displays of menus, prompts, and fill-in-the-blanks formats make it easier for end users to enter data correctly into an information system.

Processing of Data into Information

Data is typically manipulated by activities such as calculating, comparing, sorting, classifying, and summarizing. These activities organize, analyze, and manipulate data, thus converting it into information for end users. The quality of any data stored in an information system must also be *maintained* by a continual process of correcting and updating activities.

Input	Optical scanning of bar coded tags on merchandise.
Processing	Calculating employee pay, taxes, and other payroll deductions.
Output	Producing reports and displays about sales performance.
Storage	Maintaining records on customers, employees, and products.
Control	Generating audible signals to indicate proper entry of sales data.

Figure 1-7 Business examples of the basic activities of information systems.

For example, data received about a purchase can be (1) *added* to a running total of sales results, (2) *compared* to a standard to determine its eligibility for a sales discount, (3) *sorted* by arranging it in a numerical order based on a product identification number, (4) *classified* into product categories (such as food and nonfood items), and (5) *summarized* to provide a sales manager with information about sales summarized by various product categories, and (6) used to update sales records to reflect new sales transactions.

Output of Information Products

Information in various forms is transmitted to end users and made available to them in the output activity. The goal of information systems is the production of appropriate **information products** for end users. Common information products are *video displays, paper documents,* and *audio responses* that provide us with *messages, forms, reports, listings, graphics displays,* and so on. We use the information provided by these products to improve our personal and professional performances as we work in organizations and live in society.

Storage of Data, Model, and Knowledge Resources

Storage is a basic system component of information systems. Storage is the information system activity in which data and information resources are retained in an organized manner for later use. For example, just as written text material is organized into words, sentences, paragraphs, and documents, stored data is commonly organized into *fields, records, files,* and *databases.* This facilitates its later use in processing or its retrieval as output when needed by users of a system. These common *data elements* are shown in Figure 1–8.

Figure 1–8 Common data elements. This is a common method of organizing stored data in information systems.

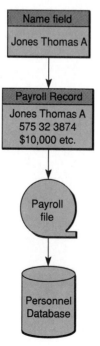

- A **field** is a grouping of characters that represent a characteristic of a person, place, thing, or event. For example, an employee's *name field.*

- A **record** is a collection of interrelated fields. For example, an employee's *payroll record* might consist of a name field, a social security number field, a department field, and a salary field.

- A **file** is a collection of interrelated records. For example, a *payroll file* might consist of the payroll *records* of all employees of a firm.

- A **database** is an integrated collection of interrelated records or files. For example, the *personnel database* of a business might contain payroll, personnel action, and employee skills files.

The vital data and information resources of an organization are typically stored by information systems in the following forms:

☐ **Databases,** which store processed and organized data needed by organizations and end users.

☐ **Model bases,** which store conceptual, mathematical, and logical models that express business relationships, computational routines, or analytical techniques.

☐ **Knowledge bases,** which store knowledge about various subjects in a variety of forms such as facts and rules.

For example, sales data can be accumulated and stored in a sales database for later processing, which produces sales analysis reports for managers. Information systems called *decision support systems* rely on model bases for decision rules and analytical techniques to help managers with decisions. Other information systems known as *expert systems* use knowledge bases to develop inferences about specific subjects to give end users expert advice. We will explore these concepts further in the next chapter.

Control of System Performance

An information system should produce feedback about its input, processing, output, and storage activities. This feedback must be monitored and evaluated to determine if the system is meeting established performance standards. Then system activities must be adjusted so that proper information products are produced for end users. For example, if *subtotals* of sales amounts in a sales report do not add up to *total sales*, then input or processing procedures would have to be changed to accumulate correctly all sales transactions captured and processed by an information system.

An information system includes four major types of resources: hardware, software, people, and data. Let's briefly discuss some basic concepts and examples of how these resources contribute to information processing. Figure 1–9 provides examples of information system resources and products.

Information System Resources

Hardware Resources

The concept of **hardware resources** should include *all physical devices and materials* used in information processing. Specifically, this should include not only **machines,** such as computers or calculators, but also all data **media**—that is, *all tangible objects on which data is recorded*, whether a sheet of paper or a magnetic disk. Examples of hardware in computer-based information systems are:

☐ Large *mainframe* computers, *minicomputers*, and *microcomputer* systems.

☐ *Computer workstations*, which use a keyboard for input of data, a video screen or printer for output of information, and *magnetic* or *optical disks for storage.*

Figure 1–9 Examples of information system resources and products.

Hardware Resources

Machines—computers, optical scanners, video monitors, magnetic disk drives, printers.
Media—floppy disks, magnetic tape, optical disks, plastic cards, paper forms.

Software Resources

Programs—operating system programs, spreadsheet programs, word processing programs, payroll programs.
Procedures—data entry procedures, error correction procedures, paycheck distribution procedures.

People Resources

Specialists—systems analysts, programmers, computer operators.
End Users—anyone else who uses information systems.

Data Resources

Product descriptions, customer records, employee files, inventory databases.

Information Products

Management reports and business documents using text and graphics displays, audio responses, and paper forms.

☐ *Telecommunications networks*, which consist of computers, workstations, communications processors, and other devices interconnected by a variety of telecommunications media to provide computing power throughout an organization.

Software Resources

The concept of **software resources** should include *all sets of information processing instructions*. This generic concept of software can be applied to all instructions needed to operate manual, mechanical, or computer-based information systems. Thus, software resources include not only the sets of operating instructions called **programs,** which direct and control computer hardware, but also the sets of information processing instructions needed by people, called **procedures.** The following are examples of such software:

☐ *System software*, such as an *operating system* program, which controls and supports the operations of a computer system.
☐ *Application software*, which are programs that direct processing for a particular use of computers by end users. Examples are an inventory program, a payroll program, or a word processing program.
☐ *Procedures*, which are operating instructions for the people who will operate and use an information system. Examples are instructions on how to fill out a paper form or use a software package.

People Resources

People are required for the operation of all information systems. These **people resources** include *specialists* and *end users*.

☐ **Specialists** are people who develop and operate information systems. They include systems analysts, programmers, computer operators, and other managerial, technical, and clerical personnel. Basically, *systems analysts* design information systems based on the information requirements of end users; *programmers* prepare computer programs based on the specifications of systems analysts; and *computer operators* operate large computer systems. The job activities of such specialists are discussed in Chapter 13.

☐ **End users** (also called *users* or *clients*) are people who use an information system or the information it produces. They can be accountants, salespeople, engineers, clerks, customers, or managers. Most of us are information system end users.

Data Resources

Data is more than the raw material of information systems. The concept of data resources has been broadened by managers and information systems professionals. They realize that data and information of many types constitute a valuable organizational resource. Thus, data and information stored in databases, model bases, and knowledge bases are now considered to be part of the **data resources** or **information resources** of an organization.

Data can take many forms. Examples include traditional *alphanumeric data*, composed of numbers and alphabetical and special characters that describe business transactions and other events and entities. *Text data*, consisting of sentences and paragraphs used in written communications, and *image data*, such as graphic shapes and figures, are also important forms of data. However, data frequently takes the form of *video data*, data presented for viewing by a variety of video display devices; *audio data*, the human voice and other sounds; *tactile data*, generated by touch-sensitive materials; and *sensor data*, provided by a variety of sensors used in the control of physical processes.

Data resources are typically recorded and stored on several types of *data media*, including paper, magnetic, optical, film, or electronic media. Examples are paper documents, magnetic disks, magnetic tape, optical disks, microfilm, and electronic circuit chips.

RECOGNIZING INFORMATION SYSTEMS

There are many kinds of information systems in the real world. Some are simple *manual* information systems, where people use simple tools such as pencils and paper, or even machines such as calculators and typewriters, to transform data into information. Others are **computer-based information systems** that use one or more types of computers and a variety of computer devices to process data automatically. These are frequently called **electronic data processing** (EDP) systems. However, whether they are manual or computer-based systems, you should be able to use an information system model and

Figure 1–10 Information system components in a computer-based information system for inventory control.

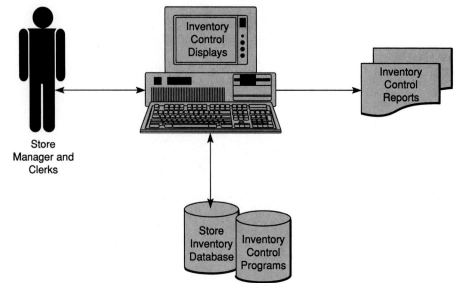

other system concepts to help you understand the information systems that you encounter in the real world. Let's see if we can do this right now by analyzing an example of a computer-based information system.

An Example of a Computer-Based Information System

Figure 1–10 illustrates some of the components you might see in a microcomputer-based information system used for inventory control by a store manager like Bill Kruse of Back Bay Hardware. Hardware resources include machines, like the microcomputer and its keyboard, video monitor, printer, and magnetic disk drives, and media consisting of magnetic disks and printer paper. Software resources include inventory control programs executed by the microcomputer and procedures followed by the store manager. People resources include the store manager and clerks who operate the system, and any information system consultants who may have helped acquire or develop its hardware and software.

Data resources (sales and inventory activity data) and various commands and inquiries are entered into the system as input through the keyboard by the store manager. Processing is accomplished by the *microprocessor*, or central processing unit of the microcomputer, under the control of inventory control programs and the procedures followed by the clerks and the store manager. Output of information products needed for inventory control is accomplished by a variety of video displays and printed reports. Storage of data and software resources is provided by magnetic disks on which are stored a database of inventory records and the inventory control programs.

Computers and Computer Systems

It is important not to confuse this example of a computer-based information system with the concept of a *computer* and a *computer system*. What is a **computer**?

A computer is a device that has the ability to accept data, internally store and automatically execute a program of instructions, perform mathematical, logical, and manipulative operations on data, and report the results.

In our previous example, the **computer system** is the integrated group of hardware devices that is used as an information processing tool by the sales manager. Thus, the computer system consists of the microcomputer main system unit (processing, storage, and control), keyboard (input), magnetic disk drives (storage), and the video monitor and printer (output).

Typically, a computer system will take the form of a *microcomputer, minicomputer,* or large *mainframe* computer. However, whether it sits on your desk or is one of many computers in an organization-wide telecommunications network, a computer system still represents only the *hardware resources* component of a computer-based information system. As we have just seen, an information system also needs software, people, and data resources. The topic of computer systems is explored in Chapter 3.

REAL WORLD CASE

Nissan Motor Company

"It's a very competitive market," says Ken Goltara, corporate manager for information systems at Nissan, of the market for its luxury car Infiniti. "We're striving to improve customer satisfaction and trying to protect dealer profits to make the customer happy and make the dealer want to be in this line of business," Goltara says. To gain an edge in that tough environment, Nissan and its suppliers spent 18 months developing an integrated network called Infinitinet, which links every dealer in the United States to the corporation's mainframe in Carson, California.

The goal of Infinitinet is to improve the front end applications—in sales, parts, and service—where the dealership comes in contact with the customer. The key to those improvements is linking the information systems at each dealership to Nissan's corporate systems. Therefore, IBM AS/400 minicomputers, connected by satellite transmission links to the corporate mainframe computer, are located at each dealership. A series of IBM PS/2 microcomputers link the

dealer's sales and business staff to the AS/400. Each PS/2 has four main modes: (1) as a standalone PC using its own software and data files, (2) connection to the applications software and database residing on the AS/400, (3) communications with applications of the corporate IBM 3090 in California and (4) as a printer for the mini. The dealer's mechanics and other service personnel use terminals that can access either the local mini or the mainframe. The figure below summarizes how car dealers use Infinitinet.

Application Questions

☐ Identify the input, processing, output, storage, and control activities in Nissan's Infinitinet information system.

☐ Identify the hardware, software, people, and data resources and the information products of this information system.

☐ What are the business benefits of Infinitinet?

Source: Adapted from Chris Sivula, "The IS Engine Driving Infiniti," *Datamation,* February 15, 1990, pp. 89–91.

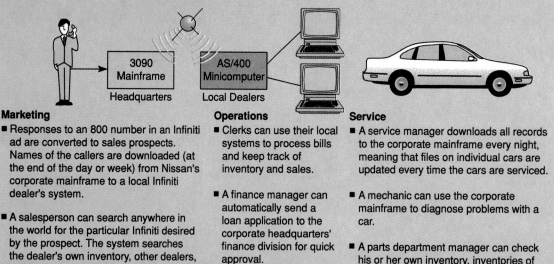

Marketing
- Responses to an 800 number in an Infiniti ad are converted to sales prospects. Names of the callers are downloaded (at the end of the day or week) from Nissan's corporate mainframe to a local Infiniti dealer's system.

- A salesperson can search anywhere in the world for the particular Infiniti desired by the prospect. The system searches the dealer's own inventory, other dealers, a shipping port in California, or the factory in Japan.

Operations
- Clerks can use their local systems to process bills and keep track of inventory and sales.

- A finance manager can automatically send a loan application to the corporate headquarters' finance division for quick approval.

Service
- A service manager downloads all records to the corporate mainframe every night, meaning that files on individual cars are updated every time the cars are serviced.

- A mechanic can use the corporate mainframe to diagnose problems with a car.

- A parts department manager can check his or her own inventory, inventories of other dealers, or Nissan's warehouse to find the quickest way to find parts.

Section III: Computers Past, Present, and Future

You have been introduced to the concepts of computer-based information system hardware, software, and people resources—and their use in processing data resources into information products. We will cover these topics in more detail in subsequent chapters. But before we go any further, we should take a brief look at how computers developed into the vital tools they are today.

It is important for you to understand the major trends that have developed in each major stage or **generation** in the development of computers so you can be prepared for the developments expected to continue into the future. The first generation of computers began in the early 1950s, the second generation in the late 1950s, the third generation in the mid-1960s, while the fourth generation began in the early 1970s and continues to the present time. A fifth generation of computers is expected to arrive during the 1990s.

Volumes could be written on the past, present, and future of computers. Instead, this section provides you with the following brief **time capsules.** Read them for an understanding of the high points of historical developments in computing, as well as the trends in computing expected to continue into the future.

TIME CAPSULES

- ☐ The Origin of Computing Machines
- ☐ Computer Pioneers
- ☐ The First Three Generations
- ☐ The Present Fourth Generation
- ☐ The Future Fifth Generation

TIME CAPSULE: THE ORIGIN OF COMPUTING MACHINES

The modern computer has many origins, some well known, some lost in antiquity. Early manual computing devices and the use of machinery to perform arithmetic operations were important advancements. However, these and other devices were not computers, though they were important contributions to the development of machine computation.

☐ The earliest data processing devices included the use of fingers, stones, and sticks for counting, and knots on a string, scratches on a rock, or notches in a stick as record-keeping devices. The Babylonians wrote on clay tablets with a sharp stick, while the ancient Egyptians developed written records on papyrus using a sharp-pointed reed as a pen and organic dyes for ink. The earliest form of manual calculating device was the *abacus*. The use of pebbles or rods laid out on a lined or grooved board were early forms of the abacus and were used for thousands of years in many civilizations. The abacus in its present form originated in China and is still used as a calculator.

☐ The use of machinery to perform arithmetic operations is frequently attributed to Blaise Pascal of France and Gottfried von Leibnitz of Germany for their development of the *adding machine* and the *calculating machine*, respectively, in the 17th century. (The programming language **Pascal** is named in honor of Blaise Pascal.) However, the inventions of Pascal and Leibnitz incorporated some ideas similar to those used in the clockwork mechanism and the odometer, both of which had been developed as far back as the Greek and Roman civilizations. It must also be recognized that the calculators of Pascal and Leibnitz—and other early mechanical data processing devices—were not reliable machines. The contributions of many persons were necessary during the next two centuries before practical, working data processing machines were developed.

☐ The use of *electromechanical punched card machines* for the automatic processing of data recorded by holes punched in paper cards was another major development in machine computation. Punched cards were developed in France by Joseph Jacquard during the 18th century to automatically control textile weaving equipment. However, their use in data processing originated with the work of the statistician Dr. Herman Hollerith during the 1880s. He was hired by the U.S. Bureau of the Census to develop new ways to process census data. The 1880 census report had not been completed until 1887, and it became evident that the processing of the 1890 census might not be completed before the 1900 census would get under way.

Dr. Hollerith developed a punched paper card for the recording of data, a hand-operated card punch, a sorting box, and a tabulator that allowed the 1890 census to be completed in less than three years. Dr. Hollerith then left the Census Bureau to start a business firm to produce punched card machines. The International Business Machines Corporation (IBM) is a descendant of Dr. Hollerith's Tabulating Machine Company.

☐ Improvements in punched card machines led to their widespread use in the late 1930s. These machines could "read" the data from punched cards when electrical impulses were generated by the action of metal brushes making electrical contact through the holes punched in a card. Data processing operations were "programmed" by an externally wired removable control panel. Electromechanical punched card machines continued to be the major method for large-scale "automatic data processing" (ADP) in business and government until the late 1950s, when they were made obsolete by the development of computers.

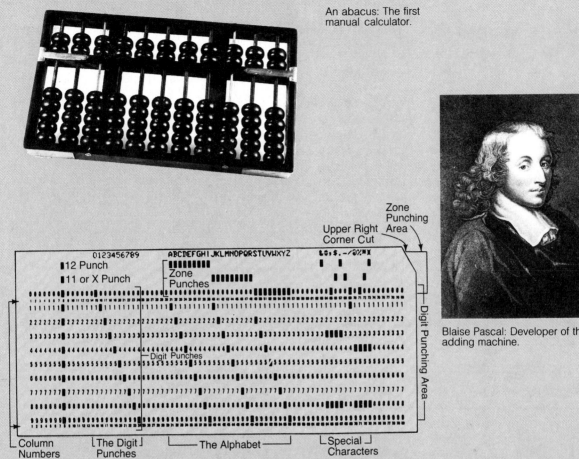

An abacus: The first manual calculator.

Blaise Pascal: Developer of the first adding machine.

A punched card: Note the explanation of the *Hollerith* coding used in such cards.

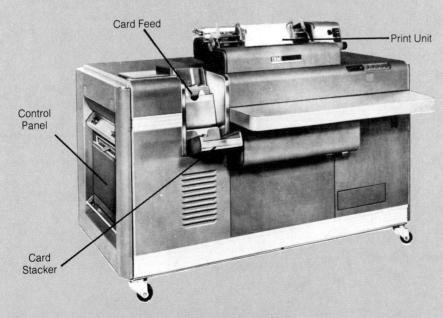

An electromechanical punched card accounting machine.

TIME CAPSULE: COMPUTER PIONEERS

Charles Babbage is generally recognized as the first person to propose the concept of the modern computer. He designed and partially built a steam-driven mechanical calculator called the "difference engine" with the help of a grant from the British government. In 1833, this English mathematician outlined in detail his plans for an "analytical engine," a mechanical steam-driven computing machine that would accept punched card input, automatically perform any arithmetic operation in any sequence under the direction of a mechanically stored program of instructions, and produce either punched card or printed output. He produced thousands of detailed drawings before his death in 1871, but the machine was never built. Babbage had designed the world's first general-purpose, stored-program, digital computer. However, his ideas were too advanced for the steam-driven technology of his time, and they had to await the development of electrical and electronic components over 100 years later.

Many of Babbage's ideas were recorded and analyzed by Lady Augusta Ada Byron, Countess of Lovelace, the daughter of Lord Byron, the famous English poet. She is considered by some to be the world's first computer programmer. The programming language **Ada** is named in her honor.

Almost 100 years passed before the ideas outlined by Babbage began to be developed. Highlights of this pioneering period include:

☐ Vannevar Bush of the Massachusetts Institute of Technology (MIT) built a large-scale electromechanical analog computer in 1925.

☐ Konrad Zuse of Germany built an electromechanical digital computer in 1941. Called the Z3, it used electrical switches (relays) to perform its computations.

☐ The first large-scale electromechanical digital computer was developed by Howard Aiken of Harvard University with the support of IBM in 1944. Aiken's Automatic Sequence Controlled Calculator, nicknamed MARK I, used electrical relays instead of mechanical gears. It relied heavily on the concepts of IBM's punched card calculator developed in the 1930s.

☐ The first working model of an electronic digital computer was built by John Atanasoff of Iowa State University in 1942. The ABC (Atanasoff-Berry Computer) used vacuum tubes instead of electrical relays to carry out its computations.

☐ The first operational electronic digital computer, the ENIAC (Electronic Numerical Integrator and Calculator), was developed by John Mauchly and J. P. Eckert of the University of Pennsylvania in 1946. THe ENIAC weighed over 30 tons and utilized over 18,000 vacuum tubes instead of the electromechanical relays of the Mark I. The ENIAC was built to compute artillery ballistic tables for the U.S. Army; it could complete in 15 seconds a trajectory computation that would take a skilled person with a desk calculator about 10 hours to complete. However, the ENIAC did not use a stored program of instructions and relied on the decimal system. Its processing was controlled externally by switches and control panels that had to be changed for each new series of computations.

☐ The first stored-program electronic computer was EDSAC (Electronic Delayed Storage Automatic Computer), developed under the direction of M. V. Wilkes at Cambridge University, England, in 1949.

☐ The EDSAC and the first American stored-program computer, the EDVAC (Electronic Discrete Variable Automatic Computer), which was completed in 1952, were based on concepts advanced in 1945 by Dr. John von Neumann of the Institute for Advanced Study in Princeton, New Jersey. He proposed that the operating instructions, or *program*, of the computer be stored in a high-speed internal storage unit, or *memory*, and that both data and instructions be represented internally by the *binary* number system (which uses only the two digits 0 and 1) rather than the decimal system. These and other computer design concepts form the basis for much of the design of today's computers.

Several other early computers and many individuals could be mentioned in a discussion of the pioneering period of computer development. However, the high points already discussed should illustrate that many persons and many ideas were responsible for the birth of the computer.

The difference engine: A mechanical calculator built by Babbage.

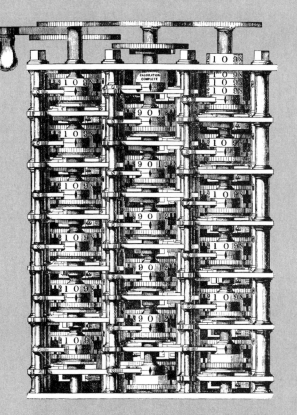

Charles Babbage: He first proposed the concept of a computer.

The ENIAC computer: The first general-purpose electronic digital computer. Also shown is one of its inventors, J. P. Eckert.

Augusta Ada Byron: Considered to be the first computer programmer.

TIME CAPSULE: THE FIRST THREE GENERATIONS

The UNIVAC I (Universal Automatic Computer), the first general-purpose electronic digital computer to be commercially available, marks the beginning of the **first generation** of computers. Highlights of this generation include:

☐ The first UNIVAC was installed at the Bureau of Census in 1951. The UNIVAC I became the first computer to process business applications when it was installed at a General Electric manufacturing plant in Louisville, Kentucky, in 1954. An innovation of the UNIVAC I was the use of *magnetic tape* as an input and output medium.

☐ Another first-generation computer, the IBM 650, was an intermediate-size computer designed for both business and scientific applications. It had a *magnetic drum* memory and used punched cards for input and output.

☐ Computers developed before the first generation were special-purpose one-of-a-kind machines, whereas 48 UNIVAC Is and almost 2,000 IBM 650s were built.

☐ The first-generation computers were quite large and produced enormous amounts of heat because of their use of **vacuum tubes.** They had large electrical power, air-conditioning, maintenance, and space requirements.

The **second generation** of computers was introduced in 1959. Highlights of this generation include:

☐ Vacuum tubes were replaced by **transistors** and other *solid state, semiconductor* devices. Transistorized circuits were a lot smaller, generated little heat, were less expensive, and required less power than vacuum tube circuits. Second-generation computers were thus significantly smaller and faster and more reliable than first-generation machines.

☐ The use of *magnetic cores* for the computer's *memory*, or internal storage and the introduction of removable *magnetic disk packs* were other major hardware developments of the second generation. Magnetic tape emerged as the major input/output and *secondary* storage medium for large computer installations, with punched cards continuing to be widely used.

The introduction of the IBM System/360 series of computers in 1964 signaled the arrival of the **third generation** of computers. Highlights of this generation include:

☐ Transistorized circuitry was replaced by **integrated circuits** in which all the elements of an electronic circuit were contained on a small silicon wafer or *chip.* These microelectronic circuits were smaller and more reliable than transistorized circuits and significantly increased the speed and reduced the size of the third-generation computers.

☐ The *family,* or *series,* concept, which provides standardization and compatibility between different models in a computer series, was developed. Manufacturers claimed to have developed computers that could handle both business and scientific applications and process programs written for other models without major modifications.

☐ The emergence of *time-sharing* (where many users at different terminals can share the same computer at the same time), *data communications* applications, and the ability to process several programs simultaneously through *multiprogramming* were other features of the third generation.

☐ The third generation marked the growth in importance of software as a means of efficiently using computers. **Operating system** programs were developed to supervise computer processing. High-level programming languages, such as FORTRAN and COBOL, greatly simplified computer programming since they allowed program instructions to be expressed in a form that more closely resembles human language or the standard notation of mathematics.

☐ **Application software packages** (prewritten programs for users) proliferated as the number of independent software companies grew rapidly. This was the result of the *unbundling* of software and hardware in 1969 by IBM and other manufacturers. They began to charge separately for software and other services instead of including them in the price of the hardware.

☐ The first **minicomputer**, the PDP–8, was marketed by the Digital Equipment Corporation in 1965. These small computers had greater computing power than larger second-generation systems and came into widespread use.

The UNIVAC I: The first commercially available electronic digital computer. Also shown is J. P. Eckert and newscaster Walter Cronkite.

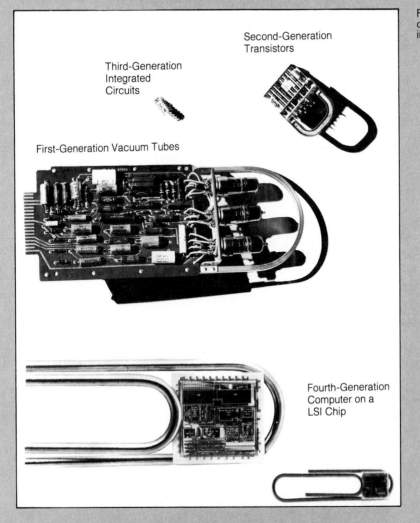

Four generations of computer circuitry. Notice the major changes in the size of these circuits.

TIME CAPSULE: THE PRESENT FOURTH GENERATION

The **fourth generation** began in the 1970s and continues to the present time. The following developments are highlights of the fourth generation:

☐ A major technological development was the use of LSI (large scale integration) semiconductor circuits for both the *logic* and *memory* circuitry of computers. LSI semiconductor technology enables thousands of electronic circuits to be placed on tiny chips of silicon. Computers thus began to use *semiconductor memory chips* instead of the *magnetic core* memories used in second- and third-generation computers.

☐ Another milestone was the development of the Intel 4004, the first commercially available **microprocessor** in 1971. All of the circuitry for the main processing unit of a computer was placed on a single chip! This was followed by the development of the Intel 8080 microprocessor in 1974, which was used in the first commercially available **microcomputer** system, the Altair 8800 in 1975. However, microcomputer sales and uses did not grow dramatically until the development of the Apple II by Steve Jobs and Steve Wozniak in 1978 and the IBM Personal Computer in 1981. By the mid-1980s millions of microcomputer systems were used in homes, schools, and businesses.

☐ Main memory capacity of fourth-generation computers increased dramatically. For example, a medium-size second-generation business computer like the IBM 1401 had a memory of 4,000 to 16,000 character positions of storage. In comparison, the fourth-generation IBM AS/400 Model B50 mid-size computer has a main memory capacity of 16 to 48 *million* characters of storage. Even microcomputers soon had memories ranging from hundreds of thousands to millions of storage positions. The cost of such memory capacity dropped in the same period from about $2 per character to only a fraction of a cent per character of storage.

☐ The trend toward increased microminiaturization significantly reduced the cost, size, and power requirements of fourth-generation computers and greatly increased their processing speeds. Processing speeds in billionths of a second and in millions of instructions per second are common. The computing power of third-generation mid-size computers costing hundreds of thousands of dollars can now be purchased with fourth-generation microcomputers costing only a few thousand dollars.

☐ Another trend was the increased use of *direct input/output* devices to provide a more natural *user interface*. Data and instructions were increasingly entered into a computer system directly through a keyboard or other input devices such as the *electronic mouse, light pens, touch screens, data tablets*, and *optical scanning wands*. Direct output of information through video displays of text and graphics and audio (voice) response devices also became commonplace.

☐ The trend toward programming languages that were easy to use and more like human languages continued. *Database management systems* and *natural* or *fourth-generation* languages not only make programming computers easier for programmers but reduce the need for traditional programming. Thus, end users do not have to tell the computer *how* to do a task, but only *what* task they want accomplished.

☐ Easy-to-use software packages for microcomputer users, such as *electronic spreadsheet* and *word processing* programs were developed. The development of the VisiCalc electronic spreadsheet program and the WordStar word processing package in 1979, and the dBASE II database management package and the Lotus 1-2-3 spreadsheet package in 1982 contributed to the purchase of millions of software packages by microcomputer users.

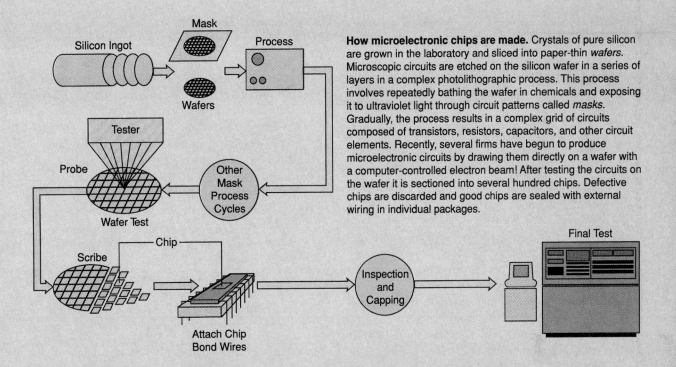

How microelectronic chips are made. Crystals of pure silicon are grown in the laboratory and sliced into paper-thin *wafers*. Microscopic circuits are etched on the silicon wafer in a series of layers in a complex photolithographic process. This process involves repeatedly bathing the wafer in chemicals and exposing it to ultraviolet light through circuit patterns called *masks*. Gradually, the process results in a complex grid of circuits composed of transistors, resistors, capacitors, and other circuit elements. Recently, several firms have begun to produce microelectronic circuits by drawing them directly on a wafer with a computer-controlled electron beam! After testing the circuits on the wafer it is sectioned into several hundred chips. Defective chips are discarded and good chips are sealed with external wiring in individual packages.

	First Generation	Second Generation	Third Generation	Fourth Generation	Fifth Generation
SIZE (Typical computers)	Room Size	Closet Size	Desk-Size Minicomputer	Typewriter-Size Microcomputer	Credit Card-Size Micro?
CIRCUITRY	Vacuum tubes	Transistors	Integrated Semi-conductor Circuits	Large-Scale Inte-grated (LSI) Semi-Conductor Circuits	Very Large-Scale Integrated (VLSI) Superconductor Circuits?
DENSITY (Components per circuit)	One	Hundreds	Thousands	Hundreds of Thousands	Millions?
SPEED (Instructions/second)	Hundreds	Thousands	Millions	Tens of Millions	Billions?
RELIABILITY (Failure of circuits)	Hours	Days	Weeks	Months	Years?
MEMORY (Capacity in characters)	Thousands	Tens of Thousands	Hundreds of Thousands	Millions	Billions?
COST (Per million instructions)	$10	$1.00	$.10	$.001	$.0001?

Trends in computer characteristics and capabilities

TIME CAPSULE: THE FUTURE FIFTH GENERATION

Developments in the present fourth computer generation indicate the continued revolutionary impact of computers on business and the rest of society. It is apparent that several major trends will continue into a future **fifth generation** of computing.

☐ *Intelligent computers* with the ability to think, see, listen, and talk are the goal of the fifth generation! These computers will depend on a *parallel processing* computer architecture that is different from the traditional *von Neumann design* of most current computers. That is, fifth-generation computers will process data and instructions in *parallel* (many at a time), instead of *serially* (one at a time) as in today's computers. The development of intelligent computer systems is one of the major goals of the science of *artificial intelligence* (AI).

☐ The fifth generation will also accelerate the trend toward direct input/output of data and instructions. Voice and visual input will be coupled with voice and visual output to make obsolete most present methods of communicating with a computer.

☐ Computer hardware costs and sizes will continue to decrease steadily. This will be a major effect of the increased use of VLSI (very large-scale integration) technology, where hundreds of thousands and even millions of circuit elements are placed on a microelectronic chip. This trend will accelerate with the development of *superconductor* circuit materials which do not need supercold temperatures to dramatically increase the speed of electronic circuits.

☐ Also making their appearance are *optical computers* that use *photonic*, or optoelectronic, circuits rather than electronic circuits. They process data using pulses of laser light instead of electronic pulses, and they operate near the speed of light. Further into the future are extremely small, fast, and powerful *biocomputers* grown from organic materials using individual cells as circuits!

☐ Computer software will continue to grow in its ease of use and versatility. Users will converse with computers in natural human languages. Application software packages will become integrated, multipurpose programs that can easily handle a variety of tasks for nontechnical users.

☐ Use of microcomputers and microprocessors will continue to increase dramatically. *Smart products* will multiply as microcomputer intelligence is built into more and more consumer, commercial, and industrial products.

☐ The office of the future will become a reality by blending information systems technology and telecommunications. Networks of computer *workstations* and other computerized office devices will accelerate the use of *office automation* systems, such as *electronic mail, voice mail, image processing*, and *teleconferencing* systems.

☐ Advanced telecommunications-based information systems will merge the transmission and processing of data, images, and voices. This will involve extensive use of computers and *fiber optics* technology in *integrated services digital networks*.

☐ Automated factories will become commonplace as information systems technology and artificial intelligence technologies such as *robotics* transform the factory floor. Factory automation results from a drive toward *computer-integrated manufacturing*, which integrates the use of computer-aided design, computer-aided manufacturing, robotics, and other manufacturing technologies to automate the entire manufacturing process.

☐ Computers and computerized workstations will become integrated into everyday business operations in offices, small business firms, wholesale and retail outlets, warehouses, and factories. Managers will rely heavily on easy-to-use *executive information systems*, while all types of end users will depend on *expert systems* based on artificial intelligence to help them perform their work assignments.

☐ Everyday use of computer-based systems in many areas—such as *electronic funds transfer* systems in banking, *point-of-sale* systems in retailing, *computer-aided systems engineering* tools to automate information systems development, *computer-assisted instruction* systems in education, *telecommuting* systems for in-home work activities, and *videotex* systems for electronic shopping, banking, and information services in the home—will increase dramatically. Thus, society as a whole will become even more reliant on computers as we enter the 21st century.

REAL WORLD CASE

Pier 1 Imports, Inc.

It takes months of dickering, careful translating, and political string-pulling to get a shipment of wicker ottomans out of Bombay. That is one reason why Pier 1 Imports, Inc., which buys 85 percent of its merchandise from exotic, relatively inaccessible ports, needs a state-of-the-art inventory management system. "We can't just re-order merchandise like that in two or three days like most retailers. It takes months to get this stuff from overseas," said Harold Muller, Jr., vice president of Pier 1's information services division.

Consequently, merchandise shortages and item overstock—both deadly to the bottom line—are constant hazards at this furnishing and clothing retailer. But Pier 1 is getting help from a new inventory management system that aids buyers in determining when and how much merchandise to import. This application is installed on the firm's personal computer–based point-of-sale (POS) system.

The IBM-compatible PCs, located in the chain's 5,000 stores and distribution centers, are linked by communications lines to an IBM 3090 mainframe computer at headquarters. The PCs communicate constantly with the mainframe, updating the master inventory file and alerting distribution centers to ship specific merchandise to stores. In turn, the mainframe-based portion of the application analyzes sales statistics and forecasts demand, alerting Pier 1 buyers when to call on suppliers in India, China, Japan, and other countries.

Pier 1 currently leaves inventory control in the hands of each store manager. Headquarters produces an inventory availability report, from which store managers can order stock based on what is selling. But that system is becoming impractical in light of Pier 1's growth. The chain had doubled in size in the last four years and plans to double again by 1993. Its active SKUs, or retail items, have ballooned to 7,000. "It's become impossible for the store manager to manage inventory effectively," said Muller, whose staff of 75 serves about 1,100 users nationwide.

Besides taking some of the burden away from managers, the system also relieves them of some of their independence. "We're taking price-change management out of their hands," Muller noted. Currently, store managers are at liberty to reject price reductions set by headquarters. Indeed, most of the time, managers ignore the price change in order to keep their own margins high, Muller said. "This slowed sales and backed up inventory at the distribution centers," he explained. With the new system, when a sales clerk punches in an item's code, the PC accesses the mainframe for the corporate price and rings it up automatically. Such regimentation also helps prevent fraud at the store level, Muller noted.

Pier 1's mainframe also plots POS-supplied customer ZIP codes and purchasing data on geographic charts. By analyzing this data, the company can tell which locations would be the best candidates for new stores. It can also determine the types of merchandise that sell best in the various demographic regions. All of this adds up to a more carefully targeted consumer market. Muller said he expects the new system to affect the bottom line in 12 to 18 months: "It will reduce inventory levels at the stores and warehouses, which will reduce our overhead."

Application Questions

☐ Identify the input, processing, output, storage, and control activities in Pier 1's inventory management information system.

☐ Identify the hardware, software, people, and data resources and the information products of this information system.

☐ How essential to Pier 1's success are its POS and inventory information systems? Explain.

Source: Adapted from Richard Pastore, "Pier 1 Pursuing Shipshape Shelves," *Computerworld*, March 5, 1990, p. 37.

SUMMARY

☐ Computer-based information systems play a vital role in the operations, management, and strategic success of business firms and other organizations in today's information society. Therefore, it is important that business end users have a knowledge of five basic areas of information systems. They should understand (1) several foundation concepts about information systems and their roles in organizations, (2) how information system solutions can be developed for business problems, (3) major concepts and developments in the technology of information systems, (4) the major applications of information systems to end user activities and business operations and management, and (5) how to meet the major challenges of managing information system resources and activities.

☐ A system is a group of interrelated components working toward the attainment of a common goal by accepting inputs and producing outputs in an organized transformation process. Feedback is information concerning the components and operations of the system. Control is the component that monitors and evaluates feedback to determine if the system is moving toward the achievement of its goal, and then makes necessary adjustments to the input and processing components to ensure that proper output is produced.

☐ The business firm should be viewed as a system in which economic resources (input) are transformed by various organizational processes (processing) into goods and services (output). Information systems thus play a vital role by providing information on the operation of the business (feedback) to management for the direction and maintenance of the firm (control). A business firm is a subsystem of society and shares inputs and outputs with other systems in its environment.

☐ An information system uses the resources of hardware (machines and media), software (programs and procedures), and people (specialists and end users) to perform input, processing, output, storage, and control activities that transform data resources into information products. Data is first collected for processing (input), then manipulated or converted into information (processing), stored for future use (storage), or communicated to its ultimate user (output) according to correct processing procedures (control).

☐ Hardware resources include both machines and media used in information processing. Software resources include both computerized instructions (programs) and instructions for people (procedures). People resources include both information systems specialists and end users. Data resources include both traditional numeric and alphabetic data, and text, image, video, audio, and sensor data. Information products produced by an information system can take a variety of forms, including paper reports, visual displays, documents, messages, graphics, and audio responses.

☐ Business end users should understand the major trends in computing that have developed and are expected to continue into the future. Major trends and developments in computers and information systems during five computer generations are summarized in the Time Capsules of Section III of this chapter.

These are the key terms and concepts of this chapter. The page number of their first explanation is in parentheses.

1. A business as a system (*14*)
2. Adaptive system (*13*)
3. Computer generations (*25*)
4. Computer system (*23*)
5. Computer-based information system (*22*)
6. Control (*12*)
7. Data (*15*)
8. Data or information processing (*15*)
9. Environment (*13*)
10. Feedback (*11*)
11. Hardware resources (*19*)
    a. Machines
    b. Media
12. Information (*15*)
13. Information system (*16*)
14. Information system activities
    a. Input (*16*)
    b. Processing (*17*)
    c. Output (*18*)
    d. Storage (*18*)
    e. Control (*19*)
15. Information system resources (*19*)
16. Interface (*13*)
17. Knowledge needed about information systems (*8*)
18. Knowledge workers (*6*)
19. Open system (*13*)
20. People resources (*21*)
    a. Specialists
    b. End users
21. Software resources (*20*)
    a. Programs
    b. Procedures
22. Subsystem (*13*)
23. System (*11*)
24. Trends in computing (*33*)

Match one of the **key terms and concepts** listed above with one of the examples or definitions listed below. Look for the best fit for answers that seem to fit more than one key term or concept. Defend your choices.

_____ 1. A system which uses hardware, software, and people resources to perform information processing activities that transform data resources into information products.

_____ 2. An information system that uses computers and their hardware and software.

_____ 3. An integrated grouping of hardware components that automatically performs information processing operations.

_____ 4. Anyone who uses an information system or the information it produces.

_____ 5. People who spend most of their workday creating, using, and distributing information.

_____ 6. You should know some fundamental concepts about information systems and their technology, development, applications, and management.

_____ 7. A group of interrelated components working together toward the attainment of a common goal.

_____ 8. Data about a system's performance.

_____ 9. Making adjustments to a system's components so that it operates properly.

_____ 10. A shared boundary between systems.

_____ 11. A system that exchanges inputs and outputs with its environment.

_____ 12. A system that can change itself or its environment in order to survive.

_____ 13. Information systems are the feedback component of this organizational system.

_____ 14. Facts or observations.

_____ 15. Data placed into a meaningful context for an end user.

_____ 16. The act of converting data into information.

_____ 17. Programs and procedures.

_____ 18. Sets of instructions for a computer.

_____ 19. Sets of instructions for people.

_____ 20. Machines and media.

_____ 21. Computer disk drives, video monitors, and printers.

_____ 22. Magnetic disks, magnetic tape, and paper forms.

_____ 23. Computer systems analysts, programmers, and operators.

_____ 24. Using the keyboard of a computer to enter data.

_____ 25. Doing loan payment calculations.

_____ 26. Printing a letter you wrote using a computer.

_____ 27. Saving a copy of the letter on a magnetic disk.

_____ 28. Having a sales receipt to document a purchase you made.

_____ 29. Major stages in the development of computers.

_____ 30. Computers are becoming smaller, faster, cheaper, and easier to use.

REAL WORLD PROBLEMS

1. Pan Am Corporation

Thomas G. Plaskett, Pan Am's CEO, uses an IBM PS/2 Model 60 microcomputer in his New York office, a Tandy 1400-LT laptop on the road, and a Tandy 2000 at home. Computers are an integral part of his work at the helm of the $3.6 billion airline. He writes notes, letters, outlines, speeches, and position papers with the help of word processing software; tracks names and phone numbers with a database manager; and analyzes financial data with an electronic spreadsheet package.

The net effect of computing on Plaskett's own job performance is something he says he's been able to monitor. "It's helped me to become a better communicator," says Plaskett. "It has helped me respond on a more timely basis to both employees and customers. It has provided me with a filing system for ideas and thoughts that I have access to instantaneously, and just made the use of information much easier." The impact on the company, says Plaskett, is harder to gauge, however. "What impact does improved communication have?" he asks rhetorically. "What impact does a faster response to a customer have? What impact does it have on the decision-making process when you are able to express your thoughts effectively and concisely? I don't know how to measure it, but I don't think there's much doubt that it has contributed to the company in a positive way."

a. How has the use of computers affected Mr. Plaskett's job performance?

b. What impact do you think it has had on his management of Pan Am? Explain.

Source: Adapted from Chris O'Connel, "The Bottom Line: He's a Better Manager," *Personal Computing,* April 1989, p. 79.

2. Wendy's International, Inc.

Aging cash registers, rising wages, and higher food prices have forced the fast-food industry to go leaner and meaner with information systems. The latest entrant in the fast-food grand prix is Wendy's International Inc., which is implementing a microcomputer-based remake of its 1,200 owned and operated stores. "We're in the midst of decentralizing management structure," said Al Huffman, director of technical services. "We need to get more information out to the stores." The program that Wendy's launched this year will place a high-powered personal computer (PC) in the back room of each store. The PC will take information from the store's IBM 3680 point-of-sale register at the end of the day. Then the PC will dial up a mainframe computer at company headquarters in Dublin, Ohio, and dump the day's data. Wendy's will use the data to plan faster and more efficient delivery of inventory and to supply 35 regional offices with critical information and decision support for store operations.

a. What does Wendy's hope to gain by installing microcomputers in its stores?

b. How do you think this will help Wendy's compete in the fast-food business?

Source: Adapted from Dennis Eskow, "Wendy's Turns to PCs to Beef Up Operations," *PC Week,* February 12, 1990, p. 121.

3. Haydel's Bakery

Haydel's Bakery of New Orleans ships its multicolored, doughnut-shaped King Cakes by Federal Express to Mardi Gras revelers celebrating vicariously from Maine to California. Recently, the bakery added an IBM AS/400 minicomputer to the distribution recipe and doubled its business, growing to a $1 million operation, according to Dave Haydel, president. In just the five-week period between Epiphany—the beginning of the Carnival season—and Fat Tuesday—the last day of Mardi Gras—the bakery shipped more than 20,000 of the 1½-foot-by-2-foot cakes.

Orders generated by the bakery's local reputation, national direct mail, and public relations efforts come in by mail or phone. The orders are entered into the minicomputer by temporary personnel who are prompted by data entry displays on their video terminals. Customer files stored on magnetic disk drives are updated immediately by sales order processing and database management programs. Then credit authorizations are processed. Once credit is approved, the system prints a mailing label, which is slapped onto a specially designed shipping carton. The day's orders are collected at 4 P.M. for overnight delivery. The computer then produces a disk containing a report on all the day's deliveries. This is sent, with a check, to Federal Express.

a. Identify some of the input, processing, output, storage, and control activities that you see occurring in Haydel's sales order processing information system.
b. Identify the hardware, software, people, and data resources used, and the information products produced by this information system.

Source: Adapted from "AS/400 Helps Bakery Spread a Flavor of New Orleans," *IBM Update*, March/April 1989, p. 16.

4. **The Movie Business**

Information systems professionals in the movie industry can't expect to do power lunches with Stephen Spielberg or dine with Meryl Streep. John Granaghan, vice president of MIS at Orion Pictures Corp., says he sees more famous people on the streets of New York than on the job. However, Hollywood has a big need for specialists in the use and management of personal computers interconnected by local area telecommunications networks, which movie companies use at production sites. There, workers use PCs to track spending and working hours, monitor budgets, and run payrolls for day workers. Others also use IS technology: animators and music composers do some of their work on PCs, and writers use them to revise scripts while a movie is being shot.

Movie companies also use computers to monitor budgets closely and to run complex financial applications unique to the industry. One application is tracking residual payments for the re-release of movies and television reruns, seeing that the right people get paid the proper amounts. Another is tracking ticket receipts: Movie companies collect a percentage of ticket prices on a sliding scale that changes as movies continue to run.

a. How dependent on computers is the movie industry? Explain.
b. Is dependency on computers unique to the movie business? Explain.

Source: Adapted from David Ludlum, "Two Cheers for Hollywood," *Computerworld*, March 26, 1990, p. 110.

5. **ABC Department Stores**

The president of ABC Department Stores asked the following questions at a recent meeting of store managers and the vice president of information systems. Match each question with one of the major areas of information systems knowledge illustrated in Figure 1–1. Explain your choices.

a. How can we use information systems to support sales floor activities and store manager decision making, and thereby outhustle the competition?
b. How can we involve store managers in building such applications?
c. Do you realize that information systems can provide instant feedback to help us integrate our efforts and more effectively meet our goals?
d. What hardware, software, telecommunications, and database management resources do we need to support our goals?
e. How are we going to manage the hardware, software, people, data, and information resources of our information systems at the store and corporate levels?

6. Jefferson State University

   Students in the College of Business Administration of Jefferson State University use its microcomputer lab for a variety of assignments. For example, a student may load a word processing program from a microcomputer's hard disk drive into main memory and then proceed to type a case study analysis. When the analysis is typed, edited, and properly formatted to an instructor's specifications, the student will save it on a floppy disk drive and print a copy on the microcomputer's printer. If the student tries to save the case study analysis using a file name he or she has already used for saving another document, the program will display a warning message and wait until it receives an additional command.

   Use the information systems model illustrated in Figure 1–6 to identify the information system components in the preceding example.

   a. Identify the input, processing, output, storage, and control activities that occurred.
   b. Identify the hardware, software, people, and data resources and the information products of this information system.

7. Analyzing an Information System

   Describe the resources, activities, and products of a manual or computerized information system that you use regularly, using the information system model illustrated in Figure 1–6. For example, you could analyze your use of an information system such as a department store POS system, a supermarket checkout system, a university registration system, or a bank ATM system. Refer to the example of the analysis of a microcomputer-based information system for inventory control (see Figure 1–10) in this chapter to help you in your analysis.

SELECTED REFERENCES

1. Checkland, Peter. *Systems Thinking, Systems Practice.* New York: John Wiley & Sons, 1981.
2. Davis, Gordon, and Margarethe Olson. *Management Information Systems: Conceptual Foundations, Structure, and Development.* New York: McGraw-Hill, 1985.
3. Galliers, Robert, ed. *Information Analysis: Selected Readings.* Sidney: Addison-Wesley Publishing, 1987.
4. Markus, M. Lynne. *Systems in Organization: Bugs and Features.* Boston: Pitman, 1984.
5. Shurkin, Joel. *Engines of the Mind: A History of the Computer.* New York: W.W. Norton, 1984.
6. Wand, Yair, and Ron Weber. "An Ontological Analysis of Some Information Systems Concepts." *Proceedings of the Ninth International Conference on Information Systems,* December 1988.
7. Weinberg, Gerald. *An Introduction to General Systems Theory.* New York: John Wiley & Sons, 1985.

INFORMATION SYSTEMS IN BUSINESS MANAGEMENT

▓ Chapter Outline

■ Learning Objectives

The purpose of this chapter is to give you an understanding of the roles played by information systems in business by analyzing (1) the operations and management support roles of information systems and (2) the role of information systems in helping an organization achieve a strategic advantage over its competitors.

Section I of this chapter presents an overview of the major roles of information systems, emphasizing their role in supporting business operations and management decision making in an organization.

Section II emphasizes competitive strategy concepts and the three major strategic roles information systems can play in gaining competitive advantages for an organization.

After reading and studying this chapter, you should be able to:

1. Give examples of how information systems can provide support for a firm's business operations, management decision making, and strategic advantage.
2. Identify how three major types of operations information systems support the operations of a business.
3. Identify the major types of management information systems, and discuss how each supports the managers of an organization.
4. Briefly explain the role of end user computing systems, expert systems, business function information systems, and integrated information systems.
5. Identify three strategic roles of information systems, and give examples of how they can provide strategic advantages to a business.

Section I: Information Systems for Operations and Management

AN OVERVIEW OF INFORMATION SYSTEMS

In Chapter 1, we stressed that information systems have a vital role to play in the success of businesses and other organizations. In this chapter, as Figure 2–1 illustrates, we will emphasize that information systems perform three major roles in an organization.

☐   Support of business operations.

☐   Support of management decision making.

☐   Support of strategic organizational advantage.

In particular, Section II will stress how information systems can play a strategic role in the success of an organization. We will also emphasize that many different types of information systems can be developed to fulfill the three roles just mentioned. Each of these types of information systems will be discussed briefly in this section and in more detail in later chapters.

The Expanding Roles of Information Systems

The roles given to the information systems function in an organization have expanded significantly over the years. Figure 2–2 summarizes these changes. Until the 1960s, the role of information systems was simple: transaction processing, record keeping, accounting, and other *electronic data processing* (EDP) applications. Then, another role was added, as the concept of *management information systems* (MIS) was conceived. This new role focused on providing managerial end users with predefined management reports that would give managers the information they needed for decision-making purposes.

By the 1970s, it was evident that the prespecified information products produced by such *information reporting systems* were failing to meet many of the decision-making needs of management. So the concept of *decision support systems* (DSS) was born. The new role for information systems was to provide managerial end users with ad hoc and interactive support of their decision-making processes. Decision support systems depend on computer workstations, database management technology, and analytical modeling software to

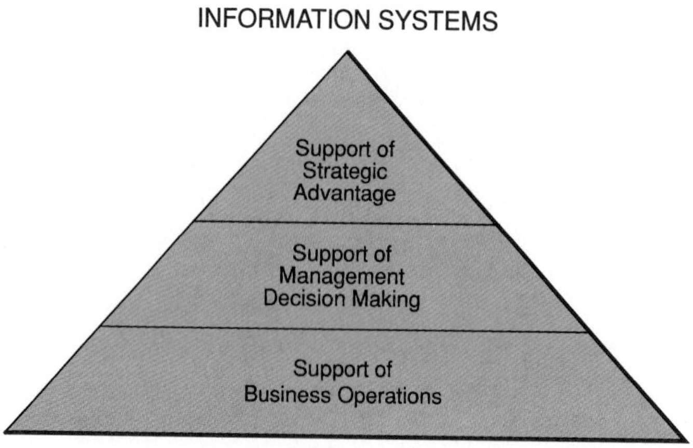

Figure 2–1 The three major roles of information systems. Information systems provide an organization with support for business operations, management decision making, and strategic advantage.

INFORMATION SYSTEMS

```
  Data Processing: 1950s–1960s

  Electronic Data Processing Systems
    Transaction processing, record keeping, and traditional accounting
    applications

  Management Reporting: 1960s–1970s

  Management Information Systems
    Management reports for prespecified information to support decision making

  Decision Support: 1970s–1980s

  Decision Support Systems
    Interactive and ad-hoc support of the decision making processes of
    individual managers

  Strategic and End User Support: 1980s–1990s

  End User Computing Systems
    Direct computing support for end user productivity
  Executive Information Systems
    Critical information for top management
  Expert Systems
    Knowledge-based expert advice to end users
  Strategic Information Systems
    Strategic products and services for competitive advantage
```

Figure 2–2 The expanding roles of information systems. Note how the roles of computer-based information systems have expanded over time. Also, note the impact of these changes on the end users and managers of an organization.

provide support tailored to the unique decision-making styles of managers as they confront specific types of problems in the real world.

In the 1980s, several new roles for information systems appeared. First, the rapid development of microcomputer processing power, application software packages, and telecommunication networks gave birth to the phenomenon of *end user computing*. Now, end users can use their own computing resources to support their job requirements, instead of waiting for the indirect support of corporate information services departments. Next, it became evident that most top corporate executives did not directly use either the reports of information reporting systems or the analytical modeling capabilities of decision support systems, so the concept of *executive information systems* (EIS) was developed. These information systems attempt to give top executives an easy way to get the critical information they want, when they want it, tailored to the formats they prefer. Third, breakthroughs were made in the development and application of *artificial intelligence* techniques to business information systems. *Expert systems* and other knowledge-based systems can now serve as consultants to end users by providing expert advice when needed to support specific job tasks.

Finally, an important new role for information systems appeared in the 1980s and is expected to continue into the 1990s. This is the concept of a **strategic role** for information systems, sometimes called *strategic information systems*. Now information systems are expected to play a direct role in helping a firm achieve its strategic objectives. This places a new responsibility on the information systems department of a business. No longer is it merely an *information utility*, a service group providing information processing services

Figure 2–3 Operations and management classifications of information systems. Note how this conceptual overview emphasizes the main purpose of information systems that support business operations or management decision making.

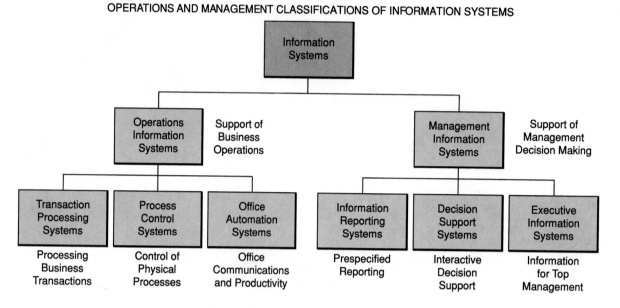

OPERATIONS AND MANAGEMENT CLASSIFICATIONS OF INFORMATION SYSTEMS

to end user departments within the firm. Now it must become a *producer of information-based products and services* that earn profits for the firm and also give it a *competitive advantage* in the marketplace.

All these changes have increased the importance of the information systems function to the success of a firm. However, they also present new managerial challenges to end users to effectively capitalize on the potential benefits of information systems.

Operations and Management Classifications

Information systems perform operational and managerial support roles in businesses and other organizations. Figure 2–3 provides a conceptual classification of information systems. It shows that some information systems can be classified conceptually as either *operations* or *management* information systems. Information systems are categorized in this manner to spotlight the major roles each can play in the operations and management of a business.

Operations information systems process data generated by and used in business operations. The major categories of these systems, and the roles they play, are as follows:

☐ **Transaction processing systems** record and process data resulting from business transactions, update databases, and produce a variety of documents and reports.

☐ Operational decisions that control physical processes are produced by **process control systems.**

☐ Office communications and productivity are supported by **office automation systems.**

The term **management information systems** has several popular meanings. Many writers use the term as a synonym for *information systems*. Others only

use it to describe information systems that provide information i
standardized reports and displays to managers. In this text we'l'
ment information systems (MIS) to describe a broad class of in
tems whose goal is to provide information and support for decis
managers. Major types of management information systems pla
roles:

☐ Prespecified and preplanned reporting to managers is a
information reporting systems.

☐ Interactive and ad hoc support for decision making by
accomplished by **decision support systems.**

☐ Critical information for top management is provided |
information systems.

Let's take a closer look now at the information systems that have always been
needed to process data generated by business operations. Such **operations
information systems** produce a variety of information products for internal and
external use, but they do not emphasize the specific information products that
can best be used by managers. Further processing by management information
systems is usually required. The role of a business firm's operations information
systems is to efficiently process business transactions, control industrial processes, support office communications and productivity, and update corporate
databases. Figure 2–4 is an example of an operations information system. It
illustrates the components and activities of a sales transaction processing system that captures sales transaction data, updates databases, and responds to
end user inquiries.

Figure 2–4 A sales transaction processing system. No
that this operations inform
tion system captures s
transactions data, up
databases, and res
end user inquirie

48

INFORMA···
SYSTEMS FOR
BUSINESS
OPERATIONS

Operations information systems include the major category of **transaction
processing systems** (TPS). Transaction processing systems were the earliest
type of information system. They evolved from manual information systems to
machine-assisted data processing systems to **electronic data processing** systems. Transaction processing systems record and process data resulting from
business transactions, such as sales, purchases, and inventory changes. They
may also process data created by making miscellaneous adjustments to the
records in a file or database, such as name and address changes to a customer
file. Transaction processing systems produce a variety of information products
for internal or external use. For example, they produce customer statements,
employee paychecks, sales receipts, purchase orders, dividend checks, tax
forms, and financial statements. They also update the databases used by an
organization for further processing by its management information systems. We
will discuss transaction processing systems in more detail in Chapter 8.

**Transaction Processing
Systems**

Operations information systems also make routine decisions that control operational processes. Examples are automatic inventory reorder and production
control decisions. Decisions such as these are called *programmed decisions*
because they are automated (programmed) by basing them on decision rules.
Decision rules outline the actions to be taken when an information system is

Process Control Systems

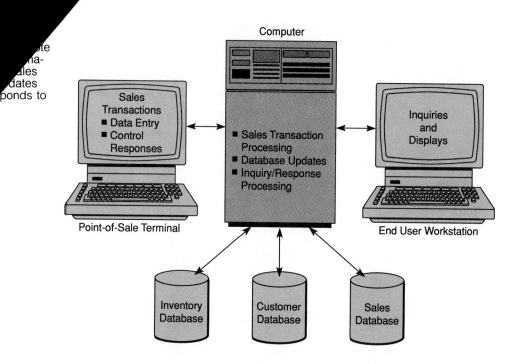

confronted with a certain set of events. This includes a category of information systems called **process control systems**, in which decisions adjusting a physical production process are automatically made by computers. Petroleum refineries and the assembly lines of automated factories use such systems. They monitor a physical process, capture and process data detected by sensors, and make real time adjustments to a process. We will discuss process control systems further in Chapter 10.

Office Automation Systems

Another major role of operations information systems is the transformation of traditional manual office methods and paper communications media by **office automation systems** (OAS). For example, instead of using typewriters to produce the paper documents mailed to customers and business associates, such systems use word processing and electronic mail systems to collect, process, store, and transmit data and information in the form of a variety of electronic office communications. Examples of typical *office automation* application categories include word processing, electronic mail, desktop publishing, teleconferencing, and document image processing. We will discuss office automation systems in detail in Chapter 7.

INFORMATION SYSTEMS FOR MANAGEMENT DECISION MAKING

The concept of **management information systems** (MIS) originated in the 1960s and became the byword (and the buzzword) of almost all attempts to relate computer technology and systems theory to data processing in organizations. During the early years of computing, it became evident that the computer was being applied to the solution of business problems in a piecemeal fashion, focusing almost entirely on the computerization of clerical and record-keeping tasks. The concept of management information systems was developed to counteract such *inefficient* development and *ineffective* use of computers by focusing instead on providing information needed for decision making by

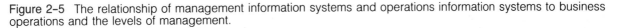

Figure 2–5 The relationship of management information systems and operations information systems to business operations and the levels of management.

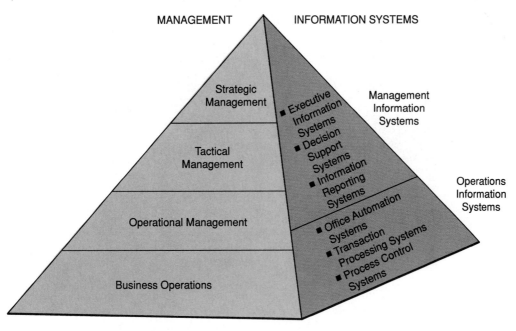

managers. Though tarnished by early failures, the MIS concept is still recognized as vital to efficient and effective information systems in organizations for two major reasons:

☐ It emphasizes the **management orientation** of information processing in business. A major goal of computer-based information systems should be the support of *management decision making*, not merely the processing of data generated by business operations.

☐ It emphasizes that a **systems framework** should be used for organizing information systems applications. Business applications of information systems should be viewed as interrelated and integrated *computer-based information systems* and not as independent data processing jobs.

Figure 2–5 illustrates the relationship of management information systems and operations information systems to business operations and management. Management information systems support the decision-making needs of strategic (top) management, tactical (middle) management, and operating (supervisory) management. Operations information systems support the information processing requirements of the day-to-day operations of a business, as well as some lower-level operations management functions.

Providing information and support for management decision making by all levels of management (from top executives to middle managers to supervisors) is a complex task. Conceptually, several major types of information systems are needed to support a variety of managerial end user responsibilities. In Chapters 8 and 9, we will discuss concepts that underlie the emergence of three major types of management information systems: (1) information reporting

Figure 2-6 The components and activities of management information systems. Note some of the resources needed to provide information reporting, decision support, strategic information, and expert advice to managerial end users.

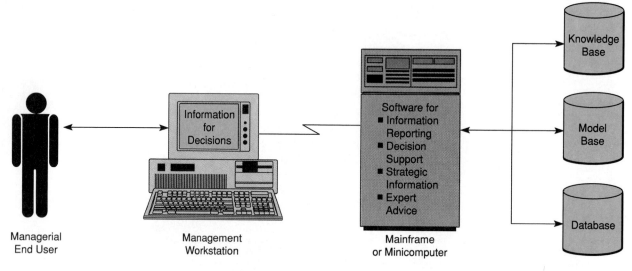

systems, (2) decision support systems, and (3) executive information systems. Figure 2–6 illustrates some of the resources needed and information products produced by several types of management information systems.

Information Reporting Systems

Information reporting systems (IRS) provide managerial end users with information products that support much of their day-to-day decision-making needs. Reports and displays produced by these systems provide information that managers have specified in advance as adequately meeting their information needs. Information reporting systems access databases containing information about internal operations that has been previously processed by transaction processing systems. Data about the business environment is obtained from external sources.

Information products provided to managers include displays and reports that can be furnished (1) on demand; (2) periodically, according to a predetermined schedule; or (3) whenever exceptional conditions occur. For example, sales managers could receive (1) instantaneous visual displays at their workstations about the sales of a particular product; (2) weekly sales analysis reports evaluating sales results by product, salesperson, and sales territory; or (3) a report produced automatically whenever a salesperson fails to produce sales results during a specified period. We will discuss information reporting systems further in Chapter 8.

Decision Support Systems

Decision support systems (DSS) are a natural progression from information reporting systems and transaction processing systems. Decision support systems are interactive, computer-based information systems that use a *model base* of decision models and specialized databases to assist the decision-making processes of managerial end users. Thus, they are different from transaction processing systems, which focus on processing the data generated by business transactions and operations. They also differ from information reporting systems, which focus on providing managers with prespecified information (reports) that could be used to help them make more effective, structured types of decisions.

Instead, decision support systems provide managerial end users with information in an *interactive session* on an *ad hoc* (as needed) basis. A DSS provides analytical modeling, data retrieval, and information presentation capabilities that allow managers to generate the information they need to make more unstructured types of decisions in an interactive, computer-based process. For example, electronic spreadsheets and other decision support software allow a managerial end user to receive interactive responses to ad hoc requests for information posed as a series of what–if questions. This differs from the prespecified responses of information reporting systems. When using a DSS, managers are exploring possible alternatives and receiving tentative information based on alternative sets of assumptions. Thus, managerial end users do not have to specify their information needs in advance. Instead, the DSS interactively helps them find the information they need. Decision support systems are discussed in Chapter 9.

Executive information systems (EIS) are management information systems tailored to the strategic information needs of top management. Top executives get the information they need from many sources, including letters, memos, periodicals, and reports produced manually as well as by computer systems. Other sources of executive information are meetings, telephone calls, and social activities. Thus, much of a top executive's information comes from noncomputer sources. Computer-generated information has not played a primary role in meeting many top executives' information needs.

Executive Information Systems

The goal of computer-based executive information systems is to provide top management with immediate and easy access to selective information about key factors that are critical to accomplishing a firm's strategic objectives. Therefore, an EIS is easy to operate and understand. Graphics displays are used extensively, and immediate access to internal and external databases is provided. EIS provide information about the current status and projected trends for key factors selected by top executives. Executive information systems are discussed again in Chapter 9.

Several major categories of information systems provide more unique or broad classifications than those we have just mentioned. That's because these information systems can support operations, management, or strategic applications. For example:

OTHER CLASSIFICATIONS OF INFORMATION SYSTEMS

☐ Expert advice for operational or managerial decision making is provided by **expert systems** and other knowledge-based information systems.

☐ Direct, hands-on support for both the operational and managerial applications of end users is provided by **end user computing systems.**

☐ Operational and managerial applications in support of basic business functions are provided by **business function information systems.**

☐ Competitive products and services to help achieve strategic objectives are provided by **strategic information systems.**

Expert Systems

The frontiers of information systems are being affected by developments in **artificial intelligence** (AI). Artificial intelligence is an area of computer science whose long-range goal is to develop computers that can think, as well as see, hear, walk, talk, and feel. AI projects involve developing natural programming languages, advanced industrial robots, and intelligent computers. A major thrust is the development of computer functions normally associated with human intelligence, such as reasoning, inference, learning, and problem solving.

One of the most practical applications of AI is the development of **expert systems.** An expert system (ES) is a *knowledge-based information system;* that is, it uses its knowledge about a specific area to act as an expert consultant to users. The components of an expert system are a *knowledge base* and software modules that perform inferences on the knowledge and offer answers to a user's questions. Expert systems are being used in many different fields, including medicine, engineering, the physical sciences, and business. For example, expert systems now help diagnose illnesses, search for minerals, analyze compounds, recommend repairs, and do financial planning. Expert system components can be built into either operations or management information systems. We will discuss artificial intelligence and expert systems further in Chapter 9.

End User Computing Systems

End user computing systems are computer-based information systems that directly support both the operational and managerial applications of end users. You should think of end user computing primarily as the direct, hands-on use of computers by end users, instead of as the indirect use provided by the hardware, software, and professional resources of an organization's information services department. In end user computing systems, end users typically use microcomputer workstations and a variety of software packages and databases for personal productivity, information retrieval, decision support, and application development. For example, users may do word processing, send electronic mail, retrieve information from a database, manipulate an analytical model, or develop a new business application. We will discuss end user computing systems in Chapter 7.

Business Function Information Systems

As a future business manager, it is important for you to realize that information systems directly support the business functions of accounting, finance, human resources management, marketing, and operations management. Such **business function information systems**, which are discussed in Chapter 10, are needed by all business functions. For example:

☐ Marketing managers need information about sales performance and trends provided by *marketing information systems.*

☐ Financial managers need information concerning financing costs and investment returns provided by *financial information systems.*

☐ Production managers need information analyzing resource requirements and worker productivity provided by a variety of *manufacturing information systems.*

☐ Personnel managers require information concerning employee compensation and professional development provided by *human resource information systems.*

It is also important to realize that most information systems in the real world are typically integrated combinations of the various conceptual types of information systems we have just mentioned. That's because the conceptual classifications of information systems that we have just discussed are designed to emphasize the many different roles of information systems.

In practice, these roles are integrated into *composite* or *cross-functional* information systems that provide a variety of functions. Thus, most information systems are designed to produce information and support decision making for various levels of management and business functions, as well as do record-keeping and transaction processing chores.

For example, a payroll system that processes employee time cards and produces employee paychecks is an operations information system. An information system that uses payroll data to produce labor analysis reports showing variances and trends in labor costs is a human resource management information system. However, in most cases, these functions are combined in an integrated payroll/labor analysis system.

Another example involves sales order/transaction processing, which is an operations information system, and sales analysis, which is a marketing management information system. However, these two systems are typically integrated in a business. The sales order processing system collects and records sales transaction data and provides input to the sales analysis system, which produces management reports concerning sales activity.

Integrated Information Systems

REAL WORLD CASE

WearGuard, Incorporated

Walk into any one of WearGuard, Inc.'s 75 stores in 10 northeastern states and the same no-nonsense, work-a-day merchandise is there: sturdy boots, thermal underwear, rubber-soled shoes, and row after row of uniforms. But, says Chief Executive Officer Richard Salem, "The computer is truly the heart of the company here, and the customer is the focus. You can't avoid putting one with the other." The firm, whose motto is "Clothes That Work Overtime," is really two businesses: a retail chain and a mail-order business that sends out 50 million catalogs per year and delivers up to 65,000 orders weekly.

WearGuard has grown from a mom-and-pop mail-order business founded in 1950—managed from notes jotted on 3 × 5 inch cards—to become the country's leading supplier of personalized work clothing, with $150 million in annual sales. "We could not have done it without computerization of marketing, distribution, and order-entry systems," said Salem, who came out of Dartmouth University's business school in 1978 with a plan to build his father's company into a direct marketing business through high tech.

The core of WearGuard's computer operation is a complex of six Prime minicomputers supporting more than 300 PC workstations. For the past year, this network has enabled WearGuard to put order-entry and customer-service operations at the fingertips of telephone order takers at their Norwell, Massachusetts, headquarters.

"The computer is used so intensively here because the secret of tomorrow's customer is on today's disk file," the CEO explained. "The machines are used everywhere here in giving feedback to our employees and helping managers monitor how well we keep the promises made to customers." "Here is a company with 2 million customers, and we have complete purchasing histories of all of them. When a customer calls, we can be interactive, quick in response, and really intelligent in answering their questions," says Salem.

Customer convenience weighs heavily on the corporate mind-set at WearGuard, where a 48-hour turnaround time is the standard promise for orders. A customer can walk into any WearGuard store on Monday, order a uniform with his name stitched over the left-hand shirt pocket, and wear it to work that Wednesday. WearGuard spent roughly $6 million to $7 million in the past few years on its systems and software, Salem said. "It might be expensive to put PCs at every desk, but the opportunity cost of not putting the right information at every hand is much greater."

Application Questions

☐ What types of information systems do you recognize in this case? Explain.

☐ How have these systems supported business operations and management at WearGuard?

☐ Has the investment in IS been worth its $6 million to $7 million price tag? Explain.

Source: Adapted from Maryfran Johnson, "Computers Work for Clothier," *Computerworld,* January 22, 1990, p. 29.

Section II: Information Systems for Strategic Advantage

Information systems can play a major role in support of the strategic objectives of an organization. This strategic role provides a firm with competitive products and services that give it a strategic advantage over its competitors in the marketplace. Let's take a closer look at several basic concepts that define the role of such **strategic information systems.**

How should a business manager think about competitive strategies? How can competitive strategies be applied to the use of information systems by an organization? Several important conceptual frameworks for understanding and applying competitive strategies have been developed by Michael Porter [5, 6], Charles Wiseman [8], and others. Figure 2-7 illustrates several important concepts. A firm can survive and succeed in the long run if it successfully develops strategies to confront five **competitive forces** that shape the structure of competition in its industry. These are (1) rivalry of competitors within its industry, (2) threats of new entrants, (3) threats of substitutes, (4) the bargaining power of customers, and (5) the bargaining power of suppliers. Several **competitive strategies** can be developed to help a firm confront these competitive forces. These include the following:

□ **Cost leadership**—becoming a low-cost producer of products and services in the industry. In addition, a firm can help its suppliers or customers reduce their own costs.

□ **Product differentiation**—developing ways to differentiate a firm's products and services from those of its competitors. This may allow a firm to focus its products or services at particular segments, or *niches*, of a market.

□ **Innovation**—finding new ways of doing business. This involves the development of new products and services or new ways of producing or distributing products and services that are fundamentally different from the way business has been conducted.

COMPETITIVE STRATEGY CONCEPTS

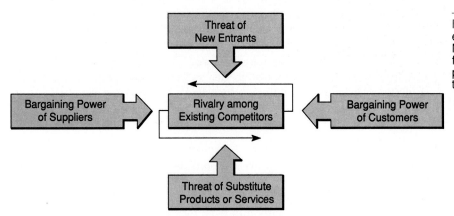

Figure 2-7 The competitive environment of an industry. Note the five competitive forces that determine the profitability and survival of the firms within an industry.

Source: Adapted from Michael E. Porter, *Competitive Advantage: Creating and Sustaining Superior Performance* (New York: Free Press, 1985), p. 5.

Figure 2-8 Examples of the application of competitive strategies to confront each of the competitive forces facing a firm. Information systems can directly support such strategic thrusts.

	Customers	Suppliers	Competitors	New Entrants	Substitutes
Strategic Objectives	Attract new customers and lock in present customers by creating switching costs	Lock in suppliers by creating switching costs	Lock out competitors by locking in customers and suppliers	Create barriers to entry into the industry	Make substitution unattractive
Cost Leadership Strategy	Offer lower prices	Help suppliers lower costs	Undercut competitor prices	Make entry investment unattractive	Make substitution economically unfeasible
Differentiation Strategy	Provide better quality, features, and service	Help suppliers improve services	Toughen competition with unique features	Complicate entry decision	Provide features of substitutes
Innovation Strategy	Provide new products and services to new markets	Provide unique supply services or acquire suppliers	Provide unmatched products and services	Enter businesses of potential entrants	Produce substitutes

Figure 2-8 provides examples of how each of these three competitive strategies can be used to confront each of the competitive forces facing a firm. Such strategic alternatives can be generated as part of a strategic management process known as *SWOT analysis,* in which managers evaluate a firm's Strengths, Weaknesses, Opportunities, and Threats prior to making strategic choices [2].

STRATEGIC ROLES FOR INFORMATION SYSTEMS

How can the preceding competitive strategy concepts be applied to the strategic role of information systems in an organization? Put another way, how can managers use investments in information systems technology to directly support a firm's competitive strategies? These questions can be answered in terms of three key strategic roles that information systems can perform in a firm. Figure 2-9 emphasizes that strategic information systems can help a firm (1) improve its operational efficiency, (2) promote organizational innovation, and (3) build strategic information resources. These three strategic roles support a firm's use of competitive strategies against the competitive forces from competitors, customers, suppliers, substitutes, and new entrants. Figure 2-10 outlines some potential results from the strategic use of information systems.

Improving Operational Efficiency

Investments in information systems technology can help make a firm's operations significantly more efficient, which could allow the firm to dramatically cut costs and improve the quality and delivery of its products and services. For example, manufacturing operations of many automobile manufacturers have been automated and significantly improved by computer-aided manufacturing technology. The distribution of cars and parts has also been improved by telecommunications systems that connect distribution facilities with automobile dealers.

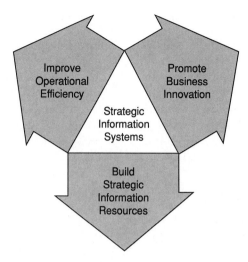

Figure 2-9 The strategic roles of information systems. Note that information systems give a firm three strategic capabilities to confront the competitive forces that surround it.

Operational efficiency allows a firm to adopt a low-cost leadership strategy. However, a firm could decide instead to increase quality and service by choosing a product differentiation strategy that stresses the unique quality of the firm's products and services. In either case, a firm would be better able to deter competitive threats. Its industry rivals and firms seeking to enter the industry using similar or substitute products would have a harder time beating an efficient competitor.

Barriers to Entry

By making investments in information systems technology that increased its operational efficiency, a firm could also erect **barriers to entry.** These could be made by increasing the amount of investment or the complexity of the technology required to compete in a market segment. Such actions would tend to discourage firms already in the industry and deter external firms from entering the industry. Thus, investment in information technology can make the stakes too high for some present or prospective players.

Figure 2-10 Examples of the strategic potential of information systems. The three strategic roles of information systems can help a firm develop the strategic results shown.

Strategic Roles of Information Systems	Some Potential Results from the Use of Strategic Information Systems		
Improving operational efficiency	Improved productivity and lowered cost of operations	Improved quality and features of products and services	Improved operational processes and work environment
Promoting organizational innovation	New products and services	New markets, businesses, and business arrangements	New production, distribution, or other organizational processes
Building strategic information resources	Databases of strategic information	Strategic information technology resources and capabilities	

Lock in Customers and Suppliers

Investments in information systems technology can also allow a business to **lock in customers and suppliers** (and lock out competitors) by building valuable new relationships with them. This can deter both customers and suppliers from abandoning a firm for its competitors or intimidating a firm into accepting less profitable relationships. Early attempts to use information systems technology in these relationships focused on significantly improving the *quality of service* to customers and suppliers in a firm's distribution, marketing, sales, and service activities. Then businesses moved to more innovative uses of information technology.

For example, many telecommunications networks were designed to provide sales people and customer service staff with up-to-date sales, shipping, inventory, and account status information for relay to their customers. Firms began to use the operational efficiency of such information systems to offer better-quality service and thereby differentiate themselves from their competitors. Then some firms began to extend these networks to their customers and suppliers in order to build innovative relationships which would lock in their business. This creates *interorganizational information systems* in which telecommunications networks electronically link the terminals and computers of businesses with their customers and suppliers.

Promoting Organizational Innovation

Investments in information systems technology can result in the production of new products, services, and processes. The use of automated teller machines (ATMs) in banking is an example of an innovative investment in information systems technology.

By employing ATMs, Citibank and several other large banks were able to gain a strategic advantage over their competitors that lasted for several years. ATMs lured customers away from other financial institutions by cutting the cost of providing bank services and increasing the convenience of such services. The more costly and less-convenient alternative would have been to establish new bank branch offices. ATMs are also an example of product differentiation since bank services are now provided in a new way. ATMs raised the cost of competition, which forced some smaller banks that could not afford the investment in new technology to merge with larger banks. ATMs represent an attractive and convenient new banking service produced and distributed to customers by making innovative changes in the delivery of bank services. Thus, information systems technology was used to develop a new distribution process for bank services.

Switching Costs

A major emphasis in strategic information systems is to build **switching costs** into the relationships between a firm and its customers or suppliers. That is, investments in information systems technology can make customers or suppliers dependent on the continued use of innovative, mutually beneficial interorganizational information systems. Thus, they become reluctant to pay the costs in time, money, effort, and inconvenience that it would take to change to a firm's competitors.

A good example is the computerized airline reservation systems offered to travel agents by several major airlines, such as the SABRE system of American Airlines and the APOLLO system of United Airlines. Once a travel agency has invested a substantial sum in installing such an interorganizational system and travel agents have been trained in its use, the agency is reluctant to switch to another airline's reservation system. Thus, what seemed to be just a more convenient and efficient way of processing airline reservations has become a strategic weapon that gives these airlines a major competitive advantage. A specialized airline reservation system raises competitive barriers and increases switching costs. It also gives the airlines a built-in advantage in gaining reservations for themselves, and provides them with a new information product that allows them to differentiate their services from other airlines. Finally, computer-based reservation services are a new source of revenue for these airlines, which charge a variety of fees to travel agencies and other airlines who use their systems.

Information systems technology enables a firm to build strategic information resources that allow it to take advantage of strategic opportunities. In many cases, this results from a firm's investing in advanced computer-based information systems to improve the efficiency of its own internal operations. Typically this means acquiring hardware and software, developing telecommunications networks, hiring information system specialists, and training end users. Then, armed with this resource base, the firm can **leverage investment in information systems technology** by developing new products and services. For example, the development by banks of remote banking services using automated teller machines was an extension of their expertise in teller terminal networks, which interconnect their branches.

Building Strategic Information Resources

A Strategic Information Base

Information systems also allow a firm to build a **strategic information base** that can provide information to support the firm's competitive strategies. Information in a firm's corporate databases has always been a valuable asset in promoting efficient operations and effective management of a firm. However, information about a firm's operations, customers, suppliers, and competitors, as well as other economic and demographic data, is now viewed as a strategic resource; that is, it is used to support strategic planning, marketing, and other strategic initiatives.

For example, many businesses are now using computer-based information about their customers to help design marketing campaigns to sell customers new products and services. This is especially true of firms that include several subsidiaries offering a variety of products and services. For example, once you become a customer of a subsidiary of Sears Roebuck and Co., you quickly become a target for marketing campaigns by their other subsidiaries, based on information provided by the Sears strategic information resource base. This is one way a firm can leverage its investment in transaction processing and customer accounting systems—by linking its databases to its strategic planning and marketing systems. This helps a firm create better marketing strategies for

Figure 2–11   The value chain of a firm. Note the examples of how strategic information systems (SIS) can be applied to a firm's basic activities to achieve competitive advantages.

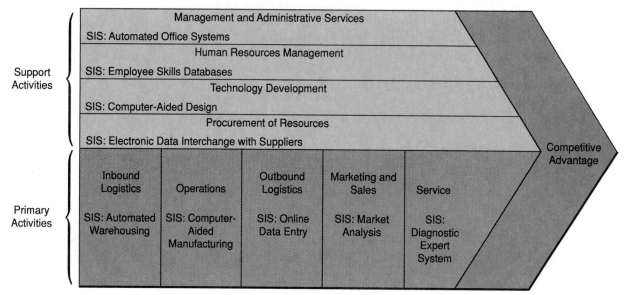

new products and services, build better barriers to entry for competitors, and find better ways to lock in customers and suppliers.

Information Systems and the Value Chain

Another important conceptual framework that can help identify strategic information systems is called the **value chain.** This concept was developed by Michael Porter [6] and is illustrated in Figure 2–11. It views a firm as a series, or chain, of basic activities that *add value* to its products and services and, thus, add a *margin of value* to the firm. In the value chain concept, some business activities are *primary activities*, others are *support activities*. This framework can highlight where competitive strategies can best be applied. That is, business managers should try to develop strategic information systems for those basic activities that add the most value to a particular firm's products or services. Figure 2–11 provides examples of how and where information systems technology can be applied to basic business activities using the value chain framework.

For example, Figure 2–11 shows that office automation systems can increase the productivity of office communications and support activities (management and administrative services); employee skills database systems can help locate and assign employees to important positions and projects (human resource management); computer-aided design systems can automate the design of products and processes (technology development); and electronic data interchange systems can provide online telecommunications links to a firm's suppliers (procurement of resources).

Other examples of strategic applications of information systems technology to basic business activities include automated warehousing systems (inbound logistics), computer-aided manufacturing systems (operations), and online order entry systems (outbound logistics). Information systems can also provide analyses of present and potential markets for goods and services (marketing and sales) and offer expert online diagnostic services to customers (the service activity).

The value chain concept can help managers decide where and how to apply the strategic capabilities of information systems technology. Information systems that improve operational efficiency, promote innovation, and build strategic resources can be applied to the specific business activities that help a firm gain strategic advantages in the marketplace.

The strategic role of information systems forces managers to look at information systems in a new light. No longer is the information systems function merely a necessary service group for processing transactions and keeping the books of a firm. It is also more than a helpful supplier of information and tools for decision making. Now the information systems function can help business managers develop competitive weapons that use information systems technology to meet challenges from the competitive forces that confront any organization.

Of course, strategic information systems are not easy to develop and implement. They may require major changes in the way a business operates and in the business's relationships with its employees, customers, suppliers, competitors, and others. The competitive advantages that strategic information systems produce can fade away, and their failure can seriously damage a firm's performance. The case studies at the end of this chapter demonstrate the challenges and problems as well as the benefits of strategic information systems. The effective use of strategic information systems presents business managers with a major managerial challenge. We will discuss the managerial and planning implications of this challenge further in Chapters 12 and 13.

A MANAGERIAL PERSPECTIVE

REAL WORLD CASE

Wal-Mart Stores, Inc.

From a featureless red brick building in Benton-ville, Arkansas, Wal-Mart Stores, Inc., quietly runs what many believe is the best retailing op-eration in the United States. That operation rests on an intense commitment to basic customer service coupled with a decade-old emphasis on information technology. The information arsenal ranges from the industry's first private satellite network to systems that monitor each store's daily sales and inventory and dispatch this data to the Wal-Mart's 17 distribution centers around the country.

"Our approach with technology is not trying to replace people but really supplementing what our people do and making them more effective," says Bob L. Martin, senior vice president of information services. "Technology is a key part of our strategic thrust," Martin says. "Much that we've done with technology is a large part of our ability to compete." Martin says with conviction that IS at Wal-Mart is "a sheer support function" and that an awareness of customers at the store level is the guiding light. "Most of the good ideas for IS applications come from our hourly associ-ates in the stores," Martin states. On the other hand, upper management is hardly uninvolved with IS strategy. Martin sits on an executive committee that meets weekly, bringing together all the company's head officers from the chief executive officer on down.

The diamond in Wal-Mart's IS crown is a private communications satellite network, con-necting over 1,800 stores and distribution cen-ters. The network provides instant data—voice and video links to all the Wal-Mart stores in the country. This includes each of the company's 17 distribution centers, which feature mainframe computer environments, and the 1,550 stores in the chain, which have IBM Series-1 minicom-puters linked to the Bentonville home office via the satellite network, as well as intelligent hand-held terminals and personal computers to run various in-store applications. "It gives us tre-mendous capability," Martin says about the sat-ellite network. It allows users to share "not just ordering or sales information, but the constant dialogue and flow of information between the operations, merchandising, and distribution functions of our company."

Outsiders believe Wal-Mart's market per-formance can be attributed to its success with "quick response," the retailing industry's equiv-alent to just-in-time manufacturing.

One surprise for the competition may be ex-pert systems, which Wal-Mart is rumored to be investigating. A more publicized feat is Wal-Mart's electronic data interchange (EDI) net-work for the electronic exchange of business transaction documents, which may be the largest in the United States. The company claims that more than 1,800 of its 5,000 suppliers use tele-communications links to send and receive busi-ness documents.

What about competitors such as Sears and K mart? Wal-Mart stands out because it was the first to realize IS was integral to their success and has been actively incorporating IS technology for the last 10 years. For Martin, IS in retailing in the coming decade will mean more of the same. "We'll eliminate processes that don't add value to the business or don't help our people serve the customer," he says. "If we can buy our peo-ple time to spend time with the customer or time to spend on the merchandise, that's value added."

Application Questions

- ☐ What types of information systems do you recognize in this case? Explain.
- ☐ What strategic IS roles is Wal-Mart imple-menting? Explain.
- ☐ What competitive forces, generic com-petitive strategies, and value chain activities are involved? Explain.

Source: Adapted from Ellis Booker, "IS Trailblazing Puts Retailer on Top," *Computerworld*, February 12, 1990, pp. 69, 73.

SUMMARY

☐ Major conceptual categories of information systems include operations information systems, such as transaction processing systems, process control systems, and automated office systems, and management information systems, such as information reporting systems, decision support systems, and executive information systems. Other major categories are end user computing systems, expert systems, strategic information systems, and business function information systems. However, in the real world, these conceptual classifications are typically integrated into information systems which provide information for managers and also perform traditional data-processing activities.

☐ Management information systems provide information needed for effective management decision making. This category includes information reporting systems, which provide prespecified information to managers on demand, according to a schedule, or on an exception basis. Decision support systems use decision models and specialized databases to provide interactive, ad hoc support for specific decisions faced by managers. Executive information systems are management information systems tailored to the strategic information needs of top management. Expert systems use a knowledge base and specialized software to act as an expert consultant to users. End user computing systems support the direct, hands-on use of computers by end users for operational and managerial applications.

☐ Information systems can play three strategic roles in businesses. They can help a business improve operational efficiency, promote organizational innovation, or build strategic information resources, thereby giving the business a competitive advantage in its relationships with customers, suppliers, competitors, new entrants, and producers of substitute products. Thus, a firm can improve productivity, lower costs, develop new products, services, and processes, lock in customers and suppliers, and build a strategic information base.

These are the key terms and concepts of this chapter. The page number of their first explanation is in parentheses.

KEY TERMS AND CONCEPTS

1. Artificial intelligence (52)
2. Business function information systems (52)
3. Competitive strategy concepts (55)
    a. Barriers to entry (57)
    b. Competitive forces (55)
    c. Competitive strategies (55)
    d. Locking in customers and suppliers (58)
    e. Switching costs (58)
4. Classification of information systems (46)
5. Decision support systems (50)
6. End user computing systems (52)
7. Executive information systems (51)
8. Expanding roles of information systems (44)
9. Expert systems (52)
10. Information reporting systems (50)
11. Integrated information systems (53)
12. Major roles of information systems (44)
13. Management information systems (46)

14. Office automation
    systems (48)
15. Operations information
    systems (46)
16. Process control systems (47)
17. Strategic information
    systems (55)
18. Strategic roles of information
    systems (56)

a. Operational
   efficiency (56)
b. Organizational
   innovation (58)
c. Strategic information
   resources (59)
19. Transaction processing
    systems (47)
20. Value chain (60)

REVIEW QUIZ

Match one of the **key terms and concepts** listed above with one of the examples or definitions listed below. Look for the best fit for answers that seem to fit more than one key term or concept. Defend your choices.

_____ 1. Information systems support an organization's operations, management, and strategic advantage.

_____ 2. Information systems can be classified into operations, management, and other categories.

_____ 3. Information systems have evolved from a data processing orientation to the support of decision making, end users, and strategic initiatives.

_____ 4. Include transaction processing, process control, and office automation systems.

_____ 5. Handle routine information processing generated by business activities.

_____ 6. Control ongoing physical processes.

_____ 7. Provide electronic office communications.

_____ 8. Include information reporting, decision support, and executive information systems.

_____ 9. Provide information for managers in a variety of structured formats.

_____ 10. Provide ad hoc, interactive support for decision making.

_____ 11. Hopes to develop computers that can see, hear, walk, talk, feel, and think.

_____ 12. Serve as consultants to end users.

_____ 13. Provide direct support for the activities of end users.

_____ 14. Support the functional areas of business in an organization.

_____ 15. Perform traditional data processing activities and also provide information to the managers of an organization.

_____ 16. A business must deal with customers, suppliers, competitors, new entrants, and substitutes.

_____ 17. Cost leadership, differentiation of products, and development of new products are examples.

_____ 18. Using investment in technology to keep firms out of an industry.

_____ 19. Making it unattractive for a firm's customers or suppliers to switch to its competitors.

_____ 20. The time, money, and effort needed for customers or suppliers to change to a firm's competitors.

_____ 21. Information systems that support operational efficiency, promote business innovation, and build strategic information resources.

_____ 22. Information systems can help a business develop new products, services, and processes.

_____ 23. Information systems can help a business significantly reduce costs and improve productivity.

_____ 24. Information systems can help a business build strategic databases of information.

_____ 25. Highlights how strategic information systems can be applied to a firm's basic activities for competitive advantage.

REAL WORLD PROBLEMS

1. K mart Corporation

   Beginning in the early 1980s, K mart Corporation made a significant commitment to make information technology the driving force behind improved retail operations. The company's retail automation program utilizes optical scanning of UPC (Universal Product Coding) bar codes on merchandise, online credit authorization, and automated layaway. This saves approximately $200 million annually, reduces customer checkout time by 23 percent and significantly improves sales over nonautomated departments. They have made K mart the world's largest user of UPC scanning, with 1,300 U.S. stores now using the technology.

   a. Is K mart's use of information technology an example of the use of strategic information systems? Explain.
   b. What generic competitive strategies are they using?

   Source: Adapted from "Call for Nominations: 1990 Partners in Leadership Award," Unpublished Announcement, Society for Information Management, February 1990.

2. Federal Express

   Federal Express Corp. watchers who think the company's grip on the airborne package business is absolute should visit Ron Ponder, the senior vice president in charge of information and telecommunications for the $6 billion package-delivery service. Ponder believes that Federal Express—though it owns more than 60 percent of the domestic overnight package-delivery business—needs to work harder to keep its customers. "Our aim is to get the smallest possible computer as close as possible to the customer," Ponder said. "The customer is our partner, and we want them to have as much access as we can without intruding on their business."

   "We are trying to find ways to smoothly make electronic connections with major accounts," said Ponder. "There are all sorts of different standards, but if we can overcome those differences, we are going to speed up a vast number of management processes." So Federal Express is testing a cigarette case–sized device for customers to transmit shipping bills to a local Federal Express office and to call for automatic package pickup. "We have concentrated in the last five years on our customer-service systems, and the revenue system and international distribution systems have been identified as strategic," said Ponder. "Internally, we talk about 'channel-device marketing,' that is, placing as small a system as close to the customer as possible."

a. What competitive strategies are involved in the Federal Express goal of placing a small computer close to their customers?
b. What are the benefits of the proposed system to Federal Express and its customers?

Source: Adapted from Dennis Eskow, "'Channel Systems' Put PCs on Front Line," *PC Week*, March 5, 1990, pp. 135–37.

3. Otis Elevator Company

Otis Elevator Company not only manufactures but services its estimated 93,000 elevators and escalators around the clock in North America. When a customer dials the toll-free OTISLINE, an operator calls up the customer's records from a giant electronic database. After logging details of the latest problem, the operator quickly locates a repairperson, who in turn is fully briefed on the situation before being sent off. In an emergency the company's repair personnel are usually on the scene within 30 minutes and, more often than not, know exactly what they have to do.

Donald Lucas, vice president of MIS at Otis, remarked that "OTISLINE has the potential to grow well beyond its current role as a service system. It could function as a customer order-entry and contract-tracking system as well. Perhaps the greatest benefit of OTISLINE has been its ability to enhance the effectiveness of the company's managers. Managers now have direct access to information from which they had previously been several levels and thousands of miles removed."

a. What type of information system is OTISLINE? Explain.
b. Does OTISLINE support business operations, management decision making, or strategic advantage? Explain your answer.

Source: "New Roles, New Processes: How IT Is Changing Organizations," *SIM Network*, January/February 1990, p. 3.

4. Ford Motor Company

Technology alone is definitely not the answer, as the Ford Motor Company found out when they set out to overhaul their warehouse procedures in 1987. Despite some 20 years of computerization, the process for supplying millions of auto parts to car dealers and parts wholesalers remained tedious, costly, and labor-intensive. At 18 huge distribution centers around the United States, hundreds of workers trudged up and down long aisles pulling auto parts off shelves to fulfill an order. A study indicated that 70 percent of the warehouse process involved just walking. Some orders, totaling thousands of parts, took days to gather.

Ford formed a team of four engineers and four systems professionals, who together spent two years overhauling the warehouse work flows. They agreed on three design objectives:

1. Take the walking out of the picking process.
2. Eliminate paper records (they made information difficult to share and update).
3. Eliminate the need to type in information on computer terminals (in order to not introduce even more errors).

The system the team designed includes miles of conveyor belts to haul parts to and from carousels containing bins of auto parts. A computer in each warehouse stores the parts orders and controls the movement of the carousels. It also knows the quantity and location of every part put on them. A warehouse might have anywhere from 30 to 60 carousels, with each parts picker having three to work from. To eliminate paper and keyboarding, workers use bar-code scanning to track, store, retrieve, and ship merchandise. This has not only made the process faster, but enables more parts to be housed in each warehouse because dead aisle space is eliminated. Ford has reduced the number of warehouses from 18 to 8, resulting in major savings in labor costs, reduced inventories, less mistakes—and millions of dollars to the bottom line.

a.   Is Ford's new warehouse system a strategic application of information systems? Explain.

b.   What benefits have resulted from the new system?

Source: "New Roles, New Processes: How IT Is Changing Organizations," *SIM Network,* January/February 1990, p. 3.

5.   Western Chemical Corporation

Western Chemical uses telecommunications systems that connect its computers to those of its customers and suppliers to capture data about sales orders and purchases. This data is processed immediately, and inventory and other databases are updated. Word processing and electronic mail services are also provided. Data generated by a chemical refinery process are captured by sensors and processed by a computer that also suggests answers to a complex refinery problem posed by an engineer. Managerial end users receive reports on a periodic, exception, and demand basis, and use computers to interactively assess the possible results of alternative decisions. Finally, top management can access text summaries and graphics displays that identify key elements of organizational performance.

a.   Identify how information systems support (1) business operations, (2) management decision making, and (3) strategic advantage at Western Chemical.

b.   Identify as many different types of information systems as you can in the preceding scenario. Explain the reasons for your selections.

6.   IBM Corporation

IBM has made massive investments in computer technology to automate its factories in a drive to become "the low-cost producer" in the computer industry. It spends billions of dollars annually for research and development to develop new production methods and new products. These include specialized microprocessors and advanced memory chips, since, unlike most of its U.S. competitors, IBM is determined not to be dependent on Japan for these vital components. IBM's factories and branch offices worldwide are connected by a telecommunications network to improve communications between its managers and other employees, as well as to provide vital information to top executives from corporate databases. Software developed for this network and other internal IBM operations (such as manufacturing expert systems) are now offered as software products for sale to its customers. IBM uses investments in information systems technology to help it protect its major market share and keep its position as a "full-service provider" of high-quality computer hardware, software, maintenance, and other services.

a. Identify how strategic information systems (1) improve operational efficiency, (2) promote innovation, and (3) build strategic information resources at IBM.
b. Identify the competitive forces involved and the competitive strategies IBM is using. Also identify instances of barriers to entry, switching costs, and leveraging investment in information technology.

7. American Airlines, Inc.
What does it take to beat your competitors to the "strategic systems" that give a company lasting advantage? To find out, *PC Week* interviewed dozens of winners, losers, and those who are still struggling to build information systems that will help their companies survive. The winners had three things going for them as American Airlines demonstrated. American Airlines Inc.'s Sabre reservation system is a classic example of a winning strategic system. But its developers had to overcome the same budget crunches, technical failures, and internal rivalries that sink systems every day. Why did American succeed?

Vision: Senior management had a vision of how to use information technology to market air travel as a commodity and sold that vision throughout the company.

Culture: American linked the marketing and technical staffs to be sure its system met the real needs of travel agents and travelers and helped the bottom line too.

Commitment: The board of directors believed in Sabre's importance and kept investing in it even when cash was tight and the system was losing money.

a. What are three keys to successful strategic information systems?
b. How did American Airlines demonstrate these keys to success?

Source: Adapted from Robert Scheir, "How Winners Build Strategic Systems" and "Inside Sabre: Surviving Budget Cuts, Software Crashes, and Conflicts," *PC Week*, November 13, 1989, p. 125–27.

8. Grand Metropolitan
Grand Metropolitan plc., a British food-services company, last year gave hand-held computers to grocery store managers to provide just-in-time ordering capabilities. To build a "channel system," they suggest managers look at three areas: (1) the kinds of information being stored, (2) telecommunications requirements, and (3) hardware investments (including those made by customers). They should then look across the "channels" formed from the company's central databases to marketing, sales, customer-support, delivery, dealer, and corporate functions.

   At Grand Metropolitan in London, Chief Information Officer Bill Brant agrees that such channel systems are going to do as much for improving internal administration as they have done for customer service. "Ultimately, what we want to achieve is a flow of information that can be bent in a lot of different directions," Brant said. "Imagine the value of a PC at the customer site if you can deliver unique and useful information along with your products and services. If you can increase the value of the customer's computer, you have increased the value of your own."

a. Are the "channel systems" mentioned above strategic information systems? Explain the reasons for your answer.
b. What are the benefits to businesses and their customers?

Source: Adapted from Dennis Eskow, "'Channel Systems' Put PCs on Front Line," *PC Week*, March 5, 1990, pp. 135–37.

SELECTED REFERENCES

1. Cash, James, Jr.; F. Warren McFarlan; James McKenney; and Michael Vitale. *Corporate Information Systems Management*, 2nd ed. Homewood, Ill.: Richard D. Irwin, Inc., 1988.
2. Hill, Charles, and Gareth Jones. *Strategic Management: An Integrated Approach*. Boston: Houghton Mifflin, 1989.
3. Johnston, H. Russell, and Michael Vitale. "Creating Competitive Advantage with Interorganizational Systems." *MIS Quarterly*, June 1988.
4. Lederer, Albert, and Aubrey Mendelow. "Convincing Top Management of the Strategic Potential of Information Systems." *MIS Quarterly*, December 1988.
5. Porter, Michael. *Competitive Advantage*. New York: The Free Press, 1985.
6. Porter, Michael, and Victor Milar. "How Information Gives You Competitive Advantage," *Harvard Business Review*, July–August 1985.
7. Reid, Richard, and William Bullers, Jr. "Strategic Information Systems Help Create Competitive Advantage." *Information Executive*, Spring 1990.
8. Wiseman, Charles. *Strategic Information Systems*. Homewood, Ill.: Richard D. Irwin, Inc., 1988.

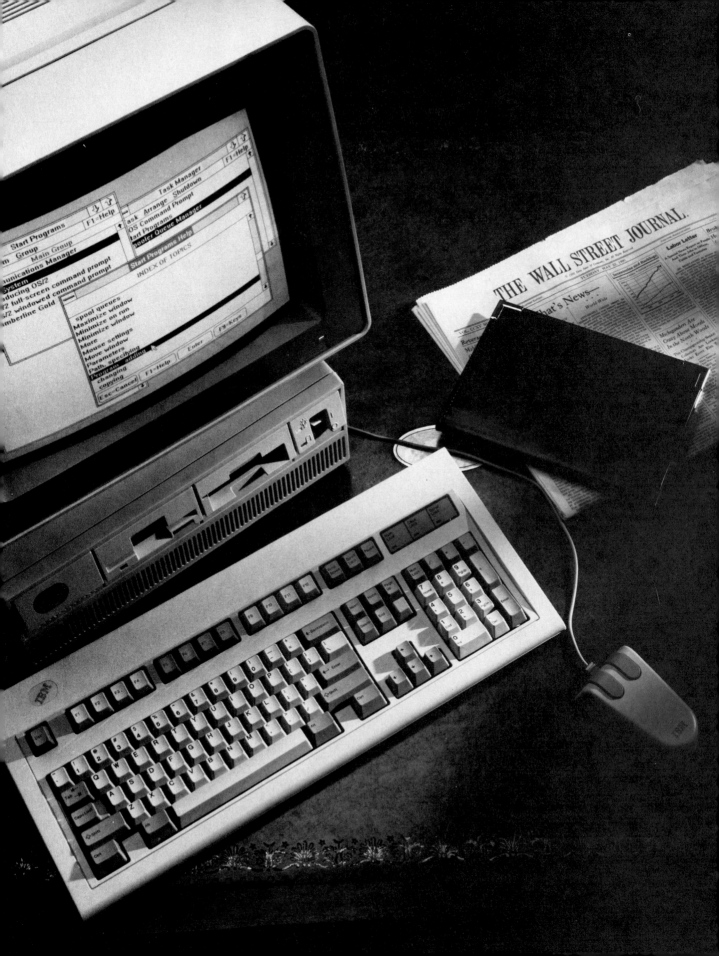

INFORMATION SYSTEMS TECHNOLOGY

MODULE

II

What should you know about information systems technology? The four chapters of this module give you an overview of the major technologies used in modern computer-based information systems and their implications for business end users.

Chapter 3, Introduction to Computer Hardware, discusses and illustrates micro, mini, and mainframe computer systems and the peripheral devices which support the *user interface* between computers and end users, and the data resources of end users and their organizations. Basic concepts about how computer systems work are then explained in Section III of the chapter.

Chapter 4, Introduction to Computer Software, describes the basic features and functions of major types of system and application software packages used to support traditional and end user computing.

Chapter 5, Introduction to Telecommunications, presents an overview of major concepts, applications, trends, and technical alternatives in telecommunications.

Chapter 6, Introduction to Database Management, emphasizes management of the data resources of computer-using organizations. It discusses basic concepts and applications of database management in computer-based information systems.

CHAPTER

3

INTRODUCTION TO COMPUTER HARDWARE

■ Chapter Outline

▨ Learning Objectives

The purpose of this chapter is to provide an introduction to computer hardware by reviewing (1) the major types and uses of computer systems and peripheral devices and (2) basic concepts of how computers work.

Section I of this chapter presents an overview of microcomputer, minicomputer, mainframe, and other types of computer systems.

Section II surveys the major characteristics and functions of computer peripheral devices used to support the user interface through visual and voice input/output methods, as well as the use of semiconductors, magnetic disks and tape, and optical disks to provide capabilities for the storage of data resources in computer systems.

Section III outlines basic CPU functions and briefly explains how computers execute instructions and represent data.

After reading and studying this chapter, you should be able to:

1. Identify the components and functions of a computer system.
2. Outline the major differences and uses of microcomputers, minicomputers, and mainframe computers.
3. Identify the major types and uses of computer peripherals for input, output, and storage.
4. Explain the benefits, limitations, and trends in major types of computer systems and peripheral devices.
5. Name the most commonly used computer storage capacity and time elements.
6. Describe how computers represent data and execute instructions.

Section I: Computer Systems: Micros, Minis, and Mainframes

THE COMPUTER SYSTEM CONCEPT

Before we examine the major types of computer systems in use today, we should emphasize what the term *computer system* means. A computer is more than an electronic data processing "black box" or collection of devices performing various information processing chores. A computer is a **system**—an interrelated combination of components that performs the basic system functions of **input, processing, output, storage,** and **control,** thus providing end users with a powerful information processing tool. Understanding a computer as a **computer system** is vital to the effective use and management of computers. You should be able to visualize any computer this way, from a microcomputer like that shown in Figure 3–1, to a large computer system whose components are interconnected by a telecommunications network and spread throughout a building or geographic area.

Figure 3–2 illustrates that a computer is a system of hardware devices organized according to the following system functions:

- ☐ **Input.** The input devices of a computer system include keyboards, touch screens, electronic "mice," optical scanners, and so on. Input devices convert data into electronic *machine readable* form for entry directly or through telecommunications links into a computer system.

- ☐ **Processing.** The *central processing unit* (CPU) is the main processing component of a computer system. (In microcomputers, it is the main **microprocessor.**) In particular, the *arithmetic-logic unit*, one of the CPU's major components, performs the arithmetic and logic functions required in computer processing.

- ☐ **Output.** The output devices of a computer system include video display units, printers, audio response units, and so on. They convert electronic information produced by the computer system into a *human-intelligible* form for presentation to end users.

- ☐ **Storage.** The storage function of a computer system takes place in the electronic circuits of the *primary storage unit* of the CPU and in *secondary storage* devices such as magnetic disk and tape units. These devices store data and program instructions until needed for processing.

- ☐ **Control.** The control unit of the CPU is the main control component of a computer system. It interprets computer program instructions and transmits directions to the other components of the computer system.

TYPES OF COMPUTER SYSTEMS

Today's computer systems display striking differences as well as basic similarities. Differences in end user needs and technological discoveries have resulted in the development of several major categories of computer systems with a variety of characteristics and capabilities. Thus, computer systems are typically classified as *microcomputers, minicomputers,* and *mainframe* com-

Courtesy IBM Corporation

Figure 3-1 A microcomputer system. This microcomputer is a system of components that includes (1) a keyboard for input, (2) microprocessors and other circuitry in its main system unit for processing and control, (3) a video monitor and printer for output, and (4) memory chips and a built-in floppy disk drive and hard magnetic disk unit for storage.

Figure 3-2 The computer system concept: A computer is a system of hardware components and functions.

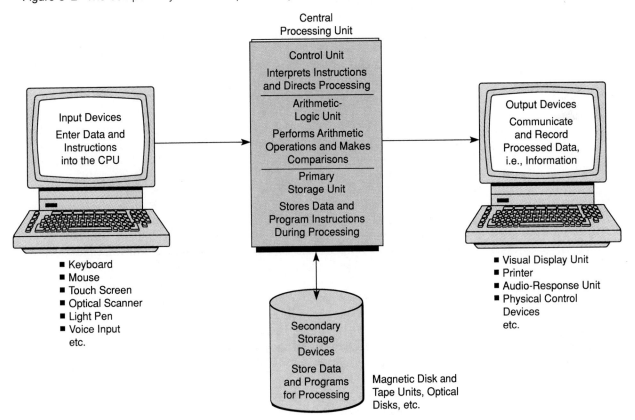

Figure 3-3 Computer system classifications. Notice the overlap among the traditional and application categories of the three major classifications of computers.

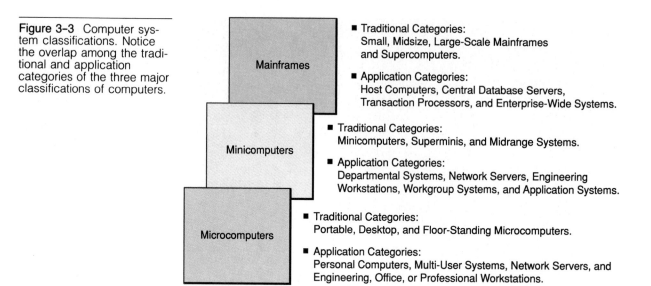

Mainframes
- Traditional Categories:
  Small, Midsize, Large-Scale Mainframes and Supercomputers.
- Application Categories:
  Host Computers, Central Database Servers, Transaction Processors, and Enterprise-Wide Systems.

Minicomputers
- Traditional Categories:
  Minicomputers, Superminis, and Midrange Systems.
- Application Categories:
  Departmental Systems, Network Servers, Engineering Workstations, Workgroup Systems, and Application Systems.

Microcomputers
- Traditional Categories:
  Portable, Desktop, and Floor-Standing Microcomputers.
- Application Categories:
  Personal Computers, Multi-User Systems, Network Servers, and Engineering, Office, or Professional Workstations.

puters. However, as Figure 3–3 illustrates, these are not precise classifications. For example, there are traditional categories such as *superminicomputers*, small, medium, and large mainframe computers, and *supercomputers*. Also, a variety of application categories, which describe major uses for various types of computers, are common. Examples are host computers, network servers, and engineering workstations.

Such categories are attempts to describe the relative *computing power* provided by these computers. This means that they may differ in their processing speed and memory capacity, as well as in the amount and capabilities of peripheral devices for input, output, and secondary storage that they can support. However, you will find microcomputers that are more powerful than some minicomputers, and minicomputers more powerful than some mainframe computers. So these computer classifications do overlap each other, as Figure 3–3 illustrates.

Speed of Computer Systems

How fast are computer systems? Computer operating speeds that were formerly measured in **milliseconds** (thousandths of a second) are now being measured in the **microsecond** (millionth of a second) and **nanosecond** (billionth of a second) range, with **picosecond** (trillionth of a second) speed being attained by some computers. Such speeds seem almost incomprehensible. For example, an average person taking one step each nanosecond would circle the earth about 20 times in one second!

Advanced micro- and minicomputers and most mainframe computers operate at nanosecond speeds and can thus process several *million instructions per second* (**MIPS**). Other measures of processing speed include *megahertz* (**MHz**), or millions of cycles per second. For example, the Intel 8088 used in the original IBM PC and similar microcomputers normally has ratings between 4.7 and 8 MHz, while the Intel 80286 microprocessor used in many IBM PS/2 and other micros typically ranges between 10 and 16 MHz. Figure 3–4 outlines the

Figure 3–4 The Intel 80486, or i486, microprocessor. This advanced microprocessor contains over one million transistors and integrates the capabilities of an 80386 microprocessor, 80387 math coprocessor, and 80385 high-speed memory chip. Compare its performance to other Intel microprocessors.

	386SX	386DX	486
Clock Speeds (MHz)	16.20	16,20,25,33	25,33,50
Performance (MIPS)	2.5-4.0	4-8	15-40
Address Bus Size	24 bit	32 bit	32 bit
Data Bus Size	16 bit	32 bit	32 bit
Memory Supported	16M bytes	4G bytes	4G bytes
Math Coprocessor	80387SX	80387	On-chip

capabilities of the Intel 80386 and 80486 microprocessors used in more powerful models of microcomputers. Notice that the Intel 80386 DX is rated from 16 to 33 MHz while the Intel 80486 or i486 microprocessor chip pictured in Figure 3–4 has a minimum rating of 25 to 33 MHz.

However, megahertz ratings can be misleading indicators of the overall or effective processing speed of microprocessors as measured in MIPS and other measures indicated in Figure 3–4. That's because processing speed depends on factors such as the size of circuitry paths or *busses* between microprocessor components, and the use of specialized microprocessors such as a *math coprocessor* to do arithmetic calculations faster. Therefore, the 80286 chip is about four times as fast as the 8088, while the 80386 chip is about two and one-half times as fast as the 80286 microprocessor. Intel's 80486 microprocessor is rated at about twice the processing speed of the 80386 microprocessor (15 to 20 MIPS). Just for comparison, an IBM Powerstation 530 engineering workstation is rated at 34.5 MIPS, while some large supercomputers have been clocked at more than 1,000 MIPS.

Figure 3–5   Computer storage capacity and time elements.

Storage Elements (approximate capacities)	Computer Time Elements
Kilobyte—One thousand bytes or characters	Millisecond—One thousandth of a second
Megabyte—One million bytes or characters	Microsecond—One millionth of a second
Gigabyte—One billion bytes or characters	Nanosecond—One billionth of a second
Terabyte—One trillion bytes or characters	Picosecond—One trillionth of a second

Capacity of Computer Systems

How large are the storage capacities of computer systems? The storage capacity of most computer hardware devices is usually expressed in terms of **bytes.** At this point, think of a byte as a term for a storage capacity that can hold one **character** of data. So for now, every time you see the word *byte*, you can substitute the term *character*. For example, suppose you have a floppy disk that has a capacity of over 360,000 bytes. This means that it can hold 360,000 alphabetic, numeric, and other characters of data. This is equivalent to about 200 double-spaced pages of typewritten material.

Storage capacities are typically measured in **kilobytes** (abbreviated as KB or K) or **megabytes** (abbreviated MB or M). Although *kilo* means 1,000 in the metric system, the computer industry uses K to represent 1,024 (2^{10}) storage positions. Therefore, a memory size of 256K, for example, is really 262,144 storage positions, rather than 256,000 positions. However, such differences are frequently disregarded in order to simplify descriptions of storage capacity. Thus, a **megabyte** is roughly 1 million bytes (1,048,576, or 2^{20}, bytes), while a **gigabyte** is roughly 1 billion bytes of storage, and a **terabyte** represents 1 trillion bytes of storage.

Typically computer primary storage capacities might range from 640K bytes (655,360 bytes) for many microcomputer memories to 10 GB (10 gigabytes, or approximately 10 billion bytes) for a very large mainframe computer system. Magnetic disk capacities might range from 360K bytes (368,640 bytes) to several megabytes for floppy disks, and over 500 megabytes for optical disks. Large mainframe magnetic disk units can supply many gigabytes of online storage. See Figure 3–5.

MICROCOMPUTER SYSTEMS

Microcomputers are the smallest but most important category of computer systems for end users. A microcomputer is typically referred to as a *personal computer*, or PC. However, microcomputers have become much more than small computers used by individual persons. Their computing power now exceeds that of the mainframes of previous computer generations at a fraction of the cost. They have thus become powerful *professional workstations* for use by end users in business firms and other organizations.

Microcomputers come in a variety of sizes and shapes for a variety of purposes, as Figure 3–6 illustrates. The classifications of *desktop* versus *porta-ble* computers, and *single-user* versus *multiuser* are widely used. That's be-

Figure 3-6   Examples of microcomputer systems.

a The IBM PS/2 Model 50Z: A professional workstation.
Courtesy IBM Corporation

b The IBM RISC 6000 Powerstation 530: An engineering
workstation.
Courtesy IBM Corporation

c The Compaq Systempro: A network server.
Courtesy Compaq Computer Corporation.

cause most microcomputers are designed to fit on top of an office desk, transforming it into an *end user workstation*. Or they are designed to be conveniently carried by end users, such as salespersons or consultants, who do a lot of traveling as part of their job assignments. Most microcomputers are *single-user* computers designed to support the work activities of a particular end user. However, powerful *multiuser machines* are available that support computing by several end users at multiple terminals, as are *network servers* that coordinate processing in *local area networks* (LANs) of microcomputers and other devices.

The typical hardware components of a microcomputer are shown in Figure 3–7. Microcomputers consist of a main **microprocessor** (a central processing unit on a chip), several support microprocessors, and associated control, primary stor-

A Microcomputer System

Figure 3-7 A hardware diagram of a microcomputer system.

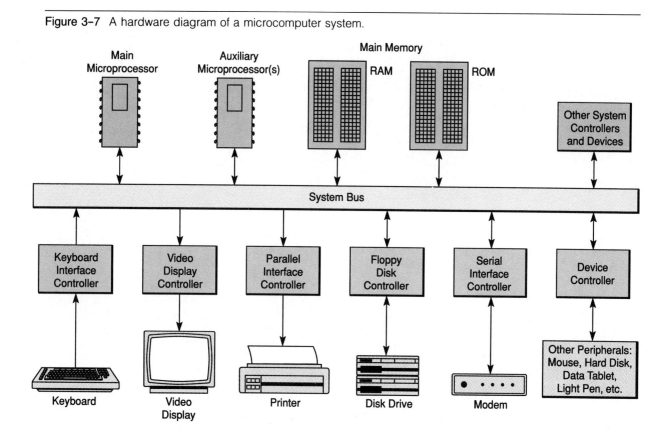

age, and input/output circuitry on one or more circuit boards, plus a variety of input/output and secondary storage devices. Thus, a microcomputer is a **computer system** that uses a variety of devices to perform the systems functions of *input, processing, output, storage,* and *control.*

Input and Output

A keyboard is the most widely used input device for microcomputers, followed by the *electronic mouse* and other devices such as touch screens, light pens, optical scanners, and voice input devices. Video display monitors and printers are the most widely used output devices in microcomputer systems. Other devices such as audio speakers and graphics plotters are also used.

Processing and Control

In most microcomputers, a *main system unit* contains circuit boards on which the main microprocessor, subsidiary processors, and other electronic devices are installed. These serve as the central processing unit and as support processors and control devices. The most popular main microprocessors for microcomputers are the Intel 8088, 80286, and 80386 for IBM and IBM-compatible microcomputers, and the Motorola 68000, 68020, and 68030 used by Apple Macintosh microcomputers.

Expansion Card Slots

80386 Main
Microprocessor

80387 Math
Coprocessor

Speaker

Cooling Fan

Hard Disk Unit

Memory Board
Sockets

Floppy Disk Drive

Figure 3–8 The main system
unit of an IBM Personal
System/2 microcomputer,
with its major components
identified.

Courtesy IBM Corporation

Storage

Primary storage is provided by semiconductor memory chips on the circuit
boards in the main system unit. Primary storage capacities typically range from
256 kilobytes to 16 megabytes of semiconductor storage, though larger capacities are possible. *Secondary storage* is provided by floppy disk drives, hard disk
drives, optical disks, and other devices, which can be part of the main system
unit or can be externally connected. They provide from several hundred
kilobytes to several hundred megabytes of online storage. Figure 3–8 shows the
microprocessors and storage devices inside a microcomputer's main system
unit.

Microcomputers are used for a wide variety of information processing jobs by
end users. Such applications are directly related to the many types of **software
packages** available for them. (We will discuss such software in Chapter 4.) The
most popular types of microcomputer applications include the following:

**Microcomputer
Applications**

☐ **Word processing**—automated electronic typing and editing. Microcomputers are used as *word processors* to prepare memos, letters,
reports, and other documents with the help of word processing and
other writing support software. Professional-looking publications can
also be produced with the use of *desktop publishing* software.

☐ **Decision support**—computerized worksheet analysis and modeling.
Microcomputers and electronic spreadsheet software allow end users
to build spreadsheet models for business situations. This assists
planning, budgeting, and analysis of business performance, and
provides interactive support for decision making.

☐ **Database management**—electronic record-keeping, interrogation, and
report generation. File and database management software allow end
users to build and maintain files and databases of business records.
They can then display information they need electronically or produce
a variety of analytical reports from the data in a database.

☐ **Graphics**—generation of charts and other graphic images. Graphics software packages, laser printers, optical scanners, and other devices allow end users to produce a variety of charts and graphics images. This visually enhances both the analysis and presentation of information in reports and other media.

☐ **Communications**—telecommunications with other end users, computers, and databanks. Telecommunications networks, software packages, and hardware (such as *modems*) allow end users to access the databases of their organization and the databanks of external information services and to use electronic mail to communicate with other end users. Microcomputer workstations can be connected to corporate mainframes to share data and software resources, or be interconnected in *local area networks* (LANs) which support end user work group activities.

☐ **Application development**—computer-supported systems and software development. Microcomputers and a variety of programming languages and computer-aided software engineering (CASE) tools are enhancing and automating many parts of the development process for new information systems.

☐ **Engineering and scientific**—computer-aided design and analysis. Powerful microcomputers are being used as *engineering workstations* for computer-aided design (CAD) to support the analysis and design process of computer-aided engineering (CAE).

☐ **Personal and home applications**—entertainment, home management, personal finance, education, and so on. The microcomputer can use a variety of video game, educational, and home management software packages to entertain, educate, and support personal and family financial management.

MINICOMPUTER SYSTEMS

Minicomputers are larger and more powerful than most microcomputers but are smaller and less powerful than most models of large *mainframe* computer systems. However, this is not a precise distinction. High-end models of microcomputer systems (*supermicros*) are more powerful than some minicomputers. High-end models of minicomputers (*superminis*) are more powerful than some small and medium-size mainframe computers. In addition, local area networks (LANs) of interconnected microcomputers have more processing power than many minicomputers and mainframe models. Thus, a controversy exists on the prospects of minicomputers remaining a separate computer category (leaving only mainframes and microcomputers of various sizes). But for now, minicomputers have a wide range of processing capabilities and hardware characteristics.

Minocomputers are designed to handle many different types of jobs and peripheral devices, and they are typically smaller and less costly than mainframe computers. Most minicomputers can also function in ordinary operating environments, do not need special air conditioning or electrical wiring, and can be placed in most offices and work areas. In addition, since they are comparatively easy to operate, the smaller models of minicomputers do not need a staff of data processing professionals but can rely on properly trained regular employees. Therefore, many organizations continue to acquire minicomputer systems. See Figure 3–9.

Figure 3-9 Examples of minicomputer systems. The AS/400 Model 40 is one of several models in IBM's minicomputer line. The DEC VAXstation 3100 packs the equivalent of a VAX 3400 minicomputer into an engineering workstation.

a The IBM AS/400 Model 40.
Courtesy IBM Corporation

b The DEC VAXstation 3100.
Courtesy Digital Equipment Corporation

Minicomputers are being used for a large number of business data processing and scientific applications. Minicomputers first became popular for use in scientific research, instrumentation systems, engineering analysis, and industrial process monitoring and control. Minicomputers can easily handle such uses because these applications are narrow in scope and do not demand the processing versatility of mainframe systems. They thus serve as industrial process-control and manufacturing plant computers, where they play a major role in computer-assisted manufacturing (CAM). Minicomputers can also take the form of powerful *engineering workstations* for computer-assisted (CAD) applications. They are also being used as *front-end* computers to help mainframe computers control data communications networks and large numbers of data-entry terminals.

Applications

Minicomputers have also become popular as *departmental* or *office* computers. They are being used for departmental computing assignments in distributed processing networks. They can also act as network servers to help control the *local area networks* (LANs) that tie together the microcomputer workstations, data entry terminals, and other computerized devices found in departments, offices, and other work groups. In addition, some larger minicomputers are used because they can provide more processing power and online storage and support more users at the same time than local area networks of microcomputers.

Mainframe computers are large, powerful computers. *Mainframes* are physically larger than micros and minis and usually have one or more central processors with faster instruction processing speeds. For example, they may be able to process from 10 to 200 million instructions per second (MIPS). Mainframes typically have larger primary storage capacities. For example, their main memory capacity can range from 16 million to several hundred million storage positions. Many mainframe models have the ability to service hundreds

MAINFRAME
COMPUTER
SYSTEMS

Figure 3–10 Large mainframe computer systems, the IBM 3090 and DEC VAX 9000.

a The IBM 3090.
Courtesy IBM Corporation

b The VAX 9000.
Courtesy Digital Equipment Corporation

of users at once. For example, a single large mainframe can process hundreds of different programs and handle hundreds of different peripheral devices (terminals, disk and tape drives, printers, etc.) for hundreds of different users at the same time.

Computer manufacturers typically produce *families*, or *product lines*, of mainframe computers that have a variety of models ranging in size from small to medium to large. This allows them to provide a range of choices to their customers, depending on their information processing needs. Most models in a family are compatible (i.e., programs written for one model can usually be run on other models of the same family, with little or no change). This allows customers to move up *(migrate)* to larger models of the same mainframe family as their needs grow. See Figure 3–10.

Applications

Mainframe computers are designed to handle the information processing needs of organizations in business, government, and education with many employees and customers, or complex computational problems. Small and medium sizes of mainframe computers can handle the processing chores of smaller organizations or the regional divisions of larger organizations. They can handle the processing of thousands of customer inquiries, employee paychecks, student registrations, sales transactions, and inventory changes, to name a few. Mainframe computers can also handle large numbers of users needing access at the same time to the centralized databases and libraries of application programs of *time-sharing* networks.

Large mainframe computer systems are used by major corporations and government agencies, which have enormous and complex data processing assignments. For example, large computers are necessary for organizations processing millions of transactions each day, such as major national banks or the national stock exchanges. Large mainframes can also handle the great volume of

Figure 3–11 The Cray 2
supercomputer.

Paul Shambroom; courtesy Cray Research Inc.

complex calculations involved in scientific and engineering analysis and simulation of complex design projects, such as the design of aircraft and spacecraft. A large computer can also act as a *host computer* for *distributed processing networks* that include many smaller computers. Thus, large mainframe computers are used in the national and international computing networks of many airlines, banks, and oil companies.

Supercomputer Systems

The term **supercomputer** has been coined to describe a category of extremely powerful mainframe computer systems specifically designed for high-speed numeric computation. A small number of supercomputers are built each year for large government research agencies, military defense systems, national weather forecasting agencies, large time-sharing networks, and large corporations. See Figure 3–11.

The leading makers of supercomputers are Cray Research, along with NEC, Fugitsu, and a few others. These supercomputers can process from 80 million to over 900 million instructions per second (MIPS). Expressed another way, they can perform arithmetic calculations at a speed of 160 million to 1.7 billion *floating-point operations per second* (FLOPS). Purchase prices for many supercomputers are in the $5 million to $25 million range. However, the development of powerful systems of interconnected microprocessors has spawned a new breed of *mini-supercomputers* with prices below $1 million. Thus, supercomputers continue to advance the state of the art for the entire computer industry.

REAL WORLD CASE

Pepperidge Farm

Pepperidge farm's baked goodies may taste mighty rich, but leaner and cheaper are the favorite flavors of the information systems division at company headquarters these days. "We're looking at our business policies and procedures and bringing them into the '90s," said MIS director Douglas Parish. The 53-year-old company has begun phasing out its IBM 3090 mainframe and moving to a network of 21 IBM Application System/400 midrange computers and 400 to 500 personal computers.

Computerization is playing a critical role in company President Richard Shea's "Project Freshness," a business mission to get the products onto store shelves at their crisp and crunchy peak. Other changes in networking and factory automation have drawn the IS department out of its traditional role "into a much more global relationship with the business," Parrish added. Five years ago, the data center was "doing the classical MIS finance and bookkeeping" on the single mainframe and a few IBM System/38 minicomputers, Parrish said. Like many IS directors, Parrish had accepted the inevitable progression to bigger and costlier machines as his computing needs grew. But while data center expenses climbed, he was watching the burgeoning wealth of software available for PCs and considering the possibilities of distributing processing to smaller computers.

So in mid-1989, the company shifted direction and started replacing all of its mainframe applications in finance, manufacturing, and decision support with AS/400-based software. Manufacturing applications have been installed on AS/400s at its nine bakery plants, and the company also added a communications package to tie together operations, marketing, and sales departments on an AS/400 at headquarters. Eventually, downsizing will shave $250,000 to $500,000 off the annual bottom line in equipment and people, Parrish said.

A subsidiary of Campbell Soup Co., Pepperidge Farm began as a mail-order home-baked bread business in 1937. Today, the business employs more than 6,000 people and produces 450 types of breads, cakes, cookies, crackers, and frozen desserts. Its 1989 operating profits were $54 million, making it one of Campbell's highest margin performers.

There are now four AS/400s at corporate headquarters and nine distributed throughout Pepperidge Farm plants in several states. One of the minis will be dedicated to sales analysis applications, which are currently processed on the mainframe.

"There is still a lot to do," Parrish said of the three-year project. "But one piece of our networking scenario is putting hand-held microcomputers into all our delivery trucks." Pepperidge Farm's 2,400 independent distributors will be working out of their trucks with Fujitsu hand-held computers and printers. "They'll be able to place all orders electronically and sell products into the supermarkets the same way," Parrish explained. "The distributor can sit down at home, figure out tomorrow's load, key it into the system and transmit it." That transmission will end up in the AT&T Mail Network, which Pepperidge Farm will poll each night and then route orders to regional bakery plants.

Application Questions

☐ Why is Pepperidge Farm switching from mainframe-based computing to a network of minicomputers and microcomputers?

☐ Why do you think Pepperidge Farm didn't use a "two-tiered" architecture of mainframes tied to networks of PCs throughout the company?

☐ What are the roles of minicomputers, personal computers, and hand-held computers at Pepperidge Farm?

Source: Adapted from Maryfran Johnson, "Recipe Calls for Low-Cal Systems," *Computerworld,* March 19, 1990, p. 37.

Section II: Computer Peripherals: Input, Output, and Storage

Peripherals is the generic name given to a variety of input/output devices (such as video display terminals) and secondary storage devices (such as magnetic disk drives) that depend on direct connections or telecommunications links to the central processing unit of a computer system. Thus, all peripherals are **online** devices, that is, they are separate from, but can be electronically connected to and controlled by a CPU. (This is the opposite of **offline** devices, which are separate from, and *not* under the control of a CPU.) The major types of peripherals and media that can be part of a computer system are discussed in this section.

There are many methods of input and output at the **user interface** between computer systems and end users. Figure 3–12 shows you the major trends in input/output media and methods that have developed over four generations of computers and are expected to continue into a future fifth generation. Figure 3–12 emphasizes that there is a major trend toward the increased use of a variety of **direct input/output devices** to provide a more natural *user interface*. More and more, data and instructions are entered into a computer system directly through a keyboard or other input devices such as *electronic mice, light pens, touch screens, data tablets,* and *optical scanning wands.* These direct input/output devices drastically reduce the need for paper source documents and their conversion to machine-readable media such as magnetic disks and tape. Direct output of information through video displays of text and graphics and audio (voice) response devices is also expected to become a dominant form of output for end users.

TRENDS IN USER INTERFACE METHODS

The most common user interface method typically involves the use of a **keyboard** for entry of data and a **video display screen** for output to users. **Computer terminals** of various types are the most widely used methods of such input and output. Technically, any input/output device connected by telecommunications links to a computer is called a *terminal.* However, most terminals use a keyboard for input and a TV-like screen for visual output, and are called

COMPUTER TERMINALS

Figure 3–12   Note the trend toward direct input and output media and methods to provide a more natural user interface.

	First Generation	Second Generation	Third Generation	Fourth Generation	Fifth Generation?
INPUT MEDIA/ METHOD	Punched Cards Paper Tape	Punched Cards	Key to Tape/Disk	Keyboard Data Entry Direct Input Devices Optical Scanning	Speech Input Tactile Input
TREND: Towards Direct Input Devices that Are Easy to Use.					
OUTPUT MEDIA/ METHOD	Punched Cards Printed Reports	Punched Cards Printed Reports	Printed Reports Video Displays	Video Displays Audio Responses Printed Reports	Graphics Displays Voice Responses
TREND: Towards Direct Output Devices that Communicate Quickly and Clearly.					

Figure 3–13 Examples of computer terminals. The video display terminals in the office are connected to the small AS/400 minicomputer in the background. The ATM is a widely used transaction terminal.

a Video display terminals.
Courtesy IBM Corporation

b An automated teller machine (ATM).
Courtesy IBM Corporation

visual (or video) **display terminals** (VDTs) or, more popularly, CRT (cathode ray tube) terminals. They allow keyed-in data to be displayed and edited before entry over telecommunications lines into minicomputer and mainframe computer systems.

Intelligent terminals have their own microprocessors and memory circuits. Many are really microcomputers used as telecommunications terminals to larger computers. Therefore, they can independently perform data entry and other information processing tasks. **Transaction terminals** are widely used in banks, retail stores, factories, and other work sites. Examples are automated teller machines (ATMs), factory transaction recorders, and retail point-of-sale (POS) terminals. These terminals use a variety of input/output methods to capture transaction data at its point of origin and transmit it over telecommunications networks to computer systems for processing. See Figure 3–13.

POINTING DEVICES

The video display screens of microcomputers and many video terminals provide a user interface that supports input as well as output. Figure 3–14 illustrates that several types of **pointing devices** can serve as an alternative to the keyboard to enable end users to issue commands, make choices, or enter data directly into a computer system. For example, pointing devices allow end users to choose from menu selections or *icons* displayed on their video screens. **Icons** are small figures that look like familiar devices, such as a file folder (for storing a file), a wastebasket (for deleting a file), a calculator (for switching to a calculator mode), and so on. Using icons helps simplify computer use since they are easier to use with pointing devices than menus and other text-based displays.

The **electronic mouse** is the most popular pointing device to move the cursor on the screen, issue commands, and make *point-and-click* icon and menu selections. It is connected to the computer and contains a roller ball, which moves the cursor in the direction the ball is rolled. By moving the mouse on a desktop, an end user can move the cursor over to an icon or menu selection

Figure 3–14 Alternatives to the keyboard: Using an electronic mouse and a touchscreen for input.

Courtesy IBM Corporation

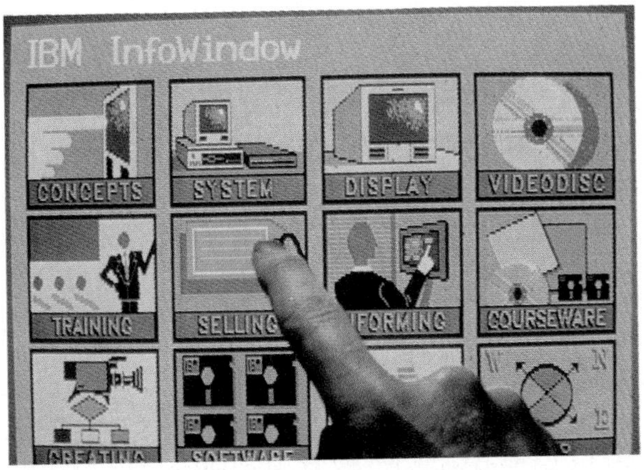

Courtesy IBM Corporation

displayed on the screen. Pressing a button on the mouse then begins the chosen activity.

The **joystick** and the **trackball** are devices that are also used to move the cursor on the display screen. A joystick looks like a small gearshift lever set in a box. Joysticks are widely used for computer-assisted design and are also popular control devices for microcomputer video games. A trackball is a stationary device that is related to the mouse. An end user turns a rollerball device with just its top exposed outside its case to move the cursor on the screen. Trackballs are becoming more popular and are built in to some microcomputer keyboards.

The **light pen** is a pen-shaped device that uses photoelectric circuitry to enter data into the computer through a video screen. A user can *write* on the video display because the light-sensitive pen enables the computer to calculate the coordinates of the points on the screen being touched by the light pen. A **graphics pen** is a form of *digitizer* which allows end users to draw or write on a pressure-sensitive **graphics tablet** and have their handwriting or graphics digitized by the computer and accepted as input.

Touch-sensitive screens are devices that allow you to use a computer by touching the surface of its video display screen. Such screens emit a grid of infrared beams, sound waves, or slight electric current which is broken when the screen is touched. The computer senses the point in the grid where the break occurs and responds with an appropriate action. For example, you could indicate your selection on a menu display by just touching the screen next to that menu item.

VIDEO OUTPUT

Cathode ray tubes (CRTs) are widely used to provide the user interface with visual displays of text and numeric data or graphic images. They use a picture tube technology basically similar to that used in home TV sets. Usually, the clarity of the display and the support of monochrome or color displays depend on the type of video monitor used and the graphics circuit board or *video adapter* installed in a microcomputer. This can provide a variety of *graphics*

Figure 3–15 Examples of video display alternatives. Note the gas plasma display of the IBM Portable 70/386, and the multiple window LCD display of the Macintosh Portable, which also includes a trackball integrated into its keyboard.

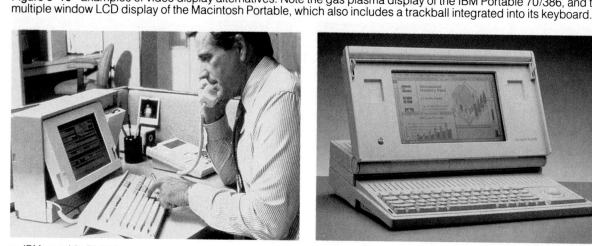

a IBM portable 70/386.
Courtesy IBM Corporation

b The Macintosh Portable.
Courtesy Apple Computer Inc.

modes of increasing capability, such as EGA (enhanced graphics adapter) or VGA (video graphics array). A high level of clarity is especially important to support the more complex graphical displays of advanced *operating environments* and software packages. These packages split the screen into multiple **window** displays or overlapping tiles and use a variety of screen images to support a graphical user interface.

Liquid crystal displays (LCDs), such as those used in electronic calculators and watches, are also being used to display computer output. Their biggest use is to provide a visual display capability for portable microcomputers and terminals. Advances in technology have improved the size, color, and clarity of such displays, which were formerly hard to see in bright sunlight or artificial light.

Plasma display devices are replacing CRT devices in providing visual displays in a limited number of applications. Plasma displays are generated by electrically charged particles of gas (plasma) trapped between glass plates. Plasma display units are becoming more popular, but are still significantly more expensive than CRT or LCD units. However, they are being used in applications where a compact, flat visual display is a critical factor, such as in some portable terminals and microcomputers. See Figure 3–15.

PRINTED OUTPUT

After video displays, **printed output** is the most common form of visual output for the user interface. Most computer systems use **printers** to produce permanent output *(hard copy)* in human-readable form. End users need such printed output if they want copies of output to take away from the computer and to share with others. Hard copy output is also frequently needed for legal documentation. Thus, computers can produce printed reports and documents such as sales invoices, payroll checks, bank statements, as well as hard copy of graphics displays. **Plotters** that draw graphics displays on paper also produce printed paper output. Figure 3–16 illustrates several types of computer printers.

Figure 3–16 Popular types of computer printers.

a A dot matrix printer.
Courtesy IBM Corporation

b A laser printer.
Courtesy IBM Corporation

Many printers (called *impact printers*) form characters and other images on paper by means of the impact of a printing mechanism that presses a printing element (such as a print wheel or cylinder) and an inked ribbon or roller against the face of a sheet or strip of paper. Multiple copies can be produced because the impact of the printing mechanism can transmit an image onto several layers of multiple-copy forms. Popular impact printers for microcomputer systems are *character printers* that use a **dot matrix** printing element consisting of short *print wires* that form a character as a grouping (or *matrix*) of dots. Speeds of several hundred characters per second are attainable. Mainframe computer systems typically use high-speed *line printers* which can print up to several thousand lines per minute. A moving metal chain or cylinder of characters is used as the printing element.

Nonimpact printers are quieter than impact printers since the sound of a printing element being struck is eliminated. However, they do not produce multiple copies like impact printers. **Laser printers** are an example of a popular nonimpact printing method for producing high-quality printed output. Laser printers allow companies to produce their own business forms as well as formal reports and manuals. Such *desktop publishing* applications are discussed in Chapter 7. Laser printers have speeds ranging from less than 5 to over 200 pages per minute. See Figure 3–17.

VOICE INPUT/OUTPUT

Voice input/output promises to be the easiest method of providing a user interface for computer data entry and conversational computing, since speech is the easiest, most natural means of human communications. Voice input/output of data has become technologically and economically feasible for a variety of applications. For example, *voice data entry terminals* allow the direct entry of data into a computer system by verbal communication of a human operator. A typical configuration might consist of one or more portable voice recognition units, microphones, and a CRT terminal for visual display of spoken input. Some voice-recognition devices place all of the required circuitry on a

Figure 3–17 Major types of computer printing methods.

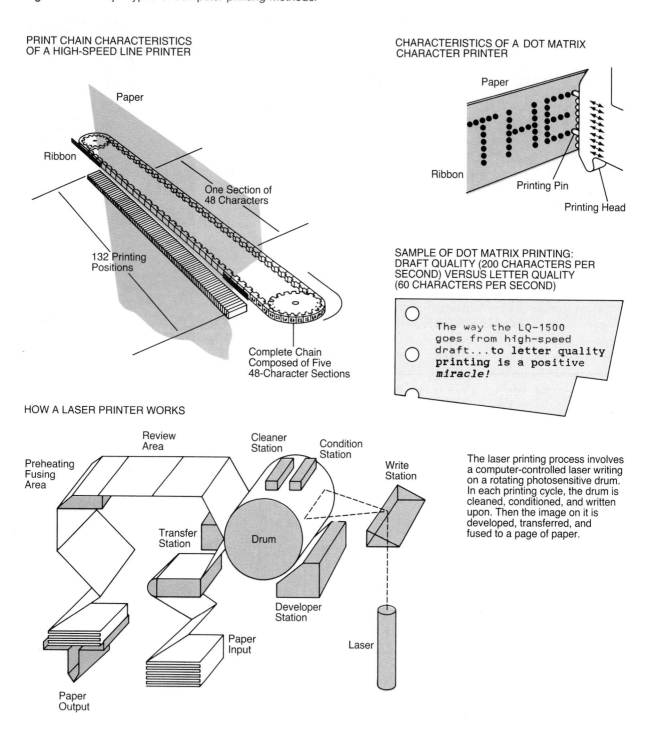

PRINT CHAIN CHARACTERISTICS
OF A HIGH-SPEED LINE PRINTER

Paper

Ribbon

One Section of
48 Characters

132 Printing
Positions

Complete Chain
Composed of Five
48-Character Sections

CHARACTERISTICS OF A DOT MATRIX
CHARACTER PRINTER

Paper

Ribbon

Printing Pin

Printing Head

SAMPLE OF DOT MATRIX PRINTING:
DRAFT QUALITY (200 CHARACTERS PER
SECOND) VERSUS LETTER QUALITY
(60 CHARACTERS PER SECOND)

The way the LQ-1500
goes from high-speed
draft...to letter quality
printing is a positive
miracle!

HOW A LASER PRINTER WORKS

Review
Area

Cleaner
Station

Condition
Station

Write
Station

Preheating
Fusing
Area

Transfer
Station

Drum

Developer
Station

Paper
Input

Laser

Paper
Output

The laser printing process involves
a computer-controlled laser writing
on a rotating photosensitive drum.
In each printing cycle, the drum is
cleaned, conditioned, and written
upon. Then the image on it is
developed, transferred, and
fused to a page of paper.

Figure 3–18 How voice recognition works.

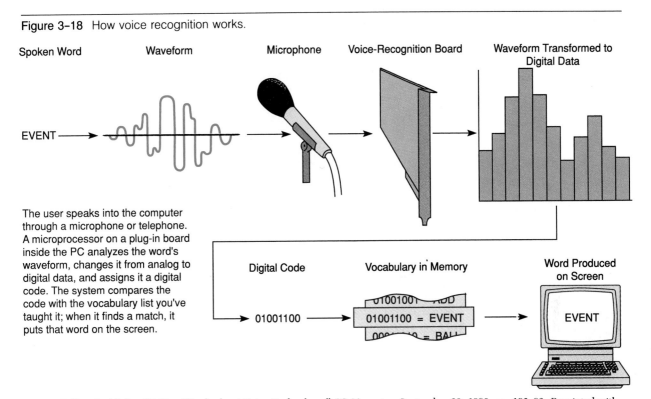

Spoken Word   Waveform   Microphone   Voice-Recognition Board   Waveform Transformed to Digital Data

EVENT

The user speaks into the computer through a microphone or telephone. A microprocessor on a plug-in board inside the PC analyzes the word's waveform, changes it from analog to digital data, and assigns it a digital code. The system compares the code with the vocabulary list you've taught it; when it finds a match, it puts that word on the screen.

Digital Code   Vocabulary in Memory   Word Produced on Screen

01001100   01001001 = ADD
01001100 = EVENT   EVENT
000...10 = BALL

Source: Jeffrey Rothfeder, "A Few Words about Voice Technology," *PC Magazine,* September 30, 1986, pp. 192–93. Reprinted with permission.

single circuit board, including a vocabulary ranging from 1,000 to 10,000 words. They are being incorporated in visual display terminals and microcomputer systems.

Voice output devices range from mainframe *audio-response* units, to voice messaging minicomputers, to *speech synthesizer microprocessors.* Speech microprocessors can be found in toys, calculators, appliances, automobiles, and a variety of other consumer, commercial, and industrial products. Voice messaging minicomputer and mainframe audio response units use voice response software that allows the computer to verbally guide an end user through the steps of a task in many types of activities. They may also allow computers to respond to verbal or touch-tone input over the telephone. Examples of applications include computerized telemarketing surveys, bank pay-by-phone bill-paying services, stock quotation services, university registration systems, and customer credit and account balance inquiries. Figure 3–18 shows how voice input works.

Voice input units rely on **voice recognition** (or *speech recognition*) microprocessors, which analyze and classify acoustic speech patterns and transform them into electronic digital codes for entry into a computer system. Most voice input systems require "training" the computer to recognize a limited vocabulary of standard words for each individual using the system. Operators train the

Figure 3–19 Using a voice input/output system for quality control in the manufacture of circuit boards.

Courtesy Interstate Electronics Corporation

system to recognize their voices by repeating each word in the vocabulary about 10 times. Trained systems regularly achieve over 99 percent word recognition.

Voice data entry devices are now being used in work situations where operators need to perform data entry without using their hands to key in data or instructions, or where it would provide faster and more accurate input. For example, voice recognition systems are being used by manufacturers for the inspection, inventory, and quality control of a variety of products, and by airlines and parcel delivery companies for voice-directed sorting of baggage and parcels. Voice recognition units for microcomputers are available that enable users to develop and use electronic spreadsheet and other standard software packages using voice input of data and commands. However, voice input for standard word processing applications is still too slow and error prone for widespread commercial use. See Figure 3–19.

OTHER INPUT/OUTPUT TECHNOLOGIES

Optical Scanning

Optical scanning devices read text or graphics and convert them into digital input for a computer. This includes **optical character recognition** (OCR) equipment which can read alphabetic, numeric, and special characters that are printed, typed, or handwritten. Optical scanning thus provides a method of direct input of data from source documents into a computer system. OCR-based systems are extensively used in the credit card billing operations of credit card companies, banks, and oil companies. They are also used to process utility bills, insurance premiums, airline tickets, and cash register machine tapes. OCR scanners are used to automatically sort mail, score tests, and process a wide variety of forms in business and government. See Figure 3–20.

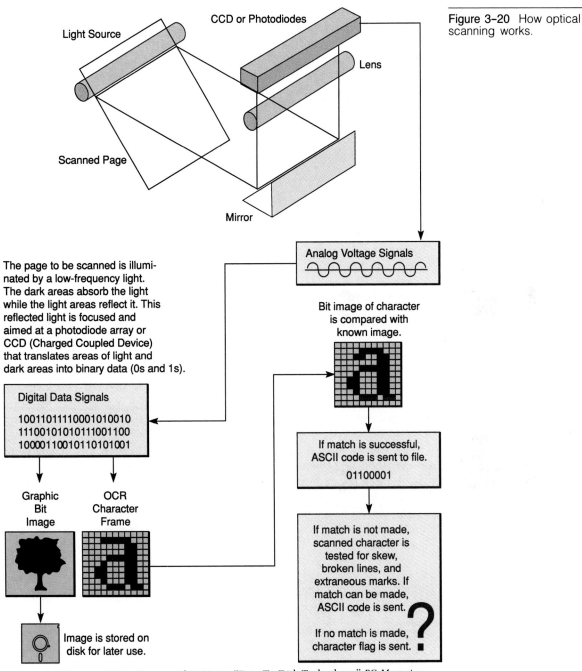

Figure 3-20 How optical scanning works.

Light Source

CCD or Photodiodes

Lens

Scanned Page

Mirror

The page to be scanned is illuminated by a low-frequency light. The dark areas absorb the light while the light areas reflect it. This reflected light is focused and aimed at a photodiode array or CCD (Charged Coupled Device) that translates areas of light and dark areas into binary data (0s and 1s).

Analog Voltage Signals

Bit image of character is compared with known image.

Digital Data Signals

10011011110001010010
11100101010111001100
10000110010110101001

If match is successful, ASCII code is sent to file.

01100001

Graphic Bit Image

OCR Character Frame

If match is not made, scanned character is tested for skew, broken lines, and extraneous marks. If match can be made, ASCII code is sent.

If no match is made, character flag is sent. ■

Image is stored on disk for later use.

Source: Tom Stanton, Diane Burns, and S. Venit, "Page To Disk Technology," *PC Magazine,* September 30, 1986, p. 134. Reprinted with permission.

Optical scanning devices such as hand-held **wands** are used to read data on merchandise tags and other media. This frequently involves reading **bar coding,** which is a code that utilizes bars to represent characters. For example, Universal Product Code (UPC) bar coding on packages of food items and other products has become commonplace because it is required for the automated checkout scanners installed at many supermarkets. Supermarket scanners emit laser beams, which are reflected off a Universal Product Code. The reflected image is converted to electronic impulses that are sent to the in-store minicomputer, where they are matched with pricing information. Pricing information is returned to the terminal, visually displayed, and printed on a receipt. See Figure 3–21.

Many scanners can read graphic images as well as text. Therefore, scanning of graphic images is especially popular in *desktop publishing* applications. There are many types of optical readers, but they all employ photoelectric devices to scan the characters being read. Reflected light patterns of the data are converted into electronic impulses that are accepted as digitized data into the computer system.

Magnetic Ink Character Recognition

Magnetic ink character recognition (MICR) technology allows the computer systems of the banking industry to magnetically read checks and deposit slips. Computers can thus sort, tabulate, and post checks to the proper checking accounts. Such processing is possible because the identification numbers of the bank and the customer's account number are preprinted on the bottom of checks with an iron oxide–based ink. The first bank receiving a check after it has been written must encode the amount of the check in magnetic ink on its lower right-hand corner. The MICR system uses 14 characters (the 10 decimal digits and 4 special symbols) of a standardized design. See Figure 3–22.

Equipment known as MICR *reader-sorters* read a check by first magnetizing the magnetic ink characters and then sensing the signal induced by each character as it passes by a reading head. Data is thus electronically captured by the computer system. The check is then sorted by directing it into one of the pockets of the reader-sorter. Reader-sorters can read over 2,400 checks per minute, with a data transfer rate of over 3,000 characters per second. See Figure 3–23.

Micrographics

The technology of **micrographics** involves three major input/output applications:

☐ **Computer-output-microfilm,** or COM, in which microfilm is used as a computer output medium. High-speed microfilm recorders are used to electronically capture the output of computer systems on microfilm, microfiche, and other *microforms.*

☐ **Computer-input-microfilm,** or CIM, where microfilm is used as an input medium. CIM systems use OCR devices to scan microfilm for high-speed input of data.

☐ **Computer-assisted-retrieval,** or CAR, in which special-purpose computer terminals are used to locate and retrieve automatically a microfilm copy of a document.

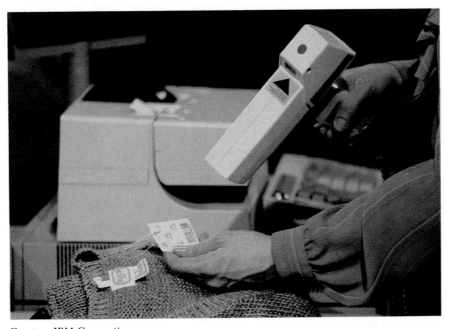

Courtesy IBM Corporation

Figure 3-21 Using an optical scanning wand to read bar coding of product data on merchandise tags.

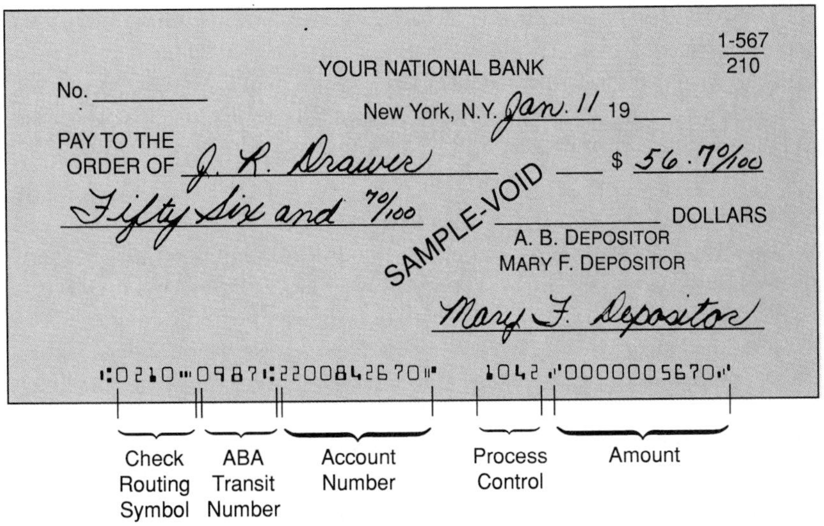

Figure 3-22 A check with MICR encoding the MICR characters on the bottom of the check on the left are pre-printed. Those on the right are encoded after a check is deposited.

Micrographics hardware includes microfilm recorders, hard copy printers, microfilm readers, and micrographics terminals. Micrographics replaces computer printing devices that are too slow and produce too much paper. COM recorders can have a data transfer rate up to 500,000 characters per second and "print" up to 60,000 lines per minute, which is much faster than most high-speed printers and equals or exceeds the output rate of magnetic tape or disk

Figure 3–23 A MICR reader-sorter. It automatically reads and sorts over 2,400 checks per minute.

Courtesy IBM Corporation

units. Microfilm output also takes up only 2 percent of the space of paper output. Micrographic output thus is a lot faster and takes up much less space than paper output. The storage, handling, and retrieval of microfilm files are substantially easier and cheaper than paper documents. However, as we will see in the next section, micrographics is being replaced by the use of optical disks for many document *image processing* applications.

TRENDS IN STORAGE METHODS

Data and information need to be stored after input, during processing, and before needed as output. For example, the information systems of many organizations still use paper documents stored in filing cabinets as a major form of storage media. However, computer-based information systems rely primarily on the *primary storage circuits* and *secondary storage* devices of computer systems to accomplish the storage function. Figure 3–24 illustrates major trends in primary and secondary storage methods. Continued developments in *very large-scale integration* (VLSI), which packs millions of electronic storage circuits on tiny semiconductor chips, are responsible for a significant increase in the main memory capacity of computers. Secondary storage capacities are also expected to escalate into the billions and trillions of characters, due primarily to the use of optical media.

Storage Media Trade-Offs

There are many types of computer storage media and devices. Figure 3–25 illustrates the speed, capacity, and cost of several alternative primary and secondary storage media. Notice the cost/speed/capacity trade-offs as one moves from semiconductor memories to moving surface magnetic media, such as magnetic disk and tape, and then to optical disks. High-speed storage media

Figure 3–24 Major trends in primary and secondary storage methods.

	First Generation	Second Generation	Third Generation	Fourth Generation	Fifth Generation?
PRIMARY STORAGE	Magnetic Drum	Magnetic Core	Magnetic Core	LSI Semiconductor Circuits	VLSI Semiconductor Circuits
TREND: Towards Large Capacities Using Smaller Microelectronic Circuits.					
SECONDARY STORAGE	Magnetic Tape Magnetic Drum	Magnetic Tape Magnetic Disk	Magnetic Disk Magnetic Tape	Magnetic Disk Floppy Disk Optical Disk	Optical Disk and Card Magnetic Disk
TREND: Towards Massive Capacities Using Magnetic and Optical Media.					

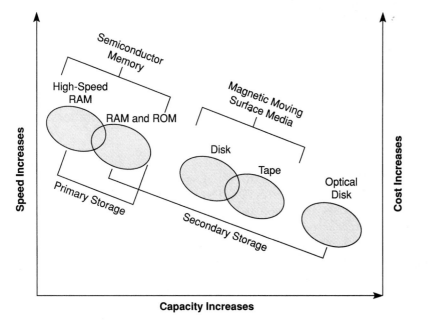

Figure 3–25 Storage media cost, speed, and capacity trade-offs. Notice how cost increases with speed, and how it decreases as capacity increases.

cost more per byte and provide lower capacities. Large capacity storage media cost less per byte but are slower. Such trade-offs are why we have different kinds of storage media.

Notice also that semiconductor memories are being used mainly for primary storage, though they are finding increasing use as high-speed secondary storage devices. Magnetic disk and tape and optical disk devices, on the other hand, are used as secondary storage media to greatly enlarge the storage capacity of a computer system. Also, since most primary storage circuits lose their contents when electrical power is interrupted, most secondary storage media provide a more permanent type of storage. However, the contents of secondary storage devices cannot be processed without first being brought into primary storage. Thus, such devices play a supporting role to the primary storage circuits of a computer system.

Figure 3–26 Sequential versus direct access storage. Magnetic tape is a typical sequential access medium. A magnetic disk is a typical direct access storage device (DASD).

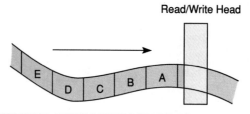

SEQUENTIAL ACCESS STORAGE DEVICE

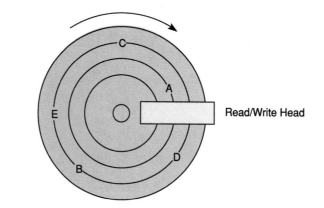

DIRECT ACCESS STORAGE DEVICE

Direct and Sequential Access

Primary storage media such as semiconductor storage chips are called **direct access,** or *random access memory* (RAM). Magnetic disk devices are frequently called *direct access storage devices* (DASDs). On the other hand, media such as magnetic tape devices are known as **sequential access** devices.

The terms *direct access* and *random access* both describe the same concept. They mean that an element of data or instructions can be directly stored and retrieved by selecting and using any of the locations on the storage media. It also means that each storage position (1) has a unique address and (2) can be individually accessed in approximately the same length of time without having to search through other storage positions. For example, each memory cell on a microelectronic semiconductor RAM chip can be individually sensed or changed in the same length of time. Also, any data record stored on a magnetic or optical disk can be accessed directly in approximately the same time period. See Figure 3–26.

Sequential access storage devices use media such a magnetic tape whose storage locations do not have unique addresses and cannot be directly addressed. Instead, data must be stored and retrieved using a sequential or serial process. Thus, data are recorded one after another in a predetermined sequence (such as a numerical or alphabetic order) on a storage medium. Locating an individual item of data requires searching much of the recorded data on the tape until the desired item is located.

SEMICONDUCTOR STORAGE

The primary storage (main memory) of most modern computers consists of microelectronic **semiconductor storage** circuits. Because of continued development in *very large-scale integration* (VLSI), millions of semiconductor storage

Courtesy IBM Corporation

Figure 3-27 A semiconductor memory chip with a capacity of 16 million bits.

circuits can be packed on silicon chips. Memory chips with capacities of 256K bits, 1 million bits (1 megabit), 4 megabits, and 16 megabits are currently used in computer systems. (A *bit* is either a 0 or a 1.) See Figure 3–27.

Some of the major attractions of semiconductor storage are small size, great speed, shock and temperature resistance, and low cost due to mass production capabilities. One major disadvantage of most semiconductor memory is its **volatility.** Uninterrupted electric power must be supplied or the contents of memory will be lost. Therefore, emergency transfer to other devices or standby electrical power (battery packs or emergency generators) is required if data must be saved. Another alternative is to permanently "burn in" the contents of semiconductor devices so that they cannot be erased by a loss of power.

There are two basic types of semiconductor memory: *random access memory* (RAM) and *read only memory* (ROM).

☐ **RAM: random access memory.** This is the most widely used primary storage medium. Each memory position can be both sensed (read) or changed (write), so it is also called direct access or read/write memory. This is a *volatile* memory.

☐ **ROM: read only memory.** This is a type of *nonvolatile* random access memory used for permanent storage. It can only be read, not "written" (i.e., changed). Frequently used control instructions in the control unit and programs in primary storage can be permanently burned in to the storage cells during manufacture. Variations include PROM (programmable read only memory) and EPROM (erasable programmable read only memory), which can be permanently or temporarily programmed after manufacture.

Semiconductor Secondary Storage

Semiconductor storage chips are used as direct access *primary and secondary storage* media for both large and small computers. This is due in large part to the development of plug-in circuit boards containing several megabytes of semiconductor storage chips (RAM cards) which can be added to a microcomputer to increase its storage capacity. This provides additional primary storage, but can also be used for secondary storage. The operating system program of the computer can be instructed to treat part of RAM as if another disk drive has been added to the system. This provides a very high speed semiconductor secondary storage capability, sometimes called a *RAM disk*. Its major limitation is its volatility since the contents of RAM are lost if power is interrupted. Peripheral devices consisting of semiconductor storage circuits are also marketed as high-speed alternatives to magnetic disk units used on mainframe computers.

MAGNETIC DISK STORAGE

Magnetic disk media and equipment are now the most common form of secondary storage for modern computer systems. They provide fast access and high storage capacities at a reasonable cost. The two basic types of magnetic disk media are conventional (hard) metal disks and flexible (floppy) diskettes. Several types of magnetic disk peripheral equipment are used as direct access storage devices (DASDs) in both small and large computer systems.

Magnetic disks are thin metal or plastic disks that resemble phonograph records and are coated on both sides with an iron oxide recording material. Several disks may be mounted together on a vertical shaft, which typically rotates the disks at speeds of 2,400 to 3,600 revolutions per minute (rpm). Electromagnetic read/write heads are positioned by access arms between the slightly separated disks to read or write data on concentric circular **tracks.** Data is recorded on tracks in the form of tiny magnetized spots which form binary digits that represent the characters of data. Thousands of bytes can be recorded on each track, and there are several hundred data tracks on each disk surface, each of which is subdivided into a number of portions called **sectors.** See Figure 3–28.

Types of Magnetic Disks

There are several types of magnetic disk arrangements, including removable disk packs and cartridges as well as fixed disk units. Removable disk devices are popular because they can be used interchangeably in magnetic disk units and stored offline when not in use. See Figure 3–29.

- □ **Floppy Disks,** or magnetic *diskettes,* are disks that consist of polyester film covered with an iron oxide compound. A single disk is mounted and rotates freely inside a protective plastic jacket, which has access openings to accommodate the read/write head of a disk drive unit.
- □ **Disk Packs** are easy to handle. For example, one type of disk pack consists of 11 14-inch-wide disks, is about 6 inches high, weighs about 20 pounds, and can store over 500 million characters.
- □ **Hard disk drives** combine magnetic disks, access arms, and read/write heads into a sealed module. These nonremovable magnetic disk assemblies allow higher speeds, greater data recording densities, and closer tolerances within a sealed, more stable environment. Removable *disk cartridge* versions are also available.

MAGNETIC TAPE STORAGE

Magnetic tape is another widely used secondary storage medium. Data is recorded in the form of magnetized spots on the iron oxide coating of a plastic tape by the read/write heads of *magnetic tape drives.* Magnetic tape is usually subdivided into horizontal tracks to accommodate the recording of bits into common computer codes. Blank spaces, known as *gaps,* are used to separate

Figure 3-28   Characteristics of magnetic disks. Notice especially the concepts of cylinders, tracks, and sectors.

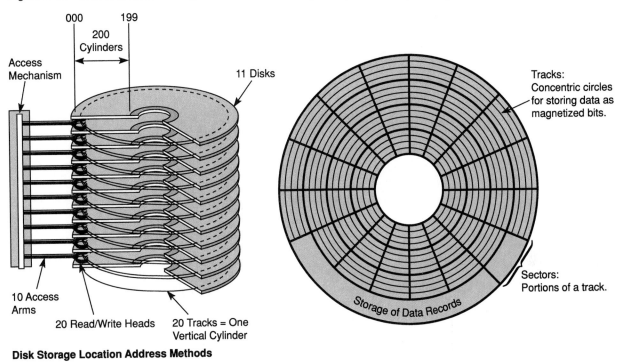

Disk Storage Location Address Methods

- By cylinder (or track), surface, and data record number.
  Example: Cylinder 199, surface 15, record 08.
- By sector and data record number.
  Example: Sector 74, record 02.

Figure 3-29   Magnetic disk media.

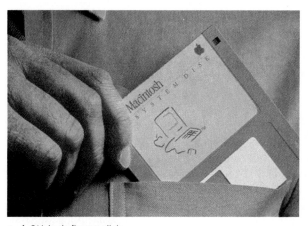

a   A 3½-inch floppy disk.
Courtesy Apple Computer Inc.

b   Hard magnetic disk drives.
Courtesy IBM Corporation

Figure 3–30 Magnetic tape data storage format. Notice how numbers, letters, and other characters can be represented on this nine-track tape.

NINE-TRACK TAPE (EBCDIC Code)

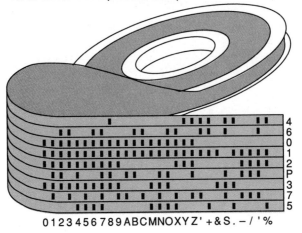

0 1 2 3 4 5 6 7 8 9 A B C M N O X Y Z ' + & S . – / ' %

individual data records or *blocks* of grouped records. Interrecord or interblock gaps are required since a certain amount of blank space between records or blocks is needed to allow for such mechanical operations as the start/stop time of a magnetic tape unit. Most files group records into blocks to conserve file space, instead of leaving gaps between each record. Figure 3–30 illustrates the format of data on magnetic tape.

Magnetic tape comes in the form of tape reels and cartridges for mainframes and minicomputers, and small cassettes and cartridges for microcomputers. Mainframe magnetic cartridges are replacing magnetic tape reels and can hold over 200 megabytes. Magnetic tape cassettes and small magnetic tape cartridges are a popular media for making backup copies of data stored on microcomputer hard disk drives. See Figure 3–31.

OPTICAL DISK STORAGE

Optical disks are a relatively new mass storage medium. Mainframe versions use 8-inch and 12-inch plastic disks with capacities of several billion bytes of information. The version for use with microcomputers is called CD-ROM (compact disk–read only memory). It uses 12-centimeter (4.7-inch) or 5¾-inch compact disks (CDs) similar to those used in stereo music systems. Each disk can store from 500 to 700 megabytes. Data are recorded by using a laser to burn permanent microscopic pits in a spiral track on a master disk from which compact disks can be mass produced. Then CD-ROM disk drives use a laser device to read the binary codes formed by those pits. See Figure 3–32.

Another optical disk technology produces *write once, read many* (WORM) disks. This allows microcomputers with the proper optical disk drive units to record their own data once on an optical disk, then be able to read it indefinitely. The major limitations of CD-ROM and WORM systems is that recorded data cannot be erased. However, **erasable optical disk** systems have now become available. This technology records and erases data by using a laser to heat a microscopic point of the disk's surface. In some versions, a magnetic coil changes the spot's reflective properties from one direction to another, thus

Courtesy IBM Corporation

Figure 3–31 Loading magnetic tape cartridges. This mainframe computer unit can automatically change cartridges during processing.

Fred Bodin

Figure 3–32 An optical data disk. This CD-ROM disk can hold over 500 million characters of information.

Figure 3–33 How an erasable optical disk works.

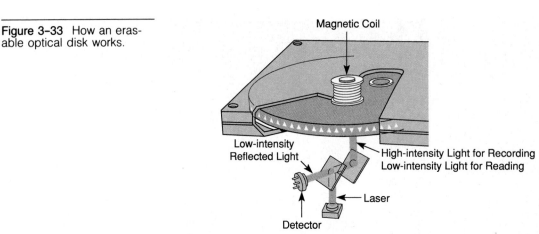

Writing Process

To prepare an optical disk to store data, a laser must first heat the area; the laser fires high-intensity light onto a microscopic area of the disk, heating it to the Curie point (roughly 300 degrees Centigrade). The magnetic property of the heated portion is easily changed at this temperature, and as the laser heats the disk, a magnetic coil emits a weak magnetic field that changes the reflective properties of the surface (corresponding to a binary one or zero, the way all computer media store data.) The disk cools instantly once the laser shuts off, and data cannot be easily changed unless the laser heats the surface again.

Reading Process

To read data, a laser shoots low-intensity light onto a spot on the disk. The reflected light waves rotate in one of two directions (polarizations), according to whether the illuminated spot was a binary one or zero. A detector next to the laser interprets the polarization of the reflected light as a binary one or zero.

Source: Adapted from Patrick Honan, "Optical Storage," *Personal Computing,* February 1989, p. 112.

recording a binary one or zero. A laser device can then read the binary codes on the disk by sensing the direction of reflected light. See Figure 3–33.

One of the major uses of optical disks is in *image processing*, where long-term *archival storage* of historical files of document images must be maintained. Financial institutions, among others, are using optical scanners to capture digitized document images and store them on WORM optical disks as an attractive alternative to microfilm media. The major use of CD-ROM disks is to provide end users with fast access to reference materials and data banks in a convenient, compact form. This includes encyclopedias, directories, manuals, periodical abstracts, part listings, and statistical databases of business and economic activity. Interactive educational and industrial training applications have also been developed for CD-ROM disks.

Thus, optical disks have emerged as a popular storage medium for image processing, and they appear to be a promising alternative to magnetic disks and tape for very large (mass) storage capabilities for organizational and end user computing systems. However, the erasable technology is still being perfected. Also, optical disk devices are significantly slower and more expensive than magnetic disk devices. As a result, optical disk systems are not expected to displace magnetic disk technology in the near future.

REAL WORLD CASE

Charles Schwab & Co. and Ohio State University

When John Stossel wants to check the value of his stock portfolio, he doesn't pick up the paper; he reaches for the phone. Stossel can also buy and sell stock and check his account balance by calling a toll-free number and pushing a few buttons on his keypad. He never speaks to a broker. "It's simple to use, and it's private," says the software engineer.

Stossel's broker is actually a Charles Schwab & Co. service called Telebroker. Many Schwab customers can now check stock prices and buy and sell securities by phone at any time of the day or night. "We're taking over 3% of the firm's trades already, and we believe we can offload as much as 20%, says Elizabeth Wilcox, senior product manager at Schwab.

Many businesses are moving into voice response systems. PC-based systems that support four telephone lines cost as little as $15,000, while high-end systems handling 48 simultaneous calls go for about $50,000. The systems turn a telephone into a computer terminal, allowing callers to execute financial transactions, place orders, register for classes, and retrieve information.

Thus, colleges and universities have latched onto the technology as a way to reduce the trials of course registration. For example, about 47,000 students at Ohio State University— nearly 90 percent of the student body—now register by phone. The Brutus registration system, named after the Buckeyes' mascot, has resulted in "phenomenal time savings for students," university registrar Eugene Schuster says. "The old process has them carrying written documents from their college office to the registration center to process an add or a drop. We've eliminated the lines and made it possible to register from your own kitchen."

Students call Brutus and punch in codes for the courses they want to take. Brutus does housekeeping work such as verifying that students have taken the required prerequisite courses and checking for additional requirements like laboratories. It will even suggest alternative times if a course is filled. The system checks and approves all fees with the callers and then reads back a summary of all that's been entered.

Of course, while the telephone has a decided edge in terms of numbers installed, in many ways it's still a lousy replacement for a computer terminal. Telephones are poor at entering text material, and voice response systems often require callers to listen to long menu lists, and don't handle interruptions and errors well.

However, voice response application can yield significant benefits. Schwab's Wilcox says that the biggest benefit of her company's Telebroker system is flexibility. Telebroker is expected to let Schwab ease into new geographic regions without having to set up a full-blown brokerage. Schwab uses AT&T as a service bureau for Telebroker, with calls coming to AT&T computers and linking to a database that Schwab provides. The service can handle 118 simultaneous calls with response times of one to three seconds.

Ohio State's Brutus is based on an Amdahl mainframe and an AT&T Conversant voice-response system. At a cost of about $200,000 for equipment, software, and a year's development time, the system hasn't been cheap. In fact, Schuster says, Brutus "has probably been a net expense for the university." The benefit, though, is an end to the crowded and error-prone paper registration system.

Application Questions

☐ What features of a touchtone telephone make it a good input/output device? What limitations does it have?

☐ Why does the use of telephone voice-response systems meet the needs of Charles Schwab & Co. and its clients? Ohio State and its students?

☐ Would (or does) a telephone voice response system work well for student registration at your university? Explain.

Source: Adapted from Paul Gillin, "Voice Data Combos: Service with a Dial," *Computerworld*, April 2, 1990, pp. 63, 74.

Section III: Computer Concepts: How Computers Work

Computers can do some amazing things, as Figure 3–34 illustrates. How they do it is the subject of this section. Of course, as a business end user, you do not need a detailed technical knowledge of computers. However, you do need to understand some basic facts and concepts about how computers work. This should help you be an informed and productive user of computer system resources. Therefore, this section presents basic concepts about the central processing unit, how computers execute instructions, and how computers represent data.

Figure 3–34 The speed and power of the computer: an example.

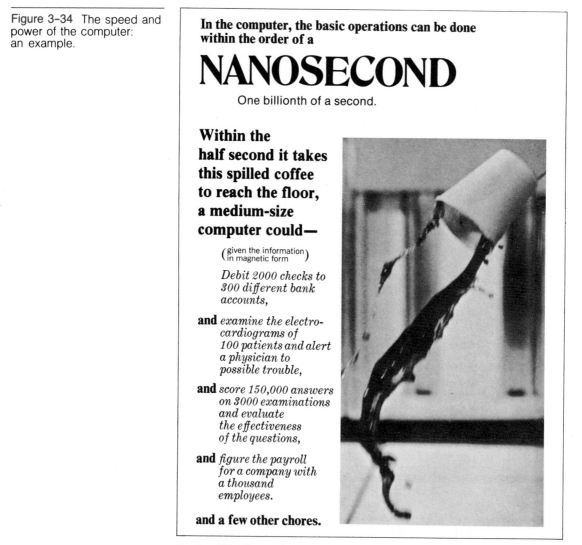

In the computer, the basic operations can be done within the order of a

NANOSECOND

One billionth of a second.

Within the half second it takes this spilled coffee to reach the floor, a medium-size computer could—

(given the information in magnetic form)

Debit 2000 checks to 300 different bank accounts,

and *examine the electro-cardiograms of 100 patients and alert a physician to possible trouble,*

and *score 150,000 answers on 3000 examinations and evaluate the effectiveness of the questions,*

and *figure the payroll for a company with a thousand employees.*

and a few other chores.

Courtesy IBM Corporation

The **central processing unit** is the most important hardware component of a computer system. It is also known as the CPU, the *central processor* or *instruction processor*, and the main *microprocessor* in a microcomputer. The three major subunits of the CPU are the *arithmetic-logic unit*, the *control unit*, and the *primary storage unit* as was illustrated in Figure 3.2. The CPU also includes specialized circuitry such as *registers* for high-speed, temporary storage of instruction and data elements, and various subsidiary processors such as those for arithmetic operations, input/output, and telecommunications support.

THE CENTRAL PROCESSING UNIT

Every other component of a computer system is controlled and directed by the CPU's **control unit.** The control unit obtains instructions from the primary storage unit. After interpreting the instructions, the control unit transmits directions to the appropriate components of the computer system, ordering them to perform the required data processing operations. The control unit tells the input and secondary storage devices what data and instructions to read into memory, and tells the arithmetic-logic unit where the data to be processed is located in memory, what operations to perform, and where in memory the results are to be stored. Finally, it directs the appropriate output devices to convert processed data into machine- or human-readable output media.

The Control Unit

Arithmetic and comparison operations occur in the **arithmetic-logic unit** (ALU). Depending on the application being processed, data may be transferred from primary storage to the arithmetic-logic unit and then returned to storage several times before processing is completed. The arithmetic-logic unit also performs such operations as shifting and moving data. Through its ability to make comparisons, it can test for various conditions during processing and then perform appropriate operations.

The Arithmetic-Logic Unit

The arithmetic-logic unit allows a computer to perform the arithmetic operations of addition, subtraction, multiplication, and division and to identify whether a number is positive, negative, or equal to zero. It can thus compare two numbers to determine which is higher than, equal to, or lower than the other. This ability of the computer to make comparisons gives it a *logic* capability. It can make logical changes from one set of program instructions to another based on the results of comparisons made during processing.

For example, in a payroll program, the computer can test if the hours worked by employees exceed 40 hours per week. Payments for such overtime would be computed using a different sequence of instructions than that used for employees without overtime. We will explain this process shortly.

The storage function of computer systems takes place in the electronic circuits of the **primary storage unit** of the CPU and in a variety of *secondary storage devices* such as magnetic disks and tape. All data and programs must be placed in the primary storage unit (also called *main memory* or *main storage*) before they can be used in processing. The primary storage unit is also used to hold data and program instructions between processing steps and after processing is completed, but before release as output.

Primary Storage

Thus, a computer can store both data and instructions internally in its memory. This internal storage enables the computer to "remember" the details of many assignments and to proceed from one assignment to another automatically since it can retain data and instructions until needed. The ability of the computer to store its operating instructions internally (the *computer program*) allows the computer to process data *automatically*, that is, without continual human intervention.

Primary storage circuitry is organized into many small groups of storage circuits called *storage positions* or *storage locations*. Primary storage is frequently compared to a group of mailboxes, where each mailbox has an address and is capable of storing one item of data. Similarly, each position of storage has a specific numerical location called an *address* so that data stored in its contents can be readily located by the computer. In most modern computers, each position of storage can usually hold at least one character, including alphabetic, numeric, and special characters.

Other CPU Designs

The CPUs of many current computer systems (from microcomputers to mainframes) use a variety of processor designs for their processing functions. For example, instead of having one CPU with a single control unit, arithmetic-logic unit, and primary storage unit (called a *uniprocessor* design), the CPUs of many computers use a **multiprocessor** design which contains several types of processing units. The major types of multiprocessor designs include:

☐ **Support processors.** This design relies on specialized microprocessors to help the main CPU perform a variety of functions. These microprocessors may be used for input/output, primary storage management, arithmetic computations, or telecommunications, thus freeing the main central processor (sometimes called the *instruction processor*) to do the major job of executing program instructions. For example, a microcomputer may use support microprocessors such as *arithmetic coprocessors, video display controllers,* or *magnetic disk controllers.* A large computer may also use support microprocessors called *channels* to control the movement of data between the CPU and input/output devices.

☐ **Coupled processors.** This multiprocessor design uses multiple CPUs or may have a CPU design consisting of multiple arithmetic-logic and control units that share the same primary storage unit. These systems can therefore execute instructions from several different programs at the same time. Some configurations may also provide what is known as a *fault tolerant* capability since the multiple CPUs provide a built-in backup to each other if one of them fails.

☐ **Parallel processors.** This multiprocessor design uses hundreds or even thousands of instruction processors organized in clusters or networks. These systems can therefore execute many instructions at a time in *parallel.* This is a major departure from the traditional design of current computers, called the *von Neumann design,* which execute instructions serially (one at a time). Many experts consider such systems the key to providing artificial intelligence capabilities to fifth-generation computers.

RISC Processors

Many advanced engineering workstations and other computers rely on a processor design called RISC (reduced instruction set computer). This contrasts with most current computers which use CISC (complex instruction set computer) processors. RISC processor designs optimize a CPU's processing speed by using a smaller *instruction set.* That is, they use a smaller number of the basic *machine instructions* that a processor is capable of executing. By keeping the instruction set simpler than CISC processors and using more complex software, a RISC processor can reduce the time needed to execute program instructions. Thus, computers that use RISC processors have become popular for computational-intensive applications in engineering and the physical sciences.

Computers work by executing the instructions in a program. The specific form of a computer instruction depends on the type of programming language and computer being used. However, in its simplest form, an instruction consists of:

HOW COMPUTERS EXECUTE INSTRUCTIONS

- □ An **operation code** that specifies what is to be done (add, compare, read, etc.).
- □ One or more **operands,** which specify the primary storage addresses of data or instructions and/or indicate which input/output and secondary storage devices will be used.

The operation code and operands of the instruction being executed, as well as data elements affected by the instruction, are moved through the special-purpose circuitry of the CPU or microprocessor during the execution of an instruction. A fixed number of electrical pulses emitted by a CPU's timing circuitry, or *internal clock,* determines the timing of such basic CPU operations as fetching and interpreting instructions. The time period to accomplish each basic operation is called a **machine cycle.** We will see examples of such basic operations shortly. The number of machine cycles required to execute an instruction varies with the complexity of the central processor's design and the instruction being executed.

During each machine cycle, electrical pulses generated by the internal clock energize special-purpose circuitry elements that sense and interpret specific instructions and data and move them (in the form of electrical pulses) between various specialized circuitry components of the CPU. One of the most important of these are **registers,** which are small high-speed storage circuit areas used for the temporary storage of an individual program instruction or an element of data during the operation of the control and arithmetic-logic units.

The execution of an instruction can be divided into two segments, the *instruction cycle* and the *execution cycle.* Simply stated, the **instruction cycle** consists of processes in which an instruction is *fetched* from primary storage and *interpreted* by the control unit. The **execution cycle** consists of *performing* the operations specified by the instruction that was interpreted. Let's look at a simplified illustration and explanation of what happens in a CPU during the instruction and execution cycles.

Executing an Instruction

Figure 3–35 illustrates and explains the execution of a typical instruction by a computer. First let's state the instruction in conversational English, then in a form more like the machine language instructions executed by computers. Then you should follow the steps used by the computer to execute this instruction as shown in Figure 3–35.

English Instruction: Add the amount of hours worked today by an employee to his or her total hours worked this week.

Computer Instruction: Add the amount stored in primary storage at address 006 to the amount contained in the *accumulator register* and store the result in primary storage location 008.

The Order of Execution

The computer automatically repeats instruction and execution cycles until the final instruction of a program is executed. Usually, instructions are sequentially executed in the order in which they are stored in primary storage. An *instruction counter*, which automatically advances in sequential order to the address of the next instruction stored in memory, is used to indicate what instruction is to be executed next.

Sometimes, a *branch instruction* is brought from storage. It tells the control unit that it may have to execute an instruction in another part of the program, instead of the next sequential instruction. This change in the sequence of instructions can be *unconditional* or *conditional*. A conditional branch is usually the result of a *test* or *comparison* instruction, which can cause a change in the sequential order of processing if a specified condition occurs. For example, in a payroll program, a different sequence of instructions is typically used for employees whose hours worked exceeded 40 hours per week. These employees have earned *overtime pay* (typically one and one-half times the regular pay rate). Thus, the payroll program could contain the following instruction:

If the total of hours worked this week is greater than 40, then execute the instruction at storage address 020 next.

Since the employee in our example in Figure 3–35 has worked 47 hours this week, the control unit would reset the instruction counter to address 020. The CPU would then branch, or "jump," to that part of the program and begin executing the instructions for computing overtime pay, rather than the instructions for computing regular pay.

HOW COMPUTERS REPRESENT DATA

The letters of the alphabet in this book are symbols that when properly organized or "coded" into the English language will represent data that you, the reader, can process into information. Thus, we can say that words, numbers, and punctuation are the human-sensible code by which data is represented in this book. Similarly, data must be represented in a machine-sensible code before it can be processed by a computer system.

The Binary Number System

Data is represented in a computer system by either the presence or absence of electronic or magnetic signals in its circuitry or in the media it uses. This is called a **binary,** or two-state, representation of data since the computer is indicating only two possible states or conditions. For example, transistors and other semiconductor circuits are either in a conducting or nonconducting state.

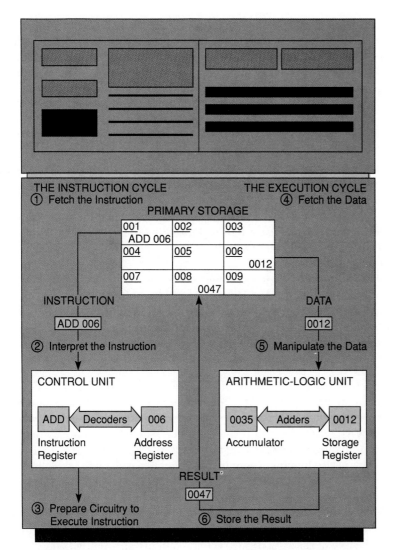

Figure 3–35 How computers execute an instruction. Notice the steps involved in this example.

THE INSTRUCTION CYCLE

1. First, an instruction is *fetched* from its location in primary storage and temporarily stored in the registers of the control unit. In this example, the instruction had been stored in primary storage location 001. The operation code part of the instruction (ADD) is moved to an instruction register, and its operand portion (006) is moved to an address register.

2. Next, the instruction is *interpreted* by the circuitry of the control unit. This involves decoding the operation code and operands of the instruction using specialized decoder circuits.

3. Finally, the control unit prepares electronic circuitry "paths" within the CPU to carry out the required operations. For example, this may involve activating the circuits that will "read" the data stored in the memory location (006) described in the instruction.

THE EXECUTION CYCLE

4. First, the data to be processed is fetched from its locations in primary storage and temporarily stored in a storage register of the arithmetic-logic unit. In this example, storage location 006 contained a value of 0012 (12 hours).

5. Next, the operations specified by the instruction are performed (addition, subtraction, comparisons, and so on). In this example, the contents of the storage register (0012) are added to the contents of an important register known as the accumulator by the use of specialized circuitry called adders. For this example, let's assume that the amount of hours worked this week (0035) was stored in the accumulator by a previous instruction.

6. Finally, the result arising from the manipulation of the data is stored in primary storage. In this example, the contents of weekly hours worked will be 0047. This amount will be transferred to primary storage at address 008 when an operand specifying this address is executed.

Media such as magnetic disks and tapes indicate these two states by having magnetized spots whose magnetic fields can have two different directions or *polarities.* These binary characteristics of computer circuitry and media are the primary reason why the **binary number system** is the basis for data representation in computers. Thus, for electronic circuits, the conducting *(ON)* state represents a *one* and the nonconducting *(OFF)* state represents a *zero.*

Therefore, the binary number system has only two symbols, 0 and 1. Thus, it is said to have a *base* of two. The familiar decimal system has a base of 10 since it uses 10 symbols (0 through 9). The binary symbol 0 or 1 is commonly called a **bit,** which is a contraction of the term *binary digit.* In the binary number system, all numbers are expressed as groups of binary digits *(bits),* that is, as groups of zeros and ones.

Just as in any other number system, the value of a binary number depends on the position or place of each digit in a grouping of binary digits. Values are based on the right-to-left position of digits in a binary number, using powers of 2 as position values, for example (. . . 2^3, 2^2, 2^1, 2^0). Therefore, the rightmost position has a value of 1 (2^0); the next position to the left has a value of 2 (2^1); the next position a value of 4 (2^2); the next, 8 (2^3); the next, 16 (2^4); and so forth. Thus, the value of any binary number consists of adding together the values of each position in which there is a binary *one* digit and ignoring those positions that contain a binary *zero* digit. Figure 3–36 gives you a simple illustration of how the binary number system can represent decimal values.

The Hexadecimal Number System

The binary number system has the disadvantage of requiring a large number of bits to express a given number value. The hexadecimal number system which is proportionately related to the binary number system, provides a shorthand method of reducing the long string of ones and zeros that make up a binary number. This is also helpful in simplifying computer codes based on the binary number system, as we will see shortly. For example, several popular computer codes use eight bit positions to represent a character. The hexadecimal equivalent would need only two positions to represent the same character. This makes it easier for professional programmers to decipher displays or printouts *(memory dumps)* of the data or instruction contents of primary storage.

Figure 3–37 shows examples of the binary and hexadecimal equivalents of the decimal numbers 0 through 20. Using the relationships in Figure 3–37, you should be able to determine that the decimal number 21 would be expressed by the binary number 10101 and the hexadecimal number 15, and so on. Several methods can be used to convert decimal numbers to a binary or hexadecimal form, or vice versa, or to use them in arithmetic operations, but they are beyond the scope of this text.

The ASCII and EBCDIC Codes

The internal circuitry of a computer needs to represent only binary ones and zeros in its operations. However, several binary-based coding systems have been devised to express the *machine language* instruction codes executed by the CPU and to represent the characters of data processed by the computer. These computer codes make the job of communicating with a computer easier and more efficient. They should be considered as shorthand methods of expressing the binary patterns within a computer.

Binary Position Values							
2^6	2^5	2^4	2^3	2^2	2^1	2^0	
64	32	16	8	4	2	1	
Binary Numbers							Examples of Equivalent Decimal Numbers
0	0	0	0	0	0	0	0
0	0	0	0	0	0	1	1
0	0	0	0	0	1	0	2
0	0	0	0	0	1	1	3
0	0	0	0	1	0	0	4
0	0	0	0	1	0	1	5
0	0	0	0	1	1	0	6
0	0	0	0	1	1	1	7
0	0	0	1	0	0	0	8
0	0	0	1	0	0	1	9
0	0	0	1	0	1	0	10
0	0	0	1	1	1	1	15
0	0	1	0	0	0	0	16
0	0	1	0	0	0	1	17
0	0	1	1	1	1	1	31
0	1	0	0	0	0	0	32
0	1	0	0	0	0	1	33
0	1	1	1	1	1	1	63
1	0	0	0	0	0	0	64
1	0	0	0	0	0	1	65

Figure 3–36 Examples of how the binary number system represents decimal values. Can you determine that the decimal number 34 is equivalent to 0100010 in binary?

Decimal	Binary	Hexadecimal
0	0	0
1	1	1
2	10	2
3	11	3
4	100	4
5	101	5
6	110	6
7	111	7
8	1000	8
9	1001	9
10	1010	A
11	1011	B
12	1100	C
13	1101	D
14	1110	E
15	1111	F
16	10000	10
17	10001	11
18	10010	12
19	10011	13
20	10100	14

Figure 3–37 Examples of the equivalents of decimal numbers in the binary and hexadecimal number systems. Can you tell that the decimal number 21 would be equivalent to 10101 in binary and 15 in hexadecimal?

Figure 3–38 Examples of
two common computer
codes: ASCII and EBCDIC.

Character	ASCII	EBCDIC
0	00110000	11110000
1	00110001	11110001
2	00110010	11110010
3	00110011	11110011
4	00110100	11110100
5	00110101	11110101
6	00110110	11110110
7	00110111	11110111
8	00111000	11111000
9	00111001	11111001
A	01000001	11000001
B	01000010	11000010
C	01000011	11000011
D	01000100	11000100
E	01000101	11000101
F	01000110	11000110
G	01000111	11000111
H	01001000	11001000
I	01001001	11001001
J	01001010	11010001
K	01001011	11010010
L	01001100	11010011
M	01001101	11010100
N	01001110	11010101
O	01001111	11010110
P	01010000	11010111
Q	01010001	11011000
R	01010010	11011001
S	01010011	11100010
T	01010100	11100011
U	01010101	11100100
V	01010110	11100101
W	01010111	11100110
X	01011000	11100111
Y	01011001	11101000
Z	01011010	11101001

The most widely used computer code is the American Standard Code for Information Interchange (**ASCII**) (pronounced *as-key*). This was originally a seven-bit code which represented 128 (2^7) different characters. However, eight-bit versions (sometimes called ASCII-8) which can represent 256 characters are now widely used. ASCII is a standardized code first developed for data communications between computers and input/output devices. However, it is used by most microcomputers and minicomputers, as well as by many larger computers. ASCII has been adopted as a standard code by national and international standards organizations. The Extended BCD Interchange Code (**EBCDIC**) (pronounced *eb-si-dick*) is used by IBM and some other mainframe computers and can provide 256 (2^8) different coding arrangements. See Figure 3–38.

Bits, Bytes, and Words

A **byte** is a basic grouping of **bits** (binary digits) that the computer operates on as a single unit. It typically consists of eight bits and is used to represent a character by the ASCII and EBCDIC coding systems. For example, each storage location of computers using EBCDIC or eight-bit ASCII codes consists of electronic circuit elements or magnetic or optical media positions that can represent at least eight binary digits. Thus, each storage location can hold one character. The capacity of a computer's primary storage and its secondary storage devices is usually expressed in terms of bytes.

A **word** is a grouping of binary digits (usually larger than a byte) that is transferred as a unit between primary storage and the registers of the arithmetic-logic unit and control unit. Thus, a computer with a 32-bit word length might have registers with a capacity of 32 bits, and transfer data and instructions within the CPU or microprocessor in groupings of 32 bits. It should process data faster than computers with a 16-bit or 8-bit word length. However, processing speed also depends on the size of a CPU's *data path* or *data bus*, which are the circuits that interconnect various CPU components. For example, a microprocessor like the Intel 80386 SX has 32-bit registers but only a 16-bit data bus. It thus only moves data and instructions 16 bits at a time. Thus, it is slower than the Intel 80386 DX microprocessor, which has 32-bit registers and data paths.

Representing Data

Figure 3–39 illustrates how data is physically represented in many modern computers. Assuming the use of the eight-bit ASCII code, Figure 3–39 shows how each character in the word "computer" can be represented by an eight-bit code. The circles represent semiconductor circuit elements or other forms of storage media. The shaded circles represent an electronic or magnetic *ON* state, while the nonshaded circles represent the *OFF* state of binary devices. Also notice that a ninth or **check bit** is *ON* to make *odd parity;* that is, an odd number of bits are turned on for each letter. If the check bit was *OFF*, this would result in *even parity;* that is, an even number of bits would be turned on.

Most computer codes include this additional *check bit.* The check bit is also known as a *parity bit* and is used for verifying the accuracy or validity of coded data. Many computers have a built-in checking capacity to detect the loss or addition of bits during the transfer of data between components of a computer system. For example, the computer may be designed to continuously check for an *odd parity,* that is, an odd number of *binary one* (electronically *ON* bit positions) in each character of data that is transferred. In such cases, a check bit is turned on when needed to ensure that an odd number of electronically *ON* bit positions is present in each character of data in storage. Thus, the check bit

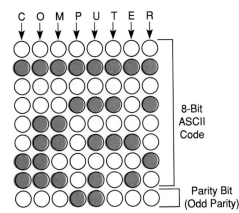

Figure 3–39 An example of how computers represent data. Note how the word "computer" is represented using the ASCII computer code.

REAL WORLD CASE

Mrs. Fields Incorporated

Mrs. Fields Inc. used PC technology to help build America's most popular gourmet cookie chain. Now Randy and Debbi Fields have placed PCs at the heart of a risky diversification into a new and potentially more stable business—full-service commercial bakeries.

By 1992, Mrs. Fields will spend $50 million on La Petite Boulangerie, a money-losing bakery-and-cafe chain it acquired in 1987. It will close nearly 100 of its 700 cookie stores and convert many of them into combination cookie and bakery shops. The gamble might seem foolish if it weren't for the company's success with cookie-store PC systems. Mrs. Fields' innovative store systems are widely credited not only with boosting cookie sales and worker productivity but also with facilitating Mrs. Fields' envied "flat" corporate structure—one with few middle-managers separating top executives from daily operations.

The Tandy 286–based PC in each cookie store is the corporate culture at Mrs. Fields. Store managers receive daily direction not from bosses but from PC-based expert systems. The systems do production and labor scheduling and screen job candidates for required skills—"all the things Debbi Fields used to do when she ran her individual store." For example, each morning a manager tells the PC what kind of day it is, such as whether it's a rainy weekend or a sunny holiday. Based on historical data, the system then spits out an hour-by-hour baking schedule. If sales are slow, the system instructs the most vivacious store employee to go outside with samples to woo customers.

While expert systems pass top management's wisdom directly to store managers without middle managers, electronic mail connects executives to stores for frequent communication. Other modules facilitate submission of reports to the company's Park City, Utah, headquarters, nearly eliminating paperwork. "When I see a person sitting at a desk filling out papers, I go crazy," said Fields, who wants to free up managers' time for human tasks like motivating em-

ployees. The company boasts an enviably low ratio of administrative staff to stores, about 150 people for 700 stores.

But can a cookie-store technology cut it in the bakery-cafe world, where inventories and consumer tastes are more complex? More important, can a cookie-cutter culture where PCs are boss pan out in the new company? The Fieldses say yes on both counts. They said the company's initial success in transferring its basic systems to La Petite were, in fact, a main factor in the decision to invest $50 million more to expand the bakery chain. Fields claims the systems "got control" of the bakery chain enough to make it profitable 14 months after its acquisition.

To supplement the cookie software, Mrs. Fields programmers are writing an expert system for bakery-cafe inventory control, as well as production-planning for soups and sandwiches. But "before we could really be effective, we had to change management positions," says VP of MIS Paul Quinn. In other words, fire managers who didn't accept the PC-based management style. As soon as the basic PC systems were in bakeries a year ago, Mrs. Fields cut La Petite's staff at headquarters from 64 to 4, ousting "corporate personnel that were shuffling a lot of papers," Quinn said. In stores, it took about eight months to weed out managers who rejected taking direction from a PC. Now that remaining managers are comfortable with the systems, top-management edicts for running the bakeries can be implemented instantly via updates to the expert systems.

Application Questions

☐ Would you like to be a store manager at Mrs. Fields? Explain why or why not based on the role of PCs in each store.

☐ What are the strategic business issues of using microcomputers at Mrs. Fields?

Source: Adapted from Don Steinburg, "Crumbling Mrs. Fields Puts Its Chips on PCs in Bakeries," *PC Week*, February 20, 1989, pp. 1, 59–61.

allows the computer to automatically determine whether the correct number of bit positions representing a character of data have been transferred.

SUMMARY

☐ A computer is a system of information processing components that performs input, processing, output, storage, and control functions. Its hardware components include input and output devices, a central processing unit, and secondary storage devices. The major functions and components of a computer system are summarized in Figure 3–2. Computer capacity and time elements are summarized in Figure 3–5.

☐ Microcomputers are used as personal computers, professional workstations, and multiuser computer systems. Microcomputers typically use a keyboard for input, a system unit containing the main microprocessor for processing and control, semiconductor RAM and ROM circuits for primary storage, floppy or hard disk drives for secondary storage, and a video display monitor and printer for output. The most popular applications for microcomputers are word processing, electronic spreadsheets, database management, graphics, communications, common business applications, and personal and home applications.

☐ Minicomputers are larger and more powerful than most microcomputers. They are used by small groups of users for many business data processing and scientific applications. Mainframe computers are larger and more powerful than most minicomputers. They are usually faster, have more memory capacity, and can support more input/output and secondary storage devices. They are designed to handle the information processing needs of organizations with many customers and employees, or complex computational problems. Supercomputers are a special category of extremely powerful mainframe computer systems designed for massive computational assignments.

☐ The execution of a computer instruction can be subdivided into an instruction cycle (when the computer prepares to execute an instruction) and an execution cycle (when it actually executes the instruction). Data is represented in a computer in a binary form because of the two-state nature of the electronic, magnetic, and optical components of the computers. Most computers use special codes based on the binary number system, including the ASCII and EBCDIC codes. Within the computer, data is usually organized into bits, bytes, and words. Each position of storage can store one byte and has a specific address so the data stored in its contents can be readily located.

☐ Refer to Figures 3–40 and 3–41 for tabular summaries of the many types of computer peripherals and media discussed in this chapter. These figures outline the functions, characteristics, advantages, and disadvantages of computer system input, output, and storage devices. They show that each device has its own cost/speed/capacity and other characteristics that give it unique advantages and disadvantages in supporting the user interface or providing storage for data resources.

Figure 3–40 A summary of important input/output methods. Notice especially the advantages and disadvantages of each method in providing hardware support of the user interface.

Peripheral Equipment	Media	Primary Functions	Typical I/O Speed Range	Major Advantages and/or Disadvantages
Video display terminals	None	Keyboard input and video output	250–50,000 characters per second output	Conventional and inexpensive, but limited display capacity and no hard copy
Printers	Paper	Printed output of paper reports and documents	Character printer: 20–600 characters per second; line printer: 200–3,000 lines per minute; page printer: 4–200 pages per minute	Hard copy, but inconvenient and bulky; many printers are relatively slow
Pointing devices	None	Input by mouse, joy-stick, light pen, touch screen, and graphics pen. Video output.	Not applicable	Input devices are easy to use and inexpensive, but may have limited applications and software support
Voice input/output devices	None	Voice input and output	Not applicable	Easiest I/O but is slow, has limited vocabulary, and accuracy problems
Optical scanners	Paper documents	Direct input from written or printed documents	100–3,600 characters per second for Optical Character Recognition (OCR) readers	Direct input from paper documents, but some limitations on input format
Magnetic ink character recognition (MICR) readers	MICR paper documents	Direct input of MICR documents	700–3,200 characters per second. 180–2,400 documents per minute.	Fast, high-reliability reading, but documents must be pre-printed and the character set is limited
Micrographics devices	Microfilm	Microfilm input or output	Computer-output microfilm (COM) recorders: 500,000 characters per second and 60,000 lines per minute	Fast, compact media, but relatively expensive peripherals

KEY TERMS AND CONCEPTS

These are the key terms and concepts of this chapter. The page number of their first explanation is in parentheses.

1. Arithmetic-logic unit *(109)*
2. Binary number system *(114)*
3. Binary representation *(112)*
4. Cathode-ray tube *(89)*
5. Central processing unit *(109)*
6. Computer codes *(114)*
   a. ASCII
   b. EBCDIC
7. Computer systems *(74)*

8. Computer terminals *(88)*
9. Control unit *(109)*
10. Direct access *(100)*
11. Direct input/output devices *(87)*
12. Electronic mouse *(88)*
13. Graphics pen and tablet *(89)*
14. Icons *(88)*
15. Input devices *(74)*

Figure 3–41 A summary of important computer storage methods. Notice the advantages and disadvantages of each type of storage device.

Peripheral Equipment	Media	Primary Functions	Typical Speed and Capacity Ranges	Major Advantages and/or Disadvantages
Magnetic disk drive	Hard disk Disk pack Disk cartridge	Secondary storage (direct access) and input/output	Access time: 10–100 milliseconds Data transfer: 200,000 to 5 million bytes per second Capacity: From 10 million to 15 billion bytes per disk drive	Large capacity, fast, direct access storage device (DASD), but relatively expensive
Floppy disk drive	Magnetic diskette 5¼- and 3½-inch diameters	Secondary storage (direct access) and input/output	Access time: 100–600 milliseconds Data transfer: 10,000–30,000 bytes per second Capacity: From 360,000 to several million bytes per disk	Small, inexpensive, and convenient, but slower and smaller capacity than other DASDs
Magnetic tape drive	Magnetic tape reel and cartridge	Secondary storage (sequential access), input/output, and disk backup	Data transfer: 15,000 to 2 million bytes per second Capacity: Up to one billion bytes per tape reel or cartridge	Inexpensive, with a fast transfer rate, but only sequential access
Optical disk drive	Optical disk: CD-ROM, WORM, and erasable	Secondary storage (direct access) and archival storage	Access time: 350–800 milliseconds Data transfer: 150,000–500,000 bytes per second Capacity: CD-ROM: up to 700 million; WORM: up to 3 billion; erasable: up to one billion bytes	Large capacity, high-quality storage of data, text, and images. Primarily a read-only medium

16. How computers execute instructions *(111)*
17. Joystick *(89)*
18. Light pen *(89)*
19. Liquid crystal displays *(90)*
20. Magnetic disk storage *(102)*
    a. Disk pack
    b. Floppy disk
    c. Hard disk
21. Magnetic tape *(102)*
22. Magnetic ink character recognition *(95)*
23. Mainframe computer *(83)*
24. Microcomputer *(78)*
25. Micrographics *(95)*
26. Microprocessor *(76)*
27. Minicomputer *(82)*
28. Multiprocessor designs *(110)*
29. Offline *(87)*
30. Online *(87)*
31. Optical character recognition *(94)*
32. Optical disk storage *(104)*
    a. CD-ROM
    b. Erasable disks
    c. WORM disks
33. Optical scanning *(94)*
34. Output devices *(75)*
35. Peripheral devices *(87)*
36. Plasma displays *(90)*
37. Plotters *(90)*
38. Pointing devices *(88)*
39. Primary storage unit *(109)*
40. Printers *(90)*
41. Registers *(100)*
42. Secondary storage *(109)*
43. Semiconductor storage *(100)*
    a. RAM
    b. ROM
44. Sequential access *(100)*
45. Storage media tradeoffs *(98)*
46. Supercomputer *(85)*
47. Storage capacity elements *(78, 116)*
    a. Bit
    b. Byte

    c. Kilobyte

    d. Megabyte

    e. Gigabyte

48. Time elements *(76)*

    a. Millisecond

    b. Microsecond

    c. Nanosecond

    d. Picosecond

49. Touch sensitive screen *(89)*

50. Trackball *(89)*
51. User interface *(87)*
52. Voice input/ouput *(91)*
53. Volatility *(101)*
54. Wand *(95)*
55. Windows *(90)*
56. Word *(117)*

REVIEW QUIZ

Match one of the **key terms and concepts** listed above with one of the examples or definitions listed below. Try to find the best fit for answers that seem to fit more than one term or concept. Defend your choices.

_____ 1. A computer performs input, processing, output, storage, and control functions.

_____ 2. Can be conceptually subdivided into an arithmetic-logic unit, control unit, and primary storage unit.

_____ 3. Performs computation and comparisons.

_____ 4. Interprets instructions and directs processing.

_____ 5. Stores instructions and data during processing.

_____ 6. Magnetic disk and tape drives are examples.

_____ 7. Video monitors and printers are examples.

_____ 8. Keyboards and optical scanners are examples.

_____ 9. Connected to and controlled by a CPU.

_____ 10. Separate from and not controlled by a CPU.

_____ 11. A central processing unit for a microcomputer.

_____ 12. Input, output, and secondary storage devices for a computer system.

_____ 13. One billionth of a second.

_____ 14. One billion characters of storage.

_____ 15. Used as a personal and professional workstation.

_____ 16. May be used as a departmental or work group computer.

_____ 17. May be used as host computers, transaction processors, and enterprise-wide systems.

_____ 18. The most powerful type of computer.

_____ 19. Computer systems can have several interconnected CPUs.

_____ 20. Computer input/output methods and devices for end users.

_____ 21. The ability to capture data or communicate information without media.

_____ 22. Most common is a device with a keyboard and a video display connected to a computer.

_____ 23. Includes electronic mice, light pens, trackballs, and joysticks.

_____ 24. Moving this along your desk top moves the cursor on the screen.

_____ 25. You can communicate with a computer by touching its display.

_____ 26. Helps you "write" on the video screen.

_____ 27. Captures data by writing on a pressure sensitive surface.

_____ 28. Promises to be the easiest, most natural way to communicate with a computer.

_____ 29. The most common video display technology.

_____ 30. Small figures are displayed to help you indicate activities to be performed.

_____ 31. The screen is divided into several sections, each with its own display.

_____ 32. Produces hard copy output such as paper documents and reports.

_____ 33. May use a mechanical arm with several pens to draw hard copy graphics output.

_____ 34. Optical scanning of bar codes and other characters.

_____ 35. Capturing data by processing light reflected from images.

_____ 36. Bank check processing uses this technology.

_____ 37. Using microfilm for input, output, and storage.

_____ 38. A hand-held device that reads bar coding.

_____ 39. Each position of storage can be accessed in approximately the same time.

_____ 40. Each position of storage can be accessed according to a predetermined order.

_____ 41. Microelectronic storage circuits on silicon chips.

_____ 42. You cannot erase the contents of these semiconductor storage circuits.

_____ 43. You can read and write data stored in these semiconductor circuits.

_____ 44. The property that determines whether data is lost or retained when power fails.

_____ 45. Uses magnetic spots on metal or plastic disks.

_____ 46. A flexible magnetic disk in a plastic jacket.

_____ 47. Adds large magnetic disk capacity to a microcomputer.

_____ 48. Uses magnetic spots on plastic tape.

_____ 49. Uses a laser to read microscopic points on plastic disks.

_____ 50. Most widely used form of permanent storage on optical disks.

_____ 51. An individual data or instruction element is stored here in the CPU.

_____ 52. Fetching and interpreting an instruction, then fetching and manipulating data.

_____ 53. Made possible by the presence, absence, or change in direction of electric current, magnetic fields, or light rays in computer circuits and media.

_____ 54. A number system with a base of two.

———— 55. A zero or a one.

———— 56. Typically equals eight bits.

———— 57. Equals 16 bits or 32 bits for most current microcomputers.

———— 58. Eight-bit codes to represent data in computers.

REAL WORLD PROBLEMS

1. **Georgia Pacific Corporation**

   Longtime IBM mainframe users such as Georgia-Pacific are saving big money by abandoning big systems, creating an unexpected market for IBM's Application System/400 midrange computers. Companies that are changing the way they do business or decentralizing their information systems are most likely to migrate downward to the AS/400. However, the substantial savings to be gained seem to be the biggest lure of all. Among the companies moving from IBM mainframes to minicomputers are Pepperidge Farm, Playboy Enterprises, Hiram Walker & Sons, Kaiser Aluminum & Chemical, U.S. Shoe, Harley-Davidson, Arco Chemical, and Johnson & Johnson.

   In Atlanta, Georgia-Pacific is winding up a two-year project designed to eliminate its IBM 3081 mainframe by replacing the machine with 20 AS/400s in a network that includes 150 IBM Personal System/2 and Compaq personal computers. In shifting to a two-tier computing strategy of minis and microcomputers, the pulp, paper, and building manufacturer's goal was to save money and jettison its mainframe technology. "Our costs in this new environment are significantly lower," said Paul Pavloff, director of information resources. "Most of the savings have been in operations and technical support areas." About two thirds of the corporate and building materials applications—including finance, accounting, distribution, sales analysis, order-entry, and inventory systems—have already been moved off an IBM 3081 mainframe onto the midrange platform.

   a. Why is Georgia Pacific switching to a two-tier strategy of minis and microcomputers and eliminating its mainframe?

   b. What are other reasons why companies may use a similar strategy?

   Source: Adapted from Maryfran Johnson, "AS/400 Irony: Some Buyers Replacing Mainframes with Low Margin Minis," *Computerworld*, February 12, 1990, pp. 1, 120.

2. **Canadian Pacific and Alamo Rent A Car, Inc.**

   "We are clearly two-tiered because three doesn't make sense," said George Sekely, vice president of computers and communications at Canadian Pacific (CP). "We need information flowing through the business, not concentrated in certain areas," he said. So CP relies on a vast network of personal computers and terminals that are tied to corporate mainframes, with no role for minicomputers. "The PCs now add so much intelligence, and provide the user friendliness and speed for transactions," Sekely said. "This is not old-fashioned personal computing, like spreadsheets. I'm talking about enhancing mainframe transactions, working in a closer way with the mainframe."

   Alamo Rent A Car, Inc., is another site with no plans for midrange systems. "It is a two-tiered universe for us," said Thomas Loane, vice president of computers and communications. "We've got thousands of terminals out there. We don't see a need for a middle [minicomputer] level. You can do an awful lot on a PC network these days."

  a. Why does Canadian Pacific rely on a two-tiered architecture of personal computers and terminals connected to mainframes?

  b. Why does Alamo Rent A Car think a middle level of minicomputers isn't needed?

  Source: Adapted from Rosemary Hamilton, "Increasingly, the Customer Leads, Big Blue Follows," *Computerworld*, February 12, 1990, pp. 1, 121.

3. Echlin, Inc.

    Echlin, Inc., a $1.3 billion automotive parts company in Branford, Connecticut, retired its IBM 4381 mainframe more than a year ago. In its place is a network of some 60 PC-based workstations, four micro-based servers, and peripherals. The network has a total or three gigabytes of hard disk storage. It supports the 10 major applications originally on the mainframe, as well as some new ones. But the information systems department still supports and administers the network and controls programming and development. Users have day-to-day operating control, while Information Systems performs such functions as backups, security, and documentation. By duplicating the control procedures of the former mainframe environment, Echlin ensures that the network is properly administered.

    Cost efficiency has improved at least three-fold by moving all systems off the mainframe. Even with all the expenses of building the PC network, designing the software, and doing the software conversions, the IS budget actually decreased slightly in the first year. This reflects terminating maintenance contracts for the mainframe, avoiding hardware upgrades, and other savings. Systems also now offer more functionality and are easier to use. They can be developed at lower cost and performance has improved. Also, systems are being implemented that could not even have been considered before because of prohibitive costs. A new executive information systems is one example. It would have been much too costly to build on a mainframe, but Echlin selected one of several commercial PC versions available.

    a. Does Echlin's microcomputer network prove that minicomputers and mainframes are no longer needed?

    b. What are some advantages and disadvantages of such a system?

    Source: Adapted from "Putting Large Systems on PC Networks," *I/S Analyzer*, January 1990, pp. 1–2.

4. Hertz International

    Hertz International introduced curbside rental-car return by customers to service agents equipped with hand-held microcomputers in 1989. In 1990, it introduced automated teller machines (ATMs) to speed up the checkout of Hertz customers at busy airports. "The curbside checkout and the ATM machines are sister systems," said Ray LaFrance, a Hertz marketing director in Wichita, Kan. Both draw their data from the same central database, he explained. "We use the hand-held computers in periods of peak volume, but they require a Hertz employee to be out there," LaFrance said. "When volume is lighter, the same customer that enjoyed curbside car return would also appreciate using the ATM machine to get an instant receipt."

Until now, a Hertz customer who used "quick return slots" put the Hertz rental agreement under a time stamp and dropped it into a mail slot. The final bill was processed that night and mailed to the customer, making the return of the form subject to the vagaries of the postal service. With the ATM machine, the car renter gets the bill back immediately.

a. What business objectives are supported by the use of hand-held computers and ATMs by Hertz?

b. What features of the ATM make it a good input/output device for this application?

Source: Adapted from Dennis Eskow, " 'Channel Systems' Put PCs on Front Line," *PC Week*, March 5, 1990, pp. 135–37.

5. Input Alternatives
Which method of input would you recommend for the following activities? Refer to Figure 3–40 to help you.

a. Entering data from printed questionnaires.
b. Entering data from telephone surveys.
c. Entering data from bank checks.
d. Entering data from merchandise tags.
e. Entering data from engineering drawings.

6. Output Alternatives
Which method of output would you recommend for the following information products? Refer to Figure 3–40 to help you.

a. Visual displays for portable microcomputers.
b. Legal documents.
c. Engineering drawings.
d. Financial results for top executives.
e. Responses for telephone transactions.

7. Storage Alternatives
Indicate which secondary storage medium you would use for each of the following storage tasks. Select from the choices at the right, using Figure 3–41 to help you.

a. Primary storage.	1. Magnetic hard disk.
b. Large capacity, permanent storage.	2. Floppy disk.
c. Large capacity, fast direct access.	3. Magnetic tape.
d. Large files for occasional processing.	4. Semiconductor chips.
e. Inexpensive, portable, direct-access storage.	5. Optical disk.

8. Apple Computer, Inc.
The Macintosh portable microcomputer from Apple features a display screen that uses an *active matrix* LCD, which means that the screen has sharper images and less image bleeding than many other portables. Instead of the Mac's traditional mouse, the portable uses an integrated trackball that can be positioned on either side of the keyboard to accom-

modate left- or right-handed users. Powered by a 16 MHz Motorola 68000 microprocessor, the laptop has 1M-byte of static random-access memory chips and a sealed lead-acid battery which provides up to 12 hours of power. A built-in telecommunications modem is also included, as is a 1.4 megabyte floppy disk drive. A 40 megabyte hard disk drive is optional. (Refer to Figure 3–15b.)

a. What system components can you identify for input, processing, output, and storage functions in the Macintosh portable?

b. Why do you think Apple used a keyboard with a built-in trackball instead of a mouse?

Source: Adapted from James Daly, "Mac-To-Go Weighs in as Big Hit," *Computerworld,* September 25, 1989, p. 6.

9. Shearson, Burlington, and Lenox

Recognition of continuous conversational speech is still too slow and error prone for most applications. However, some highly successful applications of voice recognition technology are beginning to appear. For example, a voice recognition system at brokerage house Shearson Lehman Hutton enables traders to accomplish by short verbal commands what they used to do laboriously by hand. Traders say that errors resulting from illegible or lost pieces of paper—on which important trades were communicated via pneumatic tube to clerks—more than justify the high cost of the system.

At Burlington Industries, Inc., quality control inspectors use speech recognizers to enter information about defects that are spotted on yards of textiles streaming by on frames slanted at 45 degrees. The inspectors are more accurate and have been able to shave 25 percent off the time it takes to grade the quality of the fabrics.

Lenox China, in Pomona, New Jersey, has five employees in quality control and one employee in inventory control using 1,000-word voice recognition systems developed by Dragon Systems. The voice recognition hardware, Dragon's Voice Scribe–1000, is plugged in to Compaq Deskpro 286s and IBM PC XTs with Intel 80386 add-in cards. The quality control inspectors sit at a belt production line examining each piece of china for defects. If defects are noted, the piece's disposition, routing for additional work, and other information is entered into the voice recognition system. This reduces the time collecting and then accessing information as well as eliminating completely the cost of data collection because one person can perform inspection and data collection tasks simultaneously.

a. Why are voice recognition systems used by Shearson, Burlingtron, and Lenox?

b. What are the benefits and limitations of this technology?

Source: Adapted from Alice La Plante, "Voice Recognition: Still a Long Way to Go," *Infoworld,* March 26, 1990, p. 43, and Michael Alexander, "Edging Down the Road to Voice Recognition," *Computerworld,* January 15, 1990, p. 17.

10. Mack Trucks, Inc.

Mack Trucks, Inc., of Somerset, New Jersey, recently introduced its Macspec CD-ROM. This helps Mack mechanics worldwide slash the time required to scan the vast Mack parts catalog, which is now on one CD-ROM disk instead of on paper. Using the manual system, inexperienced parts locators—those with less than three years on the job—formerly took 28 minutes to identify 10 items for a truck, while experienced ones took 14 minutes. The Macspec CD-ROM, however, lets any parts service person find those same 10 parts in just one minute and 39 seconds.

Delivering documentation digitally on a CD-ROM disk also relieves Mack Trucks dealers of the tedious job of replacing pages in mammoth paper catalogs or trying to find a misplaced page. The corporate documentation department at Mack converted 875,000 pages of paper and 23,000 pieces of art into digital form on the Macspec disk, which contains information on hundreds of thousands of trucks, most of them custom-made to user specifications. Thus CD-ROM means huge annual savings in printing and distribution costs alone—as well as faster repairs of Mack Trucks.

Mack Trucks also uses WORM technology. Research-and-development analyst Lawrence Doe finds WORM disks the appropriate mass storage media for his applications. Doe manages approximately 100 Sun Microsystems engineering workstations that imprint and recall engineering drawings to and from Sony WORM drives. "We create the drawings on the shop floor, digitize them using the computer-aided design (CAD) capabilities of the workstations, and then store them in our WORM system," he said. By using a WORM "jukebox," he was able to use a single drive and have 48 gigabytes of data online with 15 WORM disk platters.

a. What are the advantages of the CD-ROM and WORM technology for Mack Trucks?

b. What are some of the advantages and disadvantages of such optical disk technologies compared to magnetic disk and tape media?

Source: Adapted from Linda Helgerson, "What You Can Do with CD-ROM," *EDGE,* March/April 1990, pp. 31–32, and Jon Pepper, "WORM Drive Appeal Centers on Capacity, Fidelity," *PC Week,* January 1, 1990, p. 65.

SELECTED REFERENCES

1. *Computerworld, Datamation, PC Week, PC Magazine,* and *Infoworld.* (Examples of good sources for current information on computer systems hardware and other developments in information system technology.)

2. Datapro Corporation. *Datapro Reports.* (Series of regular detailed reports on selected computer systems hardware.)

3. Khosrowpour, Mehdi. *Microcomputer Systems: Management and Applications.* Boston: Boyd & Fraser, 1989.

4. Panko, Raymond. *End User Computing: Management, Applications, and Technology.* New York: John Wiley & Sons, 1988.

<table>
<tr><td>

C H A P T E R

4

</td><td>

INTRODUCTION TO COMPUTER SOFTWARE

</td></tr>
</table>

■ **Chapter Outline**

■ Learning Objectives

The purpose of this chapter is to give you an understanding of computer software by analyzing the functions, benefits, and limitations of major types of system and application software packages.

Section I of this chapter presents an overview of software types and trends and summarizes the major features and functions of operating systems, database management systems, telecommunications programs, and programming languages.

Section II surveys the major types of software available for end user computing applications, with an emphasis on microcomputer *productivity* software. Included are word processing, electronic spreadsheet, graphics, and integrated packages.

After reading and studying this chapter, you should be able to:

1. Describe two major trends occurring in computer software.
2. Identify several major types of system and application software.
3. Outline the functions of operating systems and operating environments.
4. Describe the role of database management systems, telecommunications monitors, and programming language translator programs.
5. Explain the differences between machine, assembler, high-level, and fourth-generation languages.
6. Identify and explain the purpose of several popular microcomputer software packages for end user computing.

Section I: System Software: Computer System Management

INTRODUCTION TO SOFTWARE

This chapter presents an overview of the major types of software you will depend on as you work with computers. Remember that software "gives life" to hardware. That's why you should know the characteristics and purposes of major types of software packages. All types of information systems rely on software resources in the form of programs and procedures to help computer hardware and end users transform data resources into a variety of information products. Software is needed to accomplish the input, processing, output, storage, and control activities of information systems. As we said in Chapter 1, computer programs are typically classified into two major types:

☐ **System software**—programs that manage and support the resources and operations of a computer system as it performs various information processing tasks.

☐ **Application software**—programs that direct the performance of a particular use, or *application*, of computers to meet the information processing needs of end users.

Let's begin our analysis of software by looking at an overview of the major types and functions of software available to computer users, shown in Figure 4–1. This figure summarizes the major categories of system and application

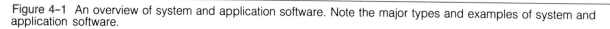

Figure 4–1 An overview of system and application software. Note the major types and examples of system and application software.

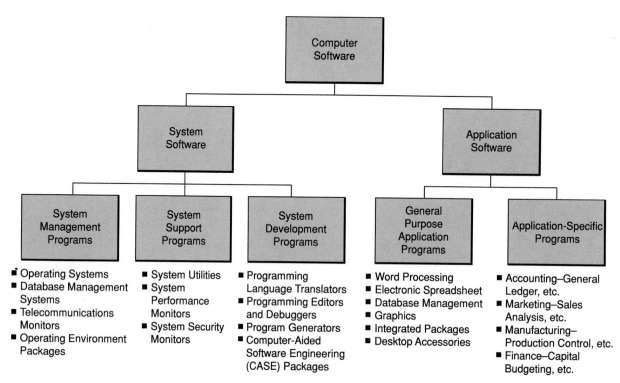

Figure 4–2 Trends in computer software. The trend in software is toward multipurpose, expert-assisted packages with natural language and graphical user interfaces.

	FIRST GENERATION	SECOND GENERATION	THIRD GENERATION	FOURTH GENERATION	FIFTH GENERATION?
Trend: Toward Conversational Natural Programming Languages.					
Software Trends	User-Written Programs Machine Languages	Packaged Programs Symbolic Languages	Operating Systems High-Level Languages	Database Management Systems Fourth-Generation Languages Microcomputer Packages	Natural Languages Multipurpose Graphic-Interface Expert-Assisted Packages
Trend: Toward Easy-to-Use Multipurpose Application Packages.					

software we will discuss in this chapter. Of course, this is a conceptual illustration. The type of software you will encounter depends, first, on the manufacturer and the model of the computer you use and, second, on what additional software is acquired to increase your computer's performance or to accomplish specific tasks for you and other end users.

Software Trends

Figure 4–2 emphasizes two major software trends important to business end users. First, there is a trend away from custom-designed, one-of-a-kind programs developed for an organization by its professional programmers or end users. Instead, the trend is toward the use of off-the-shelf software packages acquired by end users from software vendors. This trend accelerated with the development of relatively inexpensive and easy-to-use productivity software packages for microcomputers, and it continues to grow, even for minicomputer and mainframe users. This significantly reduces programming requirements, though a lot of work is still necessary to introduce software packages into an organization.

Second, there is a major trend away from (1) technical, machine-specific programming languages using binary-based or symbolic codes and (2) *procedural languages*, which use a series of brief statements and mathematical expressions to specify the sequence of instructions a computer must perform. Instead, the trend is toward *nonprocedural, natural languages* that are closer to human conversation. Thus, earlier generations of programming languages are more efficient in terms of their use of computer hardware resources. Fourth- and fifth-generation languages, on the other hand, are more efficient in their use of human resources since they are easier to program, use, and maintain.

This software trend has accelerated with the creation of easy-to-use, nonprocedural *fourth-generation languages* (4GLs). It continues to grow as developments in graphics and artificial intelligence produce *natural language and graphical interfaces* that improve the user interface features of advanced software packages. In addition, expert system modules and other artificial intelligence features are being built into a new generation of *expert-assisted* software packages.

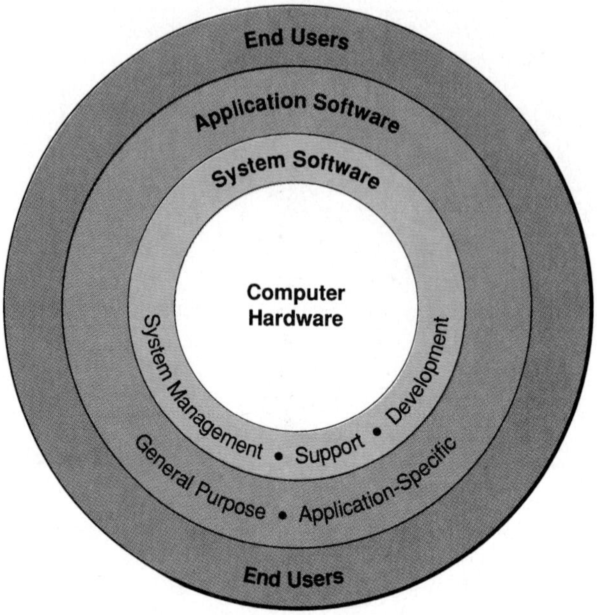

Figure 4–3 The system and
application software interface
between users and computer
hardware.

These two major trends seem to be converging to produce a fifth generation
of powerful, multipurpose, expert-assisted software packages with natural language and graphical interfaces for end users.

System Software Overview   **System software** consists of computer programs that manage and support a
computer system and its information processing activities. These programs
serve as a vital software *interface* between computer system hardware and the
application programs of users. See Figure 4–3. Note that such programs can be
grouped into three major functional categories:

☐ **System management programs**—programs that *manage* the hardware,
  software, and data resources of the computer system during its
  execution of the various information processing jobs of users. Major
  system management programs are operating systems, database management systems, and telecommunications monitors.

☐ **System support programs**—programs that *support* the operations,
  management, and users of a computer system by providing a variety of
  support services. Major support programs are system utilities, performance monitors, and security monitors.

☐ **System development programs**—programs that help users *develop*
  information system programs and procedures and prepare user programs for computer processing. Major development programs are
  language translators, programming tools, and CASE (computer-aided
  software engineering) packages.

**OPERATING
SYSTEMS**

The most important system software package for any computer is its **operating
system.** An operating system is an integrated *system* of programs that manages
the *operations* of the CPU, controls the input/output and storage resources and

activities of the computer system, and provides various support services as the computer executes the application programs of users.

The primary purpose of an operating system is to maximize the productivity of a computer system by operating it in the most efficient manner and minimizing the amount of human intervention required. An operating system also simplifies the job of computer programmers since it includes programs that perform common input/output and storage operations and other standard processing functions. If you have any hands-on experience on a computer, you know that the operating system must be loaded and activated before you can accomplish other tasks. This emphasizes that operating systems are the most indispensable component of the software interface between users and the hardware of their computer systems.

Many operating systems are designed as a collection of program *modules*, which can be organized in combinations with various capabilities around a central module, or *kernel*. Such operating systems can be tailored to fit the processing power and memory capacity of a computer system and the type of processing jobs that need to be done on it. For example, some operating system packages include a selected number of utility programs, language translator programs, and even some application programs.

Examples of popular microcomputer operating systems are DOS and OS/2 by Microsoft, which are the operating systems for the IBM PC, PS/2, and other similar microcomputers. Another example is Macintosh System 7.0, which is an operating system for the Macintosh line of Apple computers. Several versions of such popular operating systems are available. Which version you should use depends primarily on the main microprocessor in your microcomputer and on the amount of additional memory capacity required.

Figure 4–4 is an example of the programs that could be included in three major operating systems. Note that the Extended Edition of OS/2 consists of a main *kernel* program and program modules for the user interface (Presentation Manager), the programmer interface (Applications Programming Interface), telecommunications control (Communications Manager), database management (Database Manager), the interface with peripheral devices (device drivers), and various utilities. The UNIX operating system was developed by AT&T. Versions of UNIX are being used in many supermini- and super-microcomputers because UNIX is such a powerful and portable operating system. Also shown are the program modules and functions of the MVS operating system used by many IBM mainframe computers.

Operating System Management Functions

An operating system performs three major management functions in the operation of a computer system.

- ☐ **Job management**—preparing, scheduling, and monitoring *jobs* (computing assignments) for continuous processing by the computer system. Job management activities include interpreting *job control language* (JCL) statements, scheduling and selecting jobs for execution by the computer system, initiating and terminating their processing, and communicating with the computer operator concerning the status of jobs being processed.

- ☐ **Resource management**—controlling the use of computer system resources by database management, telecommunications, and other

Figure 4-4   Three major operating systems. Note the variety of program modules and their functions.

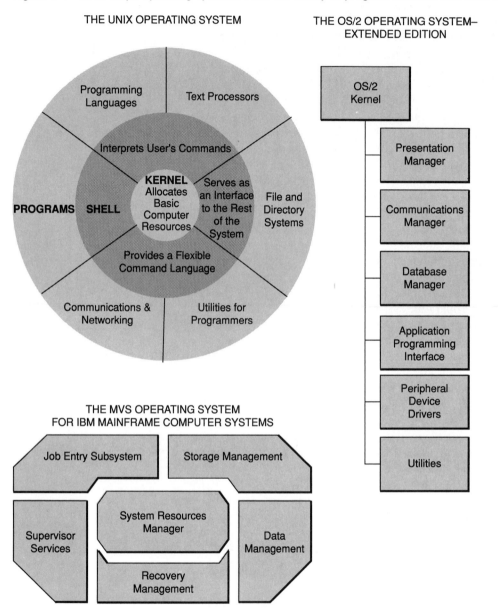

THE UNIX OPERATING SYSTEM

THE OS/2 OPERATING SYSTEM–
EXTENDED EDITION

THE MVS OPERATING SYSTEM
FOR IBM MAINFRAME COMPUTER SYSTEMS

system software and by the application programs of users. These resources include primary storage, secondary storage, CPU processing time, and input/output devices. Since these resources must be managed to accomplish various information processing tasks, this function is also called *task management*.

☐ **Data management**—controlling the input/output of data as well as their location, storage, and retrieval. Data management programs support the database processing and interrogation activities of database management system packages. They control the allocation of secondary

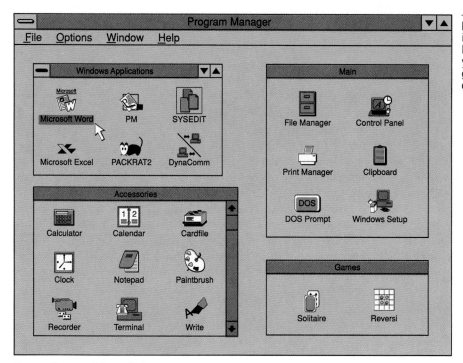

Source: Courtesy Microsoft Corporation.

Figure 4-5 Using an operating environment package. Microsoft Windows allows you to use a variety of programs in multiple window displays.

storage devices, the physical format and *cataloging* of data storage, and the movement of data between primary and secondary storage devices.

Software for the User Interface

Many operating systems are enhanced by the use of *operating environment* modules, such as OS/2's Presentation Manager, or add-on packages, such as Microsoft Windows and Desqview. These offer capabilities similar to those provided by the Apple Macintosh operating system. Operating environments enhance the user interface between computers and end users by adding a *graphics-based interface* between end users, the operating system, and their application programs. These packages serve as a *shell* to interconnect several separate application packages so that they can communicate and work together and share common data files. Operating environment packages provide icon displays and support the use of electronic mouse or other pointing devices. They also allow the output of several programs to be displayed at the same time in multiple windows. Finally, several of these packages support some type of *concurrent processing,* where several programs or tasks can be processed at the same time. See Figure 4–5.

Software for Multitasking

Mainframe and minicomputer operating systems, some microcomputer operating systems (like OS/2), and most operating environment packages provide a **multitasking** capability. Multitasking is a capability that allows end users to do two or more *operations* (for example, printing and keyboarding) or applications (for example, word processing and financial analysis) *concurrently,* that is, at the same time on the same computer. Multitasking on microcomputers has also been made possible by the development of more powerful microprocessors (like the Intel 80386) and their ability to directly address much larger memory capacities (up to 16 megabytes). This allows an operating system to subdivide primary storage into several large *partitions*, each of which can be used by a different application program.

In effect, a single computer can act as if it were several computers, or *virtual machines*, since each application program is running independently at the same time. The number of programs that can be run concurrently depends on the amount of memory that is available and the amount of processing each job demands. That's because a microprocessor (or CPU) can become overloaded with too many jobs and provide unacceptably slow response times. However, if memory and processing capacities are adequate, multitasking allows end users to easily switch from one application to another, share data files among applications, and process some applications in a *background* mode. Typically, background tasks include printing, extensive mathematical computation, or unattended telecommunications sessions. Finally, multitasking is essential for *multiuser*, or *time-sharing*, systems, where several end users share the same computer at the same time.

DATABASE MANAGEMENT SYSTEMS

A **database management system** (DBMS) is a set of computer programs that controls the creation, maintenance, and use of the databases of users and computer-using organizations. A DBMS is a software package that helps you use the integrated collections of data records and files known as databases. It allows different user application programs to easily access the same database. A DBMS also simplifies the process of retrieving information from databases in the form of displays and reports. Instead of having to write computer programs to extract information, users can ask simple questions in a *query language*. Thus, many DBMS packages provide *fourth-generation languages* (4GLs) and other application development features. Examples of popular mainframe packages are DB2 by IBM and Oracle by Oracle Corporation. We will explore the use of database management packages in modern information systems in Chapter 6.

Microcomputer DBMS Packages

Microcomputer versions of database management programs have become so popular that they are now viewed as *general-purpose application software packages* like word processing and spreadsheet programs. Packages such as dBASE IV by Ashton Tate and R:base by Microrim allow end users to set up databases of files and records on their personal computer systems and quickly store data and retrieve information. As Figure 4–6 illustrates, most microcomputer DBMS packages can perform four primary tasks:

☐ **Database creation:** Define and organize the content, relationships, and structure of the data needed to build a database.

☐ **Database interrogation:** Access the data in a database for information retrieval and report generation. Thus, you can selectively retrieve and display information and produce reports and documents.

☐ **Database maintenance:** Add, delete, update, correct, and protect the data in a database.

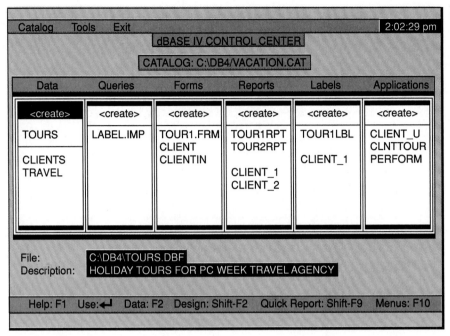

Figure 4-6 Using a DBMS package. Note how this display prompts you to create and perform other operations to a database file, create queries, forms, reports, or labels, or do applications development.

Courtesy *PC Week*.

☐ **Application development:** Develop prototypes of data entry screens, queries, forms, reports, and labels for a proposed application. Use a 4GL or application generator to develop program code.

TELECOMMUNICATIONS MONITORS

Modern information systems rely heavily on telecommunications networks, which provide electronic communication links between end user workstations, other computer systems, and databases. This requires programs called **telecommunications monitors.** They are used by a main computer (called the *host*) or in telecommunications control computers such as *front-end processors* and *network servers*. Telecommunications monitors and similar programs perform such functions as connecting or disconnecting communication links between computers and terminals, automatically checking terminals for input/output activity, assigning priorities to communications requests from terminals, and detecting and correcting transmission errors. Thus, they control and support the data communications activities occurring in a telecommunications network. We will discuss telecommunications software in more detail in Chapter 5.

Microcomputer Communications Software

Telecommunications software packages for microcomputers provide several of the control functions just mentioned. Such packages can connect a microcomputer equipped with a modem to public and private networks. Communications control packages such as Crosstalk, Access, and Smartcom provide microcomputer users with several major communications capabilities:

☐ **Terminal emulation.** The microcomputer can act as a generic *dumb terminal* that can only send, receive, and display data one line at a time. It can also act as a generic *intelligent terminal* and transmit, receive, and store entire files of data and programs. Finally, some

Figure 4–7 Using the Crosstalk telecommunications package for file transfer between computers.

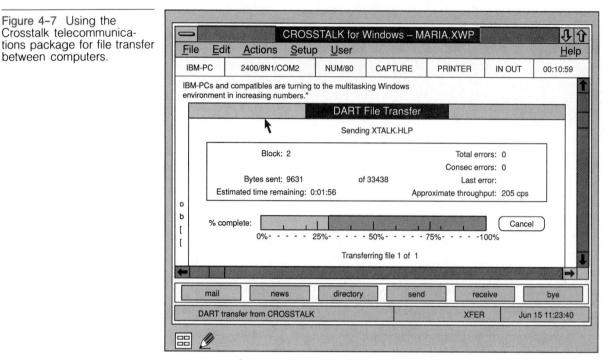

Courtesy Digital Communications Associates

packages allow a microcomputer to *emulate* (act like) a specific type of terminal, especially those used with large computer systems.

☐ **File transfer.** Files of data and programs can be *downloaded* from a host computer to a microcomputer and stored on a disk. Or files can be *uploaded* from the microcomputer to a host computer. Some programs allow files to be transferred automatically between unattended computer systems.

Telecommunication packages for microcomputers are fairly easy to use. Once you load the program, you are usually provided with a display that asks you to set communications parameters (transmission speed and mode, type of parity, etc.). Then you dial the computer system or network you want or have it done automatically for you. Most networks will provide you with a series of prompts or menus to guide you in sending or receiving messages, information, and files. See Figure 4–7.

SYSTEM SUPPORT PROGRAMS

System support programs are specialized programs that perform routine and repetitive functions and are made available to all of the users of a computer system. For example, a major category of system support involves **utility programs,** or *utilities.* They are a group of miscellaneous programs that perform various housekeeping and file conversion functions. For example, sort programs are important utility programs that perform the sorting operations on data required in many information processing applications. Utility programs also clear primary storage, load programs, record the contents of primary

| **Fourth-Generation Languages:** Use natural and nonprocedural statements |
| **High-Level Languages:** Use Englishlike statements and arithmetic notation |
| **Assembler Languages:** Use symbolic coded instructions |
| **Machine Languages:** Use binary coded instructions |

Figure 4–8 The four major levels of programming languages. They range from conversational, fourth-generation languages to the binary codes of machine languages.

storage, and convert files of data from one storage medium to another, such as from tape to disk. Many of the operating system commands used with microcomputers and other computer systems provide users with utility programs and routines for a variety of chores. Other system support programs include *performance monitors* and *security monitors* which promote the operating efficiency and security of computer system resources. These software packages will be discussed in Chapters 13 and 14.

PROGRAMMING LANGUAGES

A proper understanding of computer software requires a basic knowledge of **programming languages.** Programming languages allow programmers and end users to develop the programs of instructions that are executed by a computer. To be a knowledgeable end user, you should know the basic categories of programming languages. Many different programming languages have been developed, each with its own unique vocabulary, grammar, and uses. Programming languages can be grouped into the four major categories shown in Figure 4–8.

Machine Languages

Machine languages are the most basic level of programming languages. In the early stages of computer development, most program instructions had to be written using *binary codes* unique to each computer. This type of programming involves the difficult task of writing instructions in the form of strings of binary digits (ones and zeros) or other number systems. Programmers must have a detailed knowledge of the internal operations of the specific type of CPU they are using. They must write long series of detailed instructions to accomplish even simple processing tasks. Programming in machine language requires specifying the storage locations for every instruction and item of data used. Instructions must be included for every switch and indicator used by the program. These requirements make machine language programming a difficult and error-prone task.

A machine language program to add two numbers together in the CPU of a specific computer and store the result might take the form shown in Figure 4–9. Like many computer instructions, these instructions consist of an *operation code*, which specifies what is to be done, and an *operand*, which specifies the address of the data or device to be operated upon.

Assembler Languages

Assembler languages are the next level of programming languages. They were developed to reduce the difficulties in writing machine language programs. The use of assembler languages requires language translator programs called *assemblers*, which allow a computer to convert the instructions of such languages into machine instructions. Assembler languages are frequently called *symbolic*

Figure 4–9 Examples of four levels of programming languages. These programming language instructions might be used to compute the sum of two numbers, as expressed by the formula $X = Y + Z$. The last two levels also demonstrate how Englishlike such instructions can be if X is defined as GROSSPAY, Y as SALARY, and Z as COMMISSIONS.

Machine Language		High-Level Languages	
Operation Code	Operand	BASIC: X = Y + Z	
1010	11001	COBOL: COMPUTE X = Y + Z	
		BASIC: GROSPAY = SALARY + COMMIS	
1011	11010	COBOL: ADD SALARY, COMMISSIONS GIVING GROSSPAY	
1100	11011	Fourth-Generation Language	
Assembler Language			
Operation Code	Operand	SUM THE FOLLOWING TWO NUMBERS	
LOD	Y	COMPUTE THE GROSSPAY OF ALL SALESPERSONS BY SUMMING THEIR SALARY AND COMMISSIONS	
ADD	Z		
STR	X		

languages because symbols are used to represent operation codes and storage locations. Convenient alphabetic abbreviations called *mnemonics* (memory aids) and other symbols are used to represent operation codes, storage locations, and data elements. For example, the computation $X = Y + Z$ in an assembler language program might take the form shown in Figure 4–9.

Advantages and Disadvantages

In an assembler language, alphabetic abbreviations that are easier to remember are used in place of the actual numeric addresses of the data. This greatly simplifies programming since the programmer does not need to know the exact storage locations of data and instructions. However, assembler language is still *machine-oriented;* that is, assembler language instructions correspond closely to the machine language instructions of the particular computer model being used. Also, note that each assembler instruction corresponds to a single machine instruction, and that the same number of instructions are required in both illustrations.

Assembler languages are still widely used as a method of programming a computer in a machine-oriented language. Most computer manufacturers provide an assembler language that reflects the unique machine language *instruction set* of a particular line of computers. This feature is particularly desirable to *systems programmers,* who program systems software (as opposed to *applications programmers,* who program applications software), since it provides them with greater control and flexibility in designing a program for a particular computer. They can then produce more *efficient* software—that is, programs that require a minimum of instructions, storage, and CPU time to perform a specific processing assignment.

High-Level Languages

High-level languages are also known as *compiler languages.* The instructions of high-level languages are called *statements* and closely resemble human language or the standard notation of mathematics. Individual high-level language statements are actually *macro instructions;* that is, each individual statement generates several machine instructions when translated into machine language by high-level language translator programs called *compilers* or *interpreters*. The use of macro instructions is also common in fourth generation languages and software packages such as electronic spreadsheet and database management programs.

High-level language statements resemble the phrases or mathematical expressions required to express the problem or procedure being programmed. The *syntax* (vocabulary, punctuation, and grammatical rules) and the *semantics* (meanings) of such statements do not reflect the internal code of any particular computer. For example, the computation $X = Y + Z$ would be programmed in the high-level languages of BASIC and COBOL as shown in Figure 4–9. This figure also illustrates how close to the English language high-level language statements can be.

Advantages and Disadvantages

A high-level language is obviously easier to learn and understand than an assembler language. Also, high-level languages have less rigid rules, forms, and syntaxes, so the potential for error is reduced. However, high-level language programs are usually less efficient than assembler language programs and require a greater amount of computer time for translation into machine instructions. Most high-level languages are machine-independent, that is, they can be used on many different brands of computers. Therefore, programs written in a high-level language do not have to be reprogrammed when a new computer is installed, and computer programmers do not have to learn a new language for each computer they program. Figure 4–10 highlights some of the major high-level languages in use today. Note that the most widely used languages include COBOL for business application programs, BASIC for microcomputer end users, and FORTRAN for scientific and engineering applications.

Fourth-Generation Languages

The term **fourth-generation language** is used to describe a variety of programming languages that are more nonprocedural and conversational than prior languages. These languages are called fourth-generation languages (4GLs) to differentiate them from machine languages (first generation), assembler languages (second generation), and high-level languages (third generation). It should be noted that some industry observers have begun to use the term *fifth-generation language* to describe languages using artificial intelligence techniques to accomplish results for users.

Most fourth-generation languages are **nonprocedural languages** that encourage users and programmers to specify the *results* they want, while the computer determines the *sequence of instructions* that will accomplish those results. Users and programmers no longer have to spend a lot of time developing the sequence of instructions the computer must follow to achieve a result. Thus, fourth-generation languages have helped simplify the programming process. **Natural languages** are 4GLs that are very close to English or other human languages. Research and development activity in artificial intelligence (AI) is developing programming languages that are as easy to use as ordinary conversation in one's native tongue. Figure 4–11 outlines some of the major differences between 3GLs and 4GLs.

Figure 4–10 Highlights of high-level languages. Note the differences in the characteristics and purposes of each language.

Ada: Named after Augusta Ada Byron, considered the world's first computer programmer. Developed for the U.S. Department of Defense as a standard "high-order language" to replace COBOL and FORTRAN. It resembles an extension of Pascal.

ALGOL: (ALGOrithmic Language). An international algebraic language designed primarily for scientific and mathematical applications. It is widely used in Europe in place of FORTRAN.

APL: (A Programming Language). A mathematically oriented interactive language. It utilizes a very concise symbolic notation designed for efficient interactive programming of analytical business and scientific applications.

BASIC: (Beginner's All-Purpose Symbolic Instruction Code). A simple procedure-oriented language widely used for interactive programming on time-sharing systems and personal computing.

C: A mid-level structured language developed as part of the UNIX operating system. It resembles a machine-independent assembler language and is presently popular for system software programming and development of microcomputer packages.

COBOL: (COmmon Business Oriented Language). Designed as an Englishlike language specifically for business data processing. It is the most widely used programming language for business applications.

FORTRAN: (FORmula TRANslation). The oldest of the popular high-level languages. It was designed for solving mathematical problems in science, engineering, research, business, and education. It is still the most widely used programming language for scientific and engineering applications.

Pascal: Named after Blaise Pascal. Developed as a powerful successor to ALGOL, and designed specifically to incorporate structured programming concepts. Pascal has become a popular language for both large computers and microcomputers.

PL/1: (Programming Language/1). A general-purpose language developed to combine some of the features of COBOL, FORTRAN, ALGOL, and other languages. It is a flexible language used for business and scientific applications.

RPG: (Report Program Generator). A problem-oriented language that generates programs that produce reports and perform other data processing tasks. It is a popular language with many business minicomputer users.

Figure 4–11 Major differences between 3GLs and 4GLs.

Third-Generation Languages	Fourth-Generation Languages
Intended for use by professional programmers	May be used by a nonprogramming end user as well as a professional programmer
Requires specification of *how to perform task*	Requires specification of *what task* to perform (system determines how to perform the task)
All alternatives must be specified	Default alternatives are built in; an end user need not specify these alternatives
Requires large number of procedural instructions	Requires far fewer instructions (less than one tenth in most cases)
Code may be difficult to read, understand, and maintain	Code is easy to understand and maintain because of Englishlike commands
Language developed originally for batch operation	Language developed primarily for online use
Can be difficult to learn	Many features can be learned quickly
Difficult to debug	Errors easier to locate because of shorter programs, more structured code, and use of defaults and English-like language
Typically file-oriented	Typically database-oriented

Source: Adapted from James A. Senn, *Analysis and Design of Information Systems* (New York: McGraw-Hill, 1989), p. 228. Used with permission.

Figure 4–12 Comparing third- and fourth-generation languages. Note how brief, nonprocedural, and conversational INTELLECT is compared to BASIC, Pascal, and COBOL to accomplish the same task.

INTELLECT 4GL	BASIC
| WHAT ARE THE AVERAGE EXAM SCORES FOR STUDENTS IN MIS 200? | ```
10 REM AVERAGE EXAM SCORE PROGRAM
20 LET COUNTER = 0
30 LET TOTAL = 0
40 OPEN "STUDDATA" FOR INPUT AS #1
50 INPUT #1, SCORE
60 WHILE SCORE <> 9999
70    LET COUNTER = COUNTER + 1
80    LET TOTAL = TOTAL + SCORE
90    INPUT #1, SCORE
100 WEND
110 LET AVERAGE = TOTAL / COUNTER
120 PRINT "AVERAGE SCORE IS"; AVERAGE
130 END
``` |

COBOL (Procedure Division)

```
PROCEDURE DIVISION.
MAIN.
    PERFORM INITIALIZATION.
    PERFORM PROCESS-RECORDS UNTIL END-OF-FILE.
    PERFORM END-OF-JOB.
INITIALIZATION.
    OPEN INPUT IN-FILE.
    OPEN OUTPUT OUT-FILE.
    PERFORM READ-RECORD.
PROCESS-RECORDS.
    ADD SCORES TO STORE-SCORE.
    ADD 1 TO STORE-NUMBER.
    MOVE NAME-IN TO NAME-OUT.
    MOVE SCORE TO SCORE-OUT.
    WRITE OUT-REC FROM PRINTER-LINE
        AFTER ADVANCING 1.
    PERFORM READ-RECORD.
END-OF-JOB.
    DIVIDE STORE-NUMBER INTO STORE-SCORE GIVING
        AVERAGE.
    WRITE OUT-REC FROM AVERAGE-LINE
        AFTER ADVANCING 2 LINES.
    CLOSE IN-FILE.
    CLOSE OUT-FILE.
    STOP RUN.
READ-RECORD.
    READ IN-FILE
        AT END MOVE "Y" TO EOF-FLAG.
```

Pascal

```
PROGRAM averagescore {infile, outfile};
VAR score, sum, average, count : real ;
    infile, outfile : text;
BEGIN
    sum: = 0,0; count: 0,0;
    REPEAT
        read{infile,score};
        sum: = sum + score;
        count: = count + 1.0
    UNTIL eof{infile};
    average: = sum/count;
    write{outfile, 'Average score is', average}
END.
```

Figures 4–9 and 4–12 compare fourth-generation language statements with earlier generations. In Figure 4–12, INTELLECT, a 4GL, is compared to 3GLs BASIC, Pascal, and COBOL with respect to a simple average exam score task. Many types of software packages considered to be fourth-generation langauges are shown in Figure 4–13. These include query languages, report generators, and application generators available as separate packages or provided as part of advanced electronic spreadsheet, decision support, and database management packages.

Advantages and Disadvantages

There are major differences in the ease of use and technical sophistication of 4GL products. For instance, INTELLECT and CLOUT are natural query languages that impose no rigid grammatical rules, while SQL and FOCUS require concise structured statements. However, the ease of use of 4GLs is gained at the expense of some loss in flexibility. It is frequently difficult for an end user to override some of the prespecified formats or procedures of 4GLs. Also, the machine language code generated by a program developed by a 4GL is frequently much less efficient (in terms of processing speed and amount of storage capacity needed) than a program written in a language like COBOL.
```

Figure 4–13 Examples of
popular fourth-generation
languages.

4GL	Supplier
Query Languages and Report Writers	
QBE and SQL	IBM
CLOUT	Microrim
DATATRIEVE	DEC
EASYTRIEVE	Panasophic
HAL	Lotus Development
INTELLECT	Artificial Intelligence
Decision Support Generators	
EXPRESS	Information Resources
IFPS	Execucom
MODEL	Lloyd Bush
SAS	SAS Institute
SYSTEM W	Comshare
Application Generators	
FOCUS	Information Builders
IDEAL	Computer Associates
MANTIS	Cincom
NATURAL	Software AG
NOMAD 2	MUST International

Figure 4–13 Examples of popular fourth-generation languages.

Major failures have been reported in some large transaction processing applications programmed in a 4GL. These applications were unable to provide reasonable response times when faced with a large amount of transaction processing and end user inquiries. However, 4GLs have shown great success in end user and departmental applications without a high volume of transactions to process.

Object-Oriented Languages

Object-oriented programming (OOP) languages (humorously called OOPS—object-oriented programming systems) have been around since Xerox developed Smalltalk in the 1960s. However, object-oriented languages have become a major consideration in software development by both programmers and end users. Briefly, while most other programming languages separate data elements from the procedures or actions that will be performed upon them, OOP languages tie them together into *objects*. Thus, an *object* consists of data and the actions that can be performed on the data. For example, an object could be data about an employee and all the operations (such as payroll calculations) that might be performed upon the data. Or an object could be data in graphic form, such as a video display window, plus the display actions that might be used upon it.

In procedural languages, a program consists of procedures to perform actions on each data element. However, in object-oriented systems, programs tell objects to perform actions on themselves. For example, to have a window appear in a video display usually requires that the window be drawn upon the screen by a series of instructions in a program. However, if OOP languages have been used, a window object is sent a message to open by a program, and it appears on the screen. That's because the window object contains the program code for opening itself.

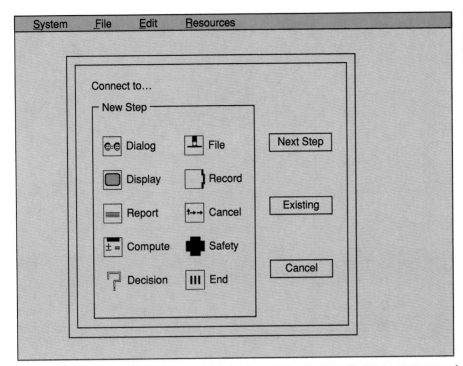

System	File	Edit	Resources

Connect to...

┌─ New Step ─────────────────────

- Dialog   File
- Display   Record
- Report   Cancel
- Compute   Safety
- Decision   End

Next Step

Existing

Cancel

Figure 4–14 The opening display of Cause, an object-oriented programming package.

Users build a Cause program, called an Effect, by creating a sequence that incorporates any of six steps represented by objects (on-screen above) called: Dialog, Display, Report, File, Decision and Compute. To assemble the program, Step objects are associated with any of four Resource objects—Window, Reports, Files, and Items (variables). Every program is built in three steps, known as Select, Discuss, and Perform.
Courtesy Maxem Corporation

Object-oriented languages like Actor, Objective C, and C + + are easier to use and more efficient for programming the graphics-oriented user interfaces required by many applications. Once objects are programmed, they are reusable. For example, programmers or end users can construct data entry displays for a new program by assembling standard objects such as windows, bars, buttons, and icons. Thus, the use of object-oriented languages for such visual programming is expected to increase. Figure 4–14 shows a display of the Cause object-oriented programming environment.

LANGUAGE TRANSLATOR PROGRAMS

Language translators (or *language processors*) are programs that translate other programs into machine language instruction codes the computer can execute. They also allow you to write your own programs by providing program creation and editing facilities. Computer programs consist of sets of instructions written in programming languages, such as BASIC or COBOL, which must be translated by a *compilation* process into the computer's own machine language before they can be processed, or *executed*, by the CPU.

Programming language translator programs are known by a variety of names. An **assembler** translates the symbolic instruction codes of programs written in an assembler language, while a **compiler** translates high-level language statements. An **interpreter** is a special type of compiler that translates and executes each program statement one at a time, instead of first producing a complete machine language program, like compilers and assemblers do. Figure 4–15

Figure 4–15 The language
translation process. A program must be translated into
machine language before it
can be executed by a com-
puter.

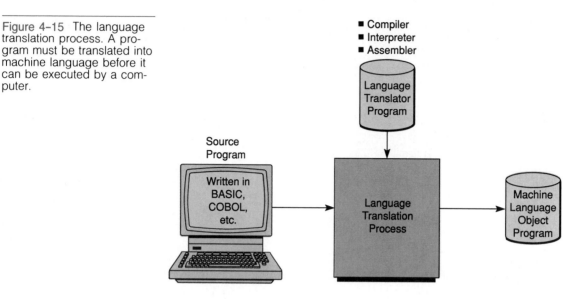

illustrates the typical language translation process. A program written in a language such as BASIC or COBOL is called a *source program*. When a source program is translated into machine language, it is called an *object program*, which can then be executed by a computer.

Programming Tools

The *programmer interface* of many language translator programs is being enhanced by a variety of built-in capabilities or add-on packages. Language translators have always provided some editing and diagnostic capabilities to help programmers identify programming errors, or *bugs*. However, many language translator programs now include powerful graphics-oriented *editors* and *debuggers*. These programs make it easier for programmers to identify and avoid errors while they are programming. Such **programming tools** provide programmers with a computer-aided programming *environment* or *workbench*. Their goal is to decrease the drudgery of programming while increasing the efficiency and productivity of programmers. Other programming tools include diagramming packages, code generators, and libraries of reusable program code and objects. Many of these same tools are part of the *toolkit* provided by integrated *computer-aided software engineering* (CASE) packages, which we will discuss in Chapter 11.

REAL WORLD CASE

The *Washington Post* and *Chicago Tribune*

Like a once-swift runner grown fat and winded, the publishing system at The *Washington Post* was having trouble getting oxygen to its extremities. Response was slowing and movement limited. With the journalistic marathon of the 1992 presidential election looming on the horizon, systems manager Ken Weiss figured it was time to get in shape—and fast. "We were tired of being left behind technologically," Weiss said from an office only a quick walk from the White House. "So now we're instituting a 10-year technological jump in six months."

Weiss's decision to replace a decade-old Raytheon editorial system with an OS/2-based network of nearly 400 IBM Personal System/2 Model 55SX personal computers is indicative of the changes blowing through the Fourth Estate. Once the bastion of proprietary minicomputer-based publishing systems, large metropolitan daily newspapers are increasingly installing PC- and workstation-based networks and catching up with the technological advances they could once only write about.

The multitasking and windowing features of OS/2 on the PCs and workstations promise to substantially streamline the news-writing task by allowing a reporter to tap into many news sources with the flick of a few buttons. The result: sharper copy and a more widely researched story. "We're seeing a transition to an environment with a PC workstation on the desk and a central processor used only as a file management machine," said John Iobst, research manager at the American Newspaper Publishers Association in Reston, Virginia.

Among the leaders of the pack is the *Chicago Tribune*, which is deeply involved in installing a text-editing system in an OS/2 environment. Software Services Manager Jim Joyce said the *Tribune* will link 400 Compaq 386SX microcomputers to 4 Tandem CLX minicomputers. The PCs, each with 6M bytes of random-access memory, will be able to run several windows at once using OS/2. For instance, a reporter or editor could draft a story on one window, view wire-service copy on a second, and query the database from a third.

Joyce explained that the old editing system—software called Edit V that uses Digital PDP-11 and Decsystem 10 minicomputers—was custom-designed for the paper in the late 1970s and had become difficult to maintain. When the new systems are implemented, Joyce said, even functions such as hyphenation and justification—whereby text is horizontally and vertically formatted into newspaper columns—will occur in the background as the writer enters text. This will free up processing capacity on the Tandem minis, which will eventually function exclusively as database servers.

Application Questions

☐ Why are the *Washington Post* and the *Chicago Tribune* switching from proprietary minicomputer systems to networks of PC workstations?

☐ What capabilities does OS/2 provide to the newspaper business?

☐ Are the capabilities provided by operating systems like OS/2 useful for other types of business activity? Explain.

Source: Adapted from James Daly and Ellis Booker, "Newspapers Take Leap into High-Tech Chase," *Computerworld*, March 19, 1990, p. 125.

Section II: Application Software: End User Applications

APPLICATION SOFTWARE FOR END USERS

Application software consists of programs that direct computers to perform specific information processing activities for end users. These programs are called *application packages* because they direct the processing required for a particular use, or *application*, that end users want accomplished. Thousands of application packages are available because there are thousands of different jobs end users want computers to do. The use of personal computers has multiplied the growth of such programs. We will briefly explain some of the most popular types of end user application packages in this section.

General-Purpose Programs

Figure 4–1 showed that application software includes a variety of programs that can be subdivided into *general-purpose* and *application-specific* categories. **General-purpose application programs** are programs that perform common information processing jobs for end users. For example, word processing programs, spreadsheet programs, database management programs, integrated packages, and graphics programs are popular with microcomputer users for home, education, business, scientific, and many other purposes. Because they significantly increase the productivity of end users, they are also known as *productivity packages*.

Application-Specific Programs

Numerous packages are available to support specific applications of end users. Major categories of such application-specific programs are:

☐ **Business application programs**—programs that accomplish the information processing tasks of important business functions or industry requirements. Examples of such business functions and their corresponding applications are accounting (general ledger), marketing (sales analysis), finance (capital budgeting), manufacturing (material requirements planning), operations management (inventory control), and human resource management (employee benefits analysis).

☐ **Scientific application programs**—programs that perform information processing tasks for the natural, physical, social, and behavioral sciences, and for mathematics, engineering, and all other areas involved in scientific research, experimentation, and development. Some broad application categories include scientific analysis, engineering design, and monitoring of experiments.

☐ **Other application programs**—there are so many other application areas of computers that we lump them all into this category. Thus, we can talk of computer applications in education, entertainment, music, art, law enforcement, medicine, and so on. Some specific examples are computer-assisted instruction programs in education, video game programs in entertainment, and computer-generated music and art programs.

Word processing packages are built around programs that automate the creation, editing, and printing of *documents* of all kinds, including letters, memos, and reports. They electronically process *text data* (words, phrases, sentences, and paragraphs) provided through the keyboard of a microcomputer or terminal. Word processing is an important part of *office automation*, which will be discussed in Chapter 7. Word processing packages such as WordPerfect, Microsoft Word, and WordStar allow end users to:

WORD
PROCESSING
PACKAGES

☐ Use a computer to create and edit a document and have each line of text automatically adjusted to fit prespecified margins.

☐ Move to any point in a document and add, delete, or change words, sentences, or paragraphs.

☐ Move a block of text from one part of a document to another and insert standard text from another document file.

☐ Check a document for spelling or grammatical errors and selectively change all occurrences of a particular word or phrase.

☐ Store a document as a document file on a magnetic disk, retrieve it any time, and print it according to a variety of predesigned formats.

Many word processing packages provide other features or can be upgraded with supplementary packages. For example, a *spelling checker* uses built-in dictionaries to identify and correct spelling errors in a document. A *thesaurus* program helps you find a better choice of words to express ideas. *Style checker* programs can identify and correct grammar and punctuation errors, as well as suggest possible improvements in your writing style. Another text productivity tool is an *idea processor* or *outliner* program. It helps organize and outline your thoughts before you prepare a document or develop a presentation. Also popular is a *mail-merge* program, which can automatically merge the names and addresses in a mailing list file with letters and other documents. Finally, many word processing programs are able to support a limited amount of *desktop publishing* activity. As we will discuss in Chapter 7, this allows end users to merge text, graphics, and illustrations on each page to produce documents that look professionally published. See Figure 4–16.

Electronic spreadsheet packages are application programs used for analysis, planning, and modeling. They provide an electronic replacement for more traditional tools such as paper worksheets, pencils, and calculators. They generate an electronic spreadsheet, which is a worksheet of rows and columns stored in the computer's memory and displayed on its video screen. You use the computer's keyboard to enter data and relationships (formulas) into the worksheet. This results in an *electronic model* of your problem. In response to your commands, the computer performs necessary calculations based on the relationships you defined in the spreadsheet. Results are immediately displayed for you to see. See Figure 4–17.

ELECTRONIC
SPREADSHEET
PACKAGES

Once an electronic spreadsheet has been developed, it can be stored for later use or printed out as a report. Popular electronic spreadsheet packages for microcomputers include Lotus 1-2-3, Excel, and QuattroPro. Mainframe and minicomputer users can also use the electronic spreadsheet modules

Figure 4–16 Using a word processing package. Note how Microsoft Word allows you to include desktop publishing features such as art, graphs, and large type in a document you are creating.

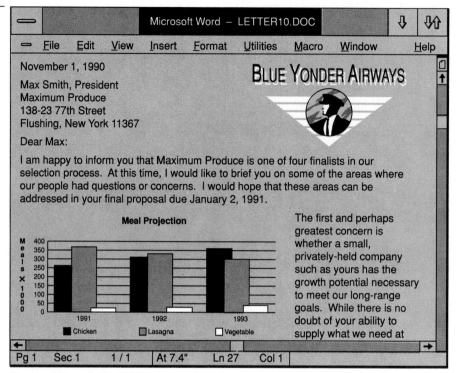

Courtesy Microsoft Corporation

Figure 4–17 Using an electronic spreadsheet. The Lotus 1-2-3/G spreadsheet package allows you to work with and display multiple related spreadsheets and graphics.

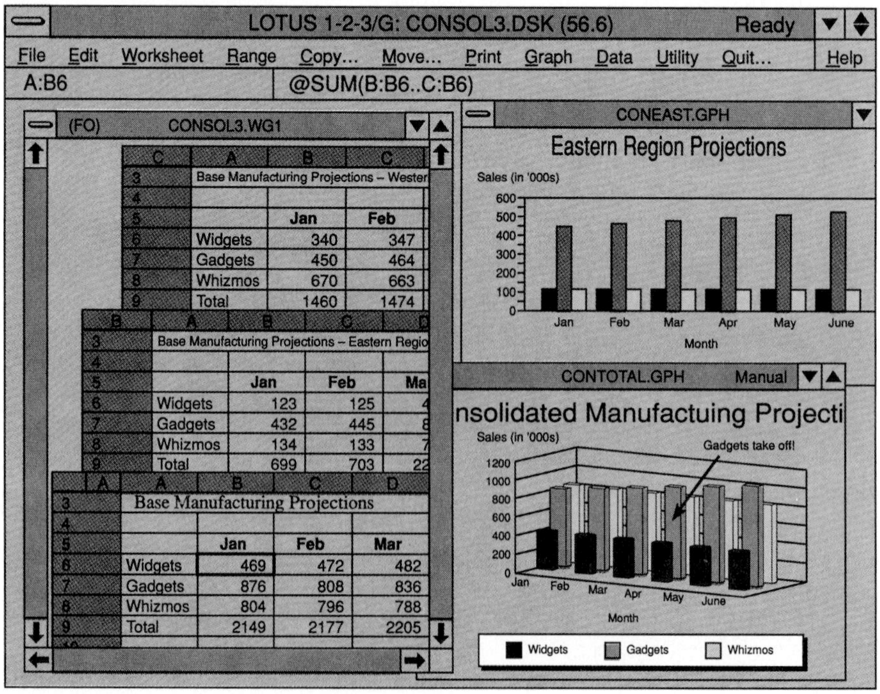

Courtesy Lotus Development Corporation

of products such as Lotus 1-2-3M, IFPS, and Focus. Special-purpose spreadsheet models called *templates* are available for most spreadsheet packages. These worksheets are developed for specific applications such as tax accounting or real estate investment.

The worksheet created by an electronic spreadsheet package is a *visual model* of the mathematical and other relationships within a particular business activity. It can thus be used to record and analyze past, present, and future activity. It is especially useful as a decision support tool to answer *what-if questions*. For example, suppose you wanted to know, **What** would happen to net profit **if** advertising expense increased by 10 percent? To answer this question, you would simply change the advertising expense formula on an income statement worksheet you had developed. The affected figures would be recalculated, and a new net profit figure would be displayed. You would then have a better insight into whether advertising expense should be increased. The use of electronic spreadsheets for end user computing and decision support will be discussed in Chapters 7 and 9.

What-If Analysis

Graphics packages convert numeric data into graphics displays such as line charts, bar charts, and pie charts. Many other types of *presentation graphics* displays are possible. Some graphics packages support freehand drawing, while desktop publishing programs provide predrawn graphics for insertion into documents. Images are displayed on your video monitor or copies can be made on your system printer or plotter. Not only are such graphic displays easier to comprehend and communicate than numeric data, but multiple-color displays can more easily emphasize strategic differences and trends in the data. Presentation graphics have proved to be much more effective than tabular presentations of numeric data for reporting and communicating in management reports or in presentations to groups of people.

Presentation graphics can be produced by graphics packages (such as Harvard Graphics and Lotus Freelance for microcomputers, and SAS Graph and Tell-A-Graph for minicomputers and mainframes) or by the graphics modules of electronic spreadsheets or integrated packages. To use such packages, you typically select the type of graph you want and enter the categories of data you want plotted. This is done in response to prompts displayed on your screen, or you can highlight the data you want graphed. The graphics program then analyzes the file of data you specify and generates the requested graphics. See Figure 4–18 for how a graphics program works.

GRAPHICS PACKAGES

Integrated packages combine the abilities of several general-purpose applications in one program. Integrated packages were developed to solve the problems caused by the inability of individual programs to communicate and work together with common files of data. However, integrated packages may require significant amounts of memory and may compromise on the speed, power, and flexibility of some of their functions in order to achieve integration. Therefore, users may prefer single-function packages for applications they use heavily.

INTEGRATED PACKAGES

Figure 4–18 Using a graphics package. The first video display shows how you would enter graphics specifications using Harvard Graphics. The second display shows the resulting bar chart.

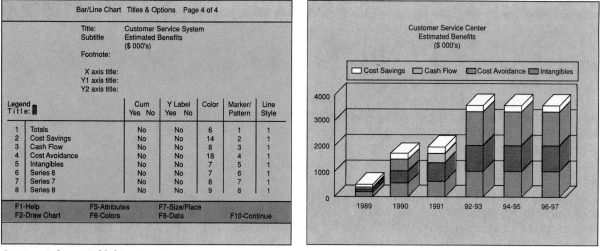

Courtesy Software Publishing Corporation

Figure 4–19 Using an integrated package. Framework III provides word processing, spreadsheet, file management, telecommunications, and graphics capabilities in one package.

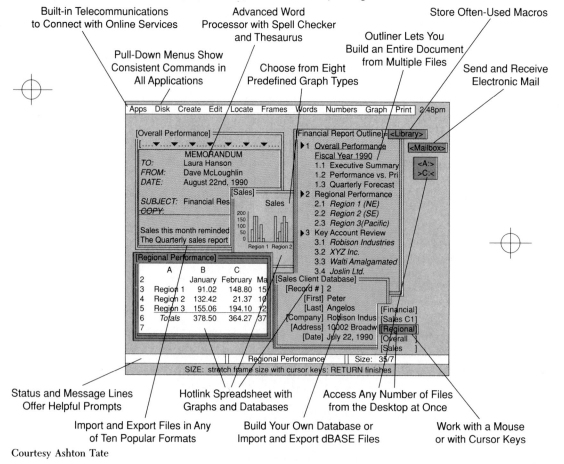

Courtesy Ashton Tate

Examples of popular integrated packages are Microsoft Works, Symphony, Framework III, PFS First Choice, and Enable. Such packages combine some of the general-purpose application software functions of electronic spreadsheets, word processing, and graphics with the system software functions of database management and telecommunications. Thus, you can process the same file of data with one package, moving from one function to the other by pressing a few keys on your keyboard. You can view displays from each function separately, or together in multiple windows on your video screen. See Figure 4–19.

OTHER END USER PACKAGES

We could spend a lot more time discussing the many application packages available to end users for use on mainframes, minicomputers, and microcomputers. As we said in Chapter 3, microcomputer application packages support managerial, professional, and business uses such as decision support, accounting, project management, investment analysis, and desktop publishing. Still other packages support end users by helping them organize random pieces of information and accomplish routine office tasks. Many other packages are available for applications such as personal finance, home management, video games, education, and information services. Figure 4–20 shows a display of a desktop accessory package for end user productivity.

These and other software packages are discussed in upcoming chapters on telecommunications, database management, end user computing, office automation, decision support and expert systems, and business function information systems. As a business end user, you should realize that the use of such application packages is a growing trend even in the minicomputer and mainframe markets. This trend is expected to continue, as application packages grow in power, flexibility, and ease of use.

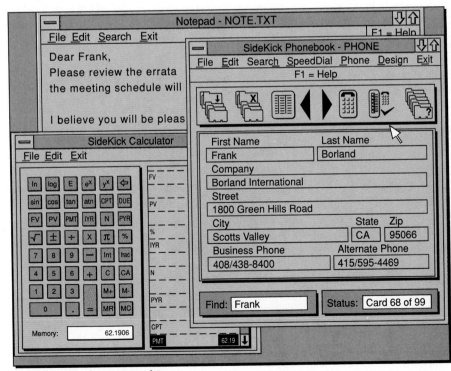

Figure 4–20 The Sidekick desktop accessory package displays pop-up windows for its notepad, calculator, phone directory, and other electronic accessories.

Courtesy Borland International Inc.

REAL WORLD CASE

Using Integrated Packages

For three years now, users at the National Broadcasting Co. have been running the LAN version of the integrated package Enable on 210 PCs linked through a Token-Ring network, and they're still delighted with their choice.

"We evaluated all of the possibilities," said Lucy Roadarmel, director of project development for the broadcasting giant in New York. "We have 250 users who are not computer experts. We needed something for them that would be both powerful and easy to use. We checked out the stand-alone programs and the integrated packages. Enable came out on top." The primary users of Enable are network sales executives. "The staff can look at the budget remaining for a particular client, the status of availabilities, and a plan we're proposing—all at the same time." NBC also uses Enable to download mainframe information, including financial and sales data and details of relations with network affiliates. "We've found no limitations with Enable," said Roadarmel. "We use it to its maximum capacity, but we've never had a reason to use anything else. And we don't have our heads buried in the sand. We never stop evaluating new software."

At another broadcaster, WNEV Channel 7, the CBS television affiliate in Boston, Ashton-Tate's Framework III is the program of choice. It is used on a local area network by every department in the building. "We have 110 people using Framework," explained Systems Manager Steve Curcuru. "Before we got it, accountants and producers didn't talk. Now, we have a real dialogue going. For example, we used the FRED programming language to assign costs to each camera site considered for the Boston Marathon. "One of the great advantages of Framework III is how you can use its electronic mail feature in combination with FRED," he continued. "We can pull down information from our mainframe and send an automatic message to a department head that he has two more employees than he's authorized, or we can download information onto a spreadsheet and distribute it automatically."

American Medical Systems, meanwhile, purchased First Choice from Software Publishing Corp. for its customers. The Minnetonka, Minnesota, firm makes surgical implants. American's customers are doctors throughout the United States who may recommend its products to patients. Gary Rose, director of marketing promotion, outlined how the policy works. "We advertise and refer leads to doctors in the readers' local areas. We give the doctors a copy of First Choice, customized with macros, to help them follow up. They can send out letters and generate lists of people for callbacks." Assessing First Choice, Rose said, "It has more capabilities than we need. Most of the doctors and their staffs have little computer background, and they have no trouble using this. They use the database, word processing, mail merge, spreadsheet, reporting, and graphics capabilities."

Glenn Sherman, systems analyst for microcomputers at Children's Hospital in Oakland, California, had similar praise for SmartWare, produced by Informix Software Inc. "I spend most of my time as a boo-boo kisser and handholder for all of the employees who use computers, and believe me, the less of that I have to do, the better," he said. "That's why I'm so glad we bought SmartWare. The learning curve is low and it's very powerful. The spreadsheet is better than Lotus, and the database is hands-down easier to use than dBase and more flexible. The support I have to give our 90 users is minimal. Project processing is the real value of a good integrated package," he added. "People can work on their own pieces of an assignment, then integrate them with other segments to complete the project in much less time."

Application Questions

☐ What features do the end users like best about these packages?

☐ Could these be found in individual application packages? Explain.

Source: Marvin Bryan, "Power and Ease of Use of Integrated Software Win Widespread Praise," PC Week, March 6, 1989, p. 103.

☐ The software resources of an information system consist of programs to direct the operation of computer hardware, and procedures to direct the activities of people who use the system. Computer software consists of two major types of programs: (1) system software, which controls and supports the operations of a computer system as it performs various information processing tasks, and (2) application software, which directs the performance of a particular use, or application, of computers to meet the information processing needs of users. Refer to Figure 4–1 for an overview of the major types of software.

☐ System software can be subdivided into system management programs, system support programs, and system development programs. System management programs manage the hardware, software, and data resources of a computer system during its execution of information processing jobs. Major system management programs are operating systems, database management programs, and telecommunications monitors. System support programs, such as utilities and performance monitors, support the operations and management of computer systems by providing a variety of support services. System development programs help users develop information processing programs and procedures and prepare user programs for computer processing. Major system development programs are language translators, programming editors and debuggers, code generators, and CASE tools.

☐ The most important system software package for any computer is its operating system. An operating system is an integrated system of programs that supervises the operation of the CPU, controls the input-output and storage functions of the computer system, and provides various support services. An operating system performs the three major functions of job management, resource management, and data management. Operating environment packages add an additional graphics interface between end users, the operating system, and application programs, and support multitasking capabilities.

☐ Database management systems control the creation, maintenance, and use of databases. A DBMS simplifies the use of the data and information in a database for both users and programmers. Telecommunications monitors control and support the telecommunication activities among the computers and terminals in a network.

☐ Programming languages are a major category of system software. They require the use of language translator programs to convert programming language instructions into machine language instruction codes. The four major levels of programming languages are machine languages, assembler languages, high-level languages, and fourth-generation languages. High-level languages such as BASIC and COBOL are the most widely used programming languages for business applications. However, natural, nonprocedural fourth-generation languages, object-oriented languages, and computer-aided programming tools are also widely used.

☐ Application software includes a variety of programs that can be segregated into general-purpose, business, scientific, and other application-specific categories. General-purpose application programs perform common information processing jobs for users. Examples are word processing, electronic spreadsheet, and graphics programs. Business application programs accomplish information processing tasks that support important business functions or industry requirements.

KEY TERMS AND CONCEPTS

These are the key terms and concepts of this chapter. The page number of their first explanation is given in parentheses.

1. Application software (*150*)
2. Application-specific programs (*150*)
3. Assembler language (*141*)
4. Data management (*136*)
5. Database management system (*138*)
6. Electronic spreadsheet package (*151*)
7. Fourth-generation language (*143*)
8. General-purpose application programs (*150*)
9. Graphics package (*153*)
10. High-level language (*142*)
11. Integrated package (*153*)
12. Job management (*135*)
13. Language translator program (*147*)
14. Machine language (*141*)
15. Multitasking (*137*)

16. Natural language (*143*)
17. Nonprocedural language (*143*)
18. Object-oriented language (*146*)
19. Operating environment package (*137*)
20. Operating system (*134*)
21. Programming tools (*148*)
22. Resource management (*135*)
23. System management programs (*134*)
24. System software (*134*)
25. System support programs (*140*)
26. Telecommunications monitor (*139*)
27. Trends in software (*133*)
28. Utility programs (*140*)
29. Word processing package (*151*)

REVIEW QUIZ

Match one of the **key terms and concepts** listed above with one of the examples or definitions listed below. Try to find the best fit for answers that seem to fit more than one term or concept. Defend your choices.

_____ 1. Programs that manage and support the operations of computers.

_____ 2. Programs that direct the performance of a specific use of computers.

_____ 3. An integrated system of programs that manages the operations of a computer system.

_____ 4. Managing the flow of information processing jobs through a computer system.

_____ 5. Managing the use of CPU time, primary and secondary storage, and input/output devices.

_____ 6. Managing the input/output, storage, and retrieval of data.

_____ 7. Manages and supports the maintenance and retrieval of data stored in databases.

_____ 8. Manages and supports telecommunications in a network.

_____   9. Translates high-level instructions into machine language instructions.

_____ 10. Performs housekeeping chores for a computer system.

_____ 11. A category of application software that performs common information processing tasks for end users.

_____ 12. Allows you to create and edit documents.

_____ 13. Creates and displays a worksheet for analysis.

_____ 14. Produces line, bar, and pie charts and other displays.

_____ 15. A program that performs several general-purpose applications in one package.

_____ 16. Serves as an end user graphics-based interface that integrates the use of the operating system and application programs.

_____ 17. Uses instructions in the form of coded strings of ones and zeros.

_____ 18. Uses instructions consisting of symbols representing operation codes and storage locations.

_____ 19. Uses instructions called statements that resemble human language or the standard notation of mathematics.

_____ 20. Might take the form of query languages and report generators.

_____ 21. Languages that tie together data and the actions that will be performed on the data.

_____ 22. You don't have to tell the computer how to do something, just what result you want.

_____ 23. As easy to use as one's native tongue.

_____ 24. Performing two or more operations or applications at the same time.

_____ 25. Includes programming editors, debuggers, and code generators.

_____ 26. Toward powerful multipurpose expert packages with easy-to-use natural language and graphical interfaces.

REAL WORLD PROBLEMS

1. High's Ice Cream Corporation

    Oscar Smith, president of High's Ice Cream Corp., based in Norfolk, Virginia, produces spreadsheets which highlight the performance of stores with poor sales results in his 33-shop chain. If, for example, company sales are down an average of 10 percent, but a particular store's sales are down 37 percent, Smith will change the font (style of characters) for that row in his spreadsheet, or put it in boldface, to draw attention to the problem. Using the PlanPerfect spreadsheet package from WordPerfect, Smith can change the font of any cell.

    Most of his spreadsheet output is in standard column form, but he also produces graphs "so that people can quickly conceptualize results," he says. "Ice cream is a weather-driven business. The temperature is more important than holidays or any amount of advertising. If the temperature is in the mid-40s this week and last week it was in the mid-60s, I'd expect all the stores to be down. If one store is way down, that really shows up in a graph." Smith is able to spot "bad crews" in stores producing below-average numbers and set goals designed to get these crews back on track. Smith combines line and area graphs to compare last year's weekly sales figures with this year's totals. Or he'll use a pie chart to compare the sales of 10 flavors. Smith also circulates a company newsletter created with word processing and desktop publishing features of WordPerfect that includes charts he generates with PlanPerfect.

a. How does Oscar Smith improve the impact of his spreadsheet output? His word processing output?

b. Why are such features becoming commonplace in many spreadsheet and word processing packages?

Source: Adapted from Michael Autonoff, "Spreadsheets with Style," *Personal Computing,* March 20, 1990, p. 72.

2. **Powercard Corporation**

"If time is money, then this thing has paid for itself," said Fred Cohen, executive vice president of Powercard Corp., a distributor of Polaroid Corp. batteries, of the Alphaworks integrated package. "We are often doing three things at once," Cohen said. "I can make an inquiry in the database, go back to a spreadsheet, or go back and forth from a module and call the main database." For Cohen, the abilty to exit the program's spreadsheet, wordprocessing, database management, or communications modules just by pressing a function key, and to enter another module and return to the same spot when finished is a big plus. He added that multiple windows and background printing features are also time-savers.

a. What are the most valuable features of Alphaworks to Fred Cohen?

b. Can end users get similar capabilities without using integrated packages? Explain.

Source: Adapted from "Integrated Packages Lend Easy Versatility," *PC Week,* January 22, 1990, p. 33.

3. **UNIX in Europe**

UNIX, the portable operating system that has cruised around the world, is dropping anchor in commercial ports around Europe. Over the last four years, European shipments of UNIX systems have steadily increased. The most symbolic and significant user in the public sector is the European Commission (EC), the governing agency of the European Economic Community (EEC). The EC is standardizing on UNIX-based workstations for administrative chores. Following the EC's lead, the governments of France, Sweden, and the United Kingdom have established their own UNIX policies. For example, every two years, the Swedish government chooses four or five vendors to satisfy all of its UNIX contracts—contracts that were worth a hefty $145 million during the most recent round. The bulk of that business went to the NCR Corporation.

Although the Dutch government has yet to make an official endorsement of UNIX, Marton van Gelderen of the Dutch UNIX User Group thinks it's only a matter of time. His reasons for the prediction are similar to those of others who have chosen the UNIX operating systems: flexibilty and portability. "When an application runs under UNIX, it will survive hardware changes," van Gelderen says. "In the UNIX environment, there really is compatibility. It is fun for the suppliers and it's also fun for the users. You can change the underlying hardware without too much disruption of day-to-day services. You can choose the hardware that best suits your particular problem."

a. Why is the UNIX operating system popular in Europe?
b. Are such capabilities found in other operating systems? Explain.

Source: Adapted from Peter Judge, "UNIX Ports in Europe," *Datamation*, February 1, 1990, p. 78.

4. Citicorp Latin American Technology Group
Paolo Paglione found himself torn between migrating to OS/2 and staying within his budget. However, Paglione, vice president of Citicorp's Latin American Technology Group (LATG), is bringing the power of OS/2 Extended Edition to Citicorp's Central and South American offices— without sacrificing his large base of PC XTs, dumb terminals, and existing DOS applications. Paglione's solution centers on Polymod 2 communications software that lets PCs act as terminals and access OS/2 applications running on a network server.

"We need to modernize and evolve into OS/2," Paglione said, "but we don't want to make a huge investment all in one shot. We'd like to keep as much of our existing hardware as possible." That hardware investment is substantial: More than 5,000 PC XTs are in use in LATG's offices in more than 10 Latin American countries. "We've spent a lot of money on XTs. We can't just throw that investment to the wind," said Paglione. At the same time, staying in the DOS universe is becoming less desirable: Paglione's users are bumping up against DOS performance limits and its infamous 640K-byte memory barrier, and bank managers are mindful that IBM and Microsoft are positioning OS/2 as the operating system of the 1990s.

a. What are the business and technology implications of switching from DOS to OS/2 operating systems for Citicorp's LATG?
b. Should other companies move from DOS to OS/2? Explain.

Source: Adapted from Gina Smith, "Bank Taps Multiuser OS/2 to Leverage Installed Base," *PC Week*, January 1, 1990, pp. 1, 6.

5. System Software
If a computer-using organization wanted to accomplish the following tasks, what system software packages would they need?

a. Control telecommunications activity with many remote terminals.
b. Manage the use of the hardware, software, and data resources of a computer system.
c. Monitor and record how computer system resources are being used.
d. Make it easier to update and interrogate company databases.
e. Monitor and control access to a computer system's sensitive resources.

6. End User Software
Identify the type of individual application software package you would need for each of the following activities:

a. Type correspondence and reports.
b. Analyze rows and columns of figures.

    c. Store and access business records.

    d. Develop line, bar, and pie charts.

    e. Transmit data to other computers.

7. Hewlett-Packard Company

New Wave, by Hewlett-Packard, is designed to provide users with a consistent, easy-to-use environment for accessing, merging, and managing computing resources among a variety of applications. New Wave's object orientation allows you to consider any document or file—along with its associated application program—as an *object*. New Wave then uses an icon- and window-based user interface and object-oriented software that allows one application to easily access and share another application's resources, such as documents, graphics, or spreadsheets. New Wave can also link applications running on an IBM PC-DOS– or OS/2-compatible personal computer so that they can access resources on a variety of networked computers and services.

    a. Does HP's New Wave sound like an operating environment or operating system? Explain.

    b. What are the benefits of New Wave's object-oriented features?

Source: Adapted from Elisabeth Horwitt, "Hewlett-Packard's Standard Equation," *Computerworld*, August 7, 1989, p. 23; and Michael Miller, "HP's New Wave: Preview of Future Operating Environments," *Infoworld*, September 18, 1989, p. 90.

8. Ron Kloss & Associates

The software industry is finally beginning to give end users a means to write and edit their own software. These users are taking programming into their own hands via a new generation of object-oriented *visual programming* tools. We're not talking about macro languages or document style sheets here. Visual tools allow users to build programs by arranging icons or designing simple diagrams on their CRT displays. For example, a visual programming package for the Apple Macintosh, called Double Helix, allows users to build database applications by positioning "tiles" on a display and then use arrows to specify how data flows, how specific data relates to other data, and what happens to it at a particular step in a program. The tiles are icons that represent sophisticated "baskets of functions" that users can predefine. For example, the *Abacus* icon can be programmed to represent a wide range of mathematic calculations. Users determine what an Abacus represents by filling out choices in menus. The icon will then insert and perform the desired functions in any program.

    Ron Kloss, president of a small advertising agency in Santa Monica, California, has built all of his business's core applications using Double Helix. The visual programming features of Double Helix are what really attracted him to the program, says Kloss. "I'm a commercial artist and photographer—it never occurred to me that I could program a computer," he says. "But I can logically assemble statements using tiles, without having to get into the semantics. There was no need even to worry what order the tasks were done in. When I look at the programs my son writes in C," says Ron, "I can't see the big picture. I know what files I need—clients, jobs, and so on—and I can assign pictures to each and then build structures for each. If I had to write regular program code, I'd have a big problem."

a. What is visual programming? How does it differ from regular programming?

b. What are the implications of object-oriented visual programming for end users?

Source: Adapted from John Rymer, "The Fine Art of Not Programming," *Personal Computing,* March 20, 1990, pp. 82–88.

SELECTED REFERENCES

1. *Business Software Review, Computerworld, PC Magazine, PC Week, Personal Computing, Software Digest.* (Examples of good sources of current information on computer software packages.)

2. Datapro Corporation. *Datapro Reports.* (Series of regular detailed reports on selected software packages.)

3. Blackford, John. "The Story of 'O'." *Personal Computing,* June 29, 1990.

4. Bobrow, Daniel. "The Object of Desire," *Datamation,* May 1, 1989.

5. Conklin, Dick. *OS/2: A Business Perspective.* New York: John Wiley & Sons, 1988.

6. McIntyre, Scott, and Lexis Higgins. "Object-Oriented Systems Analysis and Design: Methodology and Application." *Journal of Management Information Systems,* Summer 1988.

7. Methvin, David. "New Tools Help Developers Tame New Environments." *PC Week,* May 22, 1989.

8. Stamps, David. "CASE versus 4GLs." *Datamation,* August 15, 1989.

<table>
<tr><td>CHAPTER
5</td><td># INTRODUCTION TO TELECOMMUNICATIONS</td></tr>
</table>

■ Chapter Outline

▓ Learning Objectives

The purpose of this chapter is to give you an understanding of telecommunications networks, the role they play in organizations and information systems, and the challenges posed by telecommunications to business end users.

Section I discusses basic trends and concepts of telecommunications networks, and provides examples of major applications and managerial challenges of telecommunications in businesses and other organizations.

Section II reviews some of the major technical characteristics of telecommunications networks needed for a basic understanding of this technology by end users.

After reading and studying this chapter, you should be able to:

1. Identify several major trends and managerial challenges in the use and management of telecommunications networks.

2. Provide examples that illustrate how businesses and end users benefit from using telecommunications networks.

3. Identify the basic components, functions, and types of telecommunications networks.

4. Describe the primary functions of major types of telecommunications network hardware, software, and media.

Section I: An Overview of Telecommunications

INTRODUCTION

End users need to communicate electronically in today's dynamic business environment. Managers, end users, and their organizations need to exchange data and information electronically with other end users, customers, suppliers, and other organizations to perform their work activities, manage organizational resources, and compete successfully. Thus, many organizations now depend heavily on interconnected networks of computers to service the information processing needs of their end users within work groups, departments, and the entire organization. As a prospective manager, you will thus be expected to participate in decisions regarding a great variety of telecommunications options as we move toward a networked global economy. That's why we need to study the applications and technology of telecommunications.

Telecommunications is the sending of information in any form (e.g., voice, data, text, and images) from one place to another using electronic or light-emitting media. *Data communications* is a more specific term that describes the transmitting and receiving of data over communication links between one or more computer systems and a variety of input/output terminals. The terms *teleprocessing* and *telematics* may also be used since they reflect the integration of telecommunications and computer-based information processing technologies. However, all forms of telecommunications now rely heavily on computers and computerized devices. For this reason, the broader term *telecommunications* is used as a synonym for data communications activities. Therefore, in this text, we will use these terms interchangeably.

A TELECOMMUNI-CATIONS NETWORK MODEL

Before we discuss the use and management of telecommunications, we should understand the basic concept of a *telecommunications network*. Generically, a *communications network* is any arrangement where a *sender* transmits a *message* to a *receiver* over a *channel* consisting of some type of *medium*. Figure 5–1 illustrates a simple conceptual model of a **telecommunications network,** which shows that it consists of five basic categories of components:

☐ **Terminals,** such as video display terminals and other end user workstations. Of course, any input/output device that uses telecommunications networks to transmit or receive data is a terminal, including microcomputers, telephones, office equipment, and the *transaction terminals* discussed in Chapter 3.

☐ **Telecommunications processors,** which support data transmission and reception between terminals and computers. These devices, such as *modems, multiplexers,* and *front-end processors,* perform a variety of control and support functions in a telecommunications network. For example, they convert data from digital to analog and back, code and decode data, and control the accuracy and efficiency of the communications flow between computers and terminals in a telecommunications network.

☐ **Telecommunications channels and media** over which data are transmitted and received. Telecommunications *channels* use combinations of *media,* such as copper wires, coaxial cables, fiber optic cables,

Figure 5-1   The five basic categories of components in a telecommunications network: (1) terminals, (2) telecommunications processors, (3) telecommunications channels and media, (4) computers, and (5) telecommunications software.

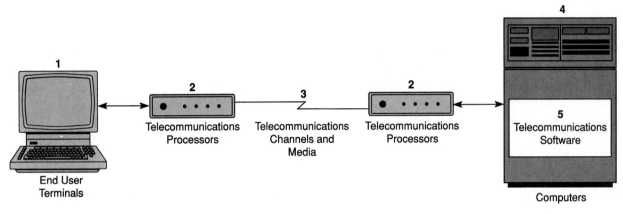

microwave systems, and communications satellite systems, to interconnect the other components of a network.

☐ **Computers** of all sizes and types are interconnected by telecommunications networks so that they can carry out their information processing assignments. For example, a mainframe computer may serve as a *host computer* for a large organization's network, assisted by microcomputers acting as *network servers* for smaller networks of end user microcomputer workstations.

☐ **Telecommunications software** consists of programs that reside in host computer systems, communications control computers, and end user computers. They control the telecommunications activities of computer systems and manage the functions of networks.

No matter how large and complex real world telecommunications networks may appear to be, these five basic categories of components must be at work to support an organization's telecommunications activities. This framework can thus be used to help end users understand the various types of telecommunications networks in use today.

TYPES OF TELECOMMUNICATIONS NETWORKS

There are many different types of telecommunications networks. However, from an end users point of view, there are two basic types: *wide area* and *local area* networks. Telecommunications networks covering a large geographic area are called *remote networks, long distance networks,* or, more popularly, **wide area networks** (WANs). Networks that cover a large city or metropolitan area *(metropolitan area networks)* can also be included in this category. Such large networks are becoming a necessity for carrying out the day-to-day activities of many business and government organizations and their end users. They are used by manufacturing firms, banks, retailers, distributors, transportation companies, government agencies, and many other types of organizations. Wide area networks allow them to transmit and receive business information across cities, regions, countries, or the world. Figure 5–2 illustrates an example of a wide area network for a major corporation, J.C. Penney Co.

Figure 5-2 J. C. Penney's wide area network (WAN).

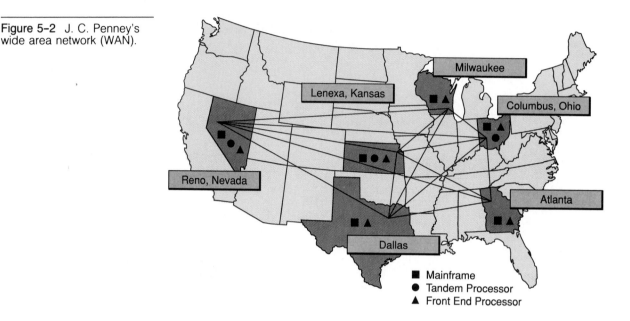

Local area networks (LANs) connect information processing devices within a limited physical area, such as an office building, manufacturing plant, or other work site. They have become a major type of telecommunications network since microcomputers were introduced into offices, departments, and other work groups. LANs use a variety of telecommunications media and communications processors to interconnect computer terminals, personal computer workstations, other computer systems, and other types of computer peripheral devices. This allows end users in a work group to share hardware, software, and data resources, and to pool their efforts when working on group projects. For example, a project team of end users whose microcomputer workstations are part of a LAN can share the use of laser printers and hard magnetic disk units, copies of electronic spreadsheet or word processing packages, and project databases. See Figure 5-3.

Most LANs use a powerful microcomputer having a large hard disk capacity called a *file server* or **network server** that contains a network operating system program that controls telecommunications and the use of network resources. For example, it distributes copies of common data files and software packages to the other microcomputers in the network, and controls access to laser printers and other network peripherals. Local area networks are connected to the computing resources and databases of wide area networks by communications processors forming a common interface called a *gateway*. LANs have thus become a popular alternative to the use of terminals connected to minicomputers or smaller mainframes for end user computing in many organizations.

APPLICATIONS OF TELECOMMUNICATIONS

Telecommunications applications provide invaluable capabilities and benefits to organizations and their end users. Figure 5-4 groups a large number of specific applications of telecommunications into the major categories of data communications, voice communications, text and messaging communications, information retrieval, image transmission, and monitoring and control. Let's take a brief look now at several major categories of telecommunications applications.

Figure 5-3 A local area network (LAN). Note how this LAN allows end users to share hardware, software, and data resources.

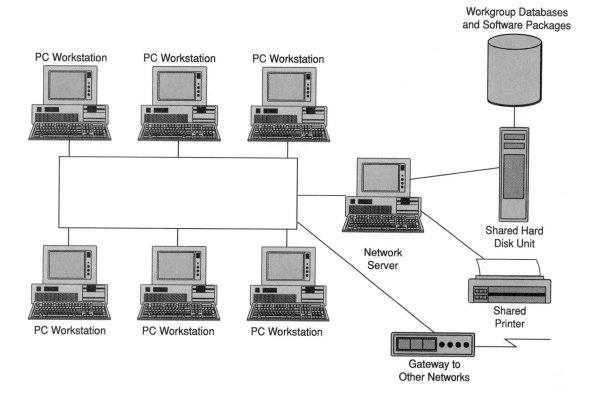

Telecommunications networks allow data generated by business transactions to be captured immediately by online terminals and transmitted from many remote sites to computer systems for processing. Transactions data can also be accumulated into *batches*, stored on magnetic disk or tape devices, and transmitted periodically to a central computer for processing from remote locations. Telecommunications networks allow business offices, banks, retail stores, and distribution centers to minimize manual data entry and expedite transaction processing, thus cutting costs, reducing errors, and improving service. In particular, **electronic data interchange** (EDI) networks support direct electronic transmission of business transaction documents among the computers of businesses and their customers and suppliers. Thus, EDI replaces the exchange of paper transaction documents such as purchase orders and sales invoices. EDI and other aspects of transaction processing systems are discussed in Chapter 8.

Transaction Processing and Inquiry/Response

Electronic funds transfer (EFT) systems in banking and retailing industries specialize in the capture and processing of money and credit transfers between businesses and customers. Bank telecommunications systems support teller terminals in all branch offices, and automated teller machines at locations throughout a city or region. Also supported are *pay-by-phone* services, which allow bank customers to use their telephones as computer terminals to electronically pay bills. Wide area networks also connect POS (point-of-sale) terminals in retail stores to bank EFT systems.

Figure 5-4   Applications of telecommunications. Note the major categories and types of applications supported by telecommunications networks.

Voice Communications	Data Communications
Standard telephone service	Online transaction processing
Voice response systems	Inquiry/response systems
Audio conferencing systems	Hardware and software sharing
Voice mail	File and database transfers
Voice recognition	Cooperative processing
Public address systems	Electronic funds transfer systems
Intercom systems	Point-of-sale systems
	Electronic document interchange
Text and Messaging Communications	**Information Retrieval**
Electronic mail	Bibliographic search services
Computer conferencing systems	News and economic database services
Electronic bulletin boards	Videotex
Multimedia document interchange	
Teletype systems	
Image Transmission	**Monitoring and Control**
Image processing	Process control systems
Facsimile	Equipment monitoring
Closed circuit television	Security surveillance
Video teleconferencing	Card-key security systems
Electronic meeting systems	Hospital patient monitoring
	Energy management

Source: Adapted from Ralph Sprague and Barbara McNurlin, ed., *Information Systems Management in Practice* (Englewood Cliffs, N.J.: Prentice-Hall, 1986), pp. 142, 144.

Inquiry/response systems allow end users to make inquiries about information stored in personal, departmental, corporate, and external databases and to receive immediate responses through telecommunications networks. This can provide up-to-date information for business operations and managerial decision making. End users can also access external data bank services providing economic, demographic, and financial data to individual and corporate users.

Distributed and Cooperative Processing

Distributed processing and *cooperative processing* are major applications of telecommunications. In **distributed processing,** information processing activities in an organization are accomplished by a network of computers interconnected by telecommunications links, instead of relying on one large *centralized* computer facility or on the *decentralized* operation of several independent computers. For example, a distributed processing network may consist of mainframes, minicomputers, and microcomputers dispersed over a geographic area and interconnected by wide area networks, or they may be distributed within end user departments and work groups in local area networks.

Cooperative processing takes this concept one step further. It allows the various types of computers in a distributed processing network to share the processing of parts of an end user's application. Application software packages are available which have common user interfaces and functions so they can operate consistently on networks of micro, mini, and mainframe computer systems. For example, an end user could use a spreadsheet package provided to his or her microcomputer workstation by a local area network server to perform financial analysis on databases managed by a mainframe computer system. This is sometimes called the **client/server model** of computing, where end user work-

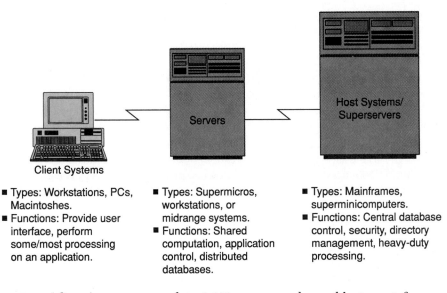

Client Systems

- Types: Workstations, PCs, Macintoshes.
- Functions: Provide user interface, perform some/most processing on an application.

- Types: Supermicros, workstations, or midrange systems.
- Functions: Shared computation, application control, distributed databases.

- Types: Mainframes, superminicomputers.
- Functions: Central database control, security, directory management, heavy-duty processing.

Figure 5–5 A client/server model for distributed and co-operative processing. Note the functions performed by different types of computers acting as clients, servers, and host systems.

stations *(clients)* are connected to LAN servers and possibly to mainframe *superservers.*

With distributed and cooperative processing, local users can handle a broad range of information processing tasks. This includes data entry, database inquiry, transaction processing, updating databases, generating reports, and providing decision support. Thus, data can be completely processed locally, where most input and output (and errors and problems) must be handled anyway, while still providing access to the resources of other computers in local area and wide area networks. This provides computer processing more tailored to the needs of end users and increases information processing efficiency and effectiveness as end users become more responsible for their own applications.

Large central-site host computers can be applied to those jobs they can best handle, such as high-volume transaction processing, communications network control, and maintenance of large corporate databases. End user workstations in a local area network can share work group databases and software provided by their LAN servers, and access host computers to receive corporate-wide management information or transmit summary transaction data reflecting local site activities. Figure 5–5 is an example of a client/server model of distributed and cooperative processing. It illustrates the information processing functions performed by different types of computers serving as *client, server,* and *host* systems in a network [4].

Office Automation and End User Computing

Telecommunications plays a vital role in office automation and end user computing. Local area networks allow end users in an office or other work site to share hardware, software, and data resources. LANs typically tie office workstations together with other office devices such as laser printers, and they may be linked to department and corporate networks. Software packages and common databases are typically shared in such networks. Services such as electronic mail, voice mail, facsimile, and teleconferencing allow end users to send and receive messages electronically in text, voice, image, or video form. Telecommunications networks also support *work group computing* where end users work together on joint projects. Networks allow them to share data, perform joint analysis, and integrate the results of individual efforts by members of the work group. We will discuss such office automation and end user computing applications in Chapter 7.

Personal Information Services

Personal information services are another major category of telecommunications applications. For example, companies such as CompuServe offer a variety of information services for a fee to anyone with an appropriately equipped personal computer. They offer such services as electronic mail, financial market information, use of software packages for personal computing, electronic games, home banking and shopping, news/sports/weather information, and a variety of specialized data banks. Gaining access to these services is easy if you have a personal computer equipped with a communications interface board, a modem, and a communications software package.

Bulletin Board Systems

Bulletin board systems (BBS) are a popular telecommunications service provided by companies such as CompuServe and thousands of business firms, organizations, and user groups. An electronic bulletin board system allows you to "post" public or private messages that other end users can read by accessing the BBS with their computers. Establishing a BBS requires at least a microcomputer with a hard disk drive, custom or packaged BBS software, and a modem and telephone line for as many simultaneous users the BBS computer can handle. Bulletin board systems serve as a central location to post and pick up messages or upload and download data files or programs 24 hours a day. A BBS helps end users ask questions, get advice, locate and share information, and get in touch with other end users. Thus, bulletin board systems are being used by many business firms as a convenient, low-cost way to enhance the flow of information among their employees and customers.

Videotex

Another way end users can get information using an information services network is **videotex.** In its simplest form *(teletext)*, videotex is a one-way, repetitive broadcast of pages of text and graphics information to your TV set. This method uses cable, telephone lines, or standard TV transmission. A control device allows you to select the page you want to display and examine. Videotex, however, is meant to be an *interactive* information service provided over phone lines or cable TV channels. End users can select specific video displays of data and information, such as electronic *Yellow Pages* and personal bank checking account registers. End users can also use a special terminal or personal computer to do banking and shopping electronically. Videotex is widely used in Europe. Many companies in the United States tried pilot programs of videotex services in the 1980s, but most efforts failed to generate sufficient consumer interest. Videotex services are currently available from several sources, including personal computer networks such as Prodigy, a joint venture of IBM and Sears, and the CompuServe Bank-at-Home and Shop-at-Home services.

In the United States, several companies have traditionally used a variety of communications media to create networks that can provide a broad range of communications services. These **common carriers** provide the wide area communications networks used by most computer-using firms and individuals. They have been authorized by government agencies to provide a selected number of communication services to the public. Examples are the former Bell operating companies, General Telephone and Electronics, Western Union, and many independent telephone companies. Some common carriers specialize in selling long-distance voice and digital data communications services in high-density areas of the country and the world. Examples of such specialized carriers are AT&T Long Distance, ITT World Communications, Southern Pacific Communications, U.S. Sprint, and MCI Communications.

Common carriers can provide several wide area telecommunications network options. For example, an organization could use regular, voice-grade, direct distance dialing (DDD), which is more expensive, slower, and less reliable than other options due to delays caused by excessive communications traffic and the noise of voice-switching circuits. Or it could sign up for a wide area telephone service (WATS) and pay a monthly fee for unlimited use of a set amount of telephone line capacity. This would be cheaper for an organization with a lot of communications activity, but it would have the same reliability problem as DDD. Or it could lease its own communications lines (called *leased lines*) from telephone companies and be guaranteed exclusive use of a low-noise, fast communications channel. However, this is an expensive alternative that is economically feasible only for large corporations and government agencies with massive data communications needs. Another expensive option is the use of a company that provides communications satellite services. Or an organization could build a *bypass* system, in which it installs its own earth stations and bypasses the common carrier networks and transmits directly to communications satellites. Once again, this is a more expensive alternative attractive only to organizations with a high volume of telecommunications traffic.

The other major communications carriers are companies called **value-added carriers.** These are third-party vendors who lease communications lines from common carriers and offer communications services to customers. Typically, messages from customers are transmitted in groupings called *packets*, via *packet-switching* networks. The networks of such carriers are known as *value-added networks* (VANs) because they add value to their leased communications lines by using communications hardware and software and their expertise to provide not only packet switching but other telecommunication services. Value-added networks also take over the responsibility for the management of the network, thus relieving their customers of the technical problems inherent in long-distance telecommunications.

Value-added carriers offer their customers, or *subscribers*, high-quality, relatively low cost service in return for a membership fee and usage charges based on the amount of communications activity accomplished. By spreading the cost of leasing the lines among many subscribers and using the capacity of the lines intensively, they are able to sell their services at attractive prices and still make a profit. Examples of value-added companies are GTE Telenet,

TELECOMMUNICATIONS CARRIERS

Common Carriers

Value-Added Carriers

General Electric's Mark Net, CompuServ, and Tymnet by Tymeshare. These VANs have become so popular that common carriers, such as the Bell operating companies, AT&T, MCI, and Western Union, and large corporations, such as IBM and RCA, now offer VAN services.

A MANAGERIAL PERSPECTIVE

Investing in telecommunications is inherently a business gamble. The technology is expensive, rapidly changing, and complex. The stakes increase as traditional marketplaces are changed by electronic delivery, as new markets open up, as some firms use communications successfully to reposition their business, and as others succeed only in creating expensive write-offs on the income statement. [6]

Statements such as this emphasize the importance of telecommunications from a managerial perspective. Thus, you should view telecommunications not only as a method of electronic communications but also as a competitive weapon, a means of organizational connectivity, and a vital investment in technology. Given this managerial perspective on the importance of telecommunications, you should develop an appreciation for (1) the potential benefits and problems of telecommunications and (2) how to plan and implement a proper role for telecommunications in an organization.

Trends in Telecommunications

Major trends occurring in the field of telecommunications have a significant impact on management decisions in this area. Informed end users should be aware of major trends in telecommunications industries, technologies, and applications that significantly increase the decision alternatives confronting computer-using organizations. See Figure 5–6.

Industry Trends

The competitive arena for telecommunications services has changed dramatically in the United States, from a few government-regulated monopolies to many fiercely competitive suppliers of telecommunications services. The breakup of AT&T and the Bell System in 1984 opened the door into the telecommunications industry for many new companies, and allowed computer and telecommunications companies to enter each other's industries. Telecommunications services are available from a variety of companies offering long-distance telephone service, communications satellites, and many other services, as well as from companies specializing in selected telecommunications equipment and services, such as cellular radio and electronic mail. Thus, the service and vendor options available to meet an organization's telecommunications needs have greatly multiplied.

Technology Trends

Telecommunications is being revolutionized by a change from *analog* to *digital* technologies. Telecommunications has always depended on voice-oriented *analog transmission* systems designed to transmit the variable electrical frequencies generated by the sound waves of the human voice. However, telecommunications technology is rapidly converting to digital transmission systems, which transmit information in the form of discrete *pulses*, as comput-

Industry Trends:	Toward a greater number of competitive vendors, carriers, and services.
Technology Trends:	Toward an integrated digital network for voice, data, text, and images with heavy use of fiber optics and satellite channels.
Applications Trends:	Toward the pervasive use of telecommunications networks in support of business operations, managerial decision making, and strategic advantage in global markets.

Figure 5–6 Major trends in telecommunications.

ers do, rather than in *waves*. Digital transmission systems greatly enhance the use of computer-based communications control devices and communications media. Compared to analog systems, digital technology provides (1) significantly higher transmission speeds, (2) the movement of larger amounts of information, (3) greater economy, and (4) much lower error rates. In addition, digital technology greatly improves the ability of telecommunications networks to carry multiple types of communications (data, voice, images, text) on the same circuits.

Another major trend in telecommunications technology is a change in communications media. Many telecommunications networks are switching from copper wire–based media (such as coaxial cable) and land-based microwave relay systems to *fiber optic* lines and communications satellite transmission. Fiber optic transmission, which uses pulses of laser-generated light, offers significant advantages in terms of reduced size and installation effort, vastly greater communications capacity, and freedom from electrical interference. Satellite transmission offers significant advantages in speed and capacity for organizations that need to transmit massive quantities of data over long distances. These trends give organizations more alternatives to overcome the limitations of their present telecommunications systems.

Application Trends

The changes in telecommunications industries and technologies just mentioned are causing a significant change in the business use of telecommunications. The trend toward more vendors, services, and advanced technologies dramatically increases the number of feasible applications. Thus, telecommunications is playing a more important role in support of the operations, management, and strategic objectives of both large and small companies. An organization's telecommunications function is no longer relegated to office telephone systems, long-distance calling arrangements, and a limited amount of data communications with corporate mainframes. Instead, it is becoming an integral part of computer-based information systems used to cut costs, improve operational processes, share resources, and develop new products and services. This makes telecommunications a more complex and important decision area for businesses which must increasingly compete in both domestic and global markets.

Figure 5–7 outlines a framework for understanding the business value of telecommunications [5]. It emphasizes that managers can use telecommunications to:

The Value of
Telecommunications

Figure 5–7 The value dimensions of telecommunications. Note how telecommunications can improve operational efficiency, business effectiveness, and organizational innovation.

| | Value | | |
Impact	Operational Efficiency	Business Effectiveness	Organizational Innovation
Compress time	Accelerate business operations and processes	Reduce information float	Create superior service
Examples:	Online transaction processing	Electronic mail	Instant credit checks
Reduce geographic limits	Generate economies of scale	Ensure control of dispersed operations	Penetrate new markets
Examples:	Online, centralized purchasing	Teleconferencing	Remote ATM banking
Restructure business relationships	Bypass intermediaries in the distribution chain	Provide expertise to remote sites	Lock in customers and suppliers
Examples:	Direct sales by phone	Remote diagnostics and maintenance	Electronic in-home shopping

Source: Adapted from Michael Hammer and Glen Mangurian, "The Changing Value of Telecommunications Technology," *Sloan Management Review*, Winter 1987, p.66.

☐ Compress the time taken to accomplish business activities.

☐ Reduce the limits placed on a firm's business activities by geographic distances.

☐ Restructure traditional business relationships with a firm's customers and suppliers and with other organizations.

These impacts of telecommunications can improve the value of a company in three major dimensions. Figure 5–7 shows that managers can use telecommunications to improve the efficiency of business operations, the effectiveness of business functions, and the extent of business innovation. For example, the use of telecommunications networks could result in the following benefits for a chain of retail stores:

☐ **Operational efficiency.** Telecommunications can provide immediate processing of sales transactions, centralized purchasing in large quantities by connections from remote stores, and direct sales by telephone.

☐ **Business effectiveness.** Telecommunications can provide electronic mail and facsimile services for instant transmission of interstore messages, teleconferencing facilities to conduct video meetings with store managers, and customer hotlines for remote diagnosis and assistance of customer service problems.

☐ **Organizational innovation.** Telecommunications can provide instant credit authorization for major purchases by customers, in-store banking through the installation of ATMs, and electronic shopping by customers from in-home terminals.

United Parcel Service

Early this year, a new sight quietly appeared on the streets of Moscow, Budapest, East Berlin, and Warsaw. Brown-uniformed drivers in shiny brown trucks from United Parcel Service (UPS) zipped through local traffic, dropping off parcels and documents at city businesses. Package delivery Western-style, had arrived in the Eastern Bloc.

This venture is the latest UPS foray in a technology-driven global expansion that began in 1987 and turned red-hot last year. Within 15 months, UPS acquired nine foreign air transport companies, built the nation's 10th-largest airline, and added 130 countries to its service area. The Greenwich, Connecticut–based firm has grown from a mostly domestic parcel carrier into a $12 billion international giant. Each day, UPS delivers an average of 12 million packages and documents (or around 2.8 billion per year) to 180 countries and territories, making it the world's largest package delivery company.

Handling routine daily activities at UPS is an awesome IS task. Today's global operation bears little resemblance to the tiny messenger firm begun in 1907. At present, the company boasts a fleet of 103,000 vehicles, 354 jets, 230,000 employees, and 1,750 facilities worldwide. And where UPS goes, its networks and computers go, so there is no shortage of integration opportunities at the company these days. Many new projects at UPS involve building or expanding the company's gargantuan web of WANs and LANs. Other projects support a corporatewide shift from centralized IBM minis and mainframes to a client/server architecture with distributed PCs.

A few examples:

☐ **Expansion of the International Shipments Processing System,** which tracks parcels moving in and out of every country in the UPS network. It handles customs documentation and automatic billing and can alert import locations hours before a package arrives. Using leased and dial-up lines as well as satellites, ISPS can zip data around the world in 2.1 seconds.

☐ **Advanced Label Imaging System,** which was designed to streamline air package tracking. The PC-based imaging system captures and processes data from UPS air labels and delivers an image via high-speed phone lines to UPS mainframes in Paramus.

☐ **Computer-to computer communications with customs.** Using ISPS, UPS has pioneered computer-to-computer communications with customs agencies in the United States, Canada, and Puerto Rico. The company is now working on deals with France, England, and West Germany.

☐ **Expanding EDI.** Electronic data interchange plays a big part in integrating UPS customers. All told, 40,000 customers now use some form of EDI. Some 300 dial directly into UPS's system and do their own billing and package tracking.

☐ **Downsizing.** In 1989, UPS replaced 93 IBM 8100 minicomputers with LANs of micros connected by gateways to their corporate mainframes.

☐ **UPSnet.** The ongoing expansion of UPSnet is the largest networking project of all. Begun last year, the wide-area network is designed to let UPS send voice, data, facsimile, video, and still images around the world. Three high-speed dedicated lines connect UPSnet to key Western European cities and local telephone companies.

Application Questions

☐ What examples of telecommunications networks and network components can you identify at UPS? Use Figure 5–1 to help you organize your answer.

☐ How is UPS using telecommunications to improve its operational efficiency, business effectiveness, and organizational innovation? Use Figure 5–7 to help you organize your answer.

Source: Adapted from Joseph Maglitta, "Eastern Europe Move Expands UPS Horizons," *Computerland,* February 19, 1990, pp. 85–87.

Section II: Technical Telecommunications Alternatives

Telecommunications is a highly technical, rapidly changing field of information systems technology. Most end users do not need a detailed knowledge of its technical characteristics. However, it is important that you understand some of the important characteristics of the basic components of telecommunications networks. This understanding will help you participate effectively in decision making regarding telecommunications alternatives. Figure 5–8 outlines key telecommunications network components and alternatives. Remember, a basic understanding and appreciation, not a detailed knowledge, is sufficient for most end users.

TELECOMMUNICATIONS MEDIA

Telecommunications channels (also called communications *lines* or *links*) are the means by which data and other forms of communications are transmitted between the sending and receiving devices in a telecommunications network. A telecommunications channel makes use of a variety of **telecommunications media.** These include twisted-pair wire, coaxial cables, and fiber optic cables, all of which physically link the devices in a network. Also included are microwave systems, communications satellite systems, and cellular radio, all of which use microwave and other radio waves to transmit and receive data. Figure 5–9 illustrates some of the major types of media used in a wide area telecommunications network.

Twisted-Pair Wire

Ordinary telephone wire, consisting of copper wire twisted into pairs *(twisted-pair wire)*, is used extensively for telecommunications. These lines are used in established communications networks throughout the world for both voice and data transmission. See Figure 5–10.

Coaxial Cable

A **coaxial cable** consists of a sturdy copper or aluminum wire wrapped with spacers to insulate and protect it. This insulation minimizes interference and distortion of the signals the cable carries. Groups of coaxial cables may be bundled together in a big cable for ease of installation. These high-quality lines can be placed underground and laid on the floors of lakes and oceans. They allow high-speed data transmission and are used instead of twisted-pair wire

---

Figure 5–8 Key telecommunications network components and alternatives.

Network Component	Examples of Alternatives
Media	Twisted-pair wire, coaxial cable, fiber optics, microwave, communications satellites, cellular radio
Processors	Modems, multiplexers, concentrators, controllers, front-end processors, private branch exchanges
Software	Telecommunications monitors, telecommunications access programs, network operating systems, end user communications packages
Channels	Analog/digital, switched/nonswitched, transmission speed, circuit/message/packet switching, simplex/duplex, asynchronous/synchronous
Topology/architecture	Point-to-point, multidrop, star/ring/bus, OSI, ISDN

lines in high-service metropolitan areas, for cable TV systems, and for short-distance connection of computers and peripheral devices. Thus, coaxial cables may also be used in local area networks.

Fiber optics uses cables consisting of one or more hair-thin filaments of glass fiber wrapped in a protective jacket. They can conduct light pulses generated by *lasers* at transmission rates as high as 2 billion bits per second. This is about 10 times greater than coaxial cable and 200 times better than twisted-pair wire lines. Fiber optic cables provide substantial size and weight reductions as well as increased speed and greater carrying capacity. A half-inch diameter fiber optic cable can carry up to 50,000 channels, compared to about 5,500 channels for a standard coaxial cable.

Fiber optic cables are not affected by and do not generate electromagnetic radiation; therefore, multiple fibers can be placed in the same cable. Fiber optic cables have a minimal need for repeaters for signal retransmissions,

Fiber Optics

Figure 5-9 An example of the telecommunications media in a wide area network. Note the use of a communications satellite, earth stations, microwave links, and fiber optic and coaxial cable.

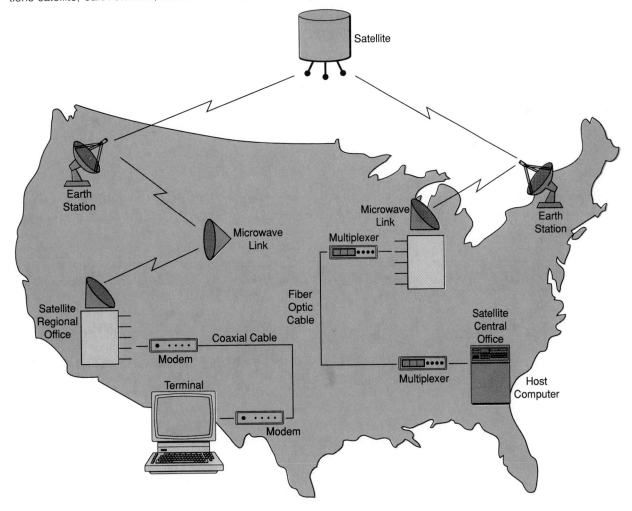

Figure 5–10 Telecommunications wire and cable alternatives.

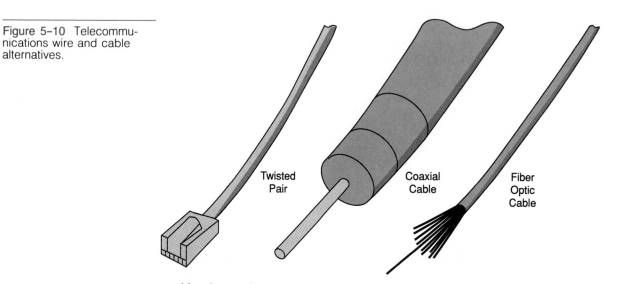

Twisted
Pair

Coaxial
Cable

Fiber
Optic
Cable

unlike electrical wire media. Fiber optics also has a much lower data error rate than other media and is harder to tap than electrical wire and cable. The biggest disadvantage of fiber optics is the difficulty of splicing the cable to make connections, though this is also a security advantage that limits line tapping. Fiber optic cables have already been installed in many parts of the United States, and they are expected to replace other communications media in many applications in the near future.

Microwave Systems

Terrestrial (earthbound) **microwave systems** transmit high-speed radio signals in a line-of-sight path between relay stations spaced approximately 30 miles apart. Microwave antennas are usually placed on top of buildings, towers, hills, and mountain peaks, and they are a familiar site in many sections of the country. They are still a popular medium for both long-distance and metropolitan area networks.

Communications Satellites

An important data communications medium is the use of **communications satellites** for microwave transmission. There are several dozen communications satellites from various nations placed into stationary "parking orbits" approximately 22,000 miles about the equator. Satellites are powered by solar panels and can transmit microwave signals at a rate of several hundred million bits per second. They serve as relay stations for communication signals transmitted from *earth stations*. Earth stations beam microwave signals to the satellites, which amplify and retransmit the signals to other earth stations thousands of miles away.

While communications satellites were used initially for voice and video transmission, they are now also used for high-speed transmission of large volumes of data. Because of time delays caused by the great distances involved, they are not suitable for interactive, real time processing. Communications satellite systems are operated by several firms, including AT&T, Western Union, American Satellite Company, and Intellsat, an international consortium of over 100 nations. Large corporate and other users are developing networks of satellite dish antennas and communications satellite services to connect their distant work areas. These networks are called *bypasses* because firms are bypassing the communications networks provided by communications carriers.

Cellular radio is a radio communications technology that divides a metropolitan area into a honeycomb of *cells*. This greatly increases the number of frequencies and users that can take advantage of mobile phone service. Each cell has its own low-power transmitter, rather than having one high-powered radio transmitter to serve an entire city. This significantly increases the number of radio frequencies available for mobile phone service. However, this technology requires a central computer and other communications equipment to coordinate and control the transmissions of thousands of mobile phone users as they drive from one cell to another. Cellular radio has become an important communications medium for mobile voice and data communications. For example, Federal Express uses cellular radio for data communications with terminals in each of its thousands of delivery vans as part of its competitive edge.

Cellular Radio

Telecommunications processors such as modems, multiplexers, concentrators, front-end processors, and other devices perform a variety of support functions between the terminals and computers in a telecommunications network. Let's take a look at some of these devices and their functions.

TELE-COMMUNICATIONS PROCESSORS

Modems are the most common type of communications processor. They convert the *digital* signals from a computer or transmission terminal at one end of a communications link into *analog* frequencies, which can be transmitted over ordinary telephone lines. A modem at the other end of the communications line converts the transmitted data back into digital form at a receiving terminal. This process is known as *modulation* and *demodulation*, and the word *modem* is a combined abbreviation of those two words. Modems come in several forms, including small stand-alone units, plug-in circuit boards, and microelectronic modem chips.

Modems

Modems are necessary because ordinary telephone lines were primarily designed to handle continuous analog signals, such as the human voice. Since data transmissions from computers are in digital form, devices are necessary to convert digital signals into appropriate analog transmission frequencies, and vice versa. However, *digital communications networks* that transmit only digital signals are rapidly being developed. Modems that only perform the digital/analog conversion function are not required for such networks. See Figure 5–11.

A multiplexer is a communications processor that allows a single communications channel to carry simultaneous data transmissions from many terminals. Thus, a single communications line can be shared by several terminals. Typ-

Multiplexers, Concentrators, and Controllers

Figure 5–11   Modems perform a modulation-demodulation process that converts digital signals to analog and back.

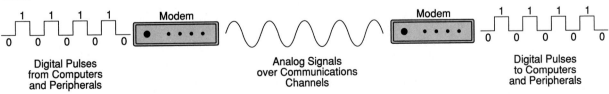

ically, a multiplexer merges the transmissions of several terminals at one end of a communications channel, while a similar unit separates the individual transmissions at the receiving end.

This is accomplished in two basic ways. In *frequency division multiplexing* (FDM), a multiplexer effectively divides a high-speed channel into multiple slow-speed channels. In *time division multiplexing* (TDM), the multiplexer divides the time each terminal can use a high-speed line into very short time slots, or time frames. The most advanced and popular type of multiplexer is the *statistical time division multiplexer*, most commonly referred to as a *statistical multiplexer*. Instead of giving all terminals equal time slots, it dynamically allocates time slots only to active terminals according to priorities assigned by a user.

Devices known as concentrators and controllers have microprocessor intelligence, stored communications programs, and buffer storage. *Concentrators* concentrate many slow-speed lines into a high-speed line through the use of buffer storage, and they also route data to its proper destination. *Controllers*, or *cluster controllers*, link groups of terminals or other devices to a communications channel. The controller *polls* the status of each terminal and transfers data from a terminal to the host computer when necessary.

Front-End Processors

A **front-end processor** is typically a minicomputer dedicated to handling the data communications control functions for large mainframe computer systems. For example, a front-end processor uses telecommunications control programs to provide temporary buffer storage, data coding and decoding, error detection, recovery, and the recording, interpreting, and processing of control information (such as characters that indicate the beginning and end of a message). It can also poll remote terminals to determine if they have a message to send or if they are ready to receive a message.

However, a front-end computer has more advanced responsibilities. It controls access to a network and allows only authorized users to use the system, assigns priorities to messages, logs all data communications activity, computes statistics on network activity, and routes and reroutes messages among alternative communication links. Thus, the front-end processor can relieve the host computer of its data communications control functions so it can concentrate on its other information processing chores.

Private Branch Exchange

The **private branch exchange** (PBX) is a communications processor that serves as a switching device between the telephone lines within a work area and the local telephone company's main telephone lines, or *trunks*. In recent years, PBXs have become electronic, computerized devices with built-in microprocessors and stored-program intelligence. They not only route telephone calls within an office but also provide other services, such as automatic forwarding of calls, conference calling, and least-cost routing of long-distance calls. Some PBX models can control communications along the terminals, computers, and other information processing devices in local area networks in offices and other work areas. Other PBXs can integrate the switching of voice, data, and images in an *integrated services digital network* (ISDN). Figure 5–12 illustrates how a PBX can handle telecommunications from a variety of computers and office devices.

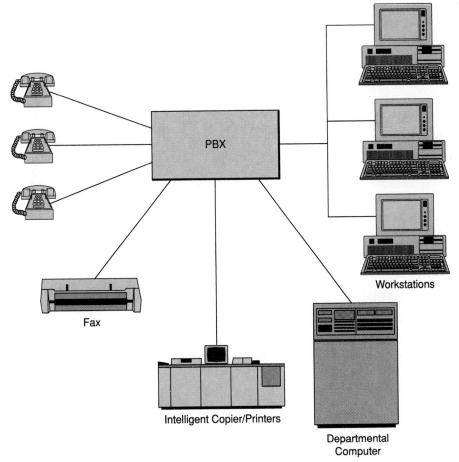

Figure 5–12 The role of a PBX as a telecommunications processor for voice, data, and image transmission in a local area network.

Workstations

Fax

Intelligent Copier/Printers

Departmental Computer

TELECOMMUNICA-TIONS SOFTWARE

Software is a vital component of all telecommunications networks. Communications control software includes programs stored in the host computer as well as programs in front-end computers and other communications processors. This software controls and supports the communications occurring in a telecommunications network. Telecommunications software packages for large computer networks are frequently called *telecommunication monitors* or *teleprocessing* (TP) *monitors*. Local area networks (LANs) rely on software called *network operating systems*. Many communications software packages are also available for microcomputers. Figure 5–13 illustrates the tasks performed by a network operating system for a local area network.

Telecommunication software packages provide a variety of communications support services. The number and type of terminals, computers, communication processors, and communications activities involved determine the capabilities of the programs required. Several major functions can be provided.

☐ **Access control.** This function establishes the connections between terminals and computers in a network. The software works with a communications processor (such as a modem) to connect and disconnect communications links and establish parameters such as transmission speed, mode, and direction. This function may also

Figure 5–13 An example of a network operating system. Note the various activities performed by the program modules making up the IBM LAN Server package.

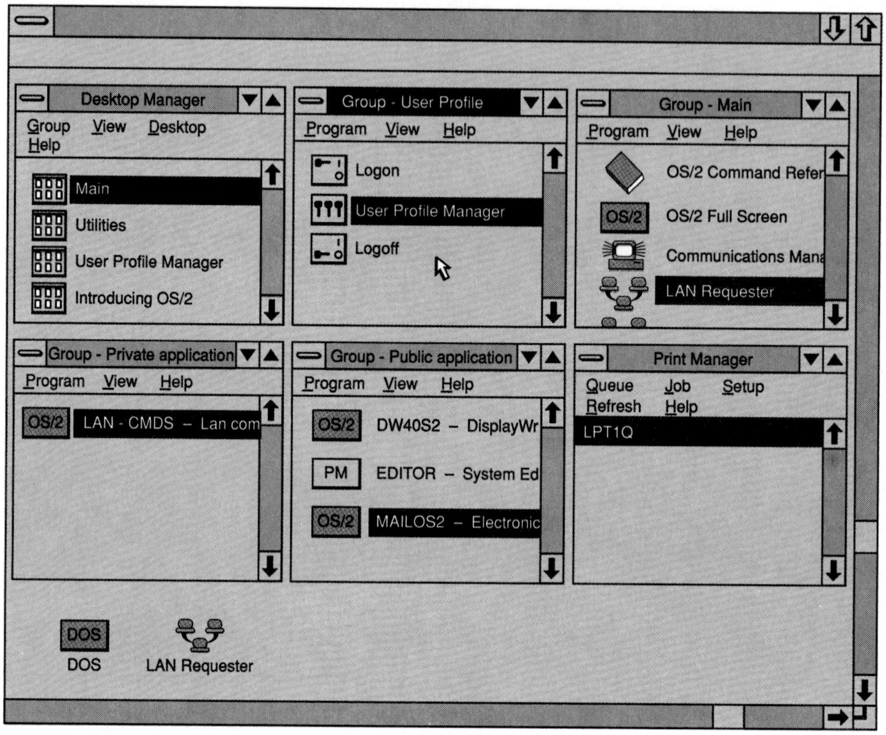

Courtesy IBM Corporation

involve automatic telephone dialing and redialing, logging on and off with appropriate account numbers and security codes, and automatic answering of telephone calls from another computer.

☐ **Transmission control.** This function allows computers and terminals to send and receive commands, messages, data, and programs. Some error checking and correction of data transmissions may also be provided. Data and programs are usually transmitted in the form of files, so this activity is frequently called *file transfer*.

☐ **Network control.** This function manages communications in a network. Software determines transmission priorities, routes (switches) messages, polls terminals in the network, and forms waiting lines (*queues*) of transmission requests. It also logs statistics of network activity and resource use and detects and corrects errors.

☐ **Error control.** This function involves detection and correction of transmission errors. Errors are usually caused by distortions in the communications channel, such as line noise and power surges. Communications software and processors control errors in transmission by several methods, including *parity checking,* as discussed in Chapter 3. Besides parity bits, additional *control codes* are usually added to the message itself. These specify such information as the destination of the data, their priority, and the beginning and end of the message, plus additional error detecting information. Most error correction methods involve retransmissions. A signal is sent back to the computer or terminal to retransmit the previous message.

Multidrop Lines　　　　　　　　　　**Point-to-Point Lines**

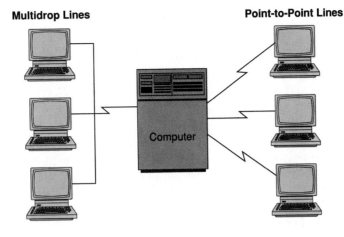

Computer

Figure 5–14 Multidrop lines allow terminals to share a communications line. Point-to-point lines provide a separate communications line for each terminal.

☐ **Security control.** This function protects a communications network from unauthorized access. Access control software and other types of programs restrict access to data and the computing resources in the network. This restriction usually involves control procedures that limit access to all or parts of a network by various categories of users. Automatic disconnection and callback procedures may also be used. Data transmissions can also be protected by coding techniques called **encryption.** Data is scrambled into a coded form before transmission and decoded upon arrival. Banks, government agencies, and others use a Data Encryption Standard as the basis for data encryption.

TELECOMMUNICATIONS NETWORK TOPOLOGIES

The two simplest types of network *topologies*, or structures, in telecommunications networks are *point-to-point lines* and *multidrop lines.* When point-to-point lines are used, each terminal is connected by its own line to a computer system. When multidrop lines are used, several terminals share each data communications line to a computer. Obviously, point-to-point lines are more expensive than multidrop lines: all of the communications capacity and equipment of a communications line is being used by a single terminal. Therefore, point-to-point lines are used only if there will be continuous communications between a computer and a terminal or other computer system. A multidrop line decreases communications costs because each line is shared by many terminals. Communications processors such as multiplexers and concentrators help many terminals share the same line. See Figure 5–14.

Star, Ring, and Bus Networks

Figure 5–15 illustrates three basic topologies used in wide area and local area telecommunications networks. A **star network** ties end user computers to a central computer. In a **ring network,** local computer processors are tied together in a ring on a more equal basis. A **bus network** is a network in which local processors share the same *bus,* or communications channel. In many cases, star networks take the form of *hierarchical networks.* In hierarchical networks, a large headquarters computer at the top of the company's hierarchy is connected to medium-size computers at the divisional level, which are connected to small computers at the departmental level or work group. A

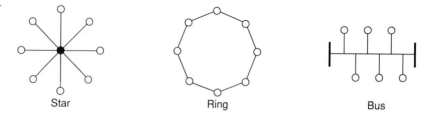

Figure 5-15 The star, ring, and bus network topologies.

variation of the ring network is the *mesh network*. This uses direct communications lines to connect some or all of the computers in the ring to each other. Another variation is the *tree network*, which joins several bus networks together.

In most cases, distributed processing networks use a combination of star, ring, and bus approaches. Obviously, the star network is more centralized, while ring and bus networks have a more decentralized approach. However, this is not always the case. For example, the central computer in a star configuration may be acting only as a **switch,** or message-switching computer, that handles the telecommunications between autonomous local computers. Figure 5-16 illustrates a network that combines star and ring approaches.

Star, ring, and bus networks differ in their performances, reliabilities, and costs. A pure star network is considered less reliable than a ring network since the other computers in the star are heavily dependent on the central host computer. If it fails, there is no backup processing and communications capability, and the local computers will be cut off from the corporate headquarters and from each other. Therefore, it is essential that the host computer be highly reliable. Having some type of *multiprocessor architecture* to provide a backup capability is a common solution. Star network variations are common because they can support the *chain-of-command* and hierarchical structures of most organizations. Ring and bus networks are most common in local area networks. Ring networks are considered more reliable and less costly for the type of communications in such networks. If one computer in the ring goes down, the other computers can continue to process their own work as well as to communicate with each other.

NETWORK ARCHITECTURES AND PROTOCOLS

Until quite recently, there was a lack of sufficient standards for the interfaces between the hardware, software, and communications channels of telecommunication networks. For this reason, it is quite common to find a lack of compatibility between the telecommunications hardware and software of different manufacturers. For example, it was very difficult to build telecommunications networks that included IBM, DEC, and Apple computer systems. This situation has hampered the use of telecommunications, increased its costs, and reduced its efficiency and effectiveness. In response, computer manufacturers and national and international organizations have developed standards called *protocols* and master plans called *network architectures* to support the development of advanced telecommunications networks.

Protocols

A **protocol** is a standard set of rules and procedures for the control of communications in a network. However, these standards may be limited to just one manufacturer's equipment, or to just one type of telecommunications. Conse-

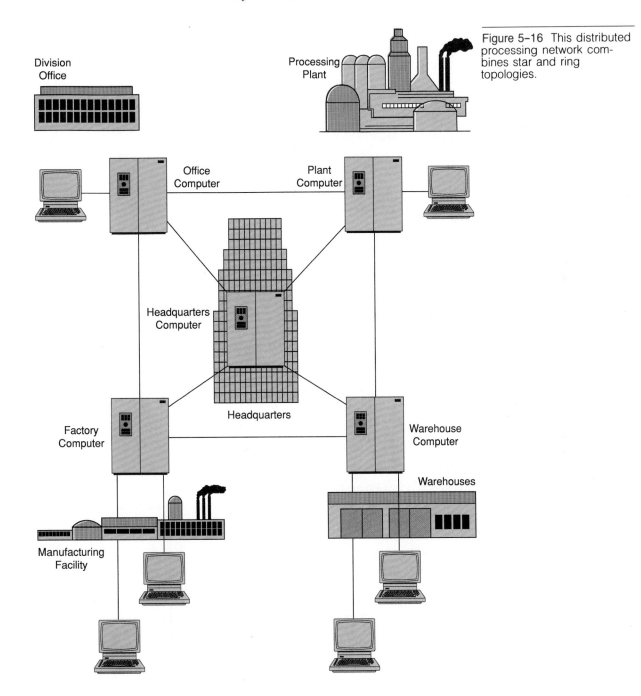

Figure 5–16 This distributed processing network combines star and ring topologies.

quently, many competing and incompatible protocols are in use today. Part of the goal of communications network architectures is to create more standardization and compatibility among communications protocols. One example of a protocol is a standard for the physical characteristics of the cables and connectors between terminals, computers, modems, and communications lines. Other examples are the protocols that establish the communications control information needed for *handshaking*, which is the process of exchanging predetermined signals and characters to establish a telecommunications session between terminals and computers. Other protocols deal with control of transmission/reception in a network, packet and other switching techniques, internetwork connections, and so on.

Network Architectures

The goal of **network architectures** is to promote an open, simple, flexible, and efficient telecommunications environment. This is accomplished by the use of standard protocols, standard communications hardware and software interfaces, and the design of a standard multilevel interface between end users and computer systems.

The OSI Model and Other Architectures

The International Standards Organization (ISO) has developed a seven-layer Open System Interconnection (OSI) model to serve as a standard for network architectures. By dividing telecommunications functions into seven distinct layers, the ISO hopes to promote the development of modular network architectures. This would assist the development, operation, and maintenance of large telecommunications networks. Network architectures currently being implemented by computer manufacturers include IBM's Systems Network Architecture (SNA) and the Digital Network Architecture (DNA) of the Digital Equipment Corporation. Another important example is the local area network architectures for computer integrated manufacturing sponsored by General Motors and Boeing called Manufacturing Automation Protocol (MAP) and Technical and Office Protocol (TOP). Figure 5–17 illustrates the functions of the seven levels of IBM's SNA as compared to the OSI model architecture.

Integrated Services Digital Network

Related to the development of network architectures is the development of a set of standards for ISDN, the Integrated Services Digital Network. This is a set of international standards needed to establish public and private digital telecommunications networks capable of handling voice, data, image, and video communications throughout the world. ISDN will replace the many types of networks in use today with a single type of digital network incorporating a standard set of communications processors to provide voice, data, image, and video services to any terminal in the network. Many communications carriers and corporations are developing and testing the communications technologies needed to implement ISDN networks. ISDN is scheduled to be implemented in major U.S. cities by the mid-1990s and in all U.S. and major international locations by 2010 [2].

COMMUNICATIONS CHANNEL CHARACTERISTICS

Transmission Speed

The communication capabilities of telecommunication channels can be classified by *band width*. This is the frequency range of the channel, which determines the channel's maximum transmission rate. Data transmission rates are typically measured in bits per second (BPS). This is sometimes referred to as the *baud rate*, though *baud* is more correctly understood as a measure of signal changes in a transmission line.

Narrowband, or *low-speed analog*, channels allow transmission rates from 300 to 1,200 BPS. They are used primarily for teletypewriters and other low-

Figure 5-17 Communications network architectures. The OSI model is recognized as an international standard. IBM's SNA is the leading network architecture for mainframe-based telecommunications networks.

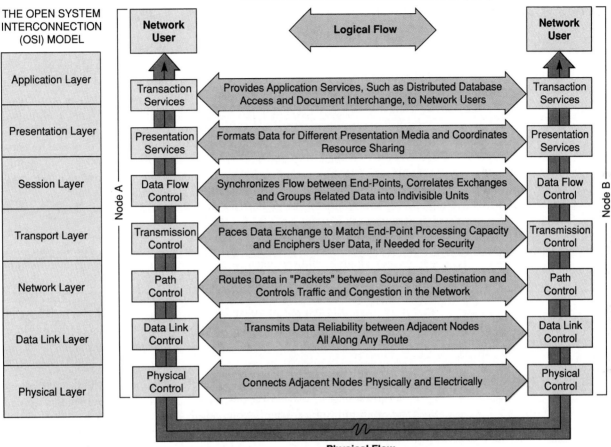

speed terminals. *Voiceband*, or *medium-speed*, channels are "voice grade" analog communication lines commonly used for voice communications. Data transmission rates from 2,400 to 9,600 BPS are attainable, with the highest rates depending on the use of specially conditioned leased lines. These medium-speed lines are typically used for CRT terminals, microcomputers, fax machines, and medium-speed printers.

Broadband, or *high-speed digital*, channels allow transmission rates at specific intervals from 19,200 BPS to several billion BPS. They typically use microwave, fiber optics, or satellite transmission. Examples are 64,000 BPS for digital telephone service and 1.54 million BPS for T1 communications channels developed by AT&T and used by many large private communications networks.

Parallel or Serial Transmission

Two basic methods of transmitting data are *parallel* and *serial* transmission. Parallel transmission involves transmitting all the bits needed to represent a character simultaneously. Serial transmission, on the other hand, involves sending each of the bits composing a character one at a time. Parallel transmission is obviously faster and more expensive than serial transmission because more telecommunications channels are required. Parallel transmission is typically used for data transfers over short distances, especially between a computer system and its peripheral devices. Serial transmission is traditionally used between computers and modems for data communications over telephone networks.

Transmission Mode

The two modes of transmitting data are called *asynchronous* and *synchronous* transmission. Asynchronous transmission transmits one character at a time, with each character preceded by a *start bit* and followed by a *stop bit*. Asynchronous transmission is normally used for low-speed transmission at rates below 2,400 BPS. Synchronous transmission transmits groups of characters at a time, with the beginning and end of a character determined by the timing circuitry of a communications processor. Synchronous transmission is normally used for high-speed transmission exceeding 2,400 BPS.

Transmission Direction

Communications channels can provide three types of data transmission directions. A *simplex* channel allows data to be transmitted in only one direction. A *half-duplex* channel allows transmission in either direction, but in only one direction at a time. This is usually sufficient for low-speed terminals (such as transaction terminals). Alternating sending and receiving is a typical characteristic of their normal communications activities. The *full duplex* channel allows data to be transmitted in both directions at the same time. It is used for high-speed communications between computer systems. See Figure 5–18.

Switching Alternatives

Regular telephone service relies on *circuit switching*, in which a circuit is opened to establish a link between a sender and receiver and remains open until the communication session is completed. In *message switching*, a message is transmitted a *block* at a time from one switching device to another. This method is sometimes called *store-and-forward* transmission because messages may be temporarily stored by the switching device before being retransmitted.

    Packet switching involves subdividing communications messages into groups called *packets*, typically 128 characters long. The packet switching network

Figure 5–18 Simplex, half-duplex, and duplex channels. Note the direction of data transmission allowed by each.

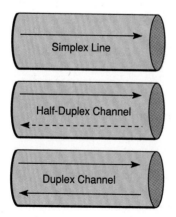

carrier uses computers and other communications processors to control the packet switching process and transmit the packets of various users over its leased lines. Packet switching networks are also known as X.25 *networks*, which is the international protocol governing the operations of public packet switching networks. Packet switching is most widely used by value-added networks.

How can terminals and other devices access and share a network to transmit and receive data? A variety of *access methods* are used to provide this capacity, including those illustrated in Figure 5–19. In the *polling* approach, a host computer or communications processor polls (contacts) each terminal in sequence to determine which terminals have messages to send. The sequence in which the terminals are polled is based on the communications traffic expected from each terminal. Thus, the transmission of each terminal is based on a "roll call" of each terminal on the line. Polling can be an effective method because

Access Methods

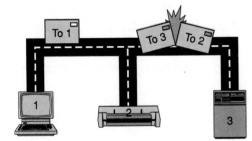

Collision avoidance and detection: Technically known as carrier-sense multiple access with collision detection, or CSMA/CD. This scheme operates like a one-lane highway with two-way traffic. Computers must monitor the network, then send a message on to the data highway in packages whenever the road appears clear. If two packages collide, they must go back and try again. Because the electronics controlling this network are simple, it is relatively inexpensive. But when traffic is heavy, it is more difficult to send a package down the highway

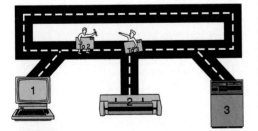

Token passing: Computer equipment attached to this kind of network must wait for a coded electrical signal, called a token, to pass by. Then the equipment attaches its information package to that token and moves it on to the data highway. After delivering the package, the token is passed along to the next device.

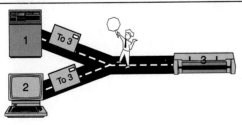

Star: All information packages must pass through a central controller, which directs them to their final destination. Because this network functions much like a central telephone switchboard, it is easy to piggyback on to existing office telephone systems without having to do any new wiring. This scheme is somewhat easier to maintain than the others because of centralized control, but if the central switch fails, the network does too.

Figure 5–19 Three competing LAN communications access methods.

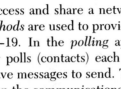

REAL WORLD CASE

Sanford C. Bernstein & Co.

A distributed client/server network in which workstations serve as windows onto Wall Street and minicomputers act as way stations for information churned out by mainframes is changing the way a 23-year-old investment firm does business. The paper, pencil, hand-held calculator, and 30-second delays in mainframe processing have given way to almost instantaneous online responses to the needs of portfolio managers at Sanford C. Bernstein & Co. Now, VAX minicomputers and servers act as way stations or nodes on an enterprisewide network. Under the architecture, data that used to be stored in a central IBM mainframe is moved to the VAXs and thus closer to the end users who repeatedly request the data.

"This is a part of a larger business revolution," said Bernstein's MIS director, George E. Reid. According to Reid, the beauty of distributed processing is that it imposes the traditional IS techniques of network management and security on what otherwise would be a chaotic jumble of workstations and personal computers. Because of its modularity, the network could be expanded to accommodate hundreds more workstations and IBM-compatible PCs.

Computers are a key to attracting new business when managing pension-fund investment accounts worth tens of millions of dollars, noted associate MIS Director Paul M. Bagnoli. The firm managed nearly $13 billion in assets in 1988. During the last two years, Bernstein's IS staff placed 220 workstations on portfolio managers' desks, dramatically changing the amount of information that can be handled on each desk, Reid said. "What now takes three or four seconds to do on the workstation used to take 20 to 30 seconds to do on a mainframe terminal," he added. "That's about a 10 to 1 magnitude of difference."

As portfolio managers answer telephone calls from clients, they can view their client's investment history, make calculations on-screen in an electronic spreadsheet, and order future stock purchases. The orders are forwarded to Bernstein traders, who can buy and sell Wall Street stocks and bonds.

At the heart of this distributed system are two VAX minicomputers that store the information downloaded nightly from an IBM mainframe in New Jersey. "The mainframe's portfolio accounting system draws in the new prices for client assets, based on the prior day's close of business," Bagnoli said. "After mainframe processing, you have an accurate picture of each client's portfolio." Once inside the VAXs, the data is then routed to multiple local-area networks located several miles away in midtown Manhattan. Each of these LANs is anchored by a VAX Microserver.

Until the current workstation technology became available, the price of such computer horsepower—available only on a mainframe—was prohibitive. Time, it seems, was on Bernstein's side. Recent price drops in computer memory, coupled with boosts in workstation performance, enabled the desktop analysis plan. However, "the network is the thing that makes it all possible," Reid observed. "You can put all of that data out on the net, and it's easy for the users to reach out and get it."

Application Questions

☐ How has Bernstein & Co.'s distributed client/server network helped to improve their business effectiveness?

☐ What is the role of each of the following in their operations: (a) wide area networks, (b) local area networks, (c) workstations, (d) LAN servers, (e) minicomputers, and (f) mainframe computers?

☐ What are the benefits and limitations of a distributed processing or client/server network compared to the use of terminals connected directly to a central mainframe?

Source: Adapted from Jean Bozman, "Client/Server Investment Pays Off," *Computerworld*, January 29, 1990, p. 25.

the speed of mainframes and communications processors allows them to poll and control transmissions by many terminals sharing the same line, especially if communications consist of brief messages and inquiries.

In the *contention* approach, line use is on a first-come, first-served basis, where a terminal can transmit data if the line is not in use, but it must wait if it is busy. One way to make contention work is a widely used method called *carrier-sense multiple access* with *collision detection* (CSMA/CD). This requires a terminal or other device to continually monitor the network and send a message only if it senses the network is not in use. If a collision is detected, the terminal must stop transmission, wait until the network is clear, and try again. This access method is used by Ethernet and some other local area networks.

Another widely used method in local area networks is *token passing*. A *token* is a special signal code sent around the network. If a terminal or other device wants to transmit a message, it must wait for the token to come by, take it off the network, and transmit its message. After transmission is completed, the token is returned to the network. This access method is used in IBM *token ring* networks and other widely used LANs, including the Datapoint and MAP *token bus* networks.

SUMMARY

☐ Modern information systems depend on computer systems interconnected by telecommunications networks to service the information processing needs of end users. Telecommunications has entered a competitive environment with many vendors, carriers, and services. It is moving toward integrated digital networks for voice, data, text, and images, and the pervasive use of this technology to support business operations, managerial decision making, and strategic advantage.

☐ There are two basic types of telecommunications networks: wide area networks (WANs) and local area networks (LANs). WANs cover a wide geographic area, while LANs interconnect end user workstations and other devices at local worksites. Such networks support a variety of applications, as outlined in Figure 5–4. This includes applications in transaction processing, inquiry/response, distributed and cooperative processing, office automation, end user computing, and personal information services.

☐ Telecommunications can help a firm compress the time taken by business activities, reduce geographic limits on business markets, and restructure business relationships. This can lead to significant improvements in operational efficiency, business effectiveness, and organizational innovation.

☐ The major components of a telecommunications network are (1) terminals, (2) telecommunications processors, (3) communications channels and media, (4) computers, and (5) telecommunications control software. Telecommunications processors include modems, multiplexers, and various devices to help enhance the capacity and efficiency of telecommunications channels. Telecommunications software consists of computer programs that control and support the communications occurring in a telecommunications network.

☐ Communications channels include such media as twisted-pair wire, coaxial cables, fiber optic cables, microwave systems, cellular radio, and communications satellite systems. Use of these channels is provided by companies called common carriers and value-added carriers who offer a variety of telecommunication services. Standards called protocols and master plans called network architectures have been developed to promote compatibility among the components of telecommunications networks.

☐ Key telecommunications network alternatives and components are summarized in Figure 5–8 for telecommunications media, processors, software, channels, and network architectures. A basic understanding of these major alternatives will help end users participate effectively in decisions involving telecommunications issues.

KEY TERMS AND CONCEPTS

These are the key terms and concepts of this chapter. The page number of their first explanation is in parentheses.

1. Bulletin board system (172)
2. Cellular radio (181)
3. Coaxial cable (178)
4. Common carriers (173)
5. Communications satellites (180)
6. Cooperative processing (170)
7. Distributed processing (170)
8. Electronic funds transfer (169)
9. Encryption (185)
10. Fiber optic cable (179)
11. Front-end processor (182)
12. Host computer (167)
13. Local area network (168)
14. Modem (181)
15. Multiplexer (181)
16. Network architecture (186)
17. Network server (168)
18. Personal information services (172)
19. Private branch exchange (182)
20. Protocol (186)
21. Telecommunications applications (176)
   a. Impact
   b. Value
22. Telecommunications channels and media (178)
23. Telecommunications network (166)
   a. Alternatives (178)
   b. Components (166)
24. Telecommunications processors (181)
25. Telecommunications control software (183)
26. Trends in telecommunications (174)
27. Value-added carriers (173)
28. Videotex (172)
29. Wide area network (167)

REVIEW QUIZ

Match one of the **key terms and concepts** listed above with one of the brief examples or definitions listed below. Try to find the best fit for answers that seem to fit more than one term or concept. Defend your choices.

_____ 1. Includes terminals, telecommunications processors, channels and media, computers, and control software.

_____ 2. A communications network covering a large geographic area.

_____ 3. A communications network in an office, a building, or other work site.

_____ 4. They provide a variety of communications networks and services to the public.

_____ 5. They lease lines from common carriers and offer specialized telecommunications services.

_____ 6. Telecommunications network resources and computing services are available for a fee to microcomputer users.

_____ 7. End users can post public or private messages for other computer users.

_____ 8. An interactive information service for home computers.

_____ 9. Systems for the capture and processing of money and credit transactions.

_____ 10. Computers at central and local sites interconnected by a network.

_____ 11. Networked computers sharing the processing of parts of an end user's application.

_____ 12. Fundamental changes have occurred in the competitive environment, the technology, and the applications of telecommunications.

_____ 13. Telecommunications can reduce geographic limits and restructure business relationships.

_____ 14. Telecommunications can improve operational efficiency, business effectiveness, and organizational innovation.

_____ 15. A microcomputer that controls the software and data resources of a local area network.

_____ 16. Coding techniques for data communications security.

_____ 17. Includes coaxial cable, microwave, fiber optics, and satellites.

_____ 18. Communications medium that uses pulses of laser light in glass fibers.

_____ 19. Supports mobile data communications in urban areas.

_____ 20. Includes modems, multiplexers, and front-end processors.

_____ 21. Includes programs for control of communications access, transmission, networks, errors, and security.

_____ 22. A common communications processor for microcomputers.

_____ 23. Helps a communications channel carry simultaneous data transmissions from many terminals.

_____ 24. The main computer in a data communications network.

_____ 25. A minicomputer dedicated to handling communications functions.

_____ 26. Handles the switching of both voice and data in a local area network.

_____ 27. A master plan for standard, multilevel interface for telecommunications networks.

_____ 28. A standard set of rules and procedures for control of communications in a network.

REAL WORLD PROBLEMS

1. K mart Corporation
   K mart has purchased 1,000 Intel 486-based Unisys Series 6000 microcomputers to run its inventory control system, KIN II. The micros will be up and running in all 2,300 stores by the end of 1994, according to David M. Carlson, senior vice president of corporation information systems. The Unisys PCs will join a lineup that includes IBM 3090 and

Amdahl 5990 mainframes at K mart's headquarters and a GTE Spacenet satellite network that links the mainframes to the store's PCs. K mart is also implementing an in-store network of hand-held terminals that will be linked to a 486 by a radio-wave network.

With KIN II, K mart is hoping to control inventory better by automating a lot of the tedious functions with which store managers contend daily. In retailing, empty shelf space is like a black hole sucking up potential profits. KIN II gives store staffs power to speed up the elimination of these merchandise holes, Carlson said. Using the hand-held unit, a clerk can scan an item's bar-code label, which is affixed to the shelf. The unit accesses the master merchandise file on the 486 micro via radio waves. When the information is relayed back, the unit will display the item's description, price, order status, and whether any new units have been received.

a. What types of telecommunications networks and network components do you recognize in KIN II?

b. What are the business benefits of KIN II for K mart?

Source: Adapted from Richard Pastore, "486-Based PCs Run K Mart's Retail Show," *Computerworld*, February 5, 1990, p. 59.

2. Qualcomm Incorporated

Imagine that you are a driver for one of the nation's largest trucking companies. Heavy snow and stormy night skies impede your vision as you attempt to make that last run for the evening. Your payload: 27,000 pounds of explosives that must be delivered on time. Suddenly, the left front tire blows out and your truck skids to a halt in a ditch! What do you do? Well, if your truck is equipped with an OmniTRACS two-way mobile communication system, you are in good shape. This satellite-based, mobile communication system provides two-way messaging between trucks and operations centers while pinpointing vehicle location.

With the OmniTRACS system, every driver has a terminal, suitable for rugged conditions, installed in the truck cab. The terminal is connected to an antenna unit that uses existing satellite frequencies to maintain a reliable connection between each truck on the network and the Qualcomm Network Management Control center earthstation in San Diego. The Network Control Center monitors and controls traffic between dispatchers, the satellite, and eventually, the trucker. For example, emergency messages on the open road can be communicated instantly to dispatch, which can then alert local authorities for assistance. Because shipping orders can be communicated to the driver in realtime, just-in-time shipments can be constantly tracked. If a delay is imminent, the shipper can be notified and adjustments to the manufacturing lines can be made. Changes to shipping orders can also be communicated directly to the driver, avoiding unnecessary travel and saving money.

a. What telecommunications network components make up the Omni-TRAC system?

b. What are the business benefits of the OmniTRAC system to trucking companies?

Source: Adapted from "Qualcomm Network: Opening the Road to Success," *Product Insight*, November 1989, pp. 16–17.

3. The National Football League

Communications parity involves much more than the transfer of bytes at the National Football League. "It is important that we make information available to each club at the same time as its competitors receive it," said Mary Oliveti, manager of information processing at NFL headquarters in New York City. A network extending across the nation linking VAX mini-computers in each of the 28 team offices of the NFL helps to ensure the fair distribution of data and allows teams to communicate electronically with each other. For example, Bill Consoli of the Los Angeles Rams IS staff says: "If we're on the road, we talk to another club over the network about accommodations, ticket requests, and even what the weather's like."

Time-sensitive information sent from the NFL main office includes roster adjustments, game statistics, and officiating changes. The number of transactions has grown to between 1,500 and 2,500 per week. This traffic includes not only waiver notices, but normal interoffice memorandums. The NFL also uses the network for other activities, such as:

- ☐ Exchange of player contracts.
- ☐ Balloting for the Pro Bowl teams.
- ☐ Maintaining officials' schedules.
- ☐ Sharing of press releases.
- ☐ Processing Super Bowl information.

a. How does the NFL use their telecommunications network?

b. Why does the NFL need their present telecommunications network? That is, couldn't they rely instead on telephone calls, fax machines, and express delivery?

Source: Adapted from "VAX Network: Leading the League into the 1990's," *Product Insight*, February 1990, pp. 20–23.

4. CBS Records

Thomas Del Otero, a program analyst with CBS Records in New York, produces catalogs listing the company's classical, rock, jazz, and other records for retailers. To do so, he downloads record information (title, musician, selection number, and so on) from CBS's mainframe using proprietary software. In the process, the software converts the data to a form Del Otero's typesetter can use and eliminates duplicate entries. The 50- to 120-page catalogs have to reflect accurately CBS's inventory. Missing entries mean lost sales, and duplicate entries portend expensive and time-consuming typesetting and printing changes. Transmitting the final file to the typesetter involved the hit-or- miss task of coordinating transmission times. Worse, Del Otero had to monitor the transfer. So he installed a two-line bulletin board system (BBS) using an old IBM PC AT.

Now the typesetter can retrieve catalog data stored on the BBS computer's hard disk whenever he's ready, and Del Otero no longer needs to baby-sit the process. The two-line BBS he installed ensures that the typesetter gets through when he's ready, even if someone else is communicating with the mainframe through the other modem. The entire catalog prep process, from mainframe to typesetter, now takes days instead of weeks, and because the BBS file incorporates the latest mainframe data, the system virtually eliminates follow-up calls to the typesetter regarding late changes. Del Otero estimates that the system will save CBS $100,000 a year.

a. What are the components of an electronic bulletin board system? How does it help CBS Records?

b. How do you think this BBS can save CBS $100,000 a year?

Source: Adapted from Russ Lockwood, "The Corporate BBS," *Personal Computing,* March 20, 1990, pp. 63–64.

5. American Express Company

How does a Fortune 500 company manage both the cost and risk justification of a still-embryonic technology such as Integrated Services Digital Network? American Express Company's answer is the same as it would be for any other service—on the basis of cost savings and quality of service improvement. So says Robert Haas, vice president of planning and engineering at American Express's Travel Related Services (TRS) Worldwide Telecommunications division in Phoenix. For example, when a customer dials in on Amex's 800 service number, the ISDN part of the connection automatically provides the caller's telephone number. The number is then used to call up the customer's file on a host and send it to the service representative's screen within seconds of the call coming in. Initial trials of the application resulted in a 16 percent improvement in performance, allowing representatives to take less time on the telephone and improving customer service as a result, Haas says.

The ISDN-based customer service application has "simplified users' lives in that they don't have to ask quite as many questions" to verify that they can talk to the caller about a particular account, says Linda Schoneberger, director of the travel division's Applied Technology Group. Transparency to customers is a key criterion by which Amex determines whether to implement a new technology or application, Schoneberger says. The only change that customers are likely to notice from Amex's ISDN implementation is the improved efficiency with which representatives can respond to queries. "If there is one thing that annoys customers, it's being asked 40 questions," she says.

a. What is the ISDN? How does it help American Express?

b. What business benefits and privacy issues arise from the automatic number identification feature provided by ISDN?

Source: Adapted from Elisabeth Horwitt, "On the Leading Edge with ISDN," *Computerworld,* January 29, 1990, pp. 49–53.

6. Metropolitan Life Insurance Co.

At Metropolitan Life Insurance Co., 1,500 business offices want to establish direct links to one another, and they don't want to burden the telecommunications network that links them to the New York insurance giant's four computer centers. In 10 years, most of the processing that takes place on the mainframe will move to personal computers, and office-to-office telecommunications will take place entirely on local area networks. Dependence on the mainframe, which today is the lifeblood of processing, will consist of file updating, shared processing, electronic mail, and accounting applications.

This isn't an easy task, according to Steve Bortnyk, manager of data communications at Met Life in New York. Currently, the company has a Systems Network Architecture (SNA) telecommunications network consisting of IBM 3090 mainframes connected to thousands of video terminals. In replacing the terminals with PCs and rerouting communications around the mainframe centers, Bortnyk has come face-to-face with the problem of network management. LAN and wide area network management issues, he says, include facilitating non-SNA telecommunications, effectively using current network management software, and connecting LANs to WANs for effective telecommunications within Met Life.

a. How is the role of telecommunications networks and computer systems changing at Metropolitan Life?

b. What network management problems must be confronted?

Source: Adapted from Mary Ryan Garcia, "Tools for Large Networks," *Computerworld*, February 5, 1990, p. 89.

7. Analyzing Telecommunications Networks

Apply the telecommunications network model illustrated in Figure 5–1 to the telecommunications network of a business, university, or other organization you know uses telecommunications.

a. Identify as many of the five basic components of a telecommunications network that might exist in this particular network. Make assumptions about the network if necessary.

b. Describe how almost all of the communication media illustrated in Figure 5–9 could be used in this network.

SELECTED REFERENCES

1. *Connectivity.* (A regular supplement to *PC Week* that is a good source for developments in telecommunications.)

2. "A Field Guide to LAN Operating Systems." *PC Magazine*, June 14, 1988.

3. *Focus on Integration.* (A regular supplement to *Computerworld* that is a good source on how organizations are using telecommunications.)

4. Francis, Bob. "Client/Server: The Model for the 90s." *Datamation*, February 15, 1990.

5. Hammer, Michael, and Glenn Mangurian. "The Changing Value of Communications Technology." *Sloan Management Review*, Winter 1987.

6. Keen, Peter. *Computing in Time: Using Telecommunications for Competitive Advantage.* New York: Ballinger Publishing Co., 1988.

7. Lockwood, Russ. "The Corporate BBS." *Personal Computing*, March 20, 1990.

8. Sprague, Ralph, and Barbara McNurlin, ed. *Information Systems Management in Practice.* Englewood Cliffs, N.J.: Prentice-Hall, 1986.

9. Stallings, William. *Business Data Communications.* New York: McMillan, 1990.

10. Stamper, David. *Business Data Communications.* 2nd ed. Redwood City, Calif.: Benjamin/Cummings Publishing Co., Inc., 1989.

INTRODUCTION TO DATABASE MANAGEMENT

■ Chapter Outline

The purpose of this chapter is to give you an understanding of how data resources are managed in information systems by analyzing basic concepts and applications of database management.

Section I of this chapter introduces the concept of data resource management and stresses the advantages of the database management approach versus the file processing approach in information systems. It also stresses the role of database management system software and the database administration function.

Section II surveys some of the more technical concepts in database management, including basic concepts of database organization and development, and methods of database and file organization and processing.

After reading and studying this chapter, you should be able to:

1. Explain the importance of data resource management and how it is implemented by methods such as database administration, data administration, and data planning.

2. Outline the advantages of the database management approach versus file processing methods.

3. Explain the uses of database management software in terms of end users, programmers, and database management applications.

4. Provide examples to illustrate each of the following concepts:
   a. Logical data elements.
   b. Fundamental database structures.
   c. Major types of databases.
   d. Database development.
   e. Sequential versus direct access organization and processing.

Section I: An Overview of Database Management

Data is a vital organizational resource. That's why organizations and their managers need to practice *data resource management*—a managerial activity that applies information systems technology and management tools to the task of managing an organization's data resources. Data resource management is an important focus for today's managers. This chapter will show you the managerial implications of some early attempts to manage data with information systems technology (*file processing*), as well as with more current technologies and methods (*database management*). We will also introduce the broader data resource management concepts of *database administration*, *data administration*, and *data planning*.

A MANAGER'S VIEW OF FILE AND DATABASE PROCESSING

How would you feel if you were an executive of a computer-using company and were told that some information you wanted about your employees was too difficult and too costly to obtain? Suppose the vice president of information services gave you the following reasons:

- ☐ The information you want is in several different files, each organized in a different way.
- ☐ Each file has been organized to be used by a different application program, none of which produces the information you want in the form you need.
- ☐ No application program is available to help get the information you want from these files.

Figure 6–1 shows a summary of the information you want and its related files and programs.

As a company executive, you would probably be frustrated and disenchanted with computer-based processing if it could not provide you with information for such a simple request. Well, that's how end users can be frustrated when an organization relies on *file processing systems* in which data are organized, stored, and processed in independent files of data records. In the **database management approach,** on the other hand, files are consolidated into a common pool, or *database*, of records available to many different application programs. In addition, an important system software package called a **database management system** (DBMS) serves as a software interface between end users and databases. This helps end users easily access the records in a database. For

Figure 6–1 An example of independent files and programs for information on employees.

Information Requested	File	Application Program
Employee salary	Payroll file	Payroll program
Educational background	Employee skills file	Skills inventory program
Salary increases and promotions	Personnel action file	Personnel action program

```
INQUIRY:    SELECT Name, Salary, Degrees, Last Promotion
            FROM Employee
            WHERE ID = 575-38-6473
RESPONSE:   Employee = 575-38-6473
            Name = Joan K. Alvarez
            Salary = $45,000
            Degrees = BA: 1974, MBA: 1976
            Last Promotion = Store Manager: 1984
```

Figure 6-2 An example of inquiry and response using a database management system program and a common employee database (instead of independent files and programs).

example, if all data about an employee were stored in a common database, you could use the *query language* feature of a DBMS and a computer terminal to easily obtain the employee information you want. See Figure 6–2.

For many years, information systems had a *file processing orientation,* as illustrated in the previous example. Data needed for each user application was stored in independent data files. Processing consisted of using separate computer programs that updated these independent data files and produced the documents and reports required by each separate user application. This file processing approach is still being used, but it has several major problems that limit its efficiency and effectiveness for end user applications.

MANAGEMENT PROBLEMS OF FILE PROCESSING

Data Duplication

Independent data files include a lot of duplicated data. The same data (such as a customer's name and address) is recorded and stored in several files. This data *redundancy* causes problems when data has to be updated since separate *file maintenance* programs have to be developed and coordinated to ensure that each file is properly updated. Of course, this proves difficult in practice, so a lot of *inconsistency* occurs among data stored in separate files. File maintenance is a time-consuming and costly process, and duplicated data increases the storage requirements of computer systems.

Lack of Data Integration

Independent data files make it difficult to provide end users with information for any ad hoc requests that require accessing data stored in several different files (as the example illustrated in Figure 6–1 emphasized). Special computer programs have to be written to retrieve data from each independent file. This is so difficult, time-consuming, and costly for some organizations that it is impossible to provide end users or management with such information. If necessary, end users have to manually extract the required information from the various reports produced by each separate application and prepare customized reports for management.

Data Dependence

In file processing systems, major components of the system—the organization of files, their physical locations on storage hardware, and the application software used to access those files—depend on one another in significant ways. For example, application programs typically contain references to the specific *format* of the data stored in the files they use. Thus, changes in the format and structure of data and records in a file require that changes be made to all of the programs that use that file. This *program maintenance* effort is a major burden of file processing systems. It proves difficult to do properly, and it results in a lot of inconsistency in the data files.

Other Problems

In file processing systems, it is easy for data elements such as stock numbers and customer addresses to be defined differently by different end users and applications. This causes serious inconsistency problems in the development of programs to access such data. In addition, the *integrity* (that is, the accuracy and completeness) of the data is suspect because there is no control over its use and maintenance by authorized end users. Such inconsistency and lack of integrity are extremely difficult to control because there is no central *dictionary* to keep track of data definitions and their authorized use in the organization. Thus, a lack of standards causes major problems in application program development and maintenance, and in the security and integrity of the data files needed by an organization.

THE DATABASE MANAGEMENT SOLUTION

The concepts *databases* and *database management* were developed to solve the problems of file processing systems. A **database** is an integrated collection of logically related records and files. It consolidates records previously stored in independent files so that it serves as a common pool of data to be accessed by many different application programs. The data stored in a database is independent of the computer programs using it and of the type of secondary storage devices on which it is stored. **Database management** involves the control of how databases are created, interrogated, and maintained to provide information needed by end users and the organization.

Figures 6–3 and 6–4 contrast the file processing and database management approaches with examples from the banking industry. Note in Figure 6–3 that it would be difficult to selectively gather information from three differently organized files (savings, installment loans, and checking accounts) about bank customers in the file processing approach. The database management approach, on the other hand, could easily handle such an assignment because of how it accomplishes the *storage* and *processing* of data.

Database Storage

Common databases are developed in the database processing approach. Each contains a directory, or *data dictionary*, which describes its data contents and interrelationships. This helps to ensure data integrity, consistency, processing efficiency, and reliability. The data needed by many different applications in an organization are consolidated and integrated into several common databases, instead of being stored in many independent data files. For example, customer records and other common types of data are needed for several different applications in banking, such as check processing, automated teller systems, bank credit cards, savings accounts, and installment loan accounting. This data can be consolidated into a common customer database, rather than being kept in separate files for each of those applications.

Database Processing

File processing involves updating and using independent data files to produce information needed for each end user's application. However, *database processing* consists of three basic activities:

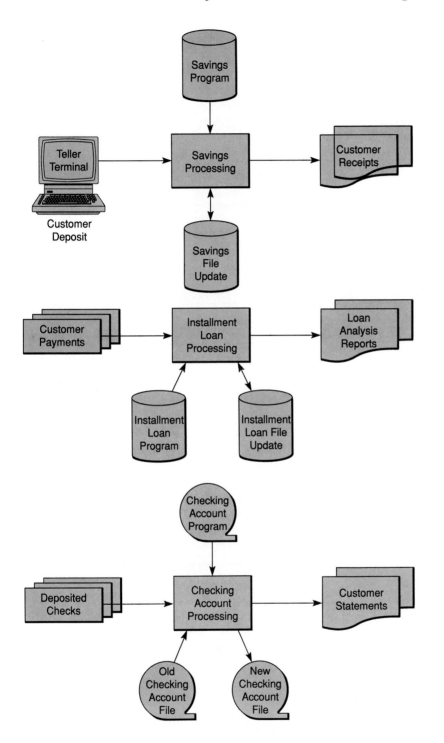

Figure 6-3 Examples of file processing systems in banking. Note the use of separate computer programs and independent data files in a file processing approach to the savings, installment loan, and checking account applications.

☐ Updating and maintaining common databases to reflect new business transactions and other events requiring changes to an organization's records.

☐ Providing information needed for each end user's application by using computer programs that share the data in common databases. This is

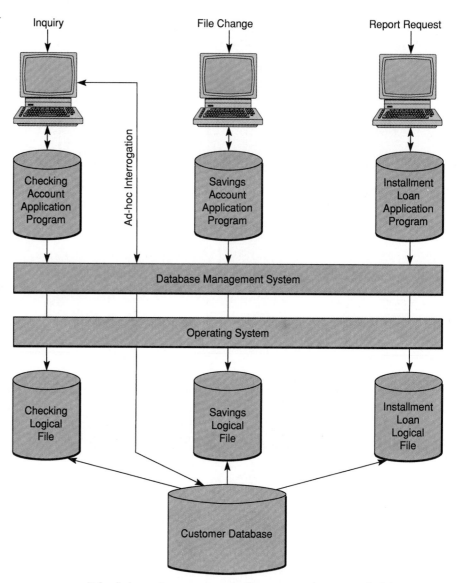

Figure 6–4 An example of a database management approach in a banking information system. Note how the savings, checking, and installment loan programs use a *database management system* to share a customer database, as if it were organized into separate logical files. Note also that the DBMS allows a user to make a direct, ad hoc interrogation of the database without using application programs.

accomplished through a common *software interface* provided by a database management system package. Thus, end users and programmers do not have to know where or how data are physically stored.

☐ Providing an inquiry/response capability through a DBMS package so that end users can easily interrogate databases and receive quick responses to their routine or ad hoc requests for information.

USING DATABASE MANAGEMENT SYSTEMS

Let's take a closer look at the capabilities provided by database management system software. A **database management system** (DBMS) is a set of computer programs that controls the creation, maintenance, and use of the databases of an organization and its end users. As we said in Chapter 4, database management packages are available for micro, mini, and mainframe computer systems. Figure 6–5 illustrates the components of a typical DBMS. The four major uses of a DBMS are illustrated in Figure 6–6. Let's take a look at each of them now.

Figure 6–5 Components of a database management system package. This figure emphasizes that a DBMS is a system of programs that perform a variety of database management functions.

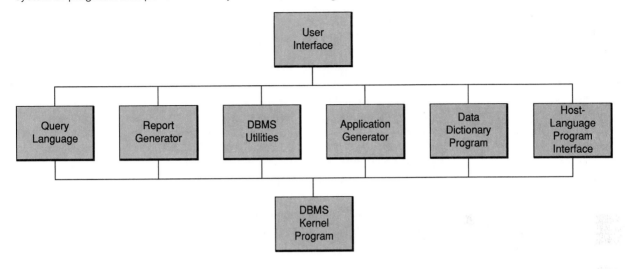

Figure 6–6 The four major uses of a DBMS package: (1) database development, (2) database interrogation and reporting, (3) application development, (4) database maintenance.

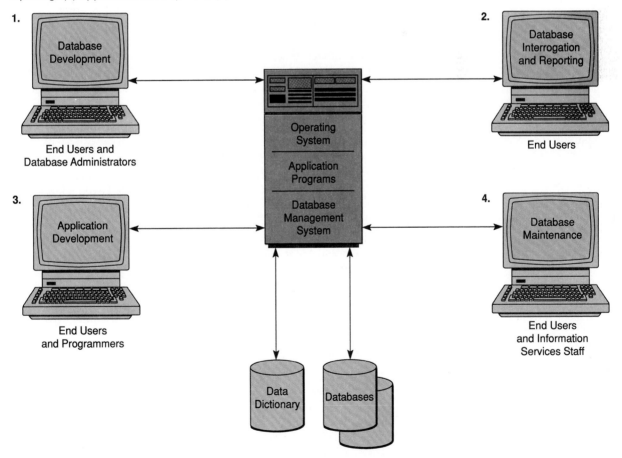

Database Development

A DBMS allows end users to easily develop the databases they need. However, a DBMS also allows organizations to place control of organizationwide database development in the hands of specialists called **database administrators** (DBAs). This improves the integrity and security of organizational databases. The database administrator uses a data definition language (DDL) to develop and specify the data contents, relationships, and structure of each database. The database administrator also uses the DDL to modify these database specifications when necessary. Such information is cataloged and stored in a database of data definitions and specifications, called a *data dictionary*, which is maintained by the DBA.

The Data Dictionary

The **data dictionary** has become a major tool of database administration. It is a software module and database containing *meta-data*, that is, data about data. The data dictionary contains meta-data about the structure, data elements, and other characteristics of an organization's databases. For example, it contains the names and descriptions of all types of data records and their interrelationships, as well as information outlining requirements for end user access, use of applications programs, and database security.

Data dictionaries can be queried by the database administrator to report the status of any aspect of a firm's meta-data. The administrator can then make changes to the definitions of selected data elements. Some *active* (versus *passive*) data dictionaries also automatically enforce standard data element definitions whenever end users and application programs use a DBMS to access an organization's databases. For example, an active data dictionary would not allow a data entry program to use a nonstandard definition of a customer record, nor would it allow a data entry operator to enter a name of a customer that exceeded the defined size of that data element. See Figure 6–7.

Database Interrogation and Reporting

You can use a DBMS to ask for information from a database and receive an immediate response in the form of video displays or printed reports. No difficult programming is required. A **query language** feature lets you easily obtain immediate responses to ad hoc inquiries: you merely key in a few short inquiries. A **report generator** feature allows you to quickly specify a report format for information you want presented as a report. See Figure 6–8.

Figure 6–2 illustrated the use of a query language for a simple request for employee information. Some query languages support the use of *natural language* inquiries. Examples of these were shown in Chapter 4. A query language that is becoming a standard for advanced database management system packages is called SQL, or *structured query language*. The basic form of an SQL query is:

```
SELECT  ...  FROM  ...  WHERE
```

For example, if a financial manager wanted to display the names of all employees who are financial analysts, he or she would use the following SQL query:

```
SELECT NAME
FROM EMPLOYEE
WHERE CLASSIFICATION = "FINANCIAL ANALYST"
```

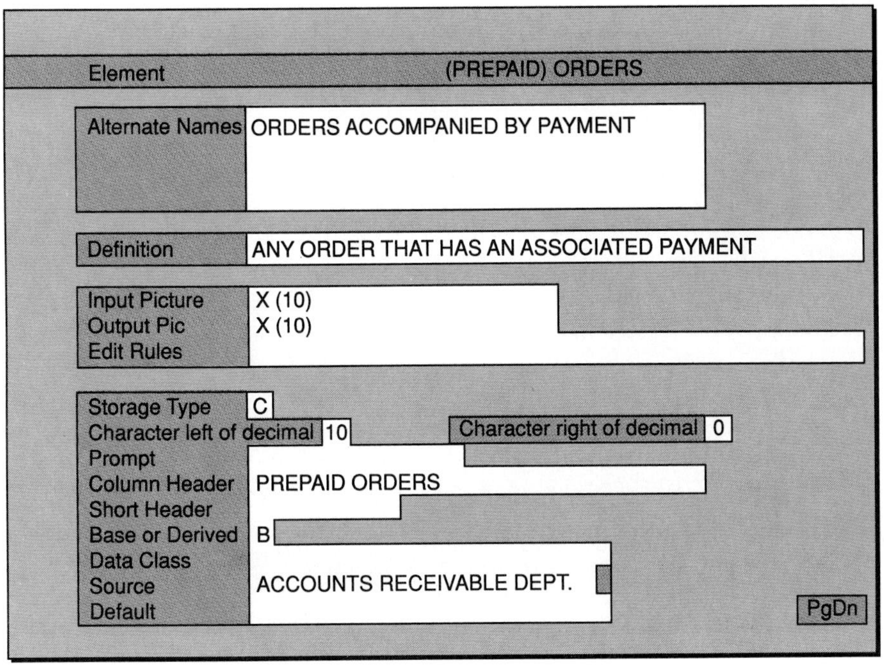

Figure 6–7 A display of part of the information in a data dictionary for an accounts receivable data element.

Courtesy Index Technology Corporation.

Application Development

A DBMS facilitates the job of programmers since they do not have to develop detailed data-handling program code using a conventional programming language (a *host* language, such as COBOL) every time they write a program. Instead, they can include *data manipulation language* (DML) statements in their application programs, which let the DBMS perform necessary data-handling activities. Programmers can also use the internal programming language provided by many DBMS packages, or a built-in application generator. Figure 6–9 shows the use of an application generator to develop an order entry program.

Database Maintenance

The databases of an organization need to be updated continually to reflect new business transactions and other events. Other miscellaneous changes must also be made to assure the accuracy of the data in the databases. This process is accomplished by transaction processing programs and other end user application packages, with the support of the DBMS. End users and information specialists can also employ various *utilities* provided by a DBMS for database maintenance.

TYPES OF DATABASES

The growth of distributed processing, end user computing, and decision support systems has caused the development of several major types of databases. Figure 6–10 illustrates five major types of databases for computer-using organizations:

☐ **Common operational databases.** These databases store detailed data needed to support the operations of the entire organization. They also may be called *subject area databases* (SADB), *transaction databases*,

Figure 6-8 Using a report generator module of the dBASE IV database management package.

A. A Report Specification Screen

B. The Report Produced

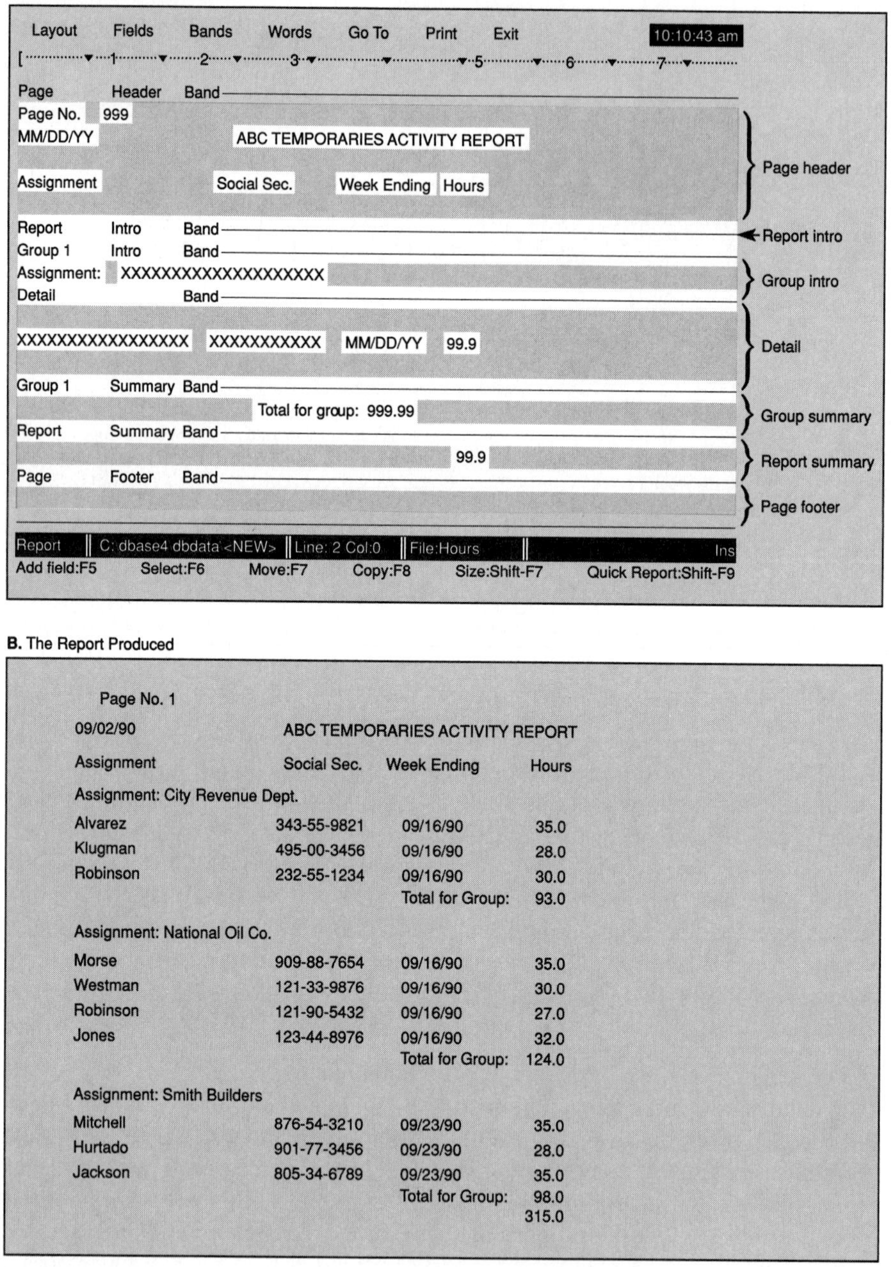

Page No. 1

09/02/90 ABC TEMPORARIES ACTIVITY REPORT

Assignment	Social Sec.	Week Ending	Hours
Assignment: City Revenue Dept.			
Alvarez	343-55-9821	09/16/90	35.0
Klugman	495-00-3456	09/16/90	28.0
Robinson	232-55-1234	09/16/90	30.0
		Total for Group:	93.0
Assignment: National Oil Co.			
Morse	909-88-7654	09/16/90	35.0
Westman	121-33-9876	09/16/90	30.0
Robinson	121-90-5432	09/16/90	27.0
Jones	123-44-8976	09/16/90	32.0
		Total for Group:	124.0
Assignment: Smith Builders			
Mitchell	876-54-3210	09/23/90	35.0
Hurtado	901-77-3456	09/23/90	28.0
Jackson	805-34-6789	09/23/90	35.0
		Total for Group:	98.0
			315.0

Source: Adapted from Edward Jones, *Using dBASE IV* (Berkeley, Calif.: Osborne-McGraw-Hill, 1988), pp. 207–24.

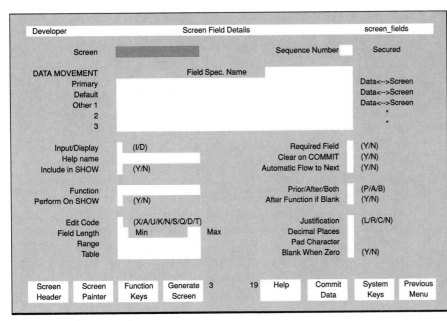

Courtesy Hewlett Packard.

Figure 6-9   Using a DBMS application generator: Allbase/4GL, from Hewlett-Packard. An analyst can develop a data entry screen display program by filling in this screen form. The application generator will generate the program code needed.

Figure 6-10   Examples of the major types of databases used by organizations and end users.

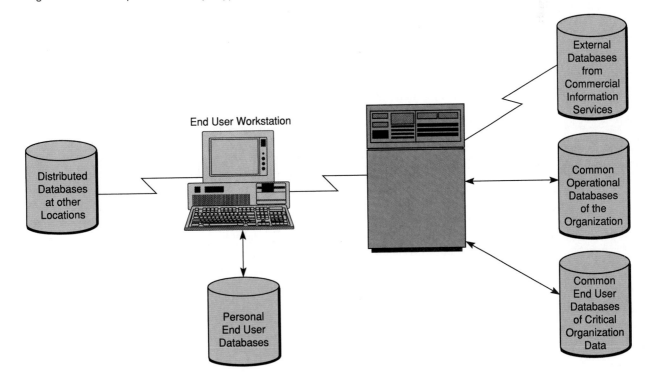

and *production databases*. Examples are a customer database, personnel database, accounting database, and other common databases containing data generated by business operations.

☐ **Common end user databases.** These databases store data and information extracted from selected operational and external databases. They consist of summarized data and information most needed by the organization's managers and other end users. They are also called *information databases* and *management databases*. These are the databases accessed by executive end users as part of *decision support systems* and *executive information systems* to support managerial decision making.

☐ **Distributed databases.** These are databases of local work groups and departments at regional offices, branch offices, manufacturing plants, and other work sites. These databases can include segments of both common operational and common user databases, as well as data generated and used only at a user's own site. Assuring that all of the data in an organization's distributed databases are consistently and concurrently updated is a major consideration of data resource management.

☐ **Personal end user databases.** These databases consist of a variety of data files developed by end users at their workstations. For example, users may have their own electronic copies of documents they generated with word processing packages or received by electronic mail. Or they may have their own data files generated from electronic spreadsheet and microcomputer DBMS packages.

☐ **External databases.** Access to large, privately owned databases, or **data banks,** is available for a fee to end users and organizations from commercial information services networks, such as Interactive Data Corporation, Dow Jones Information Services, Lockheed Information Systems, and Mead Data Central. Data is available in the form of statistics on economic and demographic activity from *statistical* data banks. Or you can receive abstracts from hundreds of newspapers, magazines, and other periodicals from *bibliographic* data banks. Some of the data bank services even offer software to help end users analyze their data. See Figure 6–11.

Text Databases

Text databases are a natural outgrowth of the use of computers to create and store documents electronically. Commercial bibliographic data banks of business, economic, and other information are stored in large text databases. Some text databases are marketed on CD-ROM optical disks for use with microcomputer systems. Major corporations and government agencies have developed large text databases containing documents of all kinds. They use *text database management systems* software to help create, store, search, retrieve, modify, and assemble documents and other information stored as text data in such databases. Microcomputer versions of such software are available to help end users manage and use text databases.

Hypertext

Hypertext is an important methodology for the construction and interactive use of text databases. A *hypertext document* is a body of text of any size in electronic form that is indexed so that it can be quickly searched by the reader. For

Figure 6–11   Examples of the statistical and bibliographic data banks offered by commercial information services.

Dow Jones Information Service. Provides statistical data banks on stock market and other financial market activity, and in-depth financial statistics on all corporations listed on the New York and American stock exchanges, plus 800 selected other companies. Its Dow Jones News/Retrieval system provides bibliographic data banks on business, financial, and general news from *The Wall Street Journal, Barron's,* the Dow Jones News Service, The Associated Press, Wall Street Week, and the 21-volume American Academic Encyclopedia.

Mead Data Central. Offers two major bibliographic data banks. *Lexis* provides legal research information, such as case law, court decisions, federal regulations, and legal articles. *Nexis* provides a full text bibliographic database of over 100 newspapers, magazines, newsletters, news services, government documents, and so on. It includes full text and abstracts from the *New York Times* and the complete 29-volume Encyclopædia Britannica. Also provided is the Advertising & Marketing Intelligence (AMI) data bank, and the National Automated Accounting Research System.

Lockheed Information Systems. Its DIALOG system offers over 75 different data banks in agriculture, business, economics, education, energy, engineering, environment, foundations, general news publications, government, international business, patents, pharmaceuticals, science, and social sciences.

CompuServe Personal computer network providing statistical data banks (business and financial market statistics) as well as bibliographic data banks (news, reference, library, and electronic encyclopedias).

example, if you highlight a term on a hypertext document displayed on your computer video screen and press a key, the computer could instantly bring up a display of a passage of text related to that term. Once you finished reading that *pop-up* display, you could return to what you were reading originally or jump to another part of the document instantly. Thus, the use of hypertext provides an environment for *interactive reading* of a document.

There are several software packages available for the development of hypertext documents. One of the most widely used is the HyperCard package for the Apple Macintosh microcomputer. In HyperCard, the basic unit of text is called a *card.* A hypertext document consists of *stacks,* or collections, of interrelated and indexed cards. Thus, hypertext document packages are known as *stackware.* Hypertext documents can be programmed to let a reader *navigate* through a document by following one or more *scripts.* This creates a hypertext document that can lead the reader through the document several different ways [4].

By definition, hypertext contains only text and a limited amount of graphics. *Hypermedia* are documents that contain multiple forms of media, including text, graphics, video, and so on. Proponents of hypertext and hypermedia expect electronic documents such as these to become as popular as more traditional paper documents such as books, magazines, and newspapers. Figure 6–12 shows part of a hypertext display, as well as a diagram of the components of the Perseus Hypermedia Project. Perseus will contain up to 100 megabytes of hypertext and 10,000 hypermedia images of the ancient Greek civilizations [1].

A MANAGERIAL PERSPECTIVE

End users should view data as an important resource that they must learn to manage properly to ensure the success and survival of their organizations. Database management is an important application of information systems technology to the management of a firm's data resources. However, other major data resource management efforts are needed in order to offset some of the problems that can result from the use of a database management approach. Those are (1) database administration, (2) data administration, and (3) data

Figure 6–12 Hypertext and hypermedia.

A. A Hypertext Display

Definition

"Hypertext" is non-sequentially linked pieces of text or other information. If the focus of such a system is on ✓ non-textual types* of information, the term hypermedia is often used instead ██████████████ ed documents, practically the only s ██████████████ s the footnote, so hypertext is often ref ██████████████ neralized footnote".

E.g. graphics, sound, moving images from videodisks, executable programs.

The things which we can link to or from are called nodes, and the whole system will form a network of nodes interconnected with links. Links may be typed and/ or have attributes, and they may be one or bi-directional. The user accesses the information in the nodes by navigating the links. ✓Frank Halasz would add to the definition that this navigation should be aided by a structural overview (which e. g. HyperCard does not have!).

This display shows the small pop-up screen which appeared when the Hypertext anchor (the finger pointing hand) was first moved to and clicked on (by use of a mouse) at the term *non-textual types*. The anchor has now been moved to the term *HyperCard*, which will be the topic of the next screen viewed.

B. Diagram of a Hypermedia System

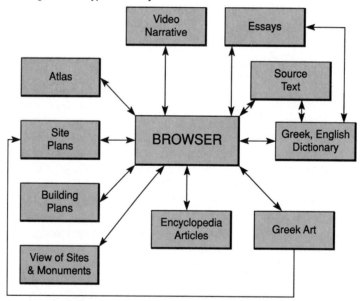

This diagram illustrates some of the categories that will appear in the Perseus Hypermedia package. A browser will serve as a central clearinghouse that allows readers to move from one part of the database to another. For example, you might select the topic "Athens" and ask to see where that appears in the Atlas or view a video clip, series of photos, or an article about Athens in the encyclopedia.

Source: Adapted from Jacob Nielsen, "The Art of Navigating through Hypertext," *Communications of the ACM*, March 1990, p. 303; and Gregory Crane, "Challenging the Individual: The Tradition of Hypermedia Databases," *Academic Computing*, January 1990, p. 35.

planning. These concepts are discussed briefly here and again in Chapter 12 and 13.

The database management approach provides managerial end users with several important benefits. Database management reduces duplication of data and integrates data so that they can be accessed by multiple programs and end users. Programs are not dependent on the format of the data and the type of secondary storage hardware being used. Users are provided with an inquiry/response capability that allows them to easily obtain information they need without having to write computer programs. Computer programming is simplified because programs are not dependent on either the logical format of the data or their physical storage location. Finally, the integrity and security of the data stored in databases can be increased since access to data and modification of the database is controlled by database management software, a data dictionary, and a database administrator function.

However, the limitations of database management arising from its increased complexity pose problems in data resource management. Developing a large database and installing a DBMS can be difficult and expensive. More hardware capability is required since storage requirements for the organization's data, overhead control data, and the DBMS programs are greater. Longer processing times may result from high-volume transaction processing applications since an extra layer of software (the DBMS) exists between application programs and the operating system. Finally, if an organization relies on one central database, its vulnerability to errors, fraud, and failures is increased. Yet problems of inconsistency of data can arise if a distributed database approach is used. Therefore, the security and integrity of an organization's databases are major concerns of an organization's data resource management effort.

Database administration is an important data resource management function responsible for the proper use of database management technology. Database administration has more operational and technical responsibilities than other data resource management functions. These include responsibilities for developing and maintaining the organization's data dictionary, designing and monitoring the performance of databases, and enforcing standards for database use and security. Database administrators work with systems analysts, programmers, and end users to provide their expertise to major systems development projects. Figure 6–13 illustrates the many important activities of database administration in support of the applications of end users and the organization.

Data administration is another vital data resource management function. It involves the establishment and enforcement of policies and procedures for managing data as a strategic corporate resource. This means that collection, storage, and dissemination of all types of data are administered in such a way that data become a standardized resource available to all end users in the organization. Thus, a data administrator must learn to work with the diverse business units and work groups in an organization, many of whom are uncomfortable with any attempt to dictate the use of "their data."

Data administration typically is an organization-wide managerial function without the operational and technical focus of database administration. Its focus

Benefits and Limitations of Database Management

Database Administration

Data Administration

Figure 6-13 The activities of the database administration function.

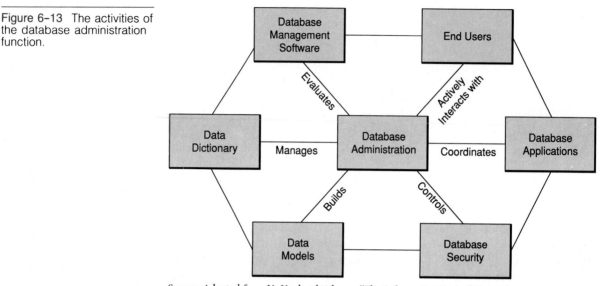

Source: Adapted from V. Venkatakrishnan, "The Information Cycle," *Datamation,* September 1983.

is the planning and control of data in support of an organization's business functions and strategic business objectives. A major thrust of data administration, therefore, is the establishment of a data planning activity for the entire organization. Data administration may also include responsibility for developing policies and setting standards for corporate database design, processing, and security arrangements, and for selecting database management and data dictionary software.

Data Planning

Data planning is a corporate planning and analysis function that focuses on data resource management. It includes the responsibility for developing an overall *information policy* and a *data architecture* for the firm's data resources that ties in with the firm's strategic mission and plans as well as the objectives and processes of its business units [2]. Data planning is thus a major component of an organization's strategic planning process. It is a formal commitment to long-range planning by an organization for the strategic use and management of its data resources. In the next section we will discuss how data planning is an important first step in developing databases for an organization.

The Seattle Symphony and Herberger Theatre Center

SQL database management technology has allowed users such as the Seattle Symphony to personalize their ticketing and fund-raising efforts to a degree never possible before, according to the symphony's systems director, Deborah Braun.

The symphony is a user of Artsoft/SQL, a database management system add-on package that was recently introduced for the entertainment industry by Hill Art & Entertainment Systems, based in Guilford, Connecticut. Hill A&E also introduced Sportsoft/SQL, a sports facility version of the product. The two packages are said to provide an integrated set of business management applications, including marketing, ticketing, accounting, fund-raising, and box office management, based on the use of Sybase, an SQL-based relational database management system. The packages thus run on a wide range of computers and local area networks.

"The biggest overall improvement is that the new system revolves around the patron as a person," Braun said. "We really like some of the ticketing features." For example, a three-dimensional seating chart allows box office telephone operators to check seating availability for not just one, but a whole series of concerts at one time. Another plus from the new system is the ability to find the best available seat "with the touch of a button instead of having to hunt around the charts," Braun said.

The difference between the new and old software's user interface is "like night and day," stated Leon Scioscia, general manager at the Herberger Theatre Center in Phoenix. The theater was an early user of the original Artsoft product and the new Artsoft/SQL. "The old system worked, but it couldn't do two different functions at the same time," Scioscia said. In contrast, the new system's windowed environment allows the user to "add, change, or delete information in a patron's record, or days and dates for performances, at any time, without having to back out of the menu to select a change mode," he added. Artsoft/SQL also provides a facility for developing scripts to guide inexperienced box office personnel through a particular procedure. This training aid is vital because "box office tellers aren't usually the kind of people who stay around a long time; we do have turnover," Scioscia said.

Both Scioscia and Braun were particularly impressed with how Sybase and Artsoft/SQL provide flexible reporting capabilities, which enables users to cross-reference subscribers according to a virtually unlimited number of variables. This is a tremendous boon to the symphony's marketing and fund-raising staffs, who are "always looking for a new base of people to hit" with targeted mailings, Braun said. Artsoft/SQL and Sybase "allows us to go into our database and use SQL queries to say, for example, 'Find all the people who came last year and saw three musical presentations,'" Scioscia said. It would then take only a few keystrokes to compile a list of such subscribers, sort it by address, and merge it with a letter inviting the people to subscribe to a special, musicals-only package, Scioscia said.

Both users also praised Artsoft/SQL's real-time database updating, a crucial feature when a dozen or so box office operators are simultaneously assigning seats for the same productions. "To my knowledge, we have not assigned the same seat to two people yet," Braun reported.

Application Questions

☐ Is this an example of the use of the database management approach? Why or why not?

☐ What five major benefits using Artsoft/SQL and Sybase are provided to the Seattle Symphony and Herberger Theatre Center?

☐ Why do you think the Artsoft/SQL package was designed to be used with the Sybase database management system?

Source: Adapted from Elisabeth Horwitt, "Entertaining the Idea of SQL-Based Systems," *Computerworld*, February 19, 1990, pp. 57, 60.

Section II: Technical Foundations of Database Management

Just imagine how difficult it would be to get any information from an information system if data were stored in an unorganized way or if there was no systematic way to retrieve it. Therefore, in all information systems, data resources must be organized and structured in some logical manner so that they can be accessed easily, processed efficiently, retrieved quickly, and managed effectively. Thus, *data structures* and *access methods* ranging from simple to complex have been devised to efficiently organize and access data stored by information systems. In this section, we will explore these and other more technical concepts of database management.

LOGICAL DATA ELEMENTS

As we first mentioned in Chapter 1, a hierarchy of several levels of data has been devised that differentiates between the most simple groupings, or *elements,* of data and more complex data elements. Thus, data are organized into **characters, fields, records, files,** and **databases,** just as writing can be organized in letters, words, sentences, paragraphs, and documents. Examples of these **logical data elements** are shown in Figure 6–14.

Character

The most basic logical data element is the **character,** which consists of a single alphabetic, numeric, or other symbol. One might argue that the *bit* or *byte* is a more elementary data element, but remember that those terms refer to the *physical* storage elements provided by the computer hardware, discussed in Chapter 3. From a user's point of view (that is, from a *logical* as opposed to a *physical* or hardware view of data), a character is the most basic element of data that can be observed and manipulated.

Figure 6–14 Examples of the logical data elements in information systems. Note especially the examples of data fields, records, files, and a database.

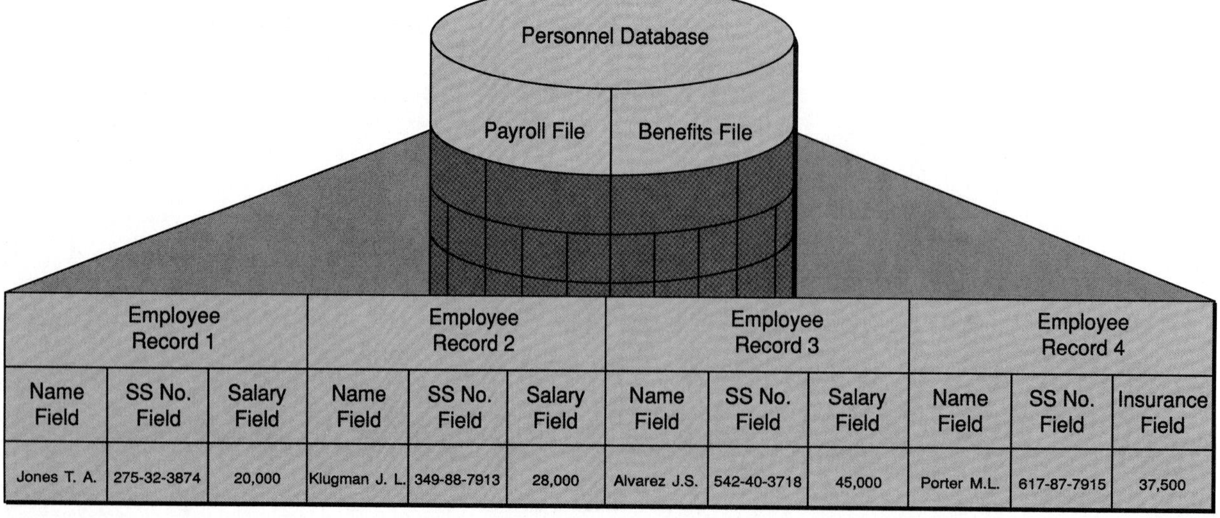

The next higher level of data is the **field,** or *data* item. A field consists of a grouping of characters. For example, the grouping of alphabetic characters in a person's name forms a *name field*, and the grouping of numeric characters in a sales amount forms a *sales amount field*. Specifically, a data field represents an **attribute** (a characteristic or quality) of some **entity** (person, place, thing, or event). For example, a person's age could be a data field that represents one of the many attributes of an individual.

Field

Related fields of data are grouped to form a **record.** Thus, a record represents a collection of attributes that describes an entity. An example is a person's payroll record, which consists of data fields such as the person's name, social security number, and rate of pay. *Fixed-length* records contain a fixed number of fixed-length data fields. *Variable-length* records contain a variable number of fields and field lengths.

Record

A group of related records is known as a data **file.** Thus, an *employee file* would contain the records of the employees of a firm. Files are frequently classified by the application for which they are primarily used, such as a *payroll file* or an *inventory file*. Files are also classified by their permanence—for example, a payroll *master file* versus a payroll *weekly transaction file*. A payroll **transaction file,** therefore, would contain records of all payroll transactions occurring during a period and would be used periodically to update the permanent records contained in a payroll **master file.** A *history file* is an obsolete transaction or master file retained for backup purposes or for long-term, historical storage, called *archival storage*. A **program file** (as opposed to a *data file*) is a file that contains a computer program, such as a spreadsheet program file.

File

A **database** is an integrated collection of logically related records and files. A database consolidates records previously stored in separate files into a common pool of data records that can be accessed by many different application programs. For example, a *personnel database* such as that illustrated in Figure 6–15, consolidates data formerly segregated in separate files such as payroll

Database

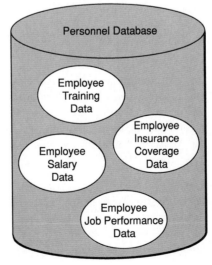

Figure 6–15 A personnel database consolidates data formerly kept in separate files.

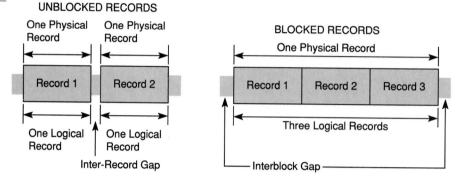

Figure 6–16 Blocked and unblocked records. Note how this illustrates the concept of logical versus physical records.

files, personnel action files, and employee skills files. Thus, a personnel database would allow easy access to different types of employee data that might be needed by a personnel manager. A database also contains a directory *(data dictionary)*, which describes its field, record, and file contents and their interrelationships. This makes it easier to change the structure of a database to meet changing end user requirements. Refer back to Figures 6–3 and 6–4 for examples of how the use of databases affects information systems in banking.

Logical and Physical Data Elements

In information systems, a distinction is made between *logical* and *physical* data elements. **Logical data elements** are units of data that are independent of the data media on which they are recorded. On the other hand, **physical data elements** are related to the data media being used to store logical records. For example, several data files and program files (logical files) may be stored on a single floppy disk, which can be considered as one physical file.

Another example: A magnetic tape or disk file may contain blank spaces *(gaps)* between groups *(blocks)* of logical records. A block of logical records on magnetic tape or disk is considered a physical record. Interrecord or interblock gaps are required since a certain amount of blank space between records or blocks is needed to allow for such mechanical operations as the start/stop time of a magnetic tape unit. Most files group logical records into blocks to conserve file space, instead of leaving gaps between each logical record. See Figure 6–16.

DATABASE STRUCTURES

The relationships among the many individual records stored in databases are based on one of several *logical data structures*, or *models*. Database management system packages are designed to use a specific data structure to provide end users with quick, easy access to information stored in databases. There are several fundamental database structures, of which the **hierarchical, network,** and **relational** models are the most widely used. Simplified illustrations of these three database structures are shown in Figure 6–17.

Hierarchical Structure

In the **hierarchical** structure, the relationships between records form a *hierarchy,* or tree structure. In this model, all records are dependent and arranged in multilevel structures, consisting of one *root* record and any number of *subordinate* levels. Thus, all of the relationships among records are *one-to-*

HIERARCHICAL STRUCTURE

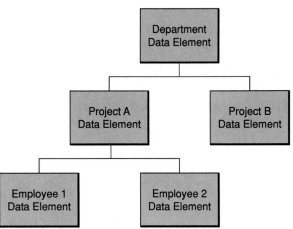

Figure 6-17 Examples of three fundamental database structures. They represent three basic ways to develop and express the relationships among the data elements in a database.

NETWORK STRUCTURE

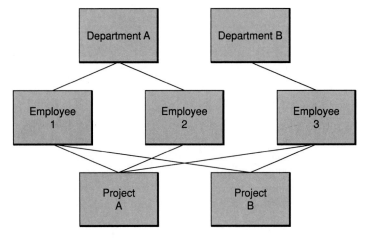

RELATIONAL STRUCTURE

Department Records

Dept No	D Name	D Loc	D Mgr
Dept A			
Dept B			
Dept C			

Employee Records

Emp No	E Name	E Title	E Salary	Dept No
Emp 1				Dept A
Emp 2				Dept A
Emp 3				Dept B
Emp 4				Dept B
Emp 5				Dept C
Emp 6				Dept B

many since each data element is related only to one element above it. The data element or record at the highest level of the hierarchy (the *department* data element in this illustration) is called the *root*. Data elements are stored and located directly by using an identifying or *key* field or by moving progressively downward from a root and along the *branches* of the tree until the desired record (for example, the employee data element) is located.

Network Structure

The **network** structure can represent more complex logical relationships. It allows *many-to-many* relationships among records—that is, the network model allows entry into a database at multiple points because any data element or record can be related to any number of other data elements. For example, in Figure 6–17, departmental records can be related to more than one employee record, and employee records can be related to more than one project record. Thus, one could locate all employee records for a particular department or all project records related to a particular employee.

Relational Structure

The **relational** model was developed in an attempt to simplify the representation of relationships among data elements in large databases. In this approach, all data elements within the database are viewed as being stored in the form of simple tables. Figure 6–17 illustrates the relational database model with two tables representing some of the relationships among departmental and employee records. Other tables, or *relations*, for this organization's database might represent the data element relationships among projects, divisions, product lines, and so on. Database management system packages based on the relational model can link data elements from various tables to provide information to users.

Object-Oriented Structure

Other database models are being developed to provide capabilities missing from the hierarchical, network, and relational structures. One example is the **object-oriented** database model. We introduced the concept of *objects* when we discussed *object-oriented programming* in Chapter 4. An object consists of data values describing the attributes and relationships of an entity, plus the methods and processes that can be performed upon the data. This capability is called *encapsulation*, and it allows the object-oriented model to better handle more complex types of data (graphics, pictures, voice, text) than other database structures. The object-oriented model also supports *inheritance*, that is, new objects can be automatically created by replicating some or all of the characteristics of one or more *parent objects*. Such capabilities have made object-oriented database management systems (OODBMS) popular in computer-aided design (CAD), and similar applications. For example, they allow designers to develop product designs, store them as objects in an object-oriented database, and replicate and modify them to create new product designs.

Evaluation of Database Structures

The hierarchical data structure is a natural model for databases used in structured, routine types of transaction processing characteristic of many business operations. Data for many of these operations can easily be represented by groups of records in a hierarchical relationship. However, there are many cases where information is needed about records that do not have hierarchical relationships. For example, it is obvious that in some organizations, employees from more than one department can work on more than one project (see Figure 6–17). A network data structure could easily handle this many-to-many relationship. It is thus more flexible than the hierarchical structure in support of databases for many types of business operations. However, like the hierarchical structure, because its relationships must be specified in advance, the network model cannot easily handle ad hoc requests for information.

Relational databases, on the other hand, allow an end user to easily receive information in response to ad hoc requests. That's because all of the relationships between the data elements in a relationally organized database do not need to be specified when the database is created, as is the case with the hierarchical and network structures. Database management software (such as Oracle, DB2, dBase IV, and Paradox) create new tables of data relationships using parts of the data from several tables. Thus, relational databases are easier for programmers to work with and easier to maintain than the hierarchical and network models. The major limitation of the relational model is that database management systems based on it cannot process large amounts of business transactions as quickly and efficiently as those based on the hierarchical and network models, in which all data relationships are prespecified. However, this performance gap is narrowing with the development of advanced relational DBMS software, including some with object-oriented capabilities. The use of database management software based on the object-oriented model is growing steadily, but this technology is still not fully developed enough for broad business use.

DATABASE DEVELOPMENT

Developing small personal databases is relatively easy using microcomputer database management packages. However, developing a large database can be a complex task. In many companies, developing and managing large corporate databases are the primary responsibility of a database administrator and database design analysts. They work with end users and systems analysts to determine (1) what data definitions should be included in the database and (2) what relationships should exist among the data elements.

Data Planning, and Modeling

As Figure 6–18 illustrates, database development should start with a top-down **data planning** process. Database administrators and designers work with corporate and end user management to develop an *enterprise model* that defines the basic business processes of the enterprise. Then they develop *entity relationship models* that define the relationships among the many entities involved in business processes. For example, Figure 6–19 illustrates some of the relationships in a purchasing/receiving system. At this point, logical *subject area databases* (SADBs) can be identified. For example, subject area databases for customers, employees, vendors, and products could support many basic business operations.

Next, end users must identify the key data elements in the SABDs that are needed to perform specific business activities. For example, they would need to identify what customer and product data are necessary in the organization's order entry process. These *user views* are the basis for a **data modeling** step where the relationships between data elements are identified. Each *data model* defines the logical relationships among the data elements needed to support a basic business process. For example, can a customer have more than one type of account with us? Can an employee have several pay rates or be assigned to several project work groups? Answering such questions will identify data relationships that have to be represented in a data model.

These data models then serve as logical frameworks (called *schemas* and *subschemas*) for the *physical design* of databases and the development of application programs to support the business processes of the organization. A

Figure 6–18 Data planning ties a model of the business enterprise to data models used to develop databases and application programs for end users in the organization.

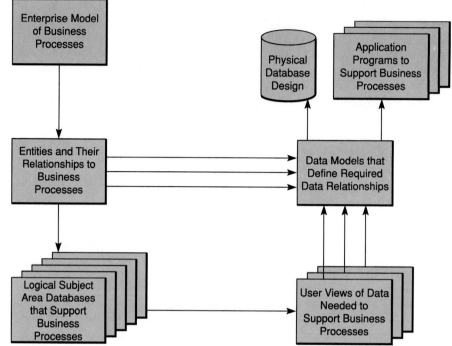

Source: Adapted from Dale Goodhue, Judith Quillard, and John Rockhart, "Managing the Data Resource: A Contingency Perspective," *MIS Quarterly*, September 1988, p. 381.

Figure 6–19 This entity relationship diagram illustrates some of the relationships among entities in a purchasing/receiving system.

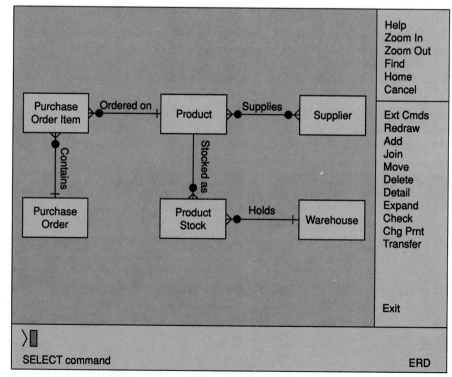

Courtesy of Texas Instruments.

schema is an overall logical view of the relationships between data in a database, while the *subschema* is a logical view of the data relationships needed to support specific end user application programs that will access that database.

Remember that data models (or schemas and subschemas) are *logical* views of the data and relationships of the database. Physical database design takes a *physical* view of the data (also called the *internal* view), which describes how data is to be physically arranged, stored, and accessed on the secondary storage devices of a computer system. For example, Figure 6–20 shows the multiple database views and software interface of a bank database processing system.

DATABASE AND FILE ORGANIZATION

Databases and files are stored on various types of storage media and are organized in a variety of ways to make it easier to *access* the data records they contain. In database and file processing, records have to be continually added, deleted, or updated to reflect business transactions. Data must also be accessed so information can be produced in response to end user requests. Thus, efficient access to data is important.

Figure 6–20 Examples of the logical and physical database views and the software interface of a database processing system in banking.

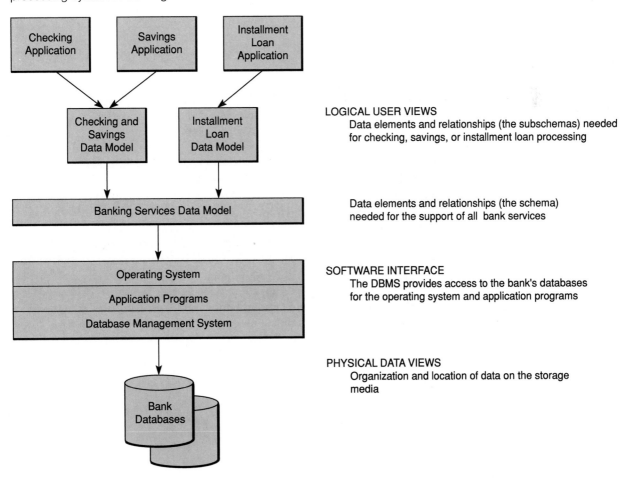

LOGICAL USER VIEWS
Data elements and relationships (the subschemas) needed for checking, savings, or installment loan processing

Data elements and relationships (the schema) needed for the support of all bank services

SOFTWARE INTERFACE
The DBMS provides access to the bank's databases for the operating system and application programs

PHYSICAL DATA VIEWS
Organization and location of data on the storage media

Sequential Organization

One of the basic ways to organize data is to use a sequential methodology, in which records are physically stored in a specified order according to an identifying field (called a *key field*) in each record. For example, payroll records could be placed in a payroll file in a numerical order based on employee social security numbers. The **sequential organization** is a method of data organization that is fast and efficient when dealing with large volumes of data that only need to be processed periodically. However, all new transactions must be sorted into their proper sequence for efficient *sequential access processing*. Also, most of the database or file may have to be searched to locate, store, or modify even a small number of data records. Thus, this method is too slow to handle applications requiring immediate updating or responses.

Direct Organization

In the **direct organization** method, records are not arranged in any particular sequence on the storage media. However, the computer must keep track of the storage location of each record, using a variety of methods, so that data can be retrieved when needed. New transactions data do not have to be sorted, and processing that requires immediate responses or updating is easily handled. There are a number of ways to access the records in the direct organization method. Let's take a look at three widely used *direct access processing* methods.

One common technique of direct access is called **key transformation.** This method performs an arithmetic computation on a key field of a record and uses the result of the calculation as an address for that record. Thus, the process is called key transformation because an arithmetic operation is applied to a key field to transform it into a storage location address. Another direct access method used to store and locate records involves the use of an **index** of record keys and related storage addresses. A new data record is stored at the next available location, and its key and address are placed in an index. The computer uses this index whenever it must access a record.

In the **indexed sequential access method** (ISAM), records are stored on magnetic disks or other direct access storage devices in a sequential order based on a key field of each record. In addition, each file includes an index which contains references to the storage location address of the key fields of each data record. Thus, an individual record can be directly located by using its key fields to search and locate its address in the file index, just as you can locate key topics in this book by looking them up in its index. As a result, if a few records must be processed quickly, the file index is used to directly access the records needed. However, the sequential organization of records provided by this method is used whenever large numbers of records must be processed on a periodic or occasional basis. For example, processing the weekly employee payroll or producing monthly statements for customers would be done using sequential access processing.

REAL WORLD CASE

Club Corporation International

To its 225,000 members, Club Corporation International means leisure, but for Clubcorp's financial and information subsidiary members, there is a serious side to business. "What we process is information that shows our managers all the strategic indicators of the operations," said Dan Barth, MIS director at Financial Management Corp. (FMC) in Dallas. With the information, officials in four regional offices are able to keep budgets in line but can also identify opportunities for expansions, club acquisitions, and new services.

FMC processes information from approximately 185 individual local country, dining, and health clubs under the Clubcorp umbrella. The firm uses 165 IBM System/36 minicomputers to post information to an IBM 4381 mainframe, and financial personnel in the regional offices snatch and analyze it on a variety of microcomputers. But before information reaches the PCs, it is fitted into meaningful form by database management software from Computer Associates International.

In the first step, FMC gleans information from the minicomputers at the individual clubs, which is processed by general ledger accounting software from McCormich & Dodge running on the mainframe. Once the company's general ledger is closed and reconciled, Barth said, it is summarized into about 100 indicators and stored in a financial database.

FMC runs two databases critical to Clubcorp's operations on its CA-Datacom/DB database management system. A membership database contains information on every member of Clubcorp, including information about their spouses, children, spending habits, and hobbies. The financial database contains four years of club history and club budgets divided into 13 periods per year. Furthermore, the 100 indicators are divided at the club level by region and by type of club within a region, according to Barth. Information about each of the company's clubs can be recaptured easily because it is identified by a three-digit number and then downloaded from the mainframe.

In addition, using the CA-Ideal fourth-generation language, FMC has built what Barth called several strategic applications that allow controllers to key into the databases and track the number of members that have been added and deleted. The four regional offices use either CA's Dataquery/PC for ad hoc queries or CA-Datacom/PC for downloading data necessary for analysis.

Using a CA-Datacom/PC procedure, regional office PCs automatically log on, download, and store data as well as export it to a spreadsheet—a process that formerly required manual entry. Further, regional managers who notice a discrepancy between expenditures within their region and the mean expenditures in the other regions can, for example, use CA-Dataquery/PC to pinpoint items that have exceeded budget.

CA-Dataquery/PC helps managers keep up with a dynamically changing industry, Barth said. "With it, we give the managers flexibility," he said. "Instead of writing an application, we give them a tool."

Application Questions

☐ Why is this an example of the use of a database management approach?

☐ What capabilities are provided by the various modules of the CA-Datacom/DB database management system?

☐ How do such capabilities help Clubcorp's managers?

Source: Adapted from Robert Moran, "There's a Flip Side to Frivolity," *Computerworld*, February 26, 1990, p. 31.

SUMMARY

☐ For many years, information systems had a file processing orientation, in which separate computer programs were used to update independent data files and produce the documents and reports required by each end user application. This caused problems of data duplication, unintegrated data, and data dependence. The concepts of databases and database management were developed to solve these problems.

☐ The database management approach affects the storage and processing of data. The data needed by different applications is consolidated and integrated into several common databases, instead of being stored in many independent data files. Also, the database management approach emphasizes updating and maintaining common databases, having users' application programs share the data in the database and providing an inquiry/response capability so end users can easily receive quick responses to requests for information.

☐ Database management systems are software packages that simplify the creation, use, and maintenance of databases. They provide software tools so end users, programmers, and database administrators can create and modify databases, interrogate a database, generate reports, do application development, and perform database maintenance.

☐ Several types of databases can exist in computer-using organizations, including common, distributed, end user, and external databases. Text databases consist of data in text form which is cataloged and indexed for quick retrieval as documents or other forms of information. Hypertext and hypermedia can be used to construct and interactively retrieve information from text and multimedia databases.

☐ Data resource management is a managerial activity that applies information systems technology and management tools to the task of managing an organization's data resources. It includes the database administration function, which focuses on developing and maintaining standards and controls for an organization's databases. Data administration, however, focuses on the planning and control of data to support business functions and strategic organizational objectives. This includes a data planning effort which focuses on developing an overall data architecture for a firm's data resources.

☐ The development of databases can be accomplished using microcomputer database management packages for small end user applications. However, the development of large corporate databases requires a top-down data planning effort. This may involve developing enterprise and entity relationship models, subject area databases, and data models which reflect the data elements and relationships needed to support the basic business processes of the organization.

☐ Data must be organized in some logical manner on physical storage devices so that they can be efficiently processed. For this reason, data is commonly organized into logical and physical data elements. Common logical data elements are characters, fields, records, files, and databases. Database structures, such as the hierarchical, network, and relational data models, are used to organize the relationships among the different types of data records stored in databases. Databases can be organized in either a sequential or direct manner, and can be maintained by either sequential access or direct access processing methods.

These are the key terms and concepts of this chapter. The page number of their first explanation is in parentheses.

1. Data administration *(215)*
2. Data dictionary *(208)*
3. Data modeling *(224)*
4. Data planning *(216)*
5. Data resource management *(202)*
6. Database administration *(215)*
7. Database administrator *(208)*
8. Database development *(208)*
9. Database management approach *(204)*
10. Database management system *(206)*
11. Database structures *(220)*
    a. Hierarchical
    b. Network
    c. Relational
    d. Object-oriented
12. Database and file organization and processing *(225)*
    a. Direct
    b. Sequential

13. File processing limitations *(203)*
    a. Data duplication
    b. Lack of data integration
    c. Data dependence
14. Hypertext *(212)*
15. Logical data elements *(218)*
    a. Character
    b. Field
    c. Record
    d. File
    e. Database
16. Query language *(208)*
17. Report generator *(208)*
18. Types of databases *(209)*
    a. Operational
    b. End user
    c. Distributed
    d. External
    e. Text

Match one of the **key terms and concepts** listed above with one of the examples or definitions listed below. Try to find the best fit for answers that seem to fit more than one term or concept. Defend your choices.

_____ 1. Marked by data duplication, unintegrated data, and dependency between programs and data formats.

_____ 2. The use of integrated collections of data records and files for data storage and processing.

_____ 3. Software that allows you to create, interrogate, and maintain a database, create reports, and develop application programs.

_____ 4. A specialist in charge of the databases of an organization.

_____ 5. This DBMS feature allows users to easily interrogate a database.

_____ 6. Defines and catalogs the data elements and data relationships in an organization's database.

_____ 7. Helps you specify and produce reports from a database.

_____ 8. Helps you construct a text database and interactively interrogate it.

_____ 9. Databases are dispersed throughout an organization.

_____ 10. Your own personal databases.

_____ 11. Databases of documents.

_____ 12. Uses information systems technology and management methods to manage an organization's data resources.

_____ 13. Developing and maintaining standards and controls for an organization's databases.

_____ 14. The planning and control of data to support organizational objectives.

_____ 15. A top-down effort that ties database development to the support of basic business processes.

_____ 16. Developing conceptual views of the relationships among data in a database.

_____ 17. A customer's name.

_____ 18. A customer's name, address, and account balance.

_____ 19. The names, addresses, and account balances of all of your customers.

_____ 20. An integrated collection of all of the data about your customers.

_____ 21. A treelike structure of records in a database.

_____ 22. A tabular structure of records in a database.

_____ 23. Database elements incorporate data values with the processes that can be performed upon the data.

_____ 24. Transactions are sorted in ascending order by social security number before processing.

_____ 25. Unsorted transactions can be used to update a master file.

REAL WORLD PROBLEMS

1. Merrill Lynch & Co.

If you are comforted by people saying that SQL and graphical interfaces are just hyped-up technologies of limited value for the next few years, you don't want to meet Danny Moeller. Moeller is a Merrill Lynch & Co. assistant vice president in charge of weaning 250 investment bankers and their secretaries from green-screened IBM Personal Computer ATs and clones onto whatever the computer platform of the future proves to be. Moving onto that platform entails two primary thrusts. The entire corporation is moving disparate mainframe databases into IBM's DB2 relational database management system environment. At the same time, the investment banking division is migrating to Microsoft Windows for applications integration and user interfaces and to a SQL Network software access to corporate databases.

Today, most bankers must exit applications they are using, log into the mainframe, and access information in several database formats. They then capture the data and re-enter it into reports in the original application. Under Windows and SQL Network, all users will be able to open multiple data windows and cut and paste data between environments. In a typical application, bankers can switch among windows to generate reports that incorporate textual background information and revenue figures drawn from DB2 using SQL Network. With the older technology, users must log off from one application, log into another, and capture information before bringing it back to be merged into the original application. Says Moeller, "We have found that the ability to concentrate on a problem while accessing necessary data is a large boost to the bankers' productivity."

a. What computing capabilities do DB2, Microsoft Windows, and the SQL Network provide?

b. How will this help Merrill's investment bankers?

Source: Adapted from Charles Von Simson, "Merrill Lynch's Moeller Steers toward Future," *Computerworld*, February 26, 1990, p. 37.

2. Parke-Davis Pharmaceuticals

Tracking the more than 10,000 chemical supplies handled by Parke-Davis Pharmaceutical Research Center can often be as aggravating as searching for a needle in a haystack. To make the process a little easier, the Research Center created a PC database application using the Oracle database management system that is designed to reliably track chemical consumption and disposal while regulating the flow of products in and out of the storerooms, explained Louis Grasso, the division's manager of research information systems. The resulting application, known as Chem-IST (Chemical Inventory Searching and Tracking system), runs on two IBM PS/2 Model 60 microcomputers. One PS/2 functions as a transaction machine, which records all materials that chemists check out of the pharmaceutical warehouse. The other lets users browse through the chemical-tracking database to see what substances are available. Information from the transaction PC is uploaded to a mainframe chemical information-management database system. Chemists use the mainframe database to extract detailed information about a chemical's physical properties and applications. The "browse" PC is then updated with this information.

Prior to the deployment of ChemIST, there was no easy way to monitor chemical inventories, said Melanie Kiburtz, senior system specialist in the division. Without such a tracking system, the center was often faced with unnecessary chemical surplus or, even worse, acute shortages of essential elements, she explained. This ineffective supply system was a cash drain on the center, Kiburtz said, which frequently had to spend significant sums of money to store surplus chemicals. ChemIST is also employed by the center to help manage the use of about 300 highly toxic chemicals that are regulated by state and federal laws, she added. The ChemIST application has been judged a success, Kiburtz said, not only for its speed and reliability, but because the chemists are willing to take the time to use the system as they check materials out of inventory.

a. What two major applications of database management technology are implemented at Parke-Davis?

b. How does this help the Research Center staff?

Source: Adapted from John Pallatto, "Oracle Database Keeps Tabs on Chemical Usage, Disposal," *PC Week*, February 26, 1990, pp. 61, 65.

3. The Bank of Montreal

The Bank of Montreal, a 1,220-branch, $87.2 billion bank, the second largest in Canada and doing business around the world, was suffering because loan customers were not coming back. Other problems included deregulation and declining customer loyalty. Top management ordered implementation of a system that would deliver information, not just process transactions. It is called the Customer and Product Information System (CPIS). Back in 1982, information on customers and products was not integrated, timely, or accurate. It was also expensive, because much of it was prepared manually. Information had to be consolidated from different locations and systems by several factors. One big problem that occurred during the development of CPIS was the assignment of uniform entity numbers to each customer's account. It took many months just to identify all of the bank accounts, because some accounts dealt with many branches.

Obstacles that had to be overcome included some senior executives who were less than enthusiastic and branch managers who were not happy to see unprofitable customers identified. Although the bank was using Cullinet's IDMS database management system, the bank switched to IBM's DB2 relational DBMS and decided to use IBM PCs as terminals throughout the bank. Three years after initial implementation, CPIS is used extensively by top management and manages $15 billion in assets. Thirteen months of historical data are online as part of a huge central database for CPIS. Bank assets have actually declined—profitably so—because so many unprofitable accounts have been identified and either closed out or charged more.

a. Why do you think the Bank of Montreal's data resource management efforts succeeded?

b. How did a data resource management approach improve the business position of the Bank of Montreal?

Source: Adapted from "Data Resource Management: Industry Survey and a Case Study of Data Architecture Implementation," *SIM Special Report*, January 1988, p. 9.

4. Unmanaged Data in Business

The problems of unmanaged data are quite real and exist in a broad range of organizations. A major bank seeking to shift its strategy toward a focus on customers finds it cannot determine how profitable individual customers are, or even what its total business is with each customer, because its customer codes are not common across branches or lines of business. A manufacturing firm with nine plants cannot negotiate favorable purchasing agreements with its major suppliers, because it cannot pool inconsistent data from these plants to find out how much it buys from each supplier. An insurance company discovers it cannot check group health insurance claims against previous claims for the same individual participant, because the structure of the data precludes it. A company attempting to merge two divisions finds that incompatibilities in data definitions and systems provide one of the greatest obstacles to attaining this important strategic action.

a. What do you think is the cause of the problems faced by these companies?

b. How could a data resource management approach provide solutions to such problems?

Source: Dale Goodhue, Judith Quillard, and John Rockart, "Managing Data Resources: A Contingency Perspective," *MIS Quarterly*, September 1988, p. 373.

5. Using the Perseus Hypermedia Database

Using the Perseus Hypermedia database package developed at Harvard University (see Figure 6–12) requires a microcomputer equipped with an add-in multimedia circuit board and a CD-ROM drive. A reader might begin by watching a video description of Apollo's temple at Delphi but halt the video at various points to probe into the text database. What do we know about Delphi in general? The reader could see Delphi on an overall map of Greece from the geographic atlas and then in a topographical map of the neighboring region and finally could zoom in to a site plan or even to plans of various buildings. If Delphi was politically important (as it was), what sources do we have that depict the kind of influence it exerted? Reading about the golden age of Athens, one might instantly call up historical sources such as Herodotus or Plutarch, read the Greek author Pausanias' description of the monuments of Athens, view plans of the buildings, and see color images of their remains as they appear today.

a. Why is Perseus called a "hypermedia" database package? What are its advantages over traditional media?

b. How could similar types of packages be useful in business?

Source: Adapted from Gregory Crane, "Challenging the Individual: The Tradition of Hypermedia Databases," *Academic Computing,* January 1990, pp. 35–36.

6. Arthur Andersen & Co.

Searching online databases is as much an art as a science. More than 3,000 databases are waiting to be tapped through your modem and personal computer, and chances are the information you seek is available in one of them. The trick, of course, is to pick the right database and pluck the critical information from it in the shortest amount of time. "The key to searching is in the planning. You should define the information you need before you start the actual search," says Paula Ingraham, assistant librarian for Arthur Andersen & Co.'s Boston office. "After that, work through the search steps on paper. By the time you get to the online database, you know exactly where you're going to get the information you need and how you're going to extract it."

With requests pouring in from four divisions—tax, audit, small business, and consulting—Ingraham has learned to ask a lot of questions to pinpoint the information someone needs. Most requesters say they want all the information she can gather on a particular industry, but that's usually overkill. "In the early days, I took the requests at their word. I went online, searched, and got everything. But it was a waste of time and money." With online meters running up to $250 per hour, the time you save by searching efficiently translates into significantly reduced costs. Some online services charge by the number of citations you pull from the database as well as by the hour, so downloading the wrong information can hit your budget twice as hard.

a. What is the key to searching online databases?

b. What are the benefits of an efficient search process?

Source: Russ Lockwood, "The Searchers: Online Heroes of the Business World," *Personal Computing,* December 1988, p. 128.

7. Bank of Boston

The Bank of Boston, 14th largest bank in the United States, is using SMS (Storage Management System), a term coined by IBM in 1988 to automate the management of its storage facilities—748 disk drives storing 900 gigabytes of data in two data centers. SMS is IBM's response to a problem that faces every major IS facility today: as the cost of storage drops, the cost of managing it rises. Even though disk drive prices are continually going down, the cost of managing those disk drives—people, floor space, electricity—is always on the rise. Storage management is not only costing more, it's also a managerial black hole. When storage is managed manually, there's really no single way to do it right. That's because once a physical disk space is assigned to one application, there's no easy way to make it available to any other application. "You could have one application blow up because it runs out of space, while unused space exists but is not accessible to it," explained John Petrella, IS project leader. A typical IS organization has anywhere from 30 to 45 percent of all online storage sitting empty.

SMS is a set of software products and a series of policies and procedures for data management. Instead of a storage administrator or a system programmer allocating a specific disk drive to a given application, allocation decisions can be made by the system based on the availability of space on disks. SMS makes it possible for the system to monitor storage levels continuously day and night to determine the optimal use of storage space. And SMS brings storage management down to the file or data set level, a finer gradation than was ever before possible. IS consulting systems engineer Bob Parsons believes SMS will help rein in storage costs—15 percent of the bank's $57 million 1989 IS budget—by reducing the number of people assigned to storage administration and by squeezing every possible byte out of existing storage facilities. The bank's goal in 1990 is to free up 90 gigabytes—about 10 percent of the bank's existing storage.

a. What role does SMS play in data resource management?
b. How will it help the Bank of Boston?

Source: Adapted from Joseph Kelley, "Automated Storage Draws Interest," *Datamation,* February 15, 1990, pp. 81–82.

8. Using a Database Management Package

Use a database management system package available on microcomputer or mainframe systems at your university to:

a. Create a Student Exam Scores file consisting of student records containing student names, social security numbers, genders, and grades on three different exams. Enter data into this file for five students.
b. Edit the Student Exam Scores file by changing a student's exam score. Add and delete student records to these files.
c. Retrieve selected data from the Student Exam Scores file. For example, find and count the records of all students whose scores on the first exam were greater than 85.
d. Produce a report showing the exam scores and total points earned by students aggregated into male and female categories. Then print an-

other report showing this information for either male or female students whose total scores exceeded 240 points.

1. Crane, Gregory. "Challenging the Individual: The Tradition of Hypermedia Databases." *Academic Computing,* January 1990.

2. Goodhue, Dale; Judith Quillard; and John Rockart. "Managing Data Resources: A Contingency Perspective." *MIS Quarterly,* September 1988.

3. Kroenke, David, and Kathleen Dolan. *Database Processing: Fundamentals, Design, Implementation.* 3rd ed. Chicago: Science Research Associates, 1988.

4. Nielsen, Jacob. "The Art of Navigating through Hypertext." *Communications of the ACM,* March 1990.

5. Rybeck, Ted. "DBMS: Next Wave Could Be an Easier Ride." *Computerworld,* March 5, 1990.

6. Shneiderman, Ben, and Greg Kearsley. *Hypertext Hands-On! An Introduction to a New Way of Organizing and Accessing Information.* Reading, Mass.: Addison-Wesley, 1989.

7. Vasta, Joseph. *Understanding Database Management Systems.* 2nd ed. Belmont, Calif.: Wadsworth, 1989.

SELECTED REFERENCES

INFORMATION SYSTEMS APPLICATIONS

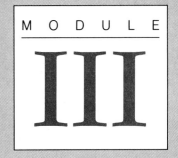

MODULE

III

How are information systems used to support end user computing, business operations, and managerial decision making? The four chapters of this module show you how such basic applications are accomplished in modern organizations.

Chapter 7, End User and Office Information Systems, discusses the resource requirements and managerial challenges of end user computing applications. It also discusses the benefits and limitations of major types of office automation information systems.

Chapter 8, Transaction Processing and Information Reporting Systems, shows the various ways that information systems support the processing of transactions generated by business operations. It also outlines basic considerations in the presentation of information and the use of information reporting systems to present information to managers.

Chapter 9, Decision Support and Expert Systems, outlines how decision support systems and executive information systems are applied to decision making situations faced by managers. It also presents basic concepts of artificial intelligence and shows how expert systems are used to support business operations and management.

Chapter 10, Business Function Information Systems, describes how information systems support the business functions of marketing, manufacturing, human resource management, accounting, and finance.

END USER AND OFFICE INFORMATION SYSTEMS

■ Chapter Outline

The purpose of this chapter is to give you an understanding of the role played in organizations by information systems in end user computing and office automation.

Section I of this chapter explores the reasons for end user computing and analyzes the resources needed to accomplish major end user computing applications. It also discusses the role of information centers and the managerial challenges posed by end user computing systems.

Section II describes major types of office automation information systems and their impact on end users and managers.

After reading and studying this chapter, you should be able to:

1. Identify the major components of an end user computing system and identify the resources needed for end user computing.

2. Give an example for each of the major application categories of end user computing.

3. Explain the role of the information center in supporting and controlling end user computing.

4. Discuss the purposes and information system activities of the major types of office automation systems.

5. Identify several types of electronic office communications and their benefits for end users.

6. Discuss the managerial challenges posed by end user computing and office automation systems.

Section I: End User Computing

INTRODUCTION

The days of relying primarily on organization-wide information systems and information systems professionals to meet our information processing needs are over. Most organizations can't keep up with the information demands of their end users. So more and more people are learning to use microcomputers and intelligent terminals as *professional workstations* to get or develop the information they need to accomplish their jobs successfully. That's what **end user computing** is all about. It's the direct, hands-on use and development of computer-based information systems by end users like yourself, instead of the indirect use provided by the hardware, software, and professional resources of an organization's information services department.

This doesn't mean you won't rely on such organizational resources. However, in end user computing, an information services department plays a supportive role to an end user's own computing resources and efforts. Figure 7–1 outlines the typical levels in an organization where traditional and end user computing are concentrated. Notice that end user computing is concentrated at the individual, work group, and departmental levels of an organization. However, you should also realize that both types of computing can be found at all levels of an organization.

COMPONENTS
OF AN END USER
COMPUTING
SYSTEM

It is important to think of end user computing in an information systems context. Figure 7–2 shows the resource components and application outputs of end user computing as an information system. It illustrates the major categories of end user computing applications and the hardware, software, people, and data resources required. As you can see, end user computing systems are

Figure 7-1 The domains of traditional and end user computing. Note the levels in an organization where each type of computing is concentrated.

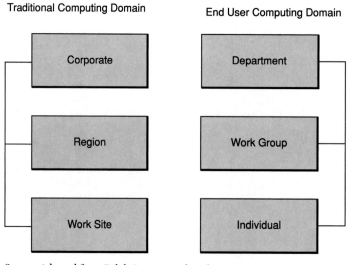

Source: Adapted from Ralph Sprague and Barbara McNurlin, *Information Systems Management in Practice,* 2nd ed. (Englewood Cliffs, N.J.: Prentice-Hall, 1989), p. 32.

computer-based information systems that directly support both the operational and managerial applications of end users.

Figure 7–2 also shows that many end users do not rely solely on their own microcomputer workstations, software packages, and databases. They can also rely on the support of software packages, databases, and computer systems at the work group, departmental, and corporate levels. In addition, many organizations provide *information centers* as another source of support for end user computing. Information center specialists serve as consultants to users who need assistance in their computing efforts. In this way, organizations hope to improve the efficiency and effectiveness of end user involvement in the information systems of their organizations.

Figure 7–2 emphasizes that hardware, software, people, and data resources are needed for end user computing. Let's briefly consider each of these resources.

The hardware resources for end user computing consist primarily of microcomputer workstations. Microcomputer systems (including their peripheral devices) provide the information processing capabilities needed for most user

RESOURCES FOR END USER COMPUTING

Hardware Resources: End User Workstations

Figure 7–2   An end user computing system. Note the major categories of end user computing applications and the hardware, software, people, and data resources required.

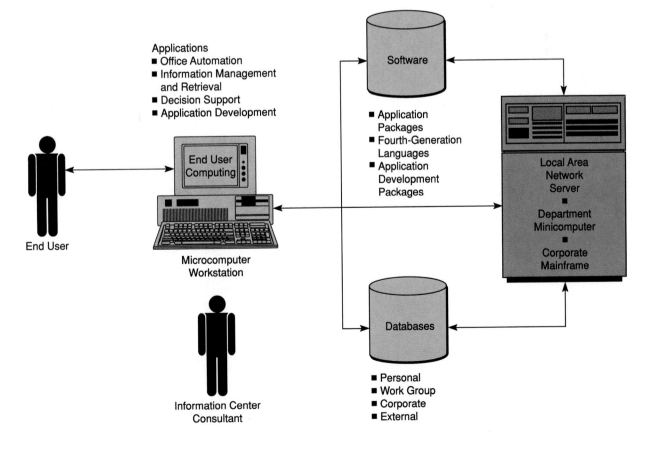

applications. Though *dumb* terminals connected to minicomputers or mainframes may also be used, they are outnumbered by microcomputers with telecommunications capabilities. Therefore, as Figure 7–2 shows, microcomputer workstations may be tied by telecommunications links to other workstations in a local area network, with a more powerful microcomputer operating as a *network server*. Or they may be connected to larger networks, using departmental minicomputers or corporate mainframes as *hosts*. These computer systems (1) help control communications in the network including serving as *gateways* between networks, (2) oversee the sharing of software packages and databases among the workstations in the network, and (3) perform *time-sharing* processing services for jobs that are too big for the workstations to handle.

Software Resources: End User Packages

Application software packages for microcomputer systems are the primary software resources needed for end user computing. These include general-purpose *productivity* packages for word processing, electronic spreadsheets, database and information management, graphics, data communications, and integrated packages, as discussed in Chapter 4. Other software resources include packages for office automation applications such as *desktop publishing*, *electronic mail*, and *office support services*. We will discuss such packages in Section II of this chapter. Of course, many other types of software can be used, depending on the business needs of specific end users. For example, users could acquire software packages to support common business functions, such as accounting applications, financial analysis and planning, sales analysis and marketing management, operations management and manufacturing applications, and so on. These applications will be discussed in Chapter 10.

Another major category of software resources shown in Figure 7–2 is that of *fourth-generation languages*. As discussed in Chapter 4, 4GL packages allow users to specify *what* information they want, rather than *how* the computer system should do it. Major categories of 4GLs include natural and structured query languages, such as Intellect and SQL, and the report generators found in many spreadsheet programs, integrated packages, database management systems, and decision support system packages. Such 4GL tools allow end users to make ad hoc inquiries and generate their own reports. The nonprocedural languages and application generators found in 4GLs, along with other application development packages, are another major software resource category. These packages allow experienced end users to interactively develop their own application programs, instead of relying on professional systems analysts and programmers.

People Resources: The Information Center

Figure 7–2 emphasizes that many organizations have made a major commitment of human resources to end user computing. This commitment usually takes the form of an **information center,** which is an organizational unit that supports the end users in an organization. The information center's biggest contribution to end user computing is a staff of *user consultants*, consisting of systems analysts, programmers, education specialists, and technicians. Their primary role is to educate and assist users in the effective use of microcomputer systems and their many software packages. They also work as consultants to end users to help them develop new applications using a variety of application development tools. We will have more to say about the role of information centers shortly.

Figure 7–2 emphasizes that end user computing relies on several major types of databases introduced in Chapter 6. *Personal databases* are created and maintained by end users to support their individual professional activities. For example, personal databases may have files of correspondence created by word processing or spreadsheets created by electronic spreadsheet packages. End users may also have access to *work group* and *corporate databases* through telecommunications network links. This allows end users to transfer data files among themselves and work group and corporate offices. Finally, end users can use the telecommunications capabilities of their workstations to access *external databases*. This allows them to access a wealth of economic and other types of information from the data banks of commercial information services.

The creation and access of these data resources make the integrity and security of end user and corporate databases a major concern of end user computing. For example, safeguards for proper access to sensitive corporate data must be developed. Also, end user databases extracted from corporate databases may become out of date or incorrect because they are not properly updated and maintained. Thus, managing end user data resources has become a major managerial challenge.

Figure 7–2 lists four major categories of end user computing applications: (1) office automation, (2) information management and retrieval, (3) decision support, and (4) application development. Before we discuss the applications that fit these categories, you should consider the implications of Figure 7–3. This figure illustrates the potential versatility and productivity end user computing can provide to end users. It emphasizes that end user computing is not confined to simple tasks and minor applications. You can utilize end user computing as much as your personal capabilities and resources can handle, professional needs dictate, and company policies allow.

END USER COMPUTING APPLICATIONS

You should also realize that much end user computing is a work group effort. This is sometimes called **work group computing.** For example, members of a work group may use a local area network to share the use of *groupware* packages for spreadsheet analysis, electronic mail, and report generation in order to accomplish group assignments. We will have more to say on this topic when discussing electronic meeting systems in Section II and group decision support systems in Chapter 9.

Office automation (OA) applications will be discussed in detail in Section II of this chapter. These applications have improved end user productivity and enhanced the ability of end users to communicate with their colleagues within their work groups and organizations and with external contacts such as customers and suppliers. This typically involves applications such as word processing, electronic mail, desktop publishing, and presentation graphics.

Office Automation

Many software packages are available to support OA applications. One simple example is the use of *activity scheduler* programs, which coordinate the scheduling of meetings, appointments, and other events. Another example is the use of *desktop accessory* software packages. These provide features such as a calculator, notepad, and appointment book that pop up in a window on the display screen of your workstation at the touch of a key. You can also compose a business letter using word processing, send electronic messages to colleagues using electronic mail, and prepare graphic displays for a formal presentation

Figure 7–3 The potential and versatility of end user computing. Note the many ways the productivity and effectiveness of end users can be enhanced.

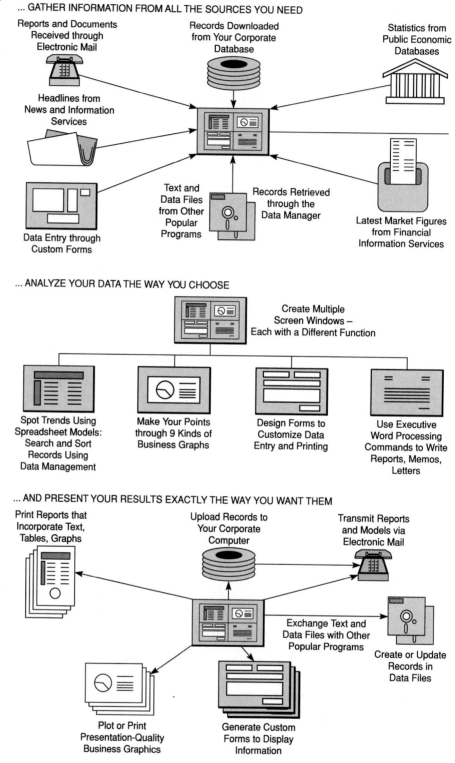

... GATHER INFORMATION FROM ALL THE SOURCES YOU NEED

Reports and Documents Received through Electronic Mail

Records Downloaded from Your Corporate Database

Statistics from Public Economic Databases

Headlines from News and Information Services

Text and Data Files from Other Popular Programs

Records Retrieved through the Data Manager

Latest Market Figures from Financial Information Services

Data Entry through Custom Forms

... ANALYZE YOUR DATA THE WAY YOU CHOOSE

Create Multiple Screen Windows – Each with a Different Function

Spot Trends Using Spreadsheet Models: Search and Sort Records Using Data Management

Make Your Points through 9 Kinds of Business Graphs

Design Forms to Customize Data Entry and Printing

Use Executive Word Processing Commands to Write Reports, Memos, Letters

... AND PRESENT YOUR RESULTS EXACTLY THE WAY YOU WANT THEM

Print Reports that Incorporate Text, Tables, Graphs

Upload Records to Your Corporate Computer

Transmit Reports and Models via Electronic Mail

Exchange Text and Data Files with Other Popular Programs

Create or Update Records in Data Files

Plot or Print Presentation-Quality Business Graphics

Generate Custom Forms to Display Information

Source: Courtesy Context Management Systems.

using the hardware, software, and telecommunication capabilities of your networked microcomputer workstation.

End users are inundated with data and information that must be organized, stored, and retrieved. Thus, one major application of end user computing is the use of database management system (DBMS) packages to manage the creation, access, and maintenance of databases and files. In Chapters 4 and 6, we discussed how DBMS packages help end users create data files and databases to store data and retrieve information. The query languages and report generators of these packages allow end users to retrieve information from personal, work group, corporate, and external databases. Query languages allow simple inquiries to be made quickly and easily by end users. Report generators help end users prepare reports that extract, manipulate, and display information in a variety of formats. In Chapter 6, we saw how end users can make inquiries using a query language like SQL and receive immediate displays of information. Figure 7–4 shows how an end user can quickly specify and generate a sales analysis report using a report generator.

Information Management and Retrieval Applications

A. Constructing the report.

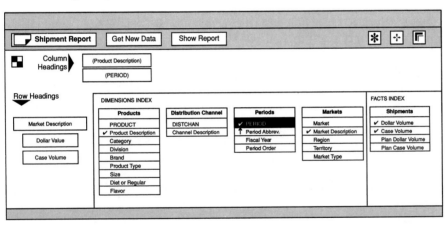

Figure 7–4   Specifying and generating a sales analysis report with the reporter module of the Metaphor System, licensed by IBM as its Data Interpretation System.

B. Part of the report produced.

	Aim Diet September, 1990	Aim Diet Small September, 1990	Aim Regular September, 1990	Aim Regular Medium September, 1990	Aim Regular Small September, 1990
Akron					
Dollar Volume	549,800.00	555,000.00	2,020,200.00	1,488,600.00	482,600.00
Case Volume	51,209.00	51,706.00	150,094.00	99,438.00	44,871.00
Albany					
Dollar Volume	1,423,000.00	1,437,000.00	2,696,400.00	1,411,400.00	1,115,600.00
Case Volume	119,207.00	120,364.00	213,565.00	98,939.00	93,447.00
Allegheny					
Dollar Volume	1,341,400.00	1,354,400.00	3,415,600.00	2,248,600.00	1,122,200.00
Case Volume	106,200.00	107,231.00	250,659.00	157,700.00	88,208.00
Anaheim					
Dollar Volume	3,352,400.00	3,455,200.00	6,988,200.00	4,138,000.00	2,616,600.00
Case Volume	294,637.00	308,696.00	46,096.00	281,487.00	229,077.00

Source: Courtesy IBM Corporation.

Another software package used for information management and retrieval is the **personal information manager** (PIM). These packages help end users store, organize, and retrieve text and numerical data in the form of notes, lists, clippings, tables, memos, letters, reports, and so on. For example, information can be entered randomly about people, companies, deadlines, appointments, meetings, projects, and financial results. The PIM package will automatically organize such data with minimal instructions from the end user. Then portions of the stored information can be retrieved in any order and in a variety of forms, depending on the relationships established among pieces of data by the software and the user. For example, information can be retrieved as a list of appointments, meetings, or other things to do; the timetable for a project; or a display of key facts and financial data about a competitor [6]. See Figure 7–5.

In Chapter 9, we will discuss how executive information systems (EISs) allow end users who are top executives of corporations to easily retrieve information tailored to their strategic information needs. So end user computing allows end users at all levels to bypass the periodic reporting process of traditional information systems. Instead, they can receive directly at their workstations much of the information they need.

Decision Support Applications

Software packages such as electronic spreadsheets, integrated packages, and other decision support system (DSS) *generators* allow end users to build and manipulate *analytical* models of business activities. End users can thus create their own decision support systems with the use of such tools and the variety of databases previously mentioned. As we will discuss in Chapter 9, this allows

Figure 7–5 An example of a personal information manager (PIM). Notice the variety of ways that information is recorded and presented in the window displays of IBM's Current PIM package.

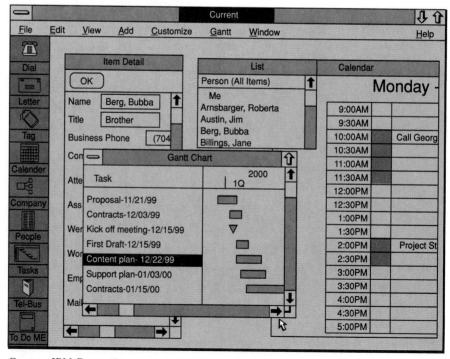

Courtesy IBM Corporation.

end users to pose *what-if* questions by entering different alternatives into a spreadsheet or other model. They can then see the results displayed immediately on their workstation screens. Thus, managerial end users can use an interactive modeling process to analyze alternatives and help them make or recommend decisions. Besides spreadsheet programs, a variety of 4GL products and financial, statistical, and mathematical analysis packages can be used by end users for decision support applications. This includes group decision support system (GDSS) software, which enhances the joint decision making of work groups and other organizational units.

Another major category of end user computing is the development of new or improved applications by users. That is, end users can develop new or improved ways to perform their jobs without the direct involvement of professional systems analysts. The primary reason for this phenomenon are the growing capabilities and availabilities of microcomputer workstations and a variety of end user application development tools. The application generation capabilities of fourth-generation languages and application software packages have been a driving force for end user development. These resources make it easier for end users to develop their own limited, but highly functional, computer-based information systems.

    Of course, many end users still need the assistance of systems analysts or information center consultants to develop effective applications with adequate performance and security controls. This is a major challenge of managing end user computing. Figure 7–6 shows how an end user can develop an application by linking together icons representing prespecified software modules (tools) which accomplish basic information processing tasks. We will have more to say about end user applications development and management in the chapters of Module IV.

End User Applications Development

An **information center** is an organizational subunit that provides hardware, software, and people support to end users in an organization. It typically has been part of an organization's information services department, but it can also be found in individual end user departments. Beginning at IBM-Canada in 1974, the concept of providing support facilities for end user computing has grown so popular that it has become a dominant factor in organizational computing [9]. Most information centers provide:

THE INFORMATION CENTER

Figure 7–6 Using an end user application development package. The Query tool is used to retrieve data, which is passed to the Spreadsheet II tool for manipulation and to the Text tool for inclusion in a prepared letter, which is sent to the printer and simultaneously to the electronic mail facility.

Courtesy IBM Corporation.

□ **Hardware support** for end users who need it by providing the use of microcomputers, intelligent terminals, advanced graphic terminals, high-speed printers, plotters, and so on.

□ **Software support** is provided by offering the temporary use of advanced software packages such as application development systems, nonprocedural languages, database management systems, and a variety of application software packages.

□ **People support** is provided by a staff of end user consultants—systems analysts and programmers who are trained to educate end users and help them apply their own computing resources to improve the efficiency and effectiveness of their work activities.

The Role of the Information Center

What do information centers do? Information centers provide a variety of services, depending on the type and size of the organization and on the age and mission of each center [5]. Figure 7–7 summarizes many of the services provided by information centers. As you can see, most of the services can be categorized as dealing with end user education and training, assistance with applications development, hardware/software sharing and evaluation, or the development of adminstrative control methods for end user applications.

Another way to view the role of the information center in an organization is shown in Figure 7–8. In this context, the information center serves as a *bridge,* or in marketing terms, a *channel* of distribution, for the delivery of information services to end user work groups [5]. This is a major benefit for departments and work groups of managerial and professional personnel, who have high information processing needs. Work groups consisting primarily of clerical personnel are served quite well by traditional information services departments. Thus, managerial and professional work groups can look to the information center as a retailer or wholesaler of information support services to fit their unique needs.

Figure 7–7   Information center services. Note the variety of services that may be provided.

Basic Services	Enhanced Services
■ Computer literacy education	■ Development of telecommunications software
■ Training on use of products	■ Data administration
■ Hardware/software sharing	■ Installing and testing new software product releases
■ Application consulting	■ Maintenance of PC equipment
■ Help center with hotline telephone service	■ Project management for user-developed systems
■ Hardware/software evaluation	■ Quality assurance of user-written software
■ Hardware and software standards	■ Prototype development for end users
■ Support for standard products	
■ Security support	

Source: Adapted from Ralph Sprague and Barbara McNurlin, *Information Systems Management in Practice,* 2nd ed. (Englewood Cliffs, N.J.: Prentice-Hall, 1989), p. 328–29.

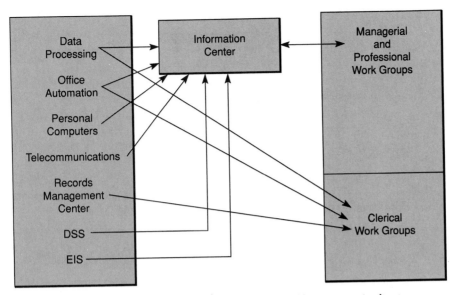

Figure 7–8 The role of the information center. An information center can serve as a bridge, or channel of distribution, for information support services to managerial and professional work groups.

Source: Adapted from Raymond Panko, *End User Computing: Management, Applications, and Technology* (New York: John Wiley & Sons, 1988), p. 130.

As we have already indicated, managers face significant challenges in managing end user computing in their organizations. Managing the hardware, software, people, and data resources of end user computing systems is a major challenge for an organization's information systems function. Workstations, computers, telecommunication networks, and software packages must be evaluated and acquired. End users must be properly trained and assisted. The integrity and security of the various types of databases that are created and available to end users must be assured. Finally, the applications end users develop and implement must be evaluated for their efficiency and effectiveness in using organizational resources and helping to meet organizational objectives.

There is no question that end user computing has improved the development and use of computer-based information systems. For the end users of an organization, it relieves the burden of end user demands on information services departments. However, end user computing can also pose major problems and risks to an organization. The development and use of applications by end users instead of by professional systems analysts is seen as a major risk factor in today's organizations. Inadequate analysis, poor design, improper implementation, and lack of controls can easily result from an end user's rush to develop and implement new applications.

So managing end user computing is not an easy job. However, it is a responsibility shared by every manager, as well as by the management of an organization's information systems function. Organizations typically make a variety of organizational, policy, and procedural changes to support and control end user computing. For example, we have previously mentioned the important role of information centers and their staffs of user consultants in the support and control of end user computing efforts. Managing end user comput-

A MANAGERIAL PERSPECTIVE

ing also requires the development of policies and procedures concerning hardware and software acquisition and applications development by end users. Corporate guidelines regulating the cost and types of hardware and software end users can purchase are common.

What managers are trying to do is to avoid the proliferation of hardware and software while assuring compatibilty with the organization's computing and telecommunications resources. Applications development guidelines encourage end users to develop well-documented information systems with built-in controls that make efficient use of computing resources and do not threaten the integrity of the organization's databases. Information center consultants and other services are provided to help end users develop applications that meet such standards. We will further discuss the managerial and control implications of the risks of end user computing in Chapters 12, 13, and 14.

REAL WORLD CASE

Hughes Aircraft Company

Once you've got the PCs on the desktops, how do you get the most out of them? That's the classic question that Virginia Johnson is trying to answer. While she does, the growth phase for PCs is slowing down a bit in the human resources department of Hughes Aircraft Company in Los Angeles, where Johnson is manager of computer services. "There are so many PCs out there not being utilized," she said. "We want to spend more money training people, getting more utilization out of the existing hardware, before we invest more capital in PCs."

Johnson was excited about PCs when she first saw them in 1982 because they allowed her more independence from the Hewlett-Packard 3000 minicomputers with which she had been working. At first, most of her PC support time was taken up teaching users how to use common tools such as word processing and graphics—"how to automate a lot of the manual things they were doing." Today, with users more sophisticated, less time is spent teaching such basic skills. Instead, the support staff carries the torch for such causes as proper data backup and the need for companywide guidelines for applications development, according to Johnson.

In the past, PC users had no guidelines for developing the systems that became vital to their business units. That led to problems when the user/developer left his or her job without leaving documentation about the system or when vital data was lost because the user hadn't backed it up. In September 1989, the corporate IS group formed an end user computing group made up of managers from throughout the aerospace company. Its job is to develop companywide guidelines for mainframe- and PC-based developers alike.

"How can we control what we give the users so we can ensure that they don't destroy themselves?" Johnson asked. "The role is more advisory versus technical support. We don't necessarily need to provide users with information but to help them understand how to use it." The group also hopes to settle on guidelines for choosing off-the-shelf applications, both to save money and to make supporting them easier.

In addition, Johnson's computer-services staff is pioneering a new approach to supporting users for everything from PCs to mainframe applications. Under the new approach, the group is divided into teams that each support a human resources function such as staffing and development or compensation, benefits, and labor relations. Previously, her staff delivered most of its support through a traditional information center. Under the new team approach, it spends more time on training, applications development, and integration of PCs, minicomputers, and mainframes.

Resistance to PCs from the traditional mainframe organization is becoming less of a problem, Johnson said. "There is a recognition this isn't going to go away." Johnson predicts that the growing power and complexity of PCs, combined with shrinking staffs at Hughes, will create more of a need for end user support personnel.

"We used to plug in a PC and you were ready to go," she said. "You don't just plug in a PS/2 and you're ready to go. We've undergone a massive head-count reduction, and people have more work to do. They have to learn to do it more efficiently, and there I see an opportunity for automation," she said.

Application Questions

☐ What end user computing problems are facing Hughes Aircraft?

☐ What changes has this caused in how end user computing is supported and controlled?

☐ Why does Virginia Johnson expect that the need for end user computing support personnel will increase?

Source: Adapted from Robert Scheier, "How Four PC Managers Traveled the Decade of Change," *PC Week,* January 1, 1990, pp. 54–55.

Section II: Office Automation

INTRODUCTION

Office automation (OA) is changing the equipment and work habits of today's end users. Of course, none of us would like to work in an office where all information processing activities are done manually. Office machines such as electric typewriters, copying machines, and dictation machines have made office work easier and more productive. But the *mechanized office* is giving way to the *automated office*. Investment in computer-based workstations and other automated equipment is transforming traditional manual office methods and paper communications media. This transformation has resulted in the development of automated information systems that rely on text processing, data processing, telecommunications, and other information systems technologies.

Office automation systems are computer-based information systems that collect, process, store, and transmit electronic messages, documents, and other forms of communications among individuals, work groups, and organizations. Such systems can increase the productivity of managerial end users and other professional and staff personnel by significantly reducing the time and effort needed to produce, access, and receive business communications. Figure 7–9 outlines the major office automation systems.

Information System Activities

You should think of office automation systems as computer-based information systems. This concept is illustrated in the *office automation system model* in Figure 7–10. Hardware resources (intelligent workstations), software resources (automated office programs), and people resources (knowledge workers) convert text, voice, and image data resources into finished information products using the information system activities of input, processing, output, storage, and control. Thus, ideas can be expressed in words, numbers, symbols, sounds, and images and entered into a computer as text, voice, or image data (input); edited and manipulated electronically (processing); stored and filed electronically, on magnetic, optical, micrographic, or paper media (storage); directed by various office automation programs (control); and communicated

Figure 7–9 An overview of office automation systems. These computer-based information systems collect, process, store, and transmit electronic office communications.

Office Automation Systems	
Office publishing systems	Word processing and desktop publishing systems
Electronic communications systems	Electronic mail, voice mail and facsimile
Electronic meeting systems	Electronic meeting, teleconferencing, and telecommuting systems
Image processing systems	Image processing, optical scanning and storage, document management, and interactive video systems
Office support systems	Electronic calendar, tickler file, notebook, and directory systems; work scheduling and task management systems

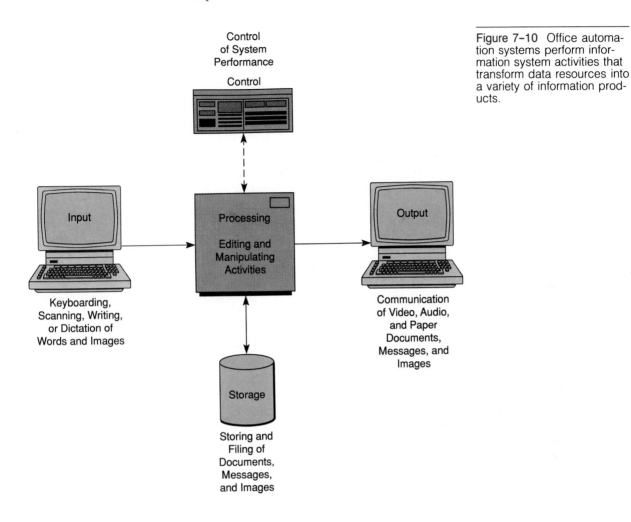

Control
of System
Performance

Control

Input

Processing

Editing and
Manipulating
Activities

Output

Keyboarding,
Scanning, Writing,
or Dictation of
Words and Images

Storage

Storing and
Filing of
Documents,
Messages,
and Images

Communication
of Video, Audio,
and Paper
Documents,
Messages, and
Images

Figure 7–10 Office automation systems perform information system activities that transform data resources into a variety of information products.

electronically in voice, video, or on paper to a recipient (output). For example, one can speak into a telephone (input) and have the voice message digitized (processing), temporarily placed on a magnetic disk (storage), then transmitted to another end user's telephone as a voice mail message when requested (output), under the direction of a voice mail program (control).

WORD PROCESSING

Word processing is the use of computer systems to automate the transformation of ideas into a readable form of communications. As we mentioned in Chapter 4, word processing involves the use of word processing software packages to manipulate **text data** (characters, words, sentences, and paragraphs) to produce information products in the form of **documents** (letters, memos, forms, and reports). Word processing was the first, and is still the most common, office automation application.

Figure 7–11 illustrates word processing activities that take place in a large office setting. These figures show how a personnel department responds to inquiries concerning employment opportunities with a personal letter which merges standard paragraphs (called *boilerplate*) with variable information specific to the person who applied for employment.

Figure 7-11 Steps in an office word processing application. Note the use of standard paragraphs to produce a personalized letter for the personnel department.

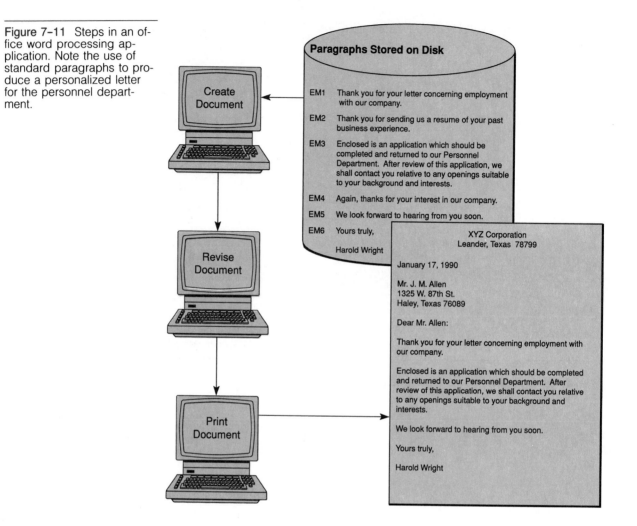

DESKTOP PUBLISHING

One of the major application areas in office automation is **desktop publishing**. Organizations can use desktop publishing systems to produce their own printed materials. They can design and print their own newsletters, brochures, manuals, and books with several type styles, graphics, and colors on each page. What constitutes a desktop publishing system? Typical hardware and software components include:

☐ A personal computer with a hard disk.
☐ A laser printer or other printer capable of high-quality graphics.
☐ Software that can do word processing, graphics, and page makeup.

Word processing packages and *page makeup packages* are available that can do word processing, graphics, and page makeup functions. For higher-quality printing, end users need to invest in a more powerful computer with advanced graphics capabilities, a more expensive graphics and page makeup package with more extensive features, and a laser or other printer with a greater variety of capabilities.

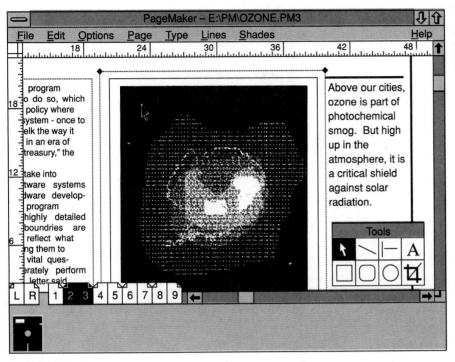

Figure 7–12 Desktop publishing in action. This video display shows the use of the PageMaker software package to design a newsletter.

Courtesy Aldus Corporation.

How does desktop publishing work? Here are the major steps in the process.

1. Prepare your text and illustrations with a word processing program and a graphics package. You can also use an optical scanner to input text and graphics from other sources.

2. Use the page makeup program to develop the format of each page. This is where desktop publishing departs from standard word processing and graphics. Your video screen becomes an *electronic pasteup board* with rulers, column guides, and other page design aids.

3. Now merge the text and illustrations into the page format you designed. The page makeup software will automatically move excess text to another column or page and help size and place illustrations and headings.

4. When the pages look the way you want them on the screen, you can store them electronically on your hard disk. Then print them on a laser printer or other printer to produce the finished printed material. See Figure 7–12.

Many word processing packages now provide limited desktop publishing features. But the desktop publishing process is not as easy as it sounds for the casual end user, especially for projects involving complex layouts. However, advances in software should make the job easier in the future, in terms of both ease of use and helping end users do a better job of graphics design for documents [1].

Figure 7–13 Electronic image management. Note the
steps involved in an EIM
system.

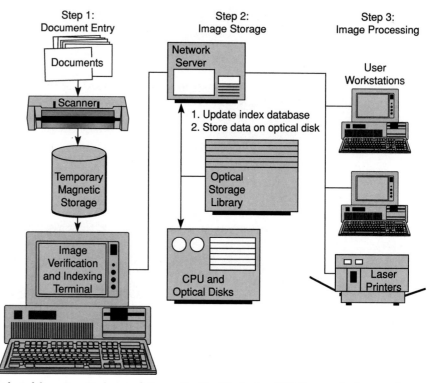

Figure 7–13 Electronic image management. Note the steps involved in an EIM system.

Adapted from Gary Cochran and Steven Neville, "Evaluating EIM Systems for Business," *Edge*, September/October 1989, p.44.

IMAGE PROCESSING

Image processing is another fast-growing area of office automation. It allows end users to electronically capture, store, process, and retrieve images of documents that may include numeric data, text, handwriting, graphics, and photographs. This application area is also known as electronic image management (EIM). A typical EIM system is illustrated in Figure 7–13.

Electronic Document Management

Electronic document management (EDM) is based on image processing technology. However, it views a document as "something that has been authored for human comprehension." Thus, an electronic document is not just an electronic image of traditional documents as described earlier. It may also take the form of a digitized "voice note" attached to an electronic mail message, or electronic images for a color graphics presentation.

Electronic document management interfaces with other office automation systems such as word processing, desktop publishing, electronic mail, and voice mail. However, one of the fastest growing EDM applications is *transaction document image processing*. Documents such as customer correspondence, sales orders, invoices, application forms, and service requests are captured electronically and routed to end users throughout the organization for processing. For example, a customer application form for a bank loan can be captured by optical scanning, indexed by the image database management system, electronically routed to various end user workstations for editing and financial and credit analysis, and then rerouted to a loan officer's workstation where the loan application decision is made. Such systems have shown productivity improvements of from 20 to 25 percent, as well as significant cost savings [3].

Interactive video systems integrate image processing with text, audio, and video processing technologies. Software for developing such *digital video interactive* (DVI) applications requires microcomputer systems with significant processing power and memory, add-on circuit boards, and hard disk and optical disk storage. This allows end users to digitally capture, edit, and combine text, pictures, and sound into multimedia business and educational presentations. For example, an interactive video session for training auto mechanics can be produced on optical disks. It could combine animated graphics displays of engine parts, electronic diagnostic charts, lists of major topics and facts, video clips of mechanics working on vehicles, and engine sounds helpful in engine diagnostics.

Interactive video sessions allow end users with microcomputers and optical disk drives to see and hear prepared material *interactively*. That is, they do not have to view a program sequentially. They can move among various segments randomly or according to preestablished paths indicated by menus and prompts. When this capability is proved by *hypertext* technology (discussed in Chapter 6), it is called *hypermedia*. Though expensive to produce, interactive video is being used for training purposes by large business firms, government agencies, and other organizations.

Interactive Video

Office automation includes a variety of *electronic communications systems*, such as **electronic mail, voice mail,** and **facsimile.** They allow organizations to send messages in text, video, or voice form or transmit copies of documents and do it in seconds, not hours or days. Such systems support the transmission and distribution of text and images in electronic form over telecommunications networks. This practice can drastically reduce the flow of paper messages, letters, memos, documents, and reports that flood our present interoffice and postal systems.

Organizations have used various forms of electronic communications for a long time. Western Union's telegram and mailgram services are examples. So are their TWX, Telex, and Teletype services, which have provided long-distance telecommunications (using printing terminals) for news media services and large organizations for many years. Another long-standing form of electronic communications is *facsimile*. This is a remote copying process in which copies of photographs, documents, and reports can be transmitted and received in hard copy from anywhere in the world. Also, we have been able for many years to use computer terminals and telecommunications channels to transmit and print reports and documents at remote sites.

However, easy-to-use, lower-cost, and more capable systems have been developed for all types of electronic messaging. Computer manufacturers and software suppliers have taken advantage of advances in computer technology to develop more powerful microcomputer workstations and telecommunications packages. Advances in telecommunications technology, such as local area networks, intelligent private branch exchanges (PBXs), and integrated services digital networks (ISDNs), are allowing the electronic merging of voice, data, and images.

ELECTRONIC COMMUNICATIONS SYSTEMS

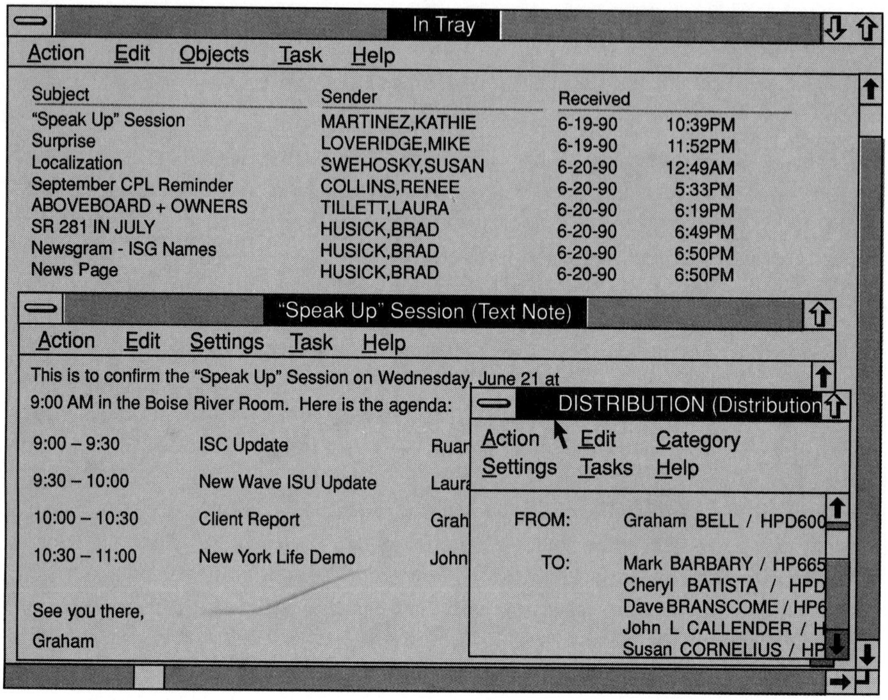

Figure 7–14 Using the New-Wave Mail electronic mail package from Hewlett-Packard.

Courtesy Hewlett-Packard.

Electronic Mail

Today, you can send an **electronic mail** (E-Mail) message to one or more individuals in an organization for storage in their *electronic mailboxes* on magnetic disk devices. Whenever they are ready, they can read their electronic mail by displaying it on the video screens at their workstations. So, with only a few minutes of effort (and a few microseconds of transmission), a message to one or many individuals can be composed, sent, and received. Thus, many organizations and work groups use their wide area and local area networks for electronic mail. Companies such as GTE, TELENET, and MCI offer E-Mail services, as do personal computer networks such as CompuServe and Prodigy. Figure 7–14 shows a video display provided by an electronic mail package.

Voice Mail

Another variation of electronic mail is **voice mail** (also called *voice store-and-forward*) where *digitized voice messages*, rather than electronic text, are used. In this method, you first dial the number of the voice mail service. In some secure systems, you may be asked to enter an identification code. Once you are accepted, you dial the voice mail number of the person you wish to contact and speak your message. Your analog message is digitized and stored on the magnetic disk devices of the voice mail computer system. Whenever users want to hear their voice mail, they simply dial their mailbox number and listen to the stored message, which the computer converts back into analog voice form.

Facsimile

As we said earlier, **facsimile** (fax) is not a new office telecommunications service. However, advantages in digital imaging technology and micro-electronics have caused a sharp drop in prices and a significant increase in

File Transmitted over
Dial-Up Telephone Lines

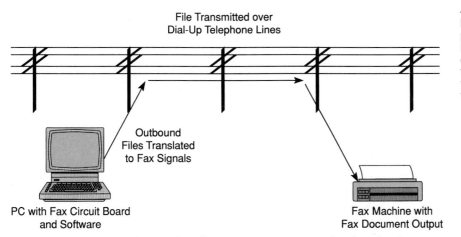

Outbound
Files Translated
to Fax Signals

PC with Fax Circuit Board
and Software

Fax Machine with
Fax Document Output

Source: Adapted from David Barcomb, *Office Automation: A Survey of Tools and Technology*, 2nd ed. (Boston: Digital Press, 1988), p. 188.

Figure 7–15 Personal computers and fax machines. Microcomputers with fax circuit boards and software can transmit document files to fax machines over standard telephone lines.

capabilities. As a consequence, sales of fax machines have skyrocketed in the last few years, and *faxing* has become a commonplace business term. Facsimile allows you to transmit images of important documents over telephone or other telecommunication links. Thus, "long-distance copying" might be an appropriate nickname for this telecommunications process.

Usually, a fax machine at one office location transmits to a fax machine at another location, with both units connected to high-speed modems. Transmission speeds for digital office fax machines range from one to four pages per minute, with quality equivalent to an office copier. A more recent development is the availability of facsimile circuit boards for microcomputers. Installing a *fax board* and using a fax software package allows a personal computer to transmit digital copies of text files to fax machines anywhere. Thus, fax machines can now become remote dial-up printers for microcomputer systems [1]. See Figure 7–15.

ELECTRONIC MEETING SYSTEMS

Why do people have to spend travel time and money to attend meetings away from their normal work locations? They don't have to if they use **electronic meeting systems** (EMS), a growing method of electronic office telecommunications. EMS involves the use of video and audio communications to allow conferences and meetings to be held with participants who may be scattered across a room, a building, a country, or the globe. Reducing the need to travel to and from meetings should save employee time, increase productivity, and reduce travel expenses and energy consumption. EMS is also being promoted as a form of group decision support systems (GDSS) because they promote more efficient and effective decision making by groups of people [2].

Teleconferencing

There are several variations of electronic meeting systems, as illustrated in Figure 7–16. In some versions, participants at remote sites key in their presentations and responses whenever convenient from their online terminals or workstations connected to a central *conference* computer. Since all participants

Figure 7–16 A taxonomy of electronic meeting system environments. Note the place of teleconferencing and other forms of EMS.

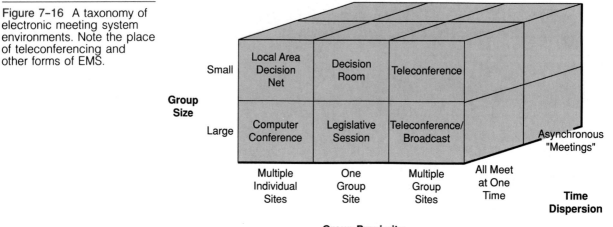

Source: Adapted from Alan R. Dennis, Joey George, Len Jessup, Jay Nunamaker, and Douglas Vogel, "Information Technology to Support Group Meetings," *MIS Quarterly,* December 1988, p. 609.

don't have to do this at the same time, this form of EMS is called *computer conferencing* and is like a form of interactive electronic mail. **Teleconferencing** is the most widely publicized form of EMS. Sessions are held in realtime, with major participants being televised while participants at remote sites take part with voice input of questions and responses.

Figure 7–16 shows that computer conferencing for small groups is called *local area decision nets.* Teleconferencing can also consist of using closed circuit television to multiple small groups, instead of television broadcasting to reach large groups of multiple sites. Group decision support systems for small groups utilize a network of workstations and large screen projection in a supported *decision room,* while a GDSS for large groups constitutes a *legislative session.* Both of these forms of electronic meeting systems provide extensive computer and video facilities for its participants.

Several major communications carriers now offer teleconferencing services for such events as sales meetings, new product announcements, and employee education and training. See Figure 7–17. However, organizations have found that teleconferencing and some forms of EMS are not as effective as face-to-face meetings, especially when important participants are not trained in how to communicate using these systems. Also, the cost of providng some electronic meeting services and facilities can be substantial and make EMS not as cost-effective as traditional meetings [1, 10].

Telecommuting

Telecommuting is the use of telecommunications by workers to replace commuting to work from their homes. It also describes the use of telecommunications to carry on work activities from temporary locations other than offices and homes. Some people refer to telecommuting as the creation of *virtual offices.* Workers use a computer terminal or microcomputer with telecommunications capability to access their company's computer network and databases. Telecommuters and their colleagues use E-mail and voice mail to communicate with each other about job assignments.

Courtesy Martin Marietta Data Systems.

Figure 7-17 An example of teleconterencing. Martin Marietta Data Systems uses teleconferencing to hold a meeting at its corporate headquarters in Bethesda, Maryland, with its aerospace facility in Denver, Colorado.

Telecommuting is being tried by several major corporations and is used by many independent professionals. It seems to be most popular with people whose jobs involve a lot of individual work, such as programmers, systems analysts, writers, consultants, and so on. It is especially helpful for handicapped persons and working parents of young children. However, studies have shown that telecommuting is not appropriate for many jobs and people. Productivity and job satisfaction seem to suffer unless workers spend several days each week at the office or other work sites with their colleagues. So telecommuting is considered only a temporary or partial work alternative for many knowledge workers [1, 10].

OFFICE SUPPORT SYSTEMS

Office support systems is an office automation category that integrates electronic calendars, tickler files, electronic mail directories, schedulers, and task management systems. Office support systems provide computer-based support services to managers and other office professionals to help them organize their work activities. These services computerize manual methods of planning such as paper calendars, appointment books, directories, file folders, memos, and notes. Microcomputer users can get some of the benefits of mainframe office support systems by using **desktop accessory** software packages, as discussed and illustrated in Chapter 4. Also available are *groupware* packages which allow members of work groups on local area networks to share office support services and OA applications such as word processing and electronic mail. Thus, office support systems help end users and work groups organize routine office tasks.

For example, you could enter the date and time of a meeting into an electronic calendar. An *electronic tickler file* will automatically remind you of important events. Electronic schedulers use the electronic calendars of several people to help you schedule meetings and other activities for them. Electronic mail directories help you contact people easily. And electronic task management packages help you plan a series of related activities so that scheduled

Figure 7–18 A display of
IBM's OfficeVision office support system. This package
supports electronic mail and
other office services on both
wide area and local area
networks.

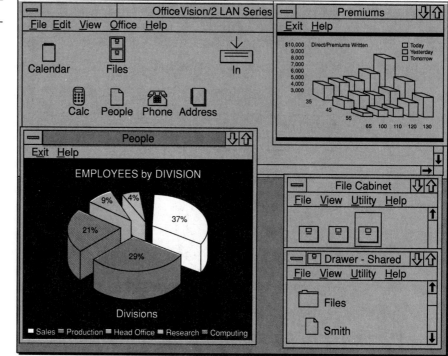

Courtesy IBM Corporation.

results are accomplished on time. Figure 7–18 shows a display from IBM's
OfficeVision office support system for wide area and local area networks of
mainframe, minicomputer, and microcomputer systems.

A MANAGERIAL PERSPECTIVE

Studies made of how knowledge workers spend their time have determined
that office automation can save a significant amount of a knowledge worker's
time (15 percent is one estimate). The major areas that can be improved include
less productive office activities such as seeking information, waiting for appointments and meetings, organizing work, scheduling, and filing. More productive
office activities, such as meetings, telephone calls, and creating documents, can
also be improved by office automation systems. Studies have also shown that
office workers have less plant and equipment invested per worker ($2,000/
worker) than factory workers ($25,000/worker) or agricultural workers ($50,000/
worker). Thus, increased investment in office automation promises increased
productivity by office workers [8, 10].

OA Benefits

Many office automation systems have been developed to achieve the benefits of
(1) more cost-effective communications and (2) more *time-effective* communications than traditional written and telephone communications methods. For
example, electronic mail and facsimile systems are designed to minimize *information float* and *telephone tag*. **Information float** is the time (at least several
days) when a written letter or other document is in transit between the sender
and receiver, and thus unavailable for any action or response. **Telephone tag** is

the process of (1) repeatedly calling people, (2) finding them unavailable, (3) leaving messages, and (4) finding out later that you were unavailable when they finally returned your calls.

Electronic mail, voice mail, and facsimile systems can eliminate the effects of mail that is lost in transit or phone lines that are frequently busy. They can also reduce the costs of labor, materials, and postage for office communications (from more than $5 for a written message to less than 50 cents for an electronic message is one estimate). Also, the amount of time wasted in regular phone calls can be reduced (by one third, according to another estimate) [8].

Office automation systems have thus proved that they can significantly improve office communication processes. Thus, office automation systems can:

- ☐ Increase the productivity of secretarial personnel and reduce the costs of creating, reviewing, revising, and distributing office documents and messages.

- ☐ Shorten the turnaround time between the preparation and receipt of messages and documents by moving information quickly and efficiently to the people who need it.

- ☐ Reduce the frustration, expense, and errors involved in revising text and images for attractive and effective documents and presentations.

- ☐ Store, retrieve, and transmit electronic documents, images, and messages quickly and efficiently.

- ☐ Increase the productivity of executives, professionals, and other knowledge workers who are heavy users of office communications. For example, most of the managerial roles discussed in Chapter 9 involve extensive information transfer activities, which can be effectively supported by office automation systems [4].

OA Limitations

Of course, these advantages are not acquired without some negative effects. First, the cost of automated office hardware is significantly higher than the equipment it replaces. Another limitation is less obvious. Office automation can disrupt traditional office work roles and work environments [10]. For example, some word processing systems have caused significant employee dissatisfaction because they give some secretaries nothing but typing to do and isolate them from other employees.

The ease of use and lack of security of many office automation systems has also caused problems. Inefficient and unauthorized use of electronic mail, voice mail, and facsimile services can significantly impair office productivity. One example is sending copies of electronic messages to people who do not need or want them. Another is "junk fax"—receiving unauthorized advertisements and unrequested documents that disrupt the normal use of an office fax machine. These problems of office automation must be solved before knowledge workers can fully accept and cooperate with a technology that significantly changes their work roles, processes, and environment. Only then will office automation's promises of increased productivity and job satisfaction be fulfilled.

REAL WORLD CASE

American Airlines

Andrew Cohen chuckles at the suggestion that office automation (OA) systems have failed to revolutionize the workplace. As manager of systems development for American Airlines Inc.'s SABRE travel information network, Cohen administers Data General's CEO office software package for about 300 users. "Now we find ourselves in the situation where we're pretty well automated. When one of our office computers goes down for some reason, which luckily doesn't happen too often, people go crazy. They've forgotten how they used to do things. You laugh but it's so true."

However, Cohen's story misses the big picture. "The larger issue," says Steve Wendler, an analyst for the Gartner Group, "is that the current generation of office systems failed to deliver on the promise of greatly improved white-collar productivity." According to Gartner Group's research, "white-collar productivity in 1987 was exactly at the same level it was in 1967. This is after all of the huge investments in PCs and integrated office systems," Wendler says. Thus, for the 1990s, vendors are focusing on office automation offerings such as IBM's OfficeVision and Data General's CEO Object Office, that they describe as a suite of services. These promise to allow users to create custom office systems for the enterprise, at last curing the white-collar productivity doldrums.

For example, office workers at Cohen's department are now testing CEO Object Office. Cohen says his division will most likely keep the package. With it, users can choose applications tied to personal productivity, such as word processing, and still access the department's minicomputer for group services, such as electronic mail.

However, American Airlines as a whole is taking a far more ambitious path to office automation. Called InterAAct, the estimated $150 million homegrown system will combine data processing, office automation, personal computing and networking into one system. Originally,

each of the airline's 70,000 employees was to have at least part-time use of one of 14,000 PCs linked in a corporatewide system, providing access to everything from spreadsheets to host-based databases.

Intel, AT&T, IBM and Tandy Corp. are supplying 386 and 386/SX workstations, the intelligent desktop computers that are key to American's new model of office computing. Hewlett-Packard's NewWave software and Microsoft Windows will provide the object-oriented, consistent graphical user interface that is central to next-generation systems. Local area networks (LANs) from Novell will provide access to printing and other services. The LANs, or in some cases individual workstations, will connect to a series of HP 2000 minicomputers for electronic mail and calendar applications. A private telecommunications network will combine InterAAct and SABRE, American's worldwide reservations network.

American Airlines is expecting the system to provide the major gains in productivity that have eluded previous generations of office systems. Management and clerical workers are expected to increase productivity by 7%. Another 2% improvement is expected as a result of giving employees more timely and accurate access to the company's data.

Application Questions

☐ What office automation capabilities are provided by the CEO Object Office and Inter-AAct Systems?

☐ Why do you think that office automation has apparently not increased white-collar productivity?

☐ Why are the new office automation products supposed to finally increase office productivity?

Source: Adapted from Chris Sivula, "The White Collar Productivity Push," *Datamation,* January 15, 1990, pp. 52–54.

SUMMARY

☐ End user computing is the direct, hands-on use of computers by end users to perform the information processing needed to accomplish their work activities. End user computing application areas include office automation, information management and retrieval, decision support, and application development. Managers face major challenges as they seek to control end user computing so that it supports the goals and protects the resources of an organization while still improving end user productivity.

☐ An end user computing system consists of hardware, software, people, and data resources. Hardware resources include microcomputer workstations, local area network servers, departmental minicomputers, and corporate mainframes. Software resources consist of application packages, fourth-generation languages, and application development packages. People resources include end users and information center consultants. Data resources include personal, work group, corporate, and external databases.

☐ Office automation systems are computer-based information systems that collect, store, and transmit electronic messages, documents, and other forms of communications. Office automation systems include word processing systems, desktop publishing systems, electronic mail, voice mail, facsimile, image processing, electronic meeting systems, and office support systems.

☐ Office automation systems increase the productivity of knowledge workers and reduce the costs of office communications. They shorten the turnaround time between the preparation and receipt of documents and messages, reduce the expense and errors involved in producing documents, and increase the productivity of executives and professionals who are heavy users of office communications. However, the cost of automated office hardware is higher than the equipment it replaces. Office automation may also disrupt traditional office work roles and work environments and impair organizational productivity.

KEY TERMS AND CONCEPTS

These are the key terms and concepts of this chapter. The page number of their first explanation is in parentheses.

1. Desktop publishing *(254)*
2. Documents *(253)*
3. Electronic document management *(256)*
4. Electronic mail *(258)*
5. Electronic meeting systems *(259)*
6. End user computing *(240)*
    a. Managerial challenges *(240)*
    b. Resources *(241)*
7. End user computing applications *(243)*
    a. Office automation *(243)*
    b. Information management and retrieval *(245)*
    c. Decision support *(246)*
    d. Applications development *(247)*
8. Facsimile *(258)*
9. Information center *(247)*
10. Information float *(262)*
11. Image processing *(256)*
12. Interactive video *(257)*
13. Office automation *(252)*
    a. Information system activities *(252)*
    b. Managerial challenges *(262)*
    c. Types of systems *(252)*
14. Office support systems *(261)*

15. Personal information manager *(246)*
16. Telecommuting *(260)*
17. Teleconferencing *(259)*
18. Telephone tag *(262)*
19. Text data *(253)*
20. User consultant *(242)*
21. Voice mail *(258)*
22. Word processing *(253)*
23. Work group computing *(243)*

REVIEW QUIZ

Match one of the **key terms and concepts** listed above with one of the brief examples of definitions listed below. Try to find the best fit for answers that seem to fit more than one term or concept. Defend your choices.

———— 1. The direct, hands-on use of computers by users.

———— 2. End user applications frequently lack adequate controls.

———— 3. Examples are microcomputers, application packages, information center consultants, and external databases.

———— 4. Managing databases and generating reports.

———— 5. Using an electronic spreadsheet for what-if analysis.

———— 6. Developing ways to use computers to perform jobs for you.

———— 7. Organizations have established these end user support groups.

———— 8. Includes word processing, desktop publishing, electronic mail, and teleconferencing systems.

———— 9. Input by optical scanning, processing of images, output by interactive video.

———— 10. Automates office work activities and communications, but may disrupt traditional work roles.

———— 11. Text data is manipulated and documents are produced.

———— 12. Characters, words, sentences, and paragraphs.

———— 13. Letters, memos, forms, and reports.

———— 14. Users can produce their own brochures and manuals.

———— 15. Use your workstation to send and receive messages.

———— 16. Use your telephone as an electronic message terminal.

———— 17. The time a document is in transit between sender and receiver.

———— 18. You and the person you want to contact repeatedly miss each other's phone calls.

———— 19. Transmitting images of documents electronically.

———— 20. Realtime televised electronic meetings at remote sites.

———— 21. Using telecommunications so you can work at home.

———— 22. End users can electronically capture, store, process, and retrieve images of documents and other visual media.

———— 23. Customer correspondence and sales orders can be optically captured and routed to end users for processing.

———— 24. Allows end users to see and hear presentations stored on optical disks in a structured or random manner.

———— 25. Helps end users store information in a variety of forms and retrieve it in many different ways.

_____ 26. Provides a variety of office automation services such as electronic calendars and meeting scheduling.

_____ 27. Members of a work group share computer resources to jointly accomplish work assignments.

REAL WORLD PROBLEMS

1. Consolidated Insurance Group, Inc.

    Consolidated Insurance Group, Inc. uses a simple ploy to dramatize the difference between its former mainframe operations and its current local area network-based environment in Wilmington, Delaware. Visitors are initially taken to the beautiful, glass-walled room housing the almost-defunct IBM 3090 Model 120E mainframe, along with "monster disk drives, like big refrigerators," said Wayne Read, the firm's assistant vice president of information systems. "Then we show them the small office with our seven LANs and disk drives the size of PCs. It's pretty powerful," Read said. The LANs were initially set up just to handle word processing and electronic mail, but IS kept finding LAN-based applications that seemed to work better or more cheaply than the mainframe versions. "Things just snowballed," Read said, particularly after management had a chance to see how well the first few applications worked on LANs and realized "we can now do things in a day that would take a week on the mainframe," Read said. Once this happened, "they gave us the green light" to implement the more complex and mission-critical applications.

    The capital expenses of the LAN-based systems come to $300,000, or 10 percent of the cost of the mainframe, Read said. Operating expenses are expected to be reduced by $1 million per year, he added. End users are the other major beneficiaries. Joseph McNally, a controller at the firm, was "ecstatic" about his new ability to download his own data into a PC application, instead of having to plod through canned reports or wait for IS to get around to his query. However, Read's group made sure that users' new freedoms did not jeopardize mission-critical applications on the new system. For example, users do not work directly with corporate files. Instead, they download what they need onto a "scratch-pad" file. This way, if they happen to delete a file, "they are only hurting themselves," Read said.

    a. Why did Consolidated Insurance switch from mainframe to LAN-based computing?

    b. How has this affected end user computing and control?

    Source: Adapted from Elisabeth Horwitt, "Insurer's Cost Cutting Policy: Out with Hosts: In with LANs," Computerworld, February 19, 1990, pp. 1, 12.

2. Canadian National Railways

    At the Canadian National Railways (CN) in Montreal, the PC revolution is over—and it has been for five years. Today, the challenge is to knot PCs more seamlessly into the company's computing strategy. "We recognized in late 1984 that PCs were becoming a part of the corporate computing architecture," said Ronan McGrath, vice president and controller for CN. "If you go back to 1981 or 82, when the PC rebels felt they couldn't get what they wanted from the traditional systems, they would build their own systems." Because the company has imposed stricter computing standards, "the kind of mechanic who is out there tinkering has largely disappeared," he said.

Early in 1985, the information-system (IS) group, led by Allan Posniak, vice president of information systems, recognized the need for a "strategic-products list" that outlined what PC-based hardware and software is compatible with the railroad's architecture. Thus, though McGrath has direct control of only about 400 of the railroad's 6,000 PCs, he sits on a senior management committee that decides on information-technology issues and is in frequent contact with executives at Compaq Computer Corp., Microsoft, and Lotus. The railroad is a frequent test site for these companies' products—as well as a major customer. "Early on, we built a very complex but successful payroll system based on PCs, and we realized all the disciplines required for information systems on the mainframe are equally required on the PC," McGrath said. Those things are not understood by the hacker-level of designer."

a. Why is "the PC revolution" over at Canadian National Railways?
b. How is CN managing end user computing?

Source: Adapted from Robert Scheier, "How Four PC Managers Traveled the Decade of Change," PC Week, January 1, 1990, p. 55.

3. Diagonal Data Corporation
The Data Access groupware package, Office Works, is more than a communications solution; it's a business solution. "If you pulled the plug on Office Works, our productivity would drop off by 20 to 30 percent," said John Shufflebarger, vice president of research and development at Diagonal Data Corporation, a software developer in Lakeland, Florida. Diagonal Data employees use most of the Office Works modules, including E-mail calendar and document control. However, electronic telephone messaging is the most important module, especially for the many sales people at the firm.

"Our phone persona is our livelihood," Shufflebarger said. "Before Office Works, our receptionist was getting writer's cramp, and the messages weren't even getting distributed—she was too busy answering the phones," he explained. Now, not only do employees get their phone messages, "but you can't ignore them either," he said. "Your screen rings like a telephone, a flashing rectangle shows up on the screen, and when you press a key, the subject line of the message appears." Also, Shufflebarger added, "Because the Office Works user interface is so intuitive, there's little need for detailed user training. We let users know the tutorial is available and tell them how to access it, but few people have had to use it."

a. What are the benefits of Office Works to Diagonal Data?
b. Would you like to work in an office that used Office Works? Explain.

Source: Adapted from Martha Tracy, "Buyers Increase Productivity with Office Works 1.1" PC Week, March 19, 1990, p. 79.

4. Price Waterhouse
Price Waterhouse has begun to link its approximately 12,000 personal computers in domestic offices via local area networks and to put the

Lotus groupware package, Notes, at the core. By pushing investment data out to departmental users quickly and efficiently, the Big Six accounting firm hopes to become a leader in the international financial industry. "It is consistent with our belief that computer technology has been going through a transition, from a support role to a strategic role that would offer leverage (on the competition)," said Sheldon Laube, Price Waterhouse's national director of information and technology. Eventually, Laube said, all the approximately 12,000 Price Waterhouse PCs in domestic office LANs will be linked with Notes. It should take two to three years to install all the 10,000 packages of Notes which the accounting firm has purchased.

Notes combines the functionality of database applications with electronic mail to enable users to customize communications used on LANs and WANs. With Notes on a LAN, a group of people working on a common project can access and annotate shared documents. Data from one server can be viewed by all others on the LAN or WAN simultaneously to enable group conferences and interaction that previously were executed by shuffling messages from client to client. Notes was chosen because of its ability to communicate and share information among all of the international offices. Laube said that, at first, he thought electronic mail was the way to do this, but that he came to realize that what he was looking for was a computer-conferencing capability.

a. Why did Price Waterhouse buy 10,000 copies of the Notes software package?

b. What capabilities of Notes were most important to Price Waterhouse?

Source: Adapted from Laurence Swasey, "Accounting Firm Builds a Notes-Based Network," *MIS Week*, January 29, 1990, pp. 1, 12.

5. Intel Corporation

Fax machines aren't just for ordering sandwiches from the local deli. Some imaginative users are turning fax machines and fax boards into strategic systems to forge vital links with suppliers and customers. At Helicopter Support Inc. in Orange, Connecticut, as many as 1,000 fax transactions per day carry price and order information to and from customers, suppliers, and government regulators around the world. At Kentucky Fried Chicken Corp. in Louisville, Kentucky, fax boards send blueprints from PCs to contractors overseas. And at Intel Corp., as many as 10,000 brochures and technical documents are faxed each week from Intel computers to customers who punch in their requests on a Touch-Tone phone.

Intel's Personal Computer Enhancement Operation (PCEO) in Hillsboro, Oregon, developed its fax-based system to reduce the number of service calls it handled manually at a cost of $10 per call, said Art King, an engineer in PCEO's new opportunity development group. Now customers call on a Touch-Tone phone and enter a code number for the product information or service bulletins they want and then type in the number of the fax machine to which they want the information sent. The whole process is completed without human intervention, said King, and costs about $1 per call in long-distance charges. Intel uses PCs with its own fax boards and a voice-synthesis card from Dialogic Corp. to read back the phone numbers and give instructions to callers.

a. Why can the use of fax produce strategic systems for a business?
b. Why is Intel's fax system an example of such strategic systems?

Source: Adapted from Robert Scheier, "Fax Provides Low Cost Links to Customers," *PC Week,* March 5, 1990, pp. 135–36.

6. North American Van Lines

Until recently, the first stop for paperwork at trucking giant North American Van Lines was a manual system dating back to the 1930s—a string of filing cabinets containing thousands of pieces of paper in color-coded folders. But now the company uses what is believed to be the first optical-based document system at a trucking company. Officials at North American said they believe the $1.05 million system will cut costs and significantly reduce the time it takes to move the 4,000 to 7,500 documents that come into its mailroom each day and then go back to customers as invoices. Best of all, they said, a customer will get immediate answers to questions about their shipment's status through terminals supplied to all customer service agents, who will be able to review all documents associated with a job.

The heart of the storage system is a Filenet OSAR-64 optical-disk jukebox and minicomputer. Able to manage up to 64 12-inch optical disks, the OSAR can hold about 3.5 million pages—the equivalent of 320 five-drawer file cabinets. "As soon as a driver walks in the door or as soon as the invoice hits the mailroom, the document will be scanned, committed to disk, and we will be able to do our financial calculations on the corporate mainframe," VP John Pentangelo said. Scanning will also make the documents immediately available to other departments, from customer service to the cargo department. The terminals—41 are now in place—are linked over a local area network at North American's headquarters in Fort Wayne, Indiana.

a. Which IS technologies are used in North American's document imaging system?
b. What are the benefits of their imaging system?

Source: Adapted from Willis Booker, "Imaging Keeps on Trucking," *Computerworld,* February 12, 1990, p. 25.

7. The Travelers Corporation

One company that is attempting to bring electronic publishing into the corporate mainstream is Hartford, Connecticut–based The Travelers Corporation, where an integrated approach to electronic publishing is now getting off the ground. "We want to control our publishing tasks from the tree to the mailbox," says Robert Bennett, second vice president at The Travelers, "From the time one of our business units has a creative thought about a product they want to produce through the time the product leaves The Travelers' premises and enters into the distribution system . . . we want to, whenever possible, electronify that process and eliminate manual intervention.

"In 1988, we spent close to $300 million on printing and publishing," continues Bennett. "Of that, 15 percent was really printing, and 85 percent was associated with all the other things that have to go on— weighing, storage, people that sort mail—in the printing and publishing process. We can cut a significant portion of that through the development of electronic publishing." Most of the company's documents, which consist of such items as insurance policies, contracts, and brochures, are created at the workstation level in a Travelers field office, either with an IBM PC AT or PS/2 using Xerox Ventura desktop publishing software. Most of the PCs are on token-ring local networks. Forms are printed on a laser printer. When a document must be moved from one workstation to another location, either for viewing, approval, or printing, Travelers employs its nationwide telecommunications network, which connects all of the field offices to each other and to corporate headquarters in Hartford. "So we're now in a position where we can have the experts compose and approve the documents and send them to their proper place for printing," Bennett says.

a. How is electronic publishing accomplished at Travelers?
b. Why does Travelers want to control their electronic publishing tasks "from the tree to the mailbox"?

Source: Adapted from Bob Frances, "A Corporate Vision for Publishing," *Datamation*, January 15, 1990, pp. 65–66.

SELECTED REFERENCES

1. Barcomb, David. *Office Automation: A Survey of Tools and Technology.* 2nd ed. Boston: Digital Press, 1988.
2. Dennis, Alan; Joey George; Len Jessup; Jay Nunamaker; and Douglas Vogel. "Information Technology to Support Group Meetings." *MIS Quarterly*, December 1988.
3. "Electronic Document Management." *I/S Analyzer*, May–June 1989.
4. Millman, Zeeva, and Jon Hartwick. "The Impact of Automated Office Systems on Middle Managers and Their Work." *MIS Quarterly*, December 1987.
5. Panko, Raymond. *End User Computing: Management, Applications, and Technology.* New York: John Wiley & Sons, 1988.
6. Radding, Alan. "So Your Users Want a PIM." *Datamation*, January 16, 1989.
7. Sanders, Bruce. "Making Groups Work." *Computerworld*," March 15, 1990.
8. Sassone, Peter, and A. Perry Schwartz. "Cost-Justifying OA." *Datamation*, February 15, 1986.
9. Sprague, Ralph, Jr., and Barbara McNurlin, ed. *Information Systems Management in Practice*, 2nd ed. Englewood Cliffs, N.J.: Prentice-Hall, 1989.
10. Strassmann, Paul. *Information Payoff: The Transformation of Work in the Electronic Age.* New York: The Free Press, 1984.

CHAPTER

8

TRANSACTION PROCESSING AND INFORMATION REPORTING SYSTEMS

■ Chapter Outline

■ Learning Objectives

The purpose of this chapter is to give you a basic understanding of how information systems support (1) the processing of business transactions and (2) the reporting needs of management.

Section I of this chapter outlines the major functions of transaction processing systems. It also discusses major changes taking place in transaction processing, such as electronic data interchange (EDI), as well as the advantages and disadvantages of basic types of transaction processing systems.

Section II discusses major considerations involved in information systems that present and report information to management. Therefore, it discusses the basic rationale, components, and information products of information reporting systems.

After reading and studying this chapter, you should be able to:

1. Identify the major activities of transaction processing systems and give examples of how they support the operations of a business.

2. Identify the advantages and disadvantages of traditional data entry versus source data automation and batch processing versus realtime processing.

3. Analyze the quality of a variety of information products using the three dimensions of information quality.

4. Discuss the purpose of the major reporting and presentation alternatives of information reporting systems.

Section I: Transaction Processing Systems

INTRODUCTION

Transaction processing systems are information systems that process data resulting from the occurrence of business transactions. Figure 8–1 illustrates this concept. *Transactions* are events that occur as part of doing business, such as sales, purchases, deposits, withdrawals, refunds, and payments. Think, for example, of the data generated whenever a business sells something to a customer on credit. Data about the customer, product, salesperson, store, and so on, must be captured and processed. This in turn causes additional transactions, such as credit checks, customer billing, inventory changes, and increases in accounts receivable balances, which generate even more data. Thus, transaction processing activities are needed to capture and process such data, or the operations of a business would grind to a halt. Therefore, transaction processing systems play a vital role in supporting the operations of an organization.

Figure 8–1   The role of transaction processing systems in a business. Note how business transactions such as sales to customers and purchases from suppliers are generated by the physical operations system of this manufacturing firm. Data describing these transactions are subsequently processed by various transaction processing systems, resulting in updated corporate databases and a variety of information products.

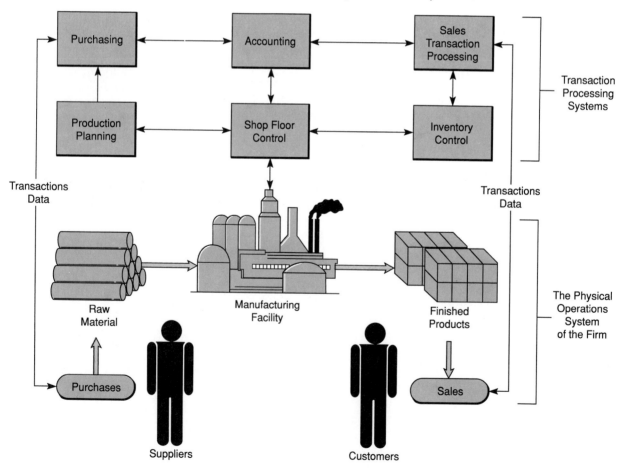

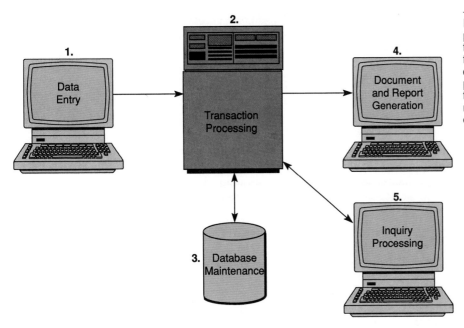

Figure 8–2 The transaction processing cycle. Note that transaction processing systems use a five-stage cycle of data entry, transaction processing, database maintenance, document and report generation, and inquiry processing activities.

Transaction processing systems capture and process data describing business transactions. Then they update the databases of the organization and produce a variety of information products for internal and external use. You should think of these activities as a cycle of basic transaction processing activities. As Figure 8–2 illustrates, transaction processing systems go through a five-stage cycle of (1) data entry activities, (2) transaction processing activities, (3) database maintenance, (4) document and report generation, and (5) inquiry processing activities. Let's take a closer look now at how each of these basic activities occurs in transaction processing systems.

The Transaction Processing Cycle

The input activity in transaction processing systems involves a **data entry** process. In this process, data is captured, or collected, by recording, coding, and editing activities. Then, data may be converted to a form that can be entered into a computer system. Data entry activities have always been a bottleneck in transaction processing. It has always been a problem getting data into computers accurately and quickly enough to match their awesome processing speeds. Thus, traditional *manual* methods of data entry that make heavy use of *data media* are being replaced by *direct automated methods*. These methods are more efficient and reliable and are known as *source data automation*. Let's take a look at these methods.

THE DATA ENTRY PROCESS

Traditional methods of data entry typically rely on the end users of an information system to capture data on **source documents** such as purchase orders, payroll time sheets, and sales order forms. These source documents are then usually accumulated into batches and transferred to data processing professionals specializing in data entry. Periodically, the source documents are subjected to several additional data entry activities:

Traditional Data Entry

☐ Have you ever heard the phrase "garbage in, garbage out" (GIGO)? That's why data must be *edited* and subjected to various *data verification* activities to ensure that it has been recorded correctly. This is a crucial part of both traditional and automated methods of data entry. For example, traditional data entry depends on visual checks of source documents and data entry displays, calculating *control totals* of selected items of data, and formatted data entry displays that warn an operator if data is entered incorrectly.

☐ The data is converted into a **machine-readable medium,** such as magnetic tape or magnetic disks. Typically, this means using such devices as key-to-tape machines and key-to-disk systems. These media are then read by input devices that enter the data into a computer system.

☐ Alternatively, the data from source documents could be entered into a computer system using a **direct input** device (such as the keyboard of a video terminal) with no use of machine-readable media.

Figure 8–3 illustrates this traditional data entry process, using sales transaction processing as an example. Note the use of sales forms as source documents and their conversion to magnetic tape media. Note also the many data entry activities involved. It should not be surprising, then, to discover that there has been a major shift away from traditional data entry. First, it requires too many activities, people, and data media. Second, it results in high costs and increases the potential for errors. Therefore, the response of both end users and the computer industry has been to move toward *source data automation*.

Source Data Automation

The use of automated methods of data entry is known as **source data automation.** Several methods have been developed to accomplish this automation, though very few completely automate the data entry process. They are all based on trying to reduce or eliminate many of the activities, people, and data media required by traditional data entry methods. Figure 8–4 is an example of source data automation. Notice that this sales transaction processing system:

☐ Captures data as *early as possible* after a transaction or other event occurs by using POS terminals.

☐ Captures transaction data as *close as possible* to the source that generates the data. Salespersons at POS terminals capture and edit data right on the sales floor.

☐ Captures data by using *machine-readable media* initially (bar-coded tags and mag stripe credit cards), instead of preparing written source documents.

☐ Capture data that rarely changes by *prerecording* it on machine-readable media or by *storing* it in the computer system.

☐ Capture data directly *without the use of data media* by optical scanning of bar codes printed on product packaging.

ELECTRONIC DATA INTERCHANGE

A fast-growing area of transaction processing is called **electronic data interchange,** or EDI. This involves the electronic transmission of business transaction data over telecommunications links between the computers of *trading partners* (organizations and their customers and suppliers). Data repre-

Figure 8-3 A traditional data entry example: sales transaction processing. Note that source documents are (1) manually edited, (2) batched, (3) converted to another medium, (4) entered into a computer system, (5) edited again, (6) corrected where necessary and reentered, (7) sorted, and (8) accepted into the computer system.

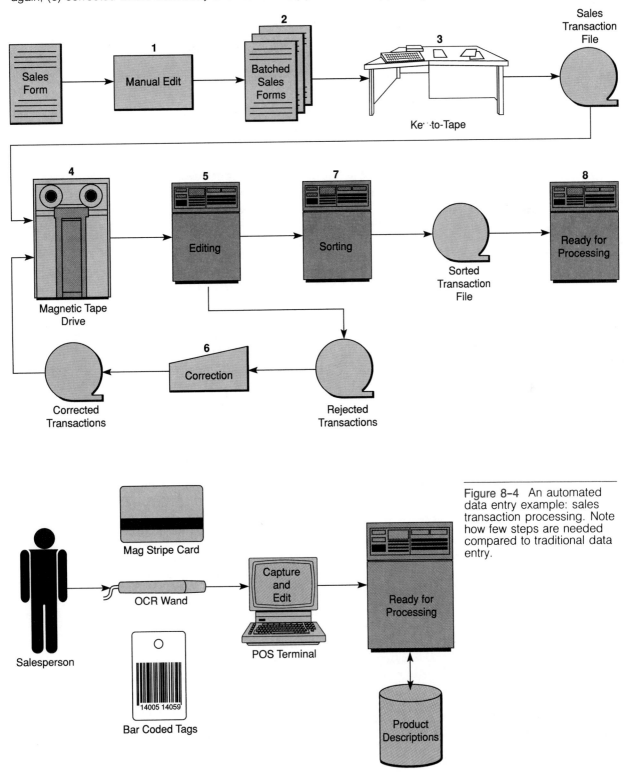

Figure 8-4 An automated data entry example: sales transaction processing. Note how few steps are needed compared to traditional data entry.

Figure 8–5 EDI alternatives.
Note that one EDI method
relies on the use of an electronic mailbox provided by a
third party, whereas the
other involves direct computer interchange between
trading partners.

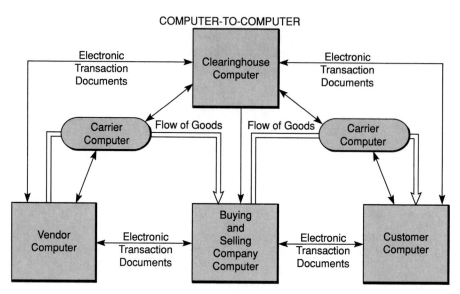

COMPUTER-TO-COMPUTER

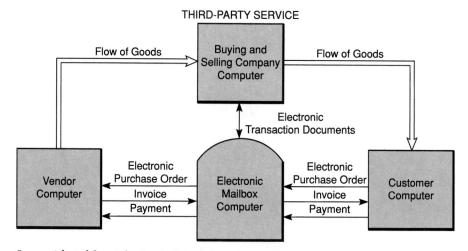

THIRD-PARTY SERVICE

Source: Adapted from John Burch, "EDI: The Demise of Paper," *Information Executive,*
Winter 1989, p. 52.

senting a variety of typical business *transaction documents* (such as purchase
orders, invoices, requests for quotations, and shipping notices) are electronically transmitted using standard document message formats. Thus, EDI is
an example of the almost complete automation of the data entry process.

Formatted transaction data is transmitted over telecommunications links
directly between computers, without paper documents or human intervention.
If necessary, EDI software is used to convert a company's own document
formats into standardized EDI formats as specified by various industry and
international protocols. Figure 8–5 illustrates two forms of EDI. One method
uses an electronic mailbox provided by a third party, usually a value-added
telecommunications carrier. The other method is direct computer connectivity

between trading partners, sometimes with the help of a *clearinghouse* organization, which provides EDI bookkeeping services for the participants [1].

Companies in the automotive, chemical, grocery, and transportation industries were the earliest users of EDI technology, but it has spread to many manufacturing and retailing companies. For example, the penetration of EDI within various industries in 1988 was estimated as follows: railroads, 90 percent; trucking, 75 percent; grocery, 50 percent; and automotive, 35 percent. Companies offering EDI services include GE Information Services, IBM, Control Data Corporation, and McDonnell Douglas [6].

EDI eliminates the printing, mailing, checking, and handling by employees of numerous multiple copy forms of business documents. Also, since standard document formats are used, the delays caused by mail or telephone communication between businesses to verify what a document means are drastically reduced. Some of the benefits that result are reductions in paper, postage, and labor costs; faster flow of transactions; reduction in errors; increases in productivity; support of just-in-time (JIT) inventory policies; reductions in inventory levels; and better customer service. For example, decreases of 25 percent to 50 percent in the total time it takes to receive, process, package, and ship customer orders are reported. Annual savings of $300 million in the grocery industry and $1.2 billion in the textile industry are expected. RCA expects the cost of processing a purchase order to drop from $50 to $4, and EDI is estimated to save $200 per automobile in the auto industry [6] .

Benefits of EDI

However, EDI is more than a way to increase efficiency, cut costs, and provide better service. In many industries, it has become an absolute business requirement. EDI is now a *strategic application* of information systems in many industries, where the message is "link up or lose out." Or as IBM vice president Edward Lucente says, "Doing business without EDI will soon be like trying to do business without a telephone. No EDI, no business." General Motors proved that point when it made EDI a requirement for its 20,000 suppliers in 1987, while the U.S. Department of Defense has made it a requirement for its suppliers as of 1991. Experts predict that, by 1995, one third of all business documents will involve EDI. Thus, EDI promises to revolutionize data entry in transaction processing systems while promoting strategic relationships between trading partners [1, 6].

Transaction processing systems process data in two basic ways: (1) **batch processing,** where transactions data is accumulated over a period of time and processed periodically, and (2) **realtime processing,** where data is processed immediately after a transaction occurs. Transaction processing systems still make heavy use of batch processing. However, the use of realtime processing for one or more stages of transaction processing is growing, and it is expected to eventually become the primary form of transaction processing.

BATCH PROCESSING

In **batch processing,** transactions data are accumulated over a period of time and processed periodically. Batch processing usually involves:

☐ Gathering *source documents* originated by business transactions, such as sales orders and invoices, into groups called *batches.*

☐ Recording transaction data on an *input medium,* such as magnetic disks or magnetic tape.

☐ Sorting the transactions in a *transaction file* in the same sequence as the records in a sequential *master file*.

☐ Processing transaction data and creating an updated master file and a variety of *documents* (such as customer invoices and paychecks) and *reports*.

☐ Capturing and storing batches of transaction data at remote sites and then transmitting it periodically to a central computer for processing. This is known as *remote job entry*, or RJE.

In batch processing, not only are the transaction data for a particular application accumulated into batches, but a number of different transaction processing jobs are processed periodically (daily, weekly, monthly). The rationale for batch processing is that the grouping of data and the periodic processing of jobs more efficiently uses computer system resources, compared to allowing data and jobs to be processed in an unorganized, random manner. Of course, this efficiency, economy, and control are accomplished by sacrificing the immediate processing of data for end users.

Example.   In a typical example of batch processing, the banking industry usually accumulates all checks deposited during the day into batches for processing each evening. Though customer bank balances are updated continually on a realtime basis to reflect electronic banking transactions (such as the use of ATMs), final daily checking account balances are confirmed, and many management reports are produced daily by batch processing systems. Figure 8–6 illustrates a batch processing system where

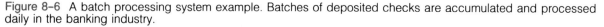

Figure 8–6   A batch processing system example. Batches of deposited checks are accumulated and processed daily in the banking industry.

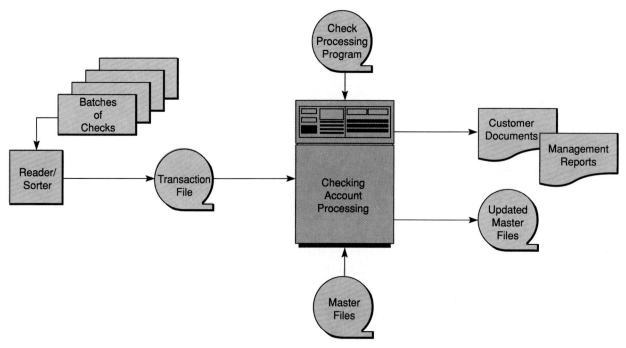

transaction data in the form of batches of deposited checks are captured each day by MICR reader/sorters, which read the data recorded in magnetic ink on the bottom of each check. The transaction data are then processed using a check processing application program that updates customer and other databases and produces a variety of customer documents and management reports.

Batch processing is an economical method when large volumes of transaction data must be processed. It is ideally suited for many applications where it is not necessary to update databases as transactions occur, and where documents and reports are required only at scheduled intervals. For example, customer statements may be prepared on a monthly basis, whereas payroll processing might be done on a weekly basis.

Advantages and Disadvantages

However, batch processing has some real disadvantages. Master files are frequently out of date between scheduled processing, as are the periodic scheduled reports that are produced. Also, immediate updated responses to inquiries cannot be made. For these reasons, more and more computer applications use realtime processing systems. However, batch processing is still widely used in transaction processing systems, and some of its disadvantages are overcome by using realtime processing for some transaction processing functions, such as data entry or inquiry processing.

In transaction processing systems, a **realtime processing** capability allows transaction data to be processed immediately after they are generated and can provide immediate output to end users. In full-fledged realtime processing, data are processed as soon as they are originated or recorded, without waiting to accumulate batches of data. Data are fed directly into the computer system from *online terminals*, without being sorted, and they are always stored *online* in *direct access files*. Files and databases are always up to date since they are updated whenever data is originated, regardless of its frequency. Responses to end users' inquiries are immediate since information stored on direct access devices can be retrieved almost instantaneously. Realtime processing depends on telecommunications networks of online terminals and computers. A summary of the important capabilities differentiating batch processing and realtime processing is shown in Figure 8–7.

REALTIME PROCESSING

Figure 8–7 Batch versus realtime processing. Note the major differences.

Characteristic	Batch Processing	Realtime Processing
Processing of transactions	Transaction data is recorded, accumulated into batches, sorted, and processed periodically.	Transaction data is processed as generated
File update	When batch is processed	When transaction is processed
Response time/turnaround time	Several hours or days after batches are submitted for processing	A few seconds after each transaction is captured

Figure 8–8 Example of a
realtime sales processing
system. Note that sales
transaction processing,
inquiries and responses, and
file updates are accom-
plished immediately using
online devices.

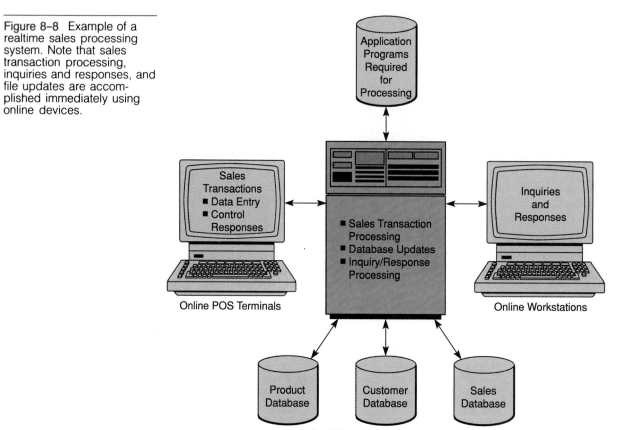

Example. An example of a realtime transaction processing system is shown in Figure 8–8. Note how POS terminals are connected by telecommunications links to a computer for immediate entry of sales data and control responses (such as customer credit verification). The online direct access customer, product, and sales databases are all immediately updated to reflect sales transactions. The application programs required for sales transaction processing, database updates, and inquiry/response processing are stored on direct access devices until needed. Finally, employees can use telecommunication links to their workstations to make inquiries and receive displays concerning customers, sales activity, inventory status, and so on.

Realtime processing is frequently called *online processing* since an online capability is required in realtime processing systems. However, use of this term can be misleading because batch processing systems can use online remote job entry devices and online direct access files in the processing of batches of data. Other terms used include *online transaction processing* (OLTP) or *online realtime* (OLRT) processing.

Part of the reluctance to use the term *realtime* stems from its former narrow meaning in which data not only had to be processed immediately, but the results of processing had to be instantly available to control an ongoing process. In the past, that definition could be used to describe only a limited number of applications, typically process control and military and spacecraft systems.

However, advances in computer hardware and software have made a realtime capability applicable to many of the functions of modern information systems. In this context, *realtime processing* means that, not only is input data processed immediately, but output results are available fast enough to meet the immediate information needs of end users. Many modern information systems can easily meet this criterion, whether they rely on microcomputer or mainframe computer systems.

Realtime processing provides immediate updating of databases and immediate responses to user inquiries. Realtime processing is particularly important for applications where there is a high frequency of changes that must be made to a database during a short time to keep it updated. Only the specific records affected by transactions or inquiries need to be processed, and several databases can be processed or updated concurrently.

Advantages and Disadvantages

   Realtime processing has its disadvantages. Because of the online, direct access nature of realtime processing, special precautions must be taken to protect the contents of databases. Thus, many realtime systems use magnetic tape files as *control logs* (to record all transactions made) or as *backup files* (by periodically making a magnetic tape copy of a file). Also, more controls have to be built into the software and processing procedures to protect against unauthorized access or the accidental destruction of data. Thus, the many advantages of realtime processing must be balanced with the extra costs and security precautions that are necessary. However, most computer-using firms are willing to pay this price since the use of realtime processing continues to increase in modern information systems.

Database maintenance is a major activity of transaction processing systems. An organization's databases must be built and maintained by its transaction processing systems so that they are always correct and up to date. (Database maintenance was discussed in Chapter 6.) Therefore, transaction processing systems update the corporate databases of an organization to reflect changes resulting from day-to-day business transactions. For example, a credit sale made to a customer will cause the customer's account balance to be increased and the amount of inventory on hand to be decreased. These and other changes must be reflected in the data records stored in the databases of the company.

DATABASE MAINTENANCE

   In addition, transaction processing systems process data resulting from miscellaneous adjustments to the records in a file or database. For example, name and address changes may have to be made to customer records, and tax withholding changes may have to be made to employee payroll records. Thus, a major role of transaction processing systems is to update and make changes to an organization's corporate databases. These databases then provide the data resources needed by information reporting systems, executive information systems, and decision support systems.

The final stage in the transaction processing cycle is the generation of information products such as documents and reports. Figure 8–9 illustrates several examples. Documents produced by transaction processing systems are called **transaction documents.** There are several major types of such documents:

DOCUMENT AND REPORT GENERATION

Figure 8–9 Examples of information products produced by transaction processing systems. Transaction documents such as customer statements must be prepared and mailed to customers on a monthly basis. The cash requirements register is a control listing that lists the checks that must be prepared in payment of amounts owed to vendors.

LANG CORPORATION

STATEMENT OF CUSTOMER ACCOUNT

CUSTOMER NO. 554386

HITTON CORPORATION
138 MARSHALL DR.
PO BOX 851
LONG PORT, CA 94134

DATE 9/30/--

| DATE | | | INVOICE | REFERENCE | DESCRIPTION | AMOUNT |
MO	DY	YR	NUMBER	NUMBER		
09	08	--	185163		PRIOR BALANCE	$7,565.46
09	10	--	075126		INVOICE	1,685.91
09	15	--		091531	PAYMENT	1,865.00CR
09	30	--			LC ADJUSTMENT	13.00CR
					LATE CHARGES	8.00

CURRENT AMOUNT	30 DAYS	60 DAYS & OVER	BALANCE DUE
$1,693.91	$696.46		$2,390.37

K KRAUSZ MANUFACTURING COMPANY
ACCOUNTS PAYABLE

CASH REQUIREMENTS REGISTER
DATE   APR 12 19

VENDOR	VENDOR NUMBER	DUE DATE	INVOICE AMOUNT	DISCOUNT	CHECK AMOUNT
SOLVAY GEN SUP	1016	4/16	$ 773.30	$ 15.47	$ 757.83
ROCHESTER PR CO	1021	4/16	1,620.18	32.40	1,587.78
CALABRIA CONT	1049	4/16	143.65	2.87	140.78
ONONDAGA STL CO	1077	4/16	5,982.82	119.66	5,863.16
BLACK & NICHOLS	1103	4/16	14.25	.71	13.54
AUSTERHOLZ INC	1240	4/16	624.77	12.50	612.27
AUSTERHOLZ INC	1240	4/16	1,833.19	36.66	1,796.53
CHRISTIE & CO	1366	4/16	745.54		754.54
WILSON & WILSON	2231	4/16	2,936.12	58.72	2,877.40
CLAR. HIGGINS	2590	4/16	1,000.00		1,000.00
HONOUR BROS	3101	4/16	97.36	1.95	95.41
BASTIANI & SON	3112	4/16	3,580.85	71.62	3,509.23
DRJ WIRE CO	3164	4/16	256.90	5.14	251.76
HASTING-WHITE	3258	4/16	1,144.42	22.89	1,121.53
DARONO ART MET	3427	4/16	32.75	.66	32.09
DARONO ART MET	3427	4/16	127.52	2.55	124.97
DARONO ART MET	3427	4/16	96.60	1.93	94.67

☐ **Action documents.** These are documents that initiate actions or transactions on the part of their recipient. For example, a purchase order authorizes a purchase from a supplier, and a paycheck authorizes a bank to pay an employee.

☐ **Information documents.** These documents relate, confirm, or prove to their recipients that transactions have occurred. Examples are sales receipts, sales order confirmations, customer invoices and statements, and credit rejection notices. Information documents can be used as *control documents* since they document the fact that a transaction has occurred.

☐ **Turnaround documents.** Some types of transaction documents are designed to be read by magnetic or optical scanning equipment. Forms produced in this manner are known as turnaround documents because they are designed to be returned to the sender. For example, many computer-printed invoices consist of a turnaround portion, which is returned by a customer along with his or her payment. The turnaround document can then be automatically processed by optical scanning devices. Thus, turnaround documents combine the functions of an action document (the turnaround portion) and an information document (the receipt portion).

Transaction processing systems also produce several types of reports and displays designed to document and monitor the results of business transactions occurring or processed during a specific time period. They are not specifically tailored for management use, though they may be used by managers. Such reports can provide an *audit trail* for control purposes. Examples are:

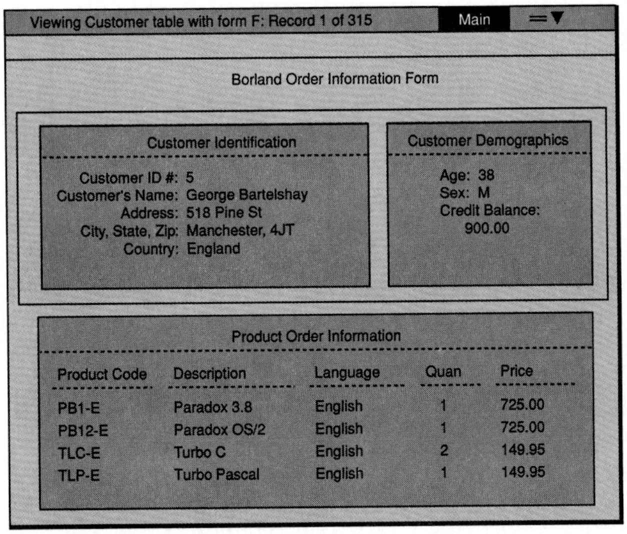

Figure 8-10 A multiple window customer order status display provided by a transaction processing system.

Courtesy Borland International Inc.

☐ **Control listings.** These are detailed reports that describe each transaction occurring during a period. They are also called *transaction logs*. For example, a listing known as a *payroll register* lists every paycheck printed on a specified payday by a payroll system.

☐ **Edit Reports.** These are reports that describe errors detected during processing. For example, a listing of invalid account numbers, missing data, and incorrect control totals would be presented in edit reports.

☐ **Accounting statements.** These are reports that legally document the financial performance or status of a business. Examples are general ledger summaries, statements of cash flow, balance sheets, and income statements.

Inquiry Processing

Transaction processing systems frequently support the realtime interrogation of online databases by end users. As we have previously mentioned, this **inquiry processing** capability can be provided by either batch or realtime processing systems. This activity of transaction processing systems depends on the use of telecommunications networks and database management query languages. It allows end users at workstations throughout an organization to make inquiries and receive responses concerning the results of transaction activity. Responses are received in a prespecified format that is displayed on an end user's video screen. For example, employees can check on the status of a sales order, the balance in an account, or the amount of stock in inventory and receive immediate responses at their workstations. See Figure 8–10.

Playtex, Sears, and DJ Distributing

Quick-response systems electronically link retailers and suppliers by means of technologies such as bar code scanners and electronic data interchange (EDI). That connection can allow just-in-time delivery of products, meaning inventory costs drop, more products can be sold at full price instead of at markdown, fewer customers leave empty-handed, and expensive store space can be devoted to sales instead of inventory. If they were used across the entire retail industry, quick-response systems could save retailers $9.6 billion a year after an initial investment of $3.6 billion and add up to savings of as much as 5.3 percent of retail sales, according to a study by Andersen Consulting, which outlines the following benefits:

☐ Boosts sales by 2 to 28 percent.
   Fewer customers walk out empty-handed.

☐ Cuts markdowns by 30 to 40 percent.
   Stores have less need to cut the price of slow-moving items.

☐ Cuts distribution costs by between one half and one quarter of 1 percent.
   Stores need fewer warehouse and stocking personnel and can cut space needed for inventory.

Playtex Apparel Inc. has been working on quick-response programs with its customers since 1985. In the last year, Playtex customers who use quick-response in their stores have increased their orders by 20 percent. At the same time, the inventory sitting in stores and warehouses has decreased by 7 percent. "Since these increased purchases are not in the store's inventory, they are increased sales, increased profitability," said Michael Baxter, manager of quick-response systems for Playtex.

Retail heavyweight Sears Roebuck & Co. used to devote 50 percent of its floor space to inventory storage. Using just-in-time inventory, it now stocks the same variety of underwear, shirts, and socks in only 20 percent of its floor space. This frees up thousands of square feet of space for sales, without the need for new construction. "At the per-square-foot cost of prime mall real estate, we see a huge profit potential in this strategy," said Tim Troy national distribution and planning director for several of Sears' clothing lines. And, he said, sales have risen 28 percent in the product lines handled via the quick-response system, using such technology as bar code scanners to update inventory and electronic purchase orders to get merchandise from suppliers.

Quick-response can work not only for large-scale suppliers such as Playtex, but also for "mom and pop" shops such as DJ Distributing in Brentwood, California, which didn't even own a PC when it began its quick-response effort. DJ now supplies the $5,000 worth of safety glasses that Pacific Bell buys each month because it was the first to accept the challenge of going online with the telecommunications provider, according to Raymond Wetteland, director of procurement systems at Pac Bell.

Once DJ had bought a PC and the EDI software, a total investment of about $2,200, the EDI software vendor wrote a program that would make it easy for DJ to exchange documents such as purchase orders with Pac Bell. But DJ still needed coaching from the bigger company before it could go online. Pac Bell spent about three weeks working with DJ to be sure both sides knew, for example, whether the word *package* referred to one pair of glasses or several pairs in one box, Wetteland said. Now, the shipping time for safety glasses has been cut from three weeks to 48 hours. "They basically captured the business because of their ability to deliver customer service and timely delivery," said Wetteland.

Application Questions

☐ What are the benefits of quick-response systems to retailers? Why do they occur?

☐ Why have quick-response systems increased sales and decreased investment at Sears and Playtex?

☐ How and why should small businesses like DJ Distributing use EDI?

Source: Adapted from Robert Scheier, "Electronic Links Save Money, Boost Sales," *PC Week,* April 2, 1990, p. 109.

Section II: Information Reporting Systems

Everyone needs information to survive and thrive. Managers and their organizations are no exception. In the previous section, we saw that transaction processing systems capture and process data which updates the corporate databases of organizations. Information reporting systems and other management information systems then process the data extracted from corporate databases to provide information to managers.

Therefore, this section will introduce you to basic concepts that underlie the quality and presentation of information to managers and other end users. This should help you understand how information reporting systems can provide high-quality information products that meet the needs of managers, executives, and the entire organization.

INTRODUCTION

In Chapter 1, we defined **information** as data (raw facts or observations) that have been transformed into a meaningful and useful form for people. Put another way, information is data placed in a context to give it value for specific end users. But what characteristics make information meaningful and useful to managers? What qualities give it value for end users? One way to answer these important questions is to consider the characteristics, or *attributes of information quality*.

Information that is outdated, inaccurate, or hard to understand would not be very meaningful, useful, or have much value to managers. They want information of high quality, that is, information whose characteristics, attributes, or qualities help make it valuable to them. It is useful to think of information as having the three dimensions of time, content, and form. Figure 8–11 summarizes important attributes of information quality and groups them into time, content, and form dimensions.

ATTRIBUTES OF INFORMATION QUALITY

Changes are occurring in information presentation methods that have significantly affected the information reporting alternatives of computer-based information systems. The goal of the changes in information presentations methods is to reduce the bottleneck of output activities that slows the speed of computerized processing, as well as to make computer-generated output more attractive and easy to use. Several important trends can be identified:

INFORMATION PRESENTATION ALTERNATIVES

☐ Replacing or supporting printed paper output with visual displays from video display terminals or voice output from audio response devices.

☐ Replacing printed paper output with machine-readable media such as magnetic tape and disks, optical disks, and microfilm media. These are faster to use for retrieval and processing and take up much less space.

☐ Reducing the amount of standardized paper reports produced on a regular basis with visual displays tailored to individual users and furnished to them instantly, but only at their request.

☐ Replacing *monochrome* displays of numeric data and text material with *color displays* of various forms of *graphics*.

Figure 8–11 The three dimensions of information quality. This outlines the attributes that should be present in high-quality management information.

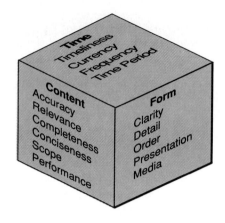

Time Dimension

Timeliness	Information should be provided when it is needed
Currency	Information should be up-to-date when it is provided
Frequency	Information should be provided as often as needed
Time Period	Information can be provided about past, present, and future time periods

Content Dimension

Accuracy	Information should be free from errors
Relevance	Information should be related to the information needs of a specific recipient for a specific situation
Completeness	All the information that is needed should be provided
Conciseness	Only the information that is needed should be provided
Scope	Information can have a broad or narrow scope, or an internal or external focus
Performance	Information can reveal performance by measuring activities accomplished, progress made, or resources accumulated

Form Dimension

Clarity	Information should be provided in a form that is easy to understand
Detail	Information can be provided in detail or summary form
Order	Information can be arranged in a predetermined sequence
Presentation	Information can be presented in narrative, numeric, graphic, or other forms
Media	Information can be provided in the form of printed paper documents, video displays, or other media

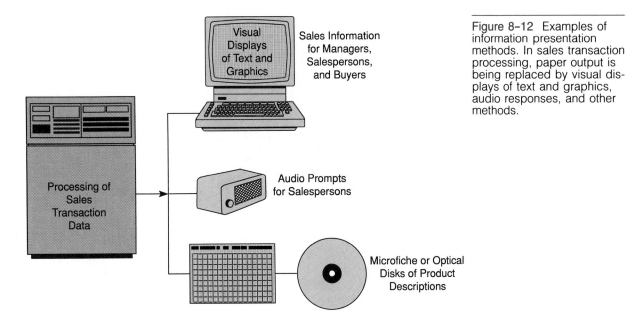

Figure 8–12 Examples of information presentation methods. In sales transaction processing, paper output is being replaced by visual displays of text and graphics, audio responses, and other methods.

Figure 8–12 provides an example of the variety of changes that have taken place in the methods, equipment, and media of modern information systems. Note that printed sales documents and reports have been replaced by visual displays, audio responses, and magnetic, optical, and microfilm media in a sales transaction processing system.

Business Graphics

Which type of output would you rather see, columns of numbers or a graphics display of the same information? Most people find it difficult to quickly and accurately comprehend numerical or statistical data that is presented in a purely numerical form (such as rows or columns of numbers). That is why *presentation graphics* methods, such as charts and graphs, are typically used in technical reports and business meetings. *Computer graphics* capabilities are provided to most end users by graphics software, which produces computer-generated video displays. Plotters and printers are also used to draw and print graphs on paper and other materials. Other devices can produce color slides and transparencies of computer-generated graphics. Most computer systems now offer end users a variety of graphics capabilities. See Figure 8–13.

Color graphics displays are replacing monochrome (one-color) displays of graphics. This may require that hardware components, such as *color graphics adapter* circuit boards, be added to microcomputers or terminals. Color displays provide a more natural user interface. This should make using video terminals a more attractive and comfortable experience and should result in fewer errors and greater productivity. Color is a very effective way of categorizing displayed information. Color helps draw attention to selected items, and it can be used to link related items in a display. For example, if an end user changes a data item that affects other data items in a display, the affected data items can change color, thus alerting the user.

Figure 8–13 Business graphics displays. Note the use of line and bar graphs, pie charts, three-dimensional graphs, and multiple window graphics.

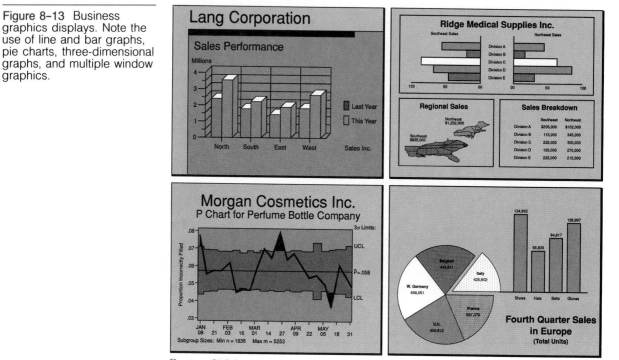

Courtesy SAS Institute Inc.

Computer graphics capabilities have been used for many years in engineering design applications, called *computer-aided design* (CAD), which are used in aircraft, automobile, machine tool, electronics, and other industries. Computer graphics techniques assist engineers in designing complex structures, researchers in analyzing volumes of data, and process control technicians in monitoring industrial processes. However, the uses of **business graphics** to help end users and managers monitor business operations and make better decisions is now being emphasized. Instead of being overwhelmed by large amounts of computer-produced data, graphics displays can assist managers in analyzing and interpreting data.

Graphics displays do not totally replace reports and displays of numbers and text material. Such methods are still needed to present the detailed information required in many applications. However, the use of line and bar graphs, pie charts, pictorial charts using a variety of symbols, and other types of presentation graphics is becoming a usual method of presenting business information. That's because trends, problems, and opportunities hidden in data are easier to spot when using graphics displays. For example, computer graphics would make it easier for a marketing manager to see complex market trends and analyze market problems and opportunities. Figure 8–14 outlines the advantages and disadvantages of various presentation graphics methods.

INFORMATION REPORTING SYSTEMS

Information reporting systems were the original type of management information system, and they are still a major category of MIS. They produce information products that support many of the day-to-day decision making

Figure 8-14   The advantages and disadvantages of four types of presentation graphics.

	Line Charts	Bar Charts	Pie Charts	Pictorial Charts
Advantages	1. Shows time and magnitude of relationships well	1. Good for comparisons	1. Good for monetary comparisons	1. Very easily understood
	2. Can show many points	2. Emphasizes one point	2. Good for part versus whole comparison	2. Easily constructed
	3. Degree of accuracy adjustable	3. Accurate	3. Very easily understood	
	4. Easily read	4. Easily read		
Disadvantages	1. Limited to less than four lines without adding complexity	1. Limited to one point	1. Limited usage	1. Limited usage
	2. Limited to two dimensions	2. Spacing can mislead	2. Limited precision	2. Limited precision
	3. Spacing can mislead		3. Tends to oversimplify	3. Tends to oversimplify

Source: John Burch and Gary Grudnitski, *Information Systems Theory and Practice*, 5th ed. (New York: John Wiley & Sons, 1989), p. 277. Used with permission.

needs of management. Reports, displays, and responses produced by such systems provide information that managers have specified in advance as adequately meeting their information needs. Such predefined information products satisfy the information needs of managers at the operational and tactical levels of the organization who are faced with more structured types of decision situations. For example, sales managers rely heavily on sales analysis reports to evaluate differences in performance among salespeople who sell the same types of products to the same types of customers. They have a pretty good idea of the kinds of information about sales results they need to manage sales performance effectively.

Figure 8-15 illustrates the components of an information reporting system. Managers can receive information at their workstations that supports their decision-making activities. This information takes the form of periodic, exception, and demand reports and immediate responses to inquiries. Application programs and database management software provide access to information in the corporate databases of the organization. Remember, these databases are maintained by transaction processing systems, as we discussed in Section I. In addition, data about the business environment is obtained from external databases when necessary.

Information Reporting Alternatives

Information reporting systems provide a variety of information products to managers. The three major reporting alternatives provided by such systems are summarized here and illustrated in Figure 8-16.

Periodic Scheduled Reports

This traditional form of providing information to managers uses a prespecified format designed to provide managers with information on a regular basis.

Figure 8–15 The information
reporting system concept.
Note especially that periodic,
exception, and demand re-
ports and responses are the
information products pro-
duced for managers by this
type of information system.

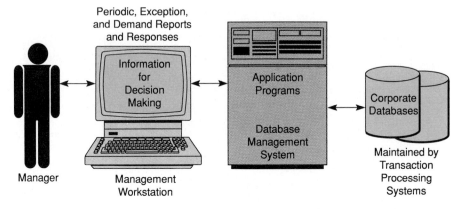

Examples of periodic scheduled reports are weekly sales analysis reports and monthly financial statements.

Exception Reports

In some cases, reports are produced only when exceptional conditions occur. In other cases, reports are produced periodically but contain information only about these exceptional conditions. For example, a credit manager is provided with a report which contains information only on customers who exceed their credit limits. Such exception reporting promotes *management by exception*, instead of overwhelming managers with periodic, detailed reports of business activity.

Demand Reports and Responses

Information is provided whenever a manager demands it. For example, DBMS query languages and report generators allow managers at online workstations to get immediate responses or reports as a result of their requests for information. Thus, managers do not have to wait for periodic reports to arrive as scheduled.

Periodic Scheduled Report available each month giving information to managers about sales for each product.

Figure 8–16 Types of management reports. Information reporting systems can produce periodic, demand, and exception reports and responses for managers.

SALES BY PRODUCT REPORT
MONTH ENDING 03/31/ --

PRODUCT	SOLD THIS MONTH	GROSS PROFIT	PROFIT PERCENT
ABRASIVES	2,720.19	271.36	10
ACIDS AND CHEMICALS	1,216.27	170.27	14
BRASS	6,220.83	435.45	7
COPPER	9,337.18	664.73	7

Exception Report listing only delinquent accounts. It is produced automatically whenever more than 10% of customers are delinquent.

DELINQUENT ACCOUNTS REPORT

CUSTOMER NAME	BALANCE	CURRENT	OVER 30 DAYS	OVER 60 DAYS	90 DAYS & OVER	CREDIT LINE
ANDERSON CORP.	3704.35	1200.00	1121.50	850.00	532.85	3500.00
ARMSTRONG INTL.	3896.68	439.61	1911.25	499.00	1046.82	3000.00
FOXBORO CORP.	2222.18	1222.18	500.00	500.00		2000.00
SMYTHE CO.	1936.05	260.40	1100.00	575.65		1500.00
WELLS HARDWARE	3195.98	469.76	325.01	151.63	2249.58	3000.00

Demand Report produced whenever a manager wants to know information about the current status of purchases made from vendors.

PURCHASE ANALYSIS BY VENDOR

VENDOR'S NUMBER	VENDOR'S NAME	AMOUNT THIS MONTH	RETURNS YEAR TO DATE	NET AMOUNT YEAR TO DATE
27	ABBOT MACHINE CO.	1286.44		3194.26
58	ACE TOOL CO.			1975.15
66	ACME ABRASIVE CO.	342.86		1505.93
324	ALLAN ALLOYS CO.		95.10	4675.22
367	AMERICAN TOOL CO.			986.74
425	ANGUS METAL WORKS			842.89
475	APEX CORPORATION	2316.84	245.73	10476.79

REAL WORLD CASE

The Benetton Group

It's been 25 years since Giuliana and Luciano Benetton sold their first sweater on a street in Northern Italy. Since then, the siblings' clothing franchise company has become a global organization whose retail reach has expanded to more than 5,000 shops in 80 countries and whose fashions have graced the likes of Princess Diana and Princess Caroline of Monaco. While many in the retail industry are struggling, Benetton Group S.p.A.—with the help of networking and electronic data interchange (EDI) technology—translated its colorful sweaters, shirts, and jeans into $1.2 billion in sales in 1989.

The IS heart of Benetton is located in Ponzano Veneto, a small Italian town just outside of Venice. It is from here that Bruno Zuccaro, the company's 49-year-old IS director, oversees the organization's IS operations. Benetton's international EDI network is one of its key IS operations. Supplied by General Electric Information Services (GEIS), the network has become the IS heart of Benetton's commercial business, according to Zuccaro.

The GEIS network is at the core of Benetton's ordering cycle, which is initiated by *agents*— Benetton's term for the independent business clients in 73 worldwide locations who act as intermediaries between the Benetton Group and retailers. Working on commission, these agents set up franchises, show twice-yearly collections to retailers, and place orders for merchandise with Benetton.

To order merchandise for his retail clients, an agent dials the GEIS network from a DOS- or Unix-based workstation and places his order using software developed by Benetton. The order handling system collects the orders and routes them to the appropriate factory. It then updates the agent's order portfolio and price lists. The system also handles electronic interchange of mail, reports, and files between the corporation and agents and among the agents themselves. The efficiency and fast turnaround of the network are crucial to getting orders right and to the retailers on time.

The data generated in the ordering process enables the Benetton Group to forecast the total number of orders early in the production cycle, Zuccaro says, so it can make faster purchasing decisions on raw materials and set up a production schedule. More important, this system allows Benetton to keep inventory low and to manufacture only what the franchises are paying for. Thus Benetton has taken away the risk and cost of carrying excess stock.

Access to Benetton's corporate mainframe and databases through the network enables agents to track orders by customer and item as well as to get online displays of what is in production, in the warehouse, or being distributed. Agents can also track customer credit, which allows them to restrict deliveries to those outlets exceeding their credit limits.

By analyzing reports based on data from point-of-sale (POS) systems installed in a number of Benetton-owned shops in Italy, the company knows what's hot and what's not, Zuccaro says. These shops, located mostly in upscale resort towns, receive merchandise earlier than the rest of Benetton's stores and keep tabs on bar coded merchandise bought by their fashion-conscious customers. Based on an analysis of style, color, and size trends, the firm notifies its agents of popular items and readies operations to handle the late orders. "Agents can place an order that can be turned around in 11 to 15 days," Zuccaro says.

Application Questions

☐ What stages of the transaction processing cycle do you recognize in this example?

☐ How does Benetton and its agents benefit from the use of an EDI network?

☐ What types of information reporting are provided to Benetton agents and managers? What are some of the attributes of this information?

Source: Adapted from Lory Zottola, "The United Systems of Benetton," *Computerworld,* April 2, 1990, p. 70.

□ Transaction processing systems are operations information systems that process data resulting from business transactions. They involve the basic activities of (1) data entry, (2) transaction processing, (3) database maintenance, (4) document and report generation, and (5) inquiry processing.

□ Traditional data entry methods in transaction processing systems requiring too many activities, people, and forms of data media are being replaced by more direct, automated methods known as source data automation. The high cost and potential for errors characteristic of traditional data entry methods can be minimized with source data automation that captures data as early and as close as possible to the source generating the data. Data is captured by using machine-readable media, prerecording data, or capturing data directly without the use of data media. Electronic data interchange methods allow the direct electronic transmission of source documents between companies.

□ Two basic processing methods used by transaction processing systems are batch processing, in which data is accumulated and processed periodically, and realtime processing, in which data is processed immediately. Transaction processing systems may use either method for one or more of their functions, but the use of realtime processing is growing.

□ Managers have to be provided with information products that possess many attributes of information quality in each of the three dimensions of time (timeliness, currency, frequency, and time period), content (accuracy, relevance, completeness, conciseness, scope, and performance), and form (clarity, detail, order, presentation, and media).

□ Information presentation methods for managers and other end users are changing. Microfilm and optical disk media are replacing paper forms of record-keeping. Standardized printed reports produced on a regular basis are being replaced by visual displays tailored to users and furnished at their request. Finally, displays of numeric data and text material are being replaced by color graphics displays.

□ Information reporting systems are management information systems that produce information products that meet many of the day-to-day information needs of management. Reports, displays, and responses provide prespecified information on demand, according to a schedule, or on an exception basis for use by managers at the operational and tactical levels of an organization.

SUMMARY

These are the key terms and concepts of this chapter. The page number of their first explanation is in parentheses.

KEY TERMS AND CONCEPTS

1. Batch processing *(279)*
2. Business graphics *(288)*
3. Control listing *(285)*
4. Edit report *(285)*
5. Electronic data interchange *(276)*
6. Information presentation alternatives *(287)*
7. Information quality *(287)*
   a. Content dimension
   b. Form dimension
   c. Time dimension
8. Information reporting alternatives *(292)*
   a. Demand
   b. Exception
   c. Periodic

9. Information reporting system *(291)*
10. Inquiry processing *(285)*
11. Realtime processing *(281)*
12. Source data automation *(276)*
13. Source document *(275)*
14. Traditional data entry *(275)*
15. Transaction *(274)*
16. Transaction document *(283)*
17. Transaction processing cycle *(275)*
18. Transaction processing systems *(274)*
19. Turnaround document *(283)*

REVIEW QUIZ

Match one of the **key terms and concepts** listed above with one of the brief examples or definitions listed below. Try to find the best fit for answers that seem to fit more than one term or concept. Defend your choices.

_____ 1. An example is making a sale or a payment.

_____ 2. Process data resulting from business transactions.

_____ 3. Data entry, transaction processing, database maintenance, document and report generation, and inquiry processing.

_____ 4. Has too many activities, people, media, costs, and errors.

_____ 5. The automatic capture of data at the time and place of transactions.

_____ 6. The electronic transmission of source documents between companies.

_____ 7. Collecting and periodically processing transaction data.

_____ 8. Processing transaction data immediately after it is captured.

_____ 9. A sales order form is an example.

_____ 10. Examples are paychecks, customer statements, and sales receipts.

_____ 11. Part of a customer's invoice is returned for automated data entry.

_____ 12. A payroll register is an example.

_____ 13. Reports that identify errors occurring during transaction processing.

_____ 14. Allows end users to check on the status of an order or the balance in an account and receive an immediate response.

_____ 15. Whether information is meaningful and useful to you.

_____ 16. Information should be provided whenever it is needed and should be up to date.

_____ 17. Information should be accurate, relevant, complete, and concise.

_____ 18. Information should be presented clearly and attractively.

_____ 19. Substituting video displays and audio responses for printed paper output.

_____ 20. Easier to understand than columns of numbers.

_____ 21. Provide information for managers in a variety of prespecified formats.

_____ 22. Information provided on a scheduled basis.

_____ 23.   Information provided on a selective basis.

_____ 24.   Information provided whenever you want it.

1. Marsh Village Pantry

Sharon Friend works in the fast lane. As manager of the Marsh Village
Pantry in Anderson, Indiana, she sees about 1,000 customers pass
through the convenience store each day. Friend supervises all store activities, from selling gasoline to stocking grocery shelves, to running the
fast-food and deli areas. Each activity can lead to a transaction, and processing these transactions can add up to a headache. Marsh Village
Pantry, a 168-store chain, is trying to make it easier to process these
transactions and cut paperwork with the personal computer-based
Xcellenet system that automates data collection across a wide area network of distributed devices.

"Before, we were doing everything via the mailman," said John Wingate, director of management information and communications systems
for the company. The system enables the company to communicate with
the stores in an orderly fashion, Wingate said. "Each store is equipped
with a PC, and the managers call up as soon as the book work is done. If
that doesn't happen by 3 P.M., the network manager software calls out to
pick up the forms and exchange electronic mail." The Xcellenet program
retrieves data from store cash registers and pulls it down to headquarters. This data is then consolidated into the company's accounting
system. According to Friend, it now takes her 15 to 20 minutes per day
to enter data, rather than the hour and a half it used to take to perform
manual calculations that are now done by the system. The company also
says that there are fewer mathematical errors in the store reports with
Xcellenet.

a. What stages of the transaction processing cycle do you recognize in
    this example? Explain.

b. What are the benefits of the Xcellenet system?

Source: Adapted from Sally Cusack, "Computerizing the Pantry," *Computerworld*, March
19, 1990, p. 62.

2. Ford Motor Company

"We consider EDI an absolute necessity," says Tom Bass, manager of
production, planning, and control for Ford. "Just by eliminating the mail
time alone, we're able to dramatically improve our rate of inventory return." When dealerships order cars, Ford breaks down the transactions
into thousands of purchasing requests matched against blanket purchase
orders for each of the suppliers involved. Before EDI, these requests
were delivered to the suppliers by mail. Today they are transferred in
electronic format to the suppliers' computers. The order process that
used to require at least a week is now completed within a matter of
hours.

EDI also improves accuracy. According to Bass, "in an EDI system,
the data is input once, by the person who knows best what the information is, rather than reentered as it proceeds through the system." In the
case of Ford, employees enter information into the EDI system immedi-

ately as orders for cars are received. The information moves directly into the suppliers' computers as requests for parts, and Ford eliminates the possibility that order entry clerks at major vendors will misplace or misread the request.

a. How does Ford use EDI?

b. What benefits accrue to Ford, its dealers, and its suppliers?

Source: Adapted from Cheryl Snapp, "EDI Aims High for Global Growth," *Datamation,* March 1, 1990, p. 77.

3. Dillard's Department Stores

Dillard's Department Stores gave its 800-plus key suppliers an ultimatum in the summer of 1989: Plug into EDI or find another buyer. Specifically, Dillard's told vendors they had until February 1, 1990, to pick up electronic data interchange (EDI) or at least submit a schedule for doing so in 1990. Ray Heflin, Dillard's director of quick response, admitted the announcement caused a bit of chaos among suppliers. But Heflin dismissed criticism of the move. EDI, he maintained, is essential to Dillard's future and the economy's health. "EDI is undoubtedly a benefit to this country," he said. However, while many vendors may agree with Heflin, they nonetheless were startled by the ultimatum.

"There was quite a bit of dissension among the ranks" of vendors when the word came down, said John Keener, MIS director at Buster Brown Apparel, Inc. "We were ready for EDI," he said. "This made us go." The company is using a personal computer–based application. He said the conversion—not counting labor—has cost "in the $10,000 range." Some small specialty wholesalers, such as leather glove–maker Fownes Bros. Co., do not have a choice. "If it were up to me, we wouldn't do it at all," said Mike Beniaminovitz, Fownes' DP manager. Though a relatively small producer, Fownes depends on its business with Dillard's. Beniaminovitz chose a PC setup using Foretell's ESP II software. He said he has spent about $7,000, excluding in-house labor. Nina Footwear Co. looked at EDI as "a necessity," EDI coordinator Larry Reines said. "All the majors are going to be doing this." However, Dillard's move surprised Nina with its suddenness and finality, Reines explained.

a. Why do you think Dillard's gave its suppliers an EDI ultimatum?

b. How and why should small suppliers respond to demands for EDI?

Source: Adapted from Jim Nash, "When Push Comes to Shove," *Computerworld,* March 5, 1990, p. 12.

4. PDX Corporation

Though the technical world has praised the number-crunching power of IBM's powerful RISC System/6000 workstation computers, the first programs ported to the new system were for a commercial application. Ken Hill, president of PDX, announced a pharmacy application using the new workstations. A former retail pharmacist, Hill spent 10 years filling prescriptions before switching careers. Knowing first-hand what tools were needed to run a pharmacy, he set out to build them. Today, PDX (which stands for Program Development in UNIX) has installations in 1,300 independent drugstore accounts and more than 2,000 in chain accounts.

In the pharmacy, all levels of government get in the act, as well as public and private insurers such as Medicaid and Blue Cross. "Online adjudication" is the way of the future in this business, according to Hill. This means that while the pharmacist fills the prescription, the computer has to recognize a valid third party for authorization "before the printer spits out the label." This eliminates druggists absorbing losses for claims rejected long after the medicine has been delivered. Pharmacies without this computer assistance will have difficulty competing, Hill believes. Besides protecting pharmacies from losses due to rejected claims, "most major third parties are requiring the pharmacists to use this technology or they won't do business with them." He says that's because it's becoming too costly to do business based on shipments of paper claims, disks, or tapes. Every state does business its own way. And every third party has roughly 2,000 to 5,000 insurance plans. "If you get a pharmacy whose business is 70 percent third-party billing and they are filling 500 prescriptions a day, you can see the problem."

a. What unique capabilities are needed by transaction processing systems for pharmacies?

b. Why is "online adjudication" becoming a business necessity for pharmacies?

Source: Adapted from "Data Congestion? PDX Prescribes RISC Remedy" *IBM Update*, March/April 1990, p. 16.

5. Godiva Chocolatier, Inc.
    Since it outfitted its field sales force with laptop computers two years ago, Godiva Chocolatier, Inc. has tasted the sweet rewards of timeliness and productivity. The $100 million leader in the premium confection business, Godiva's goal was to give its field personnel "a tool to help them make better presentations, supply more information, and be more helpful to the customer," MIS director Robert Arakelian said. The 22 field representatives currently use Gridlite Plus laptops to enter and transmit customer orders, download reports and electronic mail from the main office, and provide customers with instant order-fulfillment data.

    The laptops have cut the time required to submit certain complex multistore orders from as much as two hours to a matter of minutes. Formerly, a sales representative would call the order-fulfillment office and recite the complex order verbally. "They'd sit there for an hour saying 'Store No. 1, Product No. 1, 10 cases; Store No. 2, Product No. 1, 20 cases,'" Arakelian said. Using the laptop, the representative keys the order into a Lotus Symphony spreadsheet and transmits it to the order processing office via an internal modem and existing telephone lines. In return, the representative and the customer receive order numbers and an advisory of any problems that may affect the order's fulfillment—all on-site via the laptop. Later, the representative will attach the unit to a printer and generate a hard-copy record for the customer. The time saved on order input translates directly into more time to call on customers, Arakelian said.

a. What stages of the transaction processing cycle do you recognize in this example? Explain.

b. What are the benefits of laptop computers for Godiva's sales representatives?

Source: Adapted from Richard Pastore, "Laptops Leave Sour Taste in Sweetmaker's Mouth," *Computerworld,* January 29, 1990, p. 37.

6. Copco Papers Inc.

The irony of new order processing systems is that, in taking businesses forward, they are transporting them back in time. The idea, in effect, is to create a kind of multinational corner grocer—an individual so keenly wired into the needs, habits, preferences, and eccentricities of his customers that he knows what they want before they do. More often than not, therefore, success will be determined by the relationships service companies have: They will know their customers, their manufactured goods sources, their schedules, their prices, and their quality and will probably be online, in realtime, to their warehouses and manufacturing plants.

For example, ask Clem Wolfe, vice president of management information systems for Columbus, Ohio–based Copco Papers, Inc., what he wants more of in his order processing, and his answer is clear: "More customer information." While Wolfe is largely satisfied with the transaction processing system for customer orders installed at Copco today, he sees the next stage of the system as moving the company into the corner grocer–level of service. "What we're interested in is for managers and customer service people to have intelligent workstations rather than dumb terminals. A lot of customer information right at their fingertips." The current system has some of that information, notes Wolfe, but not enough. Ultimately, he wants sales managers and order processing personnel to have buying histories, equipment environments, receiving capabilities and schedules, and even personal information. The idea is to know each client as if each were the *only* client—even if there are thousands of them.

a. How and why should businesses develop order processing systems that make them like a "multinational corner grocer?"

b. What kinds of information attributes and information reporting does Copco want from its order processing systems?

Source: Adapted from Dennis Hamilton, "Back to the Future," *EDGE,* January/February 1990, p. 18–19.

7. Bank of Boston

The Bank of Boston has built a "control system" that uses the PCs to help manage paperwork the way a nuclear plant fights meltdowns—with boxes in a color video display that turn from green to red to signal a problem in the system. Three months ago, the bank began installing an information system to identify problems such as dividend checks being mailed late or accounts not being balanced fast enough—snafus that were costing the bank millions of dollars. Now, with a click of the mouse, managers flip through screens of data to find the details of such problems, what's being done to solve them, and who's responsible for solving them.

The IS staff interviewed managers to find out what control points they wanted in the system and what indicated that the control points were running into trouble. One accounts receivable control point, for example, is the number of bills customers are late in paying and how late their payments are. Business unit managers chose the number of late accounts and the amount of time they're past due that would turn their box yellow and then red. Now, managers throughout the bank call a central control room daily to report how all their control points are holding up. If a light has changed color, the manager must explain what's being done to fix it.

a. What types of information reporting are included in the Bank of Boston's "control system"?

b. What are the benefits of such a system to managers?

Source: Adapted from Robert Scheier, "Bank Enlists EIS in Battle to Boost Control," *PC Week*, February 5, 1990, p. 129.

8. Analyzing Transaction Processing Systems

In your day-to-day living, you are a user of many transaction processing systems, including those used by banks, department stores, super-markets, utility companies, and universities to process data generated by various end user transactions.

a. Use Figure 8.2 to help you identify the basic transaction processing activities involved in one of the transaction processing systems you use.

b. Use Figures 8.3 and 8.4 to help you identify features of traditional data entry and source data automation in this system.

c. Use Figure 8.7 to help you identify any features of batch processing and realtime processing.

d. Use Figure 8.11 to help you evaluate the quality of the information products produced by the system.

e. Use Figure 8.12 to help you identify the information presentation alternatives in the transaction processing system you chose.

f. Use the examples of periodic, exception, and demand reports shown in Figure 8.16 to help you design a mock-up of a report or display that could be produced by the system for end users or managers. Use a report generator from a database management or other software package to develop the report mock-up if possible.

g. Use Figure 8.11 to help you evaluate the information quality of your proposed report, as well as the reports shown in Figure 8.16.

SELECTED REFERENCES

1. Burch, John. "EDI: The Demise of Paper." *Information Executive*, Winter 1989.

2. Davis, Leila. "On-line Applications Grow Up." *Datamation*, January 1, 1990.

3. Fuller, David. "Advantage: EDI." *Information Executive*, Spring 1990.

4. Lehman, John. "Business Graphics: A Taxonomy for Information Systems Managers." *Data Base*, Fall 1986.

5. Payne, Robert. "Electronic Data Interchange." *Computerworld*, March 26, 1990.

6. Senn, James. "Electronic Data Interchange: An Opportunity for Fundamental Business Alliance." *SIM Network*, September/October 1988.

DECISION SUPPORT AND EXPERT SYSTEMS

■ Chapter Outline

■ Learning Objectives

The purpose of this chapter is to give you an understanding of (1) the decision making needs of managers, (2) how decision support systems provide decision making support, and (3) developments in artificial intelligence and expert systems for business applications.

Section I of this chapter emphasizes the major concepts involved in providing information to support decision making and the functions and roles of management.

Section II discusses basic concepts and components of decision support systems and executive information systems and provides examples of DSS and EIS applications.

Section III gives an overview of artificial intelligence, explores the fundamentals of expert systems, and provides examples of expert system use in business decision making situations.

After reading and studying this chapter, you should be able to:

1. Give examples of how information systems can support the functions, roles, and levels of management.

2. Give examples of how information systems can support each stage of the decision making process.

3. Identify the major components of a decision support system and explain how it differs from traditional information reporting systems.

4. Explain how decision support systems help managers do analytical modeling to support decision making.

5. Explain how executive information systems support the information needs of top management better than traditional information reporting systems.

6. Identify some of the present and future impacts of artificial intelligence on business operations and management.

7. Identify the major components of an expert system and give examples of several ways expert systems can be used in business decision making situations.

Section I: Managerial Decision Support

Information systems can significantly support managerial decision making. That is the goal which the information systems industry has been working toward since the concepts of management information systems (MIS) and decision support systems (DSS) were developed. Developing effective decision support systems requires understanding how information systems can contribute to the decision making process, as well as to the functions and roles performed by managers.

INFORMATION AND MANAGEMENT

In order to understand what information and decision support a manager needs, we need to review what *management* means. Figure 9–1 summarizes three fundamental conceptual frameworks that answer the question, What does a manager do? Let's take a closer look at each of these concepts to see how information systems can help meet the information needs of managers.

Information and the Functions of Management

Management is traditionally described as a process of leadership involving the **management functions** of planning, organizing, staffing, directing, and controlling. These functions of management were first expounded in the early 1900s by Henri Fayol of France, a pioneer of management theory [12]. They give us a valuable way to think about what managers do. A manager should *plan* the activities of his or her organization, *staff* it with personnel, *organize* its personnel and their activities, *direct* its operations, and *control* its direction by evaluating feedback and making necessary adjustments.

Information systems can assist managers by providing information needed to accomplish each of the functions of management. For example, information

Figure 9–1 What a manager does. This figure summarizes (1) the five functions of management, (2) the 10 major roles played by managers, and (3) the three levels of management activity.

The Functions of Management

Planning: establish goals and develop strategies.
Organizing: develop organizational structures.
Staffing: acquire, develop, and assign people.
Directing: lead by motivating and communicating.
Controlling: evaluate and adjust performance.

The Roles of Management

Interpersonal roles: leader, liaison, figurehead.
Informational roles: monitor, disseminator, spokesperson.
Decisional roles: entrepreneur, disturbance handler, resource allocator, negotiator.

The Levels of Management

Strategic management: strategic planning and control of overall organizational direction by top management.
Tactical management: tactical planning and control of organizational subunits by middle management.
Operational management: planning and control of day-to-day operations by supervisory management.

systems can help managers plan by providing both planning data and planning models. A typical example is the use of capital budgeting models to develop long-range plans for the major expenditures needed to build new factories or retail stores or to make other major additions to plant and equipment. Information systems could provide data on internal resource needs and external factors such as interest rates, as well as financial modeling software.

Information systems can help managers organize and staff their organizations with human resources. For example, information from a personnel database, software for personnel requirements forecasting, and an employee skills inventory can help managers organize and staff present and proposed work groups and project teams. This helps ensure that employees with the necessary skills will be available when needed. Information systems can also help managers direct their organizations. For example, the electronic mail capabilities of automated office systems make it easier for managers to communicate with people in their organizations. Finally, information systems play a major role in the control function of management. Through such information products as exception reports, they help managers recognize deviations in performance from standards and budgets. This kind of feedback helps managers adjust a firm's operations to meet organizational objectives.

Another useful management model was developed by management scholar Henry Mintzberg in the early 1970s [12]. This model views management as the performance of a variety of **managerial roles.** A manager has the authority and status to play the following roles:

Information and the Roles of Management

- ☐ **Interpersonal roles.** A manager should be (1) a *leader* of subordinates, (2) a *liaison* with the external environment, and (3) a *figurehead* when ceremonial duties arise.

- ☐ **Information roles.** A manager should be (4) a *monitor* of information on organizational performance, (5) a *disseminator* of information within the organization, and (6) a *spokesperson* to the external environment.

- ☐ **Decision roles.** A manager should be (7) an *entrepreneur* in making innovative changes that affect the organization, (8) a *disturbance handler* when unanticipated events occur, (9) a *resource allocator* in determining the distribution of financial and other resources within the organization, and (10) a *negotiator* who resolves both internal and external disputes.

What information do managers need to perform these roles? How can information systems help? Mintzberg's studies of top-level executives showed that they did not get much help from computer-based information systems. Instead, they relied primarily on verbal information gathered from telephone calls, personal contacts, and meetings. However, improvements in office automation and executive information systems have made information systems more attractive, easy to use, and helpful to top executives and other managers. For example, *electronic mail* systems allow electronic messages to be sent, stored, and forwarded among managerial and staff workstations. Executive information systems can make it easy for executives to gather critical information about organizational performance.

Figure 9–2   Information requirements by management level. The type of information required by managers is directly related to their level of management and the structure of decision situations they face.

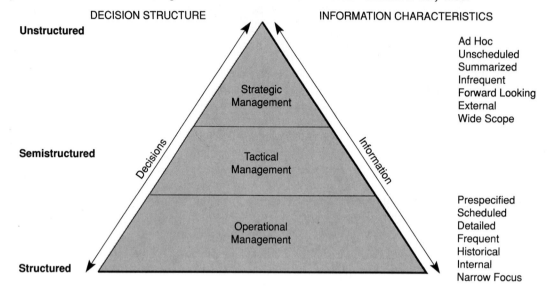

DECISION STRUCTURE

Unstructured

Semistructured

Structured

INFORMATION CHARACTERISTICS

Strategic
Management

Tactical
Management

Operational
Management

Decisions

Information

Ad Hoc
Unscheduled
Summarized
Infrequent
Forward Looking
External
Wide Scope

Prespecified
Scheduled
Detailed
Frequent
Historical
Internal
Narrow Focus

Information and the Levels of Management

The information requirements of management depend heavily on the **management level** involved. The activities of management can be subdivided into three major levels: (1) *strategic management*, (2) *tactical management*, and (3) *operational management*. These levels are related to the traditional management levels of top management, middle management, and operating, or supervisory, management. This *managerial pyramid* model of management was introduced in Chapter 2. It was popularized in the 1960s by Robert N. Anthony, another pioneer of management theory [1]. It emphasizes that management consists of planning and control activities determined by a manager's level in an organization.

Figure 9–2 is based on the work of G. Anthony Gory and Michael Scott Morton [7]. Their work emphasized that the type of information required by managers is directly related to the level of management and the amount of structure in the decision situations they face. For example, the strategic management level requires more summarized, ad hoc, unscheduled reports, forecasts, and external intelligence to support its heavy planning and policy making responsibilities. The operational management level, on the other hand, may require more regular internal reports emphasizing detailed current and historical data comparisons that support its control of day-to-day operations. Thus, higher levels of management require more ad hoc, unscheduled, infrequent summaries, with a wide, external, forward-looking scope. On the other hand, lower levels of management require more prespecified, frequently scheduled, and detailed information, with a narrow, internal, and historical focus.

INFORMATION AND DECISION MAKING

The most widely used model of the decision making process was developed by Herbert A. Simon, a Nobel prize–winning economist and scholar of management decision making. His model is a conceptual framework that divides the

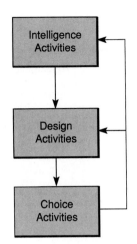

- Search for and identify conditions requiring a decision.
- Information systems should scan the internal organization and the external environment and help identify problems and opportunities.

- Develop and evaluate alternative courses of action.
- Information systems should help generate and evaluate decision alternatives.

- Select a course of action and monitor its implementation.
- Information systems should help emphasize and prioritize decision alternatives and provide feedback on the implemented decision.

Figure 9–3   A model of the decision making process. Note that the decision making process is a three-stage process of intelligence, design, and choice activities that may cycle back to previous stages. Also note how information systems can support each stage of this process.

decision making process into the following three stages [14], which are illustrated in Figure 9–3.

- ☐ **Intelligence activities.** Search the environment and identify events and conditions requiring decisions.
- ☐ **Design activities.** Develop and evaluate possible courses of action.
- ☐ **Choice activities.** Select a particular course of action and monitor its implementation.

As Figure 9–3 shows, this three-stage decision making process includes the ability to cycle back to a previous stage if the decision maker is dissatisfied with the intelligence gathered or the alternatives developed. Also note that each stage of decision making has unique information requirements.

Information for the Intelligence Stage

For example, sales analysis reports can be furnished to managers periodically, when exceptional sales situations occur, or on demand. These help managers identify the status of sales performance, sales trends, and exceptional sales conditions for the firm. Information from market research studies and external databases could also help managers identify changes in consumer preferences or competitive activity.

A major information systems capability is also needed in this stage. Managers should have the ability to make **ad hoc inquiries,** that is, unique, unscheduled, situation-specific information requests. **Prespecified reports** provided to managers periodically, on an exception basis, or even on demand are insufficient. Such information products may not give a manager enough information to recognize whether a problem or opportunity exists.

Example. A disturbing sales trend can be brought to a manager's attention by a weekly sales report that spotlights unusual or exceptional sales activity. However, the manager may need to make further inquiries to isolate the sales problem. Therefore, information systems can provide a *query language*

Figure 9–4   Examples of decisions by the type of decision structure at each level of management.

Decision Structure	Operational Management	Tactical Management	Strategic Management
Unstructured		Work group reorganization	New business planning
	Cash management	Work group performance analysis	Company reorganization
Semistructured	Credit management	Employee performance appraisal	Product planning
	Production scheduling	Capital budgeting	Mergers and acquisitions
	Daily work assignment	Program budgeting	Site location
Structured	Inventory control	Program control	

capability to allow a manager to make ad hoc inquiries of a sales database to get the sales information he or she needs.

Information for the Design Stage

The design stage of decision making involves developing and evaluating alternative courses of action. A major consideration is whether the decision situation is *structured* or *unstructured*. Figure 9–4 shows the amount of structure in typical decisions faced by each level of management [7].

Structured decisions (also called *programmable decisions*) involve situations where the procedures to follow when a decision is needed can be specified in advance. Therefore, such decisions are *structured* or *programmed* by the decision procedures, or *decision rules*, developed for them.

Example.   The inventory reorder decisions faced by most businesses are frequently quantified and automated. Inventory control software includes *decision rules* that outline the computations to perform and the steps to take when quantities in inventory are running low. Thus, one way that information systems can support structured decisions is by quantifying and automating a decision making process. In other cases, prespecified information products such as reports can provide most of the information needed by a decision maker faced with a structured decision situation.

Unstructured decisions (also called *nonprogrammable decisions*) involve decision situations where it is not possible or desirable to specify in advance most of the decision procedures to follow. Many decision situations in the real world are unstructured because they are subject to too many random or changeable events or involve too many unknown factors or relationships. At most, many decision situations are *semistructured*. That is, some decision procedures can be prespecified, but not enough to lead to a definite recommended decision.

Example.   Decisions involved in starting a new line of products or making major changes to employee benefits would probably range from unstructured to semistructured. The many unknown or changeable factors involved would require a less structured approach leading to subjective judgments by managers. Information systems can support such decisions by providing (1) the ability to make ad hoc inquiries for information in company databases and (2) the ability to reach a decision in an interactive process with the help of a decision support system.

Information systems should help managers select a proper course of action and then provide feedback on the success of the implemented decision. Of course, this assumes that enough information was gathered during the intelligence phase and that a sufficient number of alternatives were developed and evaluated during the design stage. If not, the managers may choose to return to those stages for more data or alternatives.

Information for the Choice Stage

Example.   An information system can make estimates of the net present value and payback period to rank several competing new product proposals. Other criteria, such as expected market share, number of personnel required, and training requirements, could also be used to rank alternatives. Then if a decision to introduce a new product is made, a manager can monitor the decision's effects on sales activity. If sales results are unsatisfactory, the manager must decide what actions to take to correct the problem. The decision making process then begins all over again.

REAL WORLD CASE

Chevron Corporation

During Christmas week, 1988, key officers at Chevron Corporation in San Francisco were thrown into turmoil by some decidedly unfriendly season's greetings. The Pennzoil Company was attempting a takeover. But as the company's stock fluctuated dramatically, Chief Financial Officer Marty Klitten and 45 other Chevron senior executives were able to do more than just sit by and watch: They sat by their PCs. With their executive information system (EIS) and its links to Dow Jones/Retrieval, Quotron Systems' Global Report, and E-mail, they were able to perform quick, timely analyses on stock trends—buying patterns and hourly trades—and then quickly communicate with one another. Instead of waiting for paper reports, CFO Klitten had a "window on Wall Street" that was instrumental in fending off Pennzoil's abortive bid.

"It allowed us a window that we probably would not have had otherwise," said Klitten. The resulting use of realtime stock information parallels Klitten's broader purpose in installing Chevron's EIS. "We generate a great amount of *data,* but we don't necessarily translate it that well into *information,*" he said. "We wanted to take relatively diverse systems in marketing, manufacturing, and personnel and pull them together for senior level executives."

Now presidents of Chevron's operating companies, division heads, in-house directors, and the vice chairman of the board can share information—the biggest EIS benefit, according to Klitten. A common area across their functions is personnel data, which now resides in the system so that anyone can look at an employee's work and salary history. The EIS has helped eliminate paper, Klitten says, breeding more creativity with the presentation of information and allowing for more analytical work. Recently, for exam-

ple, Chevron executives using EIS were able to analyze credit card transaction costs by location based on data collected from individual gas stations.

However, lack of organizationwide consistent information is a common complaint for EIS users. Chevron's Klitten says that because their EIS is not a universal MIS-imposed system and because the six users reporting to him have managed their EISs differently due to their varying degrees of personal interest, some departments are ahead of others. "So some of the frustration is that Department A has data that Department B doesn't have yet," says Klitten.

As today's middle-level managers who are sophisticated PC users climb corporate ladders, will they really need systems with interfaces designed for computerphobic, command-amnesic executives? Marty Klitten thinks even the most PC-literate senior executives will still need an EIS. "It's not whether individuals are afraid or not of PCs," he says, "The biggest benefit is access to information and sharing it. You don't want those who are very, very skilled with PCs spending all their time either writing programs or doing manipulations. If you're an executive, there are better things to do with your time."

Application Questions

☐ What managerial functions, roles, and levels are affected by Chevron's executive information system?

☐ What are some of the benefits and limitations of Chevron's executive information system?

☐ Will tomorrow's more computer literate executives still need an easy-to-use EIS? Explain.

Source: Adapted from Karen Frenkel, "The War for the Executive Desktop," *Personal Computing,* April 27, 1990, pp. 56–64.

Section II: Decision Support and Executive Information Systems

Decision support systems (DSS) are a major category of management information systems. They are computer-based information systems that provide interactive information support to managers during the decision making process. Decision support systems use (1) analytical models, (2) specialized databases, (3) a decision maker's own insights and judgments, and (4) an interactive, computer-based modeling process to support the making of semistructured and unstructured decisions by individual managers. Therefore, they are designed to be ad hoc, quick-response systems that are initiated and controlled by managers. Decision support systems are thus able to directly support the specific types of decisions and personal decision making styles and needs of individual managers [15].

INTRODUCTION

Decision support systems are used for a variety of applications in both business and government. When DSS are developed to solve large or complex problems that continually face an organization, they are called *institutional* DSS. Decision support systems used for strategic corporate planning are an example of this type of DSS. Other DSS applications are developed quickly to solve smaller or less complex problems that may be one-time situations facing a manager. These are called *ad hoc* DSS. The main objective of a decision support system is to provide information and decision support techniques needed to solve specific types of problems or pursue specific types of opportunities. Therefore, many DSS are developed to support the types of decisions faced by a specific industry (such as the airline, banking, or automotive industry), or by a specific functional area (such as marketing, finance or manufacturing). Let's take a brief look at a few examples to demonstrate the variety of DSS applications [15, 17].

Examples of DSS Applications

An Airline DSS

An Analytical Information Management System (AAIMS) is a decision support system used in the airline industry. It was developed by American Airlines but is used by other airlines, aircraft manufacturers, and airline financial analysts, consultants, and associations. It supports a variety of airline decisions by studying factors such as aircraft utilization, seating capacity and utilization, traffic statistics, market share, and revenue and profitability results.

A Marketing DSS

BRANDAID is a DSS used for marketing planning, especially in the packaged goods industries. It helps brand managers make pricing, sales effort, promotion, advertising, and budgeting decisions for products, product lines, and brands of products. It produces sales forecasts and profitability estimates using internal and external data about customers, competitors, retailers, and other economic and demographic information.

A Government DSS

GADS (Geodata Analysis and Display System) was developed by IBM. It constructs and displays maps and other graphics displays that support decisions affecting the geographic distribution of people and other resources. For example, it can analyze and display the geographic distribution of crimes and thus help decide how to assign police to geographic areas of a city. It has also been used for urban growth studies, defining school district boundaries, and fire department inspection and equipment deployment.

A Banking DSS

MAPP (Managerial Analysis for Profit Planning) is a DSS developed by Citibank. It was designed to support decisions involved in the financial planning, budgeting, costing, and pricing of bank products. It helps bank executives define banking products and services and identify the costs incurred in providing them. It also helps determine how resources should be shifted among bank products and services, and it prepares budgets for the bank departments producing each banking product.

COMPONENTS OF A DECISION SUPPORT SYSTEM

Figure 9–5 illustrates the components of a decision support system. Note the hardware, software, data, model, and people resources needed to provide interactive decision support for managers.

- ☐ **Hardware resources.** Personal computer workstations provide the primary hardware resource for a DSS. They can be used on a stand-alone basis or can be connected by telecommunications networks to other computer systems for access to other DSS software, model, and data resources.

- ☐ **Software resources.** DSS software packages *(DSS generators)* contain modules for database, model, and dialogue management. A **database management** module provides for the creation, interrogation, and maintenance of the DSS database using capabilities typically found in

Figure 9–5 The decision support system concept. Note that hardware, software, data, model, and people resources provide interactive decision support for managers.

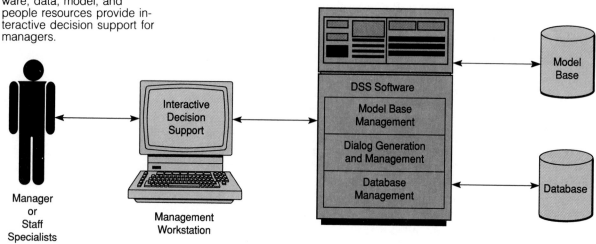

database management system packages. A **model base management** module provides the ability to create, maintain, and manipulate the mathematical models in the model base using capabilities provided by modeling packages, electronic spreadsheet packages, and user-written programs. A **dialogue generation and management** module provides an attractive user interface that supports interactive input and output by managers.

☐ **Data resources.** A DSS **database** contains data and information extracted from the databases of the organization, external databases, and a manager's personal databases. It includes summarized data most needed by the manager for specific types of decisions.

☐ **Model resources.** The **model base** includes a library of mathematical models and analytical techniques stored in a variety of program modules and files. Components of models can be combined by the model base management software to create an integrated model to support a specific decision.

☐ **People resources.** A DSS can be used by managers or their staff specialists to explore decision alternatives. Decision support systems can also be developed by such end users. However, the development of complex decision support systems and software packages is typically assigned to information systems specialists.

DSS SOFTWARE

The software resources needed by a decision support system must integrate the management and use of the model bases, databases, and dialogue generation capabilities of a decision support system. They range from full-featured **DSS generators** to more modest electronic spreadsheet and integrated packages. In any event, such software resources must support the following capabilities:

☐ **Dialogue management.** Provides the user interface that supports the dialogue between the user and the DSS, which is vital for the *interactive analytical modeling* needed. For example, user input is supported through commands, menus, queries, prompts, icons, and other data entry displays. Output to users is provided by prompts, responses, reports, and graphics displays.

☐ **Model base management.** Supports the development, revision, and control of the models in a DSS model base. Helps link models together to construct integrated models. Supports the analytical modeling needed to assist the decision making process.

☐ **Database management.** Supports the creation, use, and maintenance of a DSS database. Helps define and modify the structure of the data records and relationships in the database, the storage and retrieval of data, the updating of the database, and the control of the integrity of the database.

Figure 9–6 illustrates the structure and functions of a popular DSS generator used for financial planning, called IFPS/Plus (Interactive Financial Planning System/Plus). Several other DSS software packages (such as EXPRESS, EN-CORE, STRATEGEM, and System W) are available from independent consulting firms and computer manufacturers. Many are now available in microcomputer versions (e.g., PC/FOCUS, IFPS Personal, and ENCORE). In

Figure 9–6 An example of a DSS Generator: IFPS/Plus. Note the structure and functions of this software package for interactive decision support.

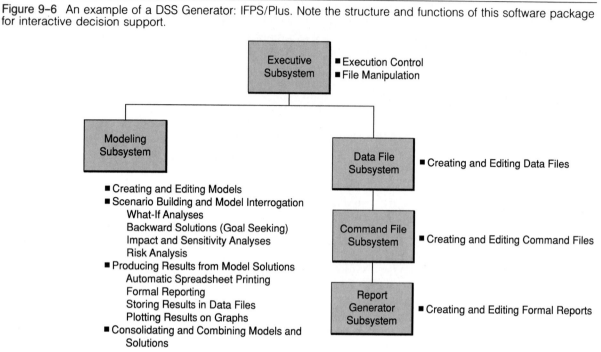

Courtesy Execucom Systems Corporation.

addition, statistical software packages (such as the SAS System and SPSS-X) are used as DSS generators for decision support that requires extensive statistical analysis. Figure 9–7 is a display provided by IFPS/Plus comparing a corporation's total sales and revenue with its net operating income.

DSS and Electronic Spreadsheets

Don't forget that even electronic spreadsheet packages (such as Lotus 1–2–3, Excel, and Quattro Pro) and integrated packages (such as Microsoft Works, Enable, and Framework) are limited DSS generators. They provide some of the model building (spreadsheet models), model manipulation (what-if analysis), database management, and dialogue management (menus, prompts, etc.) functions offered by more powerful DSS generators.

An electronic spreadsheet package allows you to build a *model* by entering the data and relationships (formulas) of a problem into the columns and rows of a worksheet format. Then you can do *what-if analysis* by making a variety of changes to data or formulas and visually evaluating the results of such changes either in worksheet or graphics displays. Spreadsheet programs also provide you with commands to manipulate the worksheet and also include built-in *functions* that perform common arithmetic, statistical, and financial computations.

Example. An electronic spreadsheet package can be used to build product performance models that incorporate some of the factors and relationships a product manager thinks are important. For example, a product breakeven analysis spreadsheet like the one shown in Figure 9–8 could be developed.

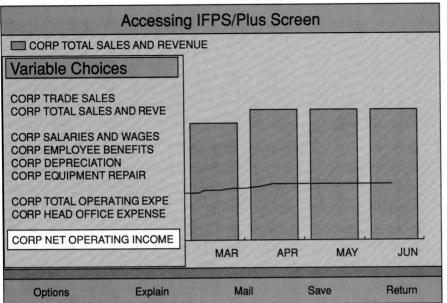

Figure 9–7 A DSS display. Comparing a corporation's total sales and revenue with its net operating income using IFPS/Plus.

Courtesy Execucom Systems Corporation.

```
A21: [W3]
VIEW  ENTER  SENSITIVITY  QUIT                                          MENU
View Breakeven Analysis in Unit Sales
        A   B     C        D      E  F  G  H      I    J      K      L  M  N
 21                    BREAKEVEN ANALYSIS IN UNIT SALES
 22     ===================================================================
 23     Price Per Unit:          $10        :  Variable Costs Per Unit:        :
 24                                          :     Manufacturing     $3 :   30% :
 25     Current Unit Sales      5000         :     Prod. Variances   $0 :    0% :
 26     ===============================       :     Sales Commiss.    $0 :    0% :
 27     Breakeven Analysis Summary:           :     Advertising       $1 :   10% :
 28                                          :     Transportation    $0 :    0% :
 29     Net Sales:              $10 :  100% :     Other Var. Cost   $0 :    0% :
 30     Total F.C.:         $38,300 :  100% :  Total V.C./Unit      $4     40% :
 31     Total V.C./Unit:        $4 :   40% :- - - - - - - - - - - - - - - - - - -
 32     Contribution/Unit:      $6 :   60% :  Total Fixed Costs:             :
 33     B/E Point: Units    6383.33 :          :     Fixed Mgf    $10,000 :   26% :
 34     B/E Point: Dollars  $63,833 :          :     General & Admin $12,300 :  32% :
 35                                          :     Mkting & Sales  $8,000 :   21% :
 36     B/E As % of Current Unit Sales:  128% :     Research & Dev. $5,500 :  14% :
 37     B/E As % of Current $ Sales:     128% :     Other F.C.    $2,500 :    7% :
 38                                          :     Other F.C.        $0 :    0% :
 39                                          :  Total F.C.      $38,300   100% :
 40     ===================================================================
                                    CMD
```

Figure 9–8 A spreadsheet display for breakeven analysis of a product.

Source: Scott Smith and William Swinyard, *Introduction to Marketing Models with Lotus 1-2-3* (Homewood, Ill.: Richard D. Irwin, 1988). Used with permission.

The product manager can then load the models with appropriate data and ask a series of what-if questions to see the effects on the spreadsheet display of a variety of alternatives. For example, What would happen to the break-even point if we cut advertising expense by 10, 20, and 25 percent? Or goal seeking questions could be used. For example, How much would we have to cut fixed costs to get a 10 percent decrease in breakeven point? As a product manager repeats this process, information is generated that helps develop and evaluate possible decision alternatives pertaining to product performance.

Thus, you can use an electronic spreadsheet package for both business analysis and decision support. It can help you solve problems that require the comparison, projection, or evaluation of alternatives. Typical business uses include sales forecasting, profit and loss analysis, product pricing, investment analysis, budget development, cash flow analysis, construction bidding, real estate investment, and bank loan analysis.

GDSS Packages

In the real world, decisions are frequently made by groups of people coming to an agreement on a particular issue. The unique needs of decision making by groups of people have spawned a variety of software packages for **group decision support systems** (GDSS). For example, extensive electronic meeting system (EMS) *toolkits* are available which provide a number of program modules to support the various group activities that may take place in a group decision making situation, such as idea generation, issue exploration, and voting. Other GDSS software may be designed to support a specific application or task, such as a package for labor management negotiations or a package that merely supports anonymous voting by members of a group. Figure 9–9 illustrates the functional components in the toolkit of an extensive EMS (or GDSS) software package developed at the University of Arizona [3, 5].

Finally, some **groupware** packages are available to support work activities by members of a work group whose workstations are interconnected by a local area network. These packages are designed to support *computer-based systems for cooperative work* (CSCW) or *collaborative work support systems* (CWSS). They support group decision making, document preparation, communications, and other work group activities. For example, they allow joint what-if analysis of an electronic spreadsheet model, joint word processing of a document, and electronic mail among members of a work group.

USING DECISION SUPPORT SYSTEMS

Using a decision support system involves an interactive **analytical modeling** process. Typically, a manager or staff specialist uses a DSS software package at his or her workstation. This allows managers to make inquiries and responses and issue commands using a keyboard, an electronic mouse, a touch screen, or, possibly, voice input. Output is typically in the form of text and graphics visual displays, but printed reports may be produced.

Using a DSS software package for decision support will result in a series of displays in response to alternative what-if changes keyed in by a manager. This differs from the demand responses of information reporting systems since managers are not demanding prespecified information. Rather, they are exploring possible alternatives. Thus, they do not have to specify their information needs in advance. Instead, the DSS interactively helps them find the informa-

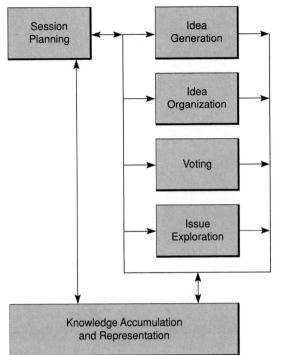

Figure 9–9 The major components of the PLEXSYS electronic meeting system software package. Note the basic types of group activities support by the modules of this GDSS package.

Source: Alan R. Dennis, Joey George, Len Jessup, Jay Nunamaker, and Douglas Vogel, "Information Technology to Support Electronic Meetings," *MIS Quarterly,* December 1988, p. 607.

tion they need to make a decision. This is the essence of the decision support system concept.

Using a decision support system involves four basic types of analytical modeling activities: (1) what-if analysis, (2) sensitivity analysis, (3) goal seeking analysis, and (4) optimization analysis [17]. Let's briefly look at each type of modeling that can be used for decision support. See Figure 9–10.

Analytical Modeling Alternatives

What-If Analysis

In what-if analysis, an end user makes changes to variables, or relationships among variables, and observes the resulting changes in the values of other variables. As we mentioned earlier, a spreadsheet user might change a revenue amount (a variable) or a tax rate formula (a relationship among variables) in a simple financial spreadsheet model. Then he or she could command the spreadsheet program to instantly recalculate all affected variables in the spreadsheet. A managerial user would be very interested in observing and evaluating any changes that occurred to the values in the spreadsheet, especially to a variable such as net profit after taxes. To many managers, net profit after taxes is an example of "the bottom line", that is, a key factor in making many types of decisions. This type of analysis would be repeated until the manager was satisfied with what the modeling revealed about the effects of various possible decisions.

Figure 9–10 Activities and examples of the major types of analytical modeling.

Type of Analytical Modeling	Activities and Examples
What-if analysis	Observing how changes to selected variables affect other variables. *Example:* What if we cut advertising by 10 percent? What would happen to sales?
Sensitivity analysis	Observing how repeated changes to a single variable affects other variables. *Example:* Let's cut advertising by $100 repeatedly so we can see its relationship to sales.
Goal seeking analysis	Making repeated changes to selected variables until a chosen variable reaches a target value. *Example:* Lets try increases in advertising until sales reach $1 million.
Optimization analysis	Finding an optimum value for selected variables given certain constraints *Example:* What's the best amount of advertising to have, given our budget and choice of media?

Sensitivity Analysis

Sensitivity analysis is a special case of what-if analysis. Typically, the value of only one variable is changed repeatedly, and the resulting changes on other variables are observed. So sensitivity analysis is really a case of what-if analysis involving repeated changes to only one variable at a time. Some DSS packages automatically make repeated small changes to a variable when asked to perform sensitivity analysis. Typically, sensitivity analysis is used when decision makers are uncertain about the assumptions made in estimating the value of certain key variables. In our previous spreadsheet example, the value of revenue could be changed repeatedly in small increments, and the effects on other spreadsheet variables observed and evaluated. This would help a manager understand the impact of various revenue levels on other factors involved in decisions being considered.

Goal Seeking Analysis

Goal seeking analysis reverses the direction of the analysis done in what-if and sensitivity analysis. Instead of observing how changes in a variable affect other variables, goal seeking analysis (also called *how can* analysis) sets a target value (a goal) for a variable and then repeatedly changes other variables until the target value is achieved. For example, a manager could specify a target value or goal of $2 million for net profit after taxes for a business venture. Then he or she could repeatedly change the value of revenue or expenses in a spreadsheet model until a result of $2 million is achieved. The manager would discover what amount of revenue or level of expenses needs to be achieved in order to reach the goal of $2 million in after-tax profits. Therefore, this form of analytical modeling would help answer the question, How can we achieve $2 million in net profit after taxes? instead of the question, What happens if we change revenue or expenses? Thus, goal seeking analysis is another important method of decision support.

Optimization Analysis

Optimization analysis is a more complex extension of goal seeking analysis. Instead of setting a specific target value for a variable, the goal is to find the optimum value for one or more target variables, given certain constraints. Then one or more other variables are changed repeatedly, subject to the specified constraints, until the best values for the target variables are discovered. For example, a manager could try to determine the highest possible level of profits that could be achieved by varying the values for selected revenue sources and expense categories. Changes to such variables could be subjected to constraints such as the limited capacity of a production process or limits to available financing. Optimization is typically accomplished by special-purpose software packages for optimization techniques such as linear programming, or by advanced DSS generators.

Executive information systems (EIS) are information systems that combine many of the features of modern information reporting systems with some of the features of decision support systems. However, their focus is on meeting the strategic information needs of top management. As we said in Chapter 2, top executives need information to support their strategic planning and control responsibilities. Thus, the goal of executive information systems is to provide top management with immediate and easy access to information about a firm's *critical success factors* (CSFs), that is, key factors that are critical to accomplishing an organization's strategic objectives. For example, the executives of a department store chain would probably consider factors such as the chain's sales promotion efforts and product line mix to be critical to its survival and success. We will discuss the use of critical success factors further in Chapter 12.

EXECUTIVE INFORMATION SYSTEMS

Studies have shown that top executives get the information they need from many sources. These include letters, memos, periodicals, and reports produced manually or by computer systems. Other major sources of executive information are meetings, telephone calls, and social activities. Thus, much of a top executive's information comes from noncomputer sources. Computer-generated information generated by traditional information reporting systems have not played a major role in meeting many top executives' information needs [12].

Rationale for EIS

Therefore, computer-based executive information systems which are extremely easy to operate and understand have been developed. EIS attempt to meet the information needs of top management not being met by other forms of management information systems. Executives and information systems specialists in major corporations are capitalizing on advances in computer technology that have made such systems feasible. Software packages are now available that support EIS on mainframe, minicomputer, and microcomputer systems. EIS are still faced with resistance by some executives and plagued by high costs. However, the use of executive information systems is expected to grow rapidly, as more top executives come to recognize their feasibility and benefits, and as less expensive microcomputer-based EIS become more available. Figure 9–11 outlines key factors needed for a successful EIS.

Figure 9-11 Key factors needed for a successful EIS.

Commitment and involvement from top-level management
If executives are not visibly 100 percent behind the project, it will not get the priority or ongoing use.

Understanding data sources
A successful EIS implementation depends on the availability of accurate and complete data. For many organizations, this could mean that a significant investment in existing business systems is needed prior to implementing EIS.

Focusing on what is important
Organization CSFs, exception reporting, accessing information with drill-down capability are a key to success of an EIS.

Response time
A successful EIS will increase in use, functionality and scope over time. Ongoing system performance monitoring is key.

Understanding of computer literacy level of executives
Dictates presentation format, degree of use of graphics, text, mouse, touch screen, etc. The EIS must be easy to use.

Learning curve for development team
Tools to be used are key, especially if developing a system. Familiar tools are best. Vendor support for an EIS package is essential.

Flexibility
Executives' needs will continue to evolve and change with time. As much flexibility as possible should be included.

Ongoing support
EIS cannot be implemented and forgotten. Continuing support is critical to satisfy changing needs.

Source: John Southcott and Bruce Hooey, "EIS: Big League Decision Support," *Edge,* November/December 1989, p.29.

Components of an EIS

As Figure 9-12 illustrates, executive workstations typically use mainframe or minicomputer systems for access to EIS software. The EIS package works with database management and telecommunications software to provide easy access to internal, external, and special databases. Executive information systems provide information about the current status and projected trends in a company's critical success factors, as determined by its top executives. A modeling capability to evaluate alternatives for decision support may also be provided by some EIS.

Of course, such information is presented in forms tailored to the preferences of the executives using these systems. For example, most executive information systems stress the use of graphics displays that are easy to understand and thus communicate clearly and quickly. Exception reporting and trend analysis displays are other information reporting methods that are typically used. Also important is a "drill-down" reporting capability that allows executives to quickly retrieve displays of information at lower levels of detail [6, 13].

Figure 9-13 shows actual displays provided by the Commander executive information system. Notice how simple and brief these displays are. Also note how they provide executives with the ability to drill down quickly to lower levels of detail in areas of particular interest to them. This *drill-down* capability is related to the *hypertext* methodology (discussed in Chapter 6), which allows end users to interactively retrieve related pieces of information from text databases. That is why many EIS packages for microcomputers are based on hypertext technology. Besides the drill-down capability, the Commander EIS also stresses *trend analysis* and *exception reporting.* Thus, an executive can quickly discover the direction key factors are heading and the extent that critical factors are deviating from expected results [18].

Figure 9–12 The executive information system concept. Note that an EIS software package relies on other major types of software to help access, evaluate, and convert data in internal, external, and special databases.

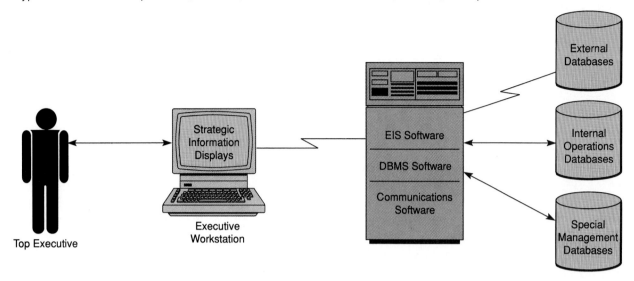

Figure 9–13 Displays provided by the Commander executive information system. Note the simplicity and clarity in which key information is provided, and the ability to drill down to lower levels of detail.

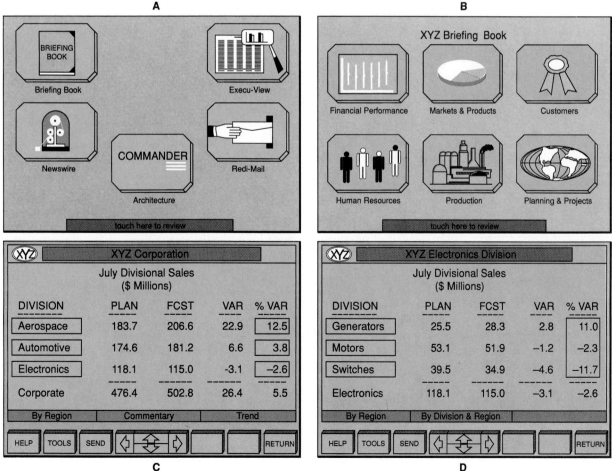

Courtesy Comshare Corporation.

REAL WORLD CASE

Frito-Lay Incorporated

Frito-Lay Incorporated, Pepsico Inc.'s snack-food subsidiary, is setting up 70 LANs around the world to run localized versions of its main-frame-based executive information systems (EIS). Built on a Commander EIS shell from Comshare Inc., the Frito-Lay system actually creates a series of highly specialized decision support system (DSS) veins running from its EIS artery.

The LAN EIS is just the latest in a series of leading-edge EIS steps taken by Frito-Lay, which for two years has been a test site for a half-dozen Comshare products. In between the initial system development and the decision to go with regional LANs, Frito-Lay also designed a no-frills version of the mainframe EIS, which is now on 10,000 hand-held computers used by sales personnel worldwide. "Of course we had to take the graphics out of the hand-held version," said Charles Feld, vice president of information management at Frito-Lay headquarters in Dallas. "For the hand-held version, we developed simple tables of data instead of graphs. But we were extremely happy to be able to get such sophisticated data as periodic sales reports on the hand-helds."

The LAN EIS will take the company a step further. "Thanks to the LANs, we have been able to tailor these systems to very localized needs without losing central corporate perspective," said Feld. "What we have now is one system each for sales, manufacturing, purchasing, and distribution. We also have what we call the *marketing workbench*, which is basically a marketing version of EIS." All of the LAN EISs run on networks using Intel 386 microcomputer servers and color workstations that can take advantage of the Commander EIS graphics. About 600 managers will have access to the LAN system by the time the last one is installed next year.

At Frito-Lay, the mainframe portion of the EIS was set up a year ago after a design meeting with top corporate managers. It was designed for Pepsico Worldwide Snacks Chairman Michael Jordan and Frito-Lay President Robert Beeby, Feld said. "About 40 managers use the EIS to monitor monthly sales reports, distribution patterns, and other data. It's a very user-friendly graphical environment." The main system gives executives touch-screen access to a range of status reports, as well as the Dow Jones News Service. One feature of the EIS, Briefing Book, breaks information down by territory with a set of maps and charts. Another feature, Execu-View, accesses multiple databases without requiring the user to know database language or commands. The system also provides electronic mail, a calendar, and other features.

The overall corporate EIS requires a mainframe. But for the individual systems used by departmental managers, a LAN is all that is needed. "We're pushing decision making down into our organization, and without the flexibility to have a host-, LAN- or PC-based EIS, we couldn't support such a vast group of users," Feld said. As the LANs are set up, Feld sends one of his five specialized LAN developers out to work with the local managers. "We are bringing local managers information their corporate managers want them to have, and we are providing services they want," said Feld. "We are out there working with them."

Application Questions

☐ What benefits does Frito-Lay expect from the LAN-based version of its EIS?

☐ Is a hand-held computer–based information system for 10,000 sales personnel really an EIS? Explain.

☐ What features of Frito-Lay's mainframe EIS mark it as an executive information system?

Source: Adapted from Dennis Eskow, "Frito-Lay Rewrites EIS History Using Regional LANs," *PC Week*, February 26, 1990, pp. 127–28.

Section III: Expert Systems

Information systems and their applications in business and society are being increasingly affected by developments in the field of artificial intelligence. Developments such as expert systems, which are the subject of this section, as well as natural languages, industrial robots, and fifth-generation computers are some examples of this impact. As a business end user, you should be aware of the importance of such developments. Businesses and other organizations are significantly increasing their attempts to assist the human intelligence and productivity of their knowledge workers with artificial intelligence tools and techniques.

But what is artificial intelligence? **Artificial intelligence** (AI) is a science and technology based on disciplines such as computer science, biology, psychology, linguistics, mathematics, and engineering. The goal of AI is to develop computers that can *think*, as well as see, hear, walk, talk, and feel. A major thrust of artificial intelligence is the development of computer functions normally associated with human intelligence, such as reasoning, inference, learning, and problem solving. That's why the term *artificial intelligence* was coined by John McCarthy at MIT in 1956. Besides McCarthy, AI pioneers included Herbert Simon and Alan Newell at Carnegie-Mellon, Norbert Wiener and Marvin Minsky at MIT, Warren McCulloch and Walter Pitts at Illinois, Frank Rosenblatt at Cornell, Alan Turing at Manchester, Edward Feigenbaum at Stanford, Roger Shank at Yale, and many others [16].

Debate has raged around artificial intelligence since serious work in the field began in the 1950s. Not only technological but moral and philosophical questions about the concept of intelligent "thinking" machines are involved. Though significant accomplishments have occurred in many areas of AI, critics claim that devising many of the algorithms needed to impart true humanlike capabilities is simply not possible. But progress continues, and only time will tell if the ambitious goals of artificial intelligence will be achieved and equal the popular images found in science fiction.

AN OVERVIEW OF ARTIFICIAL INTELLIGENCE

The Domains of Artificial Intelligence

Figure 9–14 illustrates the major domains of AI research and development. Note that AI applications can be grouped under the four major areas of cognitive science, computer science, robotics, and natural language, though these classifications do overlap each other and other classifications can be used. Also note that expert systems are just one of many important AI applications. Let's briefly review each of these major areas of AI and some of their current applications.

Cognitive Science

This area of artificial intelligence is based on research in biology, neurology, psychology, mathematics, and many allied disciplines. It focuses on researching how the human brain works and how humans think and learn. The results of such research are the basis for the development of a variety of computer-based applications in artificial intelligence.

Figure 9–14 The major application domains of artificial intelligence. Note that the many applications of AI can be grouped into the four major areas of cognitive science, computer science, robotics, and natural language.

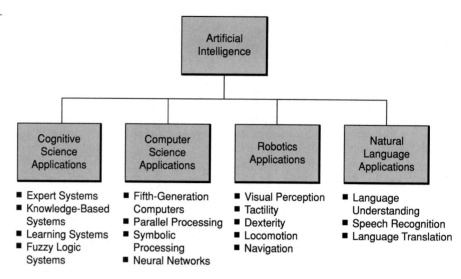

Figure 9–14 The major application domains of artificial intelligence. Note that the many applications of AI can be grouped into the four major areas of cognitive science, computer science, robotics, and natural language.

Applications in the cognitive science area of AI include the development of expert systems and other *knowledge-based systems* that add a knowledge base and some reasoning capability to information systems. Also included are adaptive *learning systems* that can modify their behaviors based on information they acquire as they operate. Chess playing systems are primitive examples of such applications, though many more applications are being implemented. *Fuzzy logic systems* can learn to recognize patterns in data that are incomplete or only partially correct, that is, *fuzzy data*. Thus, they can learn to solve unstructured problems with incomplete knowledge, as humans do [4].

Computer Science

This area of AI applications focuses on the computer hardware and system software needed to produce the powerful supercomputers required for many AI applications. At the forefront of this area are efforts to create a *fifth generation* of intelligent computers, which use the *parallel processing* architecture discussed in Chapter 3. Such computers will be designed for optimum *logical inference* processing, which depends on *symbolic processing* instead of on the numeric processing of traditional computing. Other attempts are being made to develop *neural networks*, which are *massively parallel, neurocomputer systems*. The architecture of these computer systems contains thousands of interconnected CPUs based on the human brain's meshlike neuron structure. Neural networks can process many different pieces of information simultaneously. They can "learn" by being shown sample problems and their solutions. As they start to recognize patterns, they can begin to program themselves to solve related problems on their own. That's why neural network processors and software are the primary technologies being applied to *fuzzy logic* and *adaptive learning* systems [4].

Robotics

AI, engineering, and physiology are the basic disciplines of robotics. This technology produces **robots**—machines with computer intelligence and computer-controlled, humanlike physical capabilities. This area thus includes applications designed to give robots the powers of sight, or *visual perception;* touch, or *tactile capabilities; dexterity,* or skill in handling and manipulation; *locomotion,* or the physical ability to move over any terrain; and *navigation,* or the intelligence to properly find one's way to a destination. The use of robotics in computer-aided manufacturing is discussed in Chapter 10.

Natural Language

The development of *natural languages* is considered a major area of AI applications, and it is essential to both cognitive science and robotics. Being able to talk to computers and robots in conversational human languages and have them understand us as easily as we understand each other is the goal of this area of AI. Thus, this application area involves research and development in linguistics, psychology, computer science, and other disciplines. Applications include human language understanding, speech recognition, and the computerized translation of one human language into another. This area of AI drives developments in voice input/output technology, discussed in Chapter 3, and natural programming languages, discussed in Chapter 4.

One of the most practical and widely implemented applications of artificial intelligence in business is the development of expert systems and other knowledge-based information systems. A **knowledge-based information system** (KBIS) adds a *knowledge base* to the major components found in other types of computer-based information systems. An **expert system** (ES) is a knowledge-based information system that uses its knowledge about a specific, complex application area to act as an expert consultant to end users. As we said in Chapter 2, expert systems can be used for either operational or management applications. Thus, they can be classified conceptually as either *operations* or *management* information systems, depending on whether they are giving expert advice to control operational processes or to help managerial end users make decisions.

Expert systems are only one major type of knowledge-based information system. They are related to *knowledge-based decision support systems* (KDSS), which add a knowledge base to the database and model base of traditional decision support systems. However, unlike decision support systems, expert systems provide answers to questions in a very specific problem area by making humanlike inferences about knowledge contained in a specialized knowledge base. They must also be able to explain their reasoning process and conclusions to a user. So expert systems can provide decision support to managers in the form of advice from an expert consultant in a specific problem area [17]. Figure 9–15 outlines the differences between DSS and expert systems.

The integration of expert systems into decision support systems and other types of information systems is part of a trend toward *expert-assisted information systems.* This integration adds expertise as well as a knowledge base to information systems. For example, fifth-generation computer-aided systems engineering (CASE) tools and 4GL packages are available that include expert system components. This integration promises to make the application development

KNOWLEDGE-BASED INFORMATION SYSTEMS

Expert-Assisted IS

Figure 9–15 Differences between expert systems and decision support systems.

Attribute	DSS	ES
Objectives	Assist human decision maker	Replicate a human advisor and replace him/her
Who makes the recommendations (decisions)?	The human and/or the system	The system
Major orientation	Decision making	Transfer of expertise (human-machine-human) and rendering of advice
Major query direction	Human queries the machine	Machine queries the human
Nature of support	Personal, groups, and institutional	Personal and groups
Data manipulation method	Numerical	Symbolic
Characteristics of problem area	Complex, broad	Narrow domain
Type of problems treated	Ad hoc, unique	Repetitive
Content of database	Factual knowledge	Procedural and factual knowledge
Reasoning capability	No	Yes, limited
Explanation capability	Limited	Yes

Source: Efraim Turban and Paul Watkins, "Integrating Expert Systems and Decision Support Systems," *MIS Quarterly.* June 1986, p. 123.

process easier and faster for end users and other developers who do not have a lot of systems development experience and expertise.

Another example is the integration of expert systems and decision support systems into executive information systems. For example, Figure 9–16 illustrates how the expert system capability of an *explain* feature has been built into an EIS. This executive information system can automatically select and arrange relevant data and produce explanatory text and graphics. Therefore, it can explain the meaning of previously displayed results to an executive upon request.

COMPONENTS OF AN EXPERT SYSTEM

The components of an expert system include a knowledge base and software modules that perform inferences on the knowledge and communicate answers to a user's questions. Figure 9–17 illustrates the interrelated components of an expert system. Note the following components:

☐ **Knowledge base.** The knowledge base of an expert system contains facts about a specific subject area (for example, *John is an analyst*) and *heuristics* (rules of thumb) that express the reasoning procedures of an expert on the subject (for example, *IF John is an analyst, THEN he needs a workstation*). Figure 9–18 illustrates the contents of a knowledge base in a rule-based expert system. Notice that the expert system's knowledge base consists of a *rule base* of IF-THEN rules and a *fact base* of facts and other information about a subject, which is processed by a software component called the *inference engine.*

☐ **Software resources.** These include an **inference engine** and other programs for refining knowledge and communicating with users. The inference engine program processes the rules and facts related to a

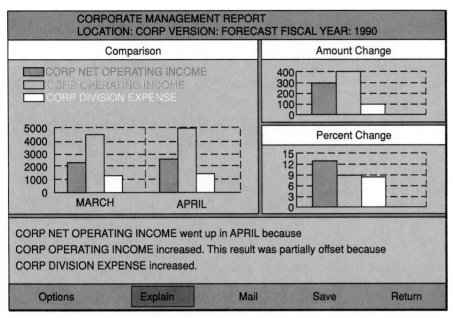

Figure 9-16 A display of an expert-assisted EIS. This executive information system can automatically explain the reasons for previously displayed results with explanatory text and graphics upon request.

Courtesy Execucom Systems Corporation.

Figure 9-17 Components of an expert system. The software modules perform inferences on a knowledge base built by an expert and/or knowledge engineer. This provides expert answers to an end user's questions in an interactive process.

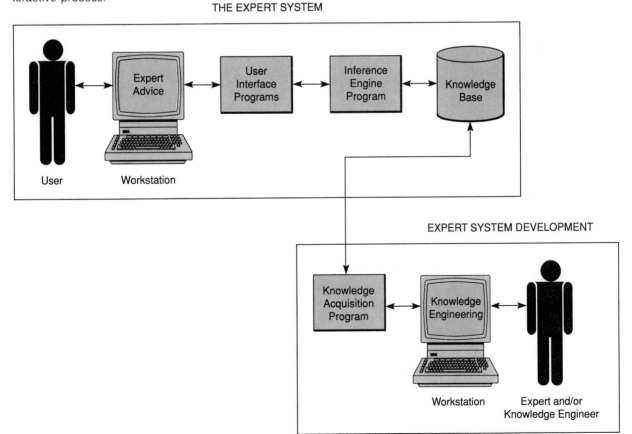

Figure 9-18 A rule-based
expert system. Note that
such systems have an in-
ference engine program that
manipulates a knowledge
base consisting of facts and
rules in order to reach conclusions.

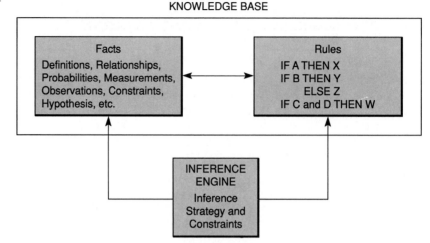

KNOWLEDGE BASE

Facts
Definitions, Relationships,
Probabilities, Measurements,
Observations, Constraints,
Hypothesis, etc.

Rules
IF A THEN X
IF B THEN Y
ELSE Z
IF C and D THEN W

**INFERENCE
ENGINE**
Inference
Strategy and
Constraints

specific problem. It then makes associations and inferences resulting
in recommended courses of action for a user.

Inferences can be made using *forward chaining* (reaching a
conclusion by applying rules to facts). For example, if a search of the
rules and facts in the knowledge base found that analysts need
workstations and John is an analyst, then the conclusion that "John
needs a workstation" would be made.

Some expert systems use *backward chaining* (justifying a proposed
conclusion by determining if it results from applying rules to facts).
For example, the hypothesis that "John should have a workstation"
would be accepted only if a search of the knowledge base found that
analysts need workstations and John is an analyst.

Other software resources include user interface programs such as a
natural language processor for communicating with end users. This
includes an explanation program to explain the reasoning process to a
user if requested. Knowledge acquisition programs are not part of an
expert system but are software tools for knowledge base development.
Other expert system development tools, such as *expert system shells*,
are also important software resources.

☐ **Hardware resources.** These include stand-alone microcomputer systems, as well as microcomputer workstations and terminals connected
to minicomputers or mainframes in a telecommunications network.
Sometimes, complex expert systems are developed with powerful,
special-purpose computers specifically designed for advanced expert
system development packages or use with the LISP or PROLOG
programming languages.

☐ **People resources.** An expert system provides expert advice to end
users. This expertise is captured in a knowledge base by a *knowledge
engineer* from facts and rules provided by an expert. Or experts and
end users can be their own knowledge engineers and use expert
system shells as development tools to build knowledge bases and
expert systems.

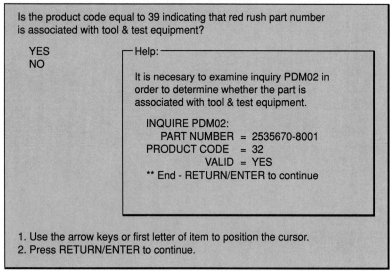

THE RED RUSH ADVISOR

Is the product code equal to 39 indicating that red rush part number is associated with tool & test equipment?

YES
NO

Help:

It is necesary to examine inquiry PDM02 in order to determine whether the part is associated with tool & test equipment.

INQUIRE PDM02:
    PART NUMBER = 2535670-8001
    PRODUCT CODE = 32
            VALID = YES
** End - RETURN/ENTER to continue

1. Use the arrow keys or first letter of item to position the cursor.
2. Press RETURN/ENTER to continue.

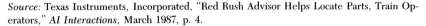

Figure 9–19 Using an expert system. Note how this expert system package asks a question and explains its reasoning to a user.

Source: Texas Instruments, Incorporated, "Red Rush Advisor Helps Locate Parts, Train Operators," *AI Interactions*, March 1987, p. 4.

EXAMPLES OF EXPERT SYSTEMS

Using an expert system involves an interactive computer-based session, in which the solution to a problem is explored, with the expert system acting as a consultant to an end user. The expert system asks questions of the user, searches its knowledge base for facts and rules, explains its reasoning process when asked, and gives expert advice to the user in the subject area being explored. For example, Figure 9–19 illustrates part of the dialogue between an expert system package for high priority (i.e., "red rush") parts ordering and a customer representative.

Expert System Applications

Expert systems are being used for many different types of applications, and the variety of applications is expected to continue to grow. However, you should realize that expert systems typically accomplish one or more generic uses. Figure 9–20 outlines seven generic categories of expert system activities, with specific examples of actual expert system applications. As you can see, expert systems are being used in many different fields, including medicine, engineering, the physical sciences, and business. Expert systems now help diagnose illnesses, search for minerals, analyze compounds, recommend repairs, and do financial planning. Let's look at a few actual examples more closely.

Airlines

United Airlines uses an expert system called *GADS* (Gate Assignment and Display System) to make airport gate assignments for its aircraft. This frame-based expert system uses the same reasoning as experienced gate controllers. For example, it knows that two adjacent gates cannot each accommodate a DC-10 at once because of the size of the planes. The system helps prevent the

Application Categories and Typical Uses
Decision management—Systems that appraise situations or consider alternatives and make recommendations based on criteria supplied during the discovery process: ■ Loan portfolio analysis ■ Employee performance evaluation ■ Insurance underwriting ■ Demographic forecasts
Diagnostic/troubleshooting—Systems that infer underlying causes from reported symptoms and history: ■ Equipment calibration ■ Help desk operations ■ Software debugging ■ Medical diagnosis
Maintenance/scheduling—Systems that prioritize and schedule limited or time-critical resources: ■ Maintenance scheduling ■ Production scheduling ■ Education scheduling ■ Project management
Intelligent text/documentation—Systems that take existing legislation or established policies and procedures and recast them into a knowledge base system: ■ Building Regulations ■ OSHA Safety Standards ■ Employee Benefits ■ EEO Employment Codes
Design/configuration—Systems that help configure equipment components, given existing constraints: ■ Computer option installation ■ Manufacturability studies ■ Communications networks ■ Optimum assembly plan
Selection/classification—Systems that help users choose products or processes, often from among large or complex sets of alternatives: ■ Material selection ■ Delinquent account identification ■ Information classification ■ Suspect identification
Process monitoring/control—Systems that monitor and control procedures or processes: ■ Machine control (including robotics) ■ Inventory control ■ Production monitoring ■ Chemical testing

Courtesy Information Builders, Inc.

long delays that can occur when weather and aircraft traffic problems disrupt gate assignments for incoming planes. Before GADS, the gate controllers used magnetic symbols that were moved around on a large metal board. Now GADS helps them use what-if analysis to head off problems long before they occur [9].

Credit Card Services

American Express uses an expert system called *Authorizer's Assistant* to help credit authorizers decide on requests for credit. With over 20 million U.S. cardholders, American Express developed the expert system to cut down on losses from incorrect credit authorizations. American Express is unique in that it has no preset credit limit, which makes credit authorization more difficult. It also has a policy of reaching approval/denial decisions within 90 seconds or less,

and a base of customers used to having their own way. Thus, the risks of a bad decision are great. Good customers can be lost if a decision to deny credit is made. Of course, a decision to approve credit could result in major losses.

Authorizer's Assistant contains the expertise of experienced credit authorizers. It helps recognize charges and charge requests that are outside of typical credit patterns. Unusual requests that do not fit this profile are declined because the probability is too high that they are not being requested by the real cardholders or will not be repaid properly. Thus, the Authorizer's Assistant is an excellent example of using an expert system to aid the decision process, boost profits through increased productivity, reduce costs through loss avoidance, and enhance product and service quality [2].

Financial Services

Expert systems for personal financial planning include PlanPower, by Applied Expert Systems, Inc. (APEX). This expert system is designed to give financial planners the benefit of the expertise of experts in tax, estate, financial planning, and portfolio management. This expert system can take into account thousands of variables to recommend the right financial products and services for an individual client. It takes into account a client's attributes, goals, and financial circumstances, such as prior investments, real estate holdings, and insurance coverages.

This expert system allows financial consultants to perform what-if analyses using its knowledge of factors such as interest and inflation rates, the client's financial situation, and a selection of 125 financial products. PlanPower then recommends a financial plan to meet the client's goals such as increasing income and capital and reducing risk and taxes [9].

Medicine

Expert systems in medicine were among the first to be developed. One classic example is Mycin, which was developed at Stanford University in the mid-1970s. Mycin diagnoses and prescribes treatment for meningitis and other bacterial infections during the first 48 hours of an infection. This is a time when symptoms are unclear and human diagnosis is difficult. Mycin was designed by painstakingly interviewing many doctors about their diagnosis and treatment practices, and it took over 20 man-years to complete. It contains over 500 rules and uses its knowledge of infectious organisms, lab test results, and patient history and symptoms to make its diagnosis and prescribe treatment. Mycin has proven more accurate than human diagnosis when tested in its area of expertise [9, 16].

DEVELOPING EXPERT SYSTEMS

As the previous examples show, many organizations are developing expert system solutions to business problems. However, before developing an expert system, the following questions need to be answered:

- ☐ What applications are suitable for expert systems?
- ☐ What benefits and limitations of expert systems should be considered?
- ☐ Should the expert system be (1) purchased as a completely developed system, (2) developed with an expert system shell, or

(3) developed from scratch as a custom system using traditional programming methods?

Obviously, expert systems are not the answer to every problem facing an organization. People using other types of information systems do quite well in many problem situations. So what types of problems are most suitable to expert system solutions? One way to answer this is to look at examples of the applications of current expert systems, including the generic tasks being accomplished, such as those that were summarized in Figure 9–20.

Once the suitability and feasibility of a proposed expert system application have been evaluated, it's time to confront the make-or-buy decision. As you saw in a previous example, complete expert system packages like PlanPower can be purchased by financial consultants and others. Many other packages are available in a variety of application areas, and the number is increasing each year. As in other make-or-buy decisions, the suitability of the expert system package for an end user's needs must be balanced against the cost in time and money of developing a custom system.

Expert System Shells

Developing large, complex expert systems typically requires the use of programming languages such as LISP or PROLOG and powerful special-purpose computers. However, the easiest way to develop your own expert system is to use an **expert system shell** as a developmental tool. An expert system shell is a software package consisting of an expert system without its *kernel*, that is, its knowledge base of facts and rules. This leaves a *shell* of software (the inference engine and user interface programs) which has generic inferencing and user interface capabilities. Other development tools (such as rule editors and user interface generators) are added to make the shell a powerful expert systems development tool.

Expert system shells are now available as relatively low-cost software packages that help users develop their own expert systems on microcomputers. They allow trained users to develop the knowledge base for a specific expert system application. For example, one shell uses a spreadsheet format to help end users develop IF-THEN rules, automatically generating rules based on examples furnished by a user. Once a knowledge base is constructed, it is used with the shell's inference engine and user interface modules as a complete expert system on a specific subject area. Expert system shells have accelerated the widespread development and use of expert systems.

Figure 9–21 shows examples of screens displayed by two popular, low-cost expert system shells for microcomputers, 1st Class and Exsys. These displays show how such packages help users define facts and develop rules to create a knowledge base. 1st Class is an *inductive* rule-based shell that creates (induces) rules based on examples furnished by the user using a spreadsheet format. Exsys is a more straightforward rule-based shell that helps the user create IF-THEN rules directly with the help of a rule editor.

Knowledge Engineering

A knowledge engineer is a professional who works with experts to capture the knowledge (facts and rules of thumb) they possess. The knowledge engineer then builds the knowledge base (and the rest of the expert system if necessary).

Figure 9–21 Using expert system shells. The top screen shows how an IF-THEN rule can be created directly with Exsys. The bottom screen shows an inductive rule-based shell, 1st-Class, being used to enter facts and generate rules via a spreadsheet format.

Using a Simple Rule-Based Shell

```
RULE NUMBER: 6

IF:

    (1)     The scope of the work is Research and analysis/
            Research and development

Then:

    (1)     Bid - Probability=7/10


---------------------------------------------------------------
CHANGE: If <I>, Then <T>, Else <E>, Note <N>, Reference <R>, Done <ENTER>
↑ for previous rule,      ↓ for next rule
```

Using an Inductive Rule-Based Shell

		new_Example,	Replicate,	Change,	Activate,	Move,	Delete		
		Files	Definitions	Examples	Methods	Rule	Advisor		
[F1=Help]		14 Examples in CPATH			[F9=Definitions]		[F10=Methods]		
(inactive)							weights - - - - ->		

		MEMO	GPA	ENJOYCOL	FREETIME	FINANCE	CAREERPATH	WEIGHT
>	1:		3.3	FAIR	*	FAIR	REALWORLD	1.0
	2:		4.0	MUCH	LITTLE	EXCELLENT	POSTGRAD	1.0
	3:		4.0	LITTLE	LITTLE	EXCELLENT	POSTGRAD	1.0
	4:		2.5	LITTLE	SOME	GOOD	REALWORLD	1.0
	5:		2.5	FAIR	SOME	EXCELLENT	REALWORLD	1.0
	6:		3.2	HATE	SOME	GOOD	REALWORLD	1.0
	7:		3.5	FAIR	SOME	EXCELLENT	POSTGRAD	1.0
	8:		3.5	FAIR	SOME	GOOD	POSTGARD	1.0
	9:		3.5	FAIR	SOME	POOR	REALWORLD	1.0
	10:		1.3	HATE	LOT	GOOD	VOCATIONAL	1.0
	11:		2.8	MUCH	SOME	POOR	REALWORLD	1.0
	12:		3.4	LITTLE	SOME	GOOD	REALWORLD	1.0
	13:		2.9	HATE	LOT	GOOD	VOCATIONAL	1.0
	14:		3.1	HATE	LITTLE	GOOD	REALWORLD	1.0

Source: Kristopher Sprague and Stephen Ruth, *Developing Expert Systems with Exsys* (Santa Cruz, Calif.: Mitchel Publishing, 1988), p. 70; and Cristopher Ruth and Stephen Ruth, *Developing Expert Systems Using 1st-Class* (Santa Cruz, Calif.: Mitchel Publishing, 1988), p. 23. Used with permission.

Thus, knowledge engineers perform a role similar to that of systems analysts in conventional information systems development. However, knowledge engineering can be a difficult assignment. Knowledge engineers must be able to understand and work with experts in many subject areas and work on projects that cannot be easily converted into facts and rules. Therefore, this new specialty requires good "people skills," as well as a background in artificial intelligence and information systems.

A MANAGERIAL PERSPECTIVE

Before deciding to acquire or develop an expert system, it is important that end users use a managerial perspective to evaluate its benefits and limitations. In particular, they must decide whether the benefits of a proposed expert system will exceed its costs [8, 11, 17].

Benefits of Expert Systems

An expert system captures the expertise of an expert or group of experts in a computer-based information system. Thus, it can outperform a single human expert in many problem situations. That's because an expert system is faster and more consistent, can have the knowledge of several experts, and does not get tired or distracted by overwork or stress.

Expert systems also help preserve and reproduce the knowledge of experts. They allow a company to preserve the expertise of an expert before he or she leaves the organization. This expertise can then be shared by reproducing the software and knowledge base of the expert system. This allows novices to be trained and supported by copies of an expert system distributed throughout an organization. Finally, expert systems can have the same competitive advantages as other types of information systems technology. That is, the effective use of expert systems can allow a firm to (1) improve the efficiency of its operations, (2) produce new products and services, (3) lock in customers and suppliers, and (4) build a knowledge-based strategic information resource.

Limitations of Expert Systems

The major limitations of expert systems arise from their limited focus, inability to learn, and developmental cost. Expert systems excel only in solving specific types of problems in a limited domain of knowledge. They fail miserably in solving problems requiring a broad knowledge and in subjective problem solving. They do well with specific types of operational or analytical tasks, but falter at subjective managerial decision making. For example, an expert system might help a financial consultant develop alternative investment recommendations for a client. But it could not adequately evaluate the nuances of current political, economic, and societal developments or the personal dynamics of a session with a client. These important factors would still have to be handled by the human consultant before a final investment decision could be reached.

Expert systems may also be difficult and costly to develop and maintain properly. The costs of the knowledge engineers, lost expert time, and hardware and software resources may be too high to offset the benefits expected from some applications. Also, expert systems can't maintain themselves. That is, they can't learn from experience but must be taught new knowledge and modified as new expertise is needed to match developments in their subject areas. However, some of these limitations can be overcome by the use of expert system shells and other developmental tools that make the job of development and maintenance easier.

REAL WORLD CASE

The Broadway

The Broadway, a subsidiary of Carter Hawley Hale Stores Inc. (CHH), is a Los Angeles–based chain of 43 department stores performing 57 million customer transactions a year in what can easily be considered the most fiercely competitive retail and fashion market in America: Southern California. In a land where conspicuous consumption is a way of life, customer service and highly qualified retail managers help to determine success or failure of a retail operation. And for the department store business, which has seen a recent spate of bankruptcies and a For Sale sign hung on Bloomingdale's, every consumer dollar won at the expense of competitors can mean the difference between ongoing White sales or a Going Out of Business sale.

At The Broadway, the everyday management of each store is handled by area sales managers (ASMs), many of whom are recent college graduates with only a few years of actual retail experience. The 645 ASMs employed by the company are expected to competently manage store salespeople; analyze sales reports; deal with customers; and plan six-month retail strategies based on market trends, fashions, and fads.

Of course, some managers were performing better than others. To create consistency, senior executives at both The Broadway and its parent company, notably Information Services Chief Vince Conant and Broadway President Richard Clayton, began exploring knowledge-based systems as a potential avenue for increasing managers' performance. The Broadway has been fully automated for some time, relying on a variety of IBM computers for interactive gift registries, credit processing, and sales transactions. In the end, Broadway selected IBM's ESE expert systems tools for mainframe development.

To begin building the knowledge base, eight of the top-producing area sales managers were recruited to provide the heuristics (rules of thumb) for a system that would become known as the Area Sales Manager Expert System Consultant. Based on knowledge-gathering sessions with these ASMs, the Broadway's systems developers came up with six modules addressing critical areas of ASM job performance: sales techniques, staffing, product knowledge, product procurement, floor layout, and motivation. Development of the system took nine weeks, which is a far cry from the standard 18 to 36 months required for AI prototyping in the early 1980s. What's more, fewer than five programmers were working on the project at any one time.

The system was tested in two Southern California Broadways during the spring of 1988. Early ASM users were given a training course in the system and then given access to use it on their own. When sales figures for the stores showed a marked uptick, The Broadway's management decided to deploy the expert system in every location. This process took about a year, and now every Broadway store is online with the ASM Expert System Consultant running on IBM mainframes. There is talk within the company of delivering the system on PCs and even installing it in every one of CHH's 114 stores nationwide.

As a user works his or her way through each of the modules, the system asks for store-specific data such as average sales per hour and current sales as compared with last year's sales. It then pinpoints areas of concern, as well as strong management strategies and characteristics. Many of The Broadway's ASMs find that the immediacy of strategy analysis based on current sales figures and general store performance helps them to make critical decisions much more quickly—something that can be very important in day-to-day retailing.

Application Questions

☐ Why is retail store management a good application of expert systems?

☐ How was the ASM system developed?

☐ What are its benefits to store managers?

Source: Adapted from Harvey P. Newquist III, "Experts at Retail," *Datamation*, April 1, 1990, p. 56.

SUMMARY

☐ Information systems can support a variety of management activities. These include the five functions of management (plan, organize, staff, direct, and control); the 10 roles of management (leader, liaison, figurehead, monitor, disseminator, spokesperson, entrepreneur, disturbance handler, resource allocator, and negotiator); and the three levels of management activity (strategic, tactical, and operational).

☐ Information systems can support the intelligence, design, and choice activities of the decision making process. To do this, information systems should (1) scan the internal organization and the external environment to produce information that helps identify problems and opportunities, (2) help generate and evaluate decision alternatives, and (3) provide information products that emphasize and prioritize decision alternatives and provide feedback on implemented decisions.

☐ Decisions can be classified as structured, semistructured, or unstructured. Structured decisions involve situations where decision procedures can be specified in advance. Unstructured decisions are subject to too many random, changeable, or unknown factors for decision procedures to be specified in advance. Information systems can provide a wide range of information products to support many types of decisions.

☐ Decision support systems are interactive, computer-based information systems that use a model base and a database to provide information tailored to support semistructured and unstructured decisions faced by individual managers. They are designed to use a decision maker's own insights and judgments in an ad hoc, interactive, analytical modeling process leading to a specific decision.

☐ A decision support system consists of hardware, software, data, model, and people resources. Hardware resources include management workstations, departmental minicomputers, and corporate mainframes. Software resources include software packages such as DSS generators and spreadsheet packages that perform database management, model base management, and dialogue generation and management. Data and model resources include a database extracted from internal, external, and personal databases, and a model base that is a collection of mathematical models and analytical techniques. People resources include managers and staff specialists who explore decision alternatives with the support of a DSS.

☐ Using a decision support system is an interactive, analytical modeling process, consisting of what-if analysis, sensitivity analysis, goal seeking analysis, or optimization analysis activities. Decision support system applications may be institutional or ad hoc, but are typically developed to support the types of decisions faced by specific industries, functional areas, and decision makers.

☐ Executive information systems are management information systems tailored to the strategic information needs of top management. They provide easily understood and used information about a company's critical success factors to top executives to support their strategic planning and control responsibilities.

☐ The major application domains of artificial intelligence include cognitive science, computer science, robotics, and natural language. The goal of AI is the development of computer functions normally associated with human physical and mental capabilities, such as robots that see, hear, talk, feel, and move, and computers capable of reasoning, learning, and problem solving.

☐ Expert systems are knowledge-based information systems that use a knowledge base about a specific, complex application area and an inference engine program to act as an expert consultant to users. An expert system consists of hardware, software, knowledge, and people resources. Hardware includes workstations and other computers. Software includes an inference engine program that makes inferences based on the facts and rules stored in a knowledge base. Other software includes user interface programs and expert system shells for expert system development. A knowledge base consists of facts about a specific subject area and heuristics (rules of thumb) that express the reasoning procedures of an expert. Users, domain experts, and knowledge engineers are the people resources of an expert system.

☐ Using an expert system involves the interactive solution of a problem with the expert system acting as a consultant to a user. Expert systems are being used for many different applications in fields such as medicine, engineering, and business, where they can support applications in business operations or managerial decision making.

☐ Expert systems can be purchased or developed if a problem situation exists that is suitable for solution by expert systems rather than by conventional experts and information processing. The benefits of expert systems (such as preservation and replication of expertise) must be balanced with their limited applicability in many problem situations. If the decision is made to develop an expert system, the use of an expert system shell should be considered.

These are the key terms and concepts of this chapter. The page number of their first explanation is in parentheses.

KEY TERMS AND CONCEPTS

1. Artificial intelligence *(322)*
   a. Application domains
   b. Objectives
2. Analytical modeling *(317)*
   a. Goal seeking analysis
   b. Optimization analysis
   c. Sensitivity analysis
   d. What-if analysis
3. Components of a DSS *(312)*
4. Decision making process *(307)*
   a. Intelligence activities
   b. Design activities
   c. Choice activities
5. Decision support system *(311)*
6. DSS generator *(313)*
7. DSS model base *(313)*
8. Functions of management *(304)*
9. Expert systems *(325)*
   a. Benefits and limitations *(334)*
   b. Components *(326)*
   c. Generic applications *(329)*
10. Executive information system *(319)*
11. Expert system shell *(332)*
12. Group decisions support system *(316)*
13. Inference engine *(326)*
14. Knowledge base *(326)*
15. Knowledge-based system *(325)*

16. Levels of management *(306)*
17. Robotics *(324)*
18. Roles of management *(305)*
19. Semistructured decisions *(308)*

20. Spreadsheet package *(314)*
21. Structured decisions *(308)*
22. Unstructured decisions *(308)*
23. Decision support versus information reporting *(307)*

REVIEW QUIZ

Match one of the **key terms and concepts** listed above with one of the examples or definitions listed below. Try to find the best fit for answers that seem to fit more than one term or concept. Defend your choices.

_____ 1. Information systems should help identify problems and opportunities.

_____ 2. Information systems should help generate and evaluate decision alternatives.

_____ 3. Information systems should help emphasize and prioritize decision alternatives.

_____ 4. Inventory reorder decisions can frequently be quantified and automated.

_____ 5. Decisions involved in starting a new line of products might involve a lot of unknown factors.

_____ 6. Managers should plan, organize, staff, direct, and control an organization.

_____ 7. A manager is a leader, liaison, monitor, spokesperson, entrepreneur, and negotiator, among other things.

_____ 8. Top managers concentrate on strategic planning for the organization, whereas operational managers control day-to-day operations.

_____ 9. Provide an interactive modeling capability tailored to the specific information needs of managers.

_____ 10. Interactive responses to ad hoc inquiries versus prespecified information.

_____ 11. A management workstation, DSS generator, database, model base, and manager or staff specialist.

_____ 12. A collection of mathematical models and analytical techniques.

_____ 13. The software component that provides database management, model base management, and dialogue generation and management.

_____ 14. A software package that uses a worksheet format to help end users do analytical modeling.

_____ 15. Analyzing the effect of changing variables and relationships and manipulating a mathematical model.

_____ 16. Changing revenues and tax rates to see the effect on net profit after taxes.

_____ 17. Changing revenues in many small increments to see revenue's effect on net profit after taxes.

_____   18. Changing revenues and expenses to find how best to achieve a specified amount of net profit after taxes.

_____   19. Changing revenues and expenses subject to certain constraints in order to achieve the highest net profit.

_____   20. Computer-based tools can enhance the effectiveness of group decision making.

_____   21. Management information systems for the strategic information needs of top management.

_____   22. Focuses on the development of computer functions normally associated with human capabilities.

_____   23. Applications in cognitive science, computer science, robotics, and natural language.

_____   24. Development of computer-based machines that possess capabilities such as sight, hearing, dexterity, and movement.

_____   25. Information systems that have a knowledge base as a major system component.

_____   26. Knowledge-based information systems that act as expert consultants to users in a specific application area.

_____   27. A workstation, user interface programs, inference engine, knowledge base, and an end user.

_____   28. Applications such as diagnosis, design, prediction, interpretation, and repair.

_____   29. They can preserve and reproduce the knowledge of experts but have a limited application focus.

_____   30. A collection of facts and reasoning procedures in a specific subject area.

_____   31. A software package that manipulates a knowledge base and makes associations and inferences leading to a recommended course of action.

_____   32. A software package used as an expert system development tool.

REAL WORLD PROBLEMS

1. American Airlines

American Airlines Inc. is moving its IBM mainframe application for flight-crew scheduling to RISC-based workstations. American's commercial mainframe system, the Crew Allocation System, is currently used by many major airlines. When American rolls out the new RISC-based Workstation Crew Allocation System (WCAS), it hopes to attract all segments of the airline industry. "We're aiming the new workstation version at the entire airline market—from commuter to large planes," said Shane Batt, a senior consultant with American's Decision Technology group in Fort Worth, Texas. "The size of our fleets is growing very rapidly, and maintaining the scheduling system on the mainframe complex has become burdensome," said Batt. The system will be used to schedule crews for American's nine fleets, each of which has a maximum of 250 aircraft.

Moving the application off the mainframe will save the airline money as well as allow scheduling analysts to improve their schedule design, said Batt. Since WCAS performs mathematical optimization, the longer the application is run, the better the results, he said. One key benefit of bringing crew scheduling to the workstation is response time. While a typical mainframe job requires nine hours, a workstation handles this task in three hours, said Batt. In addition to lower computing costs, another expected benefit is increased productivity of flight crews. The airline industry is plagued with paying crew members for layovers. With the new system, American hopes to reduce its "pay and credit" costs by scheduling crews onto other flights more quickly. American estimated the return on investment for the new application to be 70 percent per year over a five-year period.

a. Is the WCAS package an example of a decision support system?
b. What are the business benefits expected from the use of WCAS by American?

Source: Adapted from Kristina Sullivan, "American Airlines Opts for RISC PCs to Do Mainframe Job," PC Week, April 2, 1990, pp. S26, 30.

2. The University of Arizona

Imagine a conference room equipped with 24 workstations, two rear-screen projectors, and an electronic copyboard. A video projector replaces the conventional overhead projector, and the podium houses two workstations, video displays, and a bank of switches controlling the room's video, sound, and lighting systems. I am not describing NASA's mission control center, but a prototype electronic meeting room installed at the University of Arizona's College of Business and Public Administration, called the Decision and Planning Laboratory, or the Arizona Room. IBM has installed the system in 18 locations across the United States, and a study conducted at one of those sites reported a person-hour savings of more than 50 percent and a 92 percent reduction in the time required to complete a project by teams using the room. Arizona reports equally dramatic results from many groups—more than 150 corporations in all—that have used its rooms in the past few years.

What sets the Arizona system apart is a collection of software tools divided by function into five groups: Brainstorming, Issue Analysis, Prioritizing, Policy Formation, and Stakeholder Identification. My favorite meeting tool was Electronic Brainstorming. Each of us typed in ideas on our workstations. Hitting the Return key published the idea onto a central list that slowly scrolled down the large screens behind the podium. It was an interesting experience, sitting in a room full of people, all talking and typing at once. The result was an extremely large and rich list of issues and ideas—we accomplished more in 45 minutes than I would expect from several hours of a normal meeting.

a. Is the Arizona Room and its software an example of a group decision support system? Explain.
b. What are the advantages and disadvantages of conducting business meetings in such facilities?

Source: Adapted from Paul Saffo, "Same-Time, Same-Place, Groupware," Personal Computing, March 20, 1990, pp. 57–58.

3. Lockheed Aeronautical Systems Company

When Lockheed's Management and Decision Systems (MIDS) was introduced back in 1978, many of the executives who were expected to use it were skeptical. Since then, one of the prime skeptics, President Ken Cannestra, admitted that through use of his MIDS workstation, it takes him only half as long to obtain vital information. Close to 800 executives of this Lockheed Corporation division now use MIDS to manage an operation which grosses between $2 billion and $3 billion a year and builds military aircraft sold in 62 nations. One of the most helpful functions of MIDS is keeping track of key players. Thus, when any foreign official phones, the executive caller can instantly pull up background information on that individual, how much business Lockheed is doing with that nation, and the status of delivery. Because of the ready availability of information, paper reports have declined steadily.

One reason for the enthusiastic acceptance of MIDS is adherence to a key design objective—the information entered has to be unbiased. The system is designed to implement decisions, not make them. To do otherwise would make it threatening and, therefore, inhibit acceptance. Attention to details, such as standardized codes and colors, has helped make MIDS easy to use and understand.

a. Is MIDS a DSS or an EIS? Explain.

b. What are the business benefits of MIDS for Lockheed?

Source: Adapted from "Exploring the Advantages of the MIDS Executive Support System," *SIM Executive Summary,* January 1990, p. 2.

4. International Pharmaceutical Company

The chief executive officer (CEO) of a large international pharmaceutical company had a tough decision to make. A new drug the company had developed was ready to go to market pending government approval—a process which could take anywhere from 2 to 18 months. The question: Should he begin the product launch process now, penetrate the market sooner, get a jump on the competition, and hope that government approval is not delayed, or should he wait until the government gives the green light? The CEO turned to his workstation-based executive information system (EIS) to get answers to several key questions and begin his analysis.

☐ What will be the total cost of the product launch?

☐ What is the sales forecast for the new product by month, particularly during the first six months after launch?

☐ Has the product been successful in similar markets?

☐ How has the new drug performed in clinical trials, and what are leading physicians saying about its potential?

☐ What is the company's track record in dealing with government? Have similar products received quick approval?

☐ Does the competition have similar products on the market? If so, have they been successful? Do they have similar products waiting for government approval?

☐ Have the salespeople had any discussion with their customers about the product? If so, what are the customers saying?

a. What stages of decision making and what functions, roles, and levels of management are illustrated in this example?

b. Is this an example of a DSS or EIS in action? Explain.

Source: Adapted from John Southcott and Bruce Hooey, "EIS: Big League Decision Support," *EDGE*, November/December 1989, p. 28.

5. Zenith Electronics Corporation

For hands-on executives with their own ways of looking at things, there's no substitute for a computer and a good spreadsheet. At least that's the way Jerry K. Pearlman, CEO of Zenith Electronics, looks at things. Pearlman, 50, uses an electronic spreadsheet package to develop worksheets to analyze the business operations of the $2.4 billion television and computer maker. In fact, most of the spreadsheet models he uses are his own handiwork, which is how he prefers it. "There are very few spreadsheets I do that are prepared by someone else and then given to me to update or just look at," says Pearlman. "Almost all of the spreadsheets I use are models that I have generated myself because [they represent] my own way of taking an analytical look at things or because they are confidential."

Although he uses a PC less than an hour a day on average, Pearlman believes his work at the computer—coupled with that of others—often makes a profound difference in the work that is ultimately produced. "There are decisions we make now from accumulated data and manipulated data where, once or twice a week, I find myself saying, 'Amazing. We could not have made this decision 10 years ago.'"

a. Is Mr. Pearlman's use of a spreadsheet package an example of a DSS in action? Why or why not?

b. How has his use of electronic spreadsheets affected his decision making?

Source: Christopher O'Malley, "Making Software Work the Way He Does," *Personal Computing*, April 1989, p. 77.

6. Intel and Johnson Wax

A new crop of applications by corporations as diverse as Intel and Johnson Wax show how expert systems can be put to work as sales and support tools, cutting down on the time and expense of new-product training for salespeople and end users. "Cutting costs is a question of quickly bringing people up to speed on new technology, and expert systems can spread expertise very efficiently," said Larry Bielawski, author of the book, *Intelligent Systems Design*. Officials at Intel agree. As the firm expands its family of MCS-96 microprocessor controllers, crucial to its sales strategy is an expert system called ACE196, which is a PC-based expert system. The software helps users program Intel's seven new MCS-96 microprocessor controllers.

"It saved me three or four days in writing software," said Eric Overton, a research engineer who uses Intel chips in material-testing systems. "You just go through a series of windows, answering questions about how you want the chip to function, and it sets up chip configuration for you." This question-and-answer format is also used in an expert system deployed this year by Johnson Wax for salespeople in its Prism subsidiary. The salespeople are using the system to help convince restaurateurs that a new line of Warewash dishwashers and detergents will cut their water, electricity, and detergent costs.

a. Why is new product design a good expert systems application?

b. Why is new product introduction a good expert systems application?

Source: Adapted from Marc Ferranti, "Expert Systems Find Niche as Tools for Sales, Support," *PC Week,* April 16, 1990, pp. 27–28.

7. East India Hotels

The East India Hotels developed FOM-AID (Front Office Manager Aid), an expert system designed to make the expertise of key hotel managers available to others. The front office manager is a crucial person in any hotel environment. The manager's judgment, knowledge, and decision making ability have a direct bearing on the hotel's profitability, because he or she determines booking policies and practices. Much of the manager's skill is based on rule-of-thumb expertise gathered through many years in the hotel business. FOM-AID is designed for use by new front office managers or executive office staff members. By evaluating information on rooms available, booking levels, categories of bookings, and the day's special events contained in a database, the expert system recommends booking levels, reports projected occupancy rates, and recommends action on opening or closing different rate categories.

Ratan Kesvani of The Oberoi InterContinental in New Delhi served as the domain expert. Knowledge engineers conducted a series of interviews with Kesvani and periodically reviewed the knowledge base with him to gain a more accurate understanding of how he does his job. Knowledge acquisition sessions covered factors used to determine optimum room occupancy, including:

☐ Number of no-shows, cancellations, early departures, stayovers.

☐ Booking mix: how many individuals, groups, airline crews, travel agencies, and so on.

☐ Booking major events, such as conferences, seminars, trade fairs, and others.

System developers wrote a 100-rule system that evaluates occupancy factors. Sample rules include:

☐ If a weekend is expected or long holidays are possible, then occupancy increases by 15 percent.

☐ If occupancy is less than expected occupancy and the date being considered is between 7 to 15 days from now, then keep corporate categories open.

"Expert system technology can deliver the goods with a high confidence factor of 90 percent," says A. Ghosh, one of the system developers. "The other 10 percent is gut-and-gumption, which must remain with the experts." He adds that the hotel group plans to implement FOM-AID at several sites. In addition, they plan to use expert systems in other hotel operations areas, including room yield management, food and beverages cost management, and education and training.

a. Is hotel front office management a good application area for expert systems? Explain.

    b. Do you agree that using expert system technology for decision making still requires "10 percent gut-and-gumption"? Explain.

    Source: Adapted from "Indian Hotels Develop Booking Expert System," *AI Interactions,* January/February 1990, pp. 4–5.

8. Using an Electronic Spreadsheet for Decision Support
Use an electronic spreadsheet or integrated package available on the microcomputer or mainframe systems at your university.

    a. Create the ABC Company Financial Performance spreadsheet as shown in Figure 9–22. Start by entering 1,000 for 1989 revenue into a cell. Then enter formulas for other 1989 entries, assuming that expenses are 60 percent of revenue, profit is revenue minus expenses, taxes are 40 percent of profit, and profit after taxes equals profit minus taxes. Complete the 1990 and 1991 columns of the spreadsheet, assuming that 1990 revenue is 110 percent of 1989, and 1991 revenue is 120 percent of 1989. Assume that all other formula relationships for 1989 entries also apply to 1990 and 1991. Then complete the final two columns, and store and print this spreadsheet.

    b. Use the spreadsheet you created to perform **what-if analyses.** For example, change revenue, expense, or tax values or formulas in the ABC Company Financial Performance spreadsheet. (For example, increase revenue for 1989 by $1,000, increase expenses to 65 percent of revenue, and decrease taxes to 25 percent of profit.) What happens to the company's profit in each year? What might this mean to the company's management? Print the results of these changes. Write a short explanation of what happens and its implications for a manager.

    c. Create graphics displays of parts of the spreadsheet you developed. For example, develop a pie chart of profit after taxes or a bar graph of expenses. Make changes to entries in the spreadsheet and use graphics to help you perform what-if analyses.

    d. What features need to be added or improved to make this package easier to use and a more effective DSS generator? Explain.

Figure 9–22 A spreadsheet example.

ABC Company: Financial Performance				
	1989	1990	1991	Total	Average
Revenue	1000	1100	1200	3300	1100
Expenses	600	660	720	1980	660
Profit	400	440	480	1320	440
Taxes	160	176	192	528	176
Profit after taxes	240	264	288	792	264

1. Anthony, Robert. *Planning and Control Systems: A Framework for Analysis.* Cambridge: Harvard University Graduate School of Business Administration, 1965.

2. Barsanti, Joanne. "Expert Systems: Critical Success Factors for Their Implementation." *Information Executive*, Winter 1990.

3. Bostrum, Robert, and Robert Anson. "CWSS—A New Member of Your Management Team." *Information Executive*, Fall 1988.

4. Dalton, M. C. "Coming of Age—Neural Networks." *Information Executive*, Winter 1989.

5. Dennis, Alan; Joey George; Len Jessup; Jay Nunamaker; and Douglas Vogel. "Information Technology to Support Electronic Meetings." *MIS Quarterly*, December 1988.

6. Frenkel, Karen. "The War for the Executive Desktop." *Personal Computing*, April 27, 1990.

7. Gorry, G. Anthony, and Michael Scott Morton. "A Framework for Management Information Systems." *Sloan Management Review*, Fall 1971.

8. Harmon, Paul; Rex Maus; and William Morrissey. *Expert Systems Tools and Applications.* New York: John Wiley & Sons, 1988.

9. Linden, Eugene. "Putting Knowledge to Work." *Time*, March 28, 1988.

10. Main, Jeremy. "At Last, Software CEOs Can Use." *Fortune*, March 13, 1989.

11. Meyer, Marc, and Kathleen Curley. "Expert Systems Success Models." *Datamation*, September, 1989.

12. Mintzberg, Henry. *The Nature of Managerial Work.* New York: Harper and Row, 1983.

13. Rockart, John, and David DeLong. *Executive Support Systems: The Emergence of Top Management Computer Use.* Homewood, Ill.: Dow Jones-Irwin, 1988.

14. Simon, Herbert A. *The New Science of Management Decision.* Rev. ed. Englewood Cliffs, N.J.: Prentice-Hall, 1977.

15. Sprague, Ralph, and Hugh Watson, ed. *Decision Support Systems: Putting Theory into Practice.* Englewood Cliffs, N.J.: Prentice-Hall, 1986.

16. The Editors. *Artificial Intelligence.* Alexandria, Va.: Time-Life Books, Inc., 1988.

17. Turban, Efraim. *Decision Support and Expert Systems: Management Support Systems.* 2nd ed. New York: Macmillan Publishing Company, 1990.

SELECTED REFERENCES

<table>
<tr><td>

C H A P T E R

10

</td><td>

BUSINESS FUNCTION INFORMATION SYSTEMS

</td></tr>
</table>

■ **Chapter Outline**

Section I: Information Systems in Marketing, Manufacturing, and Human Resource Management

  Introduction
  Marketing Information Systems

  Sales Management, Product Management, Advertising and Promotion, Sales Forecasting, Market Research, Marketing Management

  Manufacturing Information Systems

  Computer Integrated Manufacturing, Process Control, Machine Control, Robotics, Computer-Aided Engineering

  Human Resource Information Systems

  Staffing, Training and Development, Compensation Analysis

  Real World Case: Mrs. Fields, Part II

Section II: Information Systems in Accounting and Finance

  Accounting Information Systems

  Order Processing, Inventory Control, Accounts Receivable, Accounts Payable, Payroll, General Ledger

  Financial Information Systems

  Cash and Securities Management, Capital Budgeting, Financial Forecasting, Financial Planning

  Real World Case: Barney's Stores, Inc.

Summary.   Key Terms and Concepts.   Review Quiz.   Real World Problems.
Selected References.

The purpose of this chapter is to give you an understanding of the use of information systems to support the major functional areas in business.

Section I of this chapter discusses information systems in marketing, manufacturing, and human resource management, with a special emphasis on computer integrated manufacturing.

Section II describes the most widely used types of accounting information sytems, as well as information systems needed for the effective financial management of a firm.

After reading and studying this chapter, you should be able to give examples of how information systems support the business functions of accounting, finance, human resource management, marketing, and production and operations management.

Section I: Information Systems in Marketing, Manufacturing, and Human Resource Management

INTRODUCTION

There are as many ways to use information systems in business as there are business activities to be performed, business problems to be solved, and business opportunities to be pursued. As a business end user, you should have a general understanding of the major ways information systems are used to support each of the **functions of business.** The term **business function information systems** describes the use of a variety of types of information systems (transaction processing, information reporting, decision support systems, and so on) to support a business function such as accounting, finance, marketing, or human resource management. Thus, *applications* of information systems in the functional areas of business are typically called *marketing information systems, accounting information systems, human resource information systems,* and so on.

As a business end user, you should also have a *specific* understanding of how information systems affect a particular business function (marketing, for example) or a particular industry (banking, for example) that is directly related to your *career objectives.* For example, someone whose career objective is a marketing position in banking should have a basic understanding of how information systems are used in banking and how they support the marketing activities of banks and other firms.

Figure 10–1 illustrates how information systems can be grouped into business function categories. Information systems in this chapter will be analyzed according to the business function they support to give you an appreciation of how such systems support business operations and management. However, you should remember that information systems in the real world typically are integrated combinations of functional information systems that support more than one business function. There is a strong emphasis in many organizations to

Figure 10–1 Examples of business function information systems. Note how these IS applications support the major functional areas of business.

Production/Operations	Marketing	Finance	Accounting	Human Resource Management
Computer-aided engineering	Advertising and promotion	Capital budgeting	Accounts payable	Compensation analysis
Computer-aided manufacturing	Marketing management	Cash management	Auditing	Employee skills inventory
Inventory control	Market research	Credit management	Billing and accounts receivable	Labor analysis
Material requirements planning	Product management	Financial forecasting	Budgeting	Personnel record-keeping
Process control	Sales forecasting	Financial performance analysis	Cost accounting	Personnel requirements forecasting
Purchasing and receiving	Sales management	Financing requirements analysis	Fixed asset accounting	Training and development analysis
Robotics	Sales order processing	Portfolio management	General ledger	
			Payroll	
			Tax accounting	

develop such *composite* or **cross-functional information systems.** These organizations view cross-functional information systems as a strategic way to share information resources and improve the efficiency and effectiveness of a business, thus helping it attain its strategic objectives [6, 8].

The business function of **marketing** is concerned with the planning, promotion, and sale of existing products in existing markets, and the development of new products and new markets to better serve present and potential customers. Thus, marketing performs a vital function in the operation of a business enterprise. Business firms have increasingly turned to computers to help them perform vital marketing functions in the face of the rapid changes of today's environment. Computers have been a catalyst in the development of *marketing information systems*, which integrate the information flows required by many marketing activities.

MARKETING INFORMATION SYSTEMS

Figure 10–2 illustrates how marketing information systems provide information for planning, control, and transaction processing in the marketing function. Strategic, tactical, and operational information systems assist marketing managers in product planning, pricing decisions, advertising and sales promotion strategies and expenditures, forecasting market potential for new and present products, and determining channels of distribution. Control reporting systems support the efforts of marketing managers to control the efficiency and effectiveness of the selling and distribution of products and services. Analytical reports provide information on a firm's actual performance versus planned marketing objectives. Now let's briefly review several ways that information systems support the marketing function.

Sales Management

This system provides information to help sales managers plan and monitor the performance of the sales organization. In most firms, this system produces *sales analysis reports* (such as Figure 10–3A), which analyze sales by product, product line, customer, type of customer, salesperson, and sales territory. Such reports help marketing management determine the sales performance of products and salespeople.

Product Management

Product managers need information to plan and control the performances of specific products, product lines, and brands. Computers can help provide price, revenue, cost, and growth information for existing products and new product development. Providing information and analysis for pricing decisions is a major function of this system. Information is also needed on the manufacturing and distribution resources proposed products will require. Computer-based models may be used to evaluate the performance of current products and the prospects for success of proposed products.

Advertising and Promotion

Marketing managers need information to help them achieve sales objectives at the lowest possible costs for advertising and promotion. Computers use market research information and promotion models to help (1) select media and promotional methods, (2) allocate financial resources, and (3) control and evaluate results. For example, Figure 10–3B displays a spreadsheet developed to analyze the sales response of advertising placed in a variety of magazines.

Figure 10-2 Marketing information systems provide information for the planning and control of major components of the marketing function.

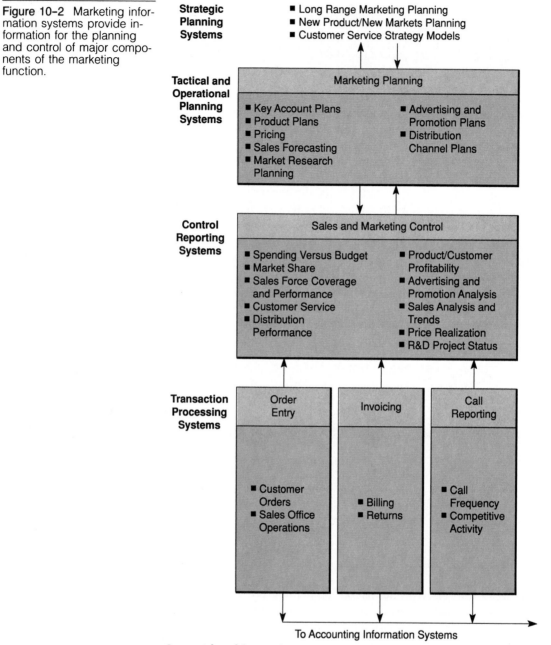

Source: Adapted from Andersen Consulting, *Foundations of Business Systems* (Hinsdale, Ill.: Dryden Press, 1989) p. 124.

Sales Forecasting

The basic functions of sales forecasting can be grouped into the two categories of short-range forecasting and long-range forecasting. Short-range forecasting deals with forecasts of sales for periods up to one year, whereas long-range forecasting is concerned with sales forecasts a year or more into the future. Marketing managers use market research data, historical sales data, promotion plans, and statistical forecasting models to generate such forecasts.

A. Sales Call Analysis

A47:								EDIT

PRESS ENTER TO CONTINUE:

	A	B	C	D	E	F	G	H
47								
48								
49	GRID SUMMARY STATISTICS FOR ALL SALESPEOPLE							
50				GRID	GRID	GRID	GRID	TOTAL
51	GRID			1	2	3	4	
52	COUNT			12	6	14	8	40
53	TOTAL SALES CALLS			222	49	48	34	353
54	TOTAL SALES			297357	135212	31491	20231	484291
55	AVERAGE SALES CALLS			18.5	8.166666	3,428571	4.25	8.825
56	AVERAGE SALES			24779.75	22535.33	2249.357	2528.875	12107.27
57	TOTAL REC. CALLS			144	60	84	32	320
58								
59								
60	STATISTICS AS A PERCENT OF ALL GRIDS							
61								
62				GRID 1	GRID 2	GRID 3	GRID 4	
63	ACCOUNTS			30.00	15.00	35.00	20.00	
64	CALLS			62.89	13.88	13.60	9.63	
65	TOTAL SALES			61.40	27.92	6.50	4.18	
66								

		CMD		CALC			SCROLL

B. Advertising Impact Analysis

M1: (W1) ':									MENU

1 2 3 MAIN

View Efficiency Computation: Page 1

	N	O	P	Q	R	S	T	U	V	W	X	Y	Z
1													
2			Exposures		Purchased		Formula:		$(E,j)*(X,jt)*(K,sjt)$				
3													
4		Media		E,j		Maximum		Average		K,sjt		Exposures	
5		Option		Value of		Sales		Sales/		Media		Purchased	
6		(Vehicle)		Exposures		Response		Capita		Efficiency			
7													
8	LIFE		0.5		$75,000		$5.00		3,780		0		
9	TIME		0.6		$210,000		$6.00		13,230		15,876		
10	NEWSWEEK		0.5		$210,000		$7.00		6,480		6,480		
11	TV GUIDE		0.6		$90,000		$9.00		5,040		3,024		
12	BUSINESS WK		0.5		$40,000		$2.00		4,500		0		
13	AZ HIGHWAYS		0.4		$200,000		$8.00		900		0		
14	SCHOOL PAPER		0.2		$32,000		$4.00		72		0		
15	DAILY HERALD		0.3		$59,500		$7.00		153		0		
16	SPORTS ILL.		0.5		$28,500		$3.00		342		0		
17	FIELD&STREAM		0.4		$27,000		$3.00		243		0		
18													
19	Totals				$972,000		$5.72		34,740		25,380		
20													

	CMD	

Figure 10-3 Examples of decision support displays and reports produced by using an electronic spreadsheet for (A) sales call analysis and (B) advertising impact analysis.

Source: Scott Smith and William Swinyard, *Marketing Models with Lotus 1-2-3* (Homewood, Ill.: Richard D. Irwin, 1988), pp. 141, 206.

The market research information system provides *marketing intelligence* to help managers make more effective marketing decisions. It also provides marketing managers with information to help them plan and control the market research projects of the firm. Computers and statistical analysis software help the market research activity collect, analyze, and maintain information on a wide variety of market variables that are subject to continual change. This includes information on customers, prospects, consumers, and competitors.

Market Research

Market, economic, and demographic trends are also analyzed. Data can be purchased in computer-readable form from external sources, or computers can help gather data through *telemarketing* and *computer-aided telephone interviewing* techniques.

Marketing Management

Marketing managers use computer-based information systems to develop short- and long-range plans outlining product sales, profit, and growth objectives. They also provide feedback concerning performance-versus-plan for each area of marketing. Marketing models in decision support systems are also used to investigate the effects of alternative marketing plans.

MANUFACTURING INFORMATION SYSTEMS

Manufacturing information systems support the **production/operations** function, which includes all activities concerned with the planning and control of the processes that produce goods or services. Thus, the production/operations function is concerned with the management of the *operational systems* of all business firms. Planning and control information systems are used for operations management and transaction processing, as illustrated in Figure 10–4. Such systems are needed by *all* firms that must plan, monitor, and control inventories, purchases, and the flow of goods and services. Therefore, firms such as transportation companies, wholesalers, retailers, and financial institutions must use production/operations information systems to plan and control their operations. In this section, we will concentrate on computer-based manufacturing applications to illustrate information systems that support the production/operations function.

Computer Integrated Manufacturing

Computer-based manufacturing information systems use several major techniques to support **computer integrated manufacturing** (CIM). Figure 10–5 illustrates that CIM is an overall concept that stresses that the goals of computer use in factory automation must be to:

- **Simplify** production processes, product designs, and factory organization as a vital foundation to automation and integration.
- **Automate** production processes and the business functions that support them with computers and robots.
- **Integrate** all production and support processes using computers and telecommunications networks [1].

Thus, computers are simplifying, automating, and integrating many of the activities needed to produce products of all kinds. For example, engineers use *computer-aided engineering* (CAE) methods, including *computer-aided design* (CAD), to design better products, and they use *computer-aided processing planning* (CAPP) to design better production processes. Computers are also used to help plan the types of material needed in the production process, which is called *material requirements planning* (MRP), and to integrate MRP with production scheduling and shop floor control, which is known as *manufacturing resource planning* (MRPII). *Computer-aided manufacturing* (CAM) is used to help manufacture products. This can be accomplished by monitoring and controlling the production process in a factory *(shop floor control)* or by directly controlling a physical process *(process control)*, a machine tool *(machine control)*, or a machine with some humanlike capabilities *(robots)*.

Figure 10–4 Production/operations management information systems for a manufacturing company. Note the levels of planning, control, and transaction processing information systems.

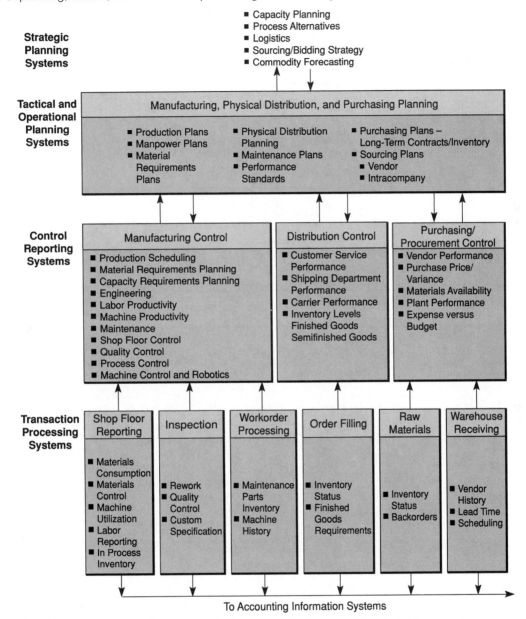

Source: Adapted from Andersen Consulting, *Foundations of Business Systems* (Hinsdale, Ill.: Dryden Press, 1989), p. 124–125.

Figure 10–6 illustrates the three major dimensions of computer integrated manufacturing. CIM focuses its simplification, automation, and integration efforts on:

☐ The three basic manufacturing functions to be performed: engineering, manufacturing administration, and factory operations.

☐ The workplace environment, from the entire enterprise, factory facility, and shop floor to small work cells, individual workstations, and equipment.

Figure 10-5 The three goals of computer integrated manufacturing.

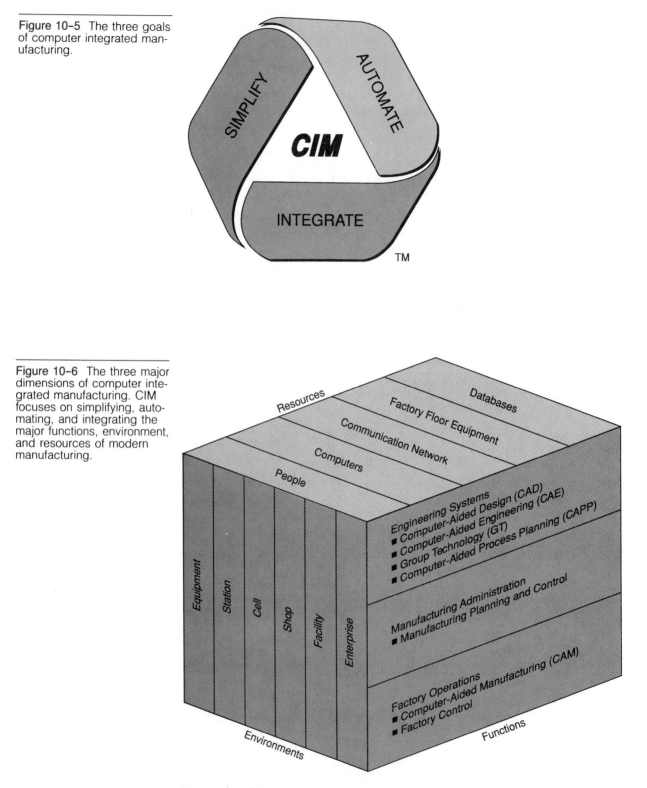

Figure 10-6 The three major dimensions of computer integrated manufacturing. CIM focuses on simplifying, automating, and integrating the major functions, environment, and resources of modern manufacturing.

Source: Adapted from Arthur Andersen & Co., *Trends in Information Technology*, 3rd. ed., 1987, p. 72.

☐ The manufacturing resources available, which are people, computers, telecommunications networks, factory floor equipment, and databases of manufacturing information [1].

Some of the benefits of computer integrated manufacturing systems are:

☐ Increased efficiency through work simplifications and automation, better production schedule planning, and better balancing of production work load to production capacity.

☐ Improved utilization of production facilities, higher productivity, and better quality control resulting from continuous monitoring, feedback, and control of factory operations, equipment, and robots.

☐ Reduced investment in inventories and facilities through work simplification, just-in-time inventory policies, and better planning and control of production and finished goods requirements.

☐ Improved customer service by drastically reducing out-of-stock situations and producing high-quality products that better meet customer requirements.

Process control is the use of computers to control an ongoing physical process. Process control computers are used to control physical processes in petroleum refineries, cement plants, steel mills, chemical plants, food product manufacturing plants, pulp and paper mills, electric power plants, and so on. Many process control computers are special-purpose minicomputer systems. A process control computer system requires the use of special sensing devices that measure physical phenomena such as temperature or pressure changes. These continuous physical measurements are converted to digital form by analog-to-digital converters and relayed to computers for processing. Process control programs use mathematical models to analyze the data generated by the ongoing process and compare them to standards or forecasts of required results. Output of a process control system can take three forms.

Process Control

☐ Periodic and on-demand reports analyzing the performance of the production process. Personal computers have become a popular method of analyzing and reporting process control data.

☐ Messages and displays about the status of the process. A human operator can then take appropriate measures to control the process.

☐ Direct control of the process by the use of control devices that adjust thermostats, valves, switches, and so on.

Machine control is the use of a computer to control the actions of a machine. This is also popularly called *numerical control*. The control of machine tools in factories is a typical numerical control application, though it also refers to the control of welding machines, weaving machines, and other industrial machinery.

Machine Control

Numerical control computer programs for machine tools convert geometric data from engineering drawings and machining instructions from process planning into a numerical code of commands that controls the actions of a machine tool. Machine control may involve the use of special-purpose microcomputers called *programmable logic controllers* (PLCs). These devices operate one or

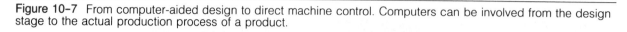

Figure 10–7 From computer-aided design to direct machine control. Computers can be involved from the design stage to the actual production process of a product.

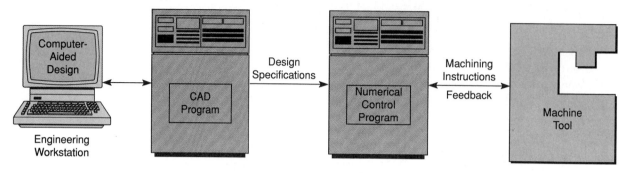

more machines according to the directions of a numerical control program. Specially equipped personal computers that can withstand a factory environment are used to develop and install numerical control programs in PLCs. They are also used to analyze production data furnished by the PLCs. This analysis helps engineers fine-tune machine performance. Figure 10–7 shows how machine control can be integrated with computer-aided design.

Robotics

An important development in machine control and computer-aided manufacturing is the creation of *smart machines* and *robots*. These devices directly control their own activities with the aid of microcomputers. **Robotics** is the technology of building and using machines (robots) with *computer intelligence* and computer-controlled *humanlike physical capabilities* (dexterity, movement, vision, and so on). As we mentioned in Chapter 9, robotics has become a major thrust of research and development efforts in the field of artificial intelligence. See Figure 10–8.

Robots are used as "steel-collar" workers to increase productivity and cut costs. For example, one robot regularly assembles compressor valves with 12 parts at the rate of 320 units per hour, which is 10 times the rate of human workers. Robots are also particularly valuable for hazardous areas or work activities. Robots follow programs loaded into separate or on-board special-purpose microcomputers. Input is received from visual and/or tactile sensors, processed by the microcomputer, and translated into movements of the robot. This typically involves moving its arms and hands to pick up and load items or perform some other work assignment such as painting, drilling, or welding. Robotics developments are expected to make robots more intelligent, flexible, and mobile by improving their computing, visual, tactile, and navigational capabilities [10].

Computer-Aided Engineering

Manufacturing engineers use **computer-aided engineering** to simulate, analyze, and evaluate the models of product designs they have developed using **computer-aided design** methods. Powerful *engineering workstations* with enhanced graphics and computational capabilities are used to analyze and design products and manufacturing facilities. Products are designed according to specifications determined in cooperation with the design efforts of marketing research and product development specialists. One of the final outputs of this design process is the *bill of materials* (specification of all required materials) used by the MRP application. The engineering subsystem is frequently respon-

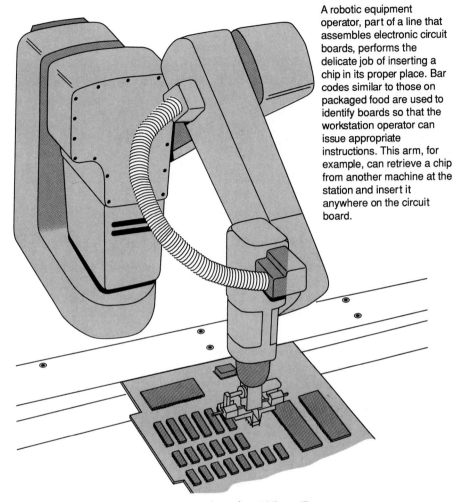

A robotic equipment operator, part of a line that assembles electronic circuit boards, performs the delicate job of inserting a chip in its proper place. Bar codes similar to those on packaged food are used to identify boards so that the workstation operator can issue appropriate instructions. This arm, for example, can retrieve a chip from another machine at the station and insert it anywhere on the circuit board.

Figure 10–8 This robot assembles electronic circuit boards.

Source: Robotics (Alexandria, Va.: Time-Life Books, 1986), p. 45.

sible for determining standards for product quality (i.e., *quality assurance*). It also is responsible for the design of the production processes needed to manufacture the products it designs. This function depends heavily on the use of computers to perform the necessary analysis and design, and it is known as *computer-aided process planning*.

Computer-aided design packages and engineering workstations are the software and hardware resources used to give engineers their engineering workstations. Engineers use these high-powered workstations for the design and testing of products, facilities, and processes. Input is by light pen, joystick, or keyboard, with the CAD package refining an engineer's initial drawings. Output is in two- or three-dimensional graphics that can be rotated to display all sides of the object being designed. The engineer can zoom in for close-up views of a specific part and even make parts of the product appear to move as they would in normal operation. The design can then be converted into a finished mathematical model of the product. This is used as the basis for production specifications and machine tool programs.

Figure 10–9 Human resource information systems support the effective and efficient use of the human resources of an organization.

	Staffing	Training/Development	Performance Review and Appraisal	Compensation Administration
Strategic information systems	Manpower planning Labor force tracking	Succession planning	Performance appraisal planning	Contract costing Salary forecasting Benefits tracking
Tactical information systems	Budget analysis Turnover analysis Turnover cost Absenteeism/performance	Training effectiveness Career matching	Performance/training correlation	Compensation effectiveness Benefit preference models
Operational information systems	Recruiting Structured interview/assessment Workforce planning Scheduling Selection models	Skill assessment	Computer-based evaluation programs	Compensation equality

Source: Adapted from David Meinert and Donald Davis, "Human Resource Decision Support Systems (HRDSS): Integrating Decision Support and Human Resource Information Systems," *Information Resources Management Journal*, Winter 1989, p. 45.

HUMAN RESOURCE INFORMATION SYSTEMS

The **human resource management** (or *personnel*) function involves the recruitment, placement, evaluation, compensation, and development of the employees of an organization. Originally, businesses used computer-based information sytems to (1) produce paychecks and payroll reports, (2) maintain personnel records, and (3) analyze the use of personnel in business operations. Many firms have gone beyond these traditional functions and have developed **human resource information systems** (HRIS), which also support (1) recruitment, selection, and hiring; (2) job placement; (3) performance appraisals; (4) employee benefits analysis; (5) training and development; and (6) health, safety, and security.

Such information systems support the concept of *human resource management*. This business function emphasizes (1) *planning* to meet the personnel needs of the business, (2) *development* of employees to their full potential, and (3) *control* of all personnel policies and programs. The goal of human resource management is the effective and efficient use of the human resources of a company. Some of the major applications of information systems that support human resource management are summarized next and illustrated in Figure 10–9.

Staffing

These information systems record and track human resources within a company to maximize their use. For example, a *personnel record-keeping* system keeps track of additions, deletions, and other changes to the records in a personnel database. Hirings and terminations and changes in job assignments and compensation are examples of information that would be used to update the personnel database. Another example is an *employee skills inventory system,* which uses the employee skills data from a personnel database to locate employees within a company who have the skills required for specific assignments and projects. Figure 10–10 includes an example of a skills inventory profile report.

Figure 10–10   A skills inventory report. This report can be used to match employee skills with specific job needs.

		Confidential	SKILLS INVENTORY PROFILE	
Jameson James L.		626	05/9x	342971
				AC105
Management/Project Ldr				
Experience				
Manager	3.0	First Preference	96	AC105
Engineering/Scientific/Tech Fields				
Electrical-Electronics				
Engineer	10 +			BC001
Circuit Design-General	8.0			BC145
Circuit Design-General		First Specialty	91	BC145
Circuit Design-Solid State	5.5			BC150
Integrated Circuits	3.5			BC280
Components Experience-BB				
Core Circuits		Design	08	CL090
DDTL		Quality Engr	28	CL160
Instruments Experience				CO140
Electrometers	4.0			
		Research or Dev Engr	21	TB100
		Research or Dev Engr	21	TD060
		Research or Dev Engr	21	TD070
		Product Test Engr	26	TD220
		Research or Dev Engr	21	TG140
		Research of Dev Engr	21	TG160
Foreign Language Proficiency				
German		Interpret	87	VE260
Russian		Summarize in English	88	VE510

Courtesy of IBM Corporation.

A final example is doing *personnel requirements forecasting* to assure a business an adequate supply of high-quality human resources. This application provides information required for forecasts of personnel requirements in each major employment category for various company departments or for new projects and other ventures being planned by management. Such long-range planning may use a computer-based simulation model to evaluate alternative plans for recruitment, reassignment, or retraining programs.

Training and Development

Information systems help human resource managers plan and control employee recruitment, training, and development programs by analyzing the success history of present programs. They also analyze the career development status of each employee to determine whether development methods such as training programs and periodic performance appraisals should be recommended. Computer-based training programs and appraisals of employee job performance are available to help support this area of human resource management.

Compensation Analysis

Information systems can help analyze the range and distribution of employee compensation (wages, salaries, incentive payments, and fringe benefits) within a company and make comparisons with compensation paid by similar firms or with various economic indicators. This information is useful for planning changes in compensation, especially if negotiations with labor unions are involved. It helps keep the compensation of a company competitive and equitable, while controlling compensation costs.

REAL WORLD CASE

Mrs. Fields, Part II

As her retail cookie business grew into hundreds of U.S. stores, Debbi Fields decided to capture her experience in expert systems that every store could access at any time. Thus was born the Retail Operations Intelligence system (ROI). Developed using IBM Expert System Environment software, the company set out to provide its store managers with software that could deliver accurate analyses of business conditions, as well as address most business predicaments of personnel situations that might arise.

From the development of basic retail systems came a host of integrated software modules that today form the core of Mrs. Fields's ROI software: Sale Reporting & Analysis, Daily Sales Capture, Labor Scheduler, Daily Production Planner, Interviewing, Skill Testing, Time Collection, and Inventory. All of these components run on in-store PCs linked into IBM AS/400 minicomputers installed in Mrs. Fields's Park City, Utah, headquarters. The minis are used for nationwide data collection and communicate with the PCs using toll-free dial-up lines.

The modules are designed to work together, but each has its own specific area of retailing expertise. For instance, the Labor Scheduler takes full advantage of Mrs. Fields's headquarters executives who have had years of employee management experience in areas like employing minimum-wage personnel, the predominant counter help at most cookie stores. The LS module schedules employees based on knowledge of labor and work force–related conditions, including the labor laws of a particular state, employee work preferences, and store characteristics. Using knowledge-processing techniques, it draws up a work schedule, including breaks, to optimize hourly employees' time. A store manager can therefore minimize overtime and provide workers with a potentially more flexible schedule.

Because many retail employees tend to stay with any particular job for less than a year, interviewing prospective employees is an ongoing task at every store. The Interviewing module of ROI is designed to help store managers assess the potential of prospective store personnel. It also provides a way to make sure that each employee is asked the same set of questions, a process that helps separate potential malcontents from future employees of the month.

For the ultimate day-to-day retail operation, there is the Daily Production Planner, an expert system that serves as an intelligent and interactive appointment book, diary, and to-do list bundled into one. All store managers log into this application about 30 minutes before the stores open and enter specific information about the day. In the case of a potentially high-traffic day for cookie sales—say Valentine's Day—the system will check traffic through the store in past years on that date and will also factor in such things as weather conditions.

The Planner creates a full-day projection of the amount of dough that must be prepared. It continues this process on an hourly basis to chart actual store traffic and progress and may make decisions on cutting back production or even offering free samples to passing customers to increase sales. All of this is designed to place the emphasis on food retailing where it counts—maximizing profit potential but minimizing leftovers and loss. At the end of a day, a Mrs. Fields store manager can measure performance against projections and then use all of those data again next year to help boost sales.

Application Questions

☐ What business functions are supported by Mrs. Fields's ROI system? Explain.

☐ Is ROI an example of a cross-functional information system? Why or why not?

☐ What benefits and limitations do you see in the ROI system for store management?

Source: Adapted from Harvey Newquist III, "Experts at Retail," *Datamation,* April 1, 1990, pp. 54–56.

Section II: Information Systems in Accounting and Finance

ACCOUNTING INFORMATION SYSTEMS

Accounting information systems are the oldest and most widely used information systems in business. They record and report business transactions and other economic events. Accounting information systems are based on the double-entry bookkeeping concept, which is hundreds of years old, and on other more recent accounting concepts such as responsibility accounting and profitability accounting. Computer-based accounting systems record and report the flow of funds through an organization on a historical basis and produce important financial statements such as balance sheets and income statements. Such systems also produce forecasts of future conditions such as projected financial statements and financial budgets. A firm's financial performance is measured against such forecasts by other accounting reports.

Operational accounting systems emphasize legal and historical record-keeping and the production of accurate financial statements. Typically, these systems include transaction processing systems such as order processing, inventory control, accounts receivable, accounts payable, payroll, and general ledger systems. *Management accounting systems* focus on the planning and control of business operations. They emphasize cost accounting reports, the development of financial budgets and projected financial statements, and analytical reports comparing actual to forecasted performance.

Figure 10–11 illustrates the interrelationships of important accounting information systems commonly computerized by both large and small businesses. Many accounting software packages are available for these applications. Let's briefly review how several of these systems support the operations and management of a business firm.

Order Processing

Order processing or *sales order processing*, is an important transaction processing system which captures and processes customer orders and produces invoices for customers and data needed for sales analysis and inventory control. In many firms, it also keeps track of the status of customer orders until goods are delivered. Computer-based sales order processing systems provide a fast, accurate, and efficient method of recording and screening customer orders and sales transactions. They also provide inventory control systems with information on accepted orders so they can be filled as quickly as possible.

Inventory Control

Inventory control systems process data reflecting changes to items in inventory. Once data about customer orders is received from an order processing system, a computer-based inventory control system records changes to inventory levels and prepares appropriate shipping documents. Then it may notify managers about items that need reordering and provide them with a variety of inventory status reports. Computer-based inventory control systems thus help a business provide high-quality service to customers while minimizing investment in inventory and inventory carrying costs. Figure 10–12 illustrates the data flows in an inventory control system. The integration of this system with other accounting information systems is quite evident in the flow of transaction documents and other forms of data.

Figure 10–11   Important accounting information systems for transaction processing and financial reporting. Note how they are related to each other in terms of input and output flows.

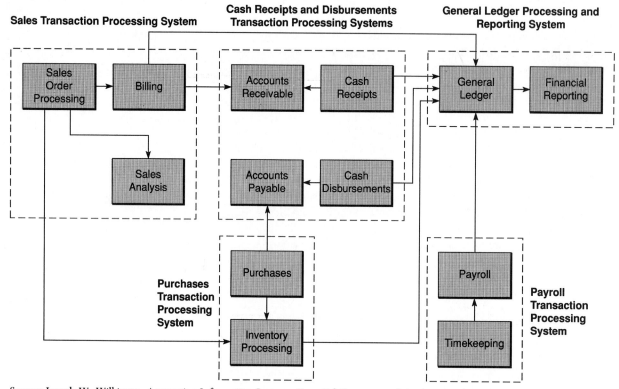

Source: Joseph W. Wilkinson, *Accounting Information Systems: Essential Concepts and Applications* (New York: John Wiley & Sons, 1989), p. 194.

Accounts Receivable

Accounts receivable systems keep records of amounts owed by customers from data generated by customer purchases and payments. They produce monthly customer statements and credit management reports, as were illustrated in Chapter 8. Computer-based accounts receivable systems stimulate prompt customer payments by preparing accurate and timely invoices and monthly statements to credit customers. They provide managers with reports to help them control the amount of credit extended and the collection of money owed. This activity helps to maximize profitable credit sales while minimizing losses from bad debts.

Accounts Payable

Accounts payable systems keep track of data concerning purchases from and payments to suppliers. They prepare checks in payment of outstanding invoices and produce cash management reports. Computer-based accounts payable systems help assure prompt and accurate payment of suppliers to maintain good relationships, ensure a good credit standing, and secure any discounts offered for prompt payment. They provide tight financial control over all cash disbursements of the business. They also provide management with informa-

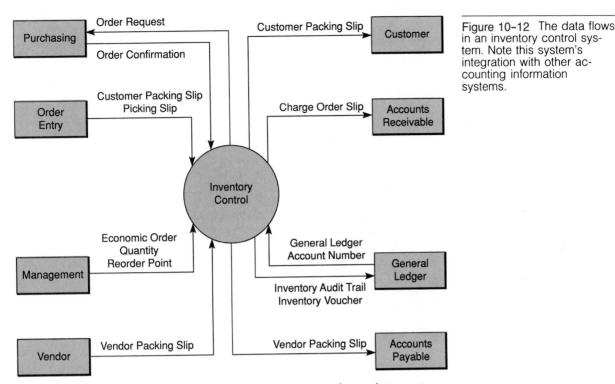

Figure 10–12 The data flows in an inventory control system. Note this system's integration with other accounting information systems.

Source: Adapted from Penney A. Kendall, *Introduction to Systems Analysis and Design: A Structured Approach* (Boston: Allyn & Bacon, 1987), p. 49.

tion needed for the analysis of payments, expenses, purchases, employee expense accounts, and cash requirements.

Payroll

Payroll systems receive and maintain data from employee time cards and other work records. They produce paychecks and other documents such as earning statements, payroll reports, and labor analysis reports. Other reports are also prepared for management and government agencies. Computer-based payroll systems help businesses make prompt and accurate payments to their employees, as well as produce reports to management, employees, and government agencies concerning earnings, taxes, and other deductions. They may also provide management with reports analyzing labor costs and productivity.

General Ledger

General ledger systems consolidate data received from accounts receivable, accounts payable, payroll, and other accounting information systems. At the end of each accounting period, they produce the general ledger trial balance, the income statement and balance sheet of the firm, and various income and expense reports for management. Computer-based general ledger systems help businesses accomplish these accounting tasks in an accurate and timely manner. They typically provide better financial controls and management reports and involve fewer personnel and lower costs than manual accounting methods.

Figure 10–13 An example of the multiwindow display of an integrated accounting package. Note the important business information it provides.

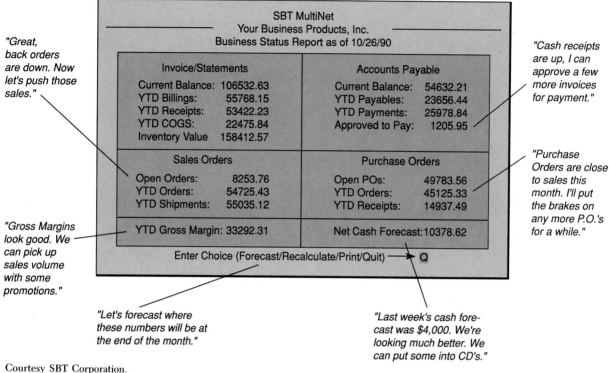

"Great, back orders are down. Now let's push those sales."

"Cash receipts are up, I can approve a few more invoices for payment."

"Purchase Orders are close to sales this month. I'll put the brakes on any more P.O.'s for a while."

"Gross Margins look good. We can pick up sales volume with some promotions."

"Let's forecast where these numbers will be at the end of the month."

"Last week's cash forecast was $4,000. We're looking much better. We can put some into CD's."

Courtesy SBT Corporation.

Figure 10–13 illustrates some of the important types of business information provided by an integrated accounting package.

FINANCIAL INFORMATION SYSTEMS

Computer-based **financial information systems** support financial managers in decisions concerning (1) the financing of a business and (2) the allocation and control of financial resources within a business. Major financial information system categories include cash and securities management, capital budgeting, financial forecasting, and financial planning. Accounting information systems are frequently included as a vital category of financial information systems. Figure 10–14 illustrates that the financial manager of a business relies on a variety of financial planning, reporting, and transaction processing information systems to make financing, investment, and accounting decisions. Let's take a brief look at the functions of these computer-based financial systems.

Cash and Securities Management

Information systems collect information on all cash receipts and disbursements within a company on a realtime or periodic basis. Such information allows businesses to deposit or invest excess funds more quickly and thus to increase the income generated by deposited or invested funds. These systems also produce daily, weekly, or monthly forecasts of cash receipts or disbursements (cash flow forecasts), which are used to spot future cash deficits or surpluses.

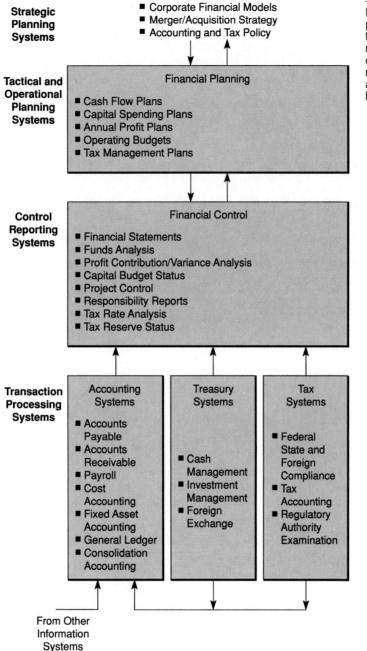

Source: Adapted from Andersen Consulting, *Foundations of Business Systems* (Hinsdale, Ill.: Dryden Press, 1989), p. 25.

Mathematical models are frequently used to determine optimal cash collection programs and to determine alternative financing or investment strategies for dealing with forecasted cash deficits or surpluses.

Many businesses invest their excess cash in short-term marketable securities (such as U.S. Treasury bills, commercial paper, or certificates of deposit) so that investment income may be earned until the funds are required. The portfolio of

Figure 10–15 Computer-based portfolio management. Note the information that can be displayed by a portfolio management package to provide investment support.

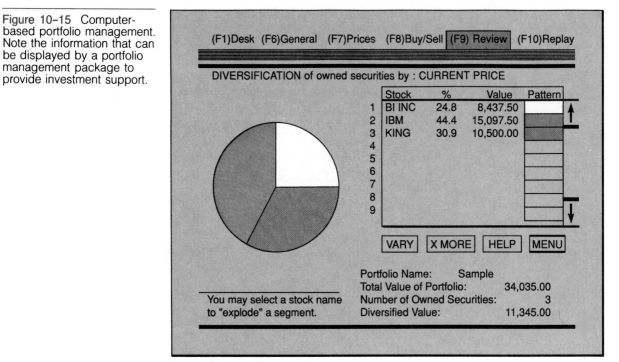

Source: Courtesy MECA, Inc.

such securities can be managed by *portfolio management* software. This helps a financial manager make buying, selling, or holding decisions for each type of security so that an optimum mix of securities is developed that minimizes risk and maximizes investment income. Figure 10–15 shows a display of a portfolio management package that can provide decision support for financial managers.

Capital Budgeting

The capital budgeting process involves evaluating the profitability and financial impact of proposed capital expenditures. Long-term expenditure proposals for plant and equipment can be analyzed using a variety of techniques incorporating present value analysis of expected cash flows and probability analysis of risk. This application makes heavy use of spreadsheet packages and other decision support system and expert system software packages that are designed for corporate financial planning.

Financial Forecasting

A business must make financial and other forecasts of economic trends. A variety of statistical forecasting packages provide analytical techniques that result in economic or financial forecasts of national and local economic conditions, wage levels, price levels, and interest rates. This forecasting may involve the use of data about the external business environment obtained from proprietary financial and demographic data banks provided by the information services mentioned in Chapter 6.

Figure 10-16   An example of a financial planning model. Note how the model allows managers to evaluate the effects of possible changes in many factors on the financial performance of a business.

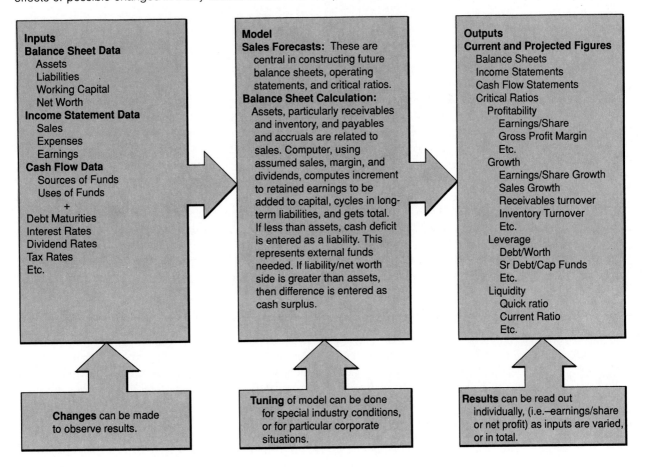

Inputs
Balance Sheet Data
    Assets
    Liabilities
    Working Capital
    Net Worth
Income Statement Data
    Sales
    Expenses
    Earnings
Cash Flow Data
    Sources of Funds
    Uses of Funds
    +
Debt Maturities
Interest Rates
Dividend Rates
Tax Rates
Etc.

Model
Sales Forecasts: These are
    central in constructing future
    balance sheets, operating
    statements, and critical ratios.
Balance Sheet Calculation:
    Assets, particularly receivables
    and inventory, and payables
    and accruals are related to
    sales. Computer, using
    assumed sales, margin, and
    dividends, computes increment
    to retained earnings to be
    added to capital, cycles in long-
    term liabilities, and gets total.
    If less than assets, cash deficit
    is entered as a liability. This
    represents external funds
    needed. If liability/net worth
    side is greater than assets,
    then difference is entered as
    cash surplus.

Outputs
Current and Projected Figures
    Balance Sheets
    Income Statements
    Cash Flow Statements
    Critical Ratios
        Profitability
            Earnings/Share
            Gross Profit Margin
            Etc.
        Growth
            Earnings/Share Growth
            Sales Growth
            Receivables turnover
            Inventory Turnover
            Etc.
        Leverage
            Debt/Worth
            Sr Debt/Cap Funds
            Etc.
        Liquidity
            Quick ratio
            Current Ratio
            Etc.

Changes can be made
to observe results.

Tuning of model can be done
for special industry conditions,
or for particular corporate
situations.

Results can be read out
individually, (i.e.—earnings/share
or net profit) as inputs are varied,
or in total.

Financial planning systems use **planning models** to evaluate the present and projected financial performance of a business or of one of its divisions or subsidiaries. They also help determine the financing needs of a business and analyze alternative methods of financing. Information concerning the economic situation, business operations, types of financing available, interest rates, and stock and bond prices are used to develop an optimal financing plan for the business. Electronic spreadsheet packages and DSS generators are frequently used to build and manipulate these models. Answers to what-if and goal seeking questions can be explored by seeing the effects of changes in data or model variables. Figure 10–16 illustrates the components of a financial planning model of a business.

Financial Planning

REAL WORLD CASE

Barney's Stores, Inc.

When cashiers at Barney's ring up sales, they are doing more than just adding purchases on cash registers: they are keying in data for market research and sales promotion. The New York–based retailer has moved beyond typical point-of-sale (POS) tasks such as price look ups and credit checks. The upscale clothing chain is using POS terminals to collect marketing data. "They're not just ringing up a sale, they're using the in-store system to help find out information about a customer," said Leo Rabinovitch, vice president of STS Systems, the Montreal-based systems-solution company that designed the Barney's system. "It's really a marketing tool."

Barney's system includes multiple cash register terminals, with a controller that runs the POS applications software and uses the OS/2 operating system. A controller is a PC used as a POS terminal configured with a hard disk, floppy disk, and modem. The controller supports POS terminal data, as well as pricing and other merchandise information; it logs and stores transaction information and also serves as a gateway to the outside world, communicating with the corporate mainframe to send out data and download pricing information and E-mail. The controller also dials out to the credit network and handles credit authorizations online.

Barney's system also includes applications software for inventory control, financial accounting, accounts receivable for store credit cards, and online credit-switching. It also handles electronic mail for messages between the stores and the main office. Thus, the system combines POS automation with computerizing the store's traditional back-office functions. The goal, said Rabinovitch, is to "automate as much of the business as possible."

STS's customer-profile system, for instance, is based on capturing customer purchases from POS terminals and using this data for promotion analysis and marketing analysis. The data can be used for everything from mailing catalogs to telephoning customers to notify them of upcoming sales. Entering the customer's name and address "automatically creates an account for that person, so the salespeople can track purchases," Rabinovitch said. On Barney's part, the business strategy is to monitor customers' buying habits and then boost sales by offering them something extra—personal service.

"Salespeople can call the customers and say, 'Why do you buy shirts from us and not suits?'" said Rabinovitch. "If you have new merchandise coming in, you can call them, or look up customers whose birthdays are coming up in the next couple of weeks, or all the customers who bought blue blazers, or all the customers who bought a certain line of clothing last year."

STS has several more applications for Barney's in the works, including some that measure employee productivity, calculate optimal sales-staff levels, and set employee goals, Rabinovitch said. "It's my belief that POS systems integrated with back-office systems produces a very powerful combination," he said. "Treating them as separate systems doesn't work as effectively in today's dynamic business environment."

Application Questions

☐ How does Barney's use its POS systems to support the marketing function?

☐ What other business functions are or will be supported? Explain.

☐ Why is it important to integrate POS systems with back-office systems in retail stores?

Source: Adapted from Paula Lovejoy, "Retailer Puts OS/2 to Work in Sophisticated POS System," *PC Week*, April 16, 1990, pp. 69, 74.

SUMMARY

☐ Marketing information systems provide information for the planning and control of the marketing function. Marketing planning information assists marketing managers in product planning, pricing decisions, planning advertising and sales promotion strategies and expenditures, forecasting the market potential for new and present products, and determining channels of distribution. Marketing control information supports the efforts of managers to control the efficiency and effectiveness of the selling and distribution of products and services. The major types of marketing information systems are sales management, product management, advertising and promotion, sales forecasting, market research, and marketing management systems.

☐ Computer-based manufacturing information systems use several major subsystems to achieve computer-aided manufacturing (CAM). Computers are automating many of the activities needed to produce products in manufacturing industries. For example, engineers use computer-aided design (CAD) to design products. Then they use material requirements planning (MRP) to help plan the types of material needed in the production process. Finally, computers may be used to directly manufacture products on the factory floor by controlling a physical process (process control), a machine tool (numerical control), or a machine with some humanlike capabilities (robotics).

☐ Human resource information systems support human resource management in organizations. They include information systems for staffing, training and development, compensation administration, and peformance appraisal.

☐ Accounting information systems record and report business transactions and events for business firms and other organizations. Operational accounting systems emphasize legal and historical record-keeping and the production of accurate financial statements. Management accounting systems focus on the planning and control of business operations. Common operational accounting information systems include order processing, inventory control, accounts receivable, accounts payable, payroll, and general ledger systems. Management accounting information systems include applications such as cost accounting and budgeting systems.

☐ Information systems in finance support financial managers in decisions regarding the financing of a business and the allocation of financial resources among competing needs within a business. Financial information systems include cash and securities management, capital budgeting, financial forecasting, and financial planning.

KEY TERMS AND CONCEPTS

These are the key terms and concepts of this chapter. The page number of their first explanation is in parentheses.

1. Accounting information systems (360)
2. Accounts payable (362)
3. Accounts receivable (362)
4. Business function information systems (348)
5. Computer-aided design (356)
6. Computer-aided engineering (356)
7. Computer-aided manufacturing (352)

8. Computer integrated manufacturing (352)

9. Cross-functional information systems (349)

10. Financial planning models (367)

11. Financial information systems (364)

12. General ledger (363)

13. Human resource information systems (358)

14. Inventory control (361)

15. Machine control (355)

16. Manufacturing information systems (352)

17. Marketing information systems (349)

18. Material requirements planning (352)

19. Order processing (361)

20. Payroll (363)

21. Process control (355)

22. Robotics (356)

REVIEW QUIZ

Match one of the **key terms and concepts** listed above with one of the examples or definitions listed below. Try to find the best fit for answers that seem to fit more than one term or concept. Defend your choices.

_____ 1. Support marketing, production, accounting, finance, and human resource management.

_____ 2. Information systems must integrate the activities and resources of business functions.

_____ 3. Include subsystems for sales management, product management, and promotion management.

_____ 4. Information systems which support manufacturing operations and management.

_____ 5. A conceptual framework whose goal is to simplify and integrate all aspects of factory automation.

_____ 6. Using computers in a variety of ways to help manufacture products.

_____ 7. Computers help the design process using advanced graphics, workstations, and software.

_____ 8. Computers help engineers evaluate products and processes.

_____ 9. Using computers to operate a petroleum refinery.

_____ 10. Using computers to operate machine tools.

_____ 11. Develops machines with computer intelligence and human-like physical capabilities that can take over some production activities from human workers.

_____ 12. Translates the production schedule into a detailed plan for all materials required.

_____ 13. Use computers to support staffing, training and development, and compensation administration.

_____ 14. Accomplish legal and historical record-keeping and gather information for the planning and control of a business.

_____ 15. Handles sales orders from computers.

_____ 16. Keeps track of items in stock.

_____ 17. Keeps track of amounts owed by customers.

_____ 18. Keeps track of purchases from suppliers.

_____ 19. Produces employee paychecks.

_____ 20. Produces the financial statements of a firm.

_____ 21. Includes systems for cash and securities management, capital budgeting, and financial forecasting.

_____ 22. Provides a decision support system capability for financial planning.

1. Database Marketing

REAL WORLD PROBLEMS

Mass marketing is dead, and niche marketing is not good enough. The theme for the 1990s is marketing to a "segment of one." "We call the 90s the age of the individual," says Robert J. Drummond, senior vice president at Epsilon Data Management, a database marketing firm in Burlington, Massachusetts. "You still have to have good products, but the message about your products is going to have to be tailored to the individual." That means creating a corporate database full of details about the buying habits of those individual customers and prospects, according to marketing experts, who call this trend-setting application "database marketing." On a more tangible level, database marketing requires a firm to extract key data from its own operational databases and then add a layer of demographic, financial, and lifestyle data obtained from outside information brokers. The marketing applications for such a database are numerous and varied. For example:

☐ Waldenbooks and B. Dalton Bookseller now copy airlines frequent-flier programs and offer "frequent-buyer" programs that recognize customers from purchases at POS scanners.

☐ Bank of America developed the Corporate Data Store, which has customer data extracted from bank card, checking, and savings accounts. It is mostly used to determine which customers are the best prospects for a new banking service or product and what characteristics the products should have.

☐ General Foods USA mails a four-color magazine to households with children age 4 to 14 that are listed in its database. The magazine includes special coupons, customized by household.

☐ Cabela's, Inc., a catalog company in Sidney, Nebraska, uses its database of customer buying habits to determine which customers should get its hunting and fishing catalogs, for example.

☐ Arby's Inc. in Atlanta, has a geographic information system loaded with demographic and lifestyle data, according to Hal Reid, vice president of franchise planning. It can be used not only to determine where to place a new fast-food outlet, but also to make marketing decisions about coupons, advertising, and store features.

a. What is database marketing? How does it differ from other types of marketing?

b. What are the benefits of database marketing? Do you think they outweigh the costs? Explain.

Source: Adapted from Mitch Betts, "Romancing the Segment of One," _Computerworld_, March 5, 1990, pp. 63–65.

2. Manufacturing at Ingersoll

The company builds the largest machines of their kind, but it's tiny bits of information that make Ingersoll Milling Machine Co. the envy of its industry. You can pick just about any computerized manufacturing technology that comes to mind, and it's probably used at Ingersoll. Flexible manufacturing systems are used to mill small machine parts in lots of one with virtually instant retooling. Numerical control systems almost eliminate human error in cutting blocks of steel into complex machine parts. And Ingersoll is well into a pilot project to fold expert systems into its operations. Helping it stay flexible is Ingersoll's unusually high level of manufacturing integration. Its diverse operations use a common database, and a computer schedules each day's activities on the company's 785,000 square feet of shop floor. A 42 MIPS Hitachi Data Systems mainframe drives the whole operation, with links between engineers on Ingersoll's 217 computer-aided design and manufacturing (CAD/CAM) terminals and such functions as purchasing, billing, order handling, payroll, and even the machines on the shop floor. For example:

☐ An engineer can create a drawing for a custom machine tool with IBM's Cadam software and simultaneously specify what parts will be needed to build it. The system consults the database, automatically cuts purchase orders for whatever parts the company needs to buy, and schedules shop time to build the parts that need to be custom-milled. The system ensures that the parts come together at the right time to minimize time spent sitting in inventory.

☐ An aggressive move into flexible manufacturing has put wire-guided vehicles into the so-called light machining area, where smaller parts are made. The vehicles shuffle pallets back and forth onto the milling machines and bide their time while the chunks of steel are shaved and drilled into finished machine parts.

☐ A "nesting" system determines the most efficient way to carve plates of steel into the pieces needed for the finished machinery. By automating this process, Ingersoll reduced manpower requirements on its torch cutting machine by 90 percent. More importantly, the system is linked into the bill-of-material, routing, payroll, cost, and master scheduling systems, minimizing the amount of time finished steel shapes are held in inventory.

a. What types of computer-aided manufacturing does Ingersoll use?

b. Does Ingersoll use computer integrated manufacturing? Explain.

Source: Adapted from Paul Gillin, "Steely Determination: Ingersoll Forges a Flexible Strategy," *Computerworld*, February 19, 1990, p. 81.

3. Human Resource Management at Pennwalt

Experience has made Robert Rubin, VP of IS at Pennwalt Corporation, a believer in the philosophy that the best way to make IS more cost-effective is to make the business process effective as well. His biggest success occurred when IS spurred personnel and payroll to combine their functions, cutting staff costs in half through attrition. The change began when IS was assigned the task of combining multiple departmental payroll systems. Rubin's staff convinced management to create a single corporate payroll system, and since personnel review was tied to payroll, record-keeping for that system was combined as well. "We had one personnel/payroll system and two clients—human resource management and treasury," Rubin says. "We then said that since they both operate off the same system, why not merge the two departments? So we did."

Although such measures are effective, they are not likely to be an easy sell. "Since hari-kari is not the favorite form of amusement in corporate America, you're not going to see middle managers recommending that their departments be merged with some other group," Rubin quips. "Only IS can take a higher level view and recommend such changes. Then it has to be done cooperatively and carefully."

a. Why were the payroll and human resource management functions combined at Pennwalt? Do you think this is a good idea? Explain.
b. What role should the IS function take in combining business functions and departments?

Source: Adapted from Michael Sullivan-Trainor, "Positive Alternatives to Slash and Burn Cost Cutting," *Computerworld,* February 26, 1990, p. 65.

4. Market Research by A. C. Nielsen

A. C. Nielsen Company installs UPC (universal product code) optical scanners, cousins of the holographic scanners used in supermarket check-out counters, in the same homes where its "people meters" track the television programs each family member watches. After a shopping trip, family members scan the UPC codes on products they've purchased so Nielsen can correlate what its surveyed families buy with the TV programming they watch. Analyzed along with records of total purchases (Nielsen and other companies can buy supermarket records collected from checkout scanners), this information can reveal key correlations between an advertiser's share of the "ad space" and its market share, even at a very local level, says Nielsen VP Jess Ray.

In its next technology upgrade, Nielsen will begin using a new kind of people meter that knows who's in the room. "It takes a digitized image of your face," Ray explains, "and one of everyone in your family. And it constantly monitors any human or breathing animal in the room. It compares these to the database of images it has stored on the system, so it can say exactly who was in the room watching the TV."

a. How does A. C. Nielsen use optical scanners for market research?
b. How will the "people meter" help their market research effort?
c. Would you like to be part of an A. C. Nielsen family? Explain.

Source: Adapted from Ned Snell, "How Hard Is Our Advertising Working," *Edge,* January/February 1990, p. 45.

5. Finance at Kidder, Peabody & Co.

In financial markets, money flows to those who find and exploit market inequities first. "The new alchemists of this process are quantitative analysts or 'quants.' They seek to capture information that may exist only for a moment," says Bernie Buda, IBM's manager of market development—trading. "They need a workstation that allows them to do this." The linking of world markets and round-the-clock trading lead to new requirements. "They need to link information on financial products and display that information in time for traders and quants to translate it into opportunity. We believe that our RISC System/6000 workstations will be the system for these customers."

However, the Wall Street investment house of Kidder, Peabody & Co. uses desktop workstations made by Sun Microsystems. Employees use the Sun machines to analyze complex securities that are sold and traded. The firm now uses 18 of these RISC workstations to analyze its fixed-income securities products, which are backed by mortgages. These products are complex, particularly in the case when you're trying to assess their risk-return properties, and their mortgages are among the most complex securities there are," said David Strauss, assistant V.P. He said the firm needs the powerful workstations' raw computer power to run simulated interest-rate models that are evaluated under hundreds of different scenarios.

a. Why do "quants" in finance need powerful workstations to be successful?

b. How does Kidder, Peabody demonstrate the need for high-powered workstations in finance?

Source: Adapted from Stephanie LaPolla, "Kidder, Peabody Profits from Move to Workstations," *PC Week*, April 2, 1990, pp. 526, 530; and "Systems for Masters of Many Trades," *IBM Update*, March/April 1990, p. 7.

6. Accounting at Reese Electric Supply

Bill Reese, president of Reese Electric Supply Inc., a lighting distributor in Johnstown, Pennsylvania, has a Novell LAN environment with eight workstations running the PC version of Great Plains Accounting Series. "We know there is better software out there for our industry niche, but there is a major difference between the cost involved with Great Plains, at $600 to $800 a module, and industry-specific software, which is $6,000 to $8,000," said Reese, whose company needs to use only a couple of accounting modules. The product's data-transfer capabilities are impressive, Reese said. After transferring database files into dBASE IV, data needed for billing customers is imported into WordPerfect, and general ledger data is imported into Lotus 1-2-3, he explained. According to Reese, the general ledger module offers options for financial reporting, including the capability to create departmental balance sheets.

a. Why did Reese Electric select Great Plains accounting software? What accounting modules do they use?

b. Why is the ability to transfer files into dBASE IV, WordPerfect, and Lotus 1-2-3 important?

Source: Adapted from "Accounting Packages Shine on Macs, PCs," *PC Week*, April 16, 1990, p. 116.

7. Marketing at Del Monte Corporation

At Del Monte, brand managers use the Metaphor database system to find meaningful patterns in reams of purchase data generated by supermarket scanners. When printed out on paper, the data can be measured in six-foot stacks. Computerization, says marketing systems manager Greta McKeon, reduces the job of digesting that mass to a manageable size. "We've gone technical because of the enormous amounts of data that are generated on our products," she says. "To try and find out manually where a problem or an opportunity exists [was] very difficult. We use the system to do reactive marketing," McKeon continues, explaining by way of example that "if you're losing volume, you go back and rework your pricing strategy."

Ed Palmer's job, however, is to figure out how to maximize profits at the supermarket level through adjustments of pricing and stock placement. In the course of that work, Palmer makes frequent forays to retailers around the country, carrying a portable data terminal equipped with an electronic wand. His purpose is to record data on shelf sizes, Del Monte items on the shelves, their dimensions, how much of which products are sold per store per week and the product's retail value. He then goes to a telephone and transmits the data into a PS/2 in his office in San Francisco. All the data will be in there when he returns to perform what-if analysis to reset the shelf based on dollar value, movement, and profits. This shelf management process represents a major step toward active management of profitability. Until as recently as 1987, "we'd kind of guess at profits," Palmer explains. Now, working in partnership with retailers, he says, food producers can stop guessing and start acting on hard information. "We have our expertise within our category, and retail has data on their activity. In partnership, we make profits together," Palmers says.

a.   Why do Del Monte brand managers use computer-based information systems for "reactive marketing"?
b.   How does computer-based shelf management help food producers like Del Monte?

Source: Adapted from Helen Pike, "From Grower to Grocer, Systems Are Taking Root," *Computerworld*, January 15, 1990, p. 67.

8.   Cross-Functional Systems at Bergen Brunswig
Bergen Brunswig Corp. may soon be reading its customers' minds. The health care distribution company's goal is to be so attuned to its customers' needs that it will anticipate orders before they're placed. "We want to be able to call buyers for a retail chain and say, 'According to our information, you're dangerously low on Tylenol. You went into your safety stock at 2 o'clock at store no. 16. Don't you think we ought to get you some?'" says Bernie Hale, vice president of distribution services at Bergen Brunswig. In such a scenario, Hale says, Bergen Brunswig would use electronic links to its customers to monitor store inventories in real-time and automatically replenish depleted supplies. The retail store manager never has to place an order.

This scenario may be futuristic, but for many manufacturers and distributors, reorganizing and integrating functions and information in the logistics environment makes good business sense. Bergen Brunswig's move toward value-added services and speedy delivery is a direct response to competitors such as McKesson Corp., which has its own automated delivery system. In fact, automation for many manufacturing and distribution companies has turned into a weapon in the battle to become the lowest cost supplier. With just-in-time delivery, manufacturers or distributors can receive a customer order in the afternoon, fill it in the evening, and deliver it the next day. The company may, in turn, require just-in-time delivery from its suppliers, further increasing inventory turn-over. For a just-in-time system to work, however, IS managers must integrate the logistics environment—shipping, receiving, warehousing, and delivery—into the manufacturing, accounting, and IS loop.

a. What strategic and cross-functional information systems can you identify in this example?

b. Why do Bergen Brunswig and other businesses need such systems?

Source: Adapted from Janet Fiderio, "Customer Closeness at Bergen Brunswig, McKesson," *Computerworld*, February 19, 1990, p. 69.

SELECTED REFERENCES

1. Arthur Anderson & Co. *Trends in Information Technology.* 3rd ed. Chicago: Author, 1987.

2. Bray, Olin. *Computer Integrated Manufacturing: The Data Management Strategy.* Bedford, Mass.: Digital Press, 1988.

3. Doll, William, and Mark Vonderembse. "Forging a Partnership to Achieve Competitive Advantage: The CIM Challenge." *MIS Quarterly,* June 1987.

4. Eliason, Alan. *Online Business Computer Applications.* 2nd ed. Chicago: Science Research Associates, 1987.

5. Greco, Alan, and Jack Hogue. "Developing Marketing Decision Support Systems in Consumer Goods Firms." *Journal of Consumer Marketing,* Winter 1990.

6. Madnick, Stuart, and Y. Richard Wang. "Evolution towards Strategic Applications of Databases through Composite Information Systems." *Journal of Management Information Systems,* Fall 1988.

7. Meinert, David, and Donald Davis. "Human Resource Decision Support Systems (HRDSS): Integrating Decision Support and Human Resource Information Systems." *Information Resources Management Journal,* Winter 1989.

8. Moad, Jeff. "Navigating Cross-Functional IS Waters." *Datamation,* March 1, 1989.

9. Ryan, Alan. "Marketing: Last Bastion of the Information Age." *Computerworld,* April 17, 1989.

10. *Robotics.* Chicago: Time-Life Books, 1986.

11. Smith, Scott, and William Swinyard. *Marketing Models with Lotus 1-2-3.* Homewood, Ill.: Richard D. Irwin, 1988.

12. Wilkinson, Joseph. *Accounting Information Systems: Essential Concepts and Applications.* New York: John Wiley & Sons, 1989.

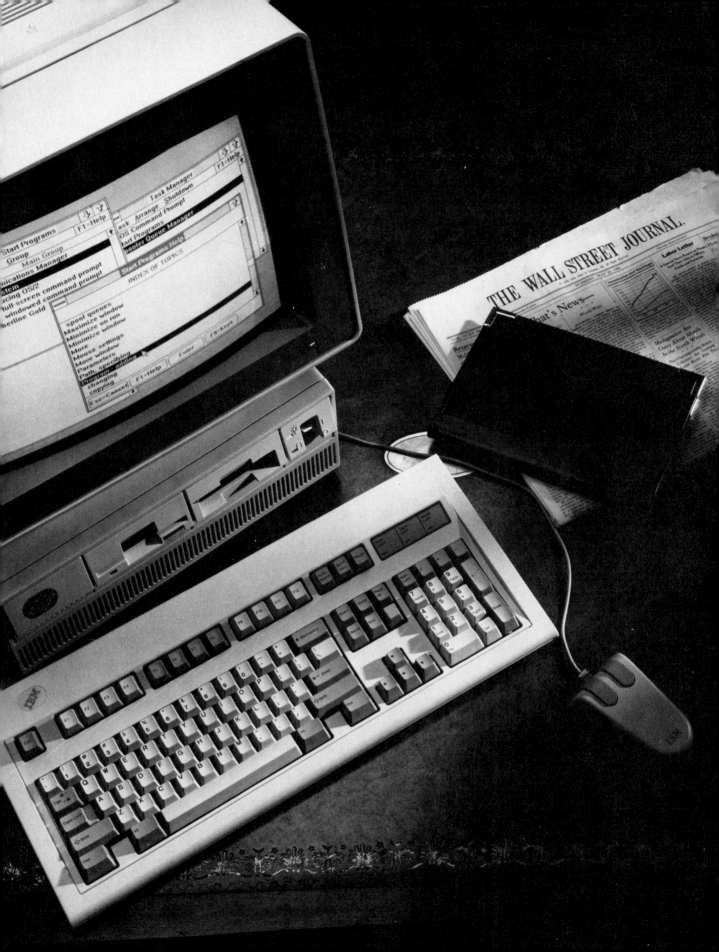

INFORMATION SYSTEMS DEVELOPMENT AND MANAGEMENT

How can information system solutions be developed to solve business problems or pursue business opportunities? What managerial challenges do information systems pose for the managers of modern organizations? The four chapters of this module are designed to emphasize how managers and end users can plan, develop, implement, and control the use of information system resources and services.

Chapter 11, Developing Information System Solutions, introduces the traditional and prototyping approaches to the development of information system solutions to business problems. It also demonstrates the use of systems development tools in a realistic case study situation.

Chapter 12, Planning and Implementing Information Systems, covers strategic, tactical, and operational information systems planning, as well as managerial issues in the implementation of information systems.

Chapter 13, Managing Information System Resources, emphasizes the impact of information technology on management and organizations, the importance of information resource management, and the managerial implications of providing information services.

Chapter 14, Controlling Information System Performance, discusses the controls needed for information system performance and security, as well as the legal and ethical implications of the control of computer crime and other societal impacts of information systems.

C H A P T E R

11

DEVELOPING INFORMATION SYSTEM SOLUTIONS

■ Chapter Outline

The purpose of this chapter is to give you an understanding of how end users can apply the methodology and tools of systems development to propose information system solutions to business problems.

Section I describes the activities involved and products produced in each of the stages of the information systems development cycle, including the prototyping approach to applications development.

Section II demonstrates the use of several tools of systems development in the context of a case study. It also explores the use of computer-aided development tools and ends with suggestions on how to get started in developing information system solutions to business problems.

After reading and studying this chapter, you should be able to:

1. Summarize the steps of the traditional information systems development life cycle.

2. Explain how computer-aided systems engineering and prototyping have affected the process of information systems development for end users and information systems specialists.

3. Use the information systems development cycle as a framework to help you propose information system solutions to simple business problems.

4. Use an information systems model as a framework to help you with the analysis and proposed design of an information system.

5. Use several systems development tools to help you create and communicate information system solutions to simple business problems.

Section I: Information Systems Development

Developing information system solutions to business problems is a major responsibility of the end users and managers of business firms, business units, departments, and other work groups. They are responsible for proposing or developing new or improved information sytems for their organizations. Managers must also frequently direct the development efforts of information systems specialists and other end users. This chapter will show you how information system solutions can be developed that meet the needs of end users, while Chapter 12 will cover planning and implementation issues.

THE SYSTEMS APPROACH

Suppose the chief executive of a firm where you are the sales manager asks you to find a better way to get information to the salespeople in your company. How would you start? What would you do? Would you just plunge ahead and hope you could come up with a reasonable solution? How would you know whether your solution was a good one for your company? Do you think there might be a systematic way to help you develop a good solution to your chief executive's request? There is. It's a problem-solving process called **the systems approach.**

The systems approach stresses a **systematic process** of problem solving. Problems and opportunities are viewed in a **systems context.** Studying a problem and formulating a solution become an organized system of interrelated activities, such as:

1. **Understand a Problem or Opportunity.**
   - ☐ Define a problem or opportunity in a systems context.
   - ☐ Gather data describing the problem or opportunity.
2. **Develop a Solution.**
   - ☐ Identify alternative solutions.
   - ☐ Evaluate each alternative solution.
   - ☐ Select the best solution.
3. **Implement a Solution.**
   - ☐ Implement the selected solution.
   - ☐ Evaluate the success of the implemented solution.

THE SYSTEMS DEVELOPMENT CYCLE

The systems approach can be applied to the solution of many types of problems. When this involves the development of information system solutions to business problems, it is called **information systems development** or **applications development.** Information systems are usually conceived, designed, and implemented using a systematic development process in which end users and specialists *design* information systems based on an *analysis* of the information requirements of an organization. Thus, a major part of this process is known as **systems analysis and design.** However, as Figure 11–1 shows, several other major activities are involved in a complete development cycle.

When the systems approach is applied to the development of information systems, a multistep process or cycle emerges. This is frequently called the *systems development cycle,* or *systems development life cycle* (SDLC). Figure 11–2 summarizes what goes on in each stage of the traditional **information**

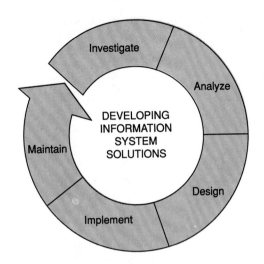

Figure 11-1 Developing information system solutions to business problems is typically a multistep process or cycle.

systems development cycle, which includes the steps of (1) *investigation,* (2) *analysis,* (3) *design,* (4) *implementation,* and (5) *maintenance.*

You should realize, however, that all of the activities involved are highly related and interdependent. Therefore, in actual practice, several developmental activities can be occurring at the same time. Also, different parts of a development project can be at different stages of the developmental cycle. For example, there may be a testing cycle, where a new system is tested and redesigned. Also typical is a maintenance cycle, where some developmental activities are performed again to improve an established system.

Finally, you should realize that developments such as *fourth-generation languages* (4GLs), *computer-aided systems engineering* (CASE), and *prototyping* are automating and changing some of the activities of information systems development. These developments are making applications development easier and enabling more end users to develop their own systems. We will discuss them shortly. Now, let's take a look at each step of this developmental process.

SYSTEMS INVESTIGATION

Do we have a business problem (or opportunity)? What is causing the problem? Would a new or improved information system help solve the problem? What would be a *feasible* information system solution to our problem? These are the questions that have to be answered in the systems investigation stage—the first step in the systems development process. This stage includes the screening, selection, and preliminary study of proposed information systems solutions to business problems.

Information Systems Planning

The investigation stage may involve the study of information systems development proposals generated by a formal **information systems planning** process, which we will discuss in Chapter 12. An IS planning process that is part of the regular *business planning* process of the organization is highly desirable. There are typically many opportunities to use information systems to support an organization's end users and its business operations, management decision making, and strategic objectives. However, in the real world, end users, departments, and the organization itself have only limited amounts of human and financial resources to allocate to the development of new information

Figure 11-2 The traditional information systems development cycle. Note that the five steps of the cycle fit into the three stages of the systems approach. Also note the products that result from each step in the cycle.

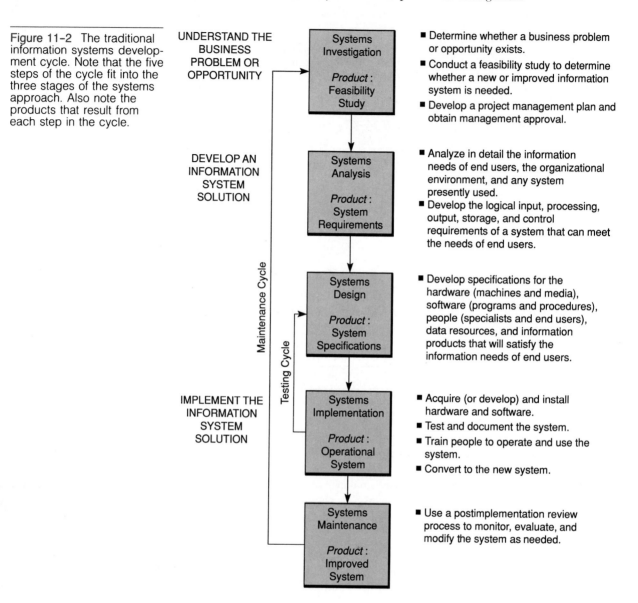

UNDERSTAND THE BUSINESS PROBLEM OR OPPORTUNITY

Systems Investigation

Product: Feasibility Study

- Determine whether a business problem or opportunity exists.
- Conduct a feasibility study to determine whether a new or improved information system is needed.
- Develop a project management plan and obtain management approval.

DEVELOP AN INFORMATION SYSTEM SOLUTION

Systems Analysis

Product: System Requirements

- Analyze in detail the information needs of end users, the organizational environment, and any system presently used.
- Develop the logical input, processing, output, storage, and control requirements of a system that can meet the needs of end users.

Systems Design

Product: System Specifications

- Develop specifications for the hardware (machines and media), software (programs and procedures), people (specialists and end users), data resources, and information products that will satisfy the information needs of end users.

IMPLEMENT THE INFORMATION SYSTEM SOLUTION

Systems Implementation

Product: Operational System

- Acquire (or develop) and install hardware and software.
- Test and document the system.
- Train people to operate and use the system.
- Convert to the new system.

Systems Maintenance

Product: Improved System

- Use a postimplementation review process to monitor, evaluate, and modify the system as needed.

Maintenance Cycle

Testing Cycle

systems, no matter how desirable they may be. Therefore, business and information systems planning helps to generate, screen, and select potential information systems for development.

Feasibility Studies

Because the process of developing a major information system can be a costly one, the systems investigation stage frequently includes a preliminary study called a **feasibility study**. A feasibility study is a preliminary study to investigate the information needs of prospective end users and the objectives, constraints, basic resource requirements, costs, benefits, and feasibility of a proposed project. Typically, the following methods of gathering information are used to collect data for a feasibility study.

☐ Interviews with employees, customers, and managers.

Organizational Feasibility	Economic Feasibility
■ How well the proposed system supports the strategic plan of the organization	■ Cost savings ■ Increased revenue ■ Decreased investment ■ Increased profits
Technical Feasibility	**Operational Feasibility**
■ Hardware and software capability, reliability, and availability	■ End user acceptance ■ Management support ■ Customer, supplier, and government requirements

Figure 11–3 Organizational, economic, technical, and operational feasibility factors. Note that there is more to feasibility than cost savings or the availability of hardware and software.

☐ Questionnaires to appropriate individuals in the organization.

☐ Personal observation of business operations and systems.

☐ Examination of documents, reports, procedures manuals, and other documentation.

☐ Inspecting accounting and management reports to collect operating statistics, cost data, and performance results.

☐ Development, manipulation, and observation of a model of the operations or systems affected by the problem or opportunity.

The findings of a feasibility study are usually formalized in a written report. It includes preliminary specifications and a developmental plan for the proposed system. This report is then submitted to the management of the firm. If management approves the recommendations of the feasibility study, the **systems analysis** stage can begin.

The Feasibility of a System

The goal of feasibility studies is to evaluate alternative systems and to propose the most feasible and desirable systems for development. The feasibility of a proposed system can be evaluated in terms of four major categories, as illustrated in Figure 11–3.

The focus of **organizational feasibility** is on how well a proposed information system supports the objectives of the organization and its strategic plan for information systems. Projects that do not directly contribute to meeting an organization's strategic objectives are typically not funded. **Economic feasibility** is concerned with whether expected cost savings, increased revenue, increased profits, reductions in required investment, and other types of benefits will exceed the costs of developing and operating a proposed system. If a project can't cover its development costs, it won't be approved, unless mandated by other considerations. **Technical feasibility** can be demonstrated if reliable hardware and software capable of meeting the needs of a proposed system can be acquired or developed by the business in the required time. Finally, **operational feasibility** is the willingness and ability of the management, employees, customers, suppliers, and others to operate, use, and support a proposed system.

SYSTEMS ANALYSIS

What is **systems analysis?** Whether you want to develop a new application quickly or are involved in a long-term project, you will need to perform several basic activities of systems analysis. Many of these activities are an extension of those used in conducting a feasibility study. Some of the same information-gathering methods are used, plus some new tools that we will discuss shortly. However, systems analysis is not a preliminary study. It is an in-depth study of end user information requirements that is needed before the design of a new information system can be completed.

Systems analysis traditionally involves a detailed study of:

☐ The information needs of the organization and its end users.

☐ The activities, resources, and products of any present information systems that will be affected.

☐ The information systems capabilities required to meet the information needs of users.

The final product of systems analysis is a set of **system requirements** for a proposed information system (these are also called the *functional specifications* or the *functional requirements*). For large development projects, this product takes the form of a *system requirements report,* which specifies the capabilities needed to meet the information needs of end users. Designing a system that meets these requirements becomes the goal of the **system design** stage.

Analysis of the Organizational Environment

An **organizational environment analysis** is an important first step in systems analysis. How can you improve an information system if you know very little about the *organizational environment* in which that system is located? You can't. That's why you have to know something about the organization, its management structure, its people, its business activities, the environmental systems it must deal with, and its current information systems. You must know this information in more detail for the specific end user work groups that will be affected by the new or improved information system being proposed. For example, you cannot design a new inventory control system for a chain of deparatment stores until you learn a lot about the company and the types of business activities that affect its inventory.

Analysis of the Present System

Before you design a new system, it is important to study any systems that will be improved or replaced. You need to analyze how such systems use hardware, software, and people resources to convert the data resources of the organization into information products for end users. You should analyze how these system resources are used to accomplish the information system activities of input, processing, output, storage, and control. Then, in the systems design stage, you can specify what these resources, products, and activities *should be* in the system you are designing.

System Requirements Analysis

This step of systems analysis is one of the most difficult. In it you must try first to determine your (or an end user's) specific information needs (this is sometimes called *needs analysis* or *user-requirements analysis*). Second, you must try to determine the information processing capabilities required for each system activity (input, processing, output, storage, control) to meet these

- **User interface requirements:** The input/output needs of end users that must be supported by the information system, including sources, formats, content, volume (average and peak) and frequency of each type of input and output.
- **Processing requirements:** Basic information-processing activities required to convert input into output. Calculations, decision rules, and other processing operations. Capacity, throughput, turnaround time, and response time needed for processing activities.
- **Storage requirements:** Organization, content, and size of databases, types and frequency of updating and inquiries, and the length and rationale for record retention or deletion.
- **Control requirements:** Accuracy, validity, safety, security, and adaptability requirements for system input, processing, output, and storage functions.

Figure 11–4 Examples of system requirements, which specify the information system capabilities required to meet the information needs of end users.

information needs (this is sometimes called *functional requirements analysis*). Finally, you should try to develop *logical* system requirements. These are end user information requirements that are not tied to the *physical* resources of hardware, software, and people that end users presently use or might use in the future. The difficulty of the requirements analysis step is one of the major reasons for the development of alternative methods of systems development. In the next section we will demonstrate several tools that help you develop and document **system requirements,** such as those shown in Figure 11–4.

Systems analysis describes *what* a system should do to meet the information needs of users. **Systems design** specifies *how* the system will accomplish this objective. Systems design consists of both *logical design* and *physical design* activities, which result in **system specifications** satisfying the system requirements developed in the systems analysis stage. End users and systems analysts can use a variety of tools and methods to do systems design, as we will demonstrate shortly.

SYSTEMS DESIGN

User Interface, Data, and Process Design

Another way to look at system design is illustrated in Figure 11–5. This concept focuses on three major products, or *deliverables*, that should result from the design stage. In this framework, systems design consists of three activities: user interface, data, and process design. This results in specifications for user interface methods and products, database structures, and processing and control procedures [1].

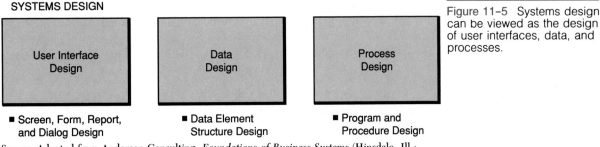

SYSTEMS DESIGN

| User Interface Design | Data Design | Process Design |

- Screen, Form, Report, and Dialog Design
- Data Element Structure Design
- Program and Procedure Design

Figure 11–5 Systems design can be viewed as the design of user interfaces, data, and processes.

Source: Adapted from Andersen Consulting, *Foundations of Business Systems* (Hinsdale, Ill.: Dryden Press, 1989), p. 101.

User Interface Design

The user interface design activity focuses on designing the interactions between end users and computer systems. It concentrates on input-output methods and the conversion of data and information between human-readable and machine-readable forms. Therefore, user interface design produces detailed specifications for information products such as display screens, interactive user/computer dialogues (including the sequence or flow of dialogue), audio responses, forms, documents, and reports.

Data Design

The data design activity focuses on the design of the logical structure of databases and files to be used by the proposed information system. Data design produces detailed descriptions of:

- ☐ The *entities* (people, places, things, events) about which the proposed information system needs to maintain information.
- ☐ The *relationships* these entities have to each other.
- ☐ The specific *data elements* (databases, files, records, etc.) that need to be maintained for each entity tracked by the information system.
- ☐ The *integrity rules* that govern how each data element is specified and used in the information system.

Process Design

The process design activity focuses on the design of the software resources, that is, the programs and procedures needed by the proposed information system. It concentrates on developing detailed specifications for the program modules that will have to be purchased as software packages or developed by custom programming. Thus, process design produces detailed program specifications and procedures needed to meet user interface and data design specifications, as well as the control and performance requirements of a proposed information system.

Logical System Design

Logical system design involves developing general specifications, or *models,* for how the basic information system activities of input, processing, output, storage, and control can transform data resources to meet end user information requirements. In the systems investigation stage, *logical design models* may have been developed in a feasibility study. These were rough or general ideas of the basic components, flows, and interrelationships of the proposed information system. For example, *data models* are typically developed to clarify end user data needs and eliminate duplication of data elements in a database design. In the systems design stage, these logical design models are refined and finalized.

Physical System Design

Physical system design involves the detailed design of user interface methods and products, database structures, and processing and control procedures. Hardware, software, and personnel specifications are developed for the proposed system. Systems analysts and end users use their knowledge of business

- **User interface specifications:** The content format and sequence of user interface products and methods such as display screens, interactive dialogues, audio responses, forms, documents, and reports.
- **Database specifications:** Content, structure, distribution, and access, response, maintenance, and retention capabilities.
- **Software specifications:** The required software package or programming specifications of the proposed system, including performance and control specifications.
- **Hardware and facilities specifications:** The physical and performance characteristics of the equipment and facilities required by the proposed system.
- **Personnel specifications:** Job descriptions of persons who will operate the system.
- **System documentation specifications:** Specifications for the documentation of system characteristics and operating procedures for end users and technical personnel provided by manuals and built-in software help features.

Figure 11–6 Examples of system specifications. Note how they specify the details of a proposed information system.

operations, information processing, and hardware and software to specify the **physical design** of an information system. Obviously, this must correspond to the input, processing, output, storage, and control specifications developed in the logical design step. The design must specify the types of hardware resources (machines and media), software resources (programs and procedures), and people resources (end users and information systems staff) that will be needed. It must specify how such resources will convert data resources (stored in files and databases they design) into information products (displays, responses, reports, and documents). These specifications are the final product of the systems design stage, and are called the **system specifications.** See Figure 11–6.

System Design Standards

A variety of system design standards exist for computer-based information systems. Conforming to such standards should thus be a major consideration of system designers. For example, IBM's Systems Application Architecture (SAA) is a leading set of design standards developed by the IBM Corporation [9]. Other systems design standards, or *application architectures*, include Application Integration Architecture (AIA), by Digital Equipment Corporation; New Wave, by Hewlett-Packard; Open Look, by AT&T; and OSF/Motif, by the Open Systems Foundation.

IBM's Systems Application Architecture is a good example of the types of design standards being promoted for computer-based information systems. It consists of three major sets of standards that promote commonality among application programs: (1) common user access, (2) common programming interfaces, and (3) common telecommunications support. The primary goal of application architectures such as SAA is to provide end users with application software with common user interfaces and functions which operate consistently on micro, mini, or mainframe computer systems. For example, Figure 11–7 illustrates design standards for workstation screen displays that conform to the common user access standards of SAA.

SYSTEMS IMPLEMENTATION AND MAINTENANCE

Once a proposed information system has been designed, it must be implemented. The **systems implementation** stage involves hardware and software acquisition, software development, testing of programs and procedures, development of documentation, and a variety of installation activities. It also involves

Figure 11-7   An example of a workstation screen display design standard.

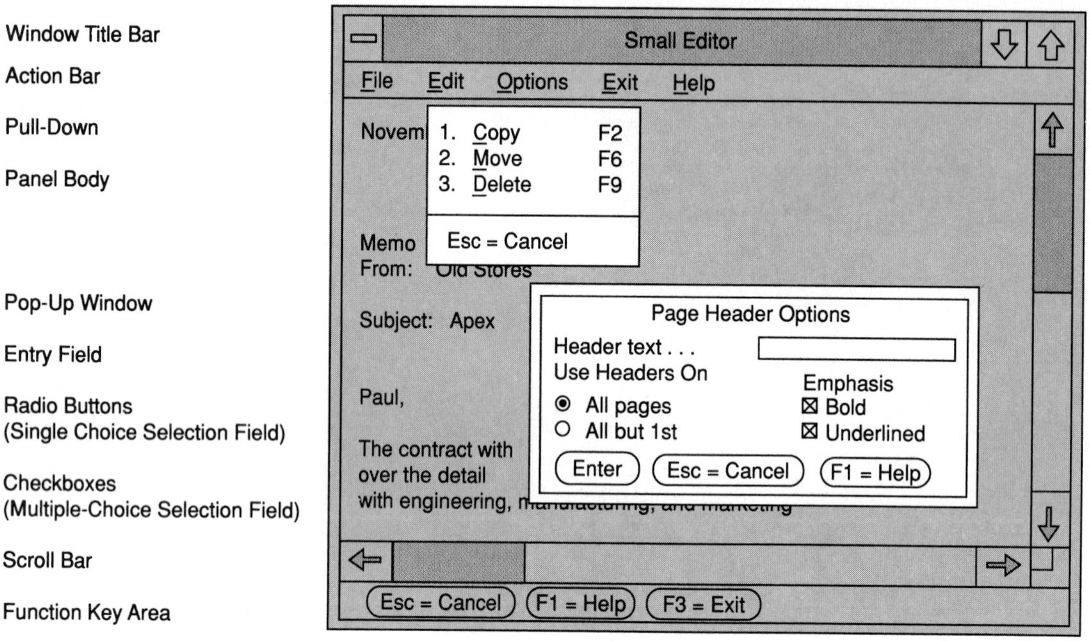

Window Title Bar

Action Bar

Pull-Down

Panel Body

Pop-Up Window

Entry Field

Radio Buttons
(Single Choice Selection Field)

Checkboxes
(Multiple-Choice Selection Field)

Scroll Bar

Function Key Area

Source: Courtesy IBM Corporation.

the education and training of end users and specialists who will operate the new system. We will discuss the activities of the systems implementation process in Chapter 12. For the present, you should realize that implementation can be a difficult process, but it is vital in assuring the success of any newly developed system. Even a well-designed system will fail if it is not properly implemented.

Systems maintenance involves the monitoring, evaluating, and modifying of a system to make desirable or necessary improvements. This includes a *postimplementation review* process to ensure that the newly implemented system meets the systems development objectives established for it. Errors in the development or use of a system are corrected by the maintenance activity. Systems maintenance also includes making modifications to a system due to changes within the business or the business environment. For example, a change in the tax laws usually requires changes to tax computations in the payroll and tax-accounting systems of a business.

COMPUTER-AIDED SYSTEMS ENGINEERING

Major changes are occurring in the traditional process of information systems development just described. That's because the SDLC process had often been too inflexible, time consuming, and expensive. In many cases, end user requirements are defined early in the process, and then end users are locked out until the system is implemented. Also, the backlog of unfilled user requests for systems development has grown to two to five years in many companies. Therefore, a **computer-aided systems engineering** (CASE) process has emerged due to the availability of a variety of software packages for systems and software development. CASE (which also stands for **computer-aided software engineering**) involves using software packages, called CASE tools, to perform

Figure 11–8 Displays of a CASE software package. The Excelerator package allows a systems analyst to interactively develop formal system specifications, use tools of analysis and design such as presentation graphs, and design the format of screens and reports.

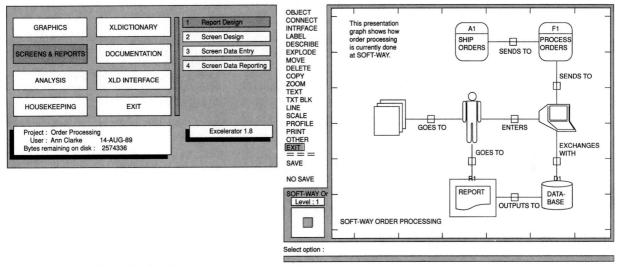

Source: Courtesy Index Technology Corporation.

many of the activities of the systems development life cycle. These might include tools to support business planning, project evaluation and management, user interface design, database design, and software development or programming. Thus, CASE tools make a computer-aided systems development process possible.

Some of the capabilities of CASE tools are also found in the application generator capabilities of end user productivity software such as electronic spreadsheet and database management packages. Since such software is available for microcomputers as well as for larger computer systems, information systems development has become a major category of end user computing. Thus, computer-aided systems engineering allows systems analysts and end users to use microcomputer workstations and CASE tools to help accomplish (and, in some cases, *automate*) activities of the systems development process. We will discuss CASE tools further in Section II. Figure 11–8 is an example of a menu display and presentation graph generated by a widely used CASE software package.

PROTOTYPING

Microcomputer workstations and a variety of CASE and other software packages allow the rapid development and testing of working models, or **prototypes,** of new applications in an interactive, iterative process involving both systems analysts and end users. **Prototyping** not only makes the development process faster and easier for systems analysts, especially for projects where end user requirements are hard to define, but it has opened up the applications development process to end users. These developments are changing the roles of end users and information systems specialists in systems development [7].

Figure 11-9 Application development with prototyping.
Note how prototyping com-
bines the steps of the
traditional systems development cycle and changes the
traditional roles of information systems specialists and
end users.

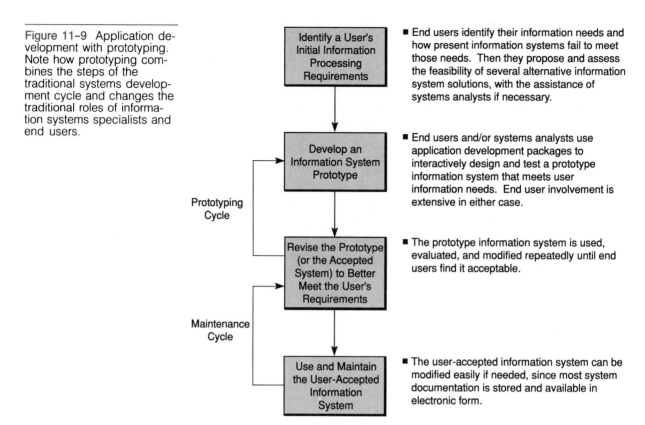

Identify a User's
Initial Information
Processing
Requirements

- End users identify their information needs and how present information systems fail to meet those needs. Then they propose and assess the feasibility of several alternative information system solutions, with the assistance of systems analysts if necessary.

Develop an
Information System
Prototype

- End users and/or systems analysts use application development packages to interactively design and test a prototype information system that meets user information needs. End user involvement is extensive in either case.

Prototyping
Cycle

Revise the Prototype
(or the Accepted
System) to Better
Meet the User's
Requirements

- The prototype information system is used, evaluated, and modified repeatedly until end users find it acceptable.

Maintenance
Cycle

Use and Maintain
the User-Accepted
Information
System

- The user-accepted information system can be modified easily if needed, since most system documentation is stored and available in electronic form.

Figure 11-10 A prototype
data entry screen for an
order-processing system.

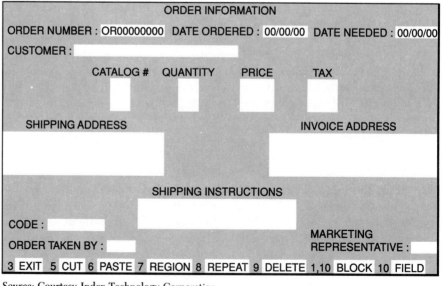

ORDER INFORMATION

ORDER NUMBER : OR00000000   DATE ORDERED : 00/00/00   DATE NEEDED : 00/00/00

CUSTOMER :

CATALOG #   QUANTITY   PRICE   TAX

SHIPPING ADDRESS   INVOICE ADDRESS

SHIPPING INSTRUCTIONS

CODE :

ORDER TAKEN BY :   MARKETING
                                    REPRESENTATIVE :

3 EXIT 5 CUT 6 PASTE 7 REGION 8 REPEAT 9 DELETE 1,10 BLOCK 10 FIELD

Source: Courtesy Index Technology Corporation.

Prototyping is a fast and iterative systems development methodology used for both large and small applications. Large, complex systems for transaction processing and information reporting still typically require using the traditional system development approach, but parts of such systems can frequently be prototyped. A prototype of an information system needed by an end user is developed quickly, using a variety of application development packages. The prototype system is then repeatedly refined until it is acceptable to an end user.

As Figure 11–9 illustrates, prototyping is an iterative, interactive process that combines steps of the traditional systems development cycle. End users with sufficient experience with application development packages can do prototyping themselves. Alternatively, an end user can work with a systems analyst to develop a prototype system in a series of interactive sessions. For example, they could develop prototypes of management reports or data entry screens such as the one illustrated in Figure 11–10. The prototype is usually modified several times until the end user finds it acceptable. Any program modules not directly produced by a program generator can then be coded using conventional programming methods. The final version of the system is then turned over to the end user for operational use.

The Prototyping Process

Sony Corporation of America

Sony Corp. of America is hustling to provide managers with the information they need to improve customer service, says Jeff Dorn, controller of Sony Component Products. "The biggest problem is that we often don't get the information we need on receipt of materials, turnaround time, value added, and delivery schedules from our factories as we need it, so we can't provide good delivery information to our customers," Dorn says. "If we aren't responsive to those needs, someone else will be."

Dorn is working with Robert Trenchard, senior VP of MIS , to develop systems for interfacing with factories and salespeople. "We're in the early end of the design process, and we found that you can really define your business quickly," Dorn says. He expects salespeople to have access to information on the availability of products when they make pitches to customers. Data on accepted orders would then flow to factories and help generate information for procurement of needed materials. Trenchard's MIS organization is adopting CASE tools in an effort to speed system development. The MIS organization studied the available tools and settled on IEF from Texas Instruments, Inc., which uses artificial intelligence-like features to develop code. Moreover, it lets systems designers use the flexibility of local workstations along with the power of a mainframe.

With IEF, code is the last thing developed. The relationships come first. That means systems developers become business experts—if systems designers are to develop models of businesses, they must understand the departments they are modeling. Addressing this need for business expertise can delay creation of code, which is one easy measure of productivity in development. "This is not easy to sell," Trenchard says. "CASE really reinforces the idea that you should think before you start writing code. So, you don't really have any software product to show for a long time."

The CASE system has boosted programmer productivity substantially. For example, it generated a program with 55,000 lines of COBOL to run an interactive executive filing system and online schedule, says Phillip Kunz, manager of data administration. In this project, Sony saw a sixfold rise in programmer productivity.

In using the system, the designer first enters statements that describe the data to be used. The designer also establishes the links between the data files to be employed. The system performs internal checks to make sure the data relationships are consistent; then, it generates code to describe the relationships. Data administration analyst David Levine says the approach speeds up his work. "Once you're used to the system, you can generate the prototype of a query menu in just a few minutes," he says. "If we didn't have the system, it would take two or three days."

The system stores the data and the description of the data, including their relationships, in a global encyclopedia or repository of corporate information. Using this kind of approach, Sony's systems analysts developed a model of how the company works, which is stored in the repository. The repository can then serve as the tool for changing and updating the systems that deliver management information. In response to a change in the way the company does business, designers alter the corporate model, then the CASE system modifies system code to conform to the changes. "A change in the company ripples through the model and the information system all the way to the documentation, which is generated automatically," Trenchard says.

Application Questions

☐ What business problems and opportunities are being solved by the development of new information systems at Sony?

☐ How does the IEF CASE tool change the role of systems developers?

☐ How does IEF improve the systems development process?

Source: Adapted from David Gabel, "A Yen for Just-in-Time Decisions Aids Sony's Drive for Coprocessing," *Computerworld*, April 10, 1989, p. SR/5.

Section II: Using Systems Development Tools

Many tools and techniques have been developed to help improve current information systems or develop new ones. Such tools help end users and systems analysts:

□ *Conceptualize, clarify, document*, and *communicate* the activities and resources of an organization and its information systems.

□ Analyze the present business operations, management decision making, and information processing activities of an organization.

□ Propose and design new or improved information systems to solve problems or pursue opportunities that have been identified.

Many **systems development tools** take the form of diagrams and other graphic representations. That's because they are easier to understand than narrative descriptions of a system. Good graphic tools can also represent the major activities and resources of a system without a lot of detail and yet be able to show various *modules* and *levels* of detail when needed. They also can be modified during the course of analysis and design, as you specify more features of a present or proposed information system. Finally, graphics and other tools serve as *documentation* methods. For example, they document the results of the analysis stage for use in the design stage, then they document the results of the design stage to assist in the implementation and maintenance of a new system.

Figure 11–11 outlines some of the major types of tools used for systems development. Notice that the tools can be grouped into four categories based on the system features each typically documents: (1) the components and flows of a system, (2) the user interface, (3) data attributes and relationships, and (4) detailed system processes. We will briefly describe these tools now and then show you examples of how a few of them are used in a realistic case study: ABC Auto Parts.

Remember that such tools can be used in every stage of system development—as analytical tools, design tools, and documentation methods. For example, system flowcharts and data flow diagrams can be used to (1) *analyze* an existing system, (2) express the *design* of a new system, and (3) provide the

SYSTEMS DEVELOPMENT TOOLS

Overview of Systems Development Tools

System Feature	Systems Development Tools Used
System components and flows	System flowcharts, presentation graphs, data flow diagrams, context diagrams, system component matrix.
User interface	Input/output layout forms and screens, dialogue flow diagrams.
Data attributes and relationships	Data dictionaries, entity-relationship diagrams, file layout forms, grid charts.
Detailed system processes	Decision trees and tables, structure charts, pseudocode, program flowcharts.

Figure 11–11 Examples of systems development tools. Note the four primary areas of use for these tools.

documentation for the implementation and maintenance of a newly developed system. You should also realize that software packages for computer-aided systems engineering (CASE) have computerized many of these tools. For example, many CASE packages will automatically draw and revise system flowcharts or data flow diagrams based on end user or analyst descriptions of a system.

System Components and Flows

These tools help you document the data flows among the resources and activities of an information system. *System flowcharts* are typically used to show the flow of data media as they are processed by hardware devices and manual activities. *Presentation graphs* are quite similar but use less technical symbols (as was shown in Figure 11–8). *Data flow diagrams* use a few simple symbols to illustrate the flow of data among external entities (such as people or organizations), processing activities, and data storage elements. A *context diagram* is the highest-level data flow diagram. A *system component matrix* provides a matrix framework to document the resources used, the activities performed, and the information products produced by an information system.

The User Interface

Designing the *interface* between end users and computer systems is a major consideration in developing new systems. *Layout forms and screens* are used to construct the formats and generic content of input-output media and methods. *Dialogue flow diagrams* analyze the flow of dialogue between computers and people. They document the flows among different display screens generated by alternative end user responses to menus and prompts.

Data Attributes and Relationships

The data resource in information systems is defined, catalogued, and designed by this category of tools. A *data dictionary* catalogs the definitions (descriptions) of the attributes (characteristics) of all data elements and their relationships to each other, as well as to external systems. *Entity-relationship diagrams* (as shown in Figure 6–19) are used to document the number and type of relationships among the entities in a system. *File layout forms* document the type, size, and names of the data elements in a system. *Grid charts* help identify the use of each type of data element in the input, output, or storage media of a system.

Detailed System Processes

This final group of tools is used to help programmers develop the detailed procedures and processes required in the design of computer programs. *Decision trees* and *decision tables* use a network or tabular form to document the complex conditional logic involved in choosing among the information processing alternatives in a system. *Structure charts* document the purpose, structure, and hierarchical relationships of the modules in a program. *Pseudocode* expresses the processing logic of a program module in a series of short phrases.

Program flowcharts are used to illustrate the detailed sequence of processing steps required in a computer program.

ABC Auto Parts is a chain of auto parts stores in southern California, with headquarters in Los Angeles. The firm has grown to 14 stores in just 10 years, an it offers a wide variety of automotive parts and accessories. Sales and profits have increased each year, but the rate of sales growth has failed to meet forecasts in the last three years. Early results for this year indicate the rate of sales growth is continuing to drop, even with the addition of two new stores last year. Adding the stores was the solution decided on by corporate management to reverse the trend in sales performance.

Now the company is faced with finding another solution to its problem. In recent meetings of corporate and store managers, the issue of computer use has been raised. ABC Auto Parts uses computers for various information processing jobs, such as sales transactions processing, analysis of sales performance, employee payroll processing, and accounting applications. However, sales transactions by customers are still written up by salespeople. Also, corporate and store managers depend on daily sales analysis reports that contain information that is always several days old.

The Retail Automation Issue

Most store managers, along with the vice presidents of marketing and information systems, argue that *retail automation* is a key to reversing ABC's sales trends. They believe using point-of-sale (POS) terminals in each store would drastically shorten the time needed by a salesperson to write up a sale. This would not only improve customer service, but it would give salespeople more time to sell to more customers. The managers call these the "selling floor" benefits that would lead to increased sales.

Another major point raised is that retail automation would allow immediate capture and processing of sales transaction data. Up-to-date sales performance information could then be made available to managers at *management workstations*, that is, personal computers connected into the company's data communications network. This would provide the capability for information on sales performance to be tailored to each manager's information needs. Currently, managers have to depend on daily sales analysis reports that all use the same report format. Too much of a manager's time is being used to generate sales performance information not provided by the system. Managers complain they don't have enough time to plan and support sales efforts unless they make decisions without enough information.

The president of ABC Auto Parts has resisted previous proposals to automate the selling process. He knows automation would involve a large initial investment and resistance to technology by some salespeople and managers. He fears the loss of salesperson/customer interactions. He also fears that managers will become too dependent on computers if they have them in their offices. However, continued disappointing sales performance has softened his position. Also the president realizes that POS systems have become commonplace in all types of retail stores. ABC's major competitors have installed such systems, and their growth continues to outpace his own firm's. The company is failing to achieve its goal of increasing its share of the automotive parts market.

Planning and Investigation

Long-range planning sessions with the managers and a management consulting group identified a strategic role for information systems in the company. A long-range strategic plan was developed that stresses the need to use information systems technology to reduce the company's cost of doing business and to enhance the products and services the firm offers. Retail automation is identified as one possible thrust of this role for information systems. Other possibilities include advanced systems in marketing, distribution, and a number of other areas. The plan also stresses that the top priorities of new information systems must be (1) support of personal selling, (2) tailoring of information to managers' needs, and (3) integration of information systems resources and services.

A group of store managers and systems analysts from the Information Services Department were commissioned to conduct a feasibility study of the retail automation options facing the firm. However, the president insisted they include the option of keeping the present system. This alternative would involve adding more salespeople to improve personal selling and customer service. Staff assistants would also be hired for each store manager. Their duties would include information analysis, freeing managers for more hands-on management.

The systems analysts made personal observations of the sales processing system in action and interviewed managers, salespeople, and other employees. The following description of the present sales processing system is a summary of information gathered by the systems analysts. The information is presented in sequential order to make it easier to follow the events that occur in a sales transaction.

The Present System

The present sales transaction processing and analysis information system at ABC Auto Parts includes the following activities:

1. When a customer wants to buy an auto part, a salesclerk writes up a sales order form. Recorded on this form is customer data, such as name, address, and account number, and product data, such as name, product number, and price. A copy of the sales order form is given to the customer as a receipt.

2. Sales order forms are sent at the end of each day to the information services department. The next day, they are recorded on magnetic tape using key-to-tape data entry devices.

3. The file of sales transactions is now ready for computer processing. One of the important information processing jobs that needs to be done is the updating of the sales files and the preparation of sales analysts' reports. One of the first jobs the store's mainframe computer does is sort the sales transactions by product number.

4. The sorted sales transactions are used by a sales processing program to update a sales *master file* to reflect the new sales. A new sales master file on magnetic tape is created.

5. Sales processing also produces a sales analysis file. This file contains historical data on previous sales performance, as well as new sales data. The computer uses this file and a sales analysis program to perform sales analysis. Sales analysis reports are produced that tell management the trends in sales performance of various products.

Based on a preliminary analysis of user requirements, the systems analysts proposed a new information system they call the *sales transaction-processing and analysis* (STPA) system. This system features a telecommunications network of point-of-sale (POS) terminals and management workstations. A brief description of part of this proposed system follows.

1. When a customer wishes to buy an auto part, the salesclerk enters customer and product data using an online POS terminal. The POS terminal has a keyboard for data entry and a video screen for display of input data, as well as data entry menus, prompts, and messages. POS terminals are connected in a telecommunications network to the store's mainframe computer, which uses a comprehensive sales transaction processing program.

2. The POS terminal prints out a sales receipt for the customer that contains customer and product data and serves as a record of the transaction.

3. Errors in data entry may cause an error indication to be displayed by the POS terminal. The salesclerk must follow various error procedures to correct such errors.

4. The POS terminal transmits sales transaction data to the store's mainframe computer. This immediately updates the sales records in the company's database, which is stored on magnetic disk units.

5. The computer performs sales analysis using the updated sales records in the company database. Afterward, sales performance information is available to corporate and store managers in a variety of report formats at their management workstations.

6. Database management software supports ad hoc database inquiries by managers, who can receive instantaneous responses about sales performance in displays at their workstations.

Many tools and techniques of systems development could have been used to help end users and systems analysts analyze the sales processing system of ABC Auto Parts and design a new one. Let's look at examples of four tools that might have been used: (1) system flowcharts, (2) data flow diagrams, (3) layout forms and screens, and (4) the system component matrix. These should help you apply the concepts discussed in Section I, and propose information system solutions to simple business problems.

A **system flowchart** is a graphic diagraming tool that documents and communicates the flow of data media and the information processing procedures taking place in an information system. This is accomplished by using a variety of labeled symbols connected by arrows to show the sequence of information processing activities. System flowcharts typically emphasize the media and hardware used and the processes that take place within an information system. They thus represent a graphic model of the *physical* information system that exists or is proposed. Figure 11–12 illustrates some common system flowchart symbols.

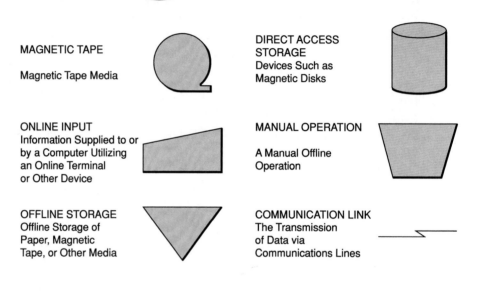

PROCESSING

A Major Computer
Processing Function

INPUT/OUTPUT

Generic Input or
Output Symbol

DOCUMENT

Paper Documents
and Reports

DISPLAY

Information Displayed
by Video Devices

MAGNETIC TAPE

Magnetic Tape Media

DIRECT ACCESS
STORAGE
Devices Such as
Magnetic Disks

ONLINE INPUT
Information Supplied to or
by a Computer Utilizing
an Online Terminal
or Other Device

MANUAL OPERATION

A Manual Offline
Operation

OFFLINE STORAGE
Offline Storage of
Paper, Magnetic
Tape, or Other Media

COMMUNICATION LINK
The Transmission
of Data via
Communications Lines

System flowcharts are widely used to communicate the overall structure and flows of a system to end users because they can offer a physical view that emphasizes the hardware and data media involved. However, in many cases, they have been displaced by data flow diagrams for use by systems analysts and by presentation graphs for communicating with end users.

Figure 11–13A shows how a system flowchart is used as a tool for the *analysis* of the existing *physical* sales processing and analysis system at ABC Auto Parts. It graphically portrays the flow of data media and the major information processing tasks taking place. Note how the flowchart symbols indicate the equipment and media used for input, output, and storage. For example, symbols and labels indicate the use of many paper documents and reports, a key-to-tape data entry device, and magnetic tape storage.

Figure 11–13B is also a system flowchart, but it is being used to illustrate the *physical design* of a *proposed* sales processing and analysis system. This proposed system will replace the system illustrated in Figure 11–13A. Note how it shows a data entry terminal, magnetic disk storage, and several printed reports. This is obviously a physical design because the hardware devices and media that will be used in the new system are specified.

Data Flow Diagrams

A **data flow diagram** (DFD) can help you identify the flow of data in a system without specifying the media or hardware involved. Data flow diagrams use a few simple symbols connected by arrows to represent such flows. Data flow

Figure 11–13 Flowcharts of the present and proposed sales transaction processing and analysis information systems at ABC Auto Parts.

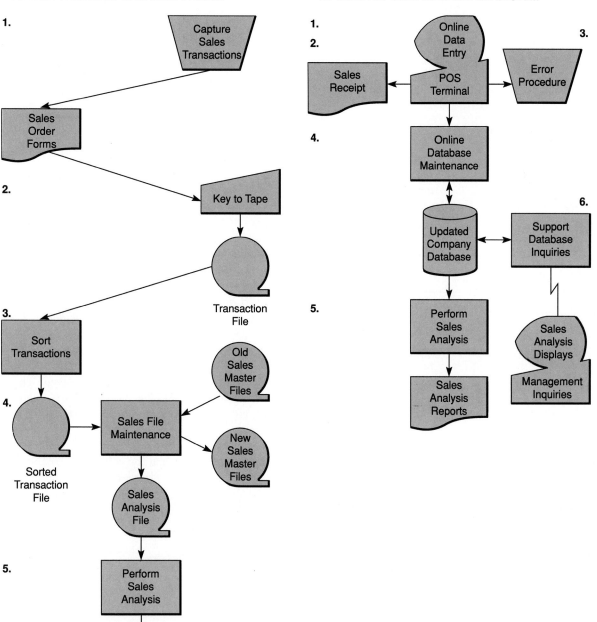

Figure 11–14 Basic data
flow diagram symbols.

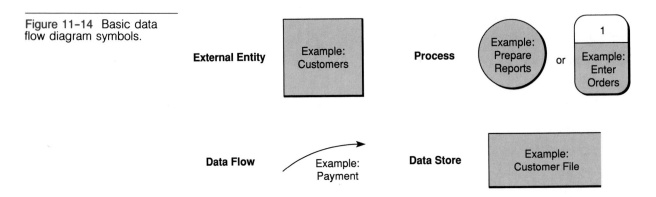

diagrams can easily illustrate the logical relationships among data, flows, external entities (sources and destinations), and stores. Figure 11–14 illustrates the
four basic symbols used in data flow diagrams.

This graphic tool is widely used for several reasons. It is simple to draw
(mostly circles connected by arrows) and easily depicts the basic components
and flows of a system. DFDs can also be drawn in increasing levels of detail,
starting with a summary high-level view and proceeding to more detailed
lower-level views. This supports a modular, structured, *top-down* view of
system data flows. For example, Figure 11–15 illustrates the highest level of
data flow diagram, called a *context diagram* or level-0 DFD.

Figure 11–16 shows how a data flow diagram can be used as a tool for both
logical analysis and *logical design* in the ABC Auto Parts example. (These are
called level-1 DFDs.) Note that a data flow diagram can portray the logical flow
of data in both present and proposed sales analysis and processing systems.
That's because it does not specify the media and equipment involved. These
DFDs only illustrate the *logical relationships* among the data flows, external
entity sources and destinations, and data stores in the sales processing and
analysis system at ABC Auto Parts.

However, data flow diagrams can also be used to represent a *physical view* of
a system. These *physical data flow diagrams* reveal the actual form of the data
media used, the people and hardware involved in processing, and the devices
in which data is stored. This is done simply by additional labeling of the
symbols for the data flows, processing, and data stores in a logical data flow

Figure 11–15 A context diagram of an order processing
system. This is the highest-
level view of this system.

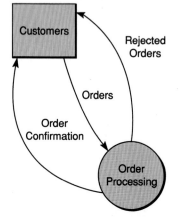

Figure 11-16   Using data flow diagrams. This graphically illustrates the logical analysis and design of a sales processing system for ABC Auto Parts.

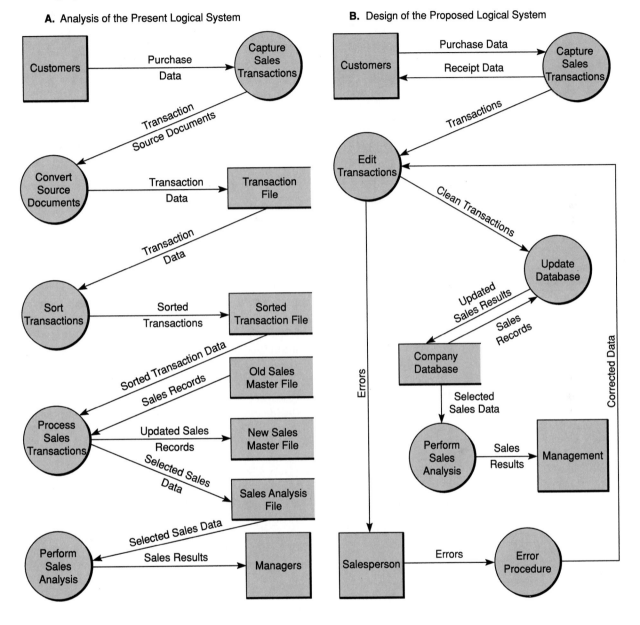

A. Analysis of the Present Logical System

B. Design of the Proposed Logical System

diagram. For example, adding labels such as *Sales Invoice* to a data flow arrow, *Data Entry by Clerks Using POS Terminals* to a processing symbol, or *Customer File on Magnetic Disk* to a data store symbol would begin to change a data flow diagram from a logical to a physical view.

You can use **layout forms and screens** to help you design the format of input, output, and storage media. They consist of electronic displays or preprinted forms on which the size and placement of titles, headings, data, and informa-

Layout Forms and
Screens

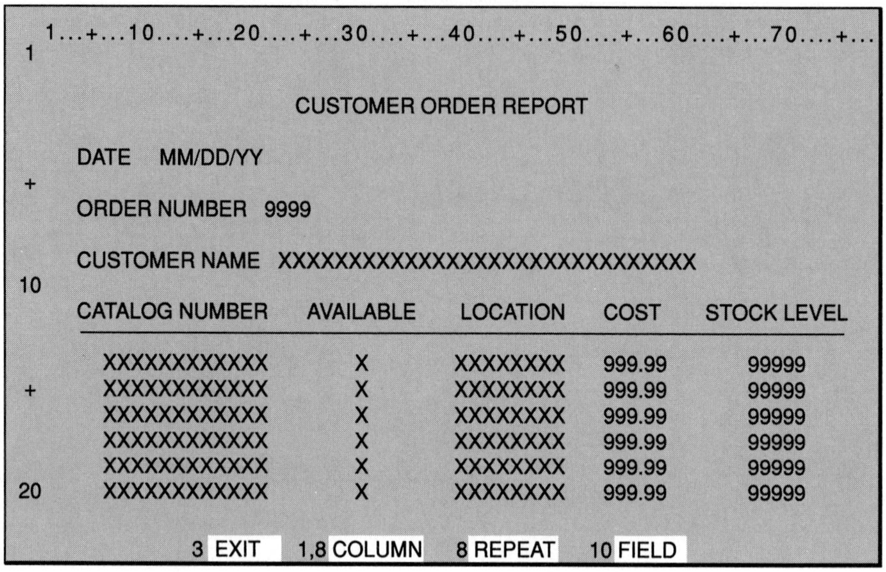

Figure 11–17 A layout
screen for the design of a
customer order report.

```
1...+...10....+...20....+...30....+...40....+...50....+...60....+...70....+...
1

                            CUSTOMER ORDER REPORT

        DATE    MM/DD/YY
+
        ORDER NUMBER   9999

        CUSTOMER NAME   XXXXXXXXXXXXXXXXXXXXXXXXXXXXXXX
10
        CATALOG NUMBER     AVAILABLE     LOCATION     COST     STOCK LEVEL

            XXXXXXXXXXX         X         XXXXXXX     999.99      99999
+           XXXXXXXXXXX         X         XXXXXXX     999.99      99999
            XXXXXXXXXXX         X         XXXXXXX     999.99      99999
            XXXXXXXXXXX         X         XXXXXXX     999.99      99999
            XXXXXXXXXXX         X         XXXXXXX     999.99      99999
20          XXXXXXXXXXX         X         XXXXXXX     999.99      99999


              3 EXIT     1,8 COLUMN     8 REPEAT     10 FIELD
```

Courtesy Index Technology Corporation.

tion can be designed. Layout forms and screens are used to design source documents, input/output and storage records and files, and output displays and reports. 4GL packages, CASE tools, and other software packages for computer-aided development of information systems provide electronic versions of layout forms. For example, screen generator packages help design *prototypes* of interrelated data entry screens and management reporting displays, along with the end user/computer dialogue that ties them together. Figure 11–17 illustrates a layout screen for the design of a display for a customer order report that could be used by ABC Auto Parts.

System Component Matrix

The **system component matrix** is based on the conceptual framework of the information system model introduced in Chapter 1. As shown in Figure 11–18, a system component matrix can be used as an *information system framework* for both systems analysis and systems design [10]. It views an information system as a matrix of components that highlights (a) how the basic information system activities of input, processing, output, storage, and control are accomplished, and (b) how the use of hardware, software, and people resources can convert data resources into information products. It poses a fundamental question that should be answered in the systems development process: What information system resources are needed to accomplish the information processing activities that can produce the information products required by end users?

Figure 11–19 illustrates the use of a system component matrix to document the basic components of the proposed sales processing and analysis system at ABC Auto Parts. Note how it spotlights the basic information processing activities needed, resources used, and products produced by this information system. Filling all of the cells in the matrix is not necessary because information for each cell may not be available or applicable. Thus, blank cells are often appropriate and unavoidable. However, duplicate cell entries can be made because many systems resources and products are used to support more than

Figure 11–18   A system component matrix used as an information system framework for systems analysis and design. It highlights the resources needed to accomplish activities that produce information products needed by end users.

Information system activities	Hardware resources		Software resources		People resources		Data resources	Information products
	Machines	Media	Programs	Procedures	Specialists	Users		
Input								
Processing								
Output								
Storage								
Control								

one activity. Still, a system component matrix serves its purpose by emphasizing the use of an information system framework for proposed information system solutions.

How can end users (and systems analysts) take advantage of computer-aided tools for systems analysis and design? In Section I, we discussed how computer-aided software engineering (CASE) tools and other packages can be used in a prototyping process of systems development. For example, end users, alone or working with systems analysts, can use these tools for developing user interface prototypes such as data entry screens or management reports. CASE tools can also help automate the use of flow charts and data flow diagrams and the creation of data dictionaries.

Figure 11–20 emphasizes that CASE packages provide many computer-based tools for both the *front end* of the systems development life cycle (analysis and design) and the *back end* of systems development (implementation and maintenance). Note that a data dictionary and systems developers such as programmers and systems analysts help integrate the use of tools at both ends of the development cycle. Integrated CASE tools (called I-CASE) are now available that can assist all of the stages of systems development. Some of these CASE tools support *joint application design* (JAD), where a group of systems analysts, programmers, and end users can jointly and interactively design new applications. Finally, if the development of new systems can be called *forward engineering*, some CASE tools support *backward engineering*. That is, they help analyze the logic of program code for old applications and convert it automatically into more efficient programs that significantly improve information system effectiveness.

As we said in Chapter 6, a data dictionary is basically a catalog or database or *meta-data*, that is, "data about data" and other information about a system. At a minimum, a data dictionary describes the characteristics of the data elements and their interrelationships. More complete dictionaries include descriptions of

USING COMPUTER-AIDED DEVELOPMENT TOOLS

Data Dictionaries and System Repositories

Figure 11–19   An example of a system component matrix for a sales processing and analysis system. Note how it emphasizes the basic activities needed, resources used, and products produced by this information system.

Information System Activities	Hardware Resources		Software Resources		People Resources		Data Resources	Information Products
	Machines	Media	Programs	Procedures	Specialists	Users		
Input	POS terminals	Bar tags mag stripe cards credit cards	Data entry program	Data entry procedures		Salesclerks Customers	Customer data Product data	Data entry displays
Processing	Mainframe computer		Sales processing program Sales analysis program	Sales transaction procedures	Computer operators	Salesclerks Managers	Customer inventory, and sales databases	Processing status displays
Output	POS terminals Management workstations	Paper reports and receipts	Report generator program Graphic programs	Output use and distribution procedures		Salesclerks Managers Customers		Sales analysis reports and displays Sales receipts
Storage	Magnetic disk drives	Magnetic disk packs	Database management program		Computer operators		Customer, inventory, and sales databases	
Control	POS terminals Management workstations	Paper documents and control reports	Performance monitor program Security monitor program	Correction procedures	Computer operators Control clerks	Salesclerks Managers Customers	Customer, inventory, sales databases	Data entry displays Sales receipts Error displays and signals

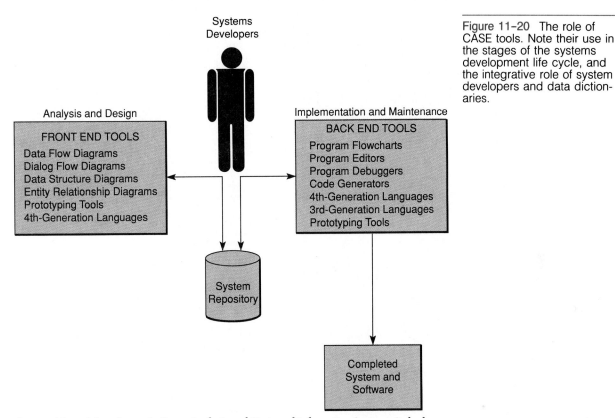

Figure 11-20 The role of CASE tools. Note their use in the stages of the systems development life cycle, and the integrative role of system developers and data dictionaries.

Source: Adapted from James A. Senn, *Analysis and Design of Information Systems*, 2nd ed. (New York: McGraw-Hill, 1989), pp. 257, 259.

data flows, data stores, and the processes that affect them. Data dictionaries may also include descriptions of hardware used and external entities (such as end users) involved in a system. Thus, they are an invaluable source of information about the data and other resources and activities of an information system. Refer back to Figure 6–7 for an example of a data dictionary entry.

Many CASE tools now include a dictionary component that ranges from limited *systems development databases* to more extensive *system encyclopedias* (as in Texas Instruments' IEF) or **system repositories** (as in IBM's AD/Cycle). These provide systems analysts with computer-aided system descriptions and cataloging facilities, beginning with their systems planning and systems analysis activities. They can continue to build and use the repository in their data design, process design, and user interface design activities. Finally, they can use the encyclopedia or repository to ensure proper implementation and maintenance of a system.

Thus, the data dictionary has become the *repository* for all the details of a system generated with other systems development tools. More important, the data dictionary itself has become a vital tool of systems development. That is, as a system repository, it integrates the use of other tools to assure consistency and compatibility in the design of the data elements, processes, user interface, and other aspects of the system being developed. For example, Figure 11–21

Figure 11–21   The CASE tools and system encyclopedias and repositories in a fully integrated CASE product: IEF, by Texas Instruments.

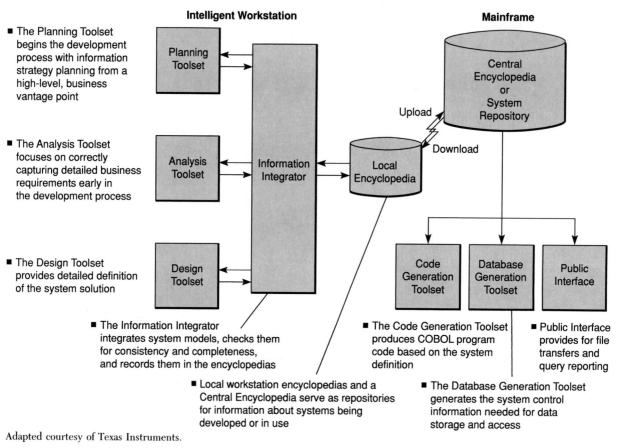

- The Planning Toolset begins the development process with information strategy planning from a high-level, business vantage point

- The Analysis Toolset focuses on correctly capturing detailed business requirements early in the development process

- The Design Toolset provides detailed definition of the system solution

- The Information Integrator integrates system models, checks them for consistency and completeness, and records them in the encyclopedias

- Local workstation encyclopedias and a Central Encyclopedia serve as repositories for information about systems being developed or in use

- The Code Generation Toolset produces COBOL program code based on the system definition

- The Database Generation Toolset generates the system control information needed for data storage and access

- Public Interface provides for file transfers and query reporting

Adapted courtesy of Texas Instruments.

presents an overall look at the tools and system encyclopedias and repositories in the IEF (Information Engineering Facility) CASE product of Texas Instruments.

COMPUTER-AIDED SYSTEMS ENGINEERING AT ABC AUTO PARTS

How could CASE tools and a prototyping methodology have been used by the IS staff at ABC Auto Parts? Let's look at a scenario of what could have happened, to help you understand the use of computer-aided development tools and a prototyping process, as discussed in this chapter.

The Prototyping Process

Systems analysts from the information services department had several prototyping sessions with selected corporate executives, store managers, and salespersons. They used CASE tools to develop prototypes for the user interface of the system. For example, they developed a series of formatted data entry screens that would be displayed by POS terminals to assist salespeople entering data about transactions. Also developed was a data dictionary of tentative database definitions for sales, customer, and inventory records. Finally, a number of tentative formats for management reports were designed with the advice of corporate and store managers.

The systems analysts then constructed a database of test data about sales, inventory, and customers. They used a CASE package that simulated the processing needed to capture data about sales transactions. Salespeople were then asked to use this prototype sales data entry system. The salespeople suggested changes to the displays that would make the process of ringing up sales easier. These improvements were easily accomplished by revising the mockups of data entry screens stored in the CASE system repository.

Next, a fourth-generation language was used to develop processing routines to process the test data and produce management reports. Store managers and corporate executives then suggested several changes in the report formats after reviewing sample reports based on test data. All of these suggestions were incorporated into a final prototype that was accepted by management. The information services staff then developed production versions of the processing programs using a COBOL program generator and a mainframe database management package. After further testing and refinement, the new sales transaction processing and analysis system was implemented on an phased, store-by-store basis by ABC Auto Parts.

DEVELOPING INFORMATION SYSTEM SOLUTIONS: GETTING STARTED

The material in this chapter should help you solve simple, real world business problems using information system solutions. How do you get started? First, review the systems approach and systems development concepts discussed in the first section of this chapter to give you an overall view of the information system solution process. Next, learn to use one or more of the tools discussed in this section (a system flowchart, data flow diagram, layout screen, or system component matrix). If you have access to computer-aided tools, you can start by learning how to use the software packages involved. Use one of these tools to try to identify the important components and requirements of the present organization and its information systems (systems analysis), and then to identify improvements or alternatives to such information systems (systems design).

A Framework for Systems Analysis and Design

The information systems concepts you learned in Chapter 1 and system component matrix introduced in this section can be used as a framework to help you get started. The following are questions you can use to begin the process of analysis and design. Also included are answers that spotlight the *generic systems components* which are typically found in most computer-based information systems in business.

Input of Data Resources

Question: How is data captured and prepared for processing? How should it be? What *data resources* are involved?

Answer: Input data is frequently collected from *source documents* (such as payroll time cards) and converted to machine-sensible data by a *keyboarding* data entry process. Other input data may be captured directly by transaction terminals (such as point-of-sale terminals) using devices such as optical scanners. Input into the system typically consists of:

☐ **Transaction data.** *Example:* Data describing sales transactions is captured by a point-of-sale terminal.

☐ **Database adjustment.** *Example:* A change in a customer's credit limit, using an online terminal in the credit department or processing a Credit Increase Request Form mailed in by a customer.

☐ **Inquiries.** *Example:* What is the balance owed on a customer's account?

☐ **Output of other systems.** *Example:* The output of a sales processing system includes data used as input by an inventory control system to reflect transactions that change the amount of inventory on hand.

Processing of Data Resources

Question: How is data manipulated and transformed into information? How should it be? What processing alternatives should be considered?

Answer: Data resources are subjected to sorting, summarizing, calculating, and other manipulation activities. Processing alternatives include batch processing and realtime processing. The results of processing are:

☐ The production of a variety of information products.

☐ The updating of information stored in databases.
Example: Sales data captured by point-of-sale terminals at retail stores are transmitted to and processed at a regional computer center. Company databases are updated, and sales documents and reports are produced.

Output of Information Products

Question: How is information communicated to users? How should it be? What **information products** should be produced?

Answer: Output typically takes the form of the following information products:

☐ **Reports.** *Example:* A sales analysis report outlining the sales made during a period by sales territory, product, and salesperson.

☐ **Documents.** *Example:* A paycheck or sales receipt.

☐ **Displays or responses.** *Example:* A video terminal displays the balance owed on a customer's account. The same information can be transmitted to a telephone by a computer audio-response unit.

☐ **Control listings.** *Example:* Each time an employee paycheck is printed, a line on a *payroll register* is also printed and recorded on magnetic tape. This helps provide an *audit trail* for control purposes.

☐ **Input to other systems.** *Example:* Part of the output of a payroll system serves as input to a labor-cost accounting system and the general ledger system of the firm.

Storage of Data Resources

Question: How are data resources organized, stored, updated, and retrieved? How should they be?

Answer: Data resources are stored for later processing. They are typically organized into files and databases. This facilitates:

☐ Supplying data needed by the organization's information system applications.

☐ The updating of files and databases to reflect the occurrence of new business transactions.

Example: The current credit balances of customers are supplied in response to inquiries from sales personnel. Also, credit sales transactions cause some customer credit balances to be increased in the customer database.

Control of System Performance

Question: How are input, processing, output, and storage activities monitored and controlled? How should they be? What control methods should be considered?

Answer: Input, processing, output, and storage activities must be controlled so that an information system produces proper information products and achieves its other objectives. (Information systems controls are explained in Chapter 14.) Typical control methods include:

☐ **Input controls.** *Example:* formatted data entry screens warn users if input data exceed specified parameters.

☐ **Processing controls.** *Example:* Software may contain checkpoint routines that check the accuracy of intermediate results during processing.

☐ **Output controls.** *Example:* End users may check the accuracy of specified control totals in reports.

☐ **Storage controls.** *Example:* Databases may be protected by security programs that require proper identification and authorization codes by end users.

Hardware, Software, and People Resources

Question: What hardware (machines and media), software (programs and procedures), and people (specialist and users) are or should be used to accomplish the input, processing, output, storage, and control activities of the information system?

Answer: Answering that question is a primary objective of systems analysis and design. If you review the answers to the previous questions, you will see that hardware, software, or people are involved in the examples used. This text is designed to help you answer that question for any information system you are studying.

REAL WORLD CASE

Chevy Chase Bank

The application process for obtaining a mortgage has always been a tedious, inexact process. The reward for weeks of trading phone calls and shuffling paper back and forth between multiple financial institutions can end up in credit rejection for the buyer and lost selling time for the home owner. Even when the loan is granted, the process can still alienate customers.

Looking to increase its market share, Chevy Chase Bank quickly concluded that its rates were competitive. But what if it could promise the participants in a real estate transaction a virtually on-the-spot mortgage commitment backed up by more accurate data? Enabling the bank to differentiate its service was the opportunity that Bob Spicer, a senior vice president and information systems director for Chevy Chase, needed. The goal was to be more responsive to consumers by providing a commitment within minutes, versus weeks, and to close the loan within a few weeks, rather than a month or more.

So Chevy Chase Bank developed a Mortgagevision loan application service that is set in motion once field-based loan officers transmit loan information to the bank's mainframe using laptop computers. In turn, it notifies the bank's mortgage underwriter, who then integrates mainframe-based data using a LAN micro workstation running the OS/2 operating system.

This is done via IBM's Easel graphics package, which provides graphical interface up front while dealing with the mainframe in the background. "Easel lets you extract information from multiple applications on multiple computers. I can bring together all the information necessary to bear on the problem into a single integrated view that is very user friendly," said Spicer. The user just points and shoots to select necessary data. Once the mortgage underwriter gets the credit and application data, it is sent off in real-time to the mortgage insurer via telecommunications links to their mainframe computer. Once the mortgage insurer has responded, Easel goes back into the mainframe to grab additional applicant credit information and then sends all collected and processed data over to a mortgage expert system, which resides on a PS/2 Model 70 microcomputer.

"We spent about a year training it. We took the problem of underwriting a loan and broke it into a number of problem sets and then trained the system to experience what we said were good and bad loans. Then we taught it how to render a final decision," Spicer explained. If the system encounters a decision it has not seen before, it logs it so that bank officers can study it to determine the proper reaction. The final decision is then relayed back to the field.

Another piece to the system puzzle utilizes a voice processing system from Syntellect Corp. Rather than chase loan officers with sometimes fruitless phone calls, users awaiting a loan decision can call into the host, punch in their applications number, and hear a computerized voice recite their current loan status.

Mortgagevision is expected to kick off a chain reaction of satisfaction from customers. Realtors, for example, can more easily qualify potential buyers. The bank, which has eliminated a lot of redundant data entry and the resulting paper float, is looking not at the prospect of fewer employees, but increased business.

Application Questions

☐ What business problems and opportunities are being handled by the use of computer-based information systems at the Chevy Chase Bank?

☐ Use one or more tools of analysis and design (system flowchart, data flow diagram, system component matrix) to analyze the mortgage loan processing system at Chevy Chase Bank.

Source: Adapted from Patricia Keefe, "Taking OS/2 Benefits to Bank," *Computerworld,* April 23, 1990, p. 37.

□ The systems approach underlies the information systems development cycle used by information systems specialists and end users to conceive, design, and implement computer-based information system solutions to business problems. The stages, activities, and products of the systems development cycle are summarized in Figure 11–2.

□ Major changes occurring in the traditional information systems development cycle include computer-aided systems engineering (CASE), software packages which computerize and automate parts of the systems development process, and prototyping tools and methodologies which promote an iterative, interactive process which develops prototypes of user interfaces and other information system components.

□ A variety of graphics methods and software packages can be used as analysis and design tools to help develop information system solutions to business problems. Graphics tools include system flowcharts, data flow diagrams, layout forms and screens, and the system component matrix. Computer-aided tools include 4GLs, CASE tools, and other application development packages.

□ An information system framework (such as the system component matrix) emphasizes that systems analysis and design must define what resources are needed to accomplish the activities that produce the information products required to meet the needs of end users.

SUMMARY

These are the key terms and concepts of this chapter. The page number of their first explanation is given in parentheses.

KEY TERMS AND CONCEPTS

1. Computer-aided systems engineering (*390*)
2. Data dictionary (*405*)
3. Data flow diagram (*400*)
4. Economic feasibility (*385*)
5. Feasibility study (*384*)
6. Layout forms and screens (*403*)
7. Logical versus physical analysis and design (*388*)
8. Operational feasibility (*385*)
9. Organizational feasibility (*385*)
10. Prototype information system (*392*)
11. Prototyping (*391*)
12. System component matrix (*404*)
13. System design standards (*389*)
14. System flowchart (*399*)
15. System repository (*407*)
16. System requirements (*387*)
17. System specifications (*388*)
18. Systems analysis (*386*)
19. Systems approach (*382*)
20. Systems design (*387*)
21. Systems development life cycle (*382*)
22. Systems development tools (*395*)
23. Systems implementation (*389*)
24. Systems investigation (*383*)
25. Systems maintenance (*390*)
26. Technical feasibility (*385*)
27. User interface, data, and process design (*387*)

Match one of the **key terms and concepts** listed above with one of the examples or definitions listed below. Try to find the best fit for answers that seem to fit more than one term or concept. Defend your choices.

REVIEW QUIZ

———————   1. A systematic problem solving process.

———————   2. A multistep process to conceive, design, and implement an information system.

———————   3. The first stage of the systems development cycle.

———————   4. Determines the organizational, economic, technical, and operational feasibility of a proposed information system.

———————   5. Cost savings and additional profits will exceed the investment required.

———————   6. Reliable hardware and software are available to implement a proposed system.

———————   7. Customers will not have trouble using a proposed system.

———————   8. The proposed system supports the strategic plan of the business.

———————   9. Studying in detail the information needs of users and any information systems presently used.

———————   10. A detailed description of end user information needs and the input, processing, output, storage, and control capabilities required to meet those needs.

———————   11. The process that results in specifications for the hardware, software, people, data resources, and information products needed by a proposed system.

———————   12. Systems analysis and design focus first on end user information needs and then on the hardware, software, and people required.

———————   13. Systems design should focus on developing input/output methods, data structures, and programs and procedures.

———————   14. Common interfaces for user access, programming, and telecommunications for application software run on all types of computers.

———————   15. A detailed description of the hardware, software, people, data resources, and information products required by a proposed system.

———————   16. Acquiring hardware and software, testing and documenting a proposed system, and training people to use it.

———————   17. Monitoring, evaluating, and modifying a system.

———————   18. Using software packages to computerize many of the activities in the systems development process.

———————   19. A working model of an information system.

———————   20. An interactive and iterative process of systems development.

———————   21. Methods used to help analyze, design, and document information systems.

———————   22. Shows you the flow of data media and information processing procedures in an information system.

———————   23. Shows you the logical flow of data in an information system without specifying the media or equipment involved.

———————   24. Shows you the content and format of displays and reports.

_____ 25. Shows you how hardware, software, people, and data resources support the input, processing, output, storage, and control activities of an information system.

_____ 26. Catalogs descriptions of data elements and relationships.

_____ 27. A database of specifications for all aspects of an organization's information systems.

1. ABC Auto Parts

   The president of ABC Auto Parts made several statements and asked several questions in a recent meeting of store managers. Match each statement or question with one of the steps of the information systems development cycle outlined in Figure 11–2. Explain your choices.

   a. What are the specific information needs of our store managers?
   b. Will the recent changes in the tax laws require us to change our computer-based payroll system?
   c. Is a new point-of-sale system a feasible solution to this store's problems?
   d. Have our employees been trained to use this POS system?
   e. What are the exact specifications for the hardware and software needed?

2. General Electric Capital Corporation

   In the case of an executive information system (EIS), less is definitely more, according to Lawrence Runge. Runge, project manager of Fleet Services Development at General Electric Capital Corp. in Stamford, Connecticut, said that when a firm is building an EIS, the easiest trap to fall into is throwing just about everything into it in the hope that the senior executives will find some use for it. Instead, he said, the users become mired in too much information and may find the system too intimidating to use. Runge said that, too often, the information systems department will try to approach an EIS project as it would tackle traditional IS projects. The traditional approach involves providing as much information as possible. Instead, Runge advised, the EIS should be simple to use and contain only highly critical information.

   A first step to EIS development is the executive interview process, in which executives work together to list the critical success factors of the company. From that list, the features of the EIS can be decided. Still, building an EIS is a continuous cycle that never ends, Runge warned. The EIS that Runge helped to build at GE Capital began as working prototypes that are continually improved and tweaked to meet the changing needs of the executives they are serving. Eventually, he said, the prototypes simply become the system. "We found our requirement specifications were impractical," he said. "But prototyping helped us to draw out the requirements. It also helped because the executives wanted immediate results and didn't have any patience for multiyear processes."

   a. Why is "less definitely more" when designing executive information systems? Is this also true for other information systems?
   b. Why was prototyping used to develop GE Capital's EIS?

   Source: Adapted from Alan Ryan, "EIS: Too Much Stuffing, and It's a Turkey," *Computerworld*, March 19, 1990, p. 71.

REAL WORLD
PROBLEMS

3. American Software Corporation

American Software took the back-door approach to CASE; that is, it began using CASE tools to offload applications development from its mainframe to personal computers. It switched to using Micro Focus's COBOL/2—a COBOL compiler, debugger, and editor—in conjunction with Excelerator, a CASE analysis and design package. American Software can now take structure charts drawn in Excelerator and use them to generate Micro Focus COBOL program code. It also can use pseudo code defined in modules developed by Excelerator to be inserted into Micro Focus COBOL programs as comments.

The move from mainframes reduced overall business application development costs by 20 percent. Response time was reduced from four seconds to less than one. In addition, the company was able to postpone an impending mainframe purchase. The quality of software has also increased. Developing on PCs has resulted in a 30 percent to 40 percent decrease in the number of code errors. American Software attributes this to better testing facilities on the PC and more sophisticated programming capabilities with the Micro Focus package.

a. How did American Software use CASE tools in systems development?

b. What benefits resulted? Why?

Source: Adapted from Andrew Topper, "CASE: A Peek at Commercial Developers Uncovers Some Clues to the Mystery," *Computerworld,* April 19, 1990, p. 63.

4. Petro-Canada

Petro-Canada, a major energy company in Calgary, Alberta, proved large systems can be developed incrementally when it developed a new materials management system. The company urgently needed to create and track purchase orders. To reach that goal quickly, the firm modified working procedures and methodologies, which included using an application generator as a prototyping aid and creating user teams to work with the designers in fashioning screens, files, and reports. The initial prototype of the purchase order system was delivered in six months, about half the time originally planned. Although it was not complete, it was functional. Adapting it to the existing system added an additional two months.

The purchase order system development was carried out independently of other subsystems, which were added later. For example, the subsystem for requisitions proved to be especially difficult to develop. The employees who ordered goods and services by filling out requisition forms were decentralized. The forms were sent to a central purchasing office and were used to generate purchase orders. Because the previous success of the purchase order system had instilled users' confidence, they were more willing to participate than they might have otherwise been in the requisition subsystem's development. Thus, refinement of the purchase order system could proceed along with the development of the requisition system.

a. Why did Petro-Canada take an incremental, prototyping approach to developing business systems?

b. How and why were end users involved?

Source: Adapted from W. Burry Foss, "Early Wins Are Key to System Success," *Datamation,* January 15, 1990, p. 81.

5. Beckman Instruments Incorporated

Business people with killer instincts aren't waiting for software vendors or information center staffers to come up with the next killer application. Instead, they're taking advantage of a new crop of applications development tools that let them write their own software. With the standard computing environment shifting from stand-alone PCs to networked work groups, user-developed applications can now move beyond custom-designed spreadsheets to create departmental business systems. That's because Structured Query Language (SQL), multitasking operating systems, and more powerful workstations give business professionals quick and easy access to corporate databases. This new access, coupled with easy-to-use development tools, lets users employ their intimate understanding of their business and solve their own problems, instead of relying on computing specialists.

Leaving information systems specialists out of the development process has its down side, however. Errors in documentation or problems with data security and integrity can undermine the effectiveness of applications developed by end users. "Applications that are department-specific have to be supported by their users, said Bernard Kaye, manager of telecommunications and teleprocessing at Beckman Instruments Inc., in Fullerton, California. "When the application has been written by the end user, it's next to impossible for a generalized support person to understand the nuances of the system." If work groups are left to their own devices in writing and maintaining systems, Kay worries that basic procedures such as documentation or backing up the network server may go unheeded. The role of the information systems support staff, he said, must therefore move away from writing systems to helping employees conform with corporate computing standards for communications protocols, hardware, and applications development.

a. How and why are business people writing their own "killer applications"?

b. What problems can arise? How can IS specialists help?

Source: Adapted from Craig Zarley, "When Users Write Their Own Applications," *PC Week,* December 16, 1989, p. 66.

6. Western Chemical Corporation

Western Chemical has an IBM AS/400 computer that runs almost around the clock. Over 10,000 customer orders a month flow through the system, drawing on a combined inventory of over 32,000 chemical products stocked at the company's warehouse. Over 60 video display terminals, many with printers, are installed at Western Chemical headquarters, and many of its dealers are connected by telecommunications links to the AS/400. Orders are received by phone or mail and entered into the system by order entry personnel at video display terminals, or they are entered directly by dealers who have installed terminals to Western Chemical. Entry of orders is assisted by formatted screens that help operators follow data entry procedures to enter required information into the system, where it is stored on the magnetic disks of the AS/400.

As the order is entered, the AS/400 checks the availability of the parts, allocates the stock, and updates customer and part databases stored on the computer's magnetic disks. It then sends the order pick list to the warehouse printer, where it is used by warehouse personnel to fill the order. The company president has a terminal in his office, as do the controller, sales manager, inventory manager, and other executives. They use database management inquiry commands to get responses and reports concerning sales orders, customers, and inventory and to review product demand and service trends.

a. What business problems and opportunities are being solved by the Western Chemical information system?
b. Use one or more tools of analysis and design (system flowchart, data flow diagram, system component matrix, etc.) to analyze the Western Chemical information system.
c. Can you think of any improvements to the system? Explain how they would help the business position of Western Chemical. Document your suggestions by making changes to the material you prepared in part (b).

7. Restaurant Data Entry Displays
Develop data entry screens that could take the place of the paper order form used at many restaurants to capture customer food orders. Assume the food servers would use a hand-held computer with a four-inch display screen. Also assume the information would be displayed on a 12-inch screen that could easily be read by the restaurant's cooks. Use your own experience and observations or interview a food server and cook. Prepare a mock-up of the proposed screen.

a. Use a paper layout form or the report generation capabilities of a database management or other software package.
b. Defend your design.

8. Laurentian Industries, Inc.
Develop a display screen mock-up or prototype for a sales manager at Laurentian Industries who must analyze sales performance. Figure 11–22 is an example of a sales analysis display. How would you improve it if you were one of their sales managers?

a. Change the display by adding or deleting some of the types of information shown. Defend your design change.
b. Improve the layout or format of the screen. Defend your design.
c. Design two or more sales analysis screens to give you sales performance information. Link them together by using an opening menu and prompts. Defend your design prototype.

LAURENTIAN INDUSTRIES , INC.
COMPARATIVE SALES ANALYSIS BY CUSTOMER
FOR EACH SALESPERSON
PERIOD ENDING 07/31/--

SLP. NO.	CUST. NO.	SALESPERSON/CUSTOMER NAME	THIS PERIOD THIS YEAR	THIS PERIOD LAST YEAR
10		A R WESTON		
	1426	HYDRO CYCLES INC	3,210.26	4,312.06
	2632	RUPP AQUA CYCLES	7,800.02	2,301.98
	3217	SEA PORT WEST CO	90.00CR	421.06
		SALESPERSON TOTALS	10,920.28	7,035.10
12		H T BRAVEMAN		
	0301	BOLLINGER ASSOCIATES	100.96	0.00

Figure 11-22   An example of a sales analysis display.

SELECTED REFERENCES

1. Andersen Consulting. *Foundations of Business Systems.* Hinsdale, Ill.: Dryden Press, 1989.

2. Carlyle, Ralph. "Is Your Data Ready for the Repository?" *Datamation*, January 1, 1990.

3. Chen, Minder; Jay Nunamaker; and E. Sue Weber. "Computer-Aided Software Engineering: Present Status and Future Directions." *Data Base*, Spring 1989.

4. Davis, Gordon. "Caution: User-Developed Systems Can Be Dangerous to Your Organization." In *End User Computing: Concepts, Issues, and Applications*, ed. R. Ryan Nelson. New York: John Wiley & Sons, 1988.

5. Konsynski, Benn. "Advances in Information Systems Design." In *The Management of Information Systems*, ed. Paul Gray, William King, Ephram McLean, and Hugh Watson. Hinsdale, Ill.: Dryden Press, 1989.

6. Kozor, Kenneth. *Humanized Information Systems Analysis and Design.* New York: McGraw-Hill, 1989.

7. Kraushaar, James, and Larry Shirland. "A Prototyping Method for Applications Development by End Users and Information System Specialists," *MIS Quarterly*, December 1987.

8. Necco, Charles; Carl Gordon; and Nancy Tsai, "Systems Analysis and Design: Current Practices." *MIS Quarterly*, December 1987.

9. Newman, William. "SAA: IBM's Commitment to the Future." *Information Executive*, Winter 1989.

10. O'Brien, James, and Craig Van Lengen. "Using an Information System Status Model for Systems Analysis and Design: A Missing Dimension." *CIS Educator Forum*, December 1988.

11. Senn, James. *Analysis and Design of Information Systems.* 2nd ed. New York: McGraw-Hill, 1989.

12. Whitten, Jeffrey; Lonnie Bentley; and Vic Barlow. *Systems Analysis and Design Methods.* 2nd ed. Homewood, Ill.: Richard D. Irwin, 1989.

PLANNING AND IMPLEMENTING INFORMATION SYSTEMS

■ **Chapter Outline**

■ Learning Objectives

The purpose of this chapter is to give you an understanding of how managers should plan and implement the use of information systems in an organization by analyzing (1) the information systems planning process and (2) the evaluation and acquisition of information system resources.

Section I of the chapter discusses the process of organizational and information systems planning at the strategic, tactical, and operational levels.

Section II explores major activities and management considerations in the implementation process for information systems.

After reading and studying this chapter, you should be able to:

1. Discuss the role of planning in organizations and the purpose of strategic, tactical, and operational planning for information systems.

2. Give examples of how planning methodologies and tools support the information systems planning process.

3. Identify the activities involved in the information systems implementation process and give examples of some of the major management techniques and issues involved.

4. Discuss several evaluation factors that should be considered in evaluating the acquisition of hardware, software, and vendor support.

Section I: Information Systems Planning

INTRODUCTION

Planning is deciding what to do before you do it. Most of us would agree that planning is an important ingredient of success. If you think about the best way to reach a goal before you begin to reach for it, you are planning, and your chances of accomplishing your goal should be enhanced. That's why organizations and their managers plan. They go through an **organizational planning process** of (1) evaluating what they have accomplished and the resources they have acquired, (2) analyzing their environment, (3) anticipating future developments, (4) deciding what goals they want to achieve, and (5) deciding what actions to take to achieve their goals.

The result of this planning process is called a **plan,** which formally articulates the actions we feel are necessary to achieve our goals. Thus, a plan is a basis for action. Plans lead to actions, actions produce results, and part of planning is learning from results. That's why we said in Chapter 9 that planning is one of the *functions of management.* In this context, the planning process should be followed by implementation, which should be followed by control measures, which provide feedback for planning. Figure 12–1 illustrates the organizational planning process.

THE ROLE OF
INFORMATION
SYSTEM PLANNING

Information systems planning is an important component of organizational planning. Information systems technology can play a vital role in the efficiency of a company's operations, the effectiveness of managerial decision making, and the success of an organization's strategic initiatives. Therefore, the IS planning process should be incorporated into the strategic, tactical, and operational planning of the organization. Figure 12–2 illustrates the activities and outputs

Figure 12–1 The organizational planning process. Note how implementation and control methods provide feedback for the planning process.

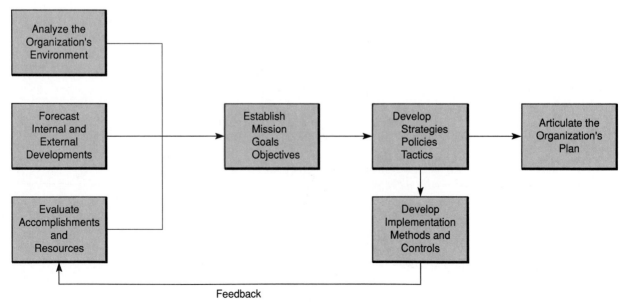

Figure 12–2 The information systems planning process. Note the activities, considerations, and outputs in strategic, tactical, and operational planning.

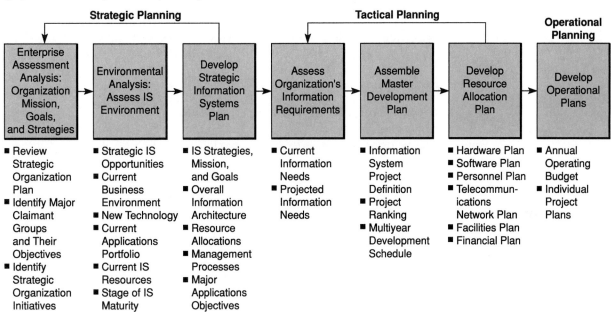

Source: Adapted from James Wetherbe, *Systems Analysis and Design*, 3rd Ed. (St. Paul, Minn.: West Publishing, 1988), p. 309.

of strategic IS planning and its interrelationship with the tactical and operational IS planning process.

A growing number of business firms are developing strategic IS for managing the information system resources of their organizations. This planning process involves a study of how information systems technology can contribute to the achievement of the goals contained in the strategic plan for the entire organization. This process is sometimes called *enterprise analysis*. The emphasis is on planning computer-based information systems that will improve the firm's performance and competitive position. Enterprise analysis frequently includes *stage analysis*. This is an analysis of the information systems needs of an organization based on its current stage in its growth cycle and its use of computers. Strategic IS planning also requires *environmental analysis*, in which the external business and technical environments and the internal organizational environment are analyzed. Assessment is made of information systems problems and opportunities and of the capabilities of hardware, software, and people resources [1, 12].

The **strategic IS plan** formulates policies, objectives, and strategies for delivering information services and allocating information systems resources. It frequently contains an analysis of a firm's information systems *application portfolio*. This analysis spotlights the types of IS applications being developed, the business functions being supported, and the resources being allocated (as a percentage of revenue or assets) to the information systems function. The strategic plan, which includes a tentative timetable for IS development projects and estimates of resource requirements and expected benefits, is then presented to top management for review and final decision [10].

Strategic Information Systems Planning

Of course, strategic IS planning is not as mechanical as it may sound. Information technology is so complex, and its rate of change so fast, that strategic planning can be quite difficult. Thus, the strategic IS plans of many companies may look three to five years into the future, but are rigorously reviewed every three to six months. Therefore, flexibility is a key attribute of strategic IS planning, given the rapid pace of technological as well as business innovation.

Benefits of Strategic IS Planning

The process of strategic information systems planning can help an organization achieve significant advantages. Business firms have found that strategic planning helps achieve benefits such as the following [1]:

☐ Pinpoints ways to achieve competitive advantage by using information systems as a strategic weapon.

☐ Stimulates the creative use of information technology and encourages innovation in applying it to the needs of the organization.

☐ Redeploys financial and human resources to the most important and strategic information systems projects for the business.

☐ Encourages the integration of existing and future information systems to eliminate information redundancies and inconsistencies and the inefficient use of information systems resources.

☐ Establishes priorities and time frames for the development of information systems in the future.

Tactical and Operational Planning

As Figure 12–2 showed, tactical and operational planning are important components of the information systems planning process. **Tactical information systems planning** starts with a specific assessment of an organization's current and projected information requirements. These requirements are then subdivided into individual project proposals for the development of new or improved information systems. These projects are then evaluated, ranked, and fitted into a multiyear development plan. Finally, a resource allocation plan is developed to specify the hardware, software, and personnel resources; telecommunications facilities; and financial commitments needed to implement the master development plan.

Operational information systems planning involves preparing annual operating budgets and planning for individual information systems development projects. Annual operating budgets specify the allocation of financial and other resources needed to support the organization's information services department in day-to-day operations and systems development and maintenance activities. This also holds true for end user departments and other work groups that do a lot of their own information processing and applications development.

Project planning is an important operational planning function. It involves the development of plans, procedures, and schedules for an information systems development project. Such planning is an important part of a **project management** effort that plans and controls the implementation of systems development projects. This is necessary if a project is to be completed on time and within its proposed budget and if it is to meet its design objectives.

Several techniques of project management produce charts to help plan and control projects. One is the Gantt chart, which specifies the times allowed for the various activities required in information systems development. Another is

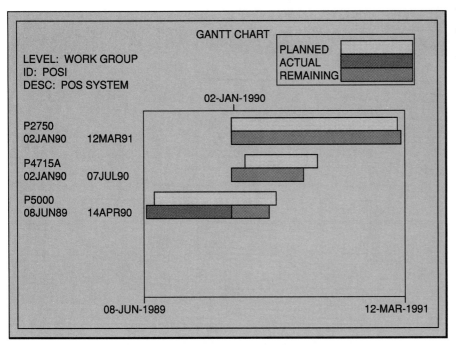

Courtesy AGS Management Systems, Inc.

Figure 12–3 A Gantt chart for a systems development project produced by a project management package.

produced by network methodologies such as the PERT system (Program Evaluation and Review Techniques), which develops a network diagram of required activities. Network methodologies view a project as a *network* of distinct tasks and milestones and specify the amount of time budgeted for the completion of each task. Figure 12–3 is an example of a Gantt chart for a systems development project prepared by a project management software package.

INFORMATION SYSTEMS PLANNING METHODOLOGIES

Many organizations have found that they need to use a formal **information systems planning methodology** to ensure that all important planning activities and products are accomplished and produced. This methodology specifies how an organization can translate its strategic goals into a detailed information systems development plan to achieve those goals. Many formal planning methodologies exist, including IBM's Business Systems Planning (BSP) and John Rockart's Critical Success Factors (CSF). We will discuss each of these methods briefly in order to give you an idea of how they help managers do strategic and tactical information systems planning.

Business Systems Planning

IBM defines **Business Systems Planning** (BSP) as a structured approach that assists an organization in developing information systems plans to satisfy its short- and long-term information requirements [6]. One of the basic premises of BSP methodology is that an organization's information system should be planned from the top down and implemented piece by piece from the bottom up. Figure 12–4 illustrates this view of the BSP approach.

Top-down planning requires that a group of top executives lay out the strategic mission and objectives of the organization to a study team composed of managers, professionals, and information systems specialists. The study team then systematically interviews manages throughout the organization to deter-

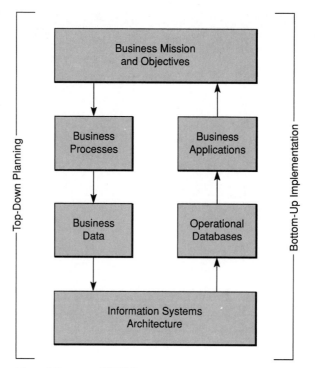

Adapted Courtesy of IBM Corporation.

mine how these objectives are implemented in the basic functions (marketing, manufacturing, etc.) and processes (order entry, shipping, receiving, etc.) of the business. Next, the team examines the types, or *classes*, of data needed to support these basic processes. Finally, it designs an *information architecture* that defines the relationships between classes of data and the business processes. The information architecture specifies the basic structure, content, and relationships of the organizational databases that provide the data needed to support basic business processes.

Bottom-up implementation involves application development activities that are performed by end users and information systems professionals. They develop information system applications (such as sales transaction processing) that rely on databases whose design was determined by the information architecture. Each application should therefore serve a business function that supports the mission and objectives of the organization.

Critical Success Factors

The **critical success factors** (CSF) approach is another important methodology for information systems planning. It can be used by itself or incorporated into other planning methodologies as a key component of their planning process. This approach was developed by John Rockart and others who were dissatisfied with the lack of emphasis on the key information needs of managers in other information systems planning methodologies [8, 9]. Its major premise is that the information requirements of an organization should be determined by its **critical success factors,** a small number of key factors that executives consider critical to the success of the enterprise. These are key areas where successful performance will assure the success of the organization and the attainment of its goals. Examples of goals and critical success factors are shown in Figure 12–5.

Organizational Goals	Critical Success Factors
For-profit companies	**Automotive industry**
Earnings per share	Styling
Return on investment	Dealer system
Market share	Cost control
New product success	Energy standards
Nonprofit hospitals	**Nonprofit hospitals**
Provide excellent health care	Differentiation from other hospitals
Meet the health care needs of the community	Cost control
	Occupancy rate
	Health care standards

Figure 12–5 Examples of goals versus critical success factors. Success in a firm's CSFs should assure the attainment of its organizational goals.

Thus, critical success factors are used as the basis for providing information to managers. Information systems are designed to continually measure performance in each CSF and report this information to management. CSFs may change over time as the organization, its industry, and its environment change. CSFs also vary from manager to manager, organization to organization, and industry to industry. Therefore, the CSF approach is used as a component of information systems planning to determine the critical success factors of individual managers as well as of the entire organization.

Figure 12–6 illustrates the activities of a CSF approach to information systems planning. Two or three different interviews are held with groups of managers to determine their individual critical success factors and their view of the CSFs for the organization. Managers are asked to identify their goals and the critical success factors that would assure the attainment of those goals. This includes consideration of the competitive strategies of the firm, its position in the industry, and its economic and political environment. Managers are asked to identify a limited number of key areas (about 5 to 10) where "things have to go right," "failure would hurt most," or they would most want information about if they had been gone for a while. These are their critical success factors.

For example, managers in the supermarket industry may consider pricing,

Figure 12–6 A critical success factors approach. Note the steps involved in defining the critical success factors of organization and implementing them in an IS architecture and portfolio.

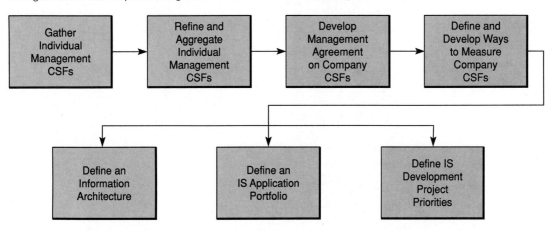

product mix, inventory turnover, and sales promotions as critical success factors. Performance in these areas could be measured by gross margin and net margin percentages, product shelf space comparisons, inventory turnover ratios, and tracking sales results with the timing and amount of sales promotions.

COMPUTER-AIDED PLANNING TOOLS

The planning process can be quite difficult and time-consuming. That's what gives organizations the "we don't have time to plan" excuse for not using a formal planning process. So vendors have developed computer-aided planning (CAP) tools to help ease the burden of planning. One example is PC Prism, from Index Technology Corporation, the makers of the Excelerator CASE tool. PC Prism is a menu-driven software package that helps end users develop strategic, tactical, and operational information systems plans. It provides generic planning features that can support other planning methodologies, such as the BSP and CSFs methodologies. PC Prism is used to define a *planning environment* (strategic, tactical, or operational) and *planning structures* such as critical success factors, organizational units, business processes, data structures, and so on. Then it is used to identify and analyze relationships between the planning structures and develop an *enterprise model* of the business. See Figure 12–7. The enterprise model then helps planners evaluate alternative planning assumptions and accomplish *data planning*, as we discussed in Chapter 6 [9].

ENTERPRISE MODEL

Figure 12–7 An enterprise model of a business developed using the PC Prism planning package.

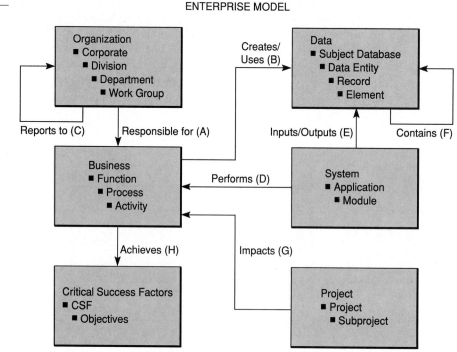

Courtesy Index Technology Corporation.

REAL WORLD CASE

AT&T Corporation

Using information technology to generate competitive marketing advantages was the challenge that faced AT&T when it set about creating a new long-distance telephone-calling card. The card, to be introduced to more than 40 million subscribers at the rate of 110,000 customers per day over 18 months, was needed to meet a court ruling that by Jan. 1, 1992, AT&T could no longer rely on regional Bell operating company billing services. However, the calling card also represents a focus for marketing new AT&T customer services and a means of warding off competition. Therefore, said Earl Hoskins, manager of AT&T Consumer Markets and Service Group, AT&T's business objectives had to be integrated into the monumental $350 million many-year information systems development effort.

"Instead of just developing individual information systems," Hoskins said, "we would have to take a holistic view and see how each system fit into the service." This, he noted, required AT&T to carry out systems development as a continuous process from the initial strategic business planning through to the production of COBOL application programs. AT&T's strategy relied on using computer-aided software engineering (CASE) tools to support competitive advantage. It is based on a concept called *computer-aided planning* (CAP). Hoskins noted that he set his sights on CAP soon after the start of the calling card development effort in late 1986. "It did not take us long," he said, "to realize that we did not understand what we were trying to do."

AT&T selected PC Prism, a strategic planning software product from Index Technology, to implement its CAP strategy. The software enabled planners to play out what-if scenarios to identify appropriate customer services for the new calling card. The planners could also define the features of needed information systems by evaluating customer needs and AT&T's internal and external goals, strategies, resources, and technology. PC Prism information and models were then converted by Index Excelerator CASE design and analysis tools into detailed business-process flow diagrams.

With the design phase of the project substantially completed, most of the 42 mainframe applications are at the stage of user-acceptance testing. The company, Hoskins said, has saved thousands of hours of programming because of better communications between system designers and end users. In addition, required changes can now be identified earlier in the systems development life cycle, when they are easier and less costly to fix. He estimated that, for every hour spent in systems planning, five to eight hours have been saved at the coding, testing, and implementing stages.

Strategic planning for the new calling card was done largely by end users, ranging from middle-level managers to corporate officers, who tested *what-if* scenarios at monitors during CAP sessions. The design factors and elements which the CAP participants gained and interrelated included the *type* of scenario, the *in-state* probable card marketplace in the 1990s, and the market *conditions* necessary for a particular in-state market to exist. To these were added political, regulatory, or competitive *events* and their probability and influence on market conditions, interrelated to *market force* business risks or opportunities. A final element was that of *response* to every identified risk or opportunity. As a result, seven possible strategies were developed to enable AT&T to drive market conditions, instead of reacting to them.

Application Questions

☐ Why did AT&T have to do strategic planning when developing a new calling card?

☐ How did PC Prism help them do strategic planning?

☐ What benefits resulted from computer-aided planning?

Source: Adapted from Mike Feuche, "AT&T Employs CASE Strategy for Competitive Edge," *MIS Week*, February 5, 1990, p. 17.

Section II: Implementing Information Systems

INTRODUCTION

Planning is important, but so is implementation; that is, doing what you planned to do. That's why some planning methodologies include implementation activities as a final step of the planning process. However, it is better to view implementation as a process that carries out the operational plans developed at the end of the information systems planning process. Therefore, implementation is an important step in assuring the successful development of information systems for end users.

The implementation process for information systems was introduced in Chapter 11 as a major step that followed the investigation, analysis, and design stages of the systems development process. Implementation involves a variety of acquisition, testing, documentation, installation, and conversion activities. It also involves the training of end users in the operation and use of a new information system. Thus, implementation is a vital step in assuring the success of new systems. Even a well-designed system can fail if it is not properly implemented. Figure 12–8 outlines the major activities of the implementation process. In this section, we will concentrate on evaluating the acquisition and installation of information system resources and other managerial implementation issues.

ACQUISITION OF HARDWARE, SOFTWARE, AND SERVICES

A major implementation activity for both end users and information systems specialists involves acquiring **information system resources** (hardware, software, and personnel) and **external services** from many sources in the computer industry. Figure 12–9 lists the top 10 mainframe, microcomputer, minicomputer, software, services, and data communications companies in 1990. Of course, there are many other firms in the computer industry that supply hardware, software, and services. For example, large companies such as Intel and Motorola produce microprocessors, memory chips, and other devices, while retail chains such as Computerland and Businessland, and thousands of consulting firms provide a range of IS services.

Figure 12–8 A summary of the implementation process. Implementation activities are needed to transform IS plans into successful information systems for end users.

Acquisition: Evaluate and acquire necessary hardware and software resources and information system services. Screen vendor proposals.

Software development: Develop any computer programs that will not be acquired externally as software packages. Make any necessary modifications to software packages that are acquired.

Training: Educate and train management, end users, and operating personnel. Use consultants or training programs to develop user competencies.

Testing: Test and make necessary corrections to the programs, procedures, and hardware used by a new system.

Documentation: Record and communicate detailed system specifications, including procedures for end users and operating personnel and examples of input/output displays and reports.

Conversion: Convert from the use of a present system to the operation of a new or improved system. This may involve operating both new and old systems in *parallel* for a trial period, operation of a *pilot* system on a trial basis at one location, *phasing in* the new system one location at a time, or an immediate *cutover* to the new system.

Figure 12-9   The top ten companies in the computer industry by major product or service categories. Note the major presence of IBM and multinational corporations.

Mainframe Systems			Minicomputer Systems			Microcomputer Systems		
Rank	Company	Revenues ($ millions)	Rank	Company	Revenues ($ millions)	Rank	Company	Revenues ($ millions)
1	IBM	12,509.0	1	IBM	6,753.0	1	IBM	8,343.0
2	Fujitsu	3,261.5	2	Digital Equipment	2,670.0	2	Apple	3,574.2
3	Hitachi	3,116.5	3	NEC	1,471.3	3	NEC	3,116.5
4	NEC	2,391.8	4	Fujitsu	1,304.6	4	Compaq	2,876.1
5	Amdahl	1,470.8	5	Unisys	1,122.0	5	Groupe Bull	1,681.0
6	Unisys	1,200.0	6	Toshiba	978.4	6	Olivetti	1,523.4
7	Groupe Bull	840.5	7	Hewlett-Packard	750.0	7	Toshiba	1,340.8
8	Cray Research	633.6	8	Tandem	709.6	8	Tandy	1,330.0
9	Siemens	611.7	9	Olivetti	607.0	9	Unisys	1,300.0
10	STC	466.1	10	Wang	570.0	10	Fujitsu	869.7

Computer Software			IS Services			Data Communications		
Rank	Company	Revenues ($ millions)	Rank	Company	Revenues ($ millions)	Rank	Company	Revenues ($ millions)
1	IBM	8,424.0	1	Elec. Data Sys.	2,477.9	1	IBM	3,000.0
2	Fujitsu	1,449.5	2	Auto. Data Proc.	1,689.5	2	AT&T	1,445.0
3	Comp. Assoc.	1,290.2	3	TRW	1,565.0	3	NTT	1,355.3
4	NEC	1,065.4	4	Computer Science	1,442.8	4	Siemens	1,345.7
5	Unisys	875.0	5	Digital Equipment	1,386.7	5	Canon	1,304.6
6	Digital Equipment	825.0	6	Arthur Andersen	1,225.7	6	Northern Telecom	1,150.0
7	Microsoft	820.8	7	IBM	1,200.0	7	Matsushita	906.0
8	Hitachi	724.8	8	Cap Gemini	1,103.4	8	Ricoh	801.1
9	Siemens	638.3	9	NTT	898.7	9	Fujitsu	797.3
10	Hewlett-Packard	600.0	10	Unisys	825.0	10	Alcatel	756.4

Source: Adapted from "Market Insights," *Datamation*, June 15, 1990, pp. 184–97.

Hardware Suppliers

The primary sources of computer hardware are the major computer manufacturers, who produce many sizes of computer systems as well as peripheral equipment and media. Other companies specialize in microcomputers, minicomputers, small computer systems, special-purpose computers, or the production of peripheral input, output, and storage devices such as video terminals or magnetic disk drives.

Two other categories of computer hardware manufacturers are the *original equipment manufacturer* (OEM) and the *plug-compatible manufacturer* (PCM). OEMs produce and sell computers by assembling components produced by other hardware suppliers. PCMs manufacture computer mainframes and peripheral devices that are specifically designed to be compatible (by just "plugging in") with the mainframes or peripherals of major computer manufacturers, especially IBM and Digital Equipment Corporation. Such firms claim that their hardware is similar to that produced by the major manufacturers but provides better performance at lower cost. For example, the Amdahl Corporation produces large mainframe computers that are marketed as lower-priced versions of IBM mainframes.

Computer retailers sell microcomputers and peripherals to individuals and small businesses. They are an important type of hardware supplier resulting from the development of microcomputer systems used as personal computers and small business computers. There are thousands of retail computer stores, including independent retailers and national chains such as Computerland, Businessland, and the Radio Shack stores of the Tandy Corporation.

Another important source of computer hardware is *computer leasing companies,* which purchase computers from computer manufacturers and lease them to computer users at rates that may be 10 percent to 20 percent lower than manufacturers' rental prices. Leasing companies are able to offer lower prices because they are willing to gamble that they can recover their costs and make a profit at the lower rates before their computers become obsolete. A final source of computer hardware is *used-computer-equipment companies,* which purchase used computers and peripheral equipment from computer users and sell them at substantial discounts.

Software Suppliers

Software can be obtained from several sources if computer users do not wish to develop their own programs. Computer manufacturers are the largest source of software in the computer industry. They supply most of the system software (such as operating systems and other control programs and service programs) for computer users and are the major source of application packages. However, independent software companies, which specialize in the development of software packages, have become major software suppliers. Microsoft Corporation and Lotus Development Corporation are prominent examples. You can also get software from computer retailers, mail-order companies, and from other computer users. *Value-added resellers* (VARs) are another important source of software (and hardware). They typically provide industry-specific software for use with the computer systems of selected manufacturers.

External Service Suppliers

The major sources of external IS services are computer manufacturers, computer service centers, computer retailers, time-sharing companies, facilities management companies, systems integrators, and independent consultants. These and other types of firms in the computer industry offer a variety of services. For example, *computer service centers* (or service bureaus) provide off-premises computer processing of customer jobs, and *time-sharing service* companies provide realtime processing services to subscribers using remote terminals. *Facilities management* companies take over complete responsibility for an organization's computer operations. *Systems integrators* assume responsibility for developing and implementing large systems development projects that may involve many vendors and subcontractors. Other services are also offered, including computer-time rental, systems design services, contract programming, consulting, education, and hardware maintenance. Many companies, especially computer manufacturers, supply several or almost all of these services.

End User Computer Suppliers

We have indicated that end users must rely on several sources in the computer industry for microcomputer hardware, software, and services. Typically, microcomputer hardware manufacturers and software companies use computer retailers and mail-order companies as their major methods of reaching microcomputer users. Many larger business and professional organizations, educational institutions, and government agencies also have employee purchase plans that provide computer hardware and software at substantial discounts. These *corporate buying plans* are arranged through negotiations with hardware manufacturers and software companies. Many department and discount stores and other retailers may offer a limited amount of computer hardware and software. Used computer hardware is typically available from previous owners and used-equipment dealers. Finally, services such as education, maintenance, and contract programming are typically offered by computer retailers and independent consultants.

How do computer-using organizations evaluate and select hardware and software? Typically, they require suppliers to present bids and proposals based on *system specifications* developed during the design stage of systems development. Minimum acceptable physical and performance characteristics for all hardware and software requirements are established. Most large business firms and all government agencies formalize these requirements by listing them in a document called an RFP (request for proposal) or RFQ (request for quotation). The RFP or RFQ is then sent to appropriate vendors, who use it as the basis for preparing a proposed purchase agreement. See Figure 12–10.

THE EVALUATION PROCESS

REQUEST FOR PROPOSAL

ABC DEPARTMENT STORES INC.

PHONE (602)323-4557   BOX 5124   PHOENIX, ARIZONA 86581-0056

REQUEST NO	PAGE	OF
0001	1	1

ACME COMPUTER SUPPLY CO.
2704 E. MCDOWELL ROAD
PHOENIX, ARIZONA 85283

TERMS: (1) YOU ARE INVITED TO BID ON GOODS AND/OR SERVICES ITEMIZED BELOW.
(2) THIS REQUEST FOR PROPOSAL IS NOT INTENDED TO BE RESTRICTIVE. BRAND NAME OR MANUFACTURER'S NAME MAY BE USED FOR PURPOSE OF DESCRIPTION AND/OR TO ESTABLISH THE QUALITY DESIRED. BIDS ARE NOT RESTRICTED TO SUCH BRAND OR MANUFACTURER.
(3) THE ATTENTION OF THE BIDDER IS DIRECTED TO THE TERMS AND CONDITIONS ON THE REVERSE SIDE WHICH ARE INCORPORATED HEREIN.

WE RESERVE THE RIGHT TO REJECT ANY AND ALL BIDS.

RETURN THIS QUOTATION TO PURCHASING DEPT. AT ABOVE ADDRESS

DATE	BUYER	REQUISITION NO.		
6/24/9X	G. WILLIAMS	0001	QUOTATION DUE DATE	7/24/9X

LINE	OBJECT CODE	QUANTITY	UNIT	PART NUMBER AND DESCRIPTION	UNIT PRICE	AMOUNT
1	08561	10	1	IMPACT DOT MATRIX PRINTER		
				MINIMUM SPECIFICATIONS:		
				FULLY COMPATIBLE WITH ALL IBM PERSONAL SYSTEM/2 MODELS		
				PRINTING SPEED: 200 CHARACTERS PER SECOND		
				PRINTING DIRECTION: BIDIRECTIONAL, LOGIC SEEKING		
				COLUMN WIDTH: 80 COLUMNS PICA		
				PAPER FEED: ADJUSTABLE SPROCKET FEED		
				PRINT HEAD: DISPOSABLE 24 PIN IMPACT DOT MATRIX		
				RIBBON TYPE: CARTRIDGE RIBBON		
				GRAPHICS CAPABILITY: HIGH-RESOLUTION GRAPHICS. SIX DENSITIES AND A GRAPHICS CHARACTER SET.		

IMPORTANT ➔	SHOW ARIZONA AND LOCAL SALES TAX WHEN APPLICABLE. IF NOT SHOWN AS SEPARATE ITEM, IT WILL BE ASSUMED TO BE INCLUDED IN UNIT AND TOTAL PRICES.	SALES TAX	
THIS IS NOT AN ORDER		**TOTAL**	

SHIPMENT WILL BE MADE	TERMS	F.O.B. POINT
Days after Receipt of Order		ABC DEPARTMENT STORES PHOENIX, ARIZONA

We quote as shown, except as otherwise noted. The undersigned agrees that this proposal is a firm offer which shall be irrevocable and open for acceptance for _____ calendar days (60 calendar days unless otherwise specified) from the date set for submission of quotes.

SIGNATURE   DATE

Figure 12–10   Example of a request for proposal (RFP). Note how it specifies the capabilities that must be met in the supplier's bid for 10-dot matrix printers.

Organizations may use a scoring system of evaluation when there are several competing proposals for a hardware or software acquisition. Each evaluation factor is given a certain number of maximum possible points. Then each competing proposal is assigned points for each factor, depending on how well it meets the specifications of end users. Scoring each evaluation factor for several proposals helps organize and document the evaluation process. It also spotlights the strengths and weaknesses of each proposal. See Figure 12–11.

A formal evaluation process reduces the possibility of buying inadequate or unnecessary computer hardware or software. Badly organized computer operations, inadequate systems development, and poor purchasing practices may cause inadequate or unnecessary acquisitions. Therefore, it is necessary to use a variety of evaluation methods to measure several key factors for computer hardware, software, and services. See Figures 12–12, 12–13, and 12–14.

Whatever the claims of hardware manufacturers and software suppliers, the performance of hardware and software must be demonstrated and evaluated. Independent hardware and software information services (such as the Datapro and Auerbach reporting services) can be used to gain detailed information and evaluations. Hardware and software should be demonstrated and evaluated. This can be done on your own premises or by visiting the operations of other

Figure 12–11   An example of a scoring system for evaluating spreadsheet software packages.

REPORT CARD High-End PC Spreadsheets	Info World weighting	Excel/Windows Version 2.1	Lotus 1-2-3 Release 2.2	Lotus 1-2-3 Release 3.0	QUATTRO PRO Version 1.0	Supercalc 5 Version 5.0
Price		$495	$495	$595	$495	$495
Performance						
Formulas/analysis	(100)	Excellent	Good	Good	Good	Good
Compatibility	(50)	Very Good	Excellent	Excellent	Excellent	Very Good
Speed	(75)	Very Good	Very Good	Very Good	Very Food	Satisfactory
Database	(75)	Very Good	Satisfactory	Very Good	Excellent	Very Good
Graphics	(75)	Good	Poor	Good	Excellent	Very Good
Output	(50)	Excellent	Very Good	Satisfactory	Very Good	Good
Macros	(50)	Excellent	Good	Good	Excellent	Good
Consolidation and linking	(50)	Very Good	Satisfactory	Excellent	Excellent	Very Good
Capacity	(50)	Good	Very Good	Very Good	Very Good	Good
Documentation	(75)	Excellent	Excellent	Excellent	Excellent	Very Good
Ease of learning	(50)	Very Good	Very Good	Very Good	Excellent	Very Good
Ease of use	(100)	Excellent	Very Good	Excellent	Very Good	Good
Error handling	(50)	Very Good	Poor	Very Good	Very Good	Very Good
Support						
Support policies	(25)	Very Good	Very Good	Very Good	Very Good	Satisfactory
Technical support	(25)	Very Good	Satisfactory	Satisfactory	Good	Satisfactory
Value	(100)	Excellent	Very Good	Excellent	Excellent	Very Good
Final Scores		**8.5**	**6.6**	**7.9**	**8.6**	**6.7**

INFO WORLD

Courtesy Info World.

Hardware Evaluation Factors	Rating
Performance What is its speed, capacity, and throughput?	
Cost What is its lease or purchase price? What will be its cost of operations and maintenance?	
Reliability What is the risk of malfunction and its maintenance requirements? What are its error control and diagnostic features?	
Availability When is the firm delivery date?	
Compatibility Is it compatible with existing hardware and software? Is it compatible with hardware provided by competing suppliers?	
Modularity Can it be expanded and upgraded by acquiring modular "add on" units?	
Technology In what year of its product life cycle is it? Does it use a new untested technology or does it run the risk of obsolescence?	
Ergonomics Has it been "human factors engineered" with the user in mind? Is it "user friendly," designed to be safe, comfortable, and easy to use?	
Connectivity Can it be easily connected to wide area and local area networks of different types of computers and peripherals?	
Environmental Requirements What are its electrical power, air-conditioning, and other environmental requirements?	
Software Is system and application software available that can best use this hardware?	
Support Are the services required to support and maintain it available?	
Overall Rating	

Figure 12–12 A summary of major hardware evaluation factors. Notice how you could use this to evaluate a computer system or peripheral device.

users who have similar types of hardware or software. Other end users are frequently the best source of information needed to evaluate the claims of manufacturers and suppliers. Vendors should be willing to provide the names of such users.

Large computer users frequently evaluate proposed hardware and software by requiring the processing of special *benchmark* test programs and test data. Users can then evaluate test results to determine which hardware device or software package displayed the best performance characteristics. Special software simulators may also be available that simulate the processing of typical jobs on several computers and evaluate their performances.

Hardware Evaluation Factors

When you evaluate computer *hardware*, you should investigate specific *physical and performance characteristics* for each hardware component to be acquired. This is true whether you are evaluating mainframes, microcomputers, or peripheral devices. Specific questions must be answered concerning many important factors. These **hardware evaluation factors** and questions are summarized in Figure 12–12.

Notice that there is much more to evaluating hardware than determining the fastest and cheapest computing device. For example, the question of possible obsolescence must be addressed by making a *technology* evaluation. The factor of *ergonomics* is also very important. **Ergonomics** is the science and technology (sometimes called *human factors engineering*), that tries to ensure that computers and other technologies are *user friendly*, that is, safe, comfortable, and easy to use. *Connectivity* is another important evaluation factor since so many computer systems are now interconnected within wide area or local area telecommunications networks.

Software Evaluation Factors

You should evaluate *software* according to many factors that are similar to those used for hardware evaluation. Thus, the factors of *performance, cost, reliability, availability, compatibility, modularity, technology, ergonomics,* and *support* should be used to evaluate proposed software acquisitions. In addition, however, the **software evaluation factors** summarized in Figure 12–13 must

Figure 12–13 A summary of selected software evaluation factors. Note that most of the hardware evaluation factors in Figure 12–12 can also be used to evaluate software packages.

Software Evaluation Factors	Rating
Efficiency Is the software a well-written system of computer instructions that does not use much memory capacity or CPU time?	
Flexibility Can it handle its processing assignments easily without major modification?	
Security Does it provide control procedures for errors, malfunctions, and improper use?	
Language Is it written in a programming language that is used by our computer programmers and users?	
Documentation Is the software well documented? Does it include helpful user instructions?	
Hardware Does existing hardware have the features required to best use this software?	
Other Factors What are its performance, cost, reliability, availability, compatibility, modularity, technology, ergonomics, and support characteristics? (Use the hardware evaluation factor questions in Figure 12–12.)	
Overall Rating	

also be considered. You should answer the questions they generate in order to properly evaluate software purchases. For example, some software packages require too much memory capacity and are notoriously slow, hard to use, or poorly documented. They are not a good selection for most end users, even if offered at attractive prices.

Most vendors or suppliers of hardware and software products offer a variety of **vendor support services** to assist you during the installation and operation of hardware and software. Assistance during installation or conversion of hardware and software, employee training, customer "hot lines," and hardware maintenance are examples of the services that should be evaluated. Some of these services are provided without cost by hardware manufacturers and software suppliers. Other types of services can be contracted for at a negotiated price. Evaluation factors and questions for vendor support services are summarized in Figure 12–14.

Evaluation of Vendor Support

Vendor Support Evaluation Factors	Rating
Performance What has been their past performance in view of their past promises?	
Systems Development Are systems analysis and programming consultants available? What are their quality and cost?	
Maintenance Is equipment maintenance provided? What is its quality and cost?	
Conversion What systems development, programming, and hardware installation services will they provide during the conversion period?	
Training Is the necessary training of personnel provided? What is its quality and cost?	
Backup Are several similar computer facilities available for emergency backup purposes?	
Accessibility Does the vendor have a local or regional office that offers sales, systems development, and hardware maintenance services? Is a customer hotline provided?	
Business Position Is the vendor financially strong, with good industry market prospects?	
Hardware Do they have a wide selection of compatible hardware devices and accessories?	
Software Do they offer a variety of useful system software and application packages?	
Overall Rating	

Figure 12–14 Vendor support evaluation factors. These factors focus on the quality of support services computer users may need.

SYSTEM TESTING

Implementation requires the *testing* of a newly developed system. This involves testing hardware devices, testing and *debugging* computer programs, and testing information processing procedures. Programs are tested using test data, which attempts to simulate all conditions that may arise during processing. In good programming practice *(structured programming)*, programs are subdivided into levels of *modules* to assist their development, testing, and maintenance. Program testing usually proceeds from higher to lower levels of program modules until the entire program is tested as a unit. The program is then tested along with other related programs in a final *systems test*. If computer-aided systems engineering methodologies are used, such program testing is minimized since automatically generated program code is more likely to be error-free.

An important part of testing is the production of tentative copies of displays, reports, and other output. These should be reviewed by end users of the proposed systems for possible design errors. Of course, testing should not occur only during the implementation stage, but throughout the systems development process. For example, input documents, screen displays, and processing procedures are examined and critiqued by end users when a prototyping methodology is used for systems design. Immediate end user testing is one of the benefits of a prototyping process.

SYSTEM DOCUMENTATION

Developing **system documentation** is an important process. Tools of systems analysis and design are used to *record* and *communicate* the results of each stage of system development. For example, the contents of feasibility studies, system requirements reports, and system specifications reports are excellent sources of system documentation. Manuals of operating procedures and sample data entry display screens, forms, and reports are other important examples. During the implementation stage, a *system documentation manual* may be prepared to finalize the documentation of a large system. When computer-aided systems engineering software is used, documentation can be created and changed easily. It can be stored on magnetic disks and retrieved, displayed on a video screen, or printed on a printer. Figure 12–15 illustrates the contents of system documentation stored by the Excelerator CASE package.

Proper documentation allows management to monitor the progress of a systems development project. It minimizes the problems that arise when changes are made in systems design. Documentation is vital for proper implementation and maintenance. Installing and operating a newly designed system or modifying an established system requires a detailed record of that system's design. Documentation is extremely important in diagnosing system errors and making system changes, especially if the end users or systems analysts who developed the system are no longer with the organization.

CONVERSION METHODS

The initial operation of a new computer-based system can be a difficult task. Such an operation is usually a **conversion** process in which the personnel, procedures, equipment, input/output forms, and database of an old information system must be converted to the requirements of a new system. Four major forms of system conversion include:

- ☐ Parallel conversion.
- ☐ Phased conversion.

Figure 12–15 The contents of system documentation organized and stored using the Excelerator CASE package.

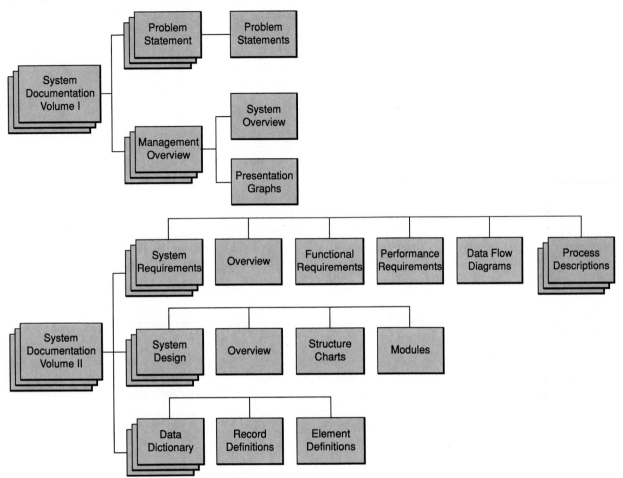

Source: Adapted courtesy of Index Technology Corporation.

   ☐ Pilot conversion.
   ☐ Plunge or direct cutover.

Conversions can be done on a *parallel* basis, whereby both the old and the new system are operated until the project development team and end user management agree to switch completely over to the new system. It is during this time that the operations and results of both systems are compared and evaluated. Errors can be identified and corrected, and the operating problems can be solved before the old system is abandoned. Installation can also be accomplished by a direct *cutover* or *plunge* to the newly developed system. It can also be done on a *phased* basis, where only a few departments, branch offices, or plant locations at a time are converted. A phased conversion allows a gradual implementation process to take place within an organization. Similar benefits accrue from using a *pilot* conversion, where one department or other work site serves as a test site. A new system can be tried out at this site until developers feel it can be implemented throughout the organization.

REAL WORLD CASE

Hospital of St. Raphael

At the Hospital of St. Raphael, physicians, nurses, laboratory technicians, and IS staff have scrubbed up and are ready to operate. The patient: the patient care information system. The disease: paper clot. After five years of study and evaluation, the New Haven hospital began implementing an automated patient care information system which will automate every patient record and eliminate the confusion of multiple paper copies of everything from admission records to drug prescriptions. Only 10 to 15 percent of U.S. hospitals have adopted such a system thus far, according to the American Hospital Association (AHA).

The software the hospital will use, Health Data Science's Ulticare, will run on five Data General minicomputers and will be accessed from 650 dumb terminals and 50 personal computers located in offices, nursing stations, and all 491 patient rooms. The IS department is recruiting 23 people to administer the system, separate from the staff of 30 that handles billing and financial applications on the hospital's IBM 4381 mainframe.

Nurses typically spend 25 percent of their day doing paperwork, according to Debbie Salerni, director of surgical critical-care nursing. "A nurse will write down little bits of information on any scrap of paper he or she can find," she said. At the end of the day, the nurse must take time to sort all this data and rewrite it into patient logs. With the new system, the physicians and nurses can log on at the terminal near the patient's bedside, entering such things as patient condition reports and prescription orders. The data is then accessible online and remains part of the patient's permanent electronic record.

Donald Myers, vice president of the hospital's medical support and information group, said that once the system is fully installed, he expects it to eliminate 64 man-years of clerical and information processing labor costs annually. However, St. Raphael will realize these benefits only "if they don't alienate nurses in the way the system is installed," warned Richard Covert, associate director of health care information and management systems for AHA. "You have to involve them in the selection and the implementation process," Covert advised.

At St. Raphael, medical professionals have been involved with the automation effort from the beginning. The principal evaluation team consisted of Myers, a pharmacist, a radiologist, a lab technician, a business office staffer, and two nurses, including Salerni. "What I liked best about Ulticare was that it's at the bedside," Salerni said. "That way, you have immediate access to what's happening to the patient."

However, hospital staff expressed several concerns—principally, system reliability, security, and user reluctance. Myers chose to address the reliability issue with redundant power supplies and CPUs. "If one application's CPU fails, the other will take over its duties," Myers said. "I think we have reliability well covered." Security measures include electronically coded terminal "keys" and passwords. Users' access profiles will be built according to their need to know.

Myers plans 30 hours of instruction for two thirds of the hospital's 2,300 employees. Automation represents a lot of work, Myers acknowledged. But his prognosis is that it will bring "an astounding change for the hospital and be good for the quality of health care."

Application Questions

☐ What implementation activities (see Figure 12–8) do you recognize in this case? Explain.

☐ How were end users involved in the implementation process?

☐ What evaluation factors (see Figures 12–12, 12–13, and 12–14) were most important in designing St. Raphael's new system? Explain.

Source: Adapted from Richard Pastore, "Hospital Discovers Cure for Paper Clot," *Computerworld,* April 9, 1990, p. 27.

Maintenance is the monitoring, evaluating, and modifying of operational information systems to make desirable or necessary improvements. The installation of a new system usually results in the phenomenon known as the *learning curve*. Personnel who operate and use the system will make mistakes simply because they are not familiar with it. Such errors usually diminish as experience is gained with a new system. However, maintenance is necessary for other failures and problems that arise during the operation of a system. End users and IS personnel must then perform a *troubleshooting* function to determine the causes of and solutions to such problems.

The maintenance activity includes a *postimplementation* review process to ensure that newly implemented systems meet the systems development objectives established for them. Errors in the development or use of a system must be corrected by the maintenance process. This includes a periodic review, or *audit*, of a system to ensure that it is operating properly and meeting its objectives. This audit is in addition to continually monitoring a new system for potential problems or necessary changes. Maintenance includes making modifications to a system due to changes in the business organization or the business environment. For example, new tax legislation, business reorganizations, or new business ventures usually require changes to current organizational information systems.

THE MAINTENANCE FUNCTION

SUMMARY

☐ Information systems planning includes strategic, tactical, and operational planning activities. Strategic information systems planning involves enterprise and environmental analysis activities that evaluate how information systems can contribute to the attainment of strategic organizational goals. It results in a strategic information systems plan that outlines a mission, goals, architecture, applications portfolio, and management philosophy for the information systems function. Tactical information systems planning evaluates current and projected information needs of the organization; defines, prioritizes, and schedules information systems development projects; and develops allocation plans for hardware, software, personnel, telecommunications, facilities, and financial resources. Operational information systems planning develops operational plans such as annual operating budgets and individual systems development project plans.

☐ Many formal planning methodologies are available to help organizations do information systems planning. Examples are Business Systems Planning and the use of a critical success factors approach. Such methodologies are used by organizations to ensure that important planning activities and products are accomplished and produced. They help organizations transform their strategic goals into an information systems development plan to achieve those goals.

☐ The implementation process for information systems consists of activities that carry out the operational plans developed during the information systems planning process. As summarized in Figure 12–8, it involves acquisition, testing, documentation, training, installation, and conversion activities that transform a newly designed information system into an operational system for end users.

☐ The computer industry is a vital source of hardware, software, and services provided by many companies. Business end users should know how to evaluate the acquisition of information system resources. Manufacturers and suppliers should be required to present proposals based on specifications developed during the design stage of systems development. A formal evaluation process reduces the possibility of incorrect or unnecessary purchases of hardware or software. Several major evaluation factors, summarized in Figures 12–12, 12–13, and 12–14 can be used to evaluate hardware, software, and vendor support.

KEY TERMS AND CONCEPTS

These are the key terms and concepts of this chapter. The page number of their first explanation is in parentheses.

1. Computer-aided planning (428)
2. Computer industry (430)
3. Conversion methods (438)
4. Documentation (438)
5. Ergonomics (436)
6. Evaluation factors
   a. Hardware (435)
   b. Software (436)
   c. Vendor support (437)
7. External services (432)
8. Implementation process (430)
9. Information systems planning
   a. Strategic (423)
   b. Tactical (424)
   c. Operational (424)
10. Organizational Planning (422)
11. Planning methodologies
    a. Business Systems Planning (425)
    b. Critical Success Factors (426)
12. Project management (424)
13. System maintenance (441)
14. System testing (438)

REVIEW QUIZ

Match one of the **key terms and concepts** listed above with one of the examples or definitions listed below. Try to find the best fit for answers that seem to fit more than one term or concept. Defend your choices.

_____ 1. Organizations evaluate their accomplishments and environment, decide on goals, and propose actions to achieve them.

_____ 2. Outlines a mission, goals, architecture, applications portfolio, and management philosophy for the information systems function.

_____ 3. Defines, prioritizes, and schedules information systems development projects for the organization.

_____ 4. Develops operating budgets for the information systems function.

_____ 5. Management of the development and implementation of new information systems.

_____ 6. A comprehensive, highly structured planning methodology for information systems planning.

_____ 7. A planning methodology that concentrates on determining a few key areas where a manager feels performance information is vital to the success of the organization.

_____ 8. Software can help develop planning structures and models.

_____ 9. Acquiring hardware and software, testing and converting to a new system, and training people to use it.

_____ 10. The source of hardware, software, and services for users.

_____ 11. Contracting with outside firms for computer processing, education, maintenance, and so on.

_____ 12. You should evaluate its performance, cost, reliability, technology, and ergonomics.

_____ 13. You should evaluate its efficiency, language, and documentation.

_____ 14. You should evaluate the maintenance and training services provided.

_____ 15. Hardware and software should be safe, comfortable, and easy to use.

_____ 16. Operate in parallel with the old system, use a test site, switch in stages, or cut over immediately to a new system.

_____ 17. Checking whether hardware and software work properly for end users.

_____ 18. A user manual communicates the design and operating procedures of a system.

_____ 19. New business ventures or legislation will probably require changes to some of our information systems.

REAL WORLD PROBLEMS

1. Lithonia Lighting

You could call Charles Darnell an old boy. He has been at Lithonia Lighting, based in Conyers, Georgia, for 26 years, and as chief information officer (CIO) and a senior vice president, he has earned his way into the company's top echelon. But listen to him talk about making information systems critical to a business's success, and he sound more like a man of the future—except that he came to these conclusions 25 years before strategic business systems and mission-critical applications became buzzwords. Darnell is not only CIO; he has also been in charge of the company's strategic planning since 1976. Given that advantage, "It was very natural for me to take and integrate the company strategy with the information strategy," he says.

Darnell consistently emphasizes that building a thorough understanding of the business is essential. For example, "Early on, I asked, What was the crux of the business? What made the business run? At that time, it was taking orders quickly and getting those orders in. So we started work on order-entry systems back when they were unheard of." Darnell forged ahead with the order-entry system in spite of some resistance, and it was instrumental in pushing Lithonia to the forefront of lighting manufacturing. Building on the confidence established by the success of the order-entry and manufacturing systems, Darnell and President James McClung were able to develop Lightlink, networked systems that tie together the disparate elements of Lithonia's business. On the strength of Lightlink, Lithonia has grown from an $18 million regional firm to a national giant with more than 5,000 employees and annual sales of $750 million. Lightlink also garnered McClung and Darnell a Partners in Leadership award from the Society for Information Management in 1988.

a. How did Lithonia "integrate the company strategy with the information strategy"?

b. Why is "a thorough understanding of the business essential for developing strategic information systems?

Source: Adapted from Carol Hildebrand, "Lighting Up IS in Business," *Computerworld,* April 9, 1990, p. 55–57.

2. Pacific Bell Company

Their titles vary company by company, but their function essentially is the same: to evaluate a company's information systems strategy within the context of its business needs and goals. They are called business analysts, strategic system planners, information systems architects, or a host of other names. The position, relatively new, is being created in more and more organizations "in recognition of how important information systems are to the long-term health of our business," in the words of one analyst, Michael J. Polosky. A 25-year veteran of Pacific Bell Co., a unit of Pacific Telesis Group, Polosky is the Bell operating company's assistant vice president of Systems Planning and Technical Services in San Ramon, California.

Question: What is specifically demanded of a business analyst?

Answer: You're involved not just in business planning but with translating overall company direction and strategies into the kind of IS technology infrastructure you need—and then seeing that it is built.

Question: What are Pacific Bell's chief system goals?

Answer: Over the years, we have designed systems that were focused on automating discrete functions in the business. But, as we implement new technology today, we find we need much more flexibility and interoperability among these systems, so we're completely rebuilding our IS infrastructure. In 1985, we put together an IS architecture which really said this is the kind of environment we need to have in order to be successful in the future. What we call our *functional business model* has, for example, identified shareable data as being very important—data that is no longer captive within applications but shareable by many applications. And so we identified that we basically must retool our major systems, and the most critical elements that we need to work on over the next three to five years. And we're beginning now to put this new IS infrastructure into place.

a. What types of planning does Michael Poloski do for Pacific Bell?

b. What change in IS planning goals has occurred at Pacific Bell?

Source: Adapted from Tom McCusker, "Why Business Analysts are Indispensible to IS," *Datamation,* January 15, 1990, pp. 76–78.

3. McDonald's Corporation

Looking for a way to bring more discipline to his group's planning process, Jim Sappington found himself in a situation that is familiar to anyone who has looked at project management software. "It all looked great," said Sappington, senior manager of the financial systems group at McDonald's Corp. "But I couldn't find something useful to do with it." The problem, he explained, was that while several vendors offered pieces of the features he also was looking for—calendar, to-do list, report writer, and electronic mail—none offered a collected group of functions that had been integrated into a single package.

Finally, Sappington settled on software from Information Research Corp., developer of a group-oriented project management software package called Syzygy. Besides project and task scheduling and organization, Syzygy includes a shared calendar feature, support for E-mail, and a database query report writer. All of the features can be shared between the personal computers running the groupware package. "That is the most powerful feature," Sappington said. "It allows us to better integrate information from a number of sources into our planning and goal setting process."

a. Why did Jim Sappington need an integrated project management package?

b. How does such a package support IS planning and implementation?

Source: Adapted from Charles Von Simson, "Burger, Fries, and Project Management," *Computerworld,* April 2, 1990, p. 39.

4. Planning for the Future
    In planning for the future, it is useful for computer-using organizations to recognize several alternative visions of how information technology will develop during the 1990s. Each will have a significantly different effect on the business impact of IS technology.

    ☐ **A future dominated by standards.** Proprietary standards fade, replaced by practical and more popular uniform, multivendor solutions. The need for compatibility slows technological advances, though. Open market prices are lower, with keen competition in application software. Biggest advantages go to small, responsive firms or large, volume producers. Far East gains world momentum at the expense of IBM.

    ☐ **A future driven by new technology.** Advances continue. Flat screens, speech recognition, image processing, superb color, expert assistants, and multimedia documents redefine user interaction. Fiber optics speeds image transmission, while parallel processing and new architectures sharply boost performance. Aggressive start-ups fuel innovation; big vendors bog down.

    ☐ **A future belonging to networking.** Use of stand-alone computers fades, as networked machines become distributed parallel processors. Location-independent data access and cooperative processing are major developments. Groupware is popular. Small firms use global marketplace for IS.

    ☐ **An affordable future.** Technology spending lags, as users rethink investments. Economic logic of moving to inexpensive distributed platforms is inescapable. End user applications are the most popular new applications. Economies of scale and good distribution are keys to success. Global stagnation fuels fierce nationalistic pride.

☐ **A future owned by big players.** Intense consolidation narrows number of broad-line IS suppliers to six large multinational giants. Need for high return on R&D investment fuels proprietary approaches, yielding better technology, integration, and functionality. Users prefer packaged solutions, centrally developed mission-critical systems. Vendors have power over suppliers and customers and raise high barriers to entry.

a. Which of the five alternative visions of the future of IT do you think is most likely to occur in the 1990s?

b. What effect will your vision of future IT developments have on IS planning for a business?

Source: Adapted from James Herman, Patricia Seybold, and Robert Weber, "Shaping the 1990's," *Computerworld,* November 27, 1989, pp. 77, 79.

5. Merrill Lynch Canada

In the high stakes world of money market securities, where single trades mean millions of dollars, every transaction counts. There's no room for system errors, lost data, or downtime. Merrill Lynch Canada in Toronto chose a PC-based network for a new trading-floor system, instead of a minicomputer or mainframe system which would have cost twice as much. The Toronto trading floor handles institutional trades of money market instruments such as municipal bonds and Treasury bills. Clients include large insurance firms and banks around the world. Transactions are very large, usually in the multimillion-dollar range, and time is short—an entire municipal-bond issue can be sold off in hours. "Trading has always been done on the back of an envelope," says Bob Jull, systems developer. "Traders yell their trades to everybody and keep a blotter on their desk with significant trades, and they write them on a big board." That's why the Presentation Manager (PM) graphical interface is a critical part of the new OS/2 application.

A trader using a mouse or keyboard picks an item off an inventory-summary screen, which automatically brings up a trade-entry screen. If other fields, such as asking price, have not changed, all the trader needs to do is enter the quantity. This updates the inventory in realtime to reflect the trade and broadcasts it to other traders. "A trader is talking to 5 or 10 people at a time, watching the Dow Jones or Reuters screen—there's a million things going on at once," Jull said. "So they don't want to have anything to do with computers and trades unless it's easy." An easy-to-use interface with a quick response time was crucial to the project's success, said Anna Ewing, assistant VP of information systems. So far the traders' response has been "very positive and very intuitive," said Ewing, who managed the project. "They're learning it without a user guide."

a. Why did Merrill Lynch Canada select OS/2 for its new trading system?

b. What are the benefits of the new system for securities traders?

Source: Adapted from Paula Lovejoy, "Investors Bank on OS/2 for Reliability and Low Costs," *PC Week,* April 16, 1990, pp. 69, 75.

6. First National Bank of Las Vegas

President Ray Litherland of the First National Bank of Las Vegas, New Mexico, knew he needed a new banking system to improve customer service and to free him for more contact with customers in his small bank (6,000 accounts) in this town of 15,000 people in the high plains of northeastern New Mexico. Litherland was looking for three things from a new system: reliability, flexibility, and support. Since his IBM PC systems had run flawlessly for years, he felt comfortable with IBM's record for reliability. After looking at other systems, he decided on an IBM minicomputer—a System/36, with eight terminals. For a software vendor, he chose Hogan Systems, whose BankVision package offered flexibility to meet changing regulatory requirements and competitive conditions. BankVision features modules for loan accounting, deposit accounting, time deposit accounting, financial accounting, electronic funds transfer support, management reporting, and safe deposit box accounting.

Litherland liked the fact that Hogan offered 24-hour telephone support and on-site conversion assistance. "Their people came in a week before conversion day, looked at our needs, and trained our people. Overall, the conversion went pretty smoothly," Litherland says. "We have cut the amount of manual work to be done. We can now offer faster and better service," he says. For example, customers now can go into any branch and get current statements printed on the spot. Similarly, bank employees now have almost instant access to customer information to answer phone queries or walk-in requests.

a. What evaluation factors for hardware, software, and vendor support (see Figures 12–12, 12–13, and 12–14) were important to Ray Litherland? Explain.

b. Why do you think the implementation process went smoothly at First National?

Source: Adapted from "Bank Keeps Customers Hours, Not Bankers Hours," *IBM Update,* March/April 1990, p. 18.

7. Portland General Electric

"We make a conscious effort to purchase packaged software whenever possible," said John Esler, information-services supervisor of technical support at Portland General Electric, a utility in Portland, Oregon. "My experience is that off-the-shelf software such as Paradox or FoxBASE is robust enough to tailor to most end user database applications without creating customized, closed end systems." Esler does not foresee a wholesale shift to end users assuming the lead in applications development. "When businesspeople have the capability to write their own systems, there's a tendency to reinvent the wheel," he explained. "How many times do people have to write their own vehicle-maintenance program, for example, when numerous packages already exist?" he asked.

At Portland General Electric, information-center account representatives are assigned to each department within the company. When a department requests a new software system, the information-center representative first determines whether a software package already exists to solve the business problem. Esler cited a recent conversion of his company's legal department from a Wang minicomputer system to a LAN.

Instead of writing a completely new system to track legal documents, the information-center representative found a software package that performed the exact functions that the utility company's lawyers needed.

a. What end user software acquisition policies are required by Portland General Electric?

b. Do you think such policies are necessary for all computer-using organizations? Explain.

Source: Adapted from Craig Zarley, "When Users Write Their Own Applications," *PC Week*, December 18, 1989, p. 66.

8. Society National Bank

Alan McClurg had it easier than some when his bank wanted to put an executive information system (EIS) in place. As the driving force behind the project, the chief financial officer offered this bit of wisdom as justification: Why spend hundreds of thousands of dollars to put technology in front of tellers who earn $5 an hour but not in front of executives who earn more than $100,000 a year? McClurg, vice president of support systems at Society National Bank in Cleveland, added, "If you don't have a corporate sponsor, do not try to do an EIS. It cannot be driven by the IS department."

Implementing an EIS, however, is no easy task. If implemented properly, an EIS can offer its users improved delivery of time-valued information and improved understanding of the business, and it will affect the kinds of decisions being made at a company. McClurg said that at Society Bank, the total cost of its EIS ran to $1.2 million, which included the purchase price of an IBM 9370 mid-size computer, 40 executive workstations (mostly Intel 80386-based personal computers and Hewlett-Packard color printers), training, Pilot Executive Software's EIS software and internal development.

a. What hardware, software, and other resources were needed to implement an EIS at Society National?

b. Why did Alan McClurg say: "If you don't have a corporate sponsor, do not try to do an EIS. It cannot be driven by the IS department?"

Source: Adapted from Alan Ryan, "Making Room at the Top for EIS," *Computerworld*, February 26, 1990, p. 14.

SELECTED REFERENCES

1. Arthur Andersen & Co. *Executive Guide to Strategic Information Planning*, 1985.

2. Brancheau, James; Larry Schuster; and Salvatore March. "Building and Implementing an Information Architecture." *Data Base, Summer, 1989.*

3. "The Datamation 100." *Datamation*, June 15, 1990.

4. Fowler, Brooks. "Planning Made Painless." *EDGE*, January/February 1990.

5. Herman, James; Patricia Seybold; and Robert Weber. "Shaping the 1990s." *Computerworld*, November 27, 1989.

6. IBM Corporation. *Information Systems Planning Guide*. 4th ed. 1984.

7. Lederer, Albert, and Vijay Sethi. "Pitfalls in Planning." *Datamation*, June 1, 1989.

8. Rockart, John. "Chief Executives Define Their Own Data Needs." *Harvard Business Review*, March-April 1979.

9. Shank, Michael; Andrew Boynton; and Robert Zmud. "Critical Success Factor Analysis as a Methodology for MIS Planning." *MIS Quarterly*, June 1985.

10. Sprague, Ralph, and Barbara McNurlin, ed. *Information Systems Management in Practice*. 2nd ed. Englewood Cliffs, N.J.: Prentice-Hall, 1989.

11. Stevens, Larry. "A Good Planner Knows How to Bend." *Computerworld*, February 20, 1989.

12. Targowski, Andrews. "Systems Planning for the Enterprise-Wide Information Management Complex: The Architectural Approach." *Journal of Management Information Systems*, Fall, 1988.

CHAPTER 13

MANAGING INFORMATION SYSTEM RESOURCES

■ Chapter Outline

■ Learning Objectives

The purpose of this chapter is to give you an understanding of the challenges computer-based information systems present to management, by analyzing (1) the managerial implications of information technology and (2) major issues in the management of information services.

Section I of this chapter discusses the impact of information systems technology on managers and organizations and the use of information resource management to improve the performance of the IS function.

Section II explores the basic issues and methods used to manage the delivery of information services in computer-using organizations.

After reading and studying this chapter, you should be able to:

1. Identify two major ways in which information technology has affected managers.

2. Explain how computer-based information systems can support either the centralization or decentralization of information systems, management, and business operations.

3. Identify the five major dimensions of the information resource management concept and explain their impact on the management of information system resources.

4. Explain how problems of information system performance can be solved by management involvement in planning and control.

5. Identify several reasons for end user resistance to information systems and discuss how and why solving such problems requires meaningful end user involvement.

6. Identify the major managerial responsibilities in each of the basic functions of an information services organization, that is, systems development, operations, and technical support.

Section I: Information Resource Management

Who should manage MIS? Managers or technicians? End users or specialists? Somebody has to. Inadequate management of information services by business firms and other organizations has been documented for many years. Thus, there is a real need for business end users to understand how to manage this vital organizational function. In this section, we will stress the concept of **information resource management.** This concept emphasizes that managing the information system resources of a business has become a major strategic responsibility of both managerial end users and information systems management. In the next section, we will analyze the basic functions performed by information services groups within an organization. We will also discuss methods of managing such functions, pointing out some of the major job responsibilities in the information systems function.

THE IMPACT OF
INFORMATION
TECHNOLOGY

When computers were first introduced into business, predictions were made that there would be significant changes in management and organizations. The information processing power and programmed decision making capability of computer-based information systems were supposedly going to cause drastic reductions in employees, including middle management. A centralized computer system would process all of the data for an organization, control all of its operations, and make most of its decisions.

This did not prove to be the case. Changes in organizational structure and types of personnel did occur, but they were not as dramatic as predicted. Naturally, highly automated systems do not require as many people as manual methods. Therefore, there have been significant reductions in the number of people required to perform manual tasks in many organizations. For example, computerized accounting systems have drastically reduced the need for clerical accounting personnel, and factory automation has greatly reduced the demand for many types of factory workers. However, these reductions were countered by dramatic increases in sales and service personnel, knowledge workers, and managers as businesses increased the depth and scope of their operations. It was also countered to some extent by the need for more technicians and professionals to develop and run the computer-based information systems of the organization [12]

Management and
Information Technology

However, **information technology** (IT), that is, the technologies in modern computer-based information systems, is once again being portrayed as a major force for organizational and managerial change. In fact, information technology is already changing decision making, management structures, and work activities in companies around the world [4]. Computing power and information resources are now more readily available to most managers. Advances in personal computing, hardware and software packages, telecommunications, database processing, office automation, decision support systems, and executive information systems have been responsible for this development. Surveys show that significant computer use has even spread from lower and middle managers to senior management. Figure 13–1 illustrates the results of a survey of computer use among CEOs in U.S. Fortune 500 companies. The survey

Figure 13-1 Managers' use of personal computers. Note what the CEOs of the Fortune 500 companies say about their use of computers.

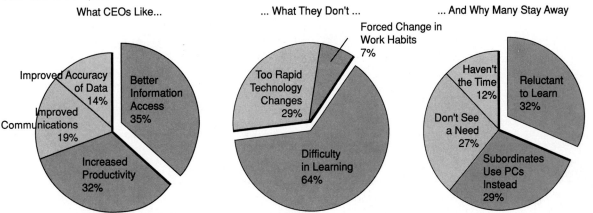

Source: Robin Nelson, "Special Report: CEO Survey," *Personal Computing*, April 1989, p. 84.

found that 21.4 percent of CEOs spent an average of one hour per day using computers.

For example, the decision support capability of information systems technology is changing the focus of managerial decision making. Managers freed from "number crunching" chores must now face tougher strategic policy questions in order to develop the realistic alternatives required for effective decision analysis. The use of telecommunications networks and realtime inquiry/response systems is another example of the impact of information technology on management. Middle managers no longer need to serve as conduits for the transmission of operations feedback or control directives between operational managers and top management. Thus, drastic reductions in the layers and numbers of middle management, and the dramatic growth of work groups consisting of *task-focused* teams of specialists, are forecast [4].

Finally, information systems technology presents managers with a major managerial challenge. Managing the information system resources of a business is no longer the sole province of information systems specialists. Instead, *information resource management* (IRM) has become a major responsibility of all managers. That is, data, information, and computer hardware, software, and personnel should be viewed as valuable resources that must be managed by all levels of management to ensure the effective use of information systems technology for the operational and strategic benefit of the entire organization.

Thus, management of the IS function is changing from *EDP management* to *information resource management* as computers become more integrated and essential to a company's operations and management. This can viewed as a movement by an organization through various stages of computer use as first conceptualized by Richard Nolan, and illustrated in Figure 13-2. In early stages, IS management is *data processing–oriented* as the computer services effort moves from a "closed shop" to a *computer utility* role, with centralized internal planning and control. In later stages, computer and information resources are managed by an organization-wide *information resource manage-*

Figure 13–2 Managing the IS function changes from EDP management to information resource management as a firm moves through stages of computer use.

Stages of Computer Use	Stage 1 Initiation	Stage 2 Contagion	Stage 3 Control	Stage 4 Integration	Stage 5 Data Administration	Stage 6 Maturity
Organizational Role of IS	The IS function is centralized and operates as a "closed shop."		IS becomes the data custodian. Computer utility established and achieves reliability.		Organizational implementation of the IRM concept. Responsibility for IS resources is placed at all appropriate organizational levels.	
IS Planning and Control	No formal planning or control.		IS planning and control is installed, including standards for software development responsibility accounting, and project management.		Corporate planning and control is installed to manage IS resources. Included are user chargebacks, steering committees, data administration, and technology management.	

ment philosophy, which is *user-oriented* and uses decentralized but integrated planning and control methods [11].

Centralization versus Decentralization

Experience has shown that modern computer-based information systems can support either the *centralization* or *decentralization* of information systems, operations, and decision making within computer-using organizations. For example, centralized information systems typically utilize computer facilities at central sites which are connected to all parts of the organization by telecommunications networks. This can allow top management to centralize some decision making formerly done by lower levels of management. It also can promote centralization of operations, which reduces the number of branch offices, manufacturing plants, warehouses, and other work sites needed by the firm.

On the other hand, distributed networks of computers at multiple work sites can allow top management to delegate more decision making to middle managers. Management can also decentralize operations by increasing the number of branch offices (or other company units) while still having access to the information and communications capabilities they need to control the overall direction of the organization.

Therefore, computer-based information systems can encourage either the centralization or decentralization of information systems, business operations, and management. The philosophy of top management, the culture of the organization, the nature of its operations, its stage of computer use, and its use of aggressive or conservative competitive strategies all play major roles with information technology in shaping the firm's organizational structure and information systems architecture [14].

A Historical Perspective

Thus, companies continue to use a variety of organizational arrangements for the delivery of information services. In the early years of computing, when computers could barely handle a single department's work load, decentralization was the only option. Then the development of large mainframe computers and telecommunications networks and terminals caused a centralization of computer hardware and software, databases, and IS specialists at the corporate level of organizations. Next, the development of minicomputers and microcomputers accelerated a trend back toward decentralization. Distributed processing networks of computers at the corporate, department, work group, and end user levels came into being. This promoted a shift of databases and IS specialists to departments and the creation of information centers to support end user computing.

Lately, the trend has been to establish tighter control over the information resources of an organization, while still serving the strategic needs of its business units. This has resulted in a centralizing trend at some organizations and the development of hybrid structures with both centralized and decentralized components. Some companies have even spun off their information systems function into independent subsidiaries that offer information processing services to external organizations as well as to their parent company [2].

Other corporations have "outsourced," i.e., turned over all or part of their IS operation to outside contractors known as *systems integrators* or *facilities management* companies. Such changes in the organizational alignment of the information systems function are expected to continue into the future. Organizations will continue to experiment with ways to both control and encourage the use of information system resources to promote end user productivity and achieve their strategic objectives.

INFORMATION RESOURCE MANAGEMENT

Information resource management (IRM) has become a popular way to emphasize a major change in the management and mission of the information systems function in many organizations. Managing the information system resources of an organization is a vital concept in today's business environment because of three major developments that are affecting how corporate management views the information systems function [2, 8].

☐ Information systems technology and its applications for users' needs are growing and changing rapidly. Hardware and software resources can now better support a wide variety of traditional and new business uses. Therefore, both end user managers and corporate executives have higher expectations for the support they receive from information systems technology.

☐ Inadequate performance and unsatisfactory use of information systems and resources are major problems in many organizations. Top management is unwilling to accept this state of affairs and is demanding new approaches to managing information services.

☐ Information systems can now give a firm a major strategic advantage over its competitors in the marketplace. Top management wants to find new and creative ways to use information resources in pursuing the strategic objectives of the firm.

Five Dimensions of IRM

Information resource management is a response to these pressures. IRM can be viewed as having five major dimensions: (1) resource management, (2) technology management, (3) distributed management, (4) functional management, and (5) strategic management. See Figure 13–3.

Figure 13-3 The information
resource management (IRM)
concept. Note that there are
five major dimensions to the
job of managing information
system resources.

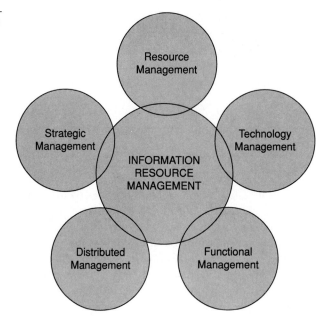

Figure 13-3 The information resource management (IRM) concept. Note that there are five major dimensions to the job of managing information system resources.

Resource Management

IRM views data, information, and computer hardware, software, and personnel as valuable resources that should be effectively and efficiently managed for the benefit of the entire organization. If plant and equipment, money, and people are considered valuable organizational resources, so should its data, information, and other information system resources. This is especially true if the organization is committed to building a strategic information resource base to be used for strategic planning and if it wants to develop innovative products and services that incorporate information systems technology [6].

Technology Management

IRM emphasizes that all technologies that process and deliver data and information must be managed as an integrated system of organizational resources. Such technologies include telecommunications and office systems, as well as computer-based information processing. These "islands of technology" are bridged by IRM and become a primary responsibility of the executive in charge of all information services, sometimes called the **chief information officer (CIO)** of the organization. Thus, the information systems function becomes "a business within a business," whose chief executive is charged with coordinating all information systems technologies for the strategic benefit of the organization [9].

Distributed Management

IRM emphasizes that managing information system resources has become a major responsibility of the management of an organization at all levels, and in all functions. It is not just the responsibility of an organization's chief informa-

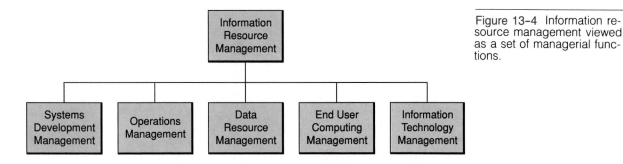

Figure 13–4 Information resource management viewed
as a set of managerial functions.

tion officer. If you're a manager, IRM is one of your responsibilities, whether you are a manager of a company, a department, a work group, or a functional area. This is especially true as developments such as distributed processing, end user computing, work group computing, and strategic information systems drive the responsibility for managing information systems out to all of an organization's functional and work group managers [12].

Functional Management

The IRM concept stresses that the management of an organization must apply common managerial functions and techniques to the management of information resources. Managers must use managerial techniques (such as planning models, management by objectives, financial budgets, project management, and functional organization) just as they do with other major resources and activities of the business. The information systems business is no longer treated as a "special case" department that is too technically complex and dynamic to be managed effectively. Instead, it is treated like other functions and expected to use the managerial techniques employed by other business units to manage the resources and activities that are unique to the information systems function. Figure 13–4 illustrates the concept of IRM as a combination of managerial functions [6].

Strategic Management

Finally, the IRM concept stresses that the information services function in the firm must be more than a provider of computer services. It must also make major contributions to the profitability and strategic objectives of the firm. Thus, the information systems function must change from an *information services utility* to a *producer of information products* that earn profits for the firm and give it a *comparative advantage* over its competitors. This topic was discussed in Chapter 2, where we saw that companies can develop strategic information systems to gain a competitive edge. Thus, information resource management focuses on developing and managing information systems that significantly improve operational efficiency, promote innovative products and services, and build a strategic information resource base that can enhance the competitiveness of the organization.

INFORMATION SYSTEMS PERFORMANCE

Computer-based information systems are developed by business firms to reduce costs, increase profits, provide better service to customers, provide better information to management, and gain competitive advantages. Using computers should reduce the cost of doing business by automating the processing of data and the control of operations. Thus, computer-based information systems should improve the competitive position and profit performance of business organizations.

However, James Martin, a visionary author and spokesman in the information systems industry, who is a consultant to chief executives of major corporations throughout the world, expresses a sentiment felt by many executives when he says:

> The extraordinary power of today's computing hardware is simply not being employed as it should be in most corporations. There is a sense of anger among much top management because in spite of their high DP costs they are not obtaining the information they want from computers and their systems are difficult to change. [8]

Thus, the promised benefits of computer-based information systems have not occurred in many documented cases. Studies by management consulting firms, computer user groups, and university researchers have shown that many businesses have not been successful in managing their computer resources and information services departments. Valuable information system resources are not being used effectively, efficiently, or economically by such businesses [5, 8]. For example:

☐ Computer-based information systems are not being used *effectively* by companies that use them primarily for record-keeping applications instead of for decision making support and strategic applications for competitive advantage.

☐ Computer-based information systems are not being used *efficiently* by information services departments that provide inadequate service to end users while failing to properly utilize their computing capacities.

☐ Many computer-based information systems are also not being used *economically*. Information processing costs have risen faster than other costs in many businesses, even though the cost of processing each unit of data is decreasing due to improvements in hardware and software technology.

Poor information systems performance can take many forms. Also, poor performance is not limited to small businesses with limited financial and human resources. Many large businesses have openly admitted their failure to manage computers effectively. What is the solution to the problem of poor performance in the information systems function? There are no quick and easy answers. However, the experiences of successful organizations reveal that the basic ingredient of high-quality information systems performance is extensive and meaningful **management and end user involvement** in the planning, development, and operation of computer-based information systems [2, 13]. This should be the key ingredient in meeting the challenge of improving the quality of information products and services.

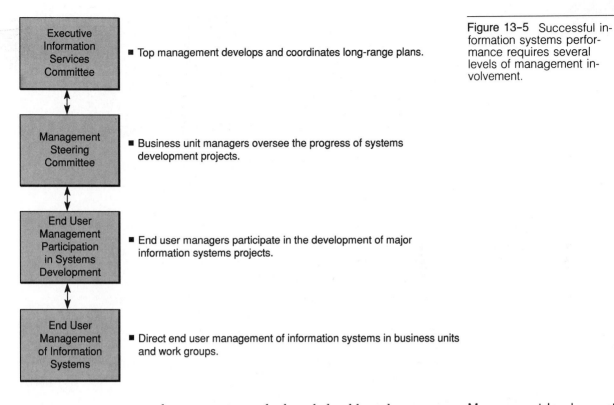

Proper management involvement requires the knowledgeable and active participation of managers in the planning and control of information system resources. Managers must practice information resource management. They must manage the hardware, software, people, data, and information resources of their business units for operational efficiency, effectiveness, and competitive advantage. Without such involvement, managers will not be able to control the quality of information systems performance. Figure 13–5 illustrates several major levels of management involvement.

Management Involvement

□ Many organizations use an *executive information services* committee of top managers to do strategic information system planning and to coordinate the development of information systems projects. This committee includes the senior management of the major divisions of the firm, as well as its chief information officer.

□ A *steering committee* of business unit managers, operating managers, and management personnel from the information services department may be created to oversee the progress of project teams. The committee meets on a regular basis to review progress made, to settle disputes, and to change priorities, if necessary.

□ Development of decision support, work group, and end user information systems is accomplished with the active participation of individual managers in prototyping and other systems development activities. Managers are also responsible for managing the quality of information services provided to their business units and work groups.

Figure 13-6 Reasons for end user resistance to computer-based information systems.

Factor	Explanation
Feelings of change	Change often threatens one's self-esteem or image in the eyes of others. Often, low self-images are brought to work and confrontation with machines threatens to reveal a person's own worst fear of incompetence.
Fear of being replaced by a machine	The computer may be perceived as an instrument that actually replaces the worker. One's own value in the workplace may be totally undermined with disastrous monetary and psychological consequences.
Fear of failure	Many workers have spent years developing the skills that have made them proficient at their jobs. Why change? If they do change, what will happen to them if they cannot perform the new task or with the new equipment?
Fear of the unknown	People need to be able to predict what they will face in the future. Established patterns are known factors, whereas new systems pose the threat of ambiguity and uncertainty.
Psychological habit	Established rules, policies, and procedures frequently become habits, and people rely on them for both guidance and protection. These habits are their security blankets. Changes frequently disrupt this security by making established habits inapplicable.
Loss of control	Computers are frequently perceived as a threat to one's power or influence. Computer systems are also commonly perceived as things over which one has no control.
Changes in interpersonal relationships	People have a strong need to interact with others. Changes that disturb existing social patterns or result in isolation are unbearable. Change can also disturb worker relationships with superiors.
Lack of understanding	Resistance to change is likely if workers don't understand its purpose.
Lack of identification	A system should not be perceived as imposed. If the change is not initially sought by workers and if the consequences of the change do not appear directly beneficial to them, their resistance is likely.

Source: Claudette Peterson and Tim Peterson, "The Darkside of Office Automation: How People Resist the Introduction of Office Automation Technology," in *Human Factors in Management Information Systems,* ed. Jane M. Carey (Norwood, N.J.: Ablex Publishing Corporation, 1988), p. 186.

End User Involvement

Any new way of doing things generates some resistance by the people affected. Thus, the introduction of computer-based information systems can generate a significant amount of fear and reluctance to change. There are many reasons for this state of affairs, some of which are explored in a discussion concerning the impact of computers on society in Chapter 14. Whatever the reasons for **end user resistance,** it is the responsibility of managers and information system professionals to find ways of reducing the conflict and resistance that arise from the development and use of information systems. Brief explanations of several major reasons for end user resistance are outlined in Figure 13–6.

Solving the problems of end user resistance requires meaningful **end user involvement** based on formal methods of (1) education and training, (2) participation in systems development, and (3) communication and coordination between end users and information systems staff.

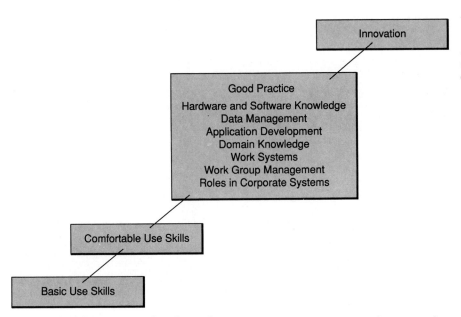

Figure 13-7   Levels of end user skills. Note the skill levels and knowledge that end users can gain with proper education and training.

Source: Adapted from Raymond Panko, *End User Computing: Management, Applications, and Technology,* (New York: John Wiley & Sons, 1988), p. 167.

Education and Training

Managers and end users must be educated in the fundamentals of information systems technology and its application to business operations and management. This basic knowledge should be supplemented by training programs for specific hardware devices, software packages, and end user applications. As we mentioned in Chapter 7, this educational role is a typical service of an organization's *information center.* Figure 13–7 shows the hierarchy of skill levels that end users can achieve with proper education and training.

End User Participation

In previous chapters, we discussed end user computing and the participation of end users in prototyping and other forms of system development. In addition, end users should be placed on project teams charged with the development of major information systems. Direct end user participation should provide the type of involvement that can improve the quality of information services and reduce the potential for end user resistance. This involvement helps assure that the design of information systems meets the needs of end users. Systems that tend to inconvenience or frustrate their users cannot be effective systems, no matter how efficiently they process data. Figure 13–8 is a tongue-in-cheek reminder of what may happen when end users are not involved in application development.

Communication and Coordination

Several methods of communication and coordination between end users and information systems professionals are employed by successful organizations. For example, some firms create *user liaison* positions or "help desks" with end

Figure 13–8 Application development without end user involvement. Effective end user applications cannot be developed without end user participation in the development of information systems.

As Stated in the System Requirements

As Outlined in the System Specifications

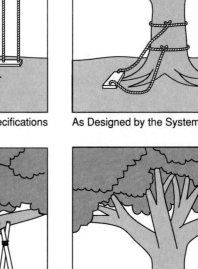

As Designed by the Systems Analyst

As Implemented by Information Services

As Operated by the End User

What the End User Really Needed

user "hot lines". Information systems specialists with titles such as *user consultant, account executive,* or *business analyst* may be assigned to end user work groups. These specialists perform a vital role by troubleshooting problems, gathering and communicating information, coordinating educational efforts, and helping end users with application development. These activities improve communication and coordination between end user work groups and the corporate information services department and avoid the runaround that can frustrate end users. Of course, the creation of information centers that provide hardware, software, and consulting services to end users is a major alternative used by many companies. Also, many firms have decentralized information systems by distributing information system resources and specialists to end user business units and work groups. This is a dramatic way to improve communication and coordination between end users and IS specialists [10].

REAL WORLD CASE

U.S. Shoe Corporation

Harvard Business School professor James Cash says that organizational redesign supported by information systems is an idea whose time has come at many major corporations. Most organizations he works with are trying to transform their enterprise into a "fast cycle" mode that permits quicker and more effective responses in the face of intensifying competitive pressure. "You don't get to be a fast-cycle company without redesigning the organization," Cash says. "Information technology is the key resource that makes it possible." Cash adds: "When it became possible to deliver information technology to every individual in a company, we began laying the foundation for truly dramatic organizational changes."

U.S. Shoe Corp. was on its way to another goal when it made that discovery. What started as a project to pare $2 million from the IS overhead expense has turned into a three-year "total quality project" that affects the entire domestic footwear business, according to Carol Biemel, vice president of IS at the Cincinnati shoe company. "Reducing costs was initially the primary objective," Biemel explains. "But it became the tip of the iceberg when the whole organization rallied around the project."

Biemel started with the premise that U.S. Shoe could cut IS costs by eliminating the mainframe in favor of departmental systems supported by smaller computers linked by local area networks. In theory, at least, Biemel predicted the company could reduce costs by as much as 40 percent. But, she says, even after they concluded it was technically possible, they had to address the fact that implementing such a change meant that every department would have to discard the systems it knew. She and her staff would have to replace those systems with new software that would work on the departmental computers. At that point, she says, the project ceased being an IS project and started being a business project.

According to Biemel, "The impetus for change arose from the question, Can information technology help us be a more efficient company?" She adds that "this involved looking at the entire business process—from taking orders to shipping shoes—to find out how we can be more competitive and eliminate unnecessary steps in the process."

For example, U.S. Shoe has implemented a pilot program linking its factory with its suppliers of insoles and outsoles. U.S. Shoe's Biemel says she figures that the new system, which eliminates the need for a warehouse and a purchasing agent, will save the company as much as $500,000 in inventory and handling this year on just those two categories of supplies. Further, the system is evolving into a full-scale just-in-time system for receiving and processing materials from suppliers.

Perhaps even more important, Biemel says, is how business changes like those at the factory are mushrooming in other parts of U.S. Shoe. IS is also using the success of the program to convince other areas of the business to consider making similar changes. For example, she is working with people in the home office who take orders and do master scheduling, hoping they can make improvements based on the changes at the factory.

Application Questions

☐ How can information technology transform an organization?

☐ How did U.S. Shoe use IT to improve its business processes?

☐ Why did U.S. Shoe's use of IT change from "an IS project to a business project"?

Source: Adapted from Katie Crane, "Systems Must Be Engaged for Proper Handling on Turns," *Computerworld*, January 29, 1990, pp. 55–57.

Section II: Managing Information Services

How do computer-using firms manage the delivery of information services to their users? In this section, we will analyze how information service groups are (1) organized into functional areas, (2) staffed by information systems specialists, and (3) managed by a variety of managerial techniques. This information should give you a good idea of the managerial responsibilities involved in providing information services to end users. Figure 13–9 outlines key management issues in information systems revealed in the 1990 survey of IS executives in the United States and Canada by the Index Group. This illustration emphasizes that the information systems function poses major managerial challenges that must be confronted by both end user managers and IS managers [16].

ORGANIZING INFORMATION SERVICES

In many large organizations, the information systems function was once a department that reported to the accounting or engineering vice presidents of the company. Now, however, the IS function typically is organized into a separate departmental or divisional unit, whose head is one of the top executives of the firm. We will use the name *information services department* for this group, though such names as information systems, computer services, data processing, EDP, MIS, and IRM department are also used. No matter what name is used, *information services departments* perform several basic functions and activities. These can be grouped into three basic functional categories: (1) **systems development,** (2) **operations,** and (3) **technical services.** Figure 13–10 illustrates this grouping of IS activities into a functional organizational structure.

ADMINISTRATION OF INFORMATION SERVICES

Many companies have created a senior management position, the **chief information officer** (CIO), to oversee all use of information technology in their organizations. Thus, all telecommunications services, office automation systems, and other IS support services are the responsibility of this executive. Also, the CIO does not direct day-to-day information service activities but concentrates on long-term planning and strategy. Thus, CIOs are responsible for implementing an information resource management role for IS. They also work with other top executives to develop strategic information systems that

---

Figure 13-9 These issues illustrate the major challenges facing information systems managers.

1. Reshaping business processes through information technology.
2. Educating senior management on information systems.
3. Instituting cross-functional information systems.
4. Aligning IS and corporate goals.
5. Doing IS strategic planning.
6. Boosting software development productivity.
7. Utilizing data resources.
8. Using IS for competitive breakthroughs.
9. Developing an information architecture.
10. Cutting IS costs.

Source: Clinton Wilder, "Re-engineering Is IS Priority," *Computerworld*, March 14, 1990, p.6.

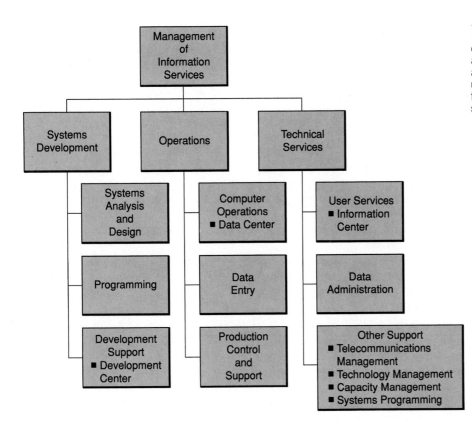

Figure 13-10 A functional organizational structure for an IS department. Note the activities that take place under each of the major functions of information services.

help make the firm more competitive in the marketplace. Several firms have filled the CIO position with executives from outside the IS field to emphasize the strategic business role of information systems.

Other administrative positions in information services might include a manager of information services and individual managers for systems development, operations, data administration, telecommunications, and end user services. Additional classifications exist in many organizations due to the recognition of seniority and the assignment of supervisory responsibilities. For example, titles such as project manager, lead systems analyst, lead programmer, and *shift supervisor* for computer operations recognize the assignment of supervisory responsibilities to these positions.

Systems development management is responsible for managing the investigation, analysis, design, implementation, and maintenance of information systems within computer-using organizations. As discussed in Chapter 11, this means managing activities such as systems analysis and design, prototyping, applications programming, project management, quality assurance, and systems maintenance for all major systems development projects. Planning, organizing, and controlling the systems development function is a major managerial responsibility. It requires the use of *project management* methods to oversee the activities of systems analysts, programmers, and end users working on a variety of projects. In addition, many systems development groups have established **development centers,** staffed with consultants to the professional pro-

**SYSTEMS
DEVELOPMENT
MANAGEMENT**

grammers and systems analysts in their organizations. Their role is to evaluate computer-aided systems engineering (CASE) tools and help information systems specialists use them to improve their applications development efforts.

OPERATIONS MANAGEMENT

Operations management is concerned with the use of hardware, software, and personnel resources in the corporate or business unit **data centers** (computer centers) of an organization. Operational activities that must be managed include data entry, equipment operations, production control, and production support. For example, data entry operators convert input source documents into machine-sensible form using a variety of data entry devices. This requires continual checking and monitoring of input data and output reports to ensure their accuracy, completeness, and timeliness. The activities of computer operators, who are responsible for the operation of large computer systems, also need supervision.

Many operations management activities are being automated by the use of software packages for computer system *performance management* and *capacity management*. These **system performance monitors** monitor the processing of computer jobs, help develop a planned schedule of computer operations that can optimize computer system performance, and produce detailed statistics that are invaluable for effective capacity planning and control. Such information is used to evaluate computer system utilization, costs, and performance. This evaluation provides information for capacity planning, production planning and control, and hardware/software acquisition planning. It is also used as the basis of *chargeback* systems, which allocate costs to users based on the information services rendered. Finally, such information is used in *quality assurance* programs, which stress quality control of service to end users. See Figure 13–11.

Many performance monitors also feature *process control* capabilities. Such packages not only monitor but also automatically control operations at large data centers. Some use built-in expert system modules based on knowledge gleaned from experts in the operation of specific computers and operating systems. These performance monitors provide more efficient computer operations than human-operated systems. They also are leading toward the goal of "lights out" data centers, where large mainframe systems can be operated unattended, especially after normal business hours.

TECHNICAL SERVICES

Technical services consist of a variety of major functions that are vital to the provision of information services and the management of information system resources. They include data administration, user services, telecommunications management, capacity management, and technology management. These functions are typically more technically specialized than the basic information services functions of systems development and operations.

Data Administration

The widespread use of common and specialized databases for corporate, work group, and end user information systems has made managing data a major dimension of information resource management. In Chapter 6, we pointed out that since the databases of an organization are used by many different applications, they need to be centrally coordinated and controlled by a *data resources management* philosophy and a *data administration* function.

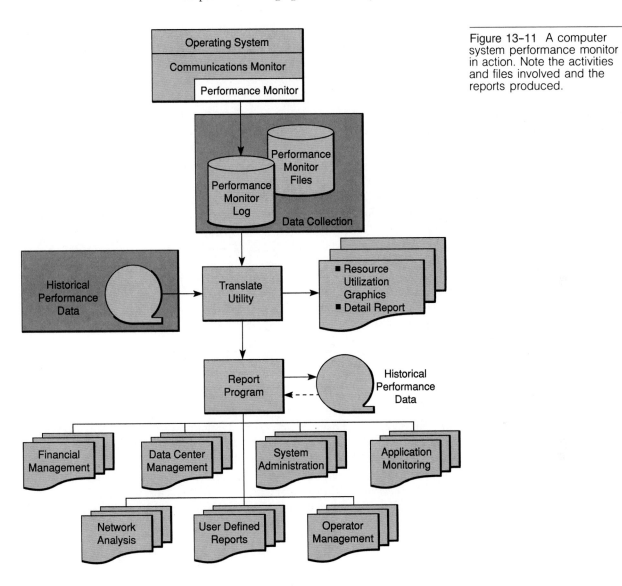

Figure 13–11 A computer system performance monitor in action. Note the activities and files involved and the reports produced.

Data administration involves the establishment and enforcement of policies and procedures for managing data as a strategic corporate resource. This means that the collection, storage, and dissemination of data are administered in such a way that data becomes a standardized resource available to all information systems in the organization. Data administration typically results in long-range data planning and the development of common databases and standards. This includes a *database administration* function to enforce the use of a common data dictionary and standards for database use and security. Figure 13–12 illustrates the relationship of the data administration function to database administration and other data resource management activities [5].

Figure 13–12 The major
responsibilities of data
administration.

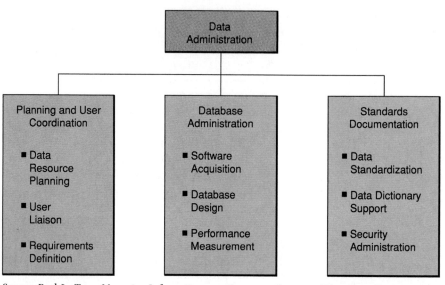

Figure 13–12 The major responsibilities of data administration.

Source: Paul L. Tom, *Managing Information as a Corporate Resource* (Glenview, Ill.: Scott, Foresman, 1987), p. 61.

User Services

As we said in Chapter 7, end users now use personal computer workstations and software packages to develop and apply computer-based information systems to their own business activities. Organizations have responded with various attempts to both support and manage this explosion of end user computing. The most important effort is the development of the **information center** concept to provide hardware, software, and staff support from within the organization. Information centers are part of a major information services function called **user services.** This function has created end user service positions such as information center manager, user consultants, business analysts, and technical support specialists.

End user computing provides both opportunities and problems for end user management. Establishing an information center in the organization or the end user department is one solution. However, policies must still be established and enforced concerning the acquisition of hardware and software by end users to assure the compatibility of such resources. Even more important is the development of applications with proper controls to promote correct performance and safeguard the integrity of corporate and departmental databases. These are the managerial challenges facing top executives, end user managers, and chief information officers. In response, many organizations have established information centers. However, others have dismantled their information centers and distributed end user support specialists to departments and other work groups [10].

Telecommunications Management

The rapid growth of telecommunications networks in computer-using firms has made **telecommunications management** a major information services function. This function manages the wide area networks for applications such as online transaction processing, inquiry/response, and electronic mail, and the local area networks for work group and end user computing. Telecommunications management is responsible for overseeing all telecommunications services provided to end users and the IS function. This may include data and voice communications, facsimile, electronic mail, voice mail, teleconferencing, tele-commuting, and electronic data interchange services.

Telecommunications managers are usually responsible for evaluating and recommending the acquisition of communications media, communications carriers, and communications hardware and software for end user, work group, and corporate telecommunications networks. They work with end user managers to improve the design, operational quality, and security of an organization's telecommunications networks and services. *Network managers* typically manage the operation of specific wide area and local area telecommunications networks. They monitor and evaluate telecommunications processors (such as network and file servers), network control software (such as network operating systems), and other common network hardware and software resources, to assure a proper level of service to the users of an organization's networks [7].

Technology Management

The management of rapidly changing technology is important to any organization. Changes in information systems technology have come swiftly and dramatically and are expected to continue into the future. Developments in information systems technology have had, and will continue to have, a major impact on the operations, costs, management work environment, and competitive position of many organizations. Therefore, many firms have established separate groups to identify, introduce, and monitor the assimilation of new information systems technologies into their organizations, especially those with a high payoff potential [2, 15].

These organizational units are called *technology management, emerging technologies,* or *advanced technology* groups. Such advanced technology groups (ATGs) typically report to the chief information systems officer and are staffed with former senior systems analysts and other specialists in information systems technology. Their job is to monitor emerging technological developments and identify innovative developments that have high potential payoffs to the firm. Then they work with end user managers and information services management to introduce new technologies into the firm. They also *audit* a firm's current applications of technology so they can recommend improvements. Figure 13–13 illustrates the forces that need to be confronted in the management of information systems technology.

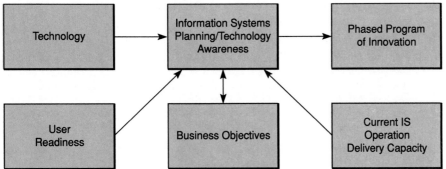

Figure 13–13 Forces to be confronted in the management of information systems technology.

Source: Adapted from James Cash, Jr., F. Warren McFarlan, James McKenney, and Michael Vitale, *Corporate Information Systems Management: Text and Cases,* 2nd ed. (Homewood, Ill.: Richard D. Irwin, 1988), p. 500.

MANAGING INFORMATION SERVICES PERSONNEL

The success or failure of an information services organization rests primarily on the quality of its people. Information systems managers consider recruiting, training, and retaining qualified personnel a major problem. Millions of persons are employed in the information services organizations of computer users. National employment surveys continually forecast shortages of qualified information services personnel. Employment opportunities in the computer field are excellent, and businesses are expected to continue to expand their use of computers. For these reasons, it is important to analyze the types of jobs and the managerial problems associated with information services personnel [3].

Figure 13–14 gives valuable insight into the variety of job types and salaries commanded by many information services personnel. Actual salaries range higher and lower than the averages shown, depending on such factors as the size and geographic location of the information services organization.

Managing information services involves the management of managerial, technical, and clerical personnel. One of the most important jobs of information service managers is to recruit qualified personnel and to develop, organize, and direct the capabilities of existing personnel. Employees must be continually trained to keep up with the latest developments in a fast-moving and highly technical field. Employee job performance must be continually evaluated and

Figure 13–14 Examples of annual salaries for information services managers and professionals in 1990.

Executives	IS Budget		
	Under $20 Mil	$20 Mil–$100 Mil	Over $100 Mil
Chief Information Officer	$120,110	$154,610	$207,140
Senior/VP of IS	124,280	142,930	183,040
Assistant VP of IS	84,380	93,060	128,130
Director of IS	87,170	107,290	120,140
Manager of IS	71,790	84,870	87,500

Operating Management	20th Percentile	Median	80th Percentile
Data Center Operations Manager	$38,000	$50,000	$67,000
Programming Development Manager	49,000	58,000	68,000
Systems Development Manager	49,000	57,000	67,000
Technical Services Manager	45,000	56,000	67,000
Systems Development			
Systems Consultant	38,000	49,000	60,000
Project Leader/Systems Analyst	38,000	45,000	54,000
Business Applications Programmer	25,000	41,000	49,000
Engineering/Scientific Programmer	27,000	44,000	53,000
Systems Software Programmer	28,000	43,900	50,000
Technical Specialists			
Technical Data Center Analyst	30,000	49,000	59,000
Database Management Analyst	28,000	49,000	57,000
Telecommunications Planner	26,000	45,000	56,000
Information Center Analyst	24,000	40,000	49,000
EDP Auditor	27,000	46,000	56,000

Adapted from Source-EDP, *Computer Salary Survey and Planning Guide*, 1990, p. 9, and *SIM Special Report*, January 1990, p. 4.

H. P. Hood, Incorporated

H. P. Hood, Inc., has launched a three-year plan to decentralize computing at the 144-year old Boston-based dairy products manufacturer. With 2,200 employees scattered throughout three major divisions and $710 million in annual sales, Hood executives feel that decentralizing will ultimately result in better overall control in process manufacturing. "Eventually, we hope to have six AS/400 minicomputers functioning as file servers to our personal computers," said Girard D. Liberty, director of MIS at Hood. The company is also installing As/400 terminals and scattering NEC and IBM PCs throughout the organization.

Hood's decision was initially dictated by the corporate purse and the cries of end users who suffered slow (five-second) response times. "We had pretty much hit the limit with the IBM 4381 midsize mainframe we were using here at headquarters," Liberty said. The response time slowdown resulted from company growth and several recent acquisitions. Hood, a subsidiary of Agway, Inc., made the decision to decentralize both management and computing functions over a year ago. The company also decided it did not want the expense of upgrading to a large IBM 3090-type platform. "It meant going the whole water-cooled data center route," Liberty said.

Decentralization forces a broader view of the business. It makes the job richer, improves customer relations and improves the IS role within the business," Liberty said. "The networking capabilities across the company will give employees a broader perspective of the entire operations." Networking the minicomputers will allow end users to generate reports, share customer profiles, and track the product transfer process, as well as provide route settlement information and better response to inquiries. The customers will benefit from local account administration functions and programs tailored to meet individual customer needs.

For example, Liberty said, individual units will be able to provide customized reports to large supermarket chains. Regional general managers will take responsibility for operations, financial reporting, general ledger, customer service, and order processing on a local level. With the 4300-type system, Hood lacked the horsepower to support such customized processing. But the greatest improvements will be realized by the company's end users, some of whom have already reported internal response times of 0.7 seconds, with the number of transactions increasing more than 20 percent.

Decentralizing activities has reduced the Hood information systems staff from 38 to 35, and Liberty notes that the only costs have occurred in technical services. "We haven't reduced the operations staff at all," he said. "Decentralizing will put us in a better position overall," Liberty concluded. "It will allow both Hood and Hood customers to better leverage their time and money."

Application Questions

☐ Why did H. P. Hood decide to decentralize its IS function?

☐ How is this being accomplished?

☐ How is decentralization of IS affecting H. P. Hood's operations and employees?

Source: Adapted from Sally Cusack, "Milking a Decentralized System," *Computerworld*, April 16, 1990, p. 33.

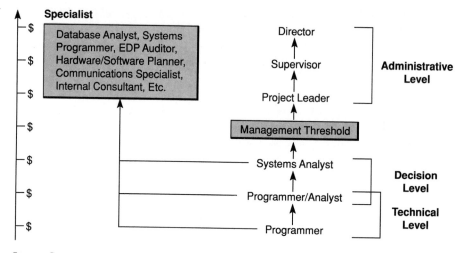

Source: Courtesy Source-EDP.

Figure 13–15 Career paths for systems development personnel. Note the traditional upward path into management and the newer path into various specialist positions.

outstanding performances rewarded with salary increases or promotions. Salary and wage levels must be set, and career paths must be designed so individuals can move to new jobs through promotion and transfer as they gain in seniority and expertise.

For example, many firms provide information services personnel with individual career paths, opportunities for merit salary increases, project leadership opportunities, and attendance at professional meetings and educational seminars. These opportunities help provide the flexible job environment needed to retain competent personnel. Challenging technological and intellectual assignments and a congenial atmosphere of fellow professionals are other major factors frequently cited in helping to retain information services personnel [3]. Figure 13–15 illustrates some of the career paths available to information systems professionals.

SUMMARY

☐ Managing the information system resources of an organization has become a major managerial responsibility known as information resource management (IRM). End user managers must learn how to manage the hardware, software, people, data, and information resources of their business units and work groups for the strategic benefit of the entire organization.

☐ Poor information system performance in many organizations is well documented and reveals that information systems are not being used effectively, efficiently, or economically by many business firms. The experiences of successful organizations reveal that the basic ingredient of high-quality information system performance is extensive and meaningful management and user involvement in the development and management of computer-based information systems.

☐ The major activities of information services organizations can be grouped into three basic functional categories: (1) systems development, (2) operations, and (3) technical services. The organizational structure, location, and staffing of an information services department must reflect these three basic functions and activities. However, many variations exist, which reflect the attempts of organizations to tailor their organizational and staffing arrangements to their particular business activities and management philosophy, as well as to the capabilities of centralized or distributed information systems.

☐ The information systems function in an organization may be headed by a chief information officer, who oversees the organization's use of information technology. Managing systems development projects requires managing the use of systems development methodologies and project management techniques. Managing computer operations involves various production planning and control techniques. Management of technical services includes data administration, the management of user services and telecommunications, and technology management.

☐ There is a wide variety of career choices and job types in many computer-using organizations that can be grouped into occupational categories that coincide with the three functional categories of systems development, operations, and technical services. Managing the technical personnel in an information services department is a major human resource management assignment.

These are the key terms and concepts of this chapter. The page number of their first explanation is in parentheses.

KEY TERMS AND CONCEPTS

1. Centralization or decentralization (*454*)
   a. Information systems
   b. Operations and management
2. Chief information officer (*464*)
3. Data administration (*466*)
4. Data center (*466*)
5. Development center (*465*)
6. End user involvement (*460*)
7. End user resistance (*460*)
8. End user services (*468*)
9. Impact of information technology on management (*452*)
10. Information center (*468*)
11. Information resource management (*455*)

12. Information services functions (*464*)
13. Information systems performance (*458*)
14. Information technology (*452*)
15. Management involvement (*459*)
16. Managing information services personnel (*470*)
17. Operations management (*466*)
18. Systems development management (*465*)
19. Technology management (*469*)
20. Technical services (*466*)
21. Telecommunications management (*468*)

Match one of the **key terms and concepts** listed above with one of the examples and definitions listed below. Try to find the best fit for answers that seem to fit more than one term or concept. Defend your choices.

REVIEW QUIZ

_____ 1. Managers have a lot of information, information processing power, and responsibility for information systems.

_____ 2. Information system resources can be distributed throughout an organization or consolidated in data centers.

——————   3. Information systems can help management increase the number of branch offices or consolidate operations.

——————   4. Managing information systems is a distributed, functional responsibility focusing on the strategic management of information systems technology and resources.

——————   5. Computer-based information systems have not been used efficiently, effectively, and economically.

——————   6. A management steering committee is an example.

——————   7. Some of the causes are ignorance, performance problems, and a lack of participation and communication.

——————   8. End user representatives on systems development teams and in prototyping sessions are examples.

——————   9. End users need information centers and other forms of liaison, consulting, and training support.

——————   10. Includes the basic functions of systems development, operations, and technical services.

——————   11. An executive that oversees all information systems technology for an organization.

——————   12. Managing systems analysis and design, computer programming, and systems maintenance activities.

——————   13. Planning and controlling information processing operations.

——————   14. Developing and enforcing data standards and doing strategic data planning.

——————   15. Corporate locations for computer operations.

——————   16. A support group for an organization's professional programmers and systems analysts.

——————   17. A support group for an organization's end users.

——————   18. Information systems are based on computer hardware, software, and telecommunications technologies.

——————   19. Rapidly changing technological developments must be anticipated, identified, and implemented.

——————   20. A category that includes user services, telecommunications management, and technology management.

——————   21. Telecommunications networks and their hardware and software must be developed, administered, and maintained.

——————   22. Recruiting and developing information systems specialists.

REAL WORLD PROBLEMS

1. MIS Hall of Fame

   Technology is great, but it takes people with a vision to put it to strategic use. The winners of the *Third Annual Awards for Achievement in Managing Information Technology* went to the following information systems executives:

   ☐ Jane E. Bailey, director of information systems for the Commonwealth of Virginia, transformed the Department of Taxation's labor-intensive operations into a computer-driven process that contributed an estimated $77 million in cost reductions and additional revenue collections in 1988, with a project cost of only $11 million.

☐ Paul F. Glaser, chairman of Citicorp's Corporate Technology and Technology Operating Committees, was among the pioneers of the ATM idea in the early 1980s and saw Citicorp's share of the New York City retail market surge from 4 percent to over 13 percent. Glaser has developed a second generation of multilingual, user friendly ATMs that have resulted in a 50 percent increase in usage.

☐ James C. Grant is executive vice president in charge of systems and technology at the Royal Bank of Canada. His projects have sought to integrate technology with business using executive training programs and new ways of improving customer service.

☐ R. W. Eaton, senior vice president and chief information officer at Levi Strauss & Co., spearheaded development of "Levilink," which speeds up and simplifies transactions from ordering to paying for Levi's products.

☐ G. Nichols Simonds, executive director of MIS at Chrysler Corp., directed development of Chrysler's Service Bay Diagnostic (SBD) system, a computerized diagnostic system for dealerships, which is projected to save Chrysler over $10 million annually in warranty costs and improve customer satisfaction.

a. Did these IS winners use information technology to improve operational efficiency or promote business innovation? Explain.

b. Are these achievements examples of strategic information systems? Information resource management? Explain.

Source: Adapted from Amy Cortese, "Eight Garner IS Impact Awards," *Computerworld,* November 20, 1989, p. 135.

2. MIS Hall of Shame
    Rona B. Stillman, chief scientist of the U.S. General Accounting Office (GAO) Information Management Technology Division, cited three examples of poor IS performance from what she called the GAO Hall of Shame. One agency planned to upgrade systems to keep up with the work load, but customers said that most of the generated reports were useless and thrown in the trash. Another agency spent a great deal of money to replace the big old message center with a big new message center, never considering eliminating the message center and using electronic mail instead. Many agencies also have technology plans , but "All we see are plans to buy new stuff to do the same wrong thing faster," Stillman said.

    The Internal Revenue Service's $1.8 billion investment in automating the examining of tax returns resulted in benefits that were 63 percent lower than the IRS had predicted, and the four-year implementation plan has turned into a 10-year period. Specifically, the IRS bought 18,000 laptop computers for field agents in 1984—a full year before the software design was even started. Thus, the software now resides on 18 different floppy disks, and the data in the laptop-based system can't always be correlated to the rest of the information the IRS has.

    In private industry, officials at Lockheed Aeronautical Systems said failure to include critical data in an executive information system (EIS) prevented the system from discovering that the weight of Lockheed's new P-7 antisubmarine aircraft was rising beyond expectations. Designers had originally counted on reusing certain parts from an earlier aircraft, the P-3. But using these parts prevented the P-7 from meeting the Navy's structural and performance requirements. As a result, Lockheed was forced to design new parts, which unexpectedly drove up the weight of the aircraft. The mistake could cost as much as $300 million and may cause the firm to report a net loss for the year.

a. What do you think were the causes of the major IS failures described above?

b. What solutions can you suggest to prevent similar failures in any organization?

Source: Adapted from Mitch Betts, "GAO Hall of Shame Cites Techno-Lemons," *Computerworld*, November 13, 1989, p. 87; Jeff Angus, "IRS Falls to Cost/Benefit Bunk," *Computerworld*, January 15, 1990, p. 19; Robert Scheier, "Lockheed Learns Costly Lesson in System Design," *PC Week*, January 29, 1990, pp. 1, 6.

3. Warner-Lambert Company

The corporate data center at Warner-Lambert Company charges the firm's divisions for its services—but the divisions are not required to use the data center. So Jim Oster, Warner-Lambert MIS director, is justifiably proud that very few of his end user clients go outside the company for IS services and of those that do, most return to the fold. The firm is a producer of health care and consumer products. Its data center serves hundreds of internal clients from 16 locations throughout the United States. Each month, the data center handles an average of 81,000 tasks and processes between 700 and 800 calls.

A major reason for the high satisfaction level, Oster says, is that the center shares system ownership. "Our technical people do not own the computers any more than the applications development staff does. They share ownership by managing projects as a service to our end user clients. Another reason is that our data center is responsive; we are getting out there, calling on clients, finding out their needs, designing solutions to meet those needs, and suggesting ways they can cut costs." All the while, the data center remains at or below budget guidelines and has consistently reduced rates to clients each year. Oster says the plan calls for no rate increase through 1992 and adds that rates actually will be lowered an average of 9.5 percent.

a. Why do you think Warner-Lambert allows its divisions to use outside vendors for their IS services?

b. How does Warner-Lambert's data center keep most end user clients from going to outside vendors?

Source: Adapted from "Data Center Keeps Customers Well Information-Processed," *IBM Update*, March/April 1990, p. 19.

4. Texaco Incorporated

Hoping to drive up quality and mend fences with users, Texaco Inc. has split its corporate information technology (IT) department into self-managed work teams and forced them to compete head-to-head with outside vendors of IS services. For the IT group, it means higher morale and lower turnover. For Texaco's 20,000 to 30,000 end user "customers," it means better, faster and less expensive service from the corporate IT department, said the department's general manager, Jim Metzger. "We're guilty of many of the traditional sins of an IT organization—doing systems without a lot of user input," said Metzger. The 800-person IT group realized that Texaco's users are no longer a captive audience but rather are customers who must be won with superior value, said Metzger. To accomplish that, the staff underwent thousands of hours of training to learn about working in teams, sharing information, and jointly setting goals. The new approach has forced the IT staff to listen to users and then sell them on the business value of technology.

Sometimes, winning means beating back the widely discussed trend toward outsourcing—turning over IS functions to outsiders. Recently, the IT department signed a three-year contract to provide a variety of mainframe, minicomputer, and software support services to Star Enterprises, a Texaco partnership that operates service stations in 26 states. Star compared Texaco's IT department costs to those of outside vendors such as Electronic Data Systems. While the IT group had some advantages as an inside supplier, "the decision was based on dollars," said Star's IS director, Gary Richardson. Metzger said that while his staff hasn't been threatened with cutbacks if it fails to compete, he realizes that, like every other department in Texaco, "if we don't provide quality service, we won't be in business."

a. How and why did Texaco change the organization and mission of its IT department?

b. What benefits have resulted?

Source: Adapted from Robert Scheier, "Texaco's IS Goes Head-to-Head with Outside Vendors—and Wins," *PC Week*, March 25, 1990, pp. 1, 6.

5. Air Products and Chemicals, Inc.

George Diehl, business manager for helium at Air Products and Chemicals, Inc., in Allentown, Pennsylvania, says that if IS executives are really going to function as full partners of business managers, there has to be face-to-face contact and shoulder-to-shoulder effort. That's the kind of relationship Diehl has developed with IS director Paul Prutzman and his staff since the company decided that selling liquid helium to a new class of customers—makers of the magnetic resonance imaging machines used in hospitals—required a joint effort from the sales force and IS. Including IS executives in sales calls was just one aspect of the partnerships the company fostered among line managers and IS professionals as it pursued the new market. Members of the two groups also held weekly breakfast meetings and developed presentations together. Through the alliance, the industrial gas division was also able to take advantage of electronic data interchange services that Diehl says helped it win the bulk of a market that did not exist five years ago.

a. Why should IS executives become partners of business managers?

b. How was this accomplished at Air Products?

Source: Adapted from David Ludlum, "The Buddy System Takes More than Handshakes and Smiles," *Computerworld*, February 12, 1990, p. 77.

6. Corning Incorporated

When novice users are stuck deep in the bowels of Lotus 1-2-3 or find themselves staring at a mute printer, who do they often ask for help? Other users, of course. Realizing that stumped users were already relying on one another for computer support anyway, Corning undertook an innovative support program in early 1988. The company's User Resource Network was designed to shift much low-level daily support of end user departments in its Corning, New York, headquarters to the departments themselves. Now, two years later, company officials say the plan is paying off—in a big way. End users get faster response, IS gets more time to work on meaty applications, and business managers get better productivity.

Two people in a department became technical mentors, joining a facilitator, or top mentor. The goal is not to make everyone a speed-demon power user but to ensure basic competency and fast problem solving. The users-helping-users idea has also sparked several changes—all positive—in how a department works. For one thing, departmental users have become more technically sophisticated and confident. Such confidence in turn has helped users think about new ways of applying technology to their daily work. Perhaps most important, however, users and IS staff alike say that being freed from trivial problems allows them to focus on more strategic tasks.

a. Why did Corning develop a "user resource network" instead of relying on an information center to support end users?

b. What benefits have resulted? Could these benefits have been provided by an information center? Explain.

Source: Adapted from Barbara Braverman and Carol Hartwig, "Users Helping Users," *Computerworld*, April 23, 1990, pp. 99–102.

7. IS Professional Profile

Do you know people like this? They prize interest and diversity in their work and want to use a variety of skills in a meaningful job. They like to guide a project from beginning to end and prefer to work autonomously—and alone. They need to see the direct impact of their efforts and want to hear what you think about their performance. They're interested in a fair wage and good benefits to keep up with inflation and the high costs of education and housing. They also want to keep on growing professionally. Recognize them yet? They are the typical analysts or programmers in your IS department—and you'd better say hello before they say goodbye for greener pastures.

Perhaps the most important personnel issue facing IS managers during the 1990s will be the impending shortage of new workers. Fewer college students are choosing majors in computer science and IS. This prospective labor shortage means that IS managers must place greater emphasis on reducing turnover of analysts and programmers. Fortunately, IS managers control the key factor that motivates programmers and analysts: the work itself. While improving feedback, pay, and benefits is important, eliminating mismatches between the employee's growth needs and the job's motivating capacity is the most important way to motivate analysts and programmers. Doing so will make IS professionals more productive while eliminating feelings that they need to leave the company to realize job satisfaction.

a. What motivates IS professionals? Why is this important for IS managers to know?

b. Do you fit the profile for IS professionals described above? Do other types of professionals have similar profiles? Explain.

Source: Adapted from J. Daniel Couger, "Motivating Analysts and Programmers," *Computerworld,* January 15, 1990, p. 73–76.

SELECTED REFERENCES

1. Carlyle, Ralph. "The Tomorrow Organization." *Datamation,* February 1, 1990.
2. Cash, James; F. Warren McFarlan; James McKenney; and Michael Vitale. *Corporate Information Systems Management: Text and Cases.* 2nd ed. Homewood, Ill.: Richard D. Irwin, 1988.
3. Couger, J. Daniel. "Motivating Analysts and Programmers." *Computerworld,* January 15, 1990.
4. Drucker, Peter. "The Coming of the New Organization." *Harvard Business Review,* January/February 1988.
5. Goodhue, Dale; Judith Quillard; and John Rockart. "Managing the Data Resource: A Contingency Perspective." *MIS Quarterly,* September 1988.
6. Guimaraes, Tor. "Information Resources Management: Improving the Focus." *Information Resources Management Journal,* Fall 1988.
7. Kerr, Susan. "Telecom Pros Evolve." *Datamation,* January 15, 1989.
8. Martin, James. *An Information Systems Manifesto.* Englewood Cliffs, N.J.: Prentice-Hall, 1984.
9. McFarlan, F. Warren, and James McKenney. "The Information Archipelago: Mazes and Bridges." *Harvard Business Review,* September/October 1982.
10. Moad, Jeff. "The Second Wave." *Datamation,* February 1, 1989.
11. Nolan, Richard. "Managing the Crisis in Data Processing." *Harvard Business Review,* March/April 1979.
12. Sprague, Ralph, and Barbara McNurlen. *Information Systems Management in Practice, 2nd ed.* Englewood Cliffs, N.J.: Prentice-Hall, 1989.
13. Tait, Peter, and Iris Vessey. "The Effect of User Involvement on System Success: A Contingency Approach." *MIS Quarterly,* March 1988.
14. Tavakolian, Hamid. "Linking the Information Technology Structure with Organizational Competitive Strategy: A Survey. *MIS Quarterly,* September, 1989.
15. Weil, Peter, and Margrethe Olson. "Managing Investment in Information Technology: Minicase Examples and Implications." *MIS Quarterly,* March 1989.
16. Wilder, Clinton. "Re-engineering Is IS Priority."*Computerworld,* March 14, 1990.

CHAPTER

14

CONTROLLING INFORMATION SYSTEMS PERFORMANCE

■ **Chapter Outline**

■ Learning Objectives

The purpose of this chapter is to give you an understanding of how business firms must control their information system resources by analyzing (1) control techniques for information systems and (2) the control implications of their impact on society, including computer crime and ethics.

Section I of this chapter discusses how the quality and security of information systems can be protected by the use of various types of information systems controls, procedural controls, and physical facility controls, as well as methods of controlling end user computing.

Section II discusses the beneficial and adverse impact of computer-based information systems on society, including the topics of computer crime and the ethical considerations involved.

After reading and studying this chapter, you should be able to:

1. Explain why information system controls are needed.

2. Outline several types of information system controls, procedural controls, and physical facility controls that can be used to assure the quality and security of information systems.

3. Discuss the impact of computer-based information systems in terms of their major beneficial and adverse effects on society.

4. Identify major types of computer crime and explain their effect on the development of information system controls.

5. Identify several ethical considerations arising from the use of computers by end users and information systems professionals.

Section I: Controls for Information System Performance and Security

WHY CONTROLS ARE NEEDED

Like any other assets, the resources of information systems hardware, software, and data need to be protected by built-in controls to assure their quality and security. That's why controls are needed. Computers have proven they can process huge volumes of data and perform complex calculations more accurately than manual or mechanical information systems. However, we know that (1) errors do occur in computer-based systems, (2) computers have been used for fraudulent purposes, and (3) computer systems and their software and data resources have been accidentally or maliciously destroyed.

There is no question that computers have had some detrimental effect on the detection of errors and fraud. Manual and mechanical information processing systems use paper documents and other media that can be visually checked by information processing personnel. Several persons are usually involved in such systems and, therefore, cross-checking procedures are easily performed. These characteristics of manual and mechanical information processing systems facilitate the direction of errors and fraud.

Computer-based information systems, on the other hand, use machine-sensible media such as magnetic disks and tape. They accomplish processing manipulations within the electronic circuitry of computer systems. The ability to check visually the progress of information processing activities and the contents of databases is significantly reduced. In addition, a relatively small number of personnel may effectively control processing activities that are critical to the survival of the organization. Therefore, the ability to detect errors and fraud can be reduced by computerization. This makes the development of various control methods a vital consideration in the design of new or improved information systems.

Effective controls are needed to ensure **information system security,** that is, the *accuracy, integrity,* and *safety* of information system activities and resources. Controls can minimize *errors, fraud,* and *destruction* in an information services organization. Effective controls provide **quality assurance** for information systems. That is, they can make a computer-based information system more free of errors and fraud and able to provide information products of higher quality than manual types of information processing. This can help reduce the potential negative impact (and increase the positive impact) that information systems can have on business survival and success and the quality of life in society.

What Controls Are Needed

Three major types of controls must be developed to assure the quality and security of information systems. These control categories, illustrated in Figure 14–1, are:

- ☐ Information system controls.
- ☐ Procedural controls.
- ☐ Physical facility controls.

INFORMATION SYSTEM CONTROLS

Information system controls are methods and devices that attempt to ensure the accuracy, validity, and propriety of information system activities. Controls

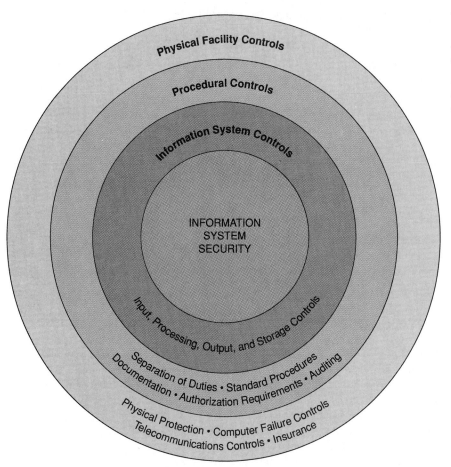

must be developed to ensure proper data entry, processing techniques, storage methods, and information output. Thus, information system controls are designed to monitor and maintain the quality and security of the input, processing, output, and storage activities of any information system. See Figure 14–2.

Remember the phrase "garbage in, garbage out" (GIGO)? That's why controls are needed for the proper entry of data into an information system. Examples include formatted data entry screens, machine-readable media, templates over the keys of key-driven input devices, and prerecorded and prenumbered forms. Realtime systems that use direct access files frequently record all entries into the system on magnetic tape control logs that preserve evidence of all system inputs.

    Computer software can include instructions to identify incorrect, invalid, or improper input data as it enters the computer system. For example, a data entry program can check for invalid codes, data fields, and transactions. Also, the computer can be programmed to conduct "reasonableness checks" to determine if input data exceeds certain specified limits or is out of sequence. This includes the calculation and monitoring of **control totals.**

    For example, a *record count* is a control total that consists of counting the total number of source documents or other input records and comparing this total to the number of records counted at other stages of data entry. If the totals

Input Controls

Figure 14–2 Types of information system controls. Note that they are designed to monitor and maintain the quality and security of the input, processing, output, and storage activities of an information system.

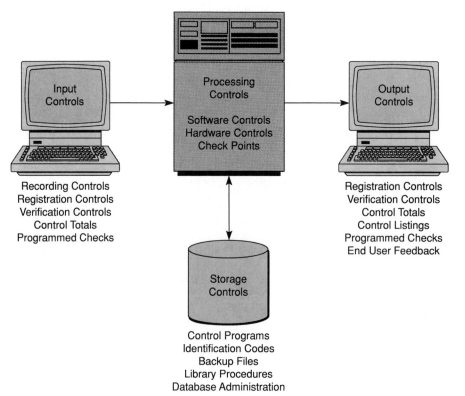

Recording Controls
Registration Controls
Verification Controls
Control Totals
Programmed Checks

Control Programs
Identification Codes
Backup Files
Library Procedures
Database Administration

Registration Controls
Verification Controls
Control Totals
Control Listings
Programmed Checks
End User Feedback

do not match, a mistake has been made. *Batch totals* and *hash totals* are other forms of control totals. A *batch total* is the sum of a specific item of data within a batch of transactions, such as the sales amounts in a batch of sales transactions. *Hash totals* are the sum of data fields that are added together only for control comparisons. For example, employee social security numbers could be added to produce a control total for the data entry of payroll documents.

Processing Controls

Once data is entered correctly into a computer system, it must be processed properly. Processing controls are developed to identify errors in arithmetic calculations and logical operations. They are also used to ensure that data are not lost or do not go unprocessed. Processing controls can include *hardware controls* and *software controls*.

Hardware Controls

Hardware controls are special checks built into the hardware to verify the accuracy of computer processing. Examples of hardware checks include:

☐ Malfunction detection circuitry within the computer that can monitor its operations. For example, *parity checks* are made to check for the loss of the correct number of bits in every byte of data processed. Another example is *echo checks*, which require that a signal be returned from a device or circuit to verify that it was properly activated. Other examples are redundant circuitry checks, arithmetic sign checks, and CPU timing and voltage checks.

☐ Redundant components. For example, multiple read-write heads on magnetic tape and disk devices check and promote the accuracy of reading and recording activities.

☐ Switches and other devices. For example, switches can be set that prohibit writing on magnetic tapes or disks. On magnetic tape reels, a removable plastic or metal ring can be removed to prevent writing on a tape. The write/protect notch on floppy disks has a similar function.

☐ Special-purpose microprocessors and associated circuitry. This may be used to support *remote diagnostics* and *maintenance*. It allows off-site technicians to diagnose and correct some problems via a telecommunications link to a computer system.

Software Controls

Some software controls are designed to assure that the right data is being processed. For example, an operating system may check the internal file labels at the beginning and end of magnetic tape and disk files. These labels contain information identifying the file and provide control totals for the data in the file. These internal file labels allow the computer to ensure that the proper file is being used and that the proper data in the file have been processed.

Another major software control is the establishment of *checkpoints* during the processing of a program. Checkpoints are intermediate points within a program where intermediate totals, listings, or *dumps* of data are written on magnetic tape or disk or listed on a printer. Checkpoints minimize the effect of processing errors or failures since processing can be restarted from the last checkpoint, rather than from the beginning of the program. They also help build an **audit trail,** which allows transactions being processed to be traced through all of the steps of processing.

Many input, processing, output, and storage controls may be provided by specialized system software packages known as **system security monitors.** These are programs that monitor and protect the use of a computer system and its resources from unauthorized use, fraud, and destruction. Such programs provide the security needed to allow only authorized users to access the system. For example, identification codes and passwords are frequently used for this purpose. Security monitors also control the use of the hardware, software, and data resources of a computer system. For example, even authorized users may be restricted to the use of certain devices, programs, and data files. Finally, such programs monitor computer use and collect statistics on any attempts at improper use. They produce reports to assist in maintaining the security of the system. See Figure 14–3.

Output Controls

How can we control the quality of the information products produced by an information system? Output controls are developed to ensure that information products are correct and complete and are transmitted to authorized users in a timely manner. For example, control totals on output are usually compared with control totals generated during the input and processing stages. Control listings can be produced that provide hard copy evidence of documents and reports produced.

Prenumbered output forms can be used to control the loss of important output documents such as stock certificates or payroll check forms. Distribution

Figure 14-3 An overview of
the features of a major software package for computer
security. This is IBM's Resource Access Control
Facility (RACF), a system security monitor.

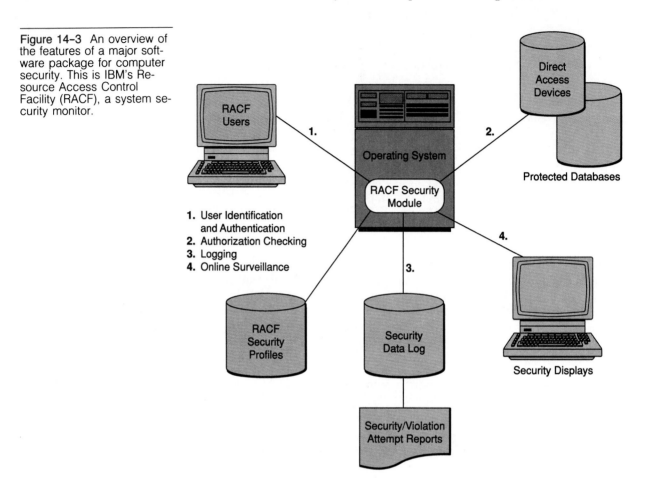

Figure 14-3 An overview of the features of a major software package for computer security. This is IBM's Resource Access Control Facility (RACF), a system security monitor.

1. User Identification and Authentication
2. Authorization Checking
3. Logging
4. Online Surveillance

lists help operations personnel ensure that only authorized users receive sensitive reports. The video displays of realtime processing systems are typically controlled by security software which controls the types of output end users are authorized to receive at their workstations and terminals. Finally, end users should provide feedback on the quality of their information products. This is an important function of systems maintenance and quality assurance activities.

Storage Controls

How can we protect our data resources? First, control responsibilities for files of computer programs and organizational databases may be assigned to a librarian or database administrator. These employees are responsible for maintaining and controlling access to the libraries and database of the organization. Second, many databases and files are protected from unauthorized or accidental use by security programs that require proper identification before they can be used. Typically, the operating system or security monitor protects the databases of realtime processing systems from unauthorized use or processing accidents. Account codes, passwords, and other identification codes are frequently used to allow access only to authorized users. A catalog of authorized users enables the computer system to identify eligible users and determine which types of information they are authorized to receive.

Typically, a three-level password system is used. First, an end user logs on to the computer system by entering his or her unique identification code, or *user ID*. The end user is then asked to enter a *password* in order to gain access into the system. Finally, to access an individual file, a unique *file name* must be entered. In some systems, the password to read the contents of a file is different from that required to write to a file (change its contents). This feature adds another level of protection to data resources [16].

Many firms also use *backup files*, which are duplicate files of data or programs. Such files may be stored off-premises, that is, in a location away from the computer center, sometimes in special storage vaults in remote locations. Many realtime processing systems use duplicate files that are updated by telecommunication links. Files are also protected by *file retention* measures, which involve storing copies of master files and transaction files from previous periods. If current files are destroyed, the files from previous periods are used to reconstruct new current files. Usually, several *generations* of files are kept for control purposes.

PROCEDURAL CONTROLS

Procedural controls are methods that specify how the information services organization should be operated for maximum security. They help an organization maintain the accuracy and integrity of IS operations.

Separation of Duties

Separation of duties is a basic principle of procedural control. It requires that the duties of systems development, computer operations, and control of data and program files be assigned to separate groups. For example, systems analysts and computer programmers may not be allowed to operate a mainframe system or make changes to data or programs being processed. In addition, the responsibility for maintaining a library of data files and program files is assigned to a librarian or database administrator. Finally, a production control section may monitor the progress of information processing jobs, data entry activities, and the quality of input/output data. This is an important *quality assurance* function.

Standard Procedures and Documentation

Standard procedures are typically developed and maintained in manuals and software help displays. Following standard procedures promotes uniformity and minimizes the chances of error and fraud. It helps employees know what is expected of them in operating procedures and output quality. It is important that procedures be developed for both normal and unusual operating conditions. For example, procedures should tell employees what to do differently when their computers are not working. Finally, systems and operations documentation must be developed and kept up-to-date to ensure the correct processing of each application. Documentation is also invaluable in the maintenance of a system as needed improvements are made.

Authorization Requirements

Request for major systems development projects, program changes, or system conversions are frequently subjected to a formal review before authorization is given. For example, program changes generated by maintenance programmers should be approved by the manager of programming after consultation with the manager of computer operations and the manager of the affected end user department. Conversion to new hardware and software, installation of newly developed information systems, and changes to existing programs should be subjected to a formal notification and scheduling procedure to minimize their detrimental effects.

Disaster Recovery

Natural and man-made disasters do happen. Hurricanes, earthquakes, fires, floods, criminal and terrorist acts, and human error can all severely damage an organization's computing resources, and thus the health of the organization itself. Many organizations, like airlines and banks, for example, are crippled by losing even a few hours of computing power. Many firms could survive only a few days without computing facilities. That's why organizations develop disaster recovery procedures and formalize them in a *disaster recovery plan*. It specifies which employees will participate in disaster recovery and what their duties will be, what hardware, software, and facilities will be used, and the priority of applications that will be processed. Arrangements with other companies for use of alternative facilities as a disaster recovery site, and offsite storage of an organization's databases are also part of an effective disaster recovery effort.

PHYSICAL FACILITY CONTROLS

Physical facility controls are methods that protect physical facilities and their contents from loss or destruction. Computer centers are subject to such hazards as accidents, natural disasters, sabotage, vandalism, unauthorized use, industrial espionage, destruction, and theft of resources. Therefore, physical safeguards and various control procedures are necessary to protect the hardware, software, and vital data resources of computer-using organizations. Figure 14–4

Figure 14–4 Recommended control strategies and methods to protect information system resources.

Control Strategy	Object	Effect	Control Methods
Containment	Control access	Reduce probability	Affect environment Reduce target attractiveness
	Isolate assets	Reduce probability	Control access to target Plug holes in defense Remove target from threat
Deterrence	Deter motives	Reduce probability	Advertise punishment Increase chances of being caught
	Prevent threats	Reduce probability	Detect early Thwart attack
	Detect results	Reduce loss	Detect all activity Review audit trails
Obfuscation	Conceal assets	Reduce probability	Cryptography Hide physical assets Control proprietary information
	Disperse assets	Reduce loss	Backup and recovery Alternative processing Multiple locations Isolation (barriers)
Recovery	Replace assets	Use other resources	Emergency procedures Backup and recovery Contingency planning
	Transfer loss	Absorb prior loss	Insurance

Source: Gerald Isaacson, "Physical Security Measures," in *The Handbook of MIS Management*, ed. Robert Umbaugh (Pennsauken, N.J.: Auerback Publishers, 1985), p. 610.

outlines major control strategies and specific control methods that are recommended to protect the information system resources of organizations and their end users.

Physical Protection Controls

Providing maximum security and disaster protection for a computer installation requires many types of controls. Only authorized personnel are allowed access to the computer center through such techniques as identification badges for information services personnel, electronic door locks, burglar alarms, security police, closed-circuit TV, and other detection systems. The computer centers are protected from disaster by such safeguards as fire detection and extinguishing systems; fireproof storage vaults for the protection of files; emergency power systems; electromagnetic shielding; and temperature, humidity, and dust control.

Biometric Controls

Biometric controls are a fast-growing area of computer security. These are security measures provided by computer devices which measure physical traits that make each individual unique. This includes voice verification, fingerprints, hand geometry, signature dynamics, keystroke analysis, retina scanning, face recognition, and genetic pattern analysis. Biometric control devices use special-purpose sensors to measure and digitize a *biometric profile* of an individual's fingerprints, voice, or other physical trait. The digitized signal is processed and compared to a previously processed profile of the individual stored on magnetic disk. If the profiles match, the individual is allowed entry into a computer facility or given access to information system resources [1].

Telecommunications Controls

The telecommunications processors and control software described in Chapter 5 play a vital role in the control of communications activity. In addition, special hardware and software can be used so data is transmitted in scrambled form and unscrambled only for authorized users. This **encryption** process transforms digital data into a scrambled code before it is transmitted and then decodes the data when it is received. Other control methods are typically used, such as the automatic disconnect and callback system illustrated in Figure 14–5.

Computer Failure Controls

"Sorry, the computer is down," is a well known phrase to many end users. A variety of controls are needed to prevent such failure or minimize its effects. Computers fail for several reasons—power failure, electronic circuitry malfunctions, mechanical malfunctions of peripheral equipment, hidden programming errors, and computer operator errors. The IS department typically takes several steps to minimize equipment failure. For example, computers with automatic and remote maintenance capabilities may be acquired. A program of *preventive maintenance* of hardware may be established. Adequate electrical supply, air-conditioning, humidity control, and fire prevention standards must also be set. A *backup computer system* capability may be arranged with other computer-using organizations, as we mentioned earlier. Major hardware or software changes should be carefully implemented to avoid problems. Finally, computer operators should have adequate training and supervision.

Many firms are acquiring **fault-tolerant** computer systems to ensure against computer failure. These systems have multiple central processors, peripherals,

Figure 14–5 A telecommunications access control system. Note how the disconnect and callback features work for authorized and nonauthorized users.

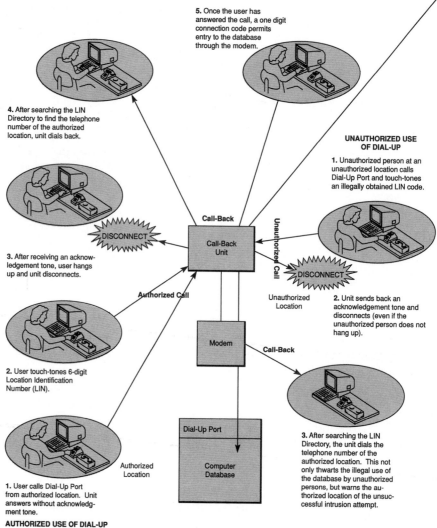

5. Once the user has answered the call, a one digit connection code permits entry to the database through the modem.

4. After searching the LIN Directory to find the telephone number of the authorized location, unit dials back.

UNAUTHORIZED USE OF DIAL-UP

1. Unauthorized person at an unauthorized location calls Dial-Up Port and touch-tones an illegally obtained LIN code.

3. After receiving an acknowledgement tone, user hangs up and unit disconnects.

Call-Back

DISCONNECT

Call-Back Unit

Unauthorized Call

DISCONNECT

Authorized Call

Unauthorized Location

2. Unit sends back an acknowledgement tone and disconnects (even if the unauthorized person does not hang up).

Modem

Call-Back

2. User touch-tones 6-digit Location Identification Number (LIN).

Dial-Up Port

Computer Database

3. After searching the LIN Directory, the unit dials the telephone number of the authorized location. This not only thwarts the illegal use of the database by unauthorized persons, but warns the authorized location of the unsuccessful intrusion attempt.

Authorized Location

1. User calls Dial-Up Port from authorized location. Unit answers without acknowledgment tone.

AUTHORIZED USE OF DIAL-UP

Source: Adapted from James A. Schweitzer, *Computer Crime and Business Information* (New York, Elsenier Science Publishing Co., 1986), p. 113.

and system software. This may provide a *fail-safe* capability where the computer system continues to operate at the same level even if there is a major hardware or software failure. However, many fault-tolerant computer systems offer a *fail-soft* capability, where the computer system can continue to operate at a reduced but acceptable level in the event of a major system failure.

CONTROLS FOR END USER COMPUTING

In Chapter 7, we outlined some of the risks of end user application development. We also discussed measures companies are taking to ensure the quality and security of end user applications. However, what many firms are beginning to realize is that in many cases, end user–developed applications are performing extremely important business functions. Instead of merely being systems for personal productivity or decision support, these applications are supporting important business activities that are critical to the success and survival of the firm. Thus, they can be called *company-critical* end user applications.

- A systems development approach that includes provisions for testing to determine whether the system is doing what it was designed to do and is consistent with company databases.
- A system notifying users when any changes in the system are planned and for testing the effect of those changes on live databases.
- A system for validating compliance with formal work procedures.
- Documentation so that a system can survive the departure of its creator.
- Means for securing the physical system, data storage media, sign-on, file systems, and printed information.
- Formal backup and recovery procedures.
- Training at least two people in the operation and maintenance of a system.
- A formal system for justifying and coordinating hardware and software acquisitions that includes a definition of the scope and purpose of the system, its business benefits, and a cost-benefit evaluation.

Figure 14–6 Controls for company-critical end user applications.

Source: Adapted from Jeff Moad, "The Second Wave," *Datamation*, February 1, 1989, p. 17.

Figure 14–6 outlines what one major company defines as the specific controls that must be observed or built in to all company-critical end user applications. What this firm and others are trying to do is protect themselves from the havoc that errors, fraud, destruction, and other hazards could cause to these critical applications and thus to the company itself. The controls involved are standard practice in applications developed by professional information services departments. However, such controls were ignored in the rush to end user computing [14].

An information services department should be periodically examined, or *audited*, by internal auditing personnel from the business firm. In addition, periodic audits by external auditors from professional accounting firms are a good business practice. Such audits should review and evaluate whether proper *information system controls, procedural controls, and physical facility controls* have been developed and implemented. There are two basic approaches for auditing the information processing activities of computer-based information systems. They are known as (1) *auditing around the computer* and (2) *auditing through the computer*.

Auditing around a computer involves verifying the accuracy and propriety of input and output without evaluating the programs used to process the data. This is a simpler and easier method that does not require that auditors have programming experience. However, this auditing method does not trace a transaction through all of its stages of processing and does not test the accuracy and integrity of computer programs. Therefore, it is recommended only as a supplement to other auditing methods.

Auditing through the computer involves verifying the accuracy and integrity of the computer programs that process the data, as well as the input and output of the computer system. Auditing through the computer requires a knowledge of computer operations and programming. Some firms employ special *EDP auditors* for this assignment. Special test data may be used to test processing accuracy and the control procedures built into the computer program. The auditors may develop special *test programs* or use *audit software packages*. See Figure 14–7.

EDP auditors use such programs to process their test data. Then they

AUDITING INFORMATION SYSTEMS

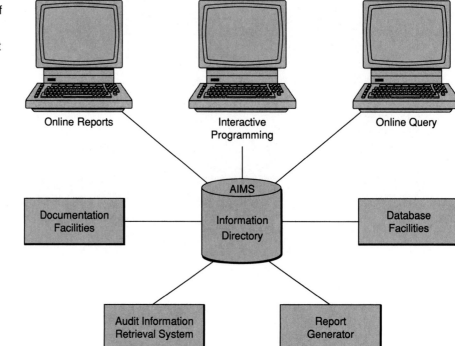

Figure 14–7 An example of the capabilities of an audit software package. This is Computer Associates' Audit Information Management System (AIMS).

compare the results produced by their audit programs with the results generated by the computer user's own programs. One of the objectives of such testing is to detect the presence of unauthorized changes, or *patches*, to programs. Unauthorized program patches may be the cause of apparently unexplainable errors or may be used for fraudulent purposes [20].

Auditing through the computer may be too costly for some computer applications. Therefore, a combination of both auditing approaches is usually employed. However, both auditing approaches must effectively contend with the changes caused by computer-based information systems to the *audit trail*.

An **audit trail** can be defined as the presence of documentation that allows a transaction to be traced through all stages of its information processing. This journey begins with a transaction's appearance on a source document and ends with its transformation into information on a final output document. The audit trail of manual information systems was quite visible and easy to trace. However, computer-based information systems have changed the form of the audit trail. Information formerly available to the auditor in the form of visual records is no longer available or is recorded on media that can be interpreted only by machines. Realtime processing systems have increased the "invisibility" of the traditional audit trail, since paper documents and historical files are frequently eliminated.

Such developments make auditing of information systems a complex but vital assignment. Therefore, auditing personnel should be included on the project team of all major systems development projects and consulted before smaller critical systems projects are implemented. In addition, auditors should be notified of major systems changes. This gives auditors the opportunity to suggest methods of preserving the audit trail, and ensures that adequate controls are designed into systems being developed or modified.

REAL WORLD CASE

Air Products and Chemicals, Inc.

Realizing that PC applications are taking center stage in its business, Air Products & Chemicals Inc. is setting mainframe-style security standards to protect those applications and the data in them. The Allentown, Pennsylvania, maker of chemicals and industrial gases learned how important PC applications are when its director of internal audit, Drew Gubanich, polled users on what software they ran. "We got back a list of hundreds of applications," Gubanich said. "When I read them, I said, 'My God, if some of this information were to get out or be lost or be destroyed, the company would have some pretty serious exposure.'"

The information on PCs included strategic plans, pricing information, and invoices. Yet many users failed to back up their data, test the applications they wrote, or write documentation for their programs so that future users could understand them. To fix that, Air Products' information center and audit staffs developed standards for everything from how to prevent PCs from being stolen, to how to do backups and test applications. According to Donna Jacobs, corporate information center manager, Air Products' intellectual investment is the $3,000 that the company spends writing, testing, and documenting applications for every $1,000 that it spends on hardware.

Corporate auditors and information center staff members developed a long list of security standards. Then they asked 40 power users for comment. The users made 150 suggestions, including requests for recommendations about specific products, such as software to detect and defeat viruses. Finally, they used an instructional videotape and a series of awareness sessions to alert PC users and their managers (all key nontechnical people) to the risks to PC applications and the ways to protect the software.

Security tips are included in a manual of suggested PC standards that Air Products distributes to all PC users. The manual comes with software that lets users analyze their security risks and decide which measures to take. It's up to end users to audit their own PC use and take the proper precautions, and it's up to their managers to make sure they comply. Gubanich still performs routine security audits, with a copy of the results going to all department managers who have been audited, and to their divisional manager, in turn.

The Air Products standards for PC security by end users include:

☐ Comply with all software licensing agreements.

☐ Guard all data and applications from unauthorized use and access.

☐ Regularly back up data and store it in secure locations.

☐ Protect PC equipment from damage and theft.

☐ Test applications thoroughly to be sure they perform as intended.

☐ Arrange for disaster recovery.

☐ Screen for viruses when using public domain software.

☐ Apply security measures when communicating with other systems.

☐ Document applications for future users.

☐ Recognize and protect the company's intellectual and physical investment in PCs.

Application Questions

☐ What security problems did PC applications pose to Air Products?

☐ How is Air Products controlling the risks of end user computing?

☐ Are Air Products security standards applicable to most organizations? Explain.

Source: Adapted from Robert Scheier, "Firm Protects Critical PC Data with Mainframe-Style Policies," *PC Week*, April 16, 1990, pp. 1, 6.

Section II: Computer Crime, Ethics, and Society

THE IMPACT OF COMPUTERS ON SOCIETY

We are in the midst of an information revolution. As we have seen in this text, the widespread use of computers has significantly magnified our ability to analyze, compute, and communicate. What should managers and end users do to help control the use of computers in business and society? To answer this question, we should analyze some of the major social and economic impacts of computers, as illustrated in Figure 14–8. **Social applications** of computers include their use in solving human and social problems such as crime and pollution. **Socioeconomic effects** of computers are the impact on society of the use of computers. For example, computerizing a production process may have an *adverse* effect of a decrease in employment opportunities and the *beneficial effect* of providing consumers with products of better quality at lower cost.

Business end users should understand the beneficial and adverse effects of computer usage on society. This will help them plan and control the development and operation of computer-based information systems within their organizations. It will also help them assure the survival and success of their organizations in a dynamic societal environment. We will now briefly explain several major aspects of the impact of computers on society. Then we will go into more depth on the issues of computer crime and ethics.

Figure 14–8 Major aspects of the computer's impact on society. Computers have had both a positive and negative effect on society in each of the areas shown.

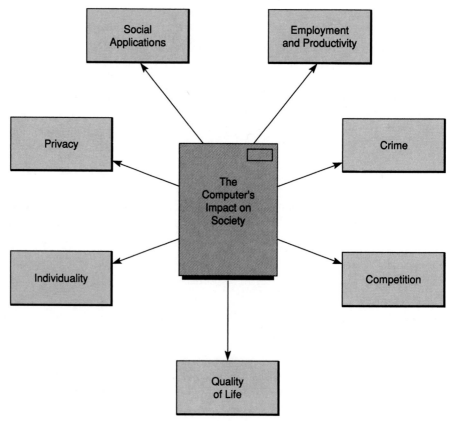

Computers can have many direct beneficial effects on society when they are used to solve human and social problems through *social applications* such as medical diagnosis, computer-assisted instruction, governmental program planning, environmental quality control, and law enforcement. Computers can be used to help diagnose an illness, prescribe necessary treatment, and monitor the progress of hospital patients. Computer-assisted instruction (CAI) allows a computer to serve as tutor since it uses conversational computing to tailor instruction to the needs of a particular student. This is beneficial to students, especially those with learning disabilities.

Social Applications

Computers can be used for crime control through various law enforcement applications that allow police to identify and respond quickly to evidence of criminal activity. Computers have been used to monitor the level of pollution in the air and in bodies of water, to detect the sources of pollution, and to issue early warnings when dangerous levels are reached. Computers are also used for the program planning of many government agencies in such areas as urban planning, population density and land use studies, highway planning, and urban transit studies. Computers are being used in job placement systems to help match unemployed persons with available jobs. These and other applications illustrate that computer-based information systems can be used to help solve the problems of society.

The impact of computers on **employment** and **productivity** is directly related to the use of computers to achieve automation. There can be no doubt that the use of computers has created new jobs and increased productivity, while also causing a significant reduction in some types of job opportunities. Computers used for office information processing or for the numerical control of machine tools are accomplishing tasks formerly performed by many clerks and machinists. Also, jobs created by computers within a computer-using organization require different types of skills and education than do the jobs eliminated. For example, factory automation has significantly upgraded the minimum skills needed to be a *factory worker* in many industries. Therefore, a general high school education is no longer adequate, and individuals within such organizations may become unemployed unless they can be retrained for new, more demanding positions or responsibilities.

Impact on Employment and Productivity

However, the computer industry has created a host of new job opportunities for the manufacture, sale, and maintenance of computer hardware and software, and for other information system services. Many new jobs, such as systems analysts and computer programmers, have been created in computer-using organizations. New jobs have also been created in service industries that provide services to the computer industry and to computer-using firms. Additional jobs have been created because computers make possible the production of complex industrial and technical goods and services that would otherwise be impossible to produce. Thus, jobs have been created by activities that are heavily dependent on computers in such areas as space exploration, microelectronic technology, and scientific research [11, 19].

The impact of computers on **competition** concerns the effect computer systems have on the size and market control of business organizations. Computers allow large firms to become more efficient or gain strategic competitive advantages.

Impact on Competition

This can have several anticompetitive effects. Small business firms that could exist because of the inefficiencies of large firms are now driven out of business or absorbed by the larger firms. The efficiency and technological superiority of the larger firms allows them to continue to grow and combine with other business firms and thus create large corporations or strategic business alliances.

It is undoubtedly true that computers allow large organizations to grow larger and become more efficient. Organizations grow in terms of people, market share, business alliances, productive facilities, and such geographic locations as branch offices and plants. Only computer-based information systems are capable of controlling the complex activities and relationships that occur. However, it should be noted that the cost and size of computer systems continue to *decrease* due to the development of microcomputers and minicomputers, and that the availability of computer and telecommunications services continues to *increase* due to the offerings of computer service bureaus, time-sharing companies, telecommunications carriers, and cooperative industry ventures. Therefore, even small firms can take advantage of the productivity, efficiency, and strategic advantages generated by computer-based systems.

Impact on Individuality

A frequent criticism of computers concerns their negative effect on the **individuality** of people. Computer-based systems are criticized as impersonal systems that dehumanize and depersonalize activities because they eliminate the human relationships present in noncomputer systems. Although it is more efficient for an information system to deal with an individual as a number than as a name, many people feel a loss of identity when they seem to be "just another number."

Another aspect of the loss of individuality is the regimentation of the individual that seems to be required. Some systems do not seem to possess any flexibility. They demand strict adherence to detailed procedures if the system is to work. The negative impact of computers on individuality is reinforced by "horror stories" that describe how inflexible and uncaring computer-based systems are when it comes to rectifying their own mistakes. Many of us are familiar with stories of how computerized customer billing systems continued to demand payment and send warning notices to a customer whose account had already been paid, despite repeated attempts by the customer to have the error corrected.

However, computer-based systems can be *ergonomically* engineered to accommodate **human factors** that minimize depersonalization and regimentation. Figure 14–9 outlines some of the human factors that are accommodated in the design of application software. People-oriented and user friendly information systems can thus be developed. The computer hardware, software, and *user interface* capabilities that make such systems possible are increasing rather than decreasing. The use of microcomputers has dramatically improved the development of people-oriented end user and work group information systems. Even everyday products and services have been improved through microprocessor-powered *smart* products [7].

Impact on the Quality of Life

Since computerized business systems increase productivity, they allow the production of better-quality goods and services at lower costs, with less effort and time. Thus, the computer is partially responsible for the high standard of living and increased leisure time many people enjoy. In addition, the computer

Figure 14–9   Human factors can be accommodated in the design of applications software to support a range of end users.

Human Factor	Human Subfactor	End User Computer Knowledge	
		Novice	Experienced
Nature of message	1. Tone	Explanatory and polite	Short and to the point
	2. Use of humor	Careful	None
	3. Bypasses	None	Allow
	4. Warnings	Many	Rarely
	5. Screen format	Menu	Inquiry
	6. Input verification	Always	Rarely
	7. Highlighting	Some (Judiciously)	Little
	8. Defaults	With explanation	Without explanation
	9. Screen discontinuation	Prompt and keyed response	Keyed response without prompt
Help function	1. Procedures	Full, unsolicited	Upon request
	2. Values		

Source: Adapted from Merle P. Martin, "Adaptive General Audience Modes: A Research Framework," in *Human Factors in Management Information Systems,* ed. Jane M. Carey (Norwood, N.J.: Ablex Publishing, 1988), p. 73.

has eliminated monotonous or obnoxious tasks in the office and the factory that formerly had to be performed by people. In many instances, this allows people to concentrate on more challenging and interesting assignments, upgrades the skill level of the work to be performed, and creates challenging jobs requiring highly developed skills in the computer industry and within computer-using organizations. Thus, computers can be said to upgrade the **quality of life** because they can upgrade the quality of working conditions and the content of work activities.

Of course, it must be remembered that some jobs created by the computer—data entry, for example—are quite repetitive and routine and can create an "electronic sweatshop" work environment, especially if computers are used to monitor worker productivity. Also, to the extent that computers are utilized in some types of automation, they must take some responsibility for the criticism of assembly line operations that require the continual repetition of elementary tasks, thus forcing a worker to work like a machine instead of like a skilled craftsperson. Such effects do have a detrimental effect on the quality of life, but they are more than offset by the less burdensome and more creative jobs created by computers [7].

Impact on Privacy

Modern computer systems make it technically and economically feasible to collect, store, integrate, interchange, and retrieve data and information quickly and easily. This characteristic has an important beneficial effect on system efficiency and effectiveness. However, the power of computers to store and retrieve information can have a negative effect on the **right to privacy** of every individual. Confidential information on individuals contained in computer databases by credit bureaus, government agencies, and private business firms could be misused and result in the invasion of privacy and other injustices. The unauthorized use of such information would seriously invade the privacy of individuals. Errors in such files could seriously hurt the credit standing or reputation of an individual.

Such developments were possible before the advent of computers. However, the speed and power of computers with centralized direct access databases and remote terminals greatly increase the potential for such injustices. The trend toward nationwide information systems with integrated databases by business firms and government agencies substantially increases the potential for the misuse of computer-stored information.

In the United States, the Federal Privacy Act strictly regulates the collection and use of personal data by governmental agencies (except for law enforcement investigative files, classified files, and civil service files). The law specifies that individuals have the right to inspect their personal records, make copies, and correct or remove erroneous or misleading information. It also specifies that federal agencies (1) must annually disclose the types of personal data files they maintain, (2) cannot disclose personal information on an individual to any other individual or agency except under certain strict conditions, (3) must inform individuals of the reasons for requesting personal information from them, (4) must retain personal data records only if it is "relevant and necessary to accomplish" an agency's legal purpose, and (5) must "establish appropriate *administrative, technical,* and *physical* safeguards to ensure the security and confidentiality of records" [17].

In 1986, the Electronic Communications Privacy Act and the Computer Fraud and Abuse Act were enacted in the United States. These federal laws attempt to enforce the privacy of computer-based files and communications. They prohibit intercepting data communications messages, stealing or destroying data, or trespassing in federal-related computer systems. Such legislation emphasizes the importance of using hardware, software, and procedural controls to maintain the confidentiality of computerized databases [5].

COMPUTER CRIME

What is computer crime? Who commits computer crimes? Who are the victims of such crimes? What are some solutions to the problems of computer crime? Informed managers and end users should know the answers to these questions. Computer crime is a growing threat caused by the criminal or irresponsible actions of a small minority of computer users who are abusing the widespread dependence on computers in our society. It thus presents a major challenge to the security of computer-based information systems and the development of effective system controls.

Computer Crime Laws

One way to understand computer crime is to see how current legislation defines it. A good example of this is the Computer Fraud and Abuse Act of 1986. This law says that computer crime involves access of *federal interest computers* (used by the federal government), or operating in interstate or foreign commerce (1) with intent to defraud, (2) resulting in more than a $1,000 loss, or (3) to gain access to certain medical computer systems. Trafficking in computer access passwords is also prohibited. Penalties for violations of this law are severe. They include 1 to 5 years in prison for a first offense, 10 years for a second offense, and 20 years for three or more offenses. Fines could range up to $250,000 or twice the value of stolen data [5].

The Data Processing Management Association (DPMA) defines computer crime more specifically. Its Model Computer Crime Act defines computer crime as (1) the unauthorized use, access, modification, and destruction of hardware, software, or data resources; (2) the unauthorized release of information; (3) the unauthorized copying of software; (4) denying an end user access to his or her own hardware, software, or data resources; (5) using or conspiring to use computer resources to commit a felony; (6) the *intent* to illegally obtain information or tangible property through the use of computers; and (7) the *intent* to establish control for the purpose of unauthorized experimentation with computer resources [10].

Another way to understand computer crime is to examine examples of major types of criminal activity involving computers. This typically involves activities such as (1) theft of money, services, programs, and data; (2) destruction of data and programs by computer "viruses"; (3) malicious access, or "hacking"; (4) violation of privacy; and (5) violations of antitrust or international law. The following examples also reveal the types of people who become computer criminals and the institutions and individuals who are victims of computer crime. Figure 14–10 illustrates the results of a survey to identify computer crime [2, 5].

Examples of Computer Crime

Money Theft

Many computer crimes involve the theft of money. Major examples are bank frauds such as the $21 million Wells Fargo Bank theft and the $10.2 million Security Pacific Bank theft where the falsifications of records in computer-based systems allowed millions to be embezzled.

Computer Viruses and Worms

One of the most insidious of computer crimes is the use of **computer viruses** or *worms*, which are programs that copy destructive routines into the computer systems of anyone who accesses "infected" computer systems or uses copies of

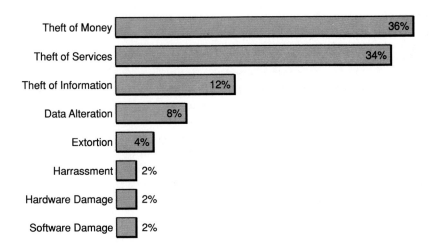

Figure 14–10 Types of computer crime. Note that theft of money and services are the most prevalent criminal acts.

Percent of Prosecutions Tracked

Source: National Center for Computer Data and RGC Associates, in Michael Alexander, "Hacker Stereotypes Changing," *Computerworld*, April 3, 1989, p. 101.

Figure 14–11 Anatomy of a computer virus infection. This example documents the contamination of the Arpanet computer network by a computer virus (or *worm*) in November 1988.

COMPUTER VIRUS CONTAMINATION ACROSS THE UNITED STATES

Infected Areas

The Arpanet communications network provided a vehicle for spreading the virus. Some computers at universities, companies, and military research facilities received and spread the virulent program, eventually forcing hundreds of users off the network. Some of the major links in the network are shown below.

How the Infection Spread

1. Virus program is written by a computer science graduate student at Cornell and designed to secretly spread to other companies.

2. The Arpanet (Advanced Research Projects Agency Network) communications network, which connects military and civilian computers, is infected.

3. The virus spreads throughout the network by mailing itself to other computers and by masquerading as a legitimate user.

4. By continually copying itself, the virus forces the host computer to dedicate all of its computing power to the new illegitimate files. The effect is to shut or slow down the computer.

5. The virus begins to send itself to other computers it has not already infected and is supposed to skip the ones where it already resides. A programming mistake causes one out of every 10 infected computers to accept it again, tying up even more computing power.

6. Users disconnect from the network to delete the virus and the files it has created and try to destroy any traces it might have left behind.

7. Users, fearing they will be reinfected, remain off-line as investigators try to sterilize the network and eliminate the virus.

Source: SRI International, *The New York Times.*

data or programs taken from such computers. (*Note:* Though *virus* is the more popular term, technically, a virus is program code that cannot run unaided but must first be inserted into another program. A *worm* is a distinct program that can run unaided.)

Thus, a computer virus or worm can destroy the programs and data of many computer users. A good example was the *contamination* of the Arpanet telecommunications network in November 1988 by a computer worm developed by a graduate student at Cornell. This is a classic example of the disruptive and destructive potential of computer viruses. See Figure 14–11. [8]

Service Theft

Service theft is the unauthorized use of computer hardware or software for one's own benefit. One example is the case of a county employee convicted of theft under New York State's criminal code for using less than $10 worth of the memory of a county computer system. Another case involved a Long Island university computer system. The manager of the computer center and his assistant used the school's computer to service commercial accounts for their own enrichment. They received at least $53,000 in revenue from one of their clients.

Program and Data Theft

Data and programs are themselves valuable property and thus are the subject of theft from computer systems. Employees have been charged with computer crime or trade secret theft on several occasions involving disputes between employee and employer as to what the employee is entitled to take upon leaving the company. Thus, computer crime is adding a new twist to acts of industrial espionage between competing firms.

Program Copying

This is another major form of program theft. Several major cases involving the unauthorized copying of software by users or competing software companies have been widely reported. These include lawsuits by software companies such as Lotus Development Corporation and Ashton-Tate against major corporations for allowing unauthorized copying of their programs, as well as lawsuits against competitors marketing supposed copies or clones that copy the "look and feel" of their popular software packages.

Data Alteration

Some changes in data allow criminals to derive significant gains, tangible or intangible. A recent prosecution in Los Angeles resulted in a guilty plea by an employee of the University of Southern California who had been taking payments from students and changing their grades in return. Other reported schemes involved changes in credit information and changes in Department of Motor Vehicles records that facilitated the theft of the cars to which the records referred.

Program Damage

Programmers familiar with a system can do considerable harm by erasing or replacing parts of major programs. A recent case involved a plan to erase the operating systems of two computers maintained by a Los Angeles corporation that operated several restaurants and fast-food outlets. In another case, a "logic bomb" was used to interfere with operations at the Department of Water and Power in Los Angeles. A *logic bomb* is a program routine that is designed and timed to disrupt the operations of a computer system.

Data Destruction

Mostly as acts of mischief, contents of files have been destroyed. In San Francisco, United States Leasing International, Inc., found that several people replaced words in their files with curse words, friends' names, and similar material. In other cases, computer viruses and worms are used maliciously to erase the data or program contents of magnetic disks and use copy routines to destroy the data of many computer users.

Malicious Access

Hacking is the unauthorized access and use of computer systems. One of the leading issues in reaction to hacking is the problem of what to do when a hacker gets access to a computer system, reads some files, but neither steals nor damages anything. This situation is becoming increasingly common in the computer crime cases that are prosecuted. In California, a court found that the typical computer crime statute language prohibiting malicious access to a computer system *did* apply to users gaining access to others' computer systems.

Violation of Privacy

A consistent fear relating to computers is that they will facilitate invasions of privacy. With the growing awareness of the dangers that computer crime poses to average citizens, it can be anticipated that invasions of privacy will increasingly be punished through the use of computer crime laws. In the United States, these include the Federal Privacy Act, the Electronic Communications Privacy Act, and other legislation enacted by individual states.

Violations of Antitrust or International Law

Computer-based information systems can violate antitrust or international laws and regulations. For example, some strategic information systems involve the sharing of telecommunications networks or other resources among organizations that are competitors in the marketplace. Such arrangements have been challenged by the U.S. Department of Justice as anticompetitive and in violation of the antitrust laws [4]. In other cases, the use of international telecommunications networks by the information systems of multinational corporations has been challenged by the nations involved as violating their national sovereignty. Information systems that cross national borders generate *transborder data flows* that may violate tariff, taxation, privacy, or labor regulations of host countries [6].

Information Systems and Computer Crime

It should now be obvious that computer-based information systems are vulnerable to many types of computer crime by criminal end users. The increased use of computers and the widespread distribution of computer power through interconnected networks of computers have significantly increased the potential for computer crime. Even the proliferation of microcomputers in business, government, education, and the rest of society provides new opportunities for computer crime. See Figure 14–12.

Thus, computer crime and computer criminals present a major challenge to end users and information systems developers. Designing effective information system controls has now become a vitally important assignment. End users, systems developers, and systems auditors must use many of the control methods discussed in the previous section to build, operate, and maintain secure systems. Only then will information systems security be a realizable goal.

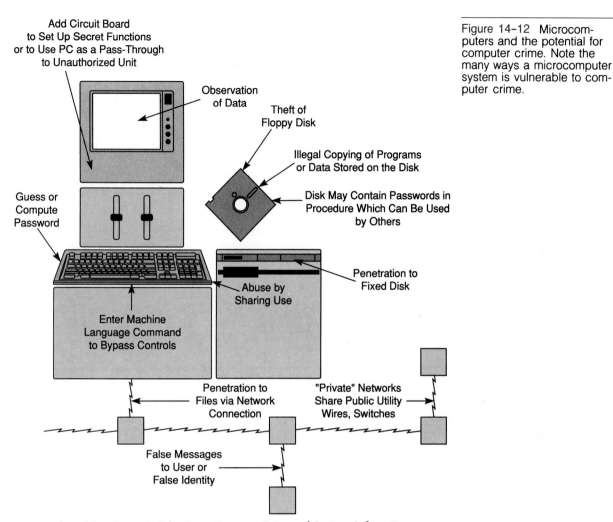

Source: Adapted from James A. Schweitzer, *Computer Crime and Business Information* (New York: Elsevier Science Publishing Co., 1986), p. 17.

Figure 14–12 Microcomputers and the potential for computer crime. Note the many ways a microcomputer system is vulnerable to computer crime.

COMPUTER ETHICS

Do end users have a *responsibility* to do something about computer crime and other abuses of computer power? This is where **computer ethics** becomes an issue. IS professionals, managers, and end users should accept their responsibilities and properly perform their role as the human resources that are vital to any information system. But what are these responsibilities? How can one be a responsible end user or IS professional?

A Code of Ethics

One way to start answering such questions is to examine the responsibilities contained in a code of professional conduct for computer professionals. A good example is the code of professional conduct of the Data Processing Management Association (DPMA). It is a national organization of professionals in the computing field. Its code of conduct outlines the ethical considerations inher-

Figure 14–13 DPMA standards of professional conduct. Note how the code stresses an IS professional's responsibilities to management, employers, other professionals, and society.

DPMA Standards of Professional Conduct

In recognition of my obligation to management I shall:

- Keep my personal knowledge up to date and ensure that proper expertise is available when needed.
- Share my knowledge with others and present factual and objective information to management to the best of my ability.
- Accept full responsibility for work that I perform.
- Not misuse the authority entrusted to me.
- Not misrepresent or withhold information concerning the capabilities of equipment, software or systems.
- Not take advantage of the lack of knowledge or inexperience of others.

In recognition of my obligation to my profession I shall:

- Be honest in all my professional relationships.
- Take appropriate action in regard to any illegal or unethical practices that come to my attention. However, I will bring charges against any person only when I have reasonable basis for believing in the truth of the allegation and without regard to personal interest.
- Endeavor to share my special knowledge.
- Cooperate with others in achieving understanding and identifying problems.
- Not use or take credit for the work of others without specific acknowledgment and authorization.
- Not take advantage of the lack of knowledge or inexperience on the part of others for personal gain.

In recognition of my obligation to society I shall:

- Protect the privacy and confidentiality of all information entrusted to me.
- Use my skill and knowledge to inform the public in all areas of my expertise.
- To the best of my ability, ensure that the products of my work are used in a socially responsible way.
- Support, respect, and abide by the appropriate local, state, provincial, and Federal laws.
- Never misrepresent or withhold information that is germane to a problem or a situation of public concern nor will I allow any such known information to remain unchallenged.
- Not use knowledge of a confidential or personal nature in any unauthorized manner to achieve personal gain.

In recognition of my obligation to my employer I shall:

- Make every effort to ensure that I have the most current knowledge and that the proper expertise is available when needed.
- Avoid conflict of interest and ensure that my employer is aware of any potential conflicts.
- Present a fair, honest, and objective viewpoint.
- Protect the proper interests of my employer at all times.
- Protect the privacy and confidentiality of all information entrusted to me.
- Not misrepresent or withhold information that is germane to the situation.
- Not attempt to use the resources of my employer for personal gain or for any purpose without proper approval.
- Not exploit the weakness of a computer system for personal gain or personal satisfaction.

Source: Adapted from Bruce E. Spiro, "Ethics in the Information Age," *Information Executive,* Fall, 1989, p. 40.

ent in the major responsibilities of a professional in the computer industry. Figure 14–13 is a summary of the DPMA code [18].

The DPMA code provides general guidelines for ethical conduct in the development and operation of information systems. End users and IS professionals would live up to their ethical responsibilities by voluntarily following such guidelines. For example, you can be a **responsible end user** by (1) acting with integrity, (2) increasing your professional competence, (3) setting high standards of personal performance, (4) accepting responsibility for your work, and (5) advancing the health, privacy, and general welfare of the public. Then you would be demonstrating ethical conduct, avoiding computer crime, and increasing the security of any information systems you develop or use.

Of course, codes of conduct are guidelines, not laws. Thus, a more obvious guide to ethical conduct in computing would be computer crime laws. In the United States, these include the Fair Credit Act, the Federal Privacy Act, the Electronic Communications Privacy Act, the Computer Fraud and Abuse Act, and other federal and state computer crime laws. End users and computer professionals should take such laws seriously. Truly ethical behavior would involve following the *spirit*, not just the *letter*, of the provisions in these laws. For example, many organizations have voluntarily developed policies forbidding the creation or use of unauthorized copies of software, as well as the unauthorized use of their computer facilities or data resources by their employers. Thus, all organizations should establish policies and individuals should act in a cooperative and mutually beneficial spirit of ethical responsibility in computing. [3, 18]

Another way to confront the topic of computer ethics is to consider the basic ethical issues that arise from the use of computer-based information systems. Richard Mason has posed four basic ethical issues, which deal with the vulnerability of people to computer-based information systems [12]. These are based on the concept that information forms the *intellectual capital* of individuals. However, information systems can rob people of their intellectual capital. For example, people can lose information without compensation and without their permission. People can also be denied access to information or be exposed to erroneous information. Mason summarizes these four ethical issues with the acronym *PAPA*—Privacy, Accuracy, Property, and Accessibility.

Ethical Issues

> Privacy. What information about one's self or one's associations must a person reveal to others, under what conditions, and with what safeguards? What things can people keep to themselves and not be forced to reveal to others?
>
> Accuracy. Who is responsible for the authenticity, fidelity, and accuracy of information? Similarly, who is to be held accountable for errors in information and how is the injured party to be made whole?
>
> Property. Who owns information? What are the just and fair prices for its exchange? Who owns the channels, especially the airways, through which information is transmitted? How should access to this scarce resource be allocated?
>
> Accessibility. What information does a person or an organization have a right or a privilege to obtain, under what conditions, and with what safeguards?

In answering these questions, Mason proposes the development of a new *social contract*, where information systems will help ensure everyone's right to fulfill his or her human potential. In this new social contract, information systems should be designed to ensure accuracy and not invade a person's

Figure 14–14 Software and intellectual rights. A code of ethics proposed by EDU-COM for colleges and universities.

Software and intellectual rights

Respect for intellectual labor and creativity is vital to academic discourse and enterprise. This principle applies to works of all authors and publishers in all media. It encompasses respect for the right to acknowledgment, right to privacy, and right to determine the form, manner, and terms of publication and distribution. Because electronic information is so volatile and easily reproduced, respect for the work and personal expression of others is especially critical in computer environments. Violations of authorial integrity, including plagiarism, invasion of privacy, unauthorized access, and trade secret and copyright violations, may be grounds for sanctions against members of the academic community.

Source: "The EDUCOM Code," *Academic Computing*, March 1989, p. 59.

privacy. Channels of information should be protected and information made accessible to avoid information illiteracy or deprivation. Finally, information systems should be designed to protect an individual's intellectual capital from unauthorized exposure, loss, or damage Developing, protecting, and enforcing this social contract then becomes the responsibility of end users, managers, and information system professionals. Figure 14–14 is a good example of an effort by an academic computing organization to articulate ethical standards for information and software as intellectual property.

Controls and Social Responsibility

It should now be obvious that end users and managers should insist that the societal and personal impact of using computers must be considered when a computer-based information system is being developed. A major management objective should be to develop systems that can be easily and effectively used by people. System objectives must also include protection of end user privacy and the defense of the system against computer crime. Control hardware, software, and procedures must be included in the systems design. The potential for misuse and malfunction of a proposed system must be analyzed with respect to its impact on all of an organization's present and potential stakeholders, individuals, and society as a whole [15].

Many of the potential negative effects of computer usage mentioned previously result from inadequacies in the design of information systems. Increased emphasis on the control capabilities of information systems would help protect us from computer criminals and various negative effects. Information systems can be designed to help prevent their own misuse and remedy their own malfunctions. Computers make it possible for us to monitor the activities of information systems and thus help prevent computerized crime and correct system malfunctions. Managers must recognize that a *socially responsible design* and *effective system controls* are the key to minimizing the negative effects of computer misuse and malfunction.

It should also be obvious that many detrimental effects of computers on society are caused by individuals and organizations that are not willing to accept the social responsibility for their actions. Like other powerful tools, computers possess the potential for great good or evil, especially in a society that has become so dependent on them. End users, managers, and information system professionals must accept the responsibility for their proper control and beneficial use.

Robert T. Morris Jr.

A jury found Robert T. Morris, Jr. guilty, and in the process turned a computer wizard into a convicted felon. However, while the verdict sends a message that society may no longer tolerate computer pranks, it is not clear whether it will deter other criminal hackers. In January 1990, a U.S. District Court in Syracuse, New York, found Morris, 24, former Cornell graduate student, guilty of illegally running a worm program on thousands of computers scattered across the country on the Arpanet Network (refer to Figure 14.11), preventing authorized users from using their computers for several hours to several days and causing them a loss of more than $150,000 in efforts to recover from the virus attack. In May 1990, Morris was sentenced to three years probation, fined $10,000, and ordered to perform 400 hours of community service and pay the costs of his probation supervision.

"If they had let him go, it would have been virus city out there, but whether this will be a deterrent over the long term is another story," said Ian Murphy, a self-described hacker and president of I Am Secure Data Systems in Philadelphia. "The hacking community would not be fazed" unless the penalty included at least a fine and community service, he said. Morris could have been imprisoned for up to five years, fined up to $250,000, and ordered to make restitution to his victims.

"A jail sentence for a first-time offender who acted without malicious intent would strike most people as heavy-handed and takes a too narrow view of the problem if you are really trying to reach young hackers," said Marc Rotenberg, an attorney and a director of Computer Professionals for Social Responsibility. "It is not enough to hold up Robert Morris and say he should go to jail. It is better that they understand why it is wrong to do what Morris did." The community service should require Morris to visit schools and talk to students about the importance of computer networks and why it is a mistake to engage in the sort of activities for which he has been convicted, Rotenberg said.

"I am with the throw-the-book-at-him crowd," said Walter Ulrich, director of information and telecommunications consulting services at Arthur D. Little, Inc. in Cambridge, Massachusetts. "Some jail time should have been required because an electronic crime is no different than any other crime, and it should be treated as such." A light sentence sends an unintended message that these sorts of violation will be tolerated, he said. A harsher sentence should have been applied, said David Newman Jr., an attorney and associate professor at George Washington University in Washington, D.C.

Legal experts said that the conviction of Morris proves that the Computer Fraud and Abuse Act of 1986 is tight enough to protect the nation's computers from tampering and attacks by viruses, worms, and other malicious programs. "It establishes a precedent that a person who creates worms and viruses can be held accountable," said Newman. "The hackers will continue to try to probe systems and get away with it, but cases like this show that they can get caught and prosecuted." The verdict also signals a change in the way that the nation views hackers and computer-related crimes, Newman said. "They are not folklore heroes; they are felons, and the fact that they used computers to do something wrong does not vindicate them."

Application Questions

- [ ] Why does the conviction of Robert Morris set an important precedent in computer crime?
- [ ] What do you think would have been an appropriate sentence for his crime?
- [ ] How should end users and their organizations protect themselves from computer viruses?

Source: Adapted from Michael Alexander, "Morris Verdict Stirs Debate," *Computerworld*, January 29, 1990, pp. 1, 6; "Three Year Probation for Morris," *Computerworld*, May 7, 1990, pp. 1, 112; and "Morris Sentence Spurs Debate," *Computerworld*, May 14, 1990, p. 128.

SUMMARY

☐ One of the most important responsibilities of the management of computer-using business firms is to assure the security and quality of its information services activities. Controls are needed that ensure the accuracy, integrity, and safety of the information system activities and resources of the organization and its end users. Such controls attempt to minimize errors, fraud, and destruction, and can be grouped into three major categories: (1) information system controls, (2) procedural controls, and (3) physical facility controls. as summarized in Figures 14–1 and 14–2.

☐ Computers have had a major impact on society and thus impose serious responsibilities upon the managers of computer-using business firms. Social applications of computers provide a direct beneficial effect to society when they are used to solve human and social problems. Computers have had a major effect on employment, productivity, and competition in the business world. Computers have had both beneficial and detrimental effects on individuality, the quality of life, and privacy.

☐ Computer crime poses a growing threat to society. Such crimes typically involve the theft, destruction, or unauthorized use of hardware software, or data resources. Several major laws have been enacted to counter computer crime.

☐ End users and managers must accept the responsibility for the proper and beneficial use of computers in their business firms and organizations. Managers must insist that effective measures be taken to ensure that the social and economic effects of computer usage are considered during the development and operation of information systems.

KEY TERMS AND CONCEPTS

These are the key terms and concepts of this chapter. The page number of their first explanation is in parentheses.

1. Auditing information systems (491)
2. Audit trail (492)
3. Control of end user computing (490)
4. Computer crime (499)
5. Computer crime laws (498)
6. Computer ethics (503)
7. Computer virus (499)
8. Fault-tolerant (489)
9. Hacking (502)
10. Human factors (496)
11. Information system controls (482)
12. Information system security (482)
13. Physical facility controls (488)
14. Procedural controls (487)
15. Quality assurance (482)
16. Social applications of computers (495)
17. Socioeconomic effects of computers (494)
    a. Competition
    b. Employment
    c. Individuality
    d. Privacy
    e. Productivity
    f. Quality of life
18. System security monitor (485)

Match one of the **key terms and concepts** listed above with one of the brief examples or definitions listed below. Try to find the best fit for answers that seem to fit more than one term or concept. Defend your choices.

_____ 1. The accuracy, integrity, and safety of information system activities and resources are protected.

_____ 2. A computer-based information system must be evaluated on the excellence of its information products and services.

_____ 3. Control totals are an example.

_____ 4. The separation of the duties of computer programmers and computer operators is an example.

_____ 5. Fire and biometric access detection systems are examples.

_____ 6. Software can control access and use of a computer system.

_____ 7. A computer system can continue to operate even after a major system failure.

_____ 8. Periodically examine the accuracy and integrity of computer processing.

_____ 9. The presence of documentation that allows a transaction to be traced through all stages of information processing.

_____ 10. Information system controls in an organization's work groups.

_____ 11. Computerized monitoring of environmental quality is an example.

_____ 12. Employees may have to retrain or transfer.

_____ 13. We can produce more goods per worker.

_____ 14. Helps big firms get bigger and small firms survive.

_____ 15. Tedious jobs are decreased and leisure time increased.

_____ 16. Personal information in computer-accessible files.

_____ 17. You are more than just a number.

_____ 18. People have a variety of needs when using computers.

_____ 19. Fraudulent transfer of funds is an example.

_____ 20. Makes it illegal to access a computer with intent to defraud.

_____ 21. Breaking and entering into a computer system.

_____ 22. A program makes copies of itself and destroys data and programs in connected computer systems.

_____ 23. IS professionals and end users should accept the responsibility to act with integrity and competence in their use of information systems.

1. Hertz Corporation and Security Pacific Bank
Biometric security systems—used to restrict access to computer systems and data centers—are more apt to be found on reruns of "Get Smart" and other once-popular television shows than in corporations. But it now looks as though biometric systems are about to move from "Mission: Impossible" into widespread, everyday use, even though they are far from foolproof. For example, Hertz Corporation opted for a voice-verification system to control entry to its data centers, as well as to limit access to its

computer systems within authorized levels, because it was among the least expensive and easiest to use, said Mark Stutte, director of MIS operations. "We looked at such devices as retina scanners, fingerprint readers, signature analyzers, and palm readers, but they were too expensive, and it became an issue of how employees would react to it," he said.

Security Pacific Bank is evaluating a voice-verification system that is now being used by bank managers at some 600 locations to ensure that fund transfers and other transactions are handled only by authorized individuals. Bank officials are normally assigned a new password each day that enables them to telephone headquarters to retrieve confidential information about their customers and conduct other banking business. "That did not seem quite secure enough, so we began to explore the possibilities of identifying remote corporate employees using voice verification," said Dave Bristow, vice president of security. "User training is critical. You have to pay close attention to the passwords they're using and make sure they're comfortable." If they are nervous, the biometric profile will not be reliable and will reject users at higher than acceptable rates, he said.

a. What are biometric security systems? What are their advantages and limitations compared to other security methods?

b. Why did Hertz and Security Pacific select voice verification systems to provide IS security?

Source: Adapted from Michael Alexander, "Biometric System Use Widening," *Computerworld,* January 8, 1990, p. 16.

2. Citicorp

If you thought no one noticed your office computer habits, guess again. Next on the list for exhaustive observation and analysis may be how and when you use a computer. These approaches, generally called *intrusion detection systems,* use expert systems technologies and behavioral profiles drawn from samplings of everyday computer use to spot activities that are out of the ordinary. Any deviations from historical use, supporters believe, could indicate security violations. For example, take financial services giant Citicorp. "We are using artificial intelligence to come up with security software . . . to set a profile on a particular user and note major variances from that profile," says Bern Flaherty, manager of corporate security. Citicorp's system compares a user's current behavior with his or her historical computer activity to determine any unusual behavior.

The technology's potential for widespread use is clear. One application monitors employees responsible for processing vendor invoices. Usage profiles establish what time of the week or month employees should be entering invoices for which vendors. "In this case, [profile analysis] is run for all inputters or verifiers since these are high-risk systems where funds are involved," says Flaherty. The company informs employees that they are being monitored, as the company sees the warnings as a deterrent. "We find it's well in our interest to publicize it a lot," Flaherty says.

    a. What are intrusion detection systems? How are they used at Citi-
corp?

    b. Would you agree to having your work activities monitored by such
systems? Explain.

Source: Adapted from Susan Kerr, "Using AI to Improve Security," *Datamation,* February
1, 1990, pp. 57–58.

3. Manufacturers Hanover Corporation

Those who sneer at the diskless micro workstation are prone to dismiss it
as little more than a mutilated personal computer or "gutless wonder."
Yet at Manufacturers Hanover Corporation (or "Manny Hanny"), the
diskless PC—when coupled with a Windows operating environment—
has blossomed into a cost-saving and control-enabling wonder. Their network of high-powered Intel 80386 microprocessor diskless boxes has
provided the financial institution with a high level of control and security
it believes would not be possible otherwise.

    "We basically deal in data, for which we have fiduciary respon-
sibilities. Yet we were losing data, and were likely to lose more, at the
same time more of it was becoming critical," Vice President Arthur
Boock explained. Worse, the industry is creating and storing valuable information on the desktop. The firm had to be able to access and control
that information. A central data repository does the trick, using a LAN
server-based file system. On the user end, electronic distribution of applications and upgrades, as well as online help, have simplified and
reduced the cost of support. "Two thirds of the cost of desktop computing is training and support," he said. Since users can now only destroy or
delete what is on their screens, the firm's financial data is essentially im-
mune to a user-instigated catastrophe.

    a. What are the security advantages to Manny Hanny of diskless PC
workstations?

    b. Do these advantages outweigh the limitations of such workstations?
Explain.

Source: Adapted from Patricia Keefe, "Doing Away with Hard Disks," *Computerworld,*
March 12, 1990, p. 39.

4. Prudential-Bache Securities

Prudential-Bache Securities in New York backs up all of its data—more
than 500,000 transactions per day—through "electronic vaulting" with
Comdisco Computing Service in Carlstadt, New Jersey. Electronic vaulting is the direct transmission of business transaction data from a
computer-using organization to a computer at an off-site location for safe-
keeping and backup storage.

    "We will be transmitting all trades on a realtime basis to Carlstadt,"
said William H. Anderson, chief information officer at the retail brokerage firm. "We will then be able to recover all the major systems of
the company, rather than a critical subset of maybe 50 percent." Should
disaster strike Prudential-Bache's data center, company employees could
move to a Comdisco "hot site" and tap directly into the data stored in
their vaulting system, recovering all but the last 15 minutes of trading
data.

a. How does electronic vaulting provide IS security for Prudential-Bache?

b. What security benefits does the Comdisco hot site provide to Prudential-Bache?

Source: Adapted from Maryfran Johnson, "Into a Safer Site," *Computerworld*, April 23, 1990, p. 29.

5. Kenneth Rosenblatt, Deputy D.A.

Computer crime is costing U.S. industry billions of dollars annually, according to some estimates, but it may take even greater losses before industry and the government devise a coherent strategy to combat it. "I think what it is going to take is people dying, unfortunately, before anything will be done about computer crime," said Kenneth Rosenblatt, deputy district attorney for the County of Santa Clara, California, and the lead attorney for the district attorney's High Technology Unit. He said that it is inevitable that high-tech tampering of corporate computer systems will cause a "hacker-induced death" before long.

The incentive to improve security will be forced upon businesses, Rosenblatt said. He predicted that there will be a spate of liability lawsuits—and, inevitably, deaths— stemming from failing to provide adequate security. "If a hacker breaks into a computer at TRW Information Services and steals personal information and uses it to injure my reputation, TRW is going to have a lawsuit on their hands," Rosenblatt said. "At some point, we're going to see lawsuits against credit bureaus for not providing adequate security." He also pointed to an instance a few years ago when hackers accessed a computer system at Sloan-Kettering Cancer Research Institute in New York and altered patient records, including information related to cancer treatment by radiation. It does not take much imagination to recognize that someone could have been killed as a result, Rosenblatt said.

a. How could computer crime lead to hacker-induced deaths and computer liability losses?

b. What should businesses and other organizations be doing to prevent such events from occurring?

Source: Adapted from Michael Alexander, "Computer Crime: Ugly Secret for Business," *Computerworld*, March 12, 1990, pp. 1, 104.

6. University of California at Los Angeles

It all started at about 3 o'clock on an otherwise quiet Wednesday afternoon. Let's let Barry Gerber, administrative director of Social Sciences Computing at the University of California at Los Angeles tell the story.

"Mike Franks, a member of my staff, rushed in to report that things seemed to be falling apart on the network in one of the computer labs. The end of the academic quarter was nearing, and the lab was packed. Nearly 70 student users were logged into the lab from inside and outside. Users couldn't run certain software. Some couldn't even log in. Many reported receiving the NewWare operating system's maddening Network Error—Abort, Retry message.

"Based on past experience and the error message, I suspected a cable break or a failure in the network operating system. I ran Novell's FCONSOLE diagnostic program to see how we were doing on server memory, and disk and LAN I/O. I couldn't find anything out of the ordinary. Meanwhile, we started getting calls from another lab. Users there reported similar experiences. It was starting to look like a disaster of major proportions. At this point, I suggested that all users log off the server, then we could bring it down and back up. It had been running for 136 days. Maybe it just needed a good memory flushing. That didn't help. After that, we shut down the labs.

"Then George Bing, another member of my staff started searching for viruses using the SCAN virus detector program. George soon reported that he'd found the Jerusalem virus on the server that provides most of the services to the lab. NetWare's own LOGIN program was infected. That, of course, was why people couldn't log in. It also was the likely source of those network errors. We began tracking down the virus and found it in two diagnostic programs I'd run. It was starting to look like I was the culprit, until we found the virus in WordPerfect's WP.EXE program file on the LAN. We soon realized that most of the damage had been done when our staff logged in with supervisors' rights from lab machines which had become infected by students who brought in infected programs.

"By 8 P.M., things were back to normal. We had to replace a number of infected files with copies from other servers or from our tape backups. Our encounter with the Jerusalem virus cost us about 25 person-hours. It also seriously disrupted the lives of a couple hundred of the students who use our labs. However, the experience taught us that we have little to fear if we're careful. We now make it a practice to check our local disks with SCAN before logging into the network, and we don't log in with supervisors' rights from lab machines unless we absolutely must."

a. How were the computer labs at UCLA infected with a computer virus? How did it spread?

b. What damage was done and what lessons were learned?

Source: Adapted from Barry Gerber, "Sometimes 'Abort, Retry' Means 'Network Virus,'" *PC Week*, April 2, 1990, p. 57.

7. Facts on File, Inc.

Corporations received a warning last June when Facts on File, Inc., a New York-based publishing company, paid a six-figure out-of-court settlement to five software vendors that, with the help of the Software Publishers Association (SPA), had filed suit on the grounds that the company had copied their software. The case was the first to be filed by multiple vendors against a corporation. SPA has also settled four other corporate piracy cases out of court with the provision that the organizations' names would not be released. Currently, the association has six cases pending against corporations.

As a result of the Facts on File case, a major accounting firm posted articles about the lawsuit on bulletin boards in all of its corporate locations with a memo from top management saying, "Don't let this ever happen to us." SPA's Saunders points out that the same firm encourages its clients to have corporatewide piracy contracts and audits. SPA has pursued software audits with two dozen companies to avoid the expense and embarrassment associated with lawsuits. With the company's cooperation, SPA sends in its own investigator to compare installed software on hard disks with corporate purchasing records. "When we find pirated software," Saunders explains, "the company has to destroy it, pay us a penalty—which is less than if we had taken them to court—and then buy legal copies of the software."

a. When can you legally copy software?

b. What are software vendors doing to combat illegal copying of their software?

Source: Adapted from Janet Mason, "Crackdown on Software Pirates," *Computerworld,* February 5, 1990, p. 111.

8. Systems Applications, Inc.

Cruise through the smoggy suburbs of Los Angeles on a windless afternoon and the amber haze staining the skies lends a sooty double entendre to the region's designation as Orange County. The causes of some of that pollution, however, could soon be on the wane, thanks to the recent introduction of cleaner-burning automobile fuels in heavily polluted areas such as Southern California and the Northeast. The development of some of these gasolines represents a victory for Systems Applications, Inc. (SAI), a small science consulting firm in the foothills of San Rafael, California.

Both Shell Oil Co. and Atlantic Richfield Co. turned to SAI for computer-modeling studies to measure the emission changes resulting from their new reblended fuels. Using an elaborate battery of nearly 100 personal computers and workstations, SAI can determine how those gases will then assimilate into the atmosphere once they leave the tailpipe. SAI can factor in environmental factors such as wind flow, cloud cover, and temperature to gauge the effect the gases will have on the atmosphere. SAI used a series of customized programs to estimate the emission changes expected from using Shell's SU 2000E gasoline in 10 cities in which it was introduced, according to emission modeling group manager Lyle Chinkin. The research determined that the typical automobile burning the SU 2000E fuel emitted about 10 percent less air pollution than one running on Shell's current premium gasoline, Chinkin said.

a. How are computers being used by SAI to help reduce environmental pollution?

b. What other uses of computers can you think of which help solve human and social problems?

Source: Adapted from James Daly, "SAI Driving toward Cleaner Air," *Computerworld,* April 30, 1990, p. 47.

SELECTED REFERENCES

1. Alexander, Michael. "Biometric System Use Widening." *Computerworld,* January 8, 1990.

2. Alexander, Michael. "Hacker Stereotypes Changing." *Computerworld,* April 3, 1989.

3. Axline, Larry, and Mark Pastin. "The High-Ethics Manager." *Information Executive,* Fall 1989.

4. Betts, Mitch. "Strategic Systems: Pitfalls in Stomping Competitors." *Computerworld,* August 7, 1989.

5. Bloombecker, J. J. "New Federal Law Bolsters Computer Security Efforts." *Computerworld,* October 17, 1986.

6. Briner, Russel, and Sidney Ewer. "Financial Information Flow and Transborder Restrictions." *Journal of Systems Management,* August 1987.

7. Carey, Jane, ed. *Human Factors in Management Information Systems.* Norwood, N.J.: Ablex Publishing, 1988.

8. Honan, Patrick. "Avoiding Virus Hysteria." *Personal Computing,* May 1989.

9. Johnson, Deborah. *Computer Ethics.* Englewood Cliffs: Prentice-Hall, 1985.

10. Johnson, Robert. "Is Your Information Protected with Due Care?" *Information Executive,* Fall 1988.

11. Martin, James. "Full Automation Will Create Jobs, Not Unemployment." *PC Week,* March 6, 1989.

12. Mason, Richard. "Four Ethical Issues of the Information Age." *MIS Quarterly,* March 1986.

13. McAfee, John. *Computer Viruses, Worms, Data Diddlers, Killer Programs and Other Threats to Your System.* New York: St. Martin's Press, 1990.

14. Metz, Galen. "User-Friendly Controls in the Information Center." *Journal of Information Systems Management,* Spring 1988.

15. Mitroff, Ian, and Richard Mason. "Deep Ethical and Epistemological Issues in the Design of Information Systems." *Expert Systems Review,* June 1988.

16. Ross, Steven, and Leslie Chalmers. "Passwords, User-IDs, and Security Codes." *Journal of Information Systems Management,* Spring 1988.

17. Schweitzer, James. *Computer Crime and Business Information.* New York: Elsevier Science Publishing Co., 1986.

18. Spiro, Bruce. "Ethics in the Information Age." *Information Executive,* Fall 1989.

19. Strassman, Paul. *Information Payoff: The Transformation of Work in the Electronic Age.* New York: Free Press, 1984.

20. Wilkenson, Joseph. *Accounting Information System: Essential Concepts and Applications.* New York: John Wiley & Sons, 1989.

GLOSSARY FOR END USERS

Accounting Information Systems Information systems that record and report business transactions, the flow of funds through an organization, and produce financial statements. This provides information for the planning and control of business operations, as well as for legal and historical record-keeping.

Active Data Dictionary A data dictionary that automatically enforces standard data element definitions whenever end users and application programs use a DBMS to access an organization's databases.

Ada A programming language named after Augusta Ada Byron, considered the world's first computer programmer. Developed for the U.S. Department of Defense as a standard high-order language.

Ad Hoc Inquiries Unique, unscheduled, situation-specific information requests.

ALGOL: ALGOrithmic Language An international procedure-oriented language that is widely used in Europe. Like FORTRAN, it was designed primarily for scientific-mathematical applications.

Algorithm A set of well-defined rules or processes for the solution of a problem in a finite number of steps.

Analog Computer A computer that operates on data by measuring changes in continuous physical variables such as voltage, resistance, and rotation. Contrast with *Digital computer.*

Analytical Modeling Interactive use of computer-based mathematical models to explore decision alternatives using what-if analysis, sensitivity analysis, goal-seeking analysis, and optimization analysis.

APL: A Programming Language A mathematically oriented language originated by Kenneth E. Iverson of IBM. Realtime and interactive versions of APL are used by many time-sharing systems.

Application Generator A software package that supports the development of an application through an interactive terminal dialogue, where the programmer/analyst defines screens, reports, computations, and data structures.

Application Portfolio A planning tool used to evaluate present and proposed information systems applications in terms of the amount of revenue or assets invested in information systems which support major business functions.

Application Software Programs that specify the information processing activities required for the completion of specific tasks of computer users. Examples are electronic spreadsheet and word processing programs or inventory or payroll programs.

Application-Specific Programs Application software packages that support specific applications of end users in business, science and engineering, and other areas.

Applications Development See *Systems development.*

Arithmetic-Logic Unit (ALU) The unit of a computing system containing the circuits that perform arithmetic and logical operations.

Artificial Intelligence (AI) A science and technology whose goal is to develop computers that can think, as well as see, hear, walk, talk, and feel. A major thrust is the development of computer functions normally associated with human intelligence, for example, reasoning, inference, learning, and problem solving. Major areas of AI research and development include cognitive science, computer science, robotics, and natural language applications.

ASCII: American Standard Code for Information Interchange A standard code used for information interchange among data processing systems, communication systems, and associated equipment

Assembler A computer program that translates an assembler language into machine language.

Assembler Language A programming language that utilizes symbols to represent operation codes and storage locations.

Asynchronous Involving a sequence of operations without a regular or predictable time relationship. Thus operations do not happen at regular timed intervals, but an operation will begin only after a previous operation is completed. In data transmission, involves the use of start and stop bits with each character to indicate the beginning and end of the character being transmitted.

Audio-Response Unit An output device of a computer system whose output consists of the spoken word. Also called a voice synthesizer.

Audit Trail The presence of media and procedures that allow a transaction to be traced through all stages of information processing, beginning with its appearance on a source document and ending with its transformation into information on a final output document.

Automatic Teller Machine (ATM) A special-purpose transaction terminal used to provide remote banking services.

Automation The automatic transfer and positioning of work by machines or the automatic operation and control of a work process by machines, that is, without significant human intervention or operation.

Auxiliary Storage Storage that supplements the primary storage of the computer. Same as *Secondary storage*.

Back-End Processor Typically a smaller general-purpose computer that is dedicated to database processing using a database management system (DBMS). Also called a database machine.

Background Processing The automatic execution of lower-priority computer programs when higher-priority programs are not using the resources of the computer system. Contrast with *Foreground processing*.

Backward-Chaining An inference process which justifies a proposed conclusion by determining if it will result when rules are applied to the facts in a given situation.

Bar Codes Vertical marks or bars placed on merchandise tags, or packaging that can be sensed and read by optical character-reading devices. The width and combination of vertical lines are used to represent data.

Barriers to Entry Technological, financial, or legal requirements which deter firms from entering an industry.

BASIC: Beginner's All-Purpose Symbolic Instruction Code A programming language developed at Dartmouth College that is popular for microcomputer and time-sharing systems.

Batch Processing A category of data processing in which data is accumulated into "batches" and processed periodically. Contrast with *Realtime processing*.

Baud A unit of measurement used to specify data transmission speeds. It is a unit of signaling speed equal to the number of discrete conditions or signal events per second. In many data communications applications it represents one bit per second.

Binary Pertaining to characteristic or property involving a selection, choice, or condition in which there are two possibilities, or pertaining to the number system that utilizes a base of two.

Bit A contraction of "binary digit." It can have the value of either 0 or 1.

Block A grouping of contiguous data records or other data elements that are handled as a unit.

Bootstrap A technique in which the first few instructions of a program are sufficient to bring the rest of itself into the computer from an input device.

Branch A transfer of control from one instruction to another in a computer program that is not part of the normal sequential execution of the instructions of the program.

Buffer Temporary storage used to compensate for a difference in rate of flow of data, or time of occurrence of events, when transmitting data from one device to another.

Bug A mistake or malfunction.

Bulletin Board System (BBS) A service of personal computer networks in which electronic messages, data files, or programs can be stored for other subscribers to read or copy.

Bundling The inclusion of software, maintenance, training, and other products or services in the price of a computer system.

Bus A set of conducting paths for movement of data and instructions that interconnects the various components of the CPU.

Business Function Information System Information systems within a business organization that support one of the traditional functions of business such as marketing, finance, or production. Business information systems can be either operations or management information systems.

Business Graphics The use of computer graphics to help end users and managers monitor business operations and make better decisions, since graphics displays can assist managers in analyzing and interpreting data.

Byte A sequence of adjacent binary digits operated on as a unit and usually shorter than a computer word. In many computer systems, a byte is a grouping of eight bits that can represent one alphabetic or special character or can be "packed" with two decimal digits.

C A low-level structured programming language developed by AT&T-Bell Laboratories. It resembles a machine-independent assembler language and is popular for software package development.

Cache Memory A high-speed temporary storage area in the CPU for storing parts of a program or data during processing.

Capacity Management The use of planning and control methods to forecast and control information processing job loads, hardware and software usage, and other computer system resource requirements.

Cathode Ray Tube (CRT) An electronic vacuum tube (television screen) that displays the output of a computer system.

CD-ROM An optical disk technology for microcomputers featuring compact disks with a storage capacity of over 500 megabytes.

Cellular Radio A radio communications technology that divides a metropolitan area into a honeycomb of cells to greatly increase the number of frequencies and thus the users that can take advantage of mobile phone service.

Central Processing Unit (CPU) The unit of a computer system that includes the circuits that control the interpretation and execution of instructions. In many computer systems, the CPU includes the arithmetic-logic unit, the control unit, and primary storage unit.

Channel A path along which signals can be sent. More specifically, a small special-purpose processor that controls the movement of data between the CPU and input/output devices.

Charge-Coupled Device (CCD) A slower serial access form of semiconductor memory that uses a silicon crystal's own structure to store data.

Chargeback Systems Methods of allocating costs to end user departments based on the information services rendered and information system resources utilized.

Check Bit A binary check digit; for example, a parity bit.

Check Digit A digit in a data field that is utilized to check for errors or loss of characters in the data field as a result of data transfer operations.

Check Point A place in a program where a check or a recording of data for restart purposes is performed.

Chief Information Officer A senior management position that oversees all information technology for a firm, concentrating on long-range information system planning and strategy.

Client/Server Network A computing environment where end user workstations (clients) are connected to micro or mini LAN servers and possibly to mainframe *superservers*.

Clock A device that generates periodic signals utilized to control the timing of a synchronous computer. Also, a register whose contents change at regular intervals in such a way as to measure time.

Coaxial Cable A sturdy copper or aluminum wire wrapped with spacers to insulate and protect it. Groups of coaxial cables may also be bundled together in a bigger cable for ease of installation.

COBOL: COmmon Business Oriented Language A widely used business data processing programming language.

CODASYL: COnference on DAta SYstems Languages The group of representatives of users and computer manufacturers who developed and maintain the COBOL language.

Code Computer instructions.

Cognitive Science An area of artificial intelligence which focuses on researching how the human brain works and how humans think and learn, in order to apply such findings to the design of computer-based systems.

Common Carrier An organization that supplies communications services to other organizations and to the public as authorized by government agencies.

Communications Satellite Earth satellites placed in stationary orbits above the equator that serve as relay stations for communications signals transmitted from earth stations.

Competitive Forces A firm must confront (1) rivalry of competitors within its industry, (2) threats of new entrants, (3) threats of substitutes, (4) the bargaining power of customers, and (5) the bargaining power of suppliers.

Competitive Strategies A firm can develop cost leadership, product differentiation, and business innovation strategies to confront its competitive forces.

Compiler A program that translates a high-level programming language into a machine-language program.

Computer A device that has the ability to accept data, internally store and execute a program of instructions, perform mathematical, logical, and manipulative operations on data, and report the results.

Computer-Aided Design (CAD) The use of computers and advanced graphics hardware and software to provide interactive design assistance for engineering and architectural design.

Computer-Aided Engineering The use of computers to simulate, analyze, and evaluate models of product designs and production processes developed using computer-aided design methods.

Computer-Aided Manufacturing (CAM) The use of computers to automate the production process and operations of a manufacturing plant. Also called factory automation.

Computer-Aided Planning (CAP) The use of software packages as tools to support the planning process.

Computer-Aided Software Engineering (CASE) Same as computer-aided systems engineering, but emphasizing the importance of software development.

Computer-Aided Systems Engineering (CASE) Using software packages to accomplish and automate many of the activities of information systems development, including software development or programming.

Computer Application The use of a computer to solve a specific problem or to accomplish a particular job for an end user. For example, common business computer applications include sales order processing, inventory control, and payroll.

Computer-Assisted Instruction (CAI) The use of computers to provide drills, practice exercises, and tutorial sequences to students.

Computer-Based Information System An information system that uses computer hardware and software to perform its information processing activities.

Computer Crime Criminal actions accomplished through the use of computer systems, especially with intent to defraud, destroy, or make unauthorized use of computer system resources.

Computer Ethics A system of principles governing the legal, professional, social, and moral responsibilities of computer specialists and end users.

Computer Generations Major stages in the historical development of computing.

Computer Industry The industry composed of firms that supply computer hardware, software, and services.

Computer-Integrated Manufacturing (CIM) An overall concept that stresses that the goals of computer use in factory automation should be to simplify, automate, and integrate production processes and other aspects of manufacturing.

Computer Program A series of instructions or statements, in a form acceptable to a computer, prepared in order to achieve a certain result.

Computer System Computer hardware as a system of input, processing, output, storage, and control components. Thus a computer system consists of input and output devices, primary and secondary storage devices, the central processing unit, the control unit within the CPU, and other peripheral devices.

Computer Terminal Any input/output device connected by telecommunications links to a computer.

Computer Virus or Worm Program code that copies its destructive program routines into the computer systems of anyone who accesses computer systems which have used the program, or anyone who uses copies of data or programs taken from such

computers. This spreads the destruction of data and programs among many computer users. Technically, a *virus* will not run unaided, but must be inserted into another program, while a *worm* is a distinct program that can run unaided.

Concentrator A special-purpose computer that accepts information from many terminals using slow-speed lines and transmits data to a main computer system over a high-speed line.

Concurrent Processing The generic term for the capability of computers to work on several tasks at the same time, that is, concurrently. This may involve specific capabilities such as overlapped processing, multiprocessing, multiprogramming, multitasking, parallel processing, and so on.

Connectivity The degree to which hardware, software, and databases can be easily linked together in a telecommunications network.

Context Diagram The highest level data flow diagram. It defines the boundaries of a system by showing a single major process and the data inputs and outputs and external entities involved.

Control (1) The systems component that evaluates feedback to determine whether the system is moving toward the achievement of its goal and then makes any necessary adjustments to the input and processing components of the system to ensure that proper output is produced. (2) A management function that involves observing and measuring organizational performance and environmental activities and modifying the plans and activities of the organization when necessary.

Control Listing A detailed report that describes each transaction occurring during a period.

Control Unit A subunit of the central processing unit that controls and directs the operations of the computer system. The control unit retrieves computer instructions in proper sequence, interprets each instruction, and then directs the other parts of the computer system in their implementation.

Conversion The process in which the hardware, software, people, and data resources of an old information system must be converted to the requirements of a new information system. This usually involves a parallel, phased, pilot, or plunge conversion process from the old to the new system.

Cooperative Processing Information processing which allows the computers in a distributed processing network to share the processing of parts of an end user's application.

Counter A device such as a register or storage location used to represent the number of occurrences of an event.

Critical Success Factors A small number of key factors that executives consider critical to the success of the enterprise. These are key areas where successful performance will assure the success of the organization and attainment of its goals.

Cross-Functional Information Systems Information systems which are integrated combinations of business function information systems, thus sharing information resources across the functional units of an organization.

Cryogenics The study and use of devices utilizing the properties of materials at super cold temperatures. The superconductive nature of such materials provides ultrahigh-speed computer logic and memory circuits.

Cursor A movable point of light displayed on most video display screens to assist the user in the input of data.

Cybernetic System A system that uses feedback and control components to achieve a self-monitoring and self-regulating capability.

Cylinder An imaginary vertical cylinder consisting of the vertical alignment of data tracks on each surface of magnetic disks, which are accessed simultaneously by the read/write heads of a disk device.

Data Facts or observations about physical phenomena or business transactions. More specifically, data are objective measurements of the *attributes* (characteristics) of *entities* such as people, places, things, and events.

Data Administration A data resource management function which involves the establishment and enforcement of policies and procedures for managing data as a strategic corporate resource.

Data Bank (1) A comprehensive collection of libraries of data. (2) A centralized common database that supports several major information systems of an organization.

Database A collection of logically related records or files. A database consolidates many records previously stored in separate files so that a common pool of data records serves many applications.

Database Administration A data resource management function which includes responsibility for developing and maintaining the organization's data dictionary, designing and monitoring the performance of databases, and enforcing standards for database use and security.

Database Administrator A specialist responsible for maintaining standards for the development, maintenance, and security of an organization's databases.

Database Management Approach An approach to the storage and processing of data in which independent files are consolidated into a common pool or database of records available to different application programs and end users for processing and data retrieval.

Database Management System (DBMS) A generalized set of computer programs that controls the creation, maintenance, and utilization of the databases of an organization.

Data Center An organizational unit which uses centralized computing resources to perform information processing activities for an organization. Also known as a computer center.

Data Communications See *Telecommunications.*

Data Design The design of the logical structure of databases and files to be used by a proposed information system. This produces detailed descriptions of the entities, relationships, data elements, and integrity rules for system files and databases.

Data Dictionary A software module and database containing descriptions and definitions concerning the structure, data elements, interrelationships, and other characteristics of an organization's databases. Also, a catalog of the definitions for the attributes of all data elements and their relationships to each other, as well as to external systems.

Data Entry The process of converting data into a form suitable for entry into a computer system. Also called data capture or input preparation.

Data Flow Diagram A graphic diagramming tool which uses a few simple symbols to illustrate the flow of data among external entities, processing activities, and data storage elements.

Data Management Control program functions that provide access to data sets, enforce data storage conventions, and regulate the use of input/output devices.

Data Model A conceptual framework which defines the logical relationships among the data elements needed to support a basic business or other process.

Data Modeling A process where the relationships between data elements are identified and defined to develop data models.

Data Planning A corporate planning and analysis function that focuses on data resource management. It includes the responsibility for developing an overall information policy and data architecture for the firm's data resources.

Data Processing The execution of a systematic sequence of operations performed upon data to transform it into information.

Data Resource Management A managerial activity that applies information systems technology and management tools to the task of managing an organization's data resources. Its three major components are database administration, data administration, and data planning.

Debug To detect, locate, and remove errors from a program or malfunctions from a computer.

Decision Making Process A process of intelligence, design, and choice activities which result in the selection of a particular course of action.

Decision Support System (DSS) An information system that utilizes decision models, a database, and a decision maker's own insights in an ad hoc, interactive analytical modeling process to reach a specific decision by a specific decision maker.

Demand Reports and Responses Information provided whenever a manager or end user demands it.

Desktop Accessory Package A software package which provides features such as a calculator, note page, alarm clock, phone directory, and appointment book that is available as a pop-up window on a computer display screen at the touch of a key.

Desktop Publishing The use of microcomputers, laser printers, and page-makeup software to produce a variety of printed materials, formerly done only by professional printers.

Development Centers Systems development consultant groups formed to serve as consultants to the professional programmers and systems analysts of an organization to improve their application development efforts.

Digital Computer A computer that operates on digital data by performing arithmetic and logical operations on the data. Contrast with *Analog computer.*

Digitizer A device that is used to convert drawings and other graphic images on paper or other materials into digital data that is entered into a computer system.

Direct Access A method of storage where each storage position has a unique address and can be individually accessed in approximately the same period of time without having to search through other storage positions.

Direct Access Storage Device (DASD) A storage device that can directly access data to be stored or retrieved, for example, a magnetic disk unit.

Direct Data Organization A method of data organization in which logical data elements are distributed randomly on or within the physical data medium. For example, logical data records distributed randomly on the surfaces of a magnetic disk file. Also called direct organization.

Direct Input/Output Devices such as terminals that allow data to be input into a computer system or output from the computer system without the use of machine-readable media.

Direct Memory Access (DMA) A type of computer architecture in which intelligent components other than the CPU (such as a channel) can directly access data in main memory.

Disk Pack A removable unit containing several magnetic disks that can be mounted on a magnetic disk storage unit.

Distributed Databases The concept of distributing databases or portions of a database at remote sites where the data is most frequently referenced. Sharing of data is made possible through a network that interconnects the distributed databases.

Distributed processing A form of decentralization of information processing made possible by a network of computers dispersed throughout an organization. Processing of user applications is accomplished by several computers interconnected by a telecommunications network rather than relying on one large centralized computer facility or on the decentralized operation of several independent computers.

Document (1) A medium on which data has been recorded for human use, such as a report or invoice. (2) In word processing, a generic term for text material such as letters, memos, reports, and so on.

Documentation A collection of documents or information that describes a computer program, information system, or required data processing operations.

Downtime The time interval during which a device is malfunctioning or inoperative.

DSS Generator A software package for a decision support system which contains modules for database, model, and dialogue management.

Dump To copy the contents of all or part of a storage device, usually from an internal device, onto an external storage device.

Duplex In communications, pertaining to a simultaneous two-way independent transmission in both directions.

EBCDIC: Extended Binary Coded Decimal Interchange Code An eight-bit code that is widely used by mainframe computers.

Echo Check A method of checking the accuracy of transmission of data in which the received data are returned to the sending device for comparison with the original data.

Economic Feasibility Whether expected costs savings, increased revenue, increased profits, reductions in required investment, and other benefits exceed the costs of developing and operating a proposed system.

EDI: Electronic Data Interchange The electronic transmission of source documents between the computers of different organizations.

Edit To modify the form or format of data, for example, to insert or delete characters such as page numbers or decimal points.

Edit Report A report that describes errors detected during processing.

EFT: Electronic Funds Transfer The development of banking and payment systems that transfer funds electronically instead of using cash or paper documents such as checks.

Electronic Data Processing (EDP) The use of electronic computers to process data automatically.

Electronic Document Management An image processing technology in which an electronic document may consist of digitized voice notes and electronic graphics images, as well as digitized images of traditional documents.

Electronic Mail The transmission, storage, and distribution of text material in electronic form over communications networks.

Electronic Meeting Systems (EMS) The use of video and audio communications to allow conferences and meetings to be held with participants who may be geographically dispersed or may be present in the same room. This may take the form of group decision support systems, teleconferencing, or other methods.

Electronic Spreadsheet Package An application program used as a computerized tool for analysis, planning, and modeling that allows users to enter and manipulate data into an electronic worksheet of rows and columns.

Emulation To imitate one system with another so that the imitating system accepts the same data, executes the same programs, and achieves the same results as the imitated system.

Encryption To scramble data or convert it, prior to transmission, to a secret code that masks the meaning of the data to unauthorized recipients. Similar to enciphering.

End User Anyone who uses an information system or the information it produces.

End User Computing Systems Computer-based information systems that directly support both the operational and managerial applications of end users. Also, the direct, hands-on use of computers by end users.

Enterprise Analysis A planning process that emphasizes how computer-based information systems will improve the performance and competitive position of a business enterprise. This includes planning how information systems can support the basic business processes, functions, and organizational units of an organization.

Enterprise Model A conceptual framework which defines the structures and relationships of business processes and data elements, as well as other planning structures, such as critical success factors, and organizational units.

Entropy The tendency of a system to lose a relatively stable state of equilibrium.

Ergonomics The science and technology emphasizing the safety, comfort, and ease of use of human-operated machines such as computers. The goal of ergonomics is to produce systems that are user friendly, that is, safe, comfortable, and easy to use. Ergonomics is also called human factors engineering.

Evaluation Criteria Key areas in which a proposed solution will be evaluated.

Exception Reports Reports produced only when exceptional conditions occur, or reports produced periodically which contain information only about exceptional conditions.

Executive Information Systems An information system that provides strategic information tailored to the needs of top management.

Expert System A computer-based information system that uses its knowledge about a specific complex application area to act as an expert consultant to users. The system consists of a knowledge base and software modules that perform inferences on the knowledge, and communicates answers to a user's questions.

Facilities Management The use of an external service organization to operate and manage the information processing facilities of an organization.

Facsimile The transmission of images and their reconstruction and duplication on some form of paper at a receiving station.

Fault-Tolerant Computer Systems Computers with multiple central processors, peripherals, and system software that are able to continue operations even if there is a major hardware or software failure.

Feasibility Study A preliminary study that investigates the information needs of end users and the objectives, constraints, basic resource requirements, cost/benefits, and feasibility of proposed projects.

Feedback (1) Data or information concerning the components and operations of a system. (2) The use of part of the output of a system as input to the system.

Fiber Optics The technology that uses cables consisting of very thin filaments of glass fibers that can conduct the light generated by lasers at frequencies that approach the speed of light.

Field A data element that consists of a grouping of characters that describe a particular attribute of an entity. For example, the name field or salary field of an employee.

Fifth-Generation The next generation of computing, which will provide computers that will be able to see, hear, talk, and think. This would depend on major advances in parallel processing, user input/output methods, and artificial intelligence.

File A collection of related data records treated as a unit. Sometimes called a data set.

File Maintenance The activity of keeping a file up-to-date by adding, changing, or deleting data.

File Processing Utilizing a file for data processing activities such as file maintenance, information retrieval, or report generation.

Financial Information Systems Information systems that support financial managers in the financing of a business and the allocation and control of financial resources. Includes cash and securities management, capital budgeting, financial forecasting, and financial planning.

Firmware The use of microprogrammed read only memory circuits in place of "hardwired" logic circuitry. See also *Microprogramming*.

Flip-Flop A circuit or device containing active elements, capable of assuming either one or two states at a given time. Synonymous with toggle.

Floating-Point Pertaining to a number representation system in which each number is represented by two sets of digits. One set represents the significant digits or fixed-point "base" of the number, while the other set of digits represents the "exponent," which indicates the precision of the radix point.

Floppy Disk A small plastic disk coated with iron oxide that resembles a small phonograph record enclosed in a protective envelope. It is a widely used form of magnetic disk media that provides a direct access storage capability for microcomputer systems.

Flowchart A graphical representation in which symbols are used to represent operations, data, flow, logic, equipment, and so on. A program flowchart illustrates the structure and sequence of operations of a program, while a system flowchart illustrates the components and flows of information systems.

Foreground Processing The automatic execution of the computer programs that have been designed to preempt the use of computing facilities. Contrast with *Background processing*.

Format The arrangement of data on a medium.

FORTRAN: FORmula TRANslation A high-level programming language widely utilized to develop computer programs that perform mathematical computations for scientific, engineering, and selected business applications.

Forward-Chaining An inference strategy that reaches a conclusion by applying rules to facts to determine if any facts satisfy a rule's conditions in a particular situation.

Fourth-Generation Languages (4GL) Programming languages that are easier to use than high-level languages like BASIC, COBOL, or FORTRAN. They are also known as nonprocedural, natural, or very high-level languages.

Frame A collection of knowledge about an entity or other concept consisting of a complex package of slots, that is, data values describing the characteristics or attributes of an entity.

Frame-Based Knowledge Knowledge represented in the form of a hierarchy or network of frames.

Front-End Processor Typically a smaller, general-purpose computer that is dedicated to handling data communications control functions in a communications network, thus relieving the host computer of these functions.

Fuzzy Logic Systems Computer-based systems that can learn to recognize patterns in data that are incomplete or only partially correct, i.e., fuzzy data. Such systems can learn to solve unstructured problems with incomplete knowledge, as humans do.

General-Purpose Application Programs Programs that can perform information processing jobs for users from all application areas. For example, word processing programs, electronic spreadsheet programs, and graphics programs can be used by individuals for home, education, business, scientific, and many other purposes.

General-Purpose Computer A computer that is designed to handle a wide variety of problems. Contrast with *Special-purpose computer*.

Generate To produce a machine-language program for performing a specific data processing task based on parameters supplied by a programmer or user.

Generator A computer program that performs a generating function.

Gigabyte One billion bytes. More accurately, 2 to the 30th power, or 1,073,741,824 in decimal notation.

GIGO A contraction of "Garbage In, Garbage Out," which emphasizes that information systems will produce erroneous and invalid output when provided with erroneous and invalid input data or instructions.

Goal Seeking Analysis Making repeated changes to selected variables until a chosen variable reaches a target value.

Graphics Pertaining to symbolic input or output from a computer system, such as lines, curves, and geometric shapes, using video display units or graphics plotters and printers.

Graphics Pen and Tablet A device that allows an end user to draw or write on a pressure sensitive tablet and have their handwriting or graphics digitized by the computer and accepted as input.

Graphics Software A program that helps users generate graphics displays.

Group Decision Making Decisions made by groups of people coming to an agreement on a particular issue.

Group Decision Support System (GDSS) A decision support system which provides support for decision making by groups of people.

Groupware Software packages which support work activities by members of a work group whose workstations are interconnected by a local area network.

Hacking The unauthorized access and use of computer systems.

Handshaking Exchange of predetermined signals when a connection is established between two communications terminals.

Hard Copy A data medium or data record that has a degree of permanence and that can be read by people or machine.

Hardware (1) Machines and media. (2) Physical equipment, as opposed to computer programs or methods of use. (3) Mechanical, magnetic, electrical, electronic, or optical devices. Contrast with *Software*.

Hash Total The sum of numbers in a data field that are not normally added, such as account numbers or other identification numbers. It is utilized as a control total, especially during input/output operations of batch processing systems.

Header Label A machine-readable record at the beginning of a file containing data for file identification and control.

Heuristic Pertaining to exploratory methods of problem solving in which solutions are discovered by evaluation of the progress made toward the final result. It is an exploratory trial-and-error approach guided by rules of thumb. Opposite of algorithmic.

Hexadecimal Pertaining to the number system with a radix of 16. Synonymous with sexadecimal.

Hierarchical Data Structure A logical data structure in which the relationships between records form a hierarchy or tree structure. The relationships among records are one-to-many, since each data element is related only to one element above it.

High-Level Language A programming language that utilizes macro instructions and statements that closely resemble human language or mathematical notation to describe the problem to be solved or the procedure to be used. Also called a compiler language.

HIPO Chart (Hierarchy + Input/Processing/Output) Also known as an IPO chart. A design and documentation tool of structured programming utilized to record input/processing/output details of hierarchical program modules.

Hollerith Pertaining to a type of code or punched card utilizing 12 rows per column and usually 80 columns per card. Named after Herman Hollerith, who originated punched card data processing.

Homeostasis A relatively stable state of equilibrium of a system.

Host Computer Typically a larger central computer that performs the major data processing tasks in a computer network.

Human Resource Information Systems (HRIS) Information systems that support human resource management activities such as recruitment, selection and hiring, job placement and performance appraisals, and training and development.

Hypermedia Documents that contain multiple forms of media, including text, graphics, video, and sound, which can be interactively searched like hypertext.

Hypertext A methodology for the construction and interactive use of text material, in which a body of text in electronic form is indexed in a variety of ways so it can be quickly searched by a reader.

Icon A small figure on a video display that looks like a familiar office or other device such as a file folder (for storing a file), a wastebasket (for deleting a file), or a calculator (for switching to a calculator mode).

Image Processing A computer-based technology which allows end users to electronically capture, store, process, and retrieve images that may include numeric data, text, handwriting, graphics, documents, and photographs. Image processing makes heavy use of optical scanning and optical disk technologies.

Impact Printers Printers that form images on paper through the pressing of a printing element and an inked ribbon or roller against the face of a sheet of paper.

Index An ordered reference list of the contents of a file or document together with keys or reference notations for identification or location of those contents.

Index Sequential A method of data organization in which records are organized in sequential order and also referenced by an index. When utilized with direct access file devices, it is known as index sequential access method or ISAM.

Inference Engine The software component of an expert system which processes the rules and facts related to a specific problem and makes associations and inferences resulting in recommended courses of action.

Information Information is data placed in a meaningful and useful context for an end user.

Information Architecture A conceptual framework that defines the basic structure, content, and relationships of the organizational databases that provide the data needed to support the basic business processes of an organization.

Information Center A support facility for the end users of an organization. It allows users to learn to develop their own application programs and to accomplish their own information processing tasks. End users are provided with hardware support, software support, and people support (trained user consultants).

Information Float The time when a document is in transit between the sender and receiver, and thus unavailable for any action or response.

Information Processing A concept that covers both the traditional concept of processing numeric and alphabetic data, and the processing of text, images, and voices. It emphasizes that the production of information products for users should be the focus of processing activities.

Information Quality The degree to which information has content, form, and time characteristics which give it value to specific end users.

Information Reporting System A management information system which produces prespecified reports, displays, and responses on a periodic, exception, or demand basis.

Information Resource Management (IRM) A management concept that views data, information, and computer resources (computer hardware, software, and personnel) as valuable organizational resources that should be efficiently, economically, and effectively managed for the benefit of the entire organization.

Information Retrieval The methods and procedures for recovering specific information from stored data.

Information System A set of people, procedures, and resources that collects, transforms, and disseminates information in an organization. Or, a system that accepts data resources as input and processes them into information products as output. Also, a system that uses the resources of hardware (machines and media), software (programs and procedures), and people (users and specialists) to perform input, processing, output, storage, and control activities that transform data resources into information products.

Information System Resources Hardware, software, people, and data are the resources of an information system.

Information System Specialist A person whose occupation is related to the providing of information system services; for example, a systems analyst, programmer, or computer operator.

Information Systems Development See *Systems development.*

Information Systems Planning A formal planning process which develops plans for developing and managing information systems that will support the goals of the organization. This includes strategic, tactical, and operational planning activities.

Information Technology (IT) Hardware, software, telecommunications, database management, and other information processing technologies used in computer-based information systems.

Input Pertaining to a device, process, or channel involved in the insertion of data into a data processing system. Opposite of *Output.*

Input/Output (I/O) Pertaining to either input or output, or both.

Input/Output Interface Hardware Devices such as I/O ports, I/O busses, buffers, channels, and input/output control units, which assist the CPU in its input/output assignments. These devices make it possible for modern computer systems to perform input, output, and processing functions simultaneously.

Inquiry Processing Computer processing which supports the realtime interrogation of online files and databases by end users.

Instruction A grouping of characters that specifies the computer operation to be performed and the values or locations of its operands.

Intangible Benefits and Costs The nonquantifiable benefits and costs of a proposed solution or system.

Integrated Circuit A complex microelectronic circuit consisting of interconnected circuit elements that cannot be disassembled because they are placed on or within a "continuous substrate" such as a silicon chip.

Integrated Packages Software that combines the ability to do several general-purpose applications (such as word processing, electronic spreadsheet, and graphics) into one program.

Intelligent Terminal A terminal with the capabilities of a microcomputer or minicomputer, which can thus perform many data processing and other functions without accessing a larger computer.

Interactive Processing A type of realtime processing in which users at online terminals can interact with the computer on a realtime basis.

Interactive Video Computer-based systems that integrate image processing with text, audio, and video processing technologies, which makes interactive multimedia presentations possible.

Interface A shared boundary, such as the boundary between two systems. For example, the boundary between a computer and its peripheral devices.

Interpreter A computer program that translates and executes each source language statement before translating and executing the next one.

Interrupt A condition that causes an interruption in a processing operation during which another task is performed. At the conclusion of this new assignment, control may be transferred back to the point where the original processing operation was interrupted or to other tasks with a higher priority.

Inverted File A file that references entities by their attributes.

Iterative Pertaining to the repeated execution of a series of steps.

Job A specified group of tasks prescribed as a unit of work for a computer.

Job Control Language (JCL) A language for communicating with the operating system of a computer to identify a job and describe its requirements.

Job Management Preparing, scheduling, and monitoring jobs for continuous processing by a computer system. This is a major system management function of an operating system.

Joystick A small lever set in a box used to move the cursor on the computer's display screen.

K An abbreviation for the prefix "kilo," which is 1,000 in decimal notation. When referring to storage capacity it is equivalent to 2 to the 10th power, or 1,024 in decimal notation.

Key One or more fields within a data record that are used to identify it or control its use.

Keyboarding Using the keyboard of a typewriter, word processor, or computer terminal.

Key-to-Disk Data entry using a keyboard device to record data directly onto a magnetic disk.

Knowledge Base A computer-accessible collection of knowledge about a subject in a variety of forms, such as facts and rules of inference, frames, and objects.

Knowledge-Based Information System An information system which adds a knowledge base to the database and other components found in other types of computer-based information systems.

Knowledge Engineer A specialist who works with experts to capture the knowledge they possess in order to develop a knowledge base for expert systems and other knowledge-based systems.

Knowledge Workers People whose primary work activities include creating, using, and distributing information.

Label One or more characters used to identify a statement or an item of data in a computer program or the contents of the data file.

Language Translator Program A program that converts the programming language instructions in a computer program into machine language code. Major types include assemblers, compilers, and interpreters.

Large-Scale Integration (LSI) A method of constructing electronic circuits in which thousands of circuits can be placed on a single semiconductor chip.

Layout Forms and Screens Tools used to construct the formats and generic content of input/output media and methods for the user interface, such as display screens and reports.

Light Pen A photoelectronic device that allows data to be entered or altered on the face of a video display terminal.

Line Printer A device that prints all characters of a line as a unit.

Liquid Crystal Displays (LCDs) Electronic visual displays that form characters by applying an electrical charge to selected silicon crystals.

List Organization A method of data organization that uses indexes and pointers to allow for nonsequential retrieval.

List Processing A method of processing data in the form of lists.

Local Area Network (LAN) A communications network that typically connects computers, terminals, and other computerized devices within a limited physical area such as an office building, manufacturing plant, or other worksite.

Locking in Customers and Suppliers Building valuable relationships with customers and suppliers which deter them from abandoning a firm for its competitors or intimidating it into accepting less profitable relationships.

Logical Data Elements Data elements that are independent of the physical data media on which they are recorded.

Logical System Design Developing general specifications for how basic information systems activities can meet end user requirements.

LOGO An interactive graphical language used as a tool for learning a variety of concepts (color, direction, letters, words, sounds, etc.) as well as learning to program and use the computer. Forms and figures are used (sprites and turtles) that a child learns to move around on the screen to accomplish tasks.

Loop A sequence of instructions in a computer program that is executed repeatedly until a terminal condition prevails.

Machine Cycle The timing of a basic CPU operation as determined by a fixed number of electrical pulses emitted by the CPU's timing circuitry or internal clock.

Machine Language A programming language where instructions are expressed in the binary code of the computer.

Macro Instruction An instruction in a source language that is equivalent to a specified sequence of machine instructions.

Magnetic Bubble An electromagnetic storage device that stores and moves data magnetically as tiny magnetic spots that look like bubbles under a microscope as they float on the surface of a special type of semiconductor chip.

Magnetic Core Tiny rings composed of iron oxide and other materials strung on wires that provide electrical current that magnetizes the cores. Data is represented by the direction of the magnetic field of groups of cores. Widely used as the primary storage media in second- and third-generation computer systems.

Magnetic Disk A flat circular plate with a magnetic surface on which data can be stored by selective magnetization of portions of the curved surface.

Magnetic Drum A circular cylinder with a magnetic surface on which data can be stored by selective magnetization of portions of the curved surface.

Magnetic Ink An ink that contains particles of iron oxide that can be magnetized and detected by magnetic sensors.

Magnetic Ink Character Recognition (MICR) The machine recognition of characters printed with magnetic ink. Primarily used for check processing by the banking industry.

Magnetic Tape A plastic tape with a magnetic surface on which data can be stored by selective magnetization of portions of the surface.

Mag Stripe Card A plastic wallet-size card with a strip of magnetic tape on one surface; widely used for credit/debit cards.

Mainframe A larger-size computer system, typically with a separate central processing unit, as distinguished from microcomputer and minicomputer systems.

Management Functions Management as a process of planning, organizing, staffing, directing, and controlling activities.

Management Information System (MIS) An information system that provides information to support managerial decision making. More specifically, an information reporting system, executive information system, or decision support system.

Management Levels Management as the performance of planning and control activities at the strategic, tactical, and operational levels of an organization.

Managerial End User A manager, entrepreneur, or managerial-level professional who personally uses information systems. Also, the manager of the department or other organizational unit that relies on information systems.

Managerial Roles Management as the performance of a variety of interpersonal, information, and decision roles.

Manual Data Processing (1) Data processing requiring continual human operation and intervention that utilizes simple data processing tools such as paper forms, pencils, and filing cabinets. (2) All data processing that is not automatic, even if it utilizes machines such as typewriters and calculators.

Manufacturing Information Systems Information systems which support the planning, control, and accomplishment of manufacturing processes. This includes concepts such as computer integrated manufacturing (CIM) and technologies such as computer-aided manufacturing (CAM) or computer-aided design (CAD).

Marketing Information Systems Information systems which support the planning, control, and transaction processing required for the accomplishment of marketing activities, such as sales management, advertising and promotion.

Mark-Sensing The electrical sensing of manually recorded conductive marks on a nonconductive surface.

Mass Storage Secondary storage devices with extra-large storage capacities such as magnetic or optical disks.

Master File A data file containing relatively permanent information, which is utilized as an authoritative reference and is usually updated periodically. Contrast with *Transaction file*.

Mathematical Model A mathematical representation of a process, device, or concept.

Media All tangible objects on which data are recorded.

Megabyte One million bytes. More accurately, 2 to the 20th power, or 1,048,576 in decimal notation.

Memory Same as *Storage*.

Menu A displayed list of items (usually the names of alternative applications, files, or activities) from which an end user makes a selection.

Menu Driven A characteristic of interactive computing systems that provides menu displays and operator prompting to assist an end user in performing a particular job.

Meta-Data Data about data, that is, data describing the structure, data elements, interrelationships, and other characteristics of a database.

Microcomputer A very small computer, ranging in size from a "computer on a chip" to a small typewriter-size unit.

Micrographics The use of microfilm, microfiche, and other microforms to record data in greatly reduced form.

Microprocessor A microcomputer central processing unit (CPU) on a chip. Without input/output or primary storage capabilities in most types.

Microprogram A small set of elementary control instructions called microinstructions or microcode.

Microprogramming The use of special software (microprograms) to perform the functions of special hardware (electronic control circuitry). Microprograms stored in a read-only storage module of the control unit interpret the machine language instructions of a computer program and decode them into elementary microinstructions, which are then executed.

Microsecond A millionth of a second.

Millisecond A thousandth of a second.

Minicomputer A small (for example, the size of a desk) electronic, digital, stored-program, general-purpose computer.

Model Base An organized collection of conceptual, mathematical, and logical models that express business relationships, computational routines, or analytical techniques. Such models are stored in the form of programs and program subroutines, command files, and spreadsheets.

Modem (MOdulator-DEModulator) A device that converts the digital signals from input/output devices into appropriate frequencies at a transmission terminal and converts them back into digital signals at a receiving terminal.

Monitor Software or hardware that observes, supervises, controls, or verifies the operations of a system.

Mouse A small device that is electronically connected to a computer and is moved by hand on a flat surface in order to move the cursor on a video screen in the same direction. Buttons on the mouse allow users to issue commands and make responses or selections.

Multiplex To interleave or simultaneously transmit two or more messages on a single channel.

Multiplexer An electronic device that allows a single communications channel to carry simultaneous data transmission from many terminals.

Multiprocessing Pertaining to the simultaneous execution of two or more instructions by a computer or computer network.

Multiprocessor Computer Systems Computer systems that use a multiprocessor architecture in the design of their central processing units. This includes the use of support microprocessors and multiple instruction processors, including parallel processor designs.

Multiprogramming Pertaining to the concurrent execution of two or more programs by a computer by interleaving their execution.

Multitasking The concurrent use of the same computer to accomplish several different information processing tasks. Each task may require the use of a different program, or the concurrent use of the same copy of a program by several users.

Nanosecond One billionth of a second.

Natural Language A programming language that is very close to human language. Also called very high-level language.

Network An interconnected system of computers, terminals, and communications channels and devices.

Network Architecture A master plan designed to promote an open, simple, flexible, and efficient telecommunications environment through the use of standard protocols, standard communications hardware and software interfaces, and the design of a standard multilevel telecommunications interface between end users and computer systems.

Network Data Structure A logical data structure which allows many-to-many relationships among data records. It allows entry into a database at multiple points, because any data element or record can be related to many other data elements.

Neural Networks Massively parallel neurocomputer systems whose architecture is based on the human brain's mesh-like neuron structure. Such networks can process many pieces of information simultaneously and can learn to recognize patterns and programs themselves to solve related problems on their own.

Node A terminal point in a communications network.

Noise (1) Random variations of one or more characteristics of an entity such as voltage, current, or data. (2) A random signal of known statistical properties of amplitude, distribution, and special density. (3) Any disturbance tending to interfere with the normal operation of a device or system.

Nonimpact Printers Printers that use specially treated paper that form characters by laser, thermal (heat), electrostatic, or electrochemical processes.

Nonprocedural Languages Programming languages that allow users and professional programmers to specify the results they want without specifying how to solve the problem.

Numerical Control Automatic control of a machine process by a computer which makes use of numerical data, generally introduced as the operation is in process. Also called machine control.

Object A data element that includes both data and the methods or processes that act on that data.

Object-Based Knowledge Knowledge represented as a network of objects.

Object-Oriented Language An object-oriented programming (OOP) language used to develop programs which create and use objects to perform information processing tasks.

Object Program A compiled or assembled program composed of executable machine instructions. Contrast with *Source program*.

Octal Pertaining to the number representation system with a radix of eight.

OEM: Original Equipment Manufacturer A firm that manufactures and sells computers by assembling components produced by other hardware manufacturers.

Office Automation (OA) The use of computer-based information systems that collect, process, store, and transmit electronic messages, documents, and other forms of office communications among individuals, work groups, and organizations.

Office Support Systems Office automation systems which integrate a variety of computer-based support services, including desktop accessories, electronic mail, and electronic task management.

Offline Pertaining to equipment or devices not under control of the central processing unit.

Online Pertaining to equipment or devices under control of the central processing unit.

Online Transaction Processing (OLTP) A realtime transaction processing system.

Operand That which is operated upon. That part of a computer instruction that is identified by the address part of the instruction.

Operating Environment Package Software packages or modules which add a graphics-based interface between end users, the operating system, and their application programs, and may also provide a multitasking capability.

Operating System The main control program of a computer system. It is a system of programs that controls the execution of computer programs and may provide scheduling, debugging, input/output control, system accounting, compilation, storage assignment, data management, and related services.

Operation Code A code that represents specific operations to be performed upon the operands in a computer instruction.

Operational Feasibility The willingness and ability of management, employees, customers, and suppliers to operate, use, and support a proposed system.

Operations Information System An information system that collects, processes, and stores data generated by the operations systems of an organization and produces data and information for input into a management information system or for the control of an operations system.

Operations System A basic subsystem of the business firm that constitutes its input, processing, and output components. Also called a physical system.

Optical Character Recognition (OCR) The machine identification of printed characters through the use of light-sensitive devices.

Optical Disks A secondary storage medium using laser technology to read tiny spots on a plastic disk. The disks are currently capable of storing billions of characters of information.

Optical Scanner A device that optically scans characters or images and generates their digital representations.

Optimization Analysis Finding an optimum value for selected variables in a mathematical model, given certain constraints.

Organizational Feasibility How well a proposed information system supports the objectives of an organization's strategic plan for information systems.

Output Pertaining to a device, process, or channel involved with the transfer of data or information out of an information processing system.

Overlapped Processing Pertaining to the ability of a computer system to increase the utilization of its central processing unit by overlapping input/output and processsing operations.

Packet A group of data and control information in a specified format that is transmitted as an entity.

Packet Switching A data transmission process that transmits addressed packets such that a channel is occupied only for the duration of transmission of the packet.

Page A segment of a program or data, usually of fixed length.

Paging A process that automatically and continually transfers pages of programs and data between primary storage and direct access storage devices. It provides computers with multiprogramming and virtual memory capabilities.

Parallel Processing Executing many instructions at the same time, that is, in parallel. Performed by advanced computers using many instruction processors organized in clusters or networks.

Parity Bit A check bit appended to an array of binary digits to make the sum of all the binary digits, including the check bit, always odd or always even.

Pascal A high-level, general-purpose, structured programming language named after Blaise Pascal. It was developed by Niklaus Wirth of Zurich in 1968.

Pattern Recognition The identification of shapes, forms, or configurations by automatic means.

PCM: Plug Compatible Manufacturer A firm that manufactures computer equipment that can be plugged into existing computer systems without requiring additional hardware or software interfaces.

Performance Monitor A software package that monitors the processing of computer system jobs, helps develop a planned schedule of computer operations that can optimize computer system performance, and produces detailed statistics that are used for computer system capacity planning and control.

Periodic Reports Providing information to managers using a prespecified format designed to provide information on a regularly scheduled basis.

Peripheral Devices In a computer system, any unit of equipment, distinct from the central processing unit, that may provide the system with outside communication.

Personal Information Manager (PIM) A software package which helps end users store, organize, and retrieve text and numerical data in the form of notes, lists, memos, and a variety of other forms.

Physical System Design Design of the user interface methods and products, database structures, and processing and control procedures for a proposed information system, including hardware, software, and personnel specifications.

Picosecond One trillionth of a second.

PILOT: Programmed Inquiry, Learning Or Teaching A special-purpose language designed to develop CAI (computer-aided instruction) programs. It is a simple interactive language that enables a person with minimal computer experience to develop and test interactive CAI programs.

PL/1: Programming Language 1 A procedure-oriented, high-level, general-purpose programming language designed to combine the features of COBOL, FORTRAN, and ALGOL.

Plasma Display Output devices that generate a visual display with electrically charged particles of gas trapped between glass plates.

Plotter A hard-copy output device that produces drawings and graphical displays on paper or other materials.

Pointer A data element associated with an index, a record, or other set of data that contains the address of a related record.

Pointing Devices Devices which allow end users to issue commands, make choices, and enter graphic or alphanumeric data directly into the computer system as an alternative to the use of the keyboard.

Point-of-Sale (POS) Terminal A computer terminal used in retail stores that serves the function of a cash register as well as collecting sales data and performing other data processing functions.

Port (1) Electronic circuitry that provides a connection point between the CPU and input/output devices. (2) A connection point for a communications line on a CPU or other front-end device.

Postimplementation Review Monitoring and evaluating the results of an implemented solution or system.

Prespecified Reports Reports whose format is specified in advance to provide managers with information periodically, on an exception basis, or on demand.

Private Branch Exchange (PBX) A switching device that serves as an interface between the many telephone lines within a work area and the local telephone company's main telephone lines or trunks. Computerized PBXs can handle the switching of both voice and data in the local area networks that are needed in such locations.

Procedure-Oriented Language A programming language designed for the convenient expression of procedures used in the solution of a wide class of problems.

Procedures Sets of instructions used by people to complete a task.

Process Control The use of a computer to control an ongoing physical process such as petrochemical production.

Process Design The design of the programs and procedures needed by a proposed information system, including detailed program specifications and procedures.

Processor A hardware device or software system capable of performing operations upon data.

Program A set of instructions that cause a computer to perform a particular task.

Programmed Decision A decision that can be automated by basing it on a decision rule that outlines the steps to take when confronted with the need for a specific decision.

Programmer A person mainly involved in designing, writing, and testing computer programs.

Programming The design, writing, and testing of a program.

Programming Language A language used to develop the instructions in computer programs.

Programming Tools Software packages or modules which provide editing and diagnostic capabilities and other support facilities to assist the programming process.

Project Management Managing the accomplishment of an information system development project according to a specific project plan, in order that a project is completed on time, within its budget, and meets its design objectives.

Prompt Messages that assist the operator in performing a particular job. This would include error messages, correction suggestions, questions, and other messages that guide an operator.

Protocol A set of rules and procedures for the control of communications in a communications network.

Prototype A working model. In particular, a working model of an information system which includes tentative versions of user input and output, databases and files, control methods, and processing routines.

Prototyping The rapid development and testing of working models, or prototypes, of new information system applications in an interactive, iterative process involving both systems analysts and end users.

Pseudocode An informal design language of structured programming that expresses the processing logic of a program module in ordinary English-language phrases.

Punched Card A card punched with a pattern of holes to represent data.

Punched Tape A tape on which a pattern of holes or cuts is used to represent data.

Query Language A high-level, English-like language provided by a database management system that enables users to easily extract data and information from a database.

Queue (1) A waiting line formed by items in a system waiting for service. (2) To arrange in or form a queue.

Random Access Same as *Direct access*.

Random Access Memory (RAM) One of the basic types of semiconductor memory used for temporary storage of data or programs during processing. Each memory position can be directly sensed (read) or changed (write) in the same length of time, irrespective of its location on the storage medium.

Read Only Memory (ROM) A basic type of semiconductor memory used for permanent storage. Can only be read, not "written," that is, changed. Variations are Programmable Read Only Memory (PROM) and Erasable Programmable Read Only Memory (EPROM).

Realtime Pertaining to the performance of data processing during the actual time a business or physical process transpires, in order that results of the data processing can be used in supporting the completion of the process.

Realtime Processing Data processing in which data is processed immediately rather than periodically. Also called online processing. Contrast with *Batch processing*.

Record A collection of related data fields treated as a unit.

Reduced Instruction Set Computer (RISC) A CPU architecture which optimizes processing speed by the use of a smaller number of basic machine instructions than traditional CPU designs.

Redundancy In information processing, the repetition of part or all of a message to increase the chance that the correct information will be understood by the recipient.

Register A device capable of storing a specified amount of data such as one word.

Relational Data Structure A logical data structure in which all data elements within the database are viewed as being stored in the form of simple tables. DBMS packages based on the relational model can link data elements from various tables as long as the tables share common data elements.

Remote Access Pertaining to communication with the data processing facility by one or more stations that are distant from that facility.

Remote Job Entry (RJE) Entering jobs into a batch processing system from a remote facility.

Report Generator A feature of database management system packages which allows an end user to quickly specify a report format for the display of information retrieved from a database.

Reprographics Copying and duplicating technology and methods.

Resource Management An operating system function which controls the use of computer system resources such as primary storage, secondary storage, CPU processing time, and input/output devices by other system software and application software packages.

Robotics The technology of building machines (robots) with computer intelligence and humanlike physical capabilities.

Routine An ordered set of instructions that may have some general or frequent use.

RPG: Report Program Generator A problem-oriented language that utilizes a generator to construct programs that produce reports and perform other data processing tasks.

Rule Statements which typically take the form of a premise and a conclusion such as IF-THEN rules, i.e., IF (condition), THEN (conclusion).

Rule-Based Knowledge Knowledge represented in the form of rules and statements of fact.

Schema An overall conceptual or logical view of the relationships between the data in a database.

Scientific Method An analytical methodology which involves (1) recognizing phenomena, (2) formulating a hypothesis about the causes or effects of the phenomena, (3) testing the hypothesis through experimentation, (4) evaluating the results of such experiments, and (5) drawing conclusions about the hypothesis.

Secondary Storage Storage that supplements the primary storage of a computer. Synonymous with *Auxiliary storage*.

Sector A subdivision of a track on a magnetic disk surface.

Security Monitor A software package which monitors the use of a computer system and protects its resources from unauthorized use, fraud, and vandalism.

Semiconductor Secondary Storage (RAM Disk) A method that uses software and control circuitry to make the main processor and the operating system program treat part of the computer's semiconductor storage (RAM) as if it were another disk drive.

Semiconductor Storage Microelectronic storage circuitry etched on tiny chips of silicon or other semiconducting material. The primary storage of most modern computers consists of microelectronic semiconductor storage chips for random access memory (RAM) and read only memory (ROM).

Semistructured Decisions Decisions involving procedures which can be partially prespecified, but not enough to lead to a definite recommended decision.

Sensitivity Analysis Observing how repeated changes to a single variable affects other variables in a mathematical model.

Sequential Access A sequential method of storing and retrieving data from a file. Contrast with *Random access*.

Sequential Data Organization Organizing logical data element according to a prescribed sequence.

Serial Pertaining to the sequential or consecutive occurrence of two or more related activities in a single device or channel.

Server A computer that supports telecommunications in a local area network, as well as the sharing of peripheral devices, software, and databases among the workstations in the network.

Service Bureau A firm offering computer and data processing services. Also called a computer service center.

Smart Products Industrial and consumer products, with "intelligence" provided by built-in microcomputers or microprocessors that significantly improve the performance and capabilities of such products.

Software Computer programs and procedures concerned with the operation of an information system. Contrast with *Hardware*.

Software Package A computer program supplied by computer manufacturers, independent software companies, or other computer users. Also known as canned programs, proprietary software, or packaged programs.

Solid State Pertaining to devices whose operation depends on the control of electric or magnetic phenomena in solids such as transistors and diodes.

Source Data Automation The use of automated methods of data entry that attempt to reduce or eliminate many of the activities, people, and data media required by traditional data entry methods.

Source Document A document that is the original formal record of a transaction, such as a purchase order or sales invoice.

Source Program A computer program written in a language that is subject to a translation process. Contrast with *Object program*.

Special-Purpose Computer A computer that is designed to handle a restricted class of problems. Contrast with *General-purpose computer*.

Spooling Simultaneous peripheral operation online. Storing input data from low-speed devices temporarily on high-speed secondary storage units, which can be quickly accessed by the CPU. Also, writing output data at high speeds onto magnetic tape or disk units from which it can be transferred to slow-speed devices such as a printer.

Stage Analysis A planning process in which the information system needs of an organization are based on an analysis of its current stage in the growth cycle of the organization and its use of information systems technology.

Standards Measures of performance developed to evaluate the progress of a system towards its objectives.

Storage Pertaining to a device into which data can be entered, in which it can be held, and from which it can be retrieved at a later time.

Strategic Information Systems Information systems that provide a firm with competitive products and services that give it a strategic advantage over its competitors in the marketplace. Also, information systems which promote business innovation, improve operational efficiency, and build strategic information resources for a firm.

Structure Chart A design and documentation technique to show the purpose and relationships of the various modules in a program.

Structured Decisions Decisions which are structured by the decision procedures or decision rules developed for them. They involve situations where the procedures to follow when a decision is needed can be specified in advance.

Structured Programming A programming methodology that uses a top-down program design and a limited number of control structures in a program to create highly structured modules of program code.

Structured Query Language (SQL) A query language that is becoming a standard for advanced database management system packages. A query's basic form is
SELECT. . . . FROM . . .
WHERE.

Structured Walk-Throughs A structured programming methodology that requires a peer review by other programmers of program design and coding to minimize and reveal errors in the early stages of programming.

Subroutine A routine that can be part of another program routine.

Subschema A subset or transformation of the logical view of the database schema that is required by a particular user application program.

Subsystem A system that is a component of a larger system.

Supercomputer A special category of large mainframe computer systems that are the most powerful available. They are designed to solve massive computational problems.

Superconductor Materials which can conduct electricity with almost no resistance. This allows the development of extremely fast and small electronic circuits. Formerly only possible at super cold temperatures near absolute zero. Recent developments promise superconducting materials near room temperature.

Switch (1) A device or programming technique for making a selection. (2) A computer that controls message switching among the computers and terminals in a telecommunications network.

Switching Costs The costs in time, money, effort, and inconvenience that it would take a customer or supplier to switch its business to a firm's competitors.

Synchronous A characteristic in which each event, or the performance of any basic operation, is constrained to start on, and usually to keep in step with, signals from a timing clock. Contrast with *Asynchronous*.

System (1) A group of interrelated or interacting elements forming a unified whole. (2) A group of interrelated components working together toward a common goal by accepting inputs and producing outputs in an organized transformation process. (3) An assembly of methods, procedures, or techniques united by regulated interaction to form an organized whole. (4) An organized collection of people, machines, and methods required to accomplish a set of specific functions.

System Component Matrix A matrix framework that documents the hardware, software, people, and data resources used, the system activities performed, and the information products produced by an information system.

System Design Standards Standards that promote the design of common system features such as user interfaces, programming interfaces, and telecommunications support.

System Flowchart A graphic diagramming tool used to show the flow of data media as they are processed by hardware devices and information processing procedures in an information system.

System Requirements The information system capabilities required to meet the information needs of end users. Also called functional requirements.

System Software Programs that control and support operations of a computer system. System software includes a variety of programs such as operating systems, database management systems, communications control programs, service and utility programs, and programming language translators.

System Specifications The product of the systems design stage. It consists of specifications for the hardware, software, facilities, personnel, databases, and the user interface of a proposed information system.

System Support Programs Programs that support the operations, management, and users of a computer system by providing a variety of support services. Examples are system utilities and performance monitors.

Systems Analysis (1) Analyzing in detail the components and requirements of a system. (2) Analyzing in detail the information needs of an organization, the characteristics and components of presently utilized information systems, and the requirements of proposed information systems.

Systems Approach A systematic process of problem solving based on the scientific method, which defines problems and opportunities in a systems context. Data is gathered describing the problem or opportunity, and alternative solutions are identified and evaluated. Then the best solution is selected and implemented, and its success evaluated.

Systems Context Recognizing systems, subsystems, and components of systems in a situation. Also called a systemic view.

Systems Design Deciding how a proposed information system will meet the information needs of end users. Includes logical and physical design activities, and user interface, data, and process design activities which produce system specifications that satisfy the system requirements developed in the systems analysis stage.

Systems Development (1) Conceiving, designing, and implementing a system. (2) Developing information systems by a process of investigation, analysis, design, implementation, and maintenance. Also called the systems development life cycle (SDLC), information systems development, or applications development.

Systems Development Tools Graphical, textual, and computer-aided tools and techniques which are used to help analyze, design, and document the development of an information system. They are typically used to represent (1) the components and flows of a system, (2) the user interface, (3) data attributes and relationships, and (4) detailed system processes.

Systems Implementation The stage of systems development in which hardware and software are acquired, developed, and installed, the system is tested and documented, people are trained to operate and use the system, and an organization converts to the use of a newly developed system.

Systems Investigation The screening, selection, and preliminary study of a proposed information system solution to a business problem.

Systems Maintenance The monitoring, evaluating, and modifying of a system to make desirable or necessary improvements.

Tangible Benefits and Costs The quantifiable benefits and costs of a proposed solution or system.

Technical Feasibility Whether reliable hardware and software capable of meeting the needs of a proposed system can be acquired or developed by an organization in the required time.

Technology Management The establishment of organizational groups to identify, introduce, and monitor the assimilation of new information system technologies into organizations.

Telecommunications Pertaining to the transmission of signals over long distances, including not only data communications but also the transmission of images and voices using radio, television, and other communications technologies.

Telecommunications Channel The part of a telecommunications network that connects the message source with the message receiver. It includes the physical equipment used to connect one location to another for the purpose of transmitting and receiving information.

Telecommunications Controller A data communications interface device (frequently a special-purpose mini or microcomputer) that can control a telecommunications network containing many terminals.

Telecommunications Control Program A computer program that controls and supports the communications between the computers and terminals in a telecommunications network.

Telecommunications Monitors Computer programs that control and support the communications between the computers and terminals in a telecommunications network.

Telecommunications Processors Multiplexers, concentrators, communications controllers, and cluster controllers that allow a communications channel to carry simultaneous data transmissions from many terminals. They may also perform error monitoring, diagnostics and correction, modulation-demodulation, data compression, data coding and decoding, message switching, port contention, buffer storage, and serving as an interface to satellite and other communications networks.

Telecommuting The use of telecommunications to replace commuting to work from one's home.

Teleconferencing The use of video communications to allow business conferences to be held with participants who are scattered across a country, continent, or the world.

Telephone Tag The process that occurs when two people who wish to contact each other by telephone repeatedly miss each other's phone calls.

Teleprocessing Using telecommunications for computer-based information processing.

Terabyte One trillion bytes. More accurately, 2 to the 40th power, or 1,009,511,627,776 in decimal notation.

Terminal A point in a system or communication network at which data can either enter or leave. Also, an input/output device at such a point in a system.

Text Data Words, phrases, sentences, and paragraphs used in documents and other forms of communication.

Throughput The total amount of useful work performed by a data processing system during a given period of time.

Time-Sharing Providing computer services to many users simultaneously while providing rapid responses to each.

Top-Down Design A methodology of structured programming in which a program is organized into functional modules, with the programmer designing the main module first and then the lower-level modules.

Touch-Sensitive Screen An input device that accepts data input by the placement of a finger on or close to the CRT screen.

Track The portion of a moving storage medium, such as a drum, tape, or disk, that is accessible to a given reading head position.

Trackball A rollerball device set in a case used to move the cursor on a computer's display screen.

Transaction An event that occurs as part of doing business, such as a sale, purchase, deposit, withdrawal, refund, transfer, payment, and so on.

Transaction Document A document produced as part of a business transaction, e.g., a purchase order, paycheck, sales receipt, or customer invoice.

Transaction File A data file containing relatively transient data to be processed in combination with a master file. Contrast with *Master file*.

Transaction Processing Cycle A cycle of basic transaction processing activities including data entry, transaction processing, database maintenance, document and report generation, and inquiry processing.

Transaction Processing System An information system that processes data arising from the occurrence of business transactions.

Transaction Terminal Terminals used in banks, retail stores, factories, and other worksites that are used to capture transaction data at its point of origin. Examples are point-of-sale (POS) terminals and automated teller machines (ATMs).

Transform Algorithm Performing an arithmetic computation on a record key and using the result of the calculation as an address for that record. Also known as key transformation or hashing.

Turnaround Document Output of a computer system (such as customer invoices and statements) that is designed to be returned to the organization as machine-readable input.

Turnaround Time The elapsed time between submission of a job to a computing center and the return of the results.

Turnkey Systems Computer systems where all of the hardware, software, and systems development needed by a user are provided.

Unbundling The separate pricing of hardware, software, and other related services.

Universal Product Code (UPC) A standard identification code using bar coding, printed on products which can be read by the optical supermarket scanners of the grocery industry.

Unstructured Decisions Decisions which must be made in situations where it is not possible to specify in advance most of the decision procedures to follow.

User Friendly A characteristic of human-operated equipment and systems that makes them safe, comfortable, and easy to use.

User Interface Design Designing the interactions between end users and computer systems, including input/output methods and the conversion of data between human-readable and machine-readable forms.

Utility Program A standard set of routines that assists in the operation of a computer system by performing some frequently required process such as copying, sorting, or merging.

Value-Added Carriers Third-party vendors who lease telecommunications lines from common carriers and offer a variety of telecommunications services to customers.

Value-Added Resellers (VARs) Companies which provide industry-specific software for use with the computer systems of selected manufacturers.

Value Chain Viewing a firm as a series or chain of basic activities that add value to its products and services and thus add a margin of value to the firm.

Videotex An interactive information service provided over phone lines or cable TV channels. Users can select specific video displays of data and information (such as electronic *Yellow Pages* or their own personal bank checking account register).

Virtual Machine Pertaining to the simulation of one type of computer system by another computer system.

Virtual Memory The use of secondary storage devices as an extension of the primary storage of the computer, thus giving the appearance of a larger main memory than actually exists.

VLSI Very Large-Scale Integration. Semiconductor chips containing hundreds of thousands of circuits.

Voice Mail A variation of electronic mail where digitized voice messages rather than electronic text are accepted, stored, and transmitted.

Voice Recognition Direct conversion of spoken data into electronic form suitable for entry into a computer system. Also called voice data entry.

Volatile Memory Memory (such as electronic semiconductor memory) that loses its contents when electrical power is interrupted.

Wand A handheld optical character recognition device used for data entry by many transaction terminals.

What-If Analysis Observing how changes to selected variables affect other variables in a mathematical model.

Wide Area Network (WAN) A data communications network covering a large geographic area.

Window One section of a computer's multiple section display screen, each of which can have a different display.

Word (1) A string of characters considered as a unit. (2) An ordered set of bits (usually larger than a byte) handled as a unit by the central processing unit.

Word Processing The automation of the transformation of ideas and information into a readable form of communication. It involves the use of computers to manipulate text data in order to produce office communications in the form of documents.

Work Group Computing End user computing in a work group environment in which members of a work group may use a local area network to share hardware, software, and databases to accomplish group assignments.

Workstation A computer terminal or micro or mini computer system designed to support the work of one person. Also, a high-powered computer to support the work of professionals in engineering, science, and other areas that require extensive computing power and graphics capabilities.

INDEX